MW01116252

International Marketing 6e

Dana-Nicoleta Lascu, Ph.D.
University of Richmond

and

George L. Hiller, J.D.
University of Richmond

⠿ Textbook Media Press

The Quality Instructors Expect
At Prices Students Can Afford

Replacing Oligarch Textbooks Since 2004

International Marketing, 6e

Dana-Nicoleta Lascu

George L. Hiller

Copyright 2019, 2016, 2013, 2010 TEXTBOOK MEDIA PRESS

First and Second Editions: Atomic Dog Publishing/Cengage

ALL RIGHTS RESERVED. No part of this work covered by the copyright hereon may be reproduced or used in any form or by any means—graphic, electronic, or mechanical, including photocopying, recording, taping, Web distribution or information storage and retrieval systems—without the written permission of the publisher.

13 DIGIT ISBN: 978-1-7322425-2-4
10 DIGIT ISBN: 1-7322425-2-6

Cover Photo Credits (left to right)

Top Row: Rawpixel.com/shutterstock.com; Ayoub kayor/shutterstock.com; Aun Photographer/shutterstock.com

Title Banner: Nestor Rizhniak/shutterstock.com

Middle: Rawpixel.com/shutterstock.com; Be Panya/shutterstock.com; szefei/shutterstock.com

Middle Bottom: Ivan Marc/shutterstock.com; LauraKick/shutterstock.com; Sorbis/shutterstock.com

Bottom: Dragon Images/shutterstock.com; Rawpixel.com/shutterstock.com; Ivan Marc/shutterstock.com

For permission to use material from this text
or product, submit a request online at

info@textbookmedia.com

Textbook Media Press
795 Dodd Road
West Saint Paul, MN 55118

Textbook Media Press is a Minnesota-based educational publisher. We deliver textbooks and supplements with the quality instructors expect, while providing students with unique media options at uniquely affordable prices.
All our publications are 100% made in the U.S.A.

Dedication

This book is dedicated to my parents, Lucia and Damian Lascu, with deep appreciation for their courage to cross the Iron Curtain, and to the memory Ofra Haza and Umm Kulthoum, the divas of music who inspired the world to unite through song.
—*Dana-Nicoleta Lascu*

This book is dedicated to my wife, Laura, and our almost fifty years of learning together about the world, and to the memory of our daughter, Allison, a real trailblazer for students and professionals with physical disabilities. She made the world a better place.
—*George L. Hiller*

Brief Table of Contents

Detailed Table of Contents

Preface

The sixth edition of *International Marketing* arrives at a time of considerable upheaval and uncertainty about international trade and globalization. The era of global trade agreements and lower tariff barriers appears to be over – or, at minimum, this trend has stalled. Notwithstanding that globalization and international trade were largely responsible for lifting millions of people out of poverty, by 2016, trade and trade agreements had become thorny political topics in Europe and in the United States. With the loss of so many manufacturing jobs in the U.S., trade had come to be considered as the main reason for the disappearance of U.S. manufacturing jobs and the stagnation of middle class wages. In addition, the global influence of multinational companies on local economies and government policies has become a major concern.

By late 2018, as the new edition of *International Marketing* was being finalized, the U.S. and China were in the midst of a major rift over U.S. complaints about China's trade policies: unfair government subsidies, currency manipulation, and the theft of intellectual property. Starting with U.S. tariff hikes on Chinese steel and aluminum exports, new tariffs have been imposed by the U.S. on billions of dollars' worth of Chinese goods. Not surprisingly, this led to retaliatory tariffs by China on key U.S. exports. In addition, the U.S. finds itself at odds with Canada and the European Union over trade and tariffs. The U.S. government is also insisting on major changes to the NAFTA agreement with Canada and Mexico, to reduce the current U.S. trade imbalances with the two countries. The U.S. has threatened to pull out of NAFTA altogether if a satisfactory agreement could not be reached. Many business leaders, academics, and public sector officials are worried about this escalation of trade disputes. Some have suggested the possibility of an all-out global trade war, not seen since the 1930s.

Notwithstanding these current controversies, international trade continues to grow. People around the world seek expanded economic opportunities, improved standards of living, and communities free from armed conflicts. Against this backdrop, the authors would like to share a quote from one of the founders of the Thunderbird School of Global Management.

"Borders frequented by trade seldom need soldiers."
Dr. William Schurz, President
Thunderbird School of Global Management 1949-52

The sixth edition of *International Marketing* has been fully updated to provide analyses about current economic and political challenges, trade disputes, and other developments in international marketing. In addition to updating the comprehensive materials about multinational firms, the new edition features important discussions about international marketing and small and medium-size exporting firms. The sixth edition also includes new coverage on services exports and the booming international e-commerce and e-payments sectors. The authors continue to expand the materials on international marketing and developing countries, with a number of new illustrations focused on Latin America and Africa.

All cases have been revised and updated to offer current company examples and overviews of industry developments. Several new cases were added. Each chapter has at least one case study that helps students apply the knowledge acquired in the chapter.

International Marketing reflects the authors' teaching philosophy: presenting vivid, real-world examples that help students to better understand international marketing theory. Professor Lascu shares her own perspectives as a product of different cultures who has experienced and observed marketing on five continents, both as an expatriate and as a local, in a free-market system and under a repressive, anti- consumerist command economy. Professor Hiller has substantial experience with international trade promotion, as well as business and management in Latin America that complements Dr. Lascu's research background and extensive work in Europe and Asia.

ANCILLARY MATERIALS

Textbook Media is pleased to offer a competitive suite of supplemental materials for instructors using its textbooks. These ancillaries include a Test Bank, PowerPoint Slides, and an Instructor's Manual. This text comes with a test bank created by the author, and it includes questions in a wide range of difficulty levels for each chapter. All Textbook Media test banks offer not only the correct answer for each question but also a rationale or explanation for the correct answer and a reference to the location in the chapter where materials addressing the question content can be found. The Test Item Files are available in files that are readily adaptable to the major Learning Management Systems. The software files allows the instructor to easily create customized or multiple versions of a test and include the option of editing or adding to the existing question bank.

A full set of PowerPoint® Slides, written by the author, is available for this text. This is designed to provide instructors with comprehensive visual aids for each chapter in the book. These slides include outlines of each chapter, highlighting important terms, concepts, and discussion points.

The Instructor's Manual for this book has also been written by the author and offers suggested syllabi for 10- and 14-week terms; lecture outlines and notes; in-class and take-home assignments; recommendations for multimedia resources such as films and Web sites; and long and short essay questions and their answers, appropriate for use on tests.

The authors express their deep gratitude for the immense support received in the process of developing the sixth edition of *International Marketing*. They would especially like to thank Tom Doran and Ed Laube for their unrelenting support and creativity and for their exacting oversight of this project for almost a decade. They would also like to thank the instructors who have used previous editions. Dana Lascu expresses thanks to her family, to Bram, Michael, and Daniel Opstelten, and to her parents, Lucia and Damian Lascu, for the formidable international experiences that this book is based on and for creating and facilitating the foundations for this text. George Hiller would like to thank his wife, Laura, for her support, and also to acknowledge his inspiring students and colleagues at the University of Richmond.

About the Authors

Dana-Nicoleta Lascu is Professor of Marketing in the Marketing Department at the University of Richmond. She has a Ph.D. in marketing from the University of South Carolina, a master's in international management from the Thunderbird School of Global Management, and a B.A. in English and French from the University of Arizona. She was a Fulbright Distinguished Chair in International Business at the Johannes Kepler University of Linz, Austria, and a Fulbright Specialist at Ider University, Mongolia, from where she holds an honorary doctorate. She is Associate Editor for the *Journal of Global Marketing*, Managing Editor for the *Journal of Global Business and Technology*, and she is on the editorial review board of several journals. She has published in *International Marketing Review, International Business Review, European Journal of Marketing, Journal of Business Research, Journal of Business Ethics, Journal of Euromarketing, Journal of East-West Business*, and *Multinational Business Review*, among others, and is the co-author of *Marketing: Essentials 5e*. Dr. Lascu has consulted with companies such as Ford Motor Company, Stihl, IDV North America, Yellow Book International and others, and was a simultaneous and consecutive translator in English, French, and Romanian in Romania and Rwanda. She also worked as an international training coordinator in the United States, teaching managerial skills to bankers, corporate managers, and government employees.

George L. Hiller is a Lecturer of International Business at the University of Richmond. He has almost 35 years of experience in export promotion, trade finance, international trade law, and economic development. He has served as an instructor at the University of Richmond business and law schools since 1991. He developed the Doing Business in Latin America course, an experiential-learning course in which teams of business and law students develop market entry strategies in Latin America for Virginia companies. He has also taught at universities in Colombia and Germany. Professor Hiller has received numerous international business education grants from the U.S. Department of Education, U.S. Department of Commerce, and other governmental and nongovernmental organizations. He also consults with colleges and universities on grant strategies. Originally from Albuquerque, New Mexico, Prof. Hiller holds an undergraduate degree in history from the University of New Mexico, master's degree from the Thunderbird School of Global Management, and law degree from the University of Richmond School of Law.

Part 1

The Introduction to
International Marketing

Chapter 1

Scope, Concepts, and Drivers
of International Marketing

Learning Objectives

After studying
this chapter,
you should be able to:

- Define international marketing and identify the different levels of international involvement.

- Describe the different company orientations and philosophies toward international marketing.

- Identify environmental and firm-specific drivers that direct firms toward international markets.

- Identify obstacles preventing firms from engaging in successful international ventures.

Chapter Outline

ArtisticPhoto/shutterstock.com

Shanghai Disneyland, which opened its doors in 2016, cost over $5 billion to build. It is a joint venture between Disney and the Shanghai Shendi Group, a 100 percent state-owned enterprise, which owns 57 percent of Shanghai Disneyland. This park has the largest castle in Disney's history, a high-speed rail system, and a large shopping center and it is expected to be one of the most successful ventures in the Disney portfolio.

Disney's experience in international markets is extensive, and the company's hard-learned lessons have paved the way to this new enterprise. Over the years, Disney has readily applied its tried and true U.S.-centered formula to its international ventures: the mouse, Cinderella, Main Street U.S.A., Frontierland, Adventureland, Tomorrowland, and, in 2018, Toy Story Land—in other words, America and its present, past, and future in a cute package of several fun-packed acres. This formula worked well in the United States and in Japan at Tokyo Disney Resort. However, exporting the concept to France and Hong Kong was not an easy task. In Europe, consumers were unhappy with the U.S. themes resonating exclusively throughout the park. Disneyland Resort Paris had to reinvent Disney and adapt it to local preferences, creating entertainment based on European fairy tales, serving food that would appeal to European consumers, and creating a more lax approach to the dress code for the park's French staff. At the Hong Kong Disneyland, which opened in 2005, attendance fell short of expectations, with visitors complaining of mistreatment; the number of attractions as well as size of the park were considered insufficient. Shortly after opening, during the Chinese New Year, the park had to close due to ticketing problems, and ticket holders forced their way in by storming through gates or climbing over them. Today, however, Hong Kong Disneyland is thriving, and, along with Disneyland Paris and the Disneyland Resort in California, it leads in the introduction of new rides and themes, such as Iron Man, and Star Wars Avengers and Marvel superheroes.

Over the years, Disney's internationalization strategy has changed from a blanket application of its winning formula described above, to a greater localization and more precise targeting to better serve consumers in its different markets, where environmental forces dictate distinct, region-specific strategies.

This chapter introduces the different internationalization philosophies of international firms and explores the motivations for going international, addressing the environmental and firm-specific drivers of international expansion. It also provides an overview of the challenges and obstacles encountered in international expansion.

1-1 The Importance of International Marketing

The United States constitutes one of the most important target markets in the world, consuming a high percentage of worldwide products and services; according to the World Bank, it is the world's largest consumer market. International firms are eager to invest in the U.S. – to the tune of about to $4 trillion, employing more than 6 million Americans. But, as wealth is on the rise worldwide due to rapid economic development, it is essential for U.S. companies to look beyond the United States for opportunities, and to tap into international markets to take advantage of global market opportunities, to keep pace with competition, and to maximize the potential of their product mix.

Throughout history, companies have become leaders of industry despite the smaller size and limited markets of their home countries. It should be noted, however, that an international presence was essential for their success. Take, for example, successful global companies from the Netherlands, a small country in Western Europe, that are giants of industry worldwide. Among them are Philips, a leading electronics manufacturer; Royal Ahold, a large retailer; Royal Dutch Shell, a major Dutch-British oil company; and Unilever, a Dutch-British leading consumer products company. Japan, also a comparatively small country, boasts a number of firms that are industry leaders. Among them are Mitsui and Mitsubishi (electronics, banking, import-export, among others), Dentsu (advertising), Sony and Panasonic (electronics), and Ito Yokado (retail).

International companies such as Apple, General Motors, Mitsubishi, Microsoft, and Procter & Gamble earn profits greater than the gross domestic product of many low-income countries. U.S.-based Fortune 500 companies employ almost thirty million workers around the world. More than 300,000 US companies export. Nearly 98 percent of these firms are smaller and medium-size companies (SMEs) with fewer than 500 employees.[1] Companies find that products in the late stage of their life cycle can experience a new life in emerging markets in middle-and low-income countries.

Avon in China

China may be the most difficult place to be an Avon Lady: The sign-up process takes many weeks, and candidates must take a written test on China's sales regulations and attend a related class. Then they have to abide by many regulations, including a cap on sales commission. But being an Avon Lady is at least an option now: China lifted its ban on direct sales in 2005, after being required to liberalize its retail industry.

In spite of these restrictions, however, Avon has been doing reasonably well in China, reporting double-digit increases in sales for the company, as it changed gears to focus primarily on store sales – until recently. In 2012, Avon was accused of breaching the U.S. Foreign Corrupt Practices Act, promoting their business interests by bribing Chinese government officials. And its reputation suffered subsequently, when Coty, the fragrance company, reneged on a buyout offer. By 2015, Avon paid nearly $350 million on legal challenges and compliance fees, more than double the penalties it incurred. And yet, despite these challenges, Avon has been able to penetrate markets in large and small cities in even the most remote areas in China. In Figure 1-1, an Avon store in Lhasa, Tibet, has a prominent central location and a local clientele vying for Western beauty products.[2]

1.1 Avon display at 13,000 feet
in Lhasa, Tibet.

To excel in international business, companies must constantly monitor the international environment for opportunities. For over two decades, privatization in countries previously dominated by government monopolies has made it possible for multinationals to compete for local energy, airline, railway, and telecommunications industries. In the future, postal services might constitute the new competitive territory of international companies. Already, in many markets, post offices are enterprising competitors to established private sector firms, increasingly and effectively competing not only for mailing services, but also for banking services.

1-2 Levels of International Marketing Involvement

All companies are affected by elements of the international marketing environment. In terms of international marketing involvement, however, companies have different degrees of commitment. A company engaging in domestic marketing has the least commitment to international marketing. This company focuses solely on domestic consumers and on the home-country environment. The home-country environment, however, is affected by developments in the international environment; furthermore, the local company is directly affected by local competition, which could come from global companies. For example, Pep-Up, Inc. provides top-grade petroleum products, including heating oil and propane, to customers living on the Eastern Shore of Virginia. The company focuses entirely on local consumers living in the area. However, the price of its heating oil and propane is affected by the price of oil and propane, which is determined by international markets.

At the next level, export marketing, a firm could be involved in exporting indirectly— the company takes orders from international clients—or directly—the company actively seeks international clients. For both export marketers and domestic marketers, the international market may constitute an extension of the domestic market and might not be given special consideration. Such firms would have an ethnocentric philosophy to internationalization, as will be shown in Section 1-3a, "Ethnocentric Orientation."

International marketing activities require a substantial focus on international consumers in a particular country or countries. (When more countries are involved, international marketing is often referred to as multinational marketing.) International marketing is thus defined as the processes involved in the creation, production, distribution, promotion, and pricing of products, services, ideas, and experiences for international markets. The international company (see Figure 1-2) is present in different countries with sales offices and subsidiaries or is an active partner in strategic alliances with local companies. It is important to note that, in this case, international activities are not coordinated across the different countries or across different regions. An international company, according to this definition, has a polycentric, or regiocentric, philosophy to internationalization, as will be seen in Sections 1-3b, "Polycentric Orientation," and 1-3c, "Regiocentric Orientation."

1.2 Coca-Cola in Estonia

1-3 Consumers North America and Europe have a strong preferences for pastries – croissants, danishes, brioches, you name it. Thus they are similar in preferences. Where they differ is in their tolerance for high prices: in Berlin upscale stores (1-3a), such pastries are about $2.00, whereas in similar stores in Helsinki (1-3b), they cost about almost $6.00.

Global marketing involves marketing activities across different countries without focusing primarily on national or regional segmentation. Global marketing is possible due to the emergence of global consumer segments with similar preferences (see Figures 1-3a and 1-3b) and due to efficient global allocation of company talent and resources. A company engaging in global marketing has a geocentric philosophy to internationalization.

It should be noted, however, that the terms defined in the preceding paragraphs are often used interchangeably by nonbusiness and business alike—even by international managers. *International, global,* and *multinational* are used to refer to any company crossing borders, without particular reference to the global strategy used. The descriptions of the levels of international marketing involvement should primarily guide one to understand when distinctions are made. Another widely-used approach to distinguishing between companies' international orientation and philosophy is the ethnocentric, polycentric, regiocentric, and geocentric (EPRG) framework.

1-3 The Ethnocentric, Polycentric, Regiocentric, and Geocentric Framework and International Marketing Concepts

Management's orientation toward the internationalization of the firm's operations affects each of the functional areas of the firm and, as such, has a direct effect on the marketing functions within the firm. Management's philosophy on international involvement affects decisions such as the firm's response to global threats and opportunities and related resource allocation. Companies' philosophies on international involvement can be described, on the basis of the EPRG framework, as ethnocentric, polycentric, regiocentric, and geocentric.[3]

1-3a Ethnocentric Orientation

Eli Lilly has been described traditionally as an ethnocentric firm; in fact, even recently, in 2017, it cut jobs to divert more funds to product research and development in an effort to bring to the marketplace high-performance pharmaceutical products. Firms with an ethnocentric orientation are guided by a *domestic market extension concept*. In general, top management of firms with an ethnocentric orientation consider that domestic strategies, techniques, and personnel are superior to foreign ones and therefore provide the most effective framework for the company's overseas involvement; consequently, international operations and customers are considered secondary to domestic operations and customers.[4]

Ethnocentric firms are likely to be highly centralized and consider that the purpose of their international operations is to identify markets that could absorb surplus domestic production; alternatively, international operations could represent a cash cow that generates revenue and necessitates only minimal attention and investment. As a result, plans for international markets are developed primarily in-house by an international division and are similar to those for the domestic market.[5]

Firms in the tobacco industry,[6] as well as firms at the forefront of technology, tend to have an ethnocentric marketing orientation. It should be mentioned that, often, ethnocentric firms approach globalization by internationalizing at the level of the function, rather than the firm; for example, the marketing department may have a geocentric strategy even if top management has an ethnocentric orientation.[7] Alternatively, in the case of Wal-Mart, while merchandise is fully adapted to local preferences, staffing clearly indicates an ethnocentric philosophy; top management come from the company's headquarters, in Arkansas.

In many cases, U.S. firms sell American brands along with their related U.S. lifestyles and traditions—for example, blue jeans and entertainment are often marketed internationally using marketing themes and strategies used in the U.S.

1-3b Polycentric Orientation

Firms with a polycentric orientation are guided by a *multidomestic market concept*. Managers of polycentric firms are very much aware of the importance of individual international markets to the success of their business and are likely to establish individual businesses, typically wholly owned subsidiaries or marketing subsidiaries, in each of the countries where they operate. The assumption the company makes is that each market is unique and needs to be addressed individually. Consequently, the company is fully decentralized and engages in minimal coordination with the headquarters.

rawpixel.com/shutterstock.com

Each subsidiary has its own marketing plans and objectives and operates autonomously as an independent profit center on an individual country basis to achieve its goals; all marketing activities are performed in each country independently of the company headquarters.[8] To address local consumer needs, marketing research is conducted independently in each overseas market, and products are fully adapted to meet these needs. Alternatively, separate product lines are developed to meet the needs of the individual markets.

In the process of developing individual strategies for each market, the company does not coordinate activities across the different countries and cannot benefit from economies of scale that such coordination would allow. Furthermore, numerous functions are duplicated, and, ultimately, final product costs are higher to the end consumer. For decades, Ford used a polycentric strategy in meeting the needs of budget-conscious consumers by developing a Ford Escort automobile for the United Kingdom that looked different from the one sold in the United States or Southeast Asia.[9] Currently, the Ford automobile addressing the needs of the budget-conscious consumer, the Ford Focus, looks identical in each market: Ford has adopted a geocentric approach to product development.

rawpixel.com/shutterstock.com

1-3c Regiocentric Orientation

Firms with a regiocentric or a geocentric orientation are guided by a *global marketing concept*. Companies adopting a regiocentric orientation view world regions as distinct markets that share economic, political, and cultural traits such that they would be viable candidates for a regionwide marketing approach. A regiocentric orientation is now possible due to the success of regional economic and political integration that allows for implementing a uniform marketing strategy in the entire region. Member countries of the European Union, for example, are candidates for Pan-European marketing strategies, whereas signatory countries of the North American Free Trade Agreement (NAFTA) lend themselves to a successful marketing strategy aimed at the North American market. PepsiCo appears to have a regiocentric orientation; Its divisions are organized on the basis of location, with regional offices coordinating all local marketing activities. For example, Pepsi's South-Eastern European operations are coordinated by its Turkey-based PepsiCo subsidiary, which devises the company's regional objectives and oversees the implementation of the company's marketing strategy in the region.

1-3b Geocentric Orientation

Firms in which top management adopts a geocentric orientation perceive the entire world—without national and regional distinctions—as a potential market with identifiable, homogeneous segments that need to be addressed with similar marketing strategies, regardless of geographic location or nationality. Coordinated management policies are designed to reflect the full integration among worldwide operations.

The objective of a geocentric company is most often to achieve a position as a low-cost manufacturer and marketer of its product line; such a firm achieves a strategic competitive advantage by developing manufacturing process-

1-4 McDonald's restaurants pepper the landscape in China, even in the more remote districts of large cities.

es that add more value per unit cost to the final product than its rivals.[10] An example of a geocentric company is McDonald's (see Figure 1-4).

McDonald's has been successful as a result of its geocentric philosophy. The company uses local products to ultimately offer a similar service to consumers from Mexico City to Mumbai. In Europe, McDonald's uses Polish potatoes, which do not lend themselves to a thin, McDonald's-style cut French fry but are touted to be the best in the region. It also uses local beef from the European regions not affected or threatened by livestock disease. The company is also sensitive to the ban on genetically-modified foods in the European Union. In India or Pakistan, for example, McDonald's serves lamb or vegetarian burgers. Throughout the world, it provides a uniform service that offers, in addition to the fast food it is known for, clean restrooms, air conditioning, and service with a smile—even in markets where a smile is a rare occurrence in a service encounter.

IBM

IBM has been going through massive reorganizations to keep abreast of the ever-changing international market; IBM is a dynamic geocentric company. Under IBM's old system, a corporate customer with operations in several countries had to contract with small IBM offices in each country, and each IBM office had its own regulations. The IBM organization was, at the time, polycentric. The reorganization placed IBM's employees into 14 customer-focused groups, such as financial services, entertainment, and oil and gas, to be able to work with a central sales office to have IBM computers installed in the entire client organization. Organizing on the basis of function, rather than on country of operations, demonstrates a geocentric market orientation. Currently, the company's main focus is on what it considers its strategic imperatives, which include analytics, cloud, mobile, social, and security products. [11]

humphrey/shutterstock.com

1-4 The Drivers of International Expansion

Few companies operate in an isolated, country-specific environment, and even fewer can effectively avoid international involvement. Local firms manufacturing for local consumers are dependent on equipment, parts, and raw materials originating abroad. They sell to clients and final consumers who have had exposure to international trade practices and to international products. A complete isolation from international influence is possible only in a closed environment such as North Korea, where consumers are shielded from international influence.

Increasingly, companies cannot afford to avoid involvement in international marketing. Avoiding international expansion could mean losing market share to competitors and missing numerous opportunities created by changes in the international environment. Among reactive motivations for going international is the desire to remain competitive and maintain global market share relative to competitors. In addition, evading trade barriers and other government regulations in the home country can motivate a company to go international.

Firms should be proactive in their approach to internationalization. A proactive rationale for internationalization can be, among others, the search for new markets, new customers, increased market share and profits, tax advantages, or lower costs, as described in the next sections.

Drivers in the business environment and firm-specific drivers, addressed in Sections 1-4a, "Drivers in the Business Environment," and 1-4b, "Firm-Specific Drivers," as well as Table 1-1, help international companies benefit from such opportunities.

Business Environment Drivers	Firm-Specific Drivers
Competition	Product life-cycle considerations
Regional economic and political integration	High new-product development costs
Technology	Standardization, economies of scale, and low-cost labor
Improvements in the transportation and telecommunication infrastructure	Experience transfers
Economic growth	
Transition to a market economy	
Converging consumer needs	

Table 1-1

1-4a Drivers in the Business Environment

Competition

Competitive pressure is often a driver of internationalization. Over time, service providers and client firms develop close relationships that last as long as the firms move together into new international markets. Service providers could include accounting, legal, banking, and advertising firms. However, the relationship is in jeopardy when the service provider does not follow the client into the new market. McCann has been, for many years, the primary advertising agency for Coca-Cola and has followed the company into new markets, as illustrated in the following example.

McCann Erickson and Coca-Cola

McCann Erickson, a leading advertising agency, has followed for many years its longtime client Coca-Cola in most countries where the company was present around the globe: McCann Erickson had been handling the Coca-Cola account in 129 countries since 1942.[12] That sometimes meant McCann Erickson lost money in countries where its accounts were limited but where, nevertheless, it chose to be present to serve the advertising needs of Coke. If McCann Erickson chose not to serve its client in a market, Coca-Cola might resort to the services of a competitor, and on the basis of its experience with the competitor, Coca-Cola might replace McCann Erickson with the competing advertising firm.

However, in spite of efforts to serve their client firm, even the most dedicated service providers can be replaced. In 2007, Coca-Cola moved the management of its dedicated Red Lounge China marketing unit from McCann Erickson to Leo Burnett, a competing advertising agency, dealing McCann a significant blow. Coca-Cola executives decided that they needed to change the way they worked with agency partners. They placed Leo Burnett in charge of teams from different agencies because company executives felt that creating independence and tension between them and their agencies would lead to better ideas and better thinking. They will likely use this strategy in other markets as well, which does not bode well for McCann Erickson.[13]

(Continued on next page...)

However, more recently, Coca-Cola and McCann have been working together on a number of blockbuster campaigns. In the final moments of the Mad Men television series, Coca-Cola's famed 1971 Hilltop ad took center stage, suggesting that a character in the series created the spot. This created much social media buzz for both Coca-Cola and McCann.[14] Another campaign, aimed at the Indian market, attempts to bring Coke to the masses through an ad series underlining the joy in everyday situations.[15]

Regional Economic and Political Integration

In addition to cultural similarities—language and religion, for example—economic and political integration play an important part in facilitating international trade. Regional trade agreements such as NAFTA, and the politically and economically integrated European Union are focused on lowering or eliminating barriers among member countries and promoting trade within the perimeter of each common market. It permits subsidiaries incorporated in the respective markets to benefit from free trade within the region and allows firms outside the integrated regions to conduct business within the common market without the impediments typically posed by crossing national borders—customs paperwork, separate tariffs for each country, and so on. For example, STIHL, the large German manufacturer of outdoor power equipment and chainsaws, has a large manufacturing facility in Virginia Beach, Virginia. Stihl uses the Virginia location to export products to buyers in North and South America, taking advantage of the free trade agreements that the United States has with countries in this region.

A company from the United States exporting products to multiple countries in the European Union, for example, will cross borders once. The company will do the customs paperwork and pay the required customs duties only once, instead of applying for an import license and paying customs duties in every country where it exports products. A subsidiary of a company from the United States incorporated in any country of the European Union is a corporate citizen of the European Union. Consequently, the subsidiary does not have to pay duties or foreign exchange costs when it crosses borders of most European Union member states because all transactions are conducted in euros. See the following example of Ford Germany.

Screenshot

Ford Germany

Although Ford is a U.S. company, Ford Germany is a citizen of Germany and the European Union. As such, Ford Germany can freely ship its Ford Focus, Ford Ka, Ford Mondeo, Ford Fusion, Ford C-Max and S-Max, Ford Transit Euroline, the Ford Ranger, and its other models to dealers in the countries of the European Union without going through customs and engaging in related paperwork. Moreover, the company does not incur any foreign exchange cost because all the transactions take place in euros.

Technology

Technology has created opportunities for firms involved in international business. In terms of media development, consumers worldwide are exposed to programming originating in other countries. Entertainment programming from the United States in particular dominates the international airways. CNN is popular with business-people around the world, and NBC eagerly exports its mix of late-night comedy and news magazines to the rest of the world.

rawpixel.com/shutterstock.com

Advertising also crosses borders, exposing consumers to brands from other countries. The Internet has revolutionized the way many companies conduct business, offering businesses instant and unlimited international exposure—something that brick-and-mortar stores and traditional manufacturers have taken years to achieve. Such exposure offers tremendous opportunities to small businesses that do not normally have the advertising budget to communicate with the international market. For example, a Havasu-owned small business in Nevada, located two hours by car and another two on horseback from Las Vegas, can advertise weekend vacation opportunities to French businesspeople in the southern state of Languedoc-Roussillon planning to attend Las Vegas conferences or to French couples in the eastern state of Alsace looking for a unique honeymoon.

Improvements in the Transportation and Telecommunication Infrastructure

Closely linked to technology are the leaps in the area of transportation and, particularly, in the technology infrastructure. In 1982, a Mercedes-Benz service station in Bujumbura, Burundi (sub-Saharan East Africa), attempting to contact the company factory in Stuttgart, Germany, to order a part, would tie up an English-or German-speaking employee for quite some time for this purpose. The employee would book the telephone call with the operator early in the morning and would typically be contacted by the afternoon. The call would be facilitated by an operator in Brussels, Belgium (calls to Burundi went via cable from Belgium to its former colonies in East Africa), who would link the factory to the service station. The quality of the connection would often be problematic, necessitating a second request for a telephone connection. An alternative would have been placing the request via telex (faxing was not an option at that time, nor was the use of e-mail or video conferencing).

Today, a telephone connection to Burundi would be handled via satellite, for just pennies, and the communication would be crisp and clear, or the company could use video teleconferencing. Job interviews using Skype or FaceTime are used in interviews with potential Western employees in the United Arab Emirates, with the only challenge encountered in the process being the time that would be convenient to both parties, as 8 A.M. in the United States is 4 P.M. in the U.A.E.

Transportation has also greatly improved. The use of containers for international intermodal (ship, truck, train) shipping greatly facilitates the transportation of physical goods, and sellers can check the exact location of the merchandise at any time. In 2018, following the latest expansion of the Panama Canal, giant Super Panamax ships carrying up to 13,000 containers dramatically changed international shipping logistics. For passenger transport, efficient and rapid air travel has become more affordable, allowing for frequent interaction between expatriate or local employphotocritical/shutterstock.com

1-5 An infrastructure that can support high-speed train travel is characteristic of large European and Asian cities.

ees and employees from the company headquarters. Alternatively, high-speed train travel on inter-city routes allows for rapid transportation in Japan, China, and many countries in the European Union (see Figure 1-5). Emerging markets are also rapidly developing their transportation infrastructure; for example, in China, high-speed trains take merely a fraction of the time it used to take to travel between Shanghai and its Pudong Airport.

Economic Growth

Economic growth constitutes an important driver of internationalization. Economic development in has led to the emergence of a strong middle class in large markets, such as those of Brazil and India, leading to increased buying power, creating great potential for international brands. Economic growth has also opened markets that were previously closed or that have had limited international competition. A case in point is China, which now welcomes foreign direct investment. Emerging economies are likely to be more open to free trade and no longer severely limit international firms from entering and operating in these markets.

Transition to a Market Economy

The transition of formerly closed economies, such as those of China, Kazakhstan, Mongolia, and Vietnam, and, more recently, Cuba, to a market economy has led to rapid economic development in these countries and has created important new markets for international brands. An important outcome of the transition to a market economy has been the deregulation and privatization of former government monopolies. For example, under the former Communist regimes and other forms of government and military rule, all industry was run by inefficient government bodies. The demise of these regimes created opportunities for multinationals such as Philip Morris, Whirlpool, Unilever, Procter & Gamble, Colgate-Palmolive, and others, to purchase or partner with local companies operating at a loss, producing low-quality goods and to turn them around into successful enterprises.

Service providers, from Accenture to Pizza Hut, have actively targeted these markets, engaging in the highest level of international commitment: foreign direct investment. Similarly, small and medium-size firms have also benefited, expanding from the saturated home-country markets into the newly-opened emerging markets.

Currently, international companies, joint ventures between multinationals and local companies, private local businesses, as well as some remnants of the former system—for example, state-owned enterprises—compete for local consumers in these transition markets. At the same time, satellite television, cellular telephones, and the Internet expose these consumers to programming, information, and advertising for international brands, shaping consumer desires and brand preferences. Companies that have, initially, ignored these markets due to the obstacles they posed to international trade — for instance, limiting consumer-goods companies' access to hard currency and restricting the repatriation of profits — have finally entered these promising markets to take advantage of the many untapped opportunities. Investing in transition economies has proved to be a brilliant strategy for company growth. Most rewards are reaped by those companies investing in the larger transition economies, such as China, Brazil, and India. Take Yum! Brands, in the following example.

Yum! Brands

Yum! Brands, the largest fast food restaurant company in terms of total number of restaurants, boasting the popular fast-food chains Taco Bell, KFC, and Pizza Hut, has not had a stellar performance in recent years in the United States. Internationally, however, its restaurant business has been booming, with the company serving 1.4 billion consumers. Yum! Brands' highest growth is in China, where KFC is a dominant player, with restaurants in more than 1,000 cities (see Figure 1-6). In fact, China's division is leading Yum!'s growth – Yum! has 6900 stores in China, — as the company continues an aggressive strategy of opening restaurants around the world.[16]

1-6 Yum! Brands is omnipresent in China and Taiwan.

Converging Consumer Needs

Exposure to global brands in one's home country and, while traveling abroad, exposure to media advertising other brands has created demand for many global products. Consumers worldwide are loyal to international brands such as Nike sneakers, Levi's jeans, Coca-Cola, Heineken beer, and Ralph Lauren shirts. Uniform consumer segments are emerging in high-income countries and low-income countries: One such segment is the youth market. Young consumers in the United States and in Southeast Asia are loyal to the same soft-drink brands, wear the same brands of clothing, listen to the same music, have the same teen idols, use the same social media, and see the same television shows. Another uniform segment is the luxury segment. Luxury consumers in Latin America, Asia, Europe, and Africa vie for the same international luxury brands. New York's Fifth Avenue and 57th street boutiques carry the same brands as those found in Place Vendôme, in Paris, on the Isle of Capri, in Italy, or on Shanghai's historic Bund.

Brand websites, social media buzz, and television exposure to international brands have created brand familiarity and, indeed, brand desire with consumers in many markets where the brand might not be available. Similarly, consumers traveling abroad encounter new product offerings and develop desires for brands that may not be available in their home country. These consumers represent a ready market for international brands. In Kazakhstan, for example, consumers dedicate a larger portion of their budget to luxury goods; Kazakhs do not have a habit of saving money and, compared to most Europeans, spend substantially more on luxury and leisure. In Almaty, even emerging luxury brands such as MSGM shoes and Marc Cross couture sold out as soon as they arrived at the point of retail when they were first introduced to Kazakh consumers.[17]

Converging consumer needs have created homogeneous segments of consumers that can be addressed similarly, regardless of their location. Figure 1-7 shows a bagel shop in Berlin. Bagels started with a Jewish baker in Vienna, who made a hard roll for the king of Poland, Jan Sobieski, in the shape of a riding stirrup-Bugel (commemorating the king's favorite pastime, riding) to thank him for protecting his countrymen from Turkish invaders. From there, the bagel made its way to Poland, Russia, and, eventually to Manhattan's Lower East Side. Surprise! The bagel made it back across the Atlantic, to Germany, where Salomon Bagels (www.salomon-bagels.de) at Berlin's trendy Potsdamer Platz is very popular. Here, the schmear (spread) consists of not just cream cheese and lox (salmon), but marmalade, hazelnut spread, honey, hummus, and Parmesan. Or one can have a pizza bagel with schinken (ham, oy!) or spinach.

1.7 Bagels are back in Berlin, serving the needs of the city's cosmopolitan consumers.

1-4b Firm-Specific Drivers

Product Life-Cycle Considerations

A main driver of international expansion is a firm's attempt to prolong the life cycle of its products and thus create higher profits for the company from a larger customer base. Products that are in late maturity, or even in the decline stage, can change their position on the global product life-cycle stage by going into markets where the product is in high demand. To illustrate this point, the cigarette industry is in either the late maturity stage or in the decline stage in many industrialized countries. By entering large emerging markets where cigarettes are in the growth stage and consumers have increasing purchase power, such as China, India, Republic of South Africa, and countries in Central Asia, the cigarette industry is in fact prolonging its product life cycle.

High New Product Development Costs

The concept of high costs for new product development is related to the product life cycle. Companies often spend long periods and significant amounts of money to develop new products. Nike, on the average, spends close to a year to develop, test, and manufacture new product designs that then last on the shelves in the United States for only six months. Despite the size and purchase power of the U.S. market, it is unlikely that Nike would fully recover its product development costs and make a profit as well if it limited its sales to this country. This is especially true for companies at the forefront of technology (manufacturers of high-tech equipment and electronics, pharmaceutical firms, and others), which need to tap large markets for long periods to recoup costs and to make a profit as well; as a result, for these companies, going international is not a choice—it is a precondition for survival.

The Audi A3 cabriolet, a small luxury sedan, was introduced in Europe in the mid 1990s, in the U.S. in 2006, and in India in late 2014. In 2015, Mercedes offered its own small luxury sedan model, the CLA, which Consumer Reports described at one point as a very nice Honda. The Audi and the

Hadrian/shutterstock.com

Mercedes brands benefited greatly from a broader launch of their small luxury models; they were able to reap greater profits worldwide by selling their offering to India's rapidly growing upper middle class. With a population of 1.2 billion and a middle class expected to make up over half a billion consumers in a decade, selling affordable luxury brands is a safe bet. It is also an astute strategy that can help recoup the costs involved in developing new models of their automobiles and thus to maximize return on investment.

Standardization, Economies of Scale, and Cheap Labor

During the maturity stage of the product life cycle, the core product is likely to achieve a standard in a particular industry: Competitors—typically an oligopoly—respond to consumer needs by offering products whose components are interchangeable and which converge toward the brand experiencing the greatest consumer demand. To offer historical illustrations, standards were established in the personal computer industry, which converged on the IBM standard; more recently, smart phones appear to have converged to the iPhone standard.

Also during maturity, firms increasingly compete on price: Typically, they attempt to lower the product manufacturing costs by achieving economies of scale in production. In addition, firms with mature brands also move manufacturing operations and facilities abroad, to developing countries, in an attempt to take advantage of significantly lower labor costs.

Increasingly, firms may not even wait for a standard to develop before they attempt to obtain economies of scale and/or move their production to low-labor-cost countries. Apple, for example, produced the iPhone in China and Taiwan from the very beginning to take advantage of low labor costs.

Even startups, which usually launch their products first in wealthy countries, are increasingly introducing products in emerging markets first, taking advantage of faster approvals and less regulatory oversight. For example, Diagnostics for All, a Boston-area startup developed miniature diagnostic tests that contain small amounts of chemicals that react with samples of blood, urine, saliva, or sweat, displaying a reading with a change of color. Their technology is revolutionary because they deliver a low-cost laboratory testing technique, in contrast to existing diagnostic machines that cost over $30,000. As hospitals in emerging markets cannot afford such expensive machines, physicians are likely to adopt this product much faster, which helps the company demonstrate that its concept works. Also, selling this product in emerging markets will keep the product off the radar of the competitors manufacturing the expensive machines. In the process of delivering this product in emerging markets first, Diagnostics for All delays expensive and lengthy clinical trials in high-income countries until it has a better control of the technology and it is more broadly accepted by the market. [18]

VGstockstudio/shutterstock.com

Experience Transfers

International firms benefit from lessons they learn in the different parts of the world. Colgate-Palmolive, for example, developed its successful Axion dishwashing paste for its Latin American market after noting that women washed dishes by hand, dunking their hands in a small tub with a few slivers of soap. The same product was then offered to consumers in Central and Eastern Europe after noting that they washed dishes using a similar method— and the product was a hit. Service providers such as Pizza Hut found that they were more successful with consumers in general, but especially with younger generations of consumers in Eastern Europe and Central Asia, if they played loud pop music in their restaurants. As a result, they started entering new markets by partnering with radio stations and clubs.

Similar experience transfers have been helpful to retailers in the process of internationalization. The Tesco Extra hypermarket (superstore) in the city of Newcastle, United Kingdom, and the popular and busy Tesco hypermarket in the southern Czech Republic, in Cesky Budeovice, are based on Tesco hypermarkets first introduced by the same U.K. retailer elsewhere in Eastern Europe. Taking advantage of experience transfers, the company is able to go to different international markets and thus reduce its dependence on any one market.

1-5 Obstacles to Internationalization

Companies attempting to establish and maintain an international presence are likely to encounter obstacles to internationalization both from within the company and from outside. Such obstacles can be financial in nature — the company might not have the finances to expand beyond national frontiers. Others are psychological — fear of an unknown international environment or of local business practices may keep the company from international engagement. These two types of barriers, however, could equally affect the company's local expansion efforts. Companies may not have the finances to expand beyond a small regional market, or they fear going into new markets where consumers may not be familiar with their products and hence may not respond to their marketing strategy. (However, it bears repeating that in 2018, some 300,000 smaller and medium-size businesses or SMEs are exporters.)

There are obstacles that are typically encountered by firms in their process of international-ization—obstacles that they are unlikely to encounter in other expansion efforts. They are the self-reference criterion, government barriers, and international competition.

1-5a Self-Reference Criterion

Of crucial importance to international operations is the ability of the firm, and especially of its marketing strategy, to adapt to the local business environment to serve well the needs of local consumers and to address the requirements of local government, industry, and channels of distribution. An impediment to adaptation is the self-reference criterion, defined as individuals' conscious and unconscious reference to their own national culture and to home-country norms and values, as well as to their knowledge and experience, in the process of making decisions in the host country. At the company level, self-reference may lead the firm to fail to understand local consumers and their needs and to fail to understand the local business culture and deal effectively with local nationals.

Self-reference can lead to a breakdown in communication between parties from different cultures. For example, an employee of a large international company from the United States has been trained by career counselors in the United States that looking one's counterpart in the eyes conveys directness and honesty. When this individual conducts business in Japan using direct eye

rawpixel.com/shutterstock.com

contact, he or she is likely to be perceived as abrasive, challenging the Japanese counterpart. Similarly, if an employee proceeds directly to transacting the business deal in Latin America or southern Europe instead of first interacting in a social setting to establish rapport, he or she would be perceived as arrogant, interested only in the bottom line, rather than in a long-term working relationship.

A first step to minimizing the effect of the self-reference criterion is selecting the appropriate personnel for international assignments. Such employees are sensitive to others and have experience working in different environments. Second, it is important to train international sales managers who travel overseas as well as in-country expatriates to focus on and be sensitive to the local culture, rather than limit their personal interactions to own-country nationals or to expatriates from countries with cultures that are similar to their own. In fact, it is advisable that firms institute an organization-wide general orientation that instills and demonstrates sensitivity to international environments and openly rejects value judgments and national stereotyping.

1-5b Ethnocentrism

Ethnocentrism is related to the self-reference criterion. Individuals who are ethnocentric judge other cultures only from the perspective of their own culture; and, importantly, they judge their own culture as superior to other cultures. As the United States has played a leading role in the world economy for the past decades, and as a U.S. management style has caught on all over the world, many U.S. managers have come to assume that the American business model is the accepted model worldwide. However, this is not the case, and ethnocentric attitudes have reduced managers' ability to assess and to react to the complexities of local environments. In fact, both ethnocentrism and the self-reference criterion impede the ability to properly assess foreign markets.

1-5c Government Barriers

National governments, especially governments in low-and middle-income countries, keep a tight control over foreign investment. They scrutinize international marketers attempting to enter the market, permitting or denying access to international firms based on criteria that are deemed important for national industry and/or security considerations.

Astrid Gast/shutterstock.com

Among formal methods used by national governments to restrict or impede entrance of international firms in the local market are tariffs and other barriers such as import quotas. Barriers may be imposed by restrictions in import license awards, by instituting foreign exchange restrictions, and by requiring a large percentage of local content for imported products, among others. Governments may decide to devalue the currency, change commercial laws, or radically change commercial regulations.

Member countries of the World Trade Organization or countries that are participants in regional economic and political integration agreements such as the North American Free Trade Agreement (NAFTA) and the European Union (EU), find it difficult to use tariffs as a means of restricting international expansion of companies in the countries' territories. Increasingly, they are using non-tariff barriers, such as cumbersome procedures for import paperwork processing, delays in granting licenses, or preference given to local service providers and product manufacturing for all contracting work.

1-5d International Competition

Although competition can be a driver of internationalization, competitors can also erect barriers to new entrants in a market. Competitors' arsenals of barriers include the following: blocking channels of distribution, binding retailers into exclusive agreements, slashing prices temporarily to prevent product adoption, or engaging in an advertising blitz that could hurt a company's initial sales in a market and cause it to retrench. With heavy competition from new and lesser-known brands in Asia, Central and Eastern Europe, and North Africa and the Middle East, Marlboro created a strong defensive strategy for its cigarettes: It slashed prices by as much as a third and advertised heavily anywhere it was legal to do so, especially on billboards in the center of different capital cities and towns in the provinces.

As an example, sales of Marlboro in southeastern Europe were hurt by various local competitors and, in particular, by a successful regional brand, Assos, from Greece. Assos was rapidly gaining a leading position in a number of markets in the region when Marlboro went on the offensive with advertising blitzes and competitive prices, limiting Assos' market share to a point where the company was forced to abandon many of its markets. Ultimately, Philip Morris, the owner of Marlboro, purchased this valiant competitor.

Summary

Define international marketing and identify the different levels of international involvement. Firms can elect to engage in different levels of international expansion. Domestic firms focus on the domestic market and ignore international possibilities. At the next level, firms can export their products overseas, taking advantage of international opportunities to increase their sales and profits. Firms involved in international marketing are serving international consumers and are present in different countries (but do not coordinate between-country activities under a regional office or subsidiary) with sales offices, subsidiaries, or in partnership with local or other international firms. Global marketing involves coordination of all marketing activities within a particular region or worldwide.

Describe the different company orientations and philosophies toward international marketing. Depending on the type of industry or service and depending on the extent to which they have an international focus, companies adopt different orientations and philosophies toward internationalization. Ethnocentric companies consider domestic strategies, techniques, and personnel as superior to foreign ones; these strategies then provide the framework for the companies' overseas operations, which are secondary to domestic operations. Companies with a polycentric orientation focus on different international markets without co-ordinating between international activities. Companies with a regiocentric orientation coordinate their operations regionally, whereas companies with a geocentric orientation coordinate their marketing and management policies worldwide, fully integrating their operations and targeting uniform segments worldwide with similar strategies.

Identify environmental and firm-specific drivers that direct firms toward international markets. A number of elements in the business environment direct firms to explore international opportunities. One such element is competitive pressure, creating the need to serve clients regardless of market attractiveness and preventing them from switching to the service of a competitor. Opportunities in the environment, such as rapid economic growth and opening emerging markets, regional economic and political integration, and the removal of trade barriers, improvements in the transportation and telecommunication infrastructure, and advancement in technology also prompt international firms to pursue international markets. The advent of technology and media influence, economic prosperity, and consumer travel are creating uniform segments of consumers with similar preferences that international firms could serve effectively with standardized strategies. Firms facing decreasing sales attributed to a mature home market can extend the life cycle of their products by going international — cigarette companies are in a late maturity stage in the United States but, most likely, they are in a late growth stage worldwide. During the maturity stage, as products start competing on price, companies benefit from going international to take advantage of cheaper and yet competent labor and new markets.

Identify obstacles preventing firms from engaging in successful international ventures. Obstacles to international marketing are the self-reference criterion—the conscious and unconscious reference to one's national culture and home-country norms and values, as well as to one's knowledge and experience, in the process of making decisions in the host country — and ethnocentrism, judging one's own culture as superior to other cultures. Additional obstacles can be the local and national governments of the host country, which could impose entry barriers or prevent the companies from repatriating profits. Finally, competition can pose barriers to entry, diminishing the chance of success in attractive potential target markets.

Key Terms

drivers in the business environment

domestic marketing

ethnocentric orientation

ethnocentrism

export marketing

firm-specific drivers

geocentric orientation

global marketing

international marketing

multinational marketing

obstacles to internationalization

polycentric orientation

regiocentric orientation

Discussion Questions

1. Discuss the differences between firm internationalization philosophies.

2. Try to work backward from a company's webpage and attempt to identify its internationalization philosophy. Look at the Procter & Gamble (www.pg.com) webpages describing the company's international involvement and its international product mix. What orientation do you believe this company has and why?

3. What are the drivers in the international business environment that lead a firm to engage in international operations? What are some of the firm-specific drivers leading to internationalization?

4. What is the "self-reference criterion"?

5. How can governments and competitors prevent a firm from entering a particular market?

Chapter Quiz

True/False

1. International marketing involves marketing activities that have a substantial focus on international consumers in a particular country or countries.

                                                                                        True

Rationale: International marketing is marketing with an international focus; it refers to the processes involved in the creation, production, distribution, promotion, and pricing of products, services, ideas, and experiences for international markets. Section 1-2, "Levels of International Marketing Involvement"

2. Firms involved in domestic marketing and export marketing are more likely to have an ethnocentric philosophy to internationalization.

                                                                                        True

Rationale: In general, these firms consider domestic strategies, techniques, and personnel to be superior to foreign ones. Section 1-2, "Levels of International Marketing Involvement"

3. Nontariff barriers have been successful in restricting the international expansion of companies.

                                                                                        True

Rationale: Various nontariff barriers can impede internationalization by increasing the cost of foreign products. Section 1-5b, "Government Barriers"

4. A regiocentric orientation calls for companies to focus on distinct markets and create country-specific marketing strategies.

                                                                                        False

Rationale: A regiocentric orientation involves creating programs for a world region with socio-cultural, political, or economic similarities. Section 1-3c, "Regiocentric Orientation"

5. Reducing the cost of labor is a basic business-environment driver.

False

Rationale: Reducing the cost of labor is a firm-specific driver.
Section 1-4b, "Firm-Specific Driver"

Multiple Choice

1. International marketing obstacles include all the following EXCEPT
     a. the self-reference criterion
     b. competition
     c. new product development costs
     d. government barriers

Answer c is correct.

Rationale: The self-reference criterion, competition, and government barriers constitute obstacles to international markets, whereas new product development costs are an incentive to go international. Section 1-5, "Obstacles to Internationalization"

2. Similarities of teenagers in the United States, France, and Malaysia create opportunities for international firms. Their similarity is in fact a business-environment driver called
     a. economic growth
     b. competition
     c. converging consumer needs
     d. regional economic and political integration

Answer c is correct.

Rationale: Teenagers in the United States belong to the broad global teenager segment, a market segment that shares many similar brand preferences. Section 1-4a, "Drivers in the Business Environment"

3. Ford Focus automobiles look identical in each market and appear to have a similar marketing mix. Which internationalization philosophy best describes the Ford Focus strategy?
     a. Geocentric orientation
     b. Ethnocentric orientation
     c. Polycentric orientation
     d. Regiocentric orientation

Answer a is correct.

Rationale: Ford Focus automobiles look identical in each market and appear to have a similar marketing mix. Section 1-3b, "Polycentric Orientation"

4. CNN is known by businesspeople around the world mainly due to this driver.
     a. Standardization
     b. Competition
     c. Technology
     d. Economic growth

Answer c is correct.

Rationale: Programming from the United States has penetrated most international markets. Technology makes it possible for CNN to broadcast its programs in key world markets. Section 1-4a, "Drivers in the Business Environment"

5. The self-reference criterion is an obstacle to
     a. government barriers

b. internationalization
c. a polycentric orientation
d. standardization

Answer b is correct.

Rationale: The self-reference criterion is individuals' reference to their own national culture and to home-country norms and values, as well as their knowledge and experience, in the process of making decisions in the host country, and it could potentially prevent individuals from adapting to the local environment and from serving well the needs of local clients. Section 1-5a, "Self-Reference Criterion"

Notes

1.*Fortune Magazine*, "Avon Ladies May Be Going the Way of the Dodo," April 14, 2015, http://fortune.com/2015/04/14/avon-battle-for-future, accessed on May 29, 2015.

2.*Fortune Magazine, 2017 Fortune Global 500*, accessed at http://fortune.com/global500/list/ on April 21, 2018. U.S. Dept. of Commerce Office of International Trade Administration, "U.S. Export Fact Sheet" April 5, 2016, accessed at https://www.trade.gov/press/press-releases/2016/export-factsheet-040516.pdf on April 21, 2018; John McCary, "U.S. Still Luring Investors," *Wall Street Journal*, June 6, 2007, A5.

3.Howard Perlmutter, "The Tortuous Evolution of the Multinational Corporation," *Columbia Journal of World Business*, January–February 1969; Wind, Y., Douglas, P.S., Perlmutter,V.H. "Guidelines for Developing International Marketing Strategies," *Journal of Marketing*, 37, 1973, pp. 14-23. David Tanganelli, "Levels of Internationalization of Multinational Spanish Firms: The Role of the Amount of Committed Equity and the Managerial Attitudes toward Foreignness," *Harvard Deusto Business Research*, Volume 6, No. 3, 2017, pp. 164-175.

4.Thomas W. Malnight, "Globalization of an Ethnocentric Firm: An Evolutionary Perspective," *Strategic Management Journal*, Vol. 16, No. 2, February 1995, pp. 119–142. Jared S. Hopkins, "Drugmaker Eli Lilly Will Cut 3,500 jobs," *Bloomberg*, September 7, 2017, accessed at https://www.bloomberg.com/news/articles/2017-09-07/lilly-to-cut-3-500-jobs-close-sites-as-drugmaker-streamlines.

5.David J. Lemak and Wiboon Arunthanes, "Global Business Strategy: A Contingency Approach," *Multinational Business Review*, Vol. 5, No. 1, Spring 1997, pp. 26–37. Alain Verbeke, Liena Kano, and Wenlong Yuan, "Inside the regional multinationals: A new value chain perspective on subsidiary capabilities," **International Business Review**, Volume 25, Issue 3, June 2016, Pages 785-793.

6.Ibid.

7.Ibid.

8. Malnight, "Globalization of an Ethnocentric Firm," pp. 119–142.

9. Ibid.

10. Lemak and Arunthanes, "Global Business Strategy", pp. 26–37.

11. Alex Dumortier, "Why International Business Machines Corp. Isn't as Safe as You Think," *The Motley Fool*, April 28, 2015, http://www.fool.com/investing/general/2015/04/28/why-international-business-machines-corp-isnt-as-s.aspx, accessed on May 20, 2015.

12. Hillary Chura, "Brands IPG as Global Ad Strategist," *Advertising Age*, Vol. 71, No. 50, December 4, 2000, p. 50.

13. Atifa Hargrave-Silk, "Leo Burnett Takes Charge of Coca-Cola China," *Media*, January 26, 2007, 1.

14. Monllos, Kristina, "Coca-Cola Knew It Would be in the Mad Men Finale, but that's About All It Knew," *Adweek*, May 18, 2015,http://www.adweek.com/news/television/coca-cola-didnt-know-what-expect-after-agreeing-let-mad-men-use-its-iconic-ad-164835 accessed on May 29, 2015.

15. BestMediaInfo, "Coca-Cola Plays Enabler of Magic Between People and Relationships in 'Share of Coke' Ad," accessed at http://bestmediainfo.com/2018/04/coca-cola-plays-enabler-of-magic-between-people-and-relationships-in-share-a-coke-ad/ on April 8, 2018.

16. Yum China, "A World With More Yum!" accessed at http://www.yum.com/company/our-brands/china on April 19, 2018. Foley, John, "Yum! Brands China Split Short on Crispy Goodness," Reuters, May 6, 2015, http://blogs.reuters.com/ breakingviews/2015/05/06/yum-brands-china-split-short-on-crispy-goodness, accessed on May 29, 2015.

17. Diderich, Joelle, "Kazakhstan's Thriving Luxury Market Continues to Gain Steam," *WWD*, November 6, 2014, accessed at http://wwd.com/business-news/designer-luxury/kazakhstans-thriving-luxury-market-continues-to-gain-steam-8022790 on May 30, 2015.

18. Govindarajan, Vijay, "Should You Launch in Emerging Markets First?", *Harvard Business Review*, August 22, 2011, accessed at https://hbr.org/2011/08/should-you-launch-in-emerg.html on June 1, 2015.

Case 1-1: Alpaca Luxe: Marketing Opportunities
in the Emerging Market of Mongolia

In the middle of a torrid Virginia summer, Gertrude Fowler, an artist on the Eastern Shore of Virginia, is reviewing the new designs of alpaca shawls made for her newest creative venture, Alpaca Luxe. With their signature fine stripes and vibrant colors, made from famously soft alpaca fiber from alpaca farms in the region, the scarves are both striking and luxurious. Alpaca Luxe works with a leading textile mill in North Carolina to make the scarves, which had been selling reasonably well in several high-end boutiques on the East Coast and in Chicago and Denver until the downturn in the economy. Her marketing team, led by John Gordon and Susan Spier, cautioned that the company's sales strategy was probably not going to be profitable in the long term and time was ripe for an expansion.

Gertrude set up a meeting to consult with John, Susan, and other marketing experts from various marketing service providers that Alpaca Luxe uses to research its target market and to design appropriate marketing strategies. At the meeting, John Gordon suggested a westward expansion – California, to him, seemed a reasonable prospect given Californians' preference for natural products and luxury offerings. Susan, who had previously worked in international marketing for a large multinational before moving to the Eastern Shore, suggested that they investigate the possibility of expanding into international markets. International expansion made sense to Gertrude, who thought that the scarves would appeal to consumers in European design capitals, such as Helsinki, Amsterdam, and Munich.

International expansion seemed to be the consensus for most of the participants in the meeting, and John and Susan were advised to evaluate such opportunities at the state government level and by contacting international trade representatives at the Department of Commerce. John and Susan quickly learned that contacting the Virginia Economic Development Partnership (VEDP), located just two hours away, in Richmond, Virginia, was a reasonable first step in exploring international expansion. Most states in the United States have similar organizations, whose charge is to aid companies in the state to explore international opportunities by identifying potential new markets, developing market entry strategies and locating possible distributors and representatives for products or services, at a very low cost to the exporter.

Approaching the Government

The meeting with the VEDP director produced mixed results. The Alpaca Luxe team described their offering in detail, emphasizing the luxury aspect of the scarves and their distinctiveness. The director offered specific insights into several European markets, which appeared to be saturated with well-known luxury brands and alpaca wool products from Bolivia and other countries in Central and South America. Yes, Europeans responded well to design appeals and Gertrude's designs were certainly appealing. But Alpaca Luxe would be attempting to penetrate saturated markets, where consumer preferences were entrenched and where the new successful market entrants appealing to the luxury segment were primarily young designers with an attitude.

By chance, at the VEDP offices, the Alpaca Luxe team met a visiting delegation from the Mongolian Ministry of Commerce on a trade mission to promote Mongolia as a travel destination and to identify U.S. businesses interested in purchasing high-quality Mongolian-sourced and processed cashmere. John and Susan initially qualified them as competitors, but, upon further discussions, they were intrigued. The luxury market in Mongolia was on the upswing and many of the leading brands had successfully entered the Mongolian market, achieving substantial market share and reaping high profits as first movers into the market. Mongolians, according to the team, appreciate European and U.S. brands, but, comparatively, there are many more European designers than designers from the United States present in Ulan Bator, the capital. True, Mongolians produce the finest quality cashmere, but Mongolian consumers would undoubtedly be interested in unique offerings, such as alpaca. Moreover, Mongolians are interested in unique designs, and the trade mission visitors deemed Gertrude Fowler's design and bright colors as particularly appealing to the Mongolian consumer.

Before consulting with Gertrude, they decided to work with the marketing analysts at VDEP to probe further into expansion opportunities in Mongolia – they knew very little about the country and they had doubts that the market could sustain many luxury brands. However, the analysts provided interesting insights.

The Mongolian Market

After more than 200 years of oppressive Chinese rule, another 70 years as a Soviet satellite, which banned any reference to the proud history of Genghis Khan and his empire – the largest contiguous empire in history – Mongolia is ready to enter the world stage as a mineral-rich country taking huge leaps in its transition to a market economy.

According to *The Wall Street Journal*, Mongolia has immense reserves of coal, copper, gold, gas, and uranium – and an ongoing exploration of oil; Mongolia's current GDP of $7 billion a year had a yearly growth of a minimum of 20 percent in 2012, with the economy doubling every three to five years. On the other hand, it only has a population of 2.8 million, half of them living in Ulan Bator, while, in the rest of the country, many are nomads, living in yurts (ger, in Mongolian), and barely getting by. The capital is besieged by hundreds of thousands of people who are practically destitute, having lost all their cattle after a recent harsh winter. Mongolia also rates high on the Transparency International Corruption Perception Index, with Mongolians considering corruption to be one of the government's most serious problems.

Mongolia's market for luxury brands is thriving. In Ulan Bator's main square, Sukhbaatar Square, where once a bronze statue of Lenin reigned, there is an influx of luxury brands — Louis Vuitton, Armani, Zegna, Hugo Boss, Burberry, and others — elegantly displayed in the stores' lavish showrooms. And the luxury Mongolian consumer segment is responding enthusiastically. According to *The Wall Street Journal*, "Culturally, Mongolians like to show off. Mongolians are very proud of themselves—there is only one me. They think they deserve exclusivity."

Mongolia's primary luxury product is the best cashmere in the world; however, domestic producers are gradually put out of business, as the government levies high taxes on them, but does not tax Chinese exporters, who buy large quantities of raw wool directly from herders, offering higher prices. The Chinese are also believed to mix the cashmere with wool, silk, or cotton, whereas Mongolian cashmere is pure and retains its cachet of a quality and exclusive product.

The Export Decision

John and Susan approached Gertrude and described to her at length their findings regarding the limitations of the European market and informed her about the insights obtained from the Mongolian Ministry of Commerce trade mission. Gertrude jumped at the idea of taking her beautiful scarves to Mongolia. She thought that the bright orange, fuschia, and purple designs would resonate well in Mongolia, with colors similar to those of traditional costumes. Plus, it would be a great opportunity for her to travel to Mongolia. She had been in Tibet the previous year and found it fascinating. Although culturally very different, Mongolia would have a similar appeal, a sort of "last frontier" of authenticity, a country that is not cluttered with tourists and Western merchandise.

Gertrude was in favor of exploring the different types of distributors who could place the scarves on the luxury retailers' shelves. In fact, she herself might approach businesses in Sukhbaatar Square and persuade them to carry her scarves. She has had much success with a hands-on approach to marketing her Alpaca Luxe brand. She could try it in Mongolia.

Sources: Adapted from Maureen Orth, "The Luxury Frontier," *The Wall Street Journal*, http://online.wsj.com/article/SB10001424052702304186404576388153101917860.html, June 24, 2011; Virginia Exports: Virginia Economic Development Partnership, http://www.exportvirginia.org, accessed on April 14, 2018; company and characters are fictional.

Analysis Suggestions

1. What are the environmental and firm-specific drivers that are driving Alpaca Luxe to explore international markets?

2. Many companies use opportunistic approaches to internationalization – executives in charge of international expansion may have visited a particular country and felt that the company's products would do well. Or they might have friends who reside in the respective country who could potentially help them do business there. Aside from personal interests or connections, what are some of the drivers of internationalization that have prompted Alpaca Luxe to consider the Mongolian market for its international expansion?

Case 1-2: Zhang National Steel Company

Liu Hong, Director of International Accounts at the Zhang National Steel Company, has just been summoned by the company's chairman. He is expected to provide viable solutions for the company that will enable it to compete effectively in an increasingly saturated international steel market. China's steel production has been growing at breakneck pace in the past decade. Its rapid growth is posing serious threats to the industry, and Zhang National, one of the larger privatized steel companies, is part of the problem.

When Mao Zedong ordered an increase in the steel production as part of the Great Leap Forward, people left their fields, abandoned their work in agriculture, and fled to the large steel mills that produced millions of tons of useless substandard steel. Today, an enterprising China is taking another great leap, investing in industrial establishments, especially in the steel industry. The old, large steel mills have been privatized, becoming more efficient and producing high-quality steel, and investors are keen on banking on new and profitable steel mills.

According to industry reports, China produced 822.7 million metric tons of crude steel in 2014, a huge increase from 101.2 million metric tons produced in 1996, when it became the largest steel-producing country in the world for the first time. Today, China accounts for almost 34 percent of the world's steel production. Adding to Zhang National Steel Company's woes, the Chinese government started imposing duties of 5 to 10 percent in 2007 on exports of more than 80 Chinese-made steel products, as well as other products containing steel, to trim its trade surplus.

Under these circumstances, Zhang National Steel Company would eventually have to cut its workforce by two-thirds. Such a move would displace many workers and their dependent families and could very likely lead to political unrest in the region, as elsewhere in China. In fact, China's State Council, its cabinet, is starting to discourage investment in new steel mills by making such investments less attractive for investors. However, such efforts at the national level are countered by local officials whose goals are to increase local job opportunities and taxes. Locally, there is a strong push for establishing new steel mills, with local governments offering incentives for such investments.

Liu Hong gazed at the steel mill's dock on the Yangtze River. Many of China's steel mills are located on the banks of this river. River access facilitates barge access of ore imports, and the Yangtze is a magnet for competitors.

The steel Zhang National produces is used primarily to meet domestic demand and feed the building boom in China's large cities. Cement-and-steel structures line the large avenues in Shanghai's Pudong district, and along many of Beijing's boulevards, massive structures line up against the hazy sky (see Figure 1-8).

However, China's economy has experienced a slow-down, and after the 2008 Olympics and the 2010 World Fair, there is not as much incentive for the national government to push construction to showcase the new China to the world. The private investors in Zhang National Steel Company are starting to ask questions about the viability of the company in the near future.

In 2018, the United States, in a move directed primarily at Chinese steel, imposed 25 percent tariffs on steel. At first, it appeared that Chinese companies could bypass the tariffs by using transshipments. The Chinese company Settle Logistics, for example, advertised on its website: "For those unfair trade barriers targeting our industries from certain countries, we can adopt other approaches to bypass those trade tariffs in order to expand markets." Settle Logistics would send the steel shipments to the U.S. via Malaysia, with paperwork that certifies that the steel originated in Malaysia. Such tariff-dodging strategies were thwarted when the U.S. granted only select exemptions to the tariffs to countries that accurately certify product origin.

Even though the United States and the European Union are raising barriers to trade with China, Chinese steel will continue to remain more affordable than locally produced steel. Moreover, India's steel consumption is rapidly increasing, and with large revenues from outsourcing, India has the hard currency to purchase this commodity to meet local demand.

Liu Hong realizes that he must present a balanced perspective on going international. The challenge is convincing the chairman and the investors that going international is essential for Zhang National Steel Company.

1-8 Steel and cement dominate Beijing's landscape.

Sources: Adapted from Brooke Ringel, "China to Encourage Even More Steel Exports," *Trade and Manufacturing Monitor*, December 20, 2017, accessed at https://www.ustrademonitor.com/2017/12/china-to-encourage-even-more-steel-exports on April 14, 2018. Trefis Team, "The Extent of Overproduction In The Chinese Steel Industry," *Forbes*, January 9, 2017, accessed at https://www.forbes.com/sites/greatspeculations/2017/01/09/the-extent-of-overproduction-in-the-chinese-steel-industry/#4241f502446e on April 14, 2018. Keith Bradsher, "Tariff Dodgers Stand to Profit Off U.S.-China Trade Dispute," *The New York Times*, April 22, 2018, accessed at https://www.nytimes.com/2018/04/22/business/china-trade-tariffs-transshipment.html on April 25, 2018.

Analysis Suggestions

1. What arguments should Liu Hong offer the company chairman in favor of internationalization? What are the business environment internationalization drivers and the firm drivers that are likely to lead to the internationalization of the firm?

2. What product life-cycle stage is the steel industry in worldwide? Should Zhang National Steel Company move its labor force overseas to China's neighboring countries? Why? Why not?

Part 2

The **International Marketing** Environment

Chapter 2

An Overview of the

International Marketing Environment

After studying
this chapter,
you should be able to:

- Provide an overview of the world economic environment and examine different perspectives on economic development.

- Address differences between countries of different levels of economic development and discuss the importance of emerging markets.

- Examine the indicators of political risk and address the approaches of international firms to political risk management.

- Describe how international law, home-country law, and host-country law affect international firm operations and address issues related to jurisdiction.

- Discuss different legal systems, intellectual property laws, and national laws with extra-territorial impact that affect international firms.

- Examine the natural and techno-logical environments and the potential and limitations they present to international firms.

Chapter Outline

Kigali

Kigali is a city of contrasts: Internet cafés, poverty, a luxurious German bakery-cum-grocery-cum-ice-cream store, persons with HIV estimated to constitute 50 percent of the local population, sporty foreigners, even better-dressed locals, and dust. The city center is busy with shops selling masks, nesting baskets, and trinkets to tourists, with many bars that stay open late, restaurants, and world-

FCG/shutterstock.com

class hotels. Blue-hued Primus beer posters and red Coca-Cola billboards have replaced colorful cigarette ads previously plastered all over the city and framing the main road to the airport. Multinationals are vying for what might become a prosperous emerging market one day, as it was in the 1980s. The present and the future are topics of discussion. Bringing up the past is not appropriate, as indicated in tourist guidebooks and security briefings for nongovernmental organization staff.

Kigali is the capital city of Rwanda, where eleven million people are jammed into a country smaller than Maryland, making it one of the world's most densely settled agrarian societies. In many places, nearly every patch of reddish earth is cultivated in a patchwork of fields that stretch up, and often over, Rwanda's countless hills. Just over a decade ago, Rwanda was the home of a 100-day ethnic slaughter in which most of the 800,000 victims were hacked to death with machetes or beaten to death with clubs. The Belgian colonists favored the Tutsi minority and used them to run the country, creating antagonism between the Hutu majority tribe and the Tutsis. Most of the killings happened as ethnic Hutu militias rampaged through steep hillside villages in search of Tutsis and those who sought to defend them.[1]

History repeats itself, and the Tutsis are in charge again. Several Hutus were tried for their crimes. But unlike in the past, identity cards no longer list ethnic group information. Side by side, at the Nyabugogo market, Tutsis and Hutus sell clothing under the metal roofs, peddle their goods in the streets, and travel crowded in the matatus—open trucks that allow people to travel standing, as they weave from hill to hill. The heart of commerce in this land-locked country is bustling Kigali. But is this city—is the country—truly ready for business again?

Countries where multiple tribes or factions have coexisted for decades without any conflict, where the president and his army have led effectively, spreading the wealth to the population and attracting direct foreign investment, can still fall victim to civil war, as in the case of Rwanda. When conflict breaks out, multinational firms promptly ship their expatriates to safety, but leave their assets open to plundering. This scenario is played out over and over in the world: Multinational companies in Chad, Rwanda, Burundi, the Congo, Sierra Leone, Haiti, Bosnia and Herzegovina, and Croatia have repeatedly experienced losses. Multinational companies are also victims of corporate terrorism, which is on the increase worldwide. The volatile political environment all over the world poses many challenges to businesses.

The legal environment can be problematic as well. Some companies operate in environments where everything is forbidden unless expressly allowed. Other companies operate in environments where everything is perceived as allowed unless expressly forbidden. Companies operating in legally ambiguous environments face ethical and legal challenges from host-country national governments, and the home-country government. They must address these challenges effectively to be able to survive.

The natural environment of international marketing also poses challenges to businesses: Geology and the shortage of natural resources, coupled with a high population growth, can negatively affect market potential. Similarly, topography can impede access to the market, and hydrology and climate can affect economic development. The shortage of natural resources, the energy crisis, and the environmental quality crisis have a strong impact on the business environment.

The technological environment of international marketing is rapidly opening access to international markets never before accessible to multinationals, bringing profits to small and medium enterprises (SMEs) that have never had such a broad exposure and access to international markets. The technological environment is also speeding the new-product development process and creating unprecedented distribution potential in industry.

This chapter focuses on elements in the environment of international marketing. We examine the effect of economic, political, legal, natural, and technological environments on the international marketing operations of firms.

2-1 The Economic Environment of International Marketing

2-1a The World Economy

It was common in the past to hear that, when the United States sneezed, the rest of the world would catch a cold. This remains true today, to a certain extent: When the United States experiences a downturn in the economy, reverberations echo throughout the world. However, many other economies are just as influential. Starting in 2012, the Greek debt crisis sent the Dow Jones tumbling, and the 2015 referendum on debt restructuring created fears that the European Union

Ivan Marc/shutterstock.com

would unravel, with the euro plunging relative to the dollar. In 2014, the Crimean Crisis involving the Russian annexation of Crimea and Sevastopol led the European Union and the United States to impose severe sanctions on Russia. At the G7 Summit in southern Germany in June 2015 additional sanctions were imposed, creating a severe economic crisis in Russia. However, the sanctions imposed also created an economic downturn in Europe, a key Russian trading partner. For example, the sanctions froze billions of dollars of defense contracts with European countries and impeded financial and energy investments. The additional sanctions imposed by the European Union and the United States in 2018, in response to Russia's malicious cyber activities around the globe, have greatly delayed manufacturing of goods by European and Australian firms using Russian-made aluminum, negatively affecting a number of industries.

Countries are becoming more and more connected by trade, capital markets, the flow of technology and information across national borders, and psychology. Rather than rising and falling separately, national economies increasingly respond to the same forces. Interdependence of countries' economies, due to increased cross-border flows of products, services, and capital has become the leading principle of globalization. [2]

Angel Soler Gollonet/shutterstock.com

However, just as political crises and sanctions can have major effects on the world economy, so can changes in trade agreements. In 2018, the United States made a major turn to re-examine international trade agreements, notably the North American Free Trade Agreement (NAFTA) with Canada and Mexico. In the same year, the United States imposed new tariffs on imports of steel and aluminum. Prompted by a populist political agenda, the changes in NAFTA and the new tariffs were met by retaliatory tariffs from other nations, notably China, on U.S. exports of agricultural products, aircraft, etc. Some argue that the era of globalization and economic interdependence may soon be weakened by efforts of more and more nations to reduce international trade.

The rise in value of one currency and fall of another have repercussions. In the past, a weak dollar benefitted U.S. businesses, and, implicitly, workers in the United States. A weak dollar made American goods and services more competitive in foreign markets, kept jobs at home, and decreased the trade deficit. However, if the dollar had continued to fall, it could have had adverse implications for foreign economies: Germany, for example, suffered when the euro continued to appreciate relative to the dollar, slowing down demand for German-made goods.[3] The Greek debt crisis, however, tilted the balance in the opposite direction, with a weakening euro that almost regained its parity with the dollar, temporarily. A strong dollar meant that consumers in the United States could afford European goods that previously were beyond their reach; instead of buying American goods, consumers in the U.S. purchased European automobiles and electronics, flocked to European luxury goods, and opted for vacations in the increasingly affordable European destinations. Changes in currency values can and do take on political overtones. For example, the United States has alleged for years that China was keeping the value of the yuan artificially low in order to stimulate exports from China. Since 2017, however, the yuan has increased in value, and the Chinese government has resisted the temptation of manipulating the currency.

In other examples, an excess of steel in the world markets, attributed to overproduction in Russia and China, led to restructuring of the industry elsewhere in the world, leaving only a few players in the world steel oligopoly. And the decrease in the U.S. corporate tax rate in January, 2018, from 35 percent to 21 percent created an optimistic outlook with reverberations worldwide. The international economy has indeed become one single unit. Major companies, as well as SMEs, simply cannot afford to limit themselves to a local, home-country focus. For example, the U.S. Chamber of Commerce regularly points out that 95 percent of the world's consumers live outside the United States.[4] The market share game is played on a world scale. The one-world commercial future is becoming a reality in which large multinationals rule. The top 100 companies in the world control more than 20 percent of foreign assets, employ six million workers, and account for as much as seven percent of total world economic activity. Multinational companies account for two-thirds of world trade, and many have economic weight. More than half of the 100 largest economies in the world are now corporations, not nations. Mitsubishi is bigger than Indonesia, Ford is bigger than Turkey and Wal-Mart is bigger than Israel; as a result, multinationals are able to break down barriers that have withstood armies, missionaries, crusaders, and politicians.[5]

2-1b The Economic Development Disparity

In the current economic environment, firms from high-income, industrialized countries and their representative governments dominate the world economy, allocating resources worldwide based on market potential, rather than based on local population needs, creating a growing wealth gap between the high- and low-income countries. Low-income countries, on the other hand, control resources (raw materials, labor) that multinationals need, and access to local consumers; they sometimes pose barriers to international business operations. Globalization has enabled millions of people in developing countries to increase their standard of living. However, in developed countries, such as the United States, globalization has resulted in the loss of many manufacturing jobs to developing countries, with a considerable impact on the U.S. economy and national elections. Businesses operating in this complex environment should understand the dynamics present in countries of different levels of economic and market development and the antecedents and consequences of those dynamics.

wong yu liang/shutterstock.com

2-2 Perspectives on Economic Development

Two models of economic development have gained acceptance in the world: a Western model, best articulated by Rostow, and the Marxist-Leninist/Maoist development model, which still constitutes a dominant development philosophy in many world markets. While the fall of communism in Europe and Asia has reduced considerably the areas dominated by the Marxist-Leninist/Maoist philosophy of economic development, prominent leaders in high-, middle-, and low-income countries alike continue to endorse this economic development model.

2-2a The Rostow Modernization Model

According to the Rostow modernization model,[6] each stage is a function of productivity, economic exchange, technological improvements, and income. Economic growth requires advancing from one stage to another. The modernization stages are:

- Traditional society
- Transitional society
- Take-off
- The drive to maturity
- High mass consumption

Traditional Society

Countries in the traditional society stage are characterized by an economic structure that is dominated by agriculture. Minimal productivity occurs, and only a few exchange transactions take place. Economic change and technological improvements are not sufficient to sustain any growth in per-capita output, which is low.

Transitional Society (Preconditions for Take-Off)

The transitional society stage is characterized by increased productivity in agriculture, and the emergence of modern manufacturing. In manufacturing, low productivity remains the norm. The pre-

Nuamfollo/shutterstock.com

conditions for take-off are the following: Society engages in secular education, establishes banks and currency, has an emerging entrepreneurial class, and the concept of manufacturing emerges, with only few sectors developing at first. Overall, there is limited production and limited output. Assuming these preconditions are met, take-off is likely in 10 to 50 years.

Take-Off

During take-off, growth becomes the norm and improvements in production lead to the emergence of leading sectors. Income rises across the board, and a new class of established entrepreneurs emerges.

The Drive to Maturity

In the drive-to-maturity stage, modern technology is fully adopted in all economic activity, and new leading sectors emerge. The economy demonstrates the technological and entrepreneurial skill to produce the products it needs. The economy looks beyond the country's borders for development, and companies begin to seek out new market opportunities in less developed countries.

High Mass Consumption

In the age of high mass consumption, leading sectors shift toward durable goods. A surge occurs in per-capita income and increased allocation to social welfare programs. The masses can afford goods beyond food, clothing, and shelter.

2-2b Alternative Models of Economic Development: The Marxist-Leninist/ Maoist Model

The Rostow model of economic development is, in fact, a Western model of development. Alternative models of economic development exist, however. One competing economic development model is the Marxist-Leninist/Maoist model. It has been embraced by intellectuals in low- and middle-income countries fending off domination by capital from high-income countries This model endorses a collective orientation, one adopted by the more traditional developing countries, and competes with market-oriented capitalism, advocating anticolonial and anti-imperialist sentiments.[7] Socialist ideas of sharing wealth, leveling inequality, eliminating homelessness, and providing basic needs such as health care, food, education, and shelter to all citizens appeal to many in the poor, developing countries that were long suppressed and exploited by colonial and imperialist powers. At the heart of this philosophy are issues of equitable distribution of income, improvement in the welfare of the masses, and economic justice.[8]

Spiroview Inc/shutterstock.com

The Marxist-Leninist/Maoist model and its dialectic materialism theories approach economic development philosophy similarly to the Rostow model in the first stage. The subsequent stages are depicted as a class struggle ending in revolution, which is needed for advancement to the next stage. Advancement is a function of the control of means of production, production outcomes, resource allocation, and the development of a mindset devoid of materialist needs. The stages of this model are described next.

The Primitive Society

The primitive society stage is similar to Rostow's traditional society. There is joint, tribal ownership of the means of production, which are minimal, primitive, and centered on very basic agricultural tasks, for the benefit of all the members of the tribe. Much of the agriculture is slash-and-burn, with the tribes moving in the quest for new fertile land. All tribal members in this egalitarian society work for the common welfare of the tribe.

The Slavery-Based Society

The slavery-based society emerges as a result of tribes taking over other tribes and enslaving their populations. Slaves are now property of the conquering tribe. Under Roman, Mesopotamian, and Egyptian rule, slaves toiled in agriculture and built infrastructures, such as access roads and irrigation systems. Tribal territory ownership is considered as a first step toward establishing private property. Trading agricultural goods and tools between tribes becomes common.

Feudalism

Under feudalism, feudal lords own armies, land, and the dwellers of the land. Land is primarily in the hands of the feudal family; production is still primarily agricultural. Guilds emerge as a production unit, manufacturing goods and training future manufacturers under apprenticeships. Trading is common and widespread, and exchange is now primarily based on gold as currency.

The Capitalist Society

The capitalist society is represented by two stages. The first stage is characterized by an emerging bourgeoisie (developed from the guild class) as a ruling class alongside the aristocracy (the former feudal family). The bourgeoisie creates lucrative means of production, and it achieves high productivity at the expense of exploited workers. Production shifts gradually from the agrarian sector to the industrial sector.

Senderistas/shutterstock.com

The second stage of capitalism is multinational imperialism. Imperialist capitalism is characterized by a capital that loses its national identity by crossing borders; in fact, the export of capital — international trade — is a central mechanism of imperialism. The international firm is a double parasite exploiting its own working class, as well as workers in low-income countries. Multinational firms represent the modality for national domination of developing countries and for the domination and subjugation of workers and peasants worldwide. The creation of international monopolies (monopolistic capitalism) represents the most advanced stage of capitalist dominance.

The Socialist Society

The socialist society is also composed of two stages. The first, transitional stage, leads to the gradual disappearance of private property, which is replaced by collective, state property. Countries in this stage typically are formally known as People's Republics—as in People's Republic of China. China's ideological elite argues that this stage can take, potentially, hundreds of years, but, at the very least, a hundred years. During this time, capitalist structures

BartlomiejMagierowski/shutterstock.com

coexist with state-owned enterprises, leading to rapid economic development. In this way, China reconciles its communist ideology and aspirations with the capitalist enterprise that fuels China's double-digit economic growth.

Socialism in the more advanced (in the direction of communism) socialist republics is characterized by state ownership of practically all the means of production. The state also controls the modes of production, allocating resources to industry, agriculture, education, and health care on the basis of societal needs. In this stage of development, the state has in place most mechanisms necessary for the transition to communism. Remnants of capitalism can co-exist with socialism. Examples include small businesses, such as home-garden cultivation and sale of produce, jewelry repair, and so on. Private property limited to one's personal home or personal automobile. In this stage, individuals continue to express and manifest some level of desire for material possessions.

The Communist Society

Although in the United States, we refer to China and North Korea as "communist," no country has ever reached communism. Under communism, all means of production and private property are under state ownership or cooperative ownership. The state is in charge of allocation of resources to sectors as needed and to individuals (goods and services) according to their needs. Communism develops "the new man," who views work as a personal need that must be satisfied, and who will work according to his or her ability. According to Marx, Engels, Lenin, and Mao, individuals cease to desire to own private property; they are no longer materialistic under communism.

Lenin argued that, during the early stages of communism, foreign capital is important in the development process as a source of advanced technology. His solution was a leasing system whereby foreign firms would participate in particular projects and regions in communist countries for a limited amount of time.[9] In practice, this concept was countered by the situation created by the Cold War and by Stalin's theory of two parallel markets (capitalist and socialist), which stressed internal integration among socialist countries for mutual economic development. According to this theory, capitalist markets were inherently weak, and socialist countries needed to fully isolate themselves from the capitalist world.[10]

The Rostow and Marxist-Leninist models are comparable, up to a point. In Figure 2-1, the models work in parallel up to the level of the drive-to-maturity stage in the Rostow model and the capitalist stage in the Marxist-Leninist model.

Figure 2-1: A Comparison of the Rostow Modernization Model and the Marxist-Leninist Model

2-3 Levels of Economic Development

There are many competing classifications of countries from an economic development perspective. Historically, the informal and frequently used classification in the Western world has referred to highly industrialized, developed countries as the First World, to socialist countries as the Second World, and to developing countries as the Third World. Of this classification, only the term "Third World" has been used widely, and it is still being used, but only rarely. Another classification, advanced by the United Nations (www.un.org), provides for three groups: LLDCs (least-developed countries and the lowest-income countries); LDCs (less-developed countries and lower-income countries); and developed countries (DCs). Yet other classifications exist. For example, the term NIC (newly industrialized country) was initially used to describe the economies of Taiwan, Singapore, South Korea, and

Hong Kong (known in the 1980s and 1990s as the "Asian Tigers"), whereas countries such as Brazil, Argentina, Chile, Peru, and the transitional economies of Central and Eastern Europe are described as emerging markets. In this textbook, we will refer to three categories of countries, based on the classification used by the World Bank (www.worldbank.org):

• **High-income Countries.** These are highly industrialized countries with well-developed industrial and service sectors. In this category fall newly industrialized countries, as well as countries that have had a developed status for many years. Countries in this category are Canada, the United States, Japan, most of the countries in Western Europe, but also the Russian Federation belongs to this category.

Although these countries present great potential because they have consumers with the highest per-capita income, they also present challenges to international firms because their markets are in the maturity stage, consumers have established preferences, and competition is intense. The World Bank refers to the countries in this category as high-income countries, with a Gross National Income (GNI) per capita in 2018 of US$12,236 or more. GNI is an indicator of income developed by the World Bank that is the dollar value of the country's yearly income divided by its population – that is, the average income of the citizens.

Simon Mayer/shutterstock.com

• **Middle-income Countries** (countries with emerging markets in the previous classification). Among the countries in this category are countries in Latin America, such as Argentina, Brazil, Uruguay, Paraguay, Peru, and Bolivia, to name a few; countries in Asia, such as China, with its immense market and a substantial middle class; and the transition economies of Central and Eastern Europe, which are rapidly privatizing state-owned industries and adopting market reforms. Important in this category are big emerging markets (BEMs), the largest emerging markets, which present the greatest potential for international trade and expansion. The World Bank refers to the countries in this category as middle-income countries, with a GNI per capita of US$1,046 to US$12,236. The middle-income country category is further divided into two income groups as follows:

◊ **Upper middle income countries.** These countries have rapidly developing economies, and especially in urban areas, they have an infrastructure that is on par with that of developed countries. Among them are countries in Latin America such as Panama, Argentina, Mexico, Brazil, Dominican Republic, Costa Rica, and the Andean trio of Argentina, Ecuador, and Peru. In this category are the transition economies of Central and Eastern Europe, new European Union member countries that have rapidly privatized state-owned industries and adopted market reforms, such as Bulgaria and Romania. According to the World Bank, countries considered upper middle income countries have a GNI per capita of US$3, 956 to US$12,235.

◊ **Lower middle income countries.** This is a diverse group of countries that includes China, much of North Africa and the Middle East, and many of the former Soviet Socialist Republics, such as Armenia, Georgia, Moldova, Tajikistan, Uzbekistan, and

Ukraine. Also included in the list from Latin America would be Bolivia, and the Central American countries of El Salvador, Honduras, Nicaragua, and Guatemala. According to the World Bank, countries in this category have a GNI per capita of US$1,006 to US$3,955.

- Low-income countries (developing countries, in the previous classification). Countries in this category are primarily agrarian, have low per-capita income levels, and are located in different regions in Asia, such as Nepal and Cambodia, and in sub-Saharan Africa, such as the Democratic Republic of Congo, Somalia, Sierra Leone, and Haiti. Many low-income countries are often neglected or underserved by large multinationals and consequently present great potential as niche markets. And yet, even the countries with the lowest per-capita income have a stratum of society that can afford even the most expensive global brands. Furthermore, because they are the primary recipients of international development aid, they present important opportunities for firms operating in the areas of infrastructure development and industrial sector development and for related consultancies.

The World Bank refers to the countries in this category as low-income countries, with a GNI per capita of less than US$1,005. It is important to note that these markets are grossly underserved by the international community and that consumer needs—even the most basic ones—in these markets are barely met by local administration. Illustration 2-1 (next page) addresses challenges faced by consumers in low-income countries.

The differences between the countries in the three categories—high-income, middle-income, and low-income —is evident: With regard to the GNP distribution worldwide, high-income, highly industrialized countries account for close to 80 percent of the world's gross national product, whereas they account for less than 15 percent of the population.

To illustrate, the United Nations Development Program monitors human development worldwide and publishes its findings in the Human Development Report. The report compares countries based on life expectancy, schooling, per-capita income, etc. Table 2-1 compares countries in the low-human-development category on those dimensions.

Table 2-1 An Illustration of Human Development in Select Low-Income Countries

HDI rank	Countries	Human Development Index (HDI)	Life expectancy at birth	Expected Years of Schooling	Gross National Income (GNI) per capital (U.S. $)
149	Syria	0.536	69.7	9.0	2,441
163	Haiti	0.493	63.1	9.1	1,657
165	Sudan	0.490	63.7	7.2	3,846
169	Afghanistan	0.479	60.7	10.1	1,871
181	Mozambique	0.418	55.5	9.1	1,098
184	Burundi	0.404	57.1	10.6	691
187	Niger	0.353	61.9	5.4	889

Source: Human Development Report, United Nations Development Programme, Human Development Statistical Tables 2015, http://hdr.undp.org/en/data, accessed on April 20, 2018.

International Marketing Illustration 2-1 Underserved Markets

In many low-income countries, children must walk miles to reach their schools. In Adaboya, Ghana, for example, children must walk three miles to attend school even though a school building is located in the village. The local school is in disrepair and cannot be used during the rainy season. An average poor child in Mali has to walk five miles to elementary school. In Portero Sula, El Salvador, villagers cannot obtain health services at the local clinic because there are no doctors or nurses on staff. In the Mutasa district of Zimbabwe, women report that they were hit by staff during delivery of their babies.

Even in markets where services are available, the quality of services and their delivery are low. Absenteeism of doctors in Bangladesh is about 74 percent. Teachers in Ethiopia are absent a large percentage of the time. Children may attend school, but there may not be any teaching activity. Plus, one billion people lack access to adequate water sources and 2.5 billion lack access to adequate sanitation.

The World Bank and the rest of the international aid community are taking forceful action to ensure that communities take concerted action to improve service delivery to these markets. For example, in El Salvador, community-managed schools, where parents are involved in their children's education and visit the school regularly, have a lower rate of absenteeism. In Bangalore, India, and in Cambodia, consumers have successfully penalized the poor delivery of services and forced local politicians and service providers to act.

For developing country consumers, priorities are highest for meeting basic needs. From a marketing perspective, however, these consumers are not a priority for most multinationals, but rather an after-thought or a niche market at best. And yet, appropriate marketing strategies for these markets can, in the long run, serve a company well. The industrialized countries of the world account for only 15 percent of the total world population, and the greatest growth potential exists in the markets that are currently underserved.

Sources: Vijay Mahajan, Marcos V. Pratini De Moraes, and Jerry Wind, "The Invisible Global Market," *Marketing Management*, Winter 2000, pp. 9, 4, 30–35; *World Development Report 2004: Making Services Work for Poor People*; World Bank Group, http:// econ.worldbank.org/wdr/wdr2004. Rasul Bailay, "Small Packets, Big Business," *Far Eastern Economic Review*, January 23, 2003, pp. 166, 3, 40–41. *The Daily Star*, "GP Users in Dhaka to Get 4G Service," February 18, 2018, accessed at https:// www.thedailystar.net/business/telecom/ grameenphone-gp-bangladesh-users-dhaka-get-fourth-generation-4g-service-15-minutes-launch-1536460 on April 30, 2018.

Anton _ Ivanov/shutterstock.com

2-3 a The Importance of Emerging Markets

Countries with emerging markets present great potential to international firms. Their attractiveness lies primarily in their rate of economic growth—seven percent per year, in the past 20 years, compared with 2.3 percent for Western Europe and North America; the following countries have been identified as prominent emerging markets by the 2018 MCSI Emerging Markets Index: [11]

- In Asia: China, India, Indonesia, Malaysia, Pakistan Philippines, South Korea, Taiwan, Thailand
- In Africa and the Middle East: Egypt, Qatar, South Africa, United Arab Emirates
- In Europe: The Czech Republic, Greece, Hungary, Poland, Russia, Turkey
- In Latin America: Brazil, Chile, Colombia, Mexico, Peru

These countries have rapidly privatized their economies and adopted the economic reforms necessary to create a stable, growing economy, and have, as a result, gained considerable wealth. For example, India, a low-income country for decades, is now a middle-income country. The Baltics — Estonia, Latvia, and Lithuania, — Poland, the Czech Republic, Slovenia, Slovakia, and the Russian Federation belonged until recently in the middle-income category; today, they are all classified as high-income countries.

Countries with emerging markets that are expected to have successful economic futures share a number of traits:[12]

- High political stability
- A sound currency
- A low level of inflation
- Privatization policies that reduce government deficit, create first-time shareholders who vote for pro-business conservative policies and diminish the power of trade unions
- Policies that facilitate repatriation of dividends and capital
- Policies that are in line with international accounting standards
- Open disclosure of directors' interests
- Policies that stress regular reporting of earnings and sales figures
- A sound and comprehensive system of corporate law
- A liquid and well-traded securities market reflecting fair prices
- A high savings rate
- Strong government support for internationalization
- A people characterized by integrity, a strong work ethic, and respect for the law

Of interest to multinationals are the big emerging markets (BEMs). These markets share all the traits of emerging markets and present the most potential because they have large populations, and, consequently, set the pace for the economy in the region. Among these countries are China and India (both with populations exceeding one billion), South Korea, Argentina, Brazil, Mexico, South Africa, Poland, and Turkey. The big emerging markets are developing rapidly and making strides toward industrialization. However, breakneck growth can be problematic, as in the case of India.

India

India's economy has been on a high-growth path in the past decade (surpassing China's), much of it attributable to its outsourcing industry serving the world's multinationals. However, rapid growth and economic development have created an overheated economy with an inflationary spiral. Food prices are quickly climbing so that the poor can barely afford it; housing prices are rising rapidly, especially in large cities; and factories are running behind in filling orders. Prices in India are rising twice as fast as in China—its rival for foreign investment and outsourcing—and considerably faster than in industrialized countries. In the fashionable neighborhoods of South Mumbai, home prices have increased by 60 percent a year in the recent years, and oil-rich investors are bidding against India's affluent business elite for these properties. A 2,000 square foot apartment with a cheap concrete floor and flimsy closets in the chic Malabar Hill neighborhood is selling for $1.5 million. Rising prices are rekindling nostalgia for the 1980s, when India was one of the most highly regulated economies.[13]

2-4 The Political Environment of International Marketing

Iran

1970: the period before the Islamic Revolution. The Iranian government focused on projects aimed at increasing industrial development and many Iranians prospered. In 1976, dissatisfied groups demonstrated against the Shah's regime. The demonstrations increased in frequency and, ultimately, resulted in the ouster of the Shah, and in challenges to Western businesses. In 1979, the government and the banking industry were paralyzed.

1979–1984. After the 1979 revolution, the new government took hostile action against foreign multinationals, arresting expatriate staff, confiscating assets. Business in general deteriorated due to the political intervention and the Iran-Iraq war.

1985. The Islamic regime consolidated and local businesses gained ground and stability.[14]

1997–2006. The European Union is Iran's largest trading partner; companies from the United States were banned from doing business with Iran. The U.S. government continued to threaten sanctions against non-U.S. companies doing business in Iran.

2007–2015. The International Atomic Energy Agency (IAEA), the U.N.'s nuclear watchdog, faulted Iran for violating nuclear agreements by intensifying its efforts to create a nuclear-fuel cycle, while diminishing the IAEA's ability to monitor its activities.[15]

2015. The United States, United Kingdom, Russia, France, China, Germany, and the European Union signed an agreement with the Islamic Republic of Iran. In exchange for lifting economic sanctions, Iran agreed to reduce its nuclear facilities. The agreement opened Iran's access to billions of dollars in oil revenue and frozen assets overseas.

2018. The United States unilaterally pulls out of the Iran nuclear deal.

Grigvovan/shutterstock.com

The preceding time line demonstrates the volatile nature of alliances. The United States enjoyed a close rapport with deposed Shah Reza Pahlavi, and U.S. businesses profited under his rule. The Islamic Revolution targeted the Shah's allies in particular: U.S. firms had all their assets confiscated, and their international executives were forced to repatriate. As a result, the United States banned the involvement of U.S. firms in Iran and threatened sanctions on foreign firms with U.S. interests if they engaged in operations in Iran. This short narrative illustrates the political uncertainties and volatility in international marketing and the legal challenges that firms face in their international operations.

Companies contemplating any international involvement must have an in-depth knowledge of the political environment in the countries where they do business. This is especially important for companies involved in foreign direct investment—companies that undertake the greatest level of risk in a foreign market. Whenever there are discussions of political risk, they typically involve the host country—the country where a company engages in business in accordance with the respective country's political and legal restrictions. It should be noted, however, that an international company

Julian Peters Photography/shutterstock.com

is also affected by political developments in its home country—the country where the parent company is headquartered. An example is the relationship between the U.S. and Cuba. Over the last twenty-five years, the U.S. commercial relationship with Cuba has reflected changing administrations in Washington. There have been occasional thaws in the relationship between the two countries, suggesting enhanced trade and investment opportunities, which have often been followed by a renewed emphasis on existing trade sanctions and embargoes.

At the basis of international law lies the concept of sovereignty. Sovereignty is defined as a country's self-determination and independence from external interference in internal affairs and complete authority over all nationals living in the country and beyond its borders (individuals and corporations). All countries in the world are sovereign, and yet all must curtail their sovereignty to coexist in the world of nations and defend their national interests. By permitting international trade and by entering into international agreements, countries limit their sovereignty. When countries perceive that international firms, governments, or organizations have infringed on their right to self-determination, they can invoke national sovereignty and take actions that erect barriers to trade or even jeopardize the presence of international companies within their borders.

Ideally, a firm crossing borders will enter an environment that is politically stable and pro-trade. But this is often not the case: A company could find that the government with which it worked hard to establish a good working relationship collapsed overnight, and its replacement could have ties with a competitor—or it could be against foreign business altogether, as was the case of Iran during the Islamic Revolution, described in the preceding paragraphs. International companies doing business in Cuba and Eastern Europe experienced a similar fate after the communist take-overs.

Similarly, the stable environment where a business has operated unfettered for decades could suddenly be at the center of a civil war that nobody had foreseen: In Rwanda, formerly known as the Switzerland of Africa for its beauty and its pro-business climate, many international businesses were forced to leave their inventory and buildings behind when the genocide began; today, the country is once again the Switzerland of Africa, welcoming business and investment to a country that is prosperous and safe. Venezuela was once a very important market for U.S. firms. However, under the Chavez and Maduro administrations, many major U.S. firms have stopped doing business in the country because of the economic and political crisis, massive devaluations of the local currency, etc. There are other examples where a protectionist measure of one government launched a series of re-taliations both by the government and by consumers: When the United States instituted measures against European protectionism by increasing duties on nonessential European exports (cheese, perfume, soap, accessories), it did not expect retaliation by Europeans against icons of U.S. business such as McDonald's and Coca-Cola. More recently, the United States has been faulted by Canada, the European Union, Australia, Brazil, Argentina, Nicara-gua, Uruguay, Guatemala, and Thailand for exceeding the agricultural subsidies limit imposed under WTO rules, through direct payments, loan deficiency payments, and other programs for products such as wheat, soybeans, corn, and sugar. With appropriate political maneuvering, however, the United States averted retaliation.[16] As discussed in previous par-agraphs, in 2018 there have been major tariffs levied between the United States and China, as well as other countries, over steel exports to the U.S.

2-4 a Evaluating Country Risks: Key Political and Economic Factors

Evaluating Political Risk

A company has several resources at its disposal to evaluate country risk: The U.S. Department of Commerce Country Commercial Guides, the World Economic Forum Annual Global Competitiveness Report, World Bank's annual country rankings on the ease of doing business, and other governmental and nongovernmental agencies' publications. These agencies provide data on country political risk that is current and regularly updated to re-flect new developments in each country around the world (see an example of country risk evaluation in Table 2-2). Some examples of useful publications providing periodic infor-mation on country risk are:

- Business periodicals such as *The Economist* and *The Wall Street Journal.*
- Commercial sources, such as Country Reports, the Economist Intelligence Unit, Ltd., Chase (particularly its guide for exporters), and AON Interactive Risk Maps. AON, for example, provides last-minute country risk ratings using a scale from 0 to 6 (see Table 2-2).

Country	Risk Score (0=No Risk, 6=Highest Risk)
Argentina	4
Brazil	3
China	3
Egypt	5
India	3
Singapore	0
Venezuela	6

Table 2-2 Country Risk Score

Political Risk Signals

A number of country risk ele-ments should be monitored on a regular basis to keep track of developments that might ultimately affect a company seeking to do business in an internation-al market. These elements are illustrat-ed in Table 2-3 (next page).

Economic Performance

A poor economic performance and forecast are likely to lead to greater levels of unrest. Of particular concern are high inflationary rates and high un-employment rates, both of which could lead to political instability. General busi-ness performance is also important. Commercial payment terms and collec-tion experience indicate the availability of hard currency reserves and access to hard currency. Currency fluctuations can be a major issue for firms seeking to develop export markets outside the home country. Default on loans is likely to be a threat to companies contemplating entrance into the market. Finally, an increase in regulatory restrictions on investment, capital, or trade flows should be closely monitored.[17]

Table 2-3 Country Risk Elements

Economic performance signal	Greece has endured years of economic austerity, and loans from the European Un-ion came with the imposition of additional austerity measures. Many Greeks have left the country in search of employment elsewhere.
Political repression signal	Russians in Ukraine constitute a large minority, over 17 percent of the population, and they feel marginalized – many, in fact, oppose Ukrainian independence and advocate for the restoration of the Russian Empire.
Internal diversity and incongruent interests	Eastern European, Turkish, and Arab migrants are flocking to the high-income countries of the European Union. They do not acculturate easily and create divergent interests in Old Europe.
Political instability and the instability of government policies	Argentina, during the administration of President Cristina Fernandez de Kirchner, from 2007-2015, witnessed severe political and economic instability, including runaway inflation and a default on government debt.

Political Repression

Repression of certain ethnic groups is a signal of potential political instability. The perceived repression of Muslims in France transformed the student riots in the last decade into quasi-ethnic uprisings. It did not help that the then secretary of the interior and former president Nicolas Sarkozy, adopted a strong stance against immigrant dissent. The coordinated terrorist attacks in Paris in 2015 and the 2016 Nice terrorist attacks might have had their roots in this repression. The repression of gypsies and Muslims in Central and Eastern Europe continues to create flare-ups. Anti-Semitism is rampant in France, and the French government is unable to subdue the inflammatory rhetoric.

General repression by the elite— especially if the elite's position is not considered legitimate[18]—is always a signal of political instability. Personality cults in particular are problematic because they bring about wide-spread antipathy. Turkmenistan offered a relatively recent example. Its past leader, Saparmurad Niyazov, made himself president for life, calling himself the Father of the Turkmen and occupying virtually every high office of the state. His rule was symbolized by a revolving gold statue of himself and by grandiose marble-clad public buildings; at the same time, the country's education and health systems deteriorated greatly, and the regime piled up a record of human rights abuses. Niyazov died a natural death in December of 2006 and was replaced by a dentist, Gurbanguly Berdymukhammedov, who kept in place most restrictions on civil society and the media. One of his first actions as president was to court the support of the political elite, continuing the patronage network, rewarding political loyalty with economic benefits. Like Mr. Niyazov, he balanced rival interests through regular personnel reshuffles, ensuring that no one faction gained the upper hand.[19]

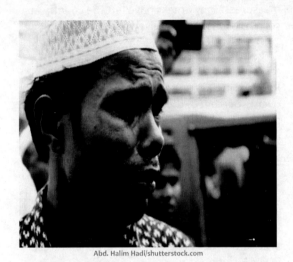
Abd. Halim Hadi/shutterstock.com

Internal Diversity and Incongruent Interests

Even if no political repression exists within a country, ethnic diversity and incongruent interests point to a history of distrust and conflict (open or simmering) in the population. There are numerous examples of repression and conflict due to diversity around the world— among the most obvious are Darfur in the Sudan and Eritrea in Ethiopia. The opening vignette also discusses the conflict between the Tutsis and the Hutus in Rwanda, a conflict that is equally alive in neighboring Burundi. Romania has a large minority of Hungarians who are actively advocating secession and annexation to Hungary of the region in Transylvania, where Hungarians represent the dominant population in a number of cities and towns. Even in highly-developed countries, substantial ethnic conflict still exists, not just between the established ethnicity—as in the case of Belgium, where the Flemish (Dutch) and Wallonians (French) often find themselves in opposition—but also between the new immigrants and Neo-Nazi nationals—as in the case of Germany, where Turkish immigrants have been targets of hate crimes. In Mexico, indigenous groups in the southern part of the country have protested against alleged repression and discrimination by the central government in Mexico City.

Political Stability and the Stability of Government Policies

Although presidents and governments change every few years, with a few exceptions, national government policies do not necessarily change radically, nor does the level of political risk. On average, Italy has had a new government for every year since World War II, and yet its commercial policies have remained unchanged. Germany has had pro-business conservatives at its helm, followed by a government with a more socialist bent, with no substantial impact on international business. Former communists have succeeded democratic presidents in Central and Eastern Europe without any substantial change in the countries' pro-business attitudes. Hong Kong has become an integral part of China, and to date this has created more opportunities than threats for international trade.

Yet political change can be a cause for concern for international firms. Companies that have operated in countries that have had decades of stability and prosperity under a one-party rule can be affected instantly by political turmoil. In Venezuela, a hard leftist regime led by Hugo Chavez from 1999 until his death in 2013 and then by his successor, Nicolas Maduro, has led to economic chaos in the country. The value of Venezuelan Bolivar has dropped to over 265,000 per U.S. dollar as of 2018. Many major U.S. firms have suspended operations in Venezuela. International trade has largely ground to a halt. Although the transition from one-party rule can be peaceful, this is often the exception. In addition to a change in the ruling party, companies should look for other signals that announce political instability: Tamil separatists in Sri Lanka, political riots in Indonesia, Rwandan refugees in Uganda and the Congo—all spell trouble for the companies operating in the respective countries.

Alexandros Michailidis/shutterstock.com

2-4b Nationalism

The expression of fierce nationalist sentiment, or nationalism, in a country where the company is operating could constitute a cause for concern to the international company. While the expression of nationalist feelings, such as pride in a country's history and accomplishments, is common in most countries, nationalist sentiment may signal attempts at separation from or isolation of a particular segment of society, which could lead to political instability in the country. This is the case, for example, of the Tamil separatist movement in Sri Lanka, which periodically leads to chaos and instability in the country. Particularly problematic for international business are expressions of anti-foreigner sentiment and anti-foreign business bias. Shared beliefs that engaging in international business represents selling one's country raise questions about the future trade environment in that country. Of special concern to international marketing managers is consumer ethnocentrism—the belief that buying foreign goods will put local companies out of business and is, consequently, morally wrong.[20] Countries where such beliefs dominate are more likely to erect barriers to international trade.

For example, Thailand experienced a military coup in 2006, resulting in new foreign-investment rules, with stringent laws of foreign ownership, requiring investors to sell holdings that exceed 50 percent ownership in Thai companies and to give up voting rights in excess of 50 percent. U.S. firms were protected from this rule by a treaty with Thailand that dates back to the Vietnam War, but European and Japanese companies were greatly affected. The Thai Foreign Business Act bans foreigners from owning majority shares in Thai businesses ranging from the media, rice farming, the production of national handicrafts, legal services, and construction. However, in 2018, the government decided to open foreign participation to industries such as next-generation cars, smart electronics, affluent medical and wellness tourism, agriculture and biotechnology, food, robotics for industry, logistics and aviation, biofuels and biochemicals, digital, and medical services.[21]

2-4c Political Risks and Risk Management in International Marketing

Nationalism and claims to national sovereignty can lead to protectionist measures, such as new tariff barriers, and can have a crippling impact on international trade and investment. Political instability can lead to the failure of the economy. All can harm the operations of any company in such a country, from hurting sales and all prospects in the market to los-ing all company assets. For example, the Brink's Company, a large multinational cash man-agement firm headquartered in Richmond, Virginia, virtually wrote off the value of their ex-tensive operations in Venezuela. Because their revenue was in Venezuelan Bolivares, the continued devaluation of the local currency effectively eliminated any transfer of local in-come to U.S. dollars. In addition, the U.S. dollar value of Brink's in-country assets in Vene-zuela dropped precipitously. The following sections present types of risks a company can experience in international markets and examples of risk management for each category of risk. [22]

Risks Related to Government Trade Policies

The host-country government can erect trade barriers, imposing tariffs and nontariff barriers on international business, such as exchange-rate controls, voluntary export re-straints and different types of quotas and export/import license requirements. A company could also find itself falling victim to a trade war, in which the host country and home coun-try reciprocally restrict the flow of goods. Or the company's home-country government can impose embargoes and sanctions on the host country, which could force the company to exit the market. All these risks are addressed at length in Chapter 3, International Trade: In-stitutional Barriers and Facilitators.

Risks Related to Government Economic Policy

Local governments can use taxes as a means to control foreign investment; during downturns in the economy, governments find that taxing foreign companies provides a source of valuable revenue. Under more extreme conditions, especially if accompanied by a radical change in the political leader-ship, change could potentially lead to the involuntary transfer of the firm's assets to local ownership. Companies face the following types of risks:

- Confiscation
- Expropriation
- Creeping expropriation
- Nationalization
- Domestication

dominika zarzycka/shutterstock.com

Confiscation

Confiscation refers to the seiz-ing of company assets and investors' assets without any compensation. In the 1940s and 1950s, most private companies operating in Central and Eastern Europe had their assets confiscated. More recently, all U.S. firms operating in Iran were confiscated af-ter the Islamic Revolution of 1979, when Shah Reza Pahlavi was dethroned. The United States subsequently imposed an embargo on all trade with Iran in 1987, which prohibited the exportation or importation of all goods and services to and from Iran.

Expropriation

Expropriation involves some reimbursement for company assets, usually not at their market value. When Fidel Castro ascended to power in Cuba and instituted a totalitarian regime, the assets of U.S. multinationals and U.S. citizens were seized. The Castro government offered payment that was deemed insufficient, and as a result, the United States imposed an embargo on trade with Cuba that is currently still in effect, although the U.S. Congress might eventually repeal it. More recently, in 2012, South Africa's African National Congress decided to end the policy of buying land from willing white farmers, advocating for land grabs with partial compensation.

Creeping Expropriation

Creeping expropriation entails opaque and overly complex rules and regulations, difficulty in navigating the local bureaucracy, and corrupt government officials. Although not explicitly, government actions discourage foreign investment, especially investment in nonessential sectors. This strategy typically imposes additional barriers on international trade.

Nationalization

Nationalization involves a takeover by the local government with the aim of creating a government-run industry. International law regards nationalization as legitimate as long as it is in the public interest and it offers fair compensation to the international company and to its investors. In 1997, the Korean government decided to nationalize the automobile company Kia Motors by converting the state-run Korea Development Bank's debt into an equity stake in the company.[23] In the aftermath of the Asian crisis, governments began nationalizing ailing banks across the region. In Indonesia, the government controls nearly all the country's biggest banks and has taken over around 75 percent of all bank assets; whereas in Japan, as a result of nationalization, the government, instead of markets, now plays a larger role in determining the flow of capital.[24]

More recently, the Argentine government nationalized the YPF Argentine oil firm, confiscating Spanish company Repsol's majority stake in the Argentine oil company — an act reminiscent of former Argentine president Juan Perón's nationalizations in the 1940s, which led to an economic downfall. As mentioned earlier, Thailand now requires European and Japanese foreign investors to sell holdings such that they would ultimately own less than 50 percent of a company; The Foreign Business Act bans foreigners from owning majority shares in Thai businesses. In another example, a decade ago, Venezuela's president, Hugo Chavez nationalized companies in the telecommunications and electricity industries and attempted to gain more control over natural gas projects. His goal was to change Venezuela into a socialist state with strong state oversight of the economy.[25]

Domestication

Domestication occurs when the local government requires a gradual transfer of ownership and management to locals. This transfer is usually completed over time, through consecutive government decrees aimed at reducing the presence of multinationals in nonessential local sectors (such as the consumer goods sector).

Companies can protect themselves against political instability by understanding the structure of a government, the political parties, and the ideologies of the ruling party, as well as the competing ideologies of the opposition. As a first step, companies must make every attempt to be exemplary corporate citizens in every country where they operate. A solid reputation for product quality and community involvement can create a general environment that is favorable toward a company's local operations.

A company also can minimize its risk by partnering with local companies, creating local expertise in product manufacturing and management, and using local suppliers. McDonald's, for example, frequently stresses the use of local ingredients in all its offerings. Similarly, companies that produce products deemed essential for local development, such as industrial products, high-technology products, or pharmaceutical products, are less vulnerable to changes in government policies than companies that manufacture goods that are considered nonessential, such as consumer goods.

Companies can obtain insurance coverage against nationalization from private insurance sources. Companies such as Global Risk Advisors insure against confiscation, expropriation, and nationalization, in addition to providing insurance against war risk; localized or subnational conflicts; kidnapping, ransom, and extortion; property terrorism; and currency inconvertibility; among others.[26] The U.S. government, through the Overseas Private Investment Corporation, or OPIC (http://www.opic.gov), also offers policies that insure companies against expropriation, nationalization, or confiscation by foreign governments. OPIC insures U.S. investments in emerging markets and developing countries against expropriation and political violence, such as revolution and war. Until recently, U.S. exporters could obtain credit insurance for short and medium-term export sales via the Export-Import Bank of the United States (https://www.exim.gov/) – note that the agency has not been fully operational since 2014.

Risks Related to Labor and Action Groups

In many countries, labor unions are very powerful and can often influence national policies. For example, layoffs by foreign companies could bring about negative feelings that could affect companies in the long term.

In early 2018, Norwegian Airlines, the fast-growing discount carrier known for offering very low-cost flights across the Atlantic, announced plans to begin domestic air service inside Argentina. Norwegian Air Argentina plans to offer flights at fares less than half those charged by Aerolineas Argentinas, the state-owned carrier that has had a monopoly on domestic flights, a state protection going back to the 1940s and President Juan Perón. As might be expected, Aerolineas Argentinas unions have threatened strikes, along with the national bus-driver unions. Many Argentine consumers currently prefer to travel using less expensive (although they take much longer!) buses instead of buying higher-priced tickets on Aerolineas Argentinas domestic flights.[27]

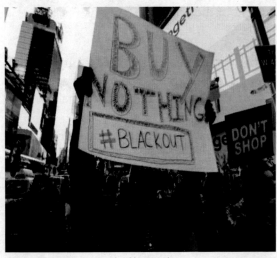

a katz/shutterstock.com

Boycotts initiated by action groups could also negatively affect companies. Esso (Exxon) was the victim of a "Boycott Esso" campaign aimed at the United States' environmental policies. These actions are not usually sanctioned by the national government; they are, however, legal.

Companies have some control over the actions of labor and action groups. Although they cannot control market demand and derived demand for labor, companies can provide severance packages that are fair, as well as invest in the services of job placement businesses in an effort to seek placement for the employees who have been terminated. To avoid negative public sentiment, companies must be politically neutral and keep a distance from local politics. Too close an association with a governing regime could elicit a negative attitude toward the company and its products. Pepsi, unfairly, is perceived as the drink that greased the hands of the former communist elite in Central and Eastern Europe, whereas Coke is associ-

ated with the new, free society. It is important for a company to be perceived as a good citizen of the country where it operates, and as a company that has created opportunities for locals and that continues to serve their interests.

wellphoto/shutterstock.com

Risks Related to Terrorism

International terrorist attacks against multinational interests gained worldwide attention with the September 11, 2001, attack on the World Trade Center in New York City. A blow to the financial nerve center of capitalism, the attacks disrupted financial operations worldwide, displaced hundreds of businesses, and stopped all travel in U.S. airspace. An "attack on the world's . . . superpower, undertaken as a consequence of specific American alliances and actions,"[28] these actions are representative of corporate terrorism with the greatest of scopes. Since then, numerous terrorist acts have attempted to kill as many people as possible in operations of various degrees of sophistication. In 2016, IntelCenter reported 2,921 terrorist incidents, averaging at one every 58 minutes, with a total of 7,795 killed and 8,428 injured.[29]

According to the 2017 Global Terrorism Index, the global economic impact of terrorism is high, costing the global economy US$84 billion in 2016. This figure, however, does not account for the indirect impacts on business, investment, and the costs associated with security agencies in countering terrorism. [30]

Companies have some control, however, in reducing their likelihood of becoming victims of terrorism by training employees in terrorism avoidance, such as briefing personnel on what to expect when entering high-risk areas and offering training for eluding roadblocks and avoiding hazardous encounters.[31] Companies can also purchase insurance against terrorist acts from private insurance companies. The hospitality and gaming industry, as well as nonprofits, have been the target of terrorist acts in recent years and have experienced the highest increase in insurance costs in recent years.[32]

2-5 The International Legal Environment

International marketing is affected by three types of law:

1. International Laws—A body of rules and regulations that countries agree to abide by. International law addresses agreements among countries with regard to trade, protection of property, and other issues in the political and economic sphere. Interna-

tional law agreements, although not enforceable, can be appropriately addressed by international law bodies.

2. **Host-Country Laws**—Laws of the different countries where the company operates. The legal system in the host country could differ substantially from that of the company's home country.

3. **Home-Country Laws**—Laws of the company's home country. Home-country laws follow the company all over the world.

U.S. companies must abide by all three types of law. For example, they must abide by international trade laws and agreements, such as WTO trade regulations; they must abide by host-country laws governing every aspect of the company's operations; and they must abide by home-country laws, such as antitrust regulations and corrupt practices regulations.

2-5a Legal Systems

Three legal systems are predominant: common law, code law, and Islamic law.

Common Law

Common law is based on prior court rulings (legal precedent). It has its roots in English common law, on which U.S. law is based. This system of law is shared by many of the countries formerly colonized by Great Britain.

Code (Civil) Law

Code law—or civil law—refers to comprehensive written laws that specify what constitutes legal behavior. Code law has its roots in Roman law. This system of law is shared by most of the countries in the world, including most of Europe, Latin America, China, Taiwan, Japan, and South Korea.

Formerly socialist countries have fully adopted civil law and are now struggling to ensure that it is properly implemented. Under the socialist system, countries of the former Soviet Union and the Eastern Bloc had a system of laws that allowed a large degree of flexibility in enforcement. All the nomenklatura, the high-ranking communist party officials and their offspring, were largely exempt from enforcement, with some exceptions. For the common person, however, activities deemed illegal, such as listening to Western radio stations or harboring a Western visitor, could place one in prison indefinitely. Selective enforcement persists even today, along with corruption, in this part of the world — and elsewhere.

Islamic Law

Islamic law (sha'ria) is a system of laws based on the interpretation of the Koran, Islam's holy book, and on interpretations of the practices and sayings of the prophet Muhammad. Islamic law establishes rules for business practices that can affect firms' operations. For example, it requires the sexes to be separate; in strict practice, this means that women cannot interact with men with whom they are not related. It also bans the consumption of products such as pork and alcohol, and it does not allow banks to offer or charge interest. Islamic law requires Muslims to pray five times a day and to fast during the month of Ramadan.

All these factors have an impact on firms' local operations wherever Islamic law constitutes the basis of the legal system—in North Africa, the Middle East, India, Indonesia, Pakistan and Malaysia, among others. For example, business activities must be organized daily around prayer time, with companies accommodating employees by stopping work and allowing for sufficient space for prayer. During Ramadan, business performance is generally limited and many international businesses rely on the foreign, non-Muslim, workforce to carry out their firms' operations during this month.

2-5b Jurisdiction

With different legal systems worldwide, and with international laws, home-country laws, and host-country laws that govern all aspects of doing business internationally, it is important to establish jurisdiction in international legal disputes. Normally, no automatic supranational jurisdiction is assigned to an international court, unless the dispute takes place between companies and/or countries in the European Union, in which case the jurisdiction lies with the European Court of Justice (www.europa.eu.int). Legal disputes that arise between governments are usually handled by the International Court of Justice (www.icj-cij.org) in the Hague, within the United Nations system. International commercial law is usually handled in the home or host country of the company, or even in a third country, depending on the place of jurisdiction for the matter under litigation. Because jurisdiction is often difficult to determine, it is advisable that each contract specifies the venue for handling the dispute and the procedure involved.

The contract should also specify whether the dispute settlement process will involve procedures other than litigation, which is often too costly and leads to negative perceptions in the international business community of the companies involved. Such procedures may be as follows:

Mediation—A nonbinding procedure that involves an independent third party. The disadvantage of mediation is that any decision of the mediator is nonbinding. The perspective of a neutral third party, however, could provide better insights into how the issue is perceived by the larger business community. Not accepting the terms of mediation could signal to firms outside the conflict that the firm in question may be at fault and might not be a reliable future partner.

Arbitration—A procedure that involves an independent third party, the outcome of arbitration is a binding decision. Agreeing to arbitration does not necessarily mean that the companies found to be at fault will adhere to the decisions; if they do not, however, it is possible that their reputation in the international business community will suffer. Arbitration is often preferred to litigation. It is a much faster procedure that is likely to cost the company much less than a lawsuit.

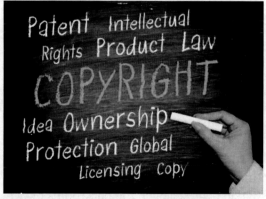

docstockmedia/shutterstock.com

2-5c Intellectual Property Rights Protection

Violation of intellectual property rights is the most significant threat to the competitiveness of companies involved in international business.[33] Intellectual property is the result of ideas and creativity transformed into products, services, and experiences that are protected for a specified period of time from unauthorized commercialization. Large multinationals with brand name products are the primary victims of intellectual property rights infringement and are leading the fight against violations. According to the Commission on the Theft of American Intellectual Property, in 2017, the cost to the U.S. economy exceeded $225 billion in counterfeit goods, pirated software, and the theft of trade secrets.

Its primary victims are the most innovative, fastest-growing industries such as software, pharmaceuticals, and entertainment (with high losses attributed to Internet piracy).[34]

Intellectual property protection takes on different forms:

1. Protecting inventor rights or those or of the firm employing him/her to use and sell the invention for a specified period —this type of intellectual property is known as a patent. In the U.S., a design is granted protection for 14 years and a utility patent for 20 years. In many countries around the world, multinationals are racing to local patent offices to apply for patents to protect and enforce their technology. In Korea, for example, local memory chip and electronics firms are embroiled in patent disputes, fending off lawsuits initiated by multinational firms such as IBM, and the stakes are high: Losers will not only suffer financial setbacks in the form of paying royalties, but will also suffer the stigma of being labeled copycats.[35] This situation will ultimately be rectified by the WTO, which has instituted uniform patent rules that all members are expected to follow.

2. Protection of the rights to an original work of art (literature, music, film, design, and other works), allowing the owner the right to reproduce, sell, perform, or film the work—this is known as copyright. In the United States, copyright protection covers the work of individuals until 70 years after death. National and international associations are actively fighting copyright infringement. For example, the International Intellectual Property Alliance, or IIPA (www.iipa.com), formed in conjunction with the Association of American Publishers, the Business Software Alliance, the Interactive Digital Software Association, the Motion Picture Association of America, the National Music Publishers' Association, and the Recording Industry Association of America. In one example, the IIPA filed petitions with the Office of the U.S. Trade Representative to investigate copyright music infringement in Brazil, Costa Rica, Guatemala, Russia, and Uruguay.[36]

3. Protection of a brand name, mark, symbol, motto, or slogan that identifies a particular manufacturer's brand and distinguishes it from the competitors' brands in the same product category—this is known as trademark. Trademark infringement occurs at many levels, starting with directly copying the product, as in the case of counterfeit Rolex watches and Prada, Gucci and Fendi purses selling for $50 in the streets of New York City, Paris, Venice, and even at the entrance of the Vatican. These counterfeits are omnipresent in Asia and in many bazaars in emerging markets. In the United States, a trademark is protected as long as it is in use and as long as the company defends it against copyright infringement.

Brand name counterfeiting involves using the brand name, as in the case of the high-quality Hermès Birkin bags selling in the backrooms of the Covered Bazaar in Istanbul, Turkey. The Birkin sells for over $10,000 at the Hermès store, although special edition might go for as much as $150,000. At the Bazaar, a perfect copy allegedly made in Turkey, with quality leather, with a key chain appropriately

ZergCSV.ZP/shutterstock.com

displayed, and all the other details and sold with an Hermès protective bag, sells for about $150, whereas a copy of mediocre quality, allegedly made in China, sells for about $50.

Design copying, which is legal, involves using a popular design without the trademark. The popular Birkin bag is also a victim of design counterfeiting, with many store displays offering bags that look very similar to the Birkin, down to the emblematic orange color. Shirts with a crocodile or polo player that do not have the respective Lacoste and Ralph Lauren names, and Peugeot watches with designs that look just like the Rolex Oyster are among the many examples of design counterfeiting.

Protection of know-how, formulas, and special blends that are not registered, and thus not protected by law—these are shared with licensees, franchisers, or other partners and are known as trade secrets. Intellectual property violations are especially problematic in China, where all products, including automobiles, are at risk, as Marketing Illustration 2-2 shows.

International Marketing Illustration 2-2 Counterfeiting Chinese Style

There is a saying in Shanghai: "We can copy anything except your mother." Soy sauce with carbonated water is sold as Pepsi, and fake designer goods are everywhere (Figure 2-2). China is the source of 86 percent of the world's counterfeit goods, with a value of about $400 billion; about 12.5 percent of Chinese exports are counterfeit goods.

Counterfeit cars first appeared in China in 1999: VW look-alikes were quickly followed by the Chery QQ, which appeared six months earlier than the Chevy Spark, the car it copied. Chery QQ was able to copy the Spark successfully because a Chinese firm somehow got hold of the blueprints. Cars bearing Honda's name ("Hongda" for motorcycles) are commonplace, and Nissan's bumpers have been under legal scrutiny.

Shuanghuan Automobile copied Audi's famous four-ring logo, then it copied the design of Honda's CR-V and called it the SR-V—and Shuanghuan is getting away with it. It also obtained an license to export the CEO, an SUV similar to the BMW X5, to Romania and Italy.

In other examples, Jiangling Motors' Landwind X7 is a copy of the Range Rover. Also, Great Wall, a producer of cars with names such as Sing, Wingle, and Sailor, copied the Toyota's Hilux and called it Deer. Great Wall is currently in litigation with Toyota for copying its Scion models and with Fiat for copying its new Panda.

Litigation with Chinese manufacturers has proved useless. Lawsuits have been thrown out on technical grounds, or because, according to the Chinese government, the foreign firm failed to properly register their designs. Foreign manufacturers, in turn, do not want to make waves, because that could prevent them from having access to China's fast-growing market. Chinese firms do not spend much on research and development, so the copied products are much more affordable, unfairly competing with the legitimate brands.

Sources: *The Economist*, "Business: The Sincerest Form of Flattery—Counterfeit Cars in China," April 7, 2007, p. 383 (8523), 76. Lujie Chen, Tao Yue, and Xiande Zhao, "Eight Ways Brands Can Fight Counterfeits in China," Harvard Business Review, May 10, 2018, accessed at https://hbr.org/2018/05/8-ways-brands-can-fight-counterfeits-in-china on May 11, 2018.

Figure 2-2: Counterfeit luggage in Shanghai: Polo, Diesel, and so on – the copies look nothing like the authentic brands.

Factors Influencing Intellectual Property Rights Violations

The degree of intellectual property rights violation is influenced by a number of market factors,[37] such as:

- Lack of appropriate legislation (e.g., for software)
- Lax enforcement, especially for local firms
- Unavailability of the authentic products, or when available, their high price provides justification for both the violators and the respective governments to allow the practice

Such violations are also influenced by cultural factors, such as:

- Values that perceive imitation as a high form of flattery
- A culture characterized by interpersonal distrust and feelings of not getting a fair deal
- A culture characterized by an emphasis on acquisition of material wealth at the expense of caring for others; in such a culture, the focus of acquisition is status brands consumed and/or displayed publicly, rather than privately
- Beliefs that technology is in the common domain and that use of others' intellectual property is appropriate

Cherries/shutterstock.com

Involvement in regional trade agreements and other trade organizations is also sought to diminish the likelihood that a country would tolerate violation of intellectual property rights. In fact, intellectual property rights used to be largely a domestic issue, with individual countries deciding on their own levels of legal protection and enforcement; today, countries that join the WTO must also sign on to the Trade-Related Aspects of Intellectual Property Rights (or TRIPS) agreement, an international agreement that sets out minimum standards for the legal protection of intellectual property.[38]

Multinationals seeking protection under TRIPS still depend on each country's patent office to grant those rights and on the countries' judicial, customs, and police services to enforce them (in the European Union, companies need only apply for EU patents). TRIPS offers rules describing the protection provided, including extending intellectual property rights to include computer programs, integrated circuits, plant varieties, and pharmaceuticals. According to TRIPS, patents can be granted for any new technological process or product, and the protection lasts 20 years from the date of application.[39]

In addition to TRIPS, and working in conjunction with the WTO, international conventions have been gaining strength. Among these conventions are the Bern Convention for copy-righted works, under the auspices of the World Intellectual Property Organization;[40] the Paris Convention for the protection of industrial property; and the Madrid Arrangement, which established the Bureau for the International Registration of Trademarks.

Helping these organizations and conventions are national governments of primarily high-income countries, which are protecting their multinationals. In the United States, the Patent and Trademark Office has an annual budget of $3.5 billion, a staff of more than

13,000, including judges presiding over patent disputes and customs representatives to fight counterfeiting.[41] To protect intellectual property rights in the Internet age, the U.S. government passed the Digital Millennium Copyright Act.

Some developing countries argue that intellectual property protection is yet another arm used to hold them in a position of economic disadvantage. According to this view, patents and copyrights impose great cost on low-income country consumers. For example, AIDS activists and the government in South Africa argued that patents were killing the country's millions of HIV-infected patients who could not afford the drugs; Mexican peasants were enraged that a U.S. company received the exclusive right to market enola beans in the United States because they have been growing the beans for generations, and the protection restricts their ability to export the beans north of the border.[42] Activists argue that intellectual property protection allows Western multinationals to set up monopolies, driving out local competing brands, diverting research and development away from the needs of developing countries, and driving up prices while preventing poor people from getting life-saving drugs, interfering with age-old farming practices, and allowing foreign "pirates" to raid local resources, such as medicinal plants, without getting permission or paying compensation.[43]

Finally, there are examples where companies, even though engaged in trademark litigation, continue to cooperate, if it serves their interests. For example, Anheuser-Busch Companies and the Czech brewer Budejovicky Budvar have had a long-standing litigation over the Budweiser name. The Czech brewer has a long history in Europe, predating Anheuser-Busch Budweiser history in the U.S. Both were bought by the Belgian company InBev, and the conflict is now moot, with InBev distributing Budvar's Czechvar Premium Czech Lager in the United States [44] (see Figure 2-3).

2-3 The Budweiser Budvar brand is very popular in upscale German restaurants.

2-5d Home-Country Legislation Affecting Multinational Firms Operating Overseas

Antitrust Laws

Antitrust laws of home and host countries are designed to prevent domestic anticompetitive activities, such as the creation of monopolies and cartels. The United States was among the first to impose its antitrust laws on firms in the United States and on U.S. firms operating abroad. Increasingly, governments of other countries are enacting and enforcing antitrust legislation that affects multinationals worldwide. In fact, antitrust enforcement in the United States often appears to be more lenient than in other developed countries. For example, the European Commission enacted rulings against and levied substantial fines on Apple, Facebook, Google, and Qualcomm, cementing the image of the European Union as the Big Tech regulator.[45]

The United States allows certain types of collusion in the case of small and medium-sized firms that might not have the resources to embark on a successful export program. The U.S. Congress passed the Export Trading Company Act in the 1980s to encourage firms to join forces in exporting by exempting them from antitrust laws.

Corruption Laws

Corruption laws of home and host countries are designed to prevent multinational corporations from using unethical means to obtain competitive advantage in a particular market. The World Bank found that businesses and individuals pay $1.5 trillion in bribes each year, about 2% of global GDP. [46] The poor pay the highest percentage of their income in bribes – in Paraguay, the poor pay 12.6 percent of their income to bribes, while high-income households pay 6.4 percent, and "every stolen dollar, euro, peso, yuan, rupee, or ruble robs the poor of an equal opportunity in life."[47]

The U.S. Foreign Corrupt Practices Act (FCPA) makes it illegal for companies and their representatives to bribe government officials and other politicians or candidates for political office. The Act also prohibits payment to third parties when a company has good reason to assume that part of that payment is being used for bribery purposes. U.S. multinational companies take such laws very seriously—some even address their commitment to reject bribery and other corruption in their mission statement (Caterpillar does so, for example)—even though forbidding these practices places U.S. firms at a disadvantage. In a number of high-profile cases, investigators found that illegal payments were made by firms operating in Canada, Colombia, Cook Islands, the Dominican Republic, Egypt, Germany, Iraq, Israel, Jamaica, Mexico, Niger, Nigeria, and Trinidad and Tobago; these payments ranged from $22,000 to $9.9 million and represented percentages of up to 20 percent of the business obtained. Seventeen companies were charged under the FCPA, with fines ranging from $10,000 to $21.8 million.[48] In addition to fines, violations of the FCPA also carry potential criminal liability and imprisonment for defendants. Even in cases where a "rogue employee" is paying bribes unbeknownst to senior management, the company may be liable.

The United States is not alone in the fight against bribery. The Organization for Economic Cooperation and Development (OECD), which consists of 30 primarily developed member countries (Australia, Austria, Belgium, Canada, the Czech Republic, Denmark, Finland, France, Germany, Greece, Hungary, Iceland, Ireland, Italy, Japan, South Korea, Luxembourg, Mexico, the Netherlands, New Zealand, Norway, Poland, Portugal, the Slovak Republic, Spain, Sweden, Switzerland, Turkey, United Kingdom, and the United States) adopted a Convention on Combating Bribery of Foreign Public Officials in International Business Transaction. Other signatories include nonmember countries Argentina, Brazil, Bulgaria, and Chile. The purpose of the Convention is to fight corruption in international business and to help level the competitive field for companies.[49]

2-6 The Natural Environment of International Marketing

The natural environment of international marketing addresses the relationship between natural resources and marketing. A country's geographic location determines optimal access to markets. Its climate determines its production and even its productivity capability. Geography facilitates or impedes relationships with other international markets. Southwestern China, for example, has been isolated from the mainland until recently, when train transportation became possible and airplane transportation became more affordable. Driving from Lhasa, Tibet, to the nearest city takes several days, as the roads are treacherous; this same distance takes less than two hours by airplane. Consequently, Western businesses only started to enter this market a decade ago, and international tourism is only now picking up.

National boundaries determine access to the local market and the movement of goods, access to natural resources, and, overall, the potential for economic development. Landlocked countries have difficulty gaining access to low-cost water transportation. In Rwanda, a land-locked country, firms mostly bring their products to market by air, as access from Uganda and Congo is often problematic due to the instability in the two countries.

2-6a Geology and the Shortage of Natural Resources

A country's access to natural resources determines whether the country can be a viable trade partner in the international market. Its geology determines the natural resources available in the country and its potential for prosperity. For example, oil in North Africa and the Middle East has brought prosperity to countries where the climate is a challenge and whose terrain contains a large desert expanse. Countries in sub-Saharan Africa that have survived at subsistence level for centuries have found new prosperity from mining gold and diamonds. Botswana and the Central African Republic have attractive markets that are actively courted by multinationals. Mongolia is referred to as "minegolia" due to the substantial copper and uranium resources recently discovered there; as a result, the country is rapidly changing, with consumers demanding a high standard of living and Western brands.

A shortage of raw materials is slowly reverberating in most world markets, including the markets of industrialized countries. Prices of oil and gas have been steadily increasing over the years, whereas access to oil and gas sources is becoming more and more limited due to geologic and political factors. Although prices have gone down recently as a result of fracking, experts believe that this trend will be short-lived, with prices continuing their upward trajectory. In the years when oil prices were high, in the 1980s and between 2008 and 2014, consumers' consumption patterns changed — in the United States, they traded in their gas-guzzling monster trucks and sports utility vehicles for fuel-efficient smaller and hybrid vehicles.

Nataliya Nazarova/shutterstock.com

2-4 Man-made canals in Holland allow for quick and inexpensive access to markets.

2-6b Topography and Access to Markets

Topography is important because it determines access to the market and affects distribution decisions. For example, Holland has a flat terrain, allowing for efficient transportation. Holland has also altered its topography to increase access by creating an effective network of man-made canals that cross the country in every direction, allowing for easier access to markets (see Figure 2-4).

On the other hand, a mountainous terrain restricts access to markets. The Andes, for example, complicate access to local consumers, which can be accomplished only at high cost. High-income countries have de-vised sophisticated access to some of the more remote areas, such as the canyons in Utah and the peaks of the Alps. On the other hand, access remains especially problematic in lower-income countries, for example, in the countries of the Brahmaputra mountain chain – see

dailin/shutterstock.com　　　　Toshio Chan/shutterstock.com

Figure 2-5　Tibet was initially reached only by air or by road from the rest of mainland China. There is now a railway that facilitates access. Nevertheless, the Brahmaputra mountain chain presents a challenge to the movement of goods and access to markets in the surrounding countries.

Figure 2-5.

2-6c Hydrology and Economic Development

Hydrology determines access to local markets as well. Ocean access allows for the affordable shipping of goods to the local target market. Rivers and lakes offer access as well as potential for the development of agriculture and manufacturing — historically, many communities were developed on river banks (see Figure 2-6). Hydroelectric power is essential for local development. In general, economic development is related to hydrology.

2-6d Climate

Climate is also an essential determinant of economic development. Arid lands, such as the desert lands of the Sahara, the Arabian Peninsula, and the southwestern United States are inhabitable only at a very high cost. In other areas, excessive rain and hurricane activity often lead to flooding and the destruction of the local infrastructure. On the other hand, a mild climate year round brings healthy crops of fruit, as well as tourists to the Amalfi Coast of Italy, the Cote d'Azur in France, and to the islands of Hawaii and the Caribbean.

Vissawes/shutterstock.com

2-6　Many communities are developed on river banks, to take advantage of access to markets.

2-6e Population and Human Capital

As mentioned earlier, one relevant aspect of the natural environment is the scarcity of natural resources, especially raw materials, in light of today's high population growth. High population growth in spite of limited natural resources has led to famine and precipitated conflict in Ethiopia, Somalia, Rwanda, and Burundi in sub-Saharan Africa. In these markets, the overall infrastructure is insufficient and cannot meet the basic needs of the population. The concentration of population in large cities of millions of inhabitants, such as Mexico City and Cairo, has taxed the infrastructure and impeded the optimal functioning of business.

Arthimedes/shutterstock.com

Today, the world's population exceeds 7.6 billion and is growing rapidly, especially in developing countries. Population growth determines the types of markets that multinational companies, as well as small and medium enterprises, can target. In high-income countries, marketers have mature markets—markets with a substantial population aged 65 and older. Population growth also has implications with regard to access to goods and services and to the environment.

The implications of population migration for international business are also considerable. Immigration from low- and middle-income countries to high-income countries has often resulted in strong anti-immigrant sentiment and instability of different degrees in countries known for their tolerance and openness to immigration, such as Belgium, Denmark, the Netherlands, France, and Sweden. Immigrants account for about 10 percent of these countries' population, of those, a large percentage are Muslim. Immigrants tend to live in run-down immigrant neighborhoods or in high-rise buildings that locals avoid and often deplore, are less likely to learn the local language, and tend to go to all-immigrant schools and remain unemployed and poor. Countries that have, historically, encouraged immigration, as in the case of Germany, which agreed to accept one million refugees in 2015, are now struggling to absorb their large immigrant populations. Many Western European countries have now passed laws restricting immigration.

The new immigrants are not fully aware of their rights or of their obligations to their adoptive country, creating difficulties for them. In Sweden, the minister of integration and gender equality, Nyamko Sabuni, an Afro-Swede, boldly proposed banning the veil for girls younger than the age of 15, subjecting schoolgirls to compulsory medical examination to protect young women from the consequence of debilitating rituals, and proposed outlawing arranged marriage and the "honor culture" of some immigrant cultures, generating anger from immigrants and gaining support from most Swedes.[50]

The challenges facing Sweden are not unusual. European media regularly addresses issues related to anti-immigrant sentiment. After France's 2006 student riots, anti-immigrant rhetoric — from government officials, no less — led to a process of national reflection and to the political change that toppled its conservative government and brought a left-leaning leadership to power for more than a decade now.

One aspect of migration that has important economic consequences for the country affected is "brain drain," the migration of trained professionals. Historically, this migration has been mostly from developing to developed countries. The migration has created shortages of qualified medical personnel in many countries in South America and Eastern Europe, among others. More recently, open borders in the European Union have created a brain drain phenomenon for countries with high taxation and unemployment. For example, the brain drain from Germany, a country with a rapidly shrinking population, has become an issue of concern to business executives and government leaders. More professionals are leaving today than in past years. A popular show on German television is Goodbye Deutschland (Goodbye Germany). The show portrays German emigrants in the process of emigrating and resettling in other countries. Over 100,000 native Germans emigrate yearly. The emigrants who leave are doctors, lawyers, and scientists. Adding to the burden of brain drain is the fact that Germany and France are less attractive to those people pursuing jobs in medicine, academic research, and engineering. The reasons emigrants give for leaving are high taxes, chronic unemployment, a rigid labor market, a stifling bureaucracy, and the hierarchical structure of professional environments such as academia and medicine. New employees have little time to pursue research and are under the thumb of their director.[51]

2-6f Environmental Quality

Concerns about the effects of the overall population growth and industry on the natural environment have led to the active regulation of business, especially in industrialized countries. For example, the European Union actively regulates the use of hormones in raising beef and the use of pesticides in agriculture. It continues to raise taxes on gasoline to reduce consumption and encourage the use of public transportation. It charges localities huge sums for refuse and actively encourages recycling at the individual and community level.

Worldwide, there is a concerted effort to reduce air and water pollution, to control the amount and disposal of nuclear waste, to reduce deforestation and land erosion, and to limit fishing and hunting activity to preserve a viable natural habitat. The effort to preserve environmental quality limits infrastructure development in protected areas and charges businesses to take responsibility of consumption by encouraging bottle reuse and recycling, by limiting packaging to its more basic forms, and by producing products that can be consumed with minimal harm to the environment. Outside the United States, Coca-Cola soft drinks and Heineken beer are sold in reusable glass bottles or in recyclable plastic bottles. Ford Motor Company competes in the international market by offering smaller automobiles with low gas consumption. And new, successful industries are emerging aimed at creating alternative energy sources and reducing the cost of electricity consumption. Windmills today populate not just the European and Asian landscape; they are increasingly present on the coast of California and on the East Coast of the United States.

Vehicular emissions are rising across the globe. Greenhouse gases are increasing even in countries where industry pollution is decreasing, due to increased car and truck use, and this is happening in spite of the popularity of environmentally friendly automobiles: hybrid cars and ethanol buses do not compensate for the effect of the large number of vehicles on the road. High taxes on cars and gasoline, such as those imposed in Denmark—where a Czech-made Skoda automobile costs twice as much as in Italy or Sweden—scare voters away, making even environmentalist politicians reluctant to propose them.[52]

Yet, in spite of these challenges, the European Union remains the world's leader in the fight against climate change. The Paris Agreement, within the United Nations Framework Convention on Climate Change, aims to respond to global climate threat by keeping global temperature rise below 2 degrees Celsius, was signed by 197 countries. Each signatory country decides on its own contribution to the reduction in global warming, and commits to regularly report on those plans and the net reductions

jaroslava V/shutterstock.com

in emissions. [53] The United States signed the Paris Agreement in 2015, but, in 2017, announced its decision to withdraw from the agreement by the year 2020.

Increasingly, environmental pollution is also attributed to developing countries, where cheap diesel generators from China are a preferred mode for providing electricity, powering home appliances, irrigation systems, allowing many in rural villages to grow crops and to connect to the world through Internet and television. In remote and roadless areas in India, China, Bangladesh, and Nepal, as many as half of the households have television sets and pay 40 cents every few days to the owner of the generator supplying the electricity for their bamboo hut. Diesel is cheap, owing to lavish government subsidies, making it difficult to introduce alternative renewable energy technologies. Efforts on the part of local government and international development organizations, such as the United Nations Development Program, to introduce expensive renewable energy have been successful for urban areas; however, the investment is not warranted in remote villages. China is offering a successful alternative: cheap rooftop water heaters that channel water through thin pipes crisscrossing a shiny surface. More than 5,000 small Chinese companies sell these water heaters to more than 30 million households. Today, China accounts for 60 percent of the market for solar water heaters. One such water heater costs $330, and it pays for itself in two years. [54]

Demand for cheap automobiles, costing less than $14,000, is huge, with many former motorcycle owners opting for an affordable automobile. Renault's Logan, manufactured in Romania, is a hit at less than $10,000: The car, sold in more than 50 countries, including India, Argentina, and Brazil, was launched in 2004. These developments carry with them bleak prospects for the environment, and governments of large emerging markets are attempting to stem the tide. In China, for example, the government imposes a graduated tax on vehicles based on their size: nine percent for a 2.5-liter engine, compared with three percent for engines less than 1.5 liters.[55]

2-7 The Technological Environment

The technological environment is changing rapidly. New product development is proceeding at breakneck pace, with thousands of patents and trademarks registered worldwide on a daily basis. The technology revolution has radically changed the face of international marketing. Hub-and-spoke networks, warehouse management systems, and electronic data interchange (EDI) systems, which allow intermediaries worldwide to share standardized inventory information, all lower firms' inventory carrying costs, facilitating the flow of products and making it easier to achieve the goal of making the distribution channel more flexible and responsive to customer needs.[56]

The number of Internet users has increased rapidly and it has reached more than half of the world's population in this decade — currently, it is at four billion.[57] The Internet allows for instant access to new international markets and creates potential for exchanges that have never been previously imagined. Multinational corporations, as well as small and medium-size enterprises, benefit from the long reach of the internet (see Table 2-5).

Africa is the highest growth market (at 10 percent) for internet penetration.[58] While five years ago, most people in the larger bustling sub-Saharan African cities had flip phones and minimal access to the Internet, today, more and more individuals have an affordable smart phone and much of the middle class is active on social media.

Table 2-5 Internet Usage and Population Statistics

World Regions	Population (2018 Est.)	Internet Users Dec. 31, 2000	Internet Users Latest Data	Penetration (% of Population)	Growth 2000-2018
Africa	1,287,914,329	4,514,400	453,329,534	35.2 %	9,941 %
Asia	4,207,588,157	114,304,000	2,023,630,194	48.1 %	1,670 %
Europe	827,650,849	105,096,093	704,833,752	85.2%	570 %
Middle East	254,438,981	3,284,800	164,037,259	64.5 %	4,893 %
North America	363,844,662	108,096,800	345,660,847	95.0%	219 %
Latin America / Caribbean	652,047,996	18,068,919	437,001,277	67.0 %	2,318 %
Oceania / Australia	41,273,454	7,620,480	28,439,277	68.9 %	273 %
WORLD TOTAL	7,634,758,428	360,985,492	4,156,932,140	54.4 %	1,052 %

Source: www.internetworldstats.com/stats.htm: Internet Usage and Population Statistics, December 31, 2017.

The Internet has profoundly changed the lives of individuals, especially in the countries with the greatest penetration — at 95% for North America, 85% for Europe, 67% for Latin America, and just at 48% in Asia, [59] but growing exponentially.

Numerous companies in the United States have been successful selling to international customers through the Internet. Nevertheless, there are some pitfalls. For example, a company may need to make use of freight forwarders, who handle transportation, insurance, and export documentation, but also substantially increase the cost to the buyer. Companies must also determine the appropriate payment mechanisms. Countries differ not only with regard to the currency they use for transactions, but also in their methods of payment; for example, Europeans tend to use the Eurocard, which is a debit card, for payments. Also, worldwide, there is a high rate of credit card theft, which increases the risk that sellers might face in the international market. Using the Internet to send Mother's Day flowers from the United States to one's mother-in-law in Eldoret, Kenya, can still be difficult, and using the telephone is not much easier because the local flower shops are reluctant to serve when it comes to accepting credit cards from unknown buyers. Nevertheless, transactions never before thought possible are today commonplace due to the advances in the past three decades.

Summary

Provide an overview of the world economic environment and examine different perspectives on economic development. Countries are becoming more and more interconnected by trade, and developments in one region have immediate repercussions in the rest of the world. There are divergent views on the economic development process: The Rostow model portrays economic development as a function of productivity, exchange, technology, and income. Alternative models portray development as a function of the control on the means of production, production outcomes, resource allocation, and the development of a mindset devoid of materialist needs and may fuel anticolonial, anticapitalist sentiment, while advocating a collective societal orientation.

Address differences between countries of different levels of economic development and discuss the importance of emerging markets. Countries belong to different development categories. Developed countries are highly industrialized, have well-developed industrial and service sectors, and present great potential for new markets, with a GNI per capita of US$12,236 or more; they also present a challenge because their markets are in the maturity stage, consumers have established preferences, and competition is intense. Countries with emerging markets are developing rapidly and have great potential, as they privatize state-owned industries and adopt market reforms; of these countries, big emerging markets present the greatest potential for international trade and expansion. These countries are middle-income countries, with a GNI per capita of US$1,046 to US$12,236. Developing countries are primarily agrarian, have a low GNI per capita (less than US$1,006), and are located in different regions in Asia and in sub-Saharan Africa; they tend to be neglected or underserved by large multinationals and thus present great potential as niche markets.

Examine the indicators of political risk and address international firm approaches to political risk management. Several indicators signal political risk: economic performance, political repression, multiple groups with incongruent interests, rampant nationalism, and political instability. Some of the risks that companies can experience in foreign markets involve some level of dispossession, such as nationalization, expropriation, and confiscation; risks related to action groups and labor, as well as corporate terrorism, are on the rise. Firms can reduce risk by being good corporate citizens, by partnering with local firms, and by purchasing risk insurance.

Describe how international law, home-country law, and host-country law affect international firm operations and address issues related to jurisdiction. International companies are subject to multiple sets of laws: laws of the host country, laws of the home country—such as anticompetitiveness (antitrust) laws and corruption laws—and international laws, which could be laws of a regional governance body, such as the European Union, or laws of an international body, such as the World Trade Organization. Under this complex scenario, jurisdiction often becomes a problem; it is advisable that firms entering into agreements agree on jurisdiction and on the procedure needed for conflict resolution.

Discuss different legal systems, intellectual property laws, and national laws with extra-territorial impact that affect international firms. The three primary types of legal systems are common law, which is based on prior court rulings, with roots in English common law; code law, or civil law, which draws on comprehensive written laws that specify what constitutes legal behavior, with roots in Roman law; and Islamic law, a system of law based on the interpretation of Islam's holy book and the practices and sayings of the prophet Muhammad. One issue facing multinationals today is the violation of intellectual property rights, which constitutes a great threat to firms' competitiveness. Protection of patents, copyrights, trademarks, and trade secrets is difficult to enforce due to lax attitudes attributed to cultural values and to economic and political motivations of national governments. This type of protection might have better prospects now that more countries have become members of the World Trade Organization and are signatories of the TRIPS agreement.

Examine the natural and technological environments and the potential and limitations they present to international firms. Geography can offer opportunity for international business, or it can restrict access to the marketplace. Geography facilitates the relationship with other international markets, if those markets are located in the proximity of the home country or if the markets are located in the proximity of ports that allow easy access. Alternatively, geographical location that is remote from other international markets and that does not allow easy access impedes relationships. Geology determines the natural resources available in the country and its potential for prosperity, and climate and hydrology have a direct impact on a country's economic development. Population growth determines the types of markets that multinational companies, as well as small and medium enterprises, can target. In the high-income countries, marketers have a more mature market to contend with— markets with a substantial population aged 65 and older. Population growth also has implications with regard to the access to goods and services and to the environment. The environment is continuously challenged by business interests; these challenges have led to extensive legislation aimed at limiting the negative impact of business on the environment. The technological environment is continuously evolving, rapidly opening international markets never before accessible to multinationals and creating a viable future for small and medium enterprises that never had such a broad exposure. The technological environment is also speeding the new product development process and creating unprecedented distribution potential in industry.

Key Terms

antitrust laws

arbitration

big emerging markets (BEMs)

bourgeoisie

capitalism

code law

common law

communism

confiscation

copyright

corruption laws

creeping expropriation

domestication

drive to maturity stage

emerging markets

expropriation

feudalism

Foreign Corrupt Practices Act (FCPA)

high mass consumption

home-country laws

host-country laws

imperialism

intellectual property rights

international laws

Islamic law

Jurisdiction

low-income countries

Marxist-Leninist development model

Mediation

middle-income countries

monopolistic capitalism

nationalism

nationalization

Overseas Private Investment Corporation (OPIC)

patent

political risk

primitive society

Rostow modernization model

slavery-based society

socialism

take-off

trade secrets

trademark

traditional society

Trade-Related Aspects of Intellectual Property Rights (TRIPS)

transitional society

upper middle income countries

Discussion Questions

1. Compare the Rostow and the Marxist-Leninist models of economic development. How do you explain the two models in light of developments over the past decade in Central and Eastern Europe? Why do developing countries continue to embrace the Marxist-Leninist model of economic development?

2. Describe indicators of political risk. Examine current events and identify some of the political risks that multinational companies face in the world today.

3. Discuss two home-country laws that affect U.S. businesses operating internationally.

4. What are some examples of violations of international property rights? Give some examples of counterfeiting.

Chapter Quiz

True/False

1. Crises in one region of the world are likely to influence economic performance worldwide.

True

Rationale: Interdependence has become the leading principle of globalization. Section 2-1a, "The World Economy"

2. Low-income countries fully control national resources (raw materials, labor), control access to local consumers, and often pose barriers to international business operations.

True

Rationale: Low-income countries attempt to lessen the development gap by controlling these factors. Section 2-1b, "The Economic Development Disparity"

3. In the Rostow model, advancement is a function of the control of means of production, production outcomes, resources allocation, and the development of a mind-set devoid of materialist needs.

False

Rationale: According to the Rostow model, each stage is a function of productivity, economic exchange, technological improvements, and income. Section 2-2a, "The Rostow Modernization Model"

4. The key political risk signals are ethnic diversity and incongruent interests.

True

Rationale: Political repression in particular is indicative of political risk. Section 2-4a, "Political Risk: An Overview"

5. Common law is defined as a body of written laws specifying what constitutes legal behavior.

False

Rationale: Code law is defined as a body of written laws specifying what constitutes legal behavior. Section 2-5a, "Legal Systems"

6. The Foreign Corrupt Practices Act makes it legal for companies to bribe government officials and candidates to political office under certain circumstances.

False

Rationale: The Foreign Corrupt Practices Act does not permit companies to bribe government officials and candidates to political office, regardless of the common level of corruption in the respective business environment. Section 2-5d, "Home-Country Legislation Affecting Multinational Firms Operating Overseas"

7. A country's geology can determine whether the country can be a viable trade partner in the international market.

True

Rationale: A country's access to natural resources determines whether the country can be a viable trade partner in the international market. Section 2-6a, "Geology and the Shortage of Natural Resources"

Multiple Choice

1. The Rostow modernization model addresses all of the following EXCEPT
a. high mass consumption.
b. the drive to maturity.
c. transitional society.
d. the capitalist society.

Answer d is correct.

Rationale: The capitalist society is not addressed in the Rostow model. Section 2-2a, "The Rostow Modernization Model"

2. A stage in which modern technology is fully adopted in all economic activity and new leading sectors emerge is known as the _____ stage.
a. drive to maturity
b. high mass consumption
c. take-off
d. transitional society

Answer a is correct.

Rationale: According to the Rostow model, the drive to maturity is facilitated by a focus on technology. Section 2-2a, "The Rostow Modernization Model"

3. A stage in economic development characterized by leading sectors shifting toward durable goods is a
a. transitional society.
b. take-off.
c. high mass consumption.
d. drive to maturity.

Answer c is correct.

Rationale: According to the Rostow model, the high mass consumption stage is characterized by a focus on the production of durable goods that would satisfy broad market segments. Section 2-2a, "The Rostow Modernization Model"

4. _____ countries are characterized by consumers with established preferences and intense competition.
a. High-income
b. Nationalized
c. Emerging
d. Low-income

Answer a is correct.

Rationale: High-income countries have the highest per-capita income. Consumers from developed countries have the means to purchase products and consequently have established preferences. Companies compete heavily for these consumers. Section 2-3, "Levels of Economic Development"

5. _____ can impede the optimal functioning of business, tax the infrastructure, and lead to the scarcity of natural resources, especially raw materials.
a. Economic development
b. Population growth
c. Technology
d. All of the above

Answer b is correct.

Rationale: High population growth in spite of limited natural resources has led to famine and precipitated conflict worldwide. High population growth has taxed the infrastructure and impeded the optimal functioning of business. Section 2-6e, "Population"

Notes

1. Antiadvertising Agency, "Beer here!: The Poster and the Public Notice in Rural Rwanda," March 24, 2010, http://antiadvertisingagency.com/%E2%80%9Cbeer-here%E2%80%9D-the-poster-and-the-public-notice-in-rural-rwanda. Craig Timberg, "In Rwanda, Suicides Haunt Search for Justice and Closure," *Washington Post Foreign Service,* Friday, February 17, 2006, A01. *New Times,* "No, Kigali is not a stroke of luck; it was built by dedicated hands,"accessed at http://www.newtimes.co.rw/opinions/editorial-no-kigali-not-stroke-luck-it-was-built-dedicated-hands on April 29, 2018.

2. Michael J. Mandel, "In a One-World Economy, a Slump Sinks All Boats," *Business Week,* Industrial Technology Edition, No. 3738, June 25, 2001, pp. 38–39. Marius-Răzvan Surugiu and Camelia Surugiu, "Globalization and Economic Interdependence between European Countries: Implications for Businesses and Marketing Framework," Procedia Economics and Finance 32, 2015, pp. 131 – 138.

3. Jeremy W. Peters, "Rising Exports: Putting Dent in Trade Gap," *The Wall Street Journal,* May 14, 2007, A1, A16.

4. U.S. Chamber of Commerce, "95% of the World Consumers Live Outside the United States," May 15, 2012. Accessed at https://www.uschamber.com/ad/95-worlds-consumers-live-outside-united-states on April 26, 2018.

5. Russell W. Belk, "Hyperreality and Globalization: Culture in the Age of Ronald McDonald," *Journal of International Consumer Marketing,* Vol. 8, No. 3/4, 1996, pp. 23–37; and Leslie Sklair, "Competing Models of Globalization: Theoretical Frameworks and Research Agendas," working paper, London School of Economics and Political Science, University of London, London, United Kingdom. Frances Maguire, "Multinationals: The New Master of the Universe," *The Banker,* January 1, 2006, p. 1.

6. Walt W. Rostow, *The Stages of Economic Growth: A Non-Communist Manifesto,* London and New York: Cambridge University Press, 1960; ———, "The Concept of a National Market and Its Economic Growth Implications," in *Marketing and Economic Development,* ed. P. D. Bennett, Chicago: American Marketing Association, 1965, pp. 11 –20; and —— *The Stages of Economic Growth,* Second Edition, London: Cambridge University Press, 1971.

7. Barkley Rosser, Jr., and Marina V. Rosser, "Islamic and Neo-Confucian Perspectives on the New Traditional Economy," *Eastern Economic Journal,* Vol. 24, No. 2, Spring 1998, pp. 217–227.

8. Ali Farazmand, "Development and Comparative Public Administration: Past, Present, and Future," *Public Administration Quarterly,* Vol. 20, No. 3, Fall 1996, pp. 343–364.

9. Rosser and Rosser, "Islamic and Neo-Confucian Perspectives," pp. 217–227.

10. Roger Hayter and Sun Sheng Han, "Reflections on China's Open Policy Towards Foreign Direct Investment, *Regional Studies,* Vol. 32, No. 1, February 1998, pp. 1–16.

11. Adapted from Leonidas Barbopoulos, Andrew Marshall, Cameron MacInnes, and Patrick McColgan, "Foreign Direct Investment in Emerging Markets and Acquirers' Value Gains," *International Business Review,* Vol. 23, No. 3, June 2014, pp. 604-619, Robert Lloyd George, *The Handbook of Emerging Markets: A Country-By-Country Guide to the World's Fastest Growing Economies,* Chicago, IL: Probus Publications, 1994. *The Economist,* "Defining Emerging Markets," October 7, 2017. Accessed at https://www.economist.com/news/special-report/21729866-self-fulfilling-prophecy-defining-emerging-markets on April 17, 2018.

12. Ibid.

13. Keith Bradsher, "India Finds Its Economy on the Verge of Overheating," *The New York Times,* February 10, 2007, B1, B9. Rishi Iyengar, "India Is Growing Faster than China Again," CNN.com, accessed at http://money.cnn.com/2018/02/28/news/economy/india-economy-gdp-7-2-growth/index.html on April 28, 2018.

14. Adapted from Amjad Hadjikhani, "Political Risk for Project-Selling Firms: Turbulence in Relationships between Business and Non-Business Actors," *Journal of Business & Industrial Marketing,* Vol. 13, No. 3, 1998, pp. 235–239.

15. Jay Solomon, "Politics & Economics: New Sanctions Are Possible As U.N. Report Faults Iran," *The Wall Street Journal,* May 24, 2007, A7.

16. Courtney Tower, "Canada Wants WTO Panel in U.S. Farm Aid Case, *Journal of Commerce*, June 11, 2007, p. 1.

17. Richard B. Loth, "How to Evaluate Country Risk," *Credit and Financial Management*, Vol. 88, No. 6, June 1986, p. 27.

18. Ilan Alon and Matthew A. Martin, "A Normative Model of Macro Political Risk Assessment," *Multinational Business Review*, Vol. 6, No. 2, Fall 1998, pp. 10–19.

19. *Economist.com*, "Turkmenistan's New Father," January 24, 2007, 1. Max Bearak, "Central Asian Dictator or Schwarzenegger in 'Commando'," *The Washington Post*, August 3, 2017, accessed at https://www.washingtonpost.com/news/worldviews/wp/2017/08/03/central-asian-dictator-or-schwarzenegger-in-commando-hard-to-tell/?utm_term=.846882374538 on May 4, 2018.

20. Terence A. Shimp and Subhash Sharma, "Consumer Ethnocentrism: Construction and Validation of the CETSCALE," *Journal of Marketing Research*, Vol. 24, No. 3, August 1987, pp. 280–289.

21. Thomas Fuller, "Thailand May Add Measures to Restrict Foreign Investment," *Wall Street Journal*, January 10, 2007, C11. *The Straits Times*, "Thailand to Consider Opening Some Service Businesses to More Foreign Investment," March 26, 2018, accessed at https://www.straitstimes.com/asia/se-asia/thailand-to-consider-opening-some-service-businesses-to-more-foreign-investment-report on May 5, 2018.

22. *Richmond Times-Dispatch*, "Currency Action Pummels Brink's,"April 15, 2014. Accessed at http://www.richmond.com/business/currency-action-pummels-brink-s/article_e2ec5b45-f33f-5845-89b5-f448697e7c00.html on April 16, 2018.

23. Sohn Young-Ju, "Saving Kia," *Business Korea*, Vol. 15, No. 1, January 1998.

24. Henny Sender, "Reflation Is No Panacea," *Far Eastern Economic Review*, Vol. 161, No. 48, November 26, 1998, p. 93.

25. Thomas Fuller, "Thailand May Add Measures to Restrict Foreign Investment," *The Wall Street Journal*, January 10, 2007, C11; Simon Romero, "Chavez Begins New Term Vowing Socialism," *The New York Times*, January 11, 2007, A14.

26. Taos Turner, "Argentina Wants Cheap Flights, But Not Too Cheap," *The Wall Street Journal*, December 23, 2017. Accessed at https://www.wsj.com/articles/argentina-wants-cheap-flightsbut-not-too-cheap-1514030401 on April 21, 2018.

27. Michael Gips, "Businesses Bearing Brunt of Terrorism," *Security Management*, Vol. 45, No. 8, August 2001, p. 18; David S. Cloud, "Bush Team Says Data Were Wrong on Terror Deaths," *The Wall Street Journal*, June 23, 2004, B2.

28. Steve Lohr, "Financial District Vows to Rise from the Ashes," *The New York Times*, September 14, 2001, A6; Susan Sontag, "The Talk of the Town, Tuesday, and After," *The New Yorker*, September 24, 2001, p. 32.

29. IntelCenter, Global Incident Location Statistics, 2016, accessed at https://intelcenter.com/reports/global-location-stats/2016/index.html on May 2, 2018.

30. Global Terrorism Index 2017, accessed at https://lnt.ma/wp-content/uploads/2017/11/global-terrorism-index-2017.pdf on May 7, 2018.

31."Counter-Terrorism Driver Training May Thwart Executive Kidnapping," *Best's Review*, Vol. 98, No. 2, June 1997, p. 95.

32. Rob Lenihan, "Insurance Market Evolving to Handle Terrorism Risks: Marsh," *Business Insurance*, April 10, 2018, accessed at http://www.businessinsurance.com/article/20180410/NEWS06/912320483/Insurance-market-evolving-to-handle-terrorism-risks-Marsh-report on May 7, 2018.

33. Ilkka A. Ronkainen and Jose-Luis Guerrero-Cusumano, "Correlates of Intellectual Property Violation," *Multinational Business Review*, Vol. 9, No. 1, Spring 2001, pp. 59–65.

34. The Commission on the Theft of American Intellectual Property, "The Theft of American Intellectual Property: Reassessments of the Challenge and United States Policy," p. 9, February 2017. Accessed at http://www.ipcommission.org/report/IP_Commission_Report_Update_2017.pdf on April 21, 2018.

35. "Copycats Beware," *Business Korea,* Vol. 18, No. 3, March 2001, pp. 44–45.

36. Heather R. Goldstein, David M. Lange, Andrew E. Roth, and James D. Lawrence, "International Intellectual Property Alliance Points USTR Toward Brazil, Costa Rica, Guatemala, Russia, Uruguay," *Intellectual Property & Technology Law Journal,* Vol. 12, No. 11, November 2000, p. 27.

37. Ronkainen and Guerrero-Cusumano, "Correlates of Intellectual Property Violation," pp. 59–65.

38. "Special: The Right to Good Ideas, Patents and the Poor," *The Economist,* Vol. 359, No. 8227, June 23, 2001, pp. 21–23. World Trade Organization, "Uruguay Round Agreement: TRIPS," accessed at https://www.wto.org/english/docs_e/legal_e/27-trips_03_e.htm on May 2, 2018.

39. Ibid.

40. Ronkainen and Guerrero-Cusumano, "Correlates of Intellectual Property Violation," pp. 59–65.

41. "Special: The Right to Good Ideas, Patents and the Poor," *The Economist,* Vol. 359, No. 8227, June 23, 2001, pp. 21–23. World Trade Organization, "Uruguay Round Agreements TRIPS," accessed at https://www.wto.org/english/docs_e/legal_e/27-trips_03_e.htm on May 2, 2018. United States Patent and Trademark Office, "Fiscal Year 2019 Budget," accessed at https://www.uspto.gov/about-us/performance-and-planning/budget-and-financial-information on May 2, 2018.

42. Ibid.

43. Ibid.

44. *The New York Times,* "Czech Republic: Busch-Budvar Thaw," January 9, 2007, C1. Prague TV, "Tips for Three Beer Capitals," March 10, 2018, accessed at https://prague.tv/en/s72/Directory/c207-Travel/n13515-Tips-for-trips-Three-Czech-beer-capitals on May 2, 2018.

45. Sarah Lyall, *"Who Strikes Fear Into Silicon Valley? Margrethe Vestager, Europe's Antitrust Enforcer," The New York Times,* May 5, 2018, accessed at https://www.nytimes.com/2018/05/05/world/europe/margrethe-vestager-silicon-valley-data-privacy.html on May 2, 2018.

46. *The World Bank,* "Combatting Corruption," September 26, 2017, accessed at http://www.worldbank.org/en/topic/ governance/brief/anti-corruption on May 3, 2018.

47. Ibid

48. Jack G. Kaikati, George M. Sullivan, John M. Virgo, T. R. Carr, and Katherine S. Virgo, "The Price of International Business Morality: Twenty Years Under the Foreign Corrupt Practices Act," *Journal of Business Ethics,* Vol. 26, No. 3, August 2000, pp. 213–222.

49. Organization for Economic Co-operation and Development (OECD), www.oecd.org. Accessed on May 2, 2018,

50. Sarah Lyall, "Sweden's Lightning Rod in a Storm over Assimilation," *The New York Times,* January 13, 2007, A4.

51. Mark Landler, "Germany Agonizes Over a Brain Drain." *New York Times,* February 6, 2007, A10. The Local, "Here are the 10 Countries Germans Immigrate to," August 10, 2017, accessed at https://www.thelocal.de/20170810/here-are-the-top-countries-where-germans-immigrate-to on May 2, 2018.

52. Elisabeth Rosenthal, "Car Boom Puts Europe on Road to a Smoggy Future," *The New York Times,* January 7, 2007, Section 1, 3.

53. United Nations Climate Change, "The Paris Agreement," accessed at https://unfccc.int/process-and-meetings/the-paris-agreement/the-paris-agreement on May 3, 2018.

54. Keith Bradsher, "India and China Explore Alternatives, but Too Often Diesel Generator Rules," *The New York Times,* January 9, 2007, C1, C7.

55. Joseph B. White, "For GM in China, Tiny Is Mighty; Wuling Venture Plans Expansion as Sales of Small Cars Surge," *The Wall Street Journal,* April 20, 2007, A9.

56. Sue Abdinnour-Helm, "Network Design in Supply Chain Management," *International Journal of Agile Management Systems,* Vol. 1, No. 2, 1999, pp. 99–106.

57. *We Are Social*, "Digital in 2018: World's Internet Users Pass the 4 Billion Mark," accessed at https://wearesocial.com/blog/2018/01/global-digital-report-2018 on May 2, 2018.

58. Internet World Stats, "Internet Usage and Population Statistics," December 31, 2017, accessed at https://www.internetworldstats.com/stats.htm on May 5, 2018.

59. Ibid.

60. Munich Re "Munich Re as a Career," accessed at https://www.munichre.com/en/career/munich-re-as-an-employer/overview/index.html on May 3, 2018.

61. "Finance and Economics: Premium Rates; Reinsurance," *The Economist*, February 9, 2002, p. 79.

62. Munich Re, "History", accessed at https://www.munichre.com/en/group/company/history/index.html on May 3, 2018.

63. Munich Re, "Corporate Responsibility," accessed at https://www.munichre.com/en/group/focus/climate-change/strategic-approach/corporate-responsibility/index.html?QUERYSTRING=corporate%20responsibility on July 7, 2015

64. Ibid.

65. *Best's Special Report*, "Global Reinsurance – Segment Review," September 2017, accessed at http://www.bestweek.com/europe/promo/ReinsurersRepositionMktDistruption.pdf on May 3, 2018.

66. "Reinsurer Munich Re Posts US $1.06B Loss, Keeps Damage Estimates from Attacks," *Canoe Money*, http:// www.canoe.ca/MoneyEarnings/nov29_munichre-ap.html, November 29, 2001, pp. 1–2 (web); February 21, 2002.

67. "Reinsurers Double Terrorist Claims," CNN money, http://money.cnn.com/2001/09/20/europe/insurance/ index.htm, September 20, 2001, p. 1 (web); February 21, 2002.

68. "Munich Re Posts $1.1B Loss," http://europe.cnn.com/.

69. "After the Terrorist Attacks: US Rating Agencies Affirm Their Top Rating for Munich Re," *Munich American News*, http://www.marclife.com/news01/mr100501.htm, October 5, 2001, p. 1 (web); February 21, 2002.

70. "Reinsurer Munich Re Posts US $1.06B Loss, Keeps Damage Estimate from Attacks," p. 2 (web).

71. Meg Green, "Extreme Weather Patterns Pose Greater Insurance Risk," *Best's Review*, Vol. 104, No. 11, March 2004, p. 69.

72. Green, "Extreme Weather Patterns," p. 69.

73. Oliver Ralph, "Munich Re Slides 5% After Profits Blown Off-Course by Hurricanes, *Financial Times*, February 5, 2018, accessed on May 5, 2018.

Case 2-1 Munich Re—Terrorism-Related Risk Management and Ecological Issues

Introduction

Munich Re (in German, Münchener Rückversicherungs-Gesellschaft) is the second largest reinsurance company. It has had its ups and downs, handling costly, massive catastrophes, but all the while, taking in profits for its innovative insurance products and maintaining its AAA rating. Its performance over the years has been impressive, despite devastating, catastrophic events, such as the September 11, 2001, terrorist attacks and the powerful hurricanes of 2017 in the U.S. and Caribbean, which wiped out its profits and created setbacks for its stock value.

As a reinsurance firm, Munich Re relies on insurance firms to minimize losses. It allows for costs attributed to insurance losses to be distributed among multiple companies; as such, the reinsurance industry makes it possible for insurance companies to take risks they otherwise would not take,[60] creating new opportunities for increased revenue and market share. The amount of risk assumed by reinsurers varies with the market. When the market is optimistic, reinsurers are more likely to assume greater risks; more capital is available, so the companies are capable of underwriting additional risk.[61]

Munich Re has been consistently rethinking its product mix and has actively pursued sustained insurance-product-related innovation in many facets of its activity. This case focuses primarily on two aspects of innovative risk management at Munich Re: terrorism risk management and ecological risk management.

Company Background

Munich Re was founded in 1880 by Carl Thieme, who, with a vision far ahead of his time, created the reinsurance business: He convinced investors of the insurance companies' need for reinsurance as a means for redistributing risk (and loss) among insurance firms, thus allowing them to take advantage of opportunities that otherwise they could not afford to consider.[62] Munich Re is headquartered in downtown Munich, Germany, where it covers a couple of square blocks with impressive older and contemporary architecture.

Inside the Munich Re complex, a Japanese garden offers an environment of meditation. Underground, all the buildings are connected with active corridors where color and light set a theatrical stage; here, a second "downtown"—the downtown of Munich Re employees— exists in parallel to the bustling street, Leopoldstrasse. The environment projects a strong spirit of innovation, the very theme of Munich Re's corporate culture.[63] In addition to its quest for product innovation, Munich Re was the first German company to introduce English working hours in the nineteenth century, requiring shorter days from its employees and granting them greater leisure time; the company is also among a few in Germany that provide benefits such as access to a holiday home in the Alps and an on-site daycare—the Munich Re Giants Childcare Center.[64]

The Munich Re Product

With a dependable brand, international presence, diversified product offering, and 42 offices around the world, Munich Re has attracted customers and investors alike, and today it is the second largest reinsurance company in the world. In the 2017 *Best Review* rankings, it recorded consolidated gross premiums of $33,154 million, closely following Swiss Re, with gross premiums of $35,622.[65]

The company offers several different types of insurance services, such as Alternative Risk-Financing and Risk-Transfer Solutions (ART), Agricultural Insurance, Managed Care Services, and Life Insurance. ART, including Finite Risk Reinsurance and Integrated Risk Management, supplements conventional reinsurance as a means of maximizing risk retention and discovering additional financial resources. This is an area that Munich Re has pioneered and that is in especially great demand today, after the September 11, 2001, terrorist attacks. Finite Risk Reinsurance allows the company to undertake more risk by using innovative financing techniques, rather than simply by transferring risk from the insured to the insurer.

Integrated Risk Management merges insurance risks with the risks involved in financial markets—for example, in currency and interest rate fluctuation. The objective of Integrated Risk Management is to achieve both the reinsurer's goals of the lowest possible risk and the client's goals of highest possible security and support. Munich Re provides a number of other insurance services, covering all aspects of the economy. For example, Agricultural Insurance is a service that Munich Re has developed to protect commercial farmers in times of catastrophe and natural disaster. Its Managed Care Services, part of the Munich Re Health Division, are involved in evaluating each potential medical procedure that it insures to determine if, in fact, the procedure is essential. Finally, the company's Life Insurance services give the company access to final consumers—a different market than its traditional

Insurance Losses and Firm Profits

Munich Re, much like other reinsurance companies, has had numerous challenges, many dealing with medical advances and genetics decoding, and others with natural disasters. For example, Munich Re had to absorb the costs involved in the recall of Lipobay, a cholesterol-reducing drug that was linked to death among users; a large typhoon in Taiwan; a chemical plant explosion in France, and the powerful 2017 hurricanes in the U.S. and Caribbean, among others.[66]

These losses, in comparison, are dwarfed by the losses incurred at the the September 11, 2001, terrorist attacks. Total damages for the reinsurance industry were more than $3 billion for the disaster.[67] Munich Re's claims totaled $1.84 billion.[68] Compared with competitors, Munich Re has handled the aftermath of September 11 well, and A.M. Best and Standard & Poor's concluded that their ratings of A++ and AAA/Stable, respectively, were still appropriate for Munich Re, based on the company's performance by the end of 2001.[69] The company's losses were offset by an increase in premium income by 20 percent; moreover, Munich Re found itself with less competition, as smaller reinsurers had incurred losses that caused them to leave the industry altogether.[70] In 2002, Munich Re experienced further losses, as natural catastrophes rose sharply due to heat waves, forest fires, severe floods in Asia and Europe, as well as tornadoes in the Midwestern United States.[71] Since 2001, tens of thousands of people were killed in natural catastrophes, what with more than 500 tornadoes in the Midwest of the United States, California wildfires, hurricanes, and snow and ice storms. In Europe, the company lost more than $13 billion due to heat waves alone.[72] More recently, the company saw its profits practically wiped out in 2017, after the powerful hurricanes in the U.S. and Caribbean. And, yet, despite losses, Munich Re remains a top performer, with a profit of over $400 million in 2017, the year of this most recent loss. [73]

Analysis Suggestions

1. Address the political risk signals that bring about terrorist actions. How can companies reduce their likelihood of becoming victims of terrorism?

2. How does Munich Re manage risk from political turmoil and natural disasters?

Case 2-2 Doing Business in Cuba... One Day Soon

As a small business operating in the Orlando area, Deco1 has served successfully middle class Hispanics' interior decorating needs. Its work has been featured in regional magazines illustrating its minimalist, yet colorful designs, which appeal to the region's Hispanic population. One of the largest target markets is the Cuban American market in the region.

Deco1's owner, Terry Kaminer, was born in Cuba, but came to the United States with her parents in the 1960s, and Terry has been active in the Cuban community in the Orlando area. One of her dreams is one day to return "home" and to teach Cubans how to live simply with good, attractive design.

Cuba's highly centralized socialist economic system is still recovering from the loss of substantial Soviet subsidies, from hurricanes, and from a massive brain drain of its best and brightest. China is increasingly reluctant to underwrite Cuba's economy, and the country's infrastructure is in dire need of an upgrade.

In the past two years, Cuba has made strides in embracing a more market-oriented economy under its new leader, Raul Castro, the brother of Cuba's long-time leader, Fidel Castro, as head of the State. There is now a fledgling real estate market and individuals are able to buy and sell automobiles and homes. For the first time, small private businesses are allowed to hire employees and pay their workers' social security contributions — a total of 350,000 business licenses have been granted for private enterprise. The government opened idle land to farmers and cooperatives, and it allows individuals to open lines of credit with no legal ceilings on how much individuals can borrow.

At the same time, Cuba is instituting austerity measures, shrinking the buying power of the ration card that Cubans receive to purchase subsidized products, cutting unemployment benefits, and dismissing up to a million individuals working for the state. Cuba is currently in a difficult position: The United States has, until recently, refused to change its strict policies, maintaining an economic, commercial, and financial blockade. As a result, Cuba is not a member of any international financial institution, and the U.S. blockade made it impossible to obtain any additional lines of credit, which led Cuba to default on its payments to foreign creditors in 2008. Currently, Cuba earns hard currency by exporting nickel, sugar, and professional services (medical) and receives income from tourism and remittances from Cubans living abroad. With the hard currency it imports everything, from food to manufactured goods and capital goods.

However, with all the difficulties Cuba continues to encounter and the insistence of the Cuban government on maintaining a Soviet-style economic and political system, Terry Kaminer's acquaintances in the Cuban-American community are preparing for a radical change and for open borders with the United States. On July 1, 2015, President Barack Obama announced the formal resumption of diplomatic relations with Cuba. Many Cuban Americans are actively looking at the possibility of investing in small businesses with the help of relatives living in Cuba. Terry is wondering about the prospects of Deco1 in Cuba. With the prospects of increasing tourism and prosperity, more Cubans will be interested in building new homes, and interior design will be on their radar screen. And yet, what if the Cuban government insists on maintaining the status quo, enforcing the existing economic and political dictatorship?

Analysis Suggestions

1. Address Cuba's current situation in light of the different models of economic development discussed in the chapter. Is Cuba socialist? Capitalist?

2. Discuss the viability of Terry's small business in the new Cuba. Are Cubans going to turn to interior design businesses anytime soon?

Sources: Jeff Jacoby, "Cubans Pay the Price for Obama's 'Engagement' with the Castros," *The Boston Globe*, July 7, 2015, accessed at https://www.bostonglobe.com/opinion/2015/07/07/obama-engagement-with-cuba-rulers-comes-expense-its-people/hdT49OQfjH7Y2UjCobhEtJ/story.html on July 7, 2015. Ted Piccone, "Cuba Is Changing Slowly but Surely," Brookings Institution, January 19, 2012, http:// www.brookings.edu/research/reports/2012/01/19-cuba-piccone CTC, http://www.marxist.com/where-is-cuba-going-capitalism-or-socialism.htm; CNBC, "Inside Cuba Market Economy Takes Hold in Socialist State Under Raul," http:// www.cnbc.com/id/46855968/ Inside_Cuba_Market_Economy_Takes_Hold_in_Socialist_State; http://www.workers.org/2012/world/ cuba_060, (accessed July 10, 2012).

This page is intentionally blank.

Chapter 3

International Trade: Institutional Barriers and Facilitators

Learning Objectives

After studying
this chapter,
you should be able to:

- Identify different trade barriers imposed on international trade and the arguments used by governments to erect and maintain these barriers.

- Provide an overview of key international organizations facilitating international trade directly or by promoting economic development.

- Identify government efforts involved in promoting economic development and trade.

- Describe other trade facilitators, such as foreign trade zones, offshore assembly plants, and special economic zones, and the U.S. Trade bills.

Chapter Outline

Businesses face numerous
barriers when entering international markets. They are imposed by the local government, by local and international competition, by the local channel members,
and by logistics and other firms offering
marketing support. Factors in the economic, political, financial, and legal environment also create barriers for businesses expanding internationally — as discussed in Chapter 2, "An Overview of the
International Marketing Environment."

Olena Hromova/shutterstock.com

Even regional organizations, such as free trade areas, common markets, or political unions can impose barriers to entry. For example, one of the first nicknames that the European
Union acquired when it was established was "Fortress Europe," for its potential to restrict
access of foreign companies to its large market. Fortunately, that was not the case: the European Union has proven itself to be a staunch supporter of free trade.

The reduction in trade barriers constitutes a main goal of multinationals, smaller exporters, and their representative governments. In addition to participating in numerous regional treaties, governments have joined forces to create forums for discussion of trade issues and mechanisms for the reduction of trade restrictions. One such organization, the
World Trade Organization (WTO), has had a significant positive impact on trade, reining in
protectionist measures, and opening formerly closed markets to international companies.
Nevertheless, despite its accomplishments, this organization has met substantial opposition
from groups that perceive globalization as the promotion of large multinational companies'
interests to the detriment of developing countries and of the environment. This chapter focuses on protectionist actions and on important facilitators of international trade; it also
addresses the opposition to trade expansion by governmental and nongovernmental bodies.

Protection of local markets from foreign companies constitutes an important mandate for national and local governments alike. Many political careers have been built and
defended on populist, market-protection rhetoric. "We will not sell our country" is one of
the slogans of resistance to foreign economic and political dominance. Such slogans have
been used against multinationals that are rapidly taking over emerging markets, and bringing with them a consumption culture perceived to go against local culture and traditions.
These multinationals are seen as eliminating small local producers and service providers,
bankrupting formerly productive factories, and replacing abundant local labor with more
efficient advanced technology, increasing local unemployment and disrupting political stability.

Some of the arguments for protectionism are indeed valid. The infant industry argument is aimed at protecting an emerging national industry from powerful international competitors, which could easily squeeze out a newcomer merely with brand name resonance
and with pricing strategies that a new industry could not possibly sustain in the long term.
The argument stressing the industrialization of developing countries also is valid for similar
reasons. The national defense argument is regarded as justified in international trade forums and is widely accepted as a reasonable argument for protectionism.

There is also the argument for environmental protection and protection of natural resources and the need for maintaining standards for the benefit of all humankind. This line of arguments is also well justified. The problem with this defense arises when the standards imposed are simply protectionist measures that unfairly require foreign competition to go through an excessive, costly, and unwarranted bureaucratic exercise. It is particularly problematic when these requirements are imposed on and enforced for international firms but not imposed on or enforced for local firms, or when they are imposed on local firms to a lesser degree.

Consumers pay a high price for protectionism. Arguments for protectionism ignore the economic advantages of free trade and the importance of adopting open market mechanisms for optimal market performance. History has demonstrated that a government's right and authority to pick and choose winners among industries and firms could be corrupted and distorted by local influential firms, by populist power-seeking politicians appealing to voters fearing losing their jobs, and by favor-seeking lobby groups.[1] Argentines, for example, pay more for locally-assembled air conditioners and cellular telephones, while imports are subjected to high tariffs, leading to the creation of a black market, or to cross-border shopping in neighboring Chile. The annual cost to Argentine taxpayers to subsidize these assembly jobs is in excess of $72,000 per employee.[2] In another example, when the U.S. imposed steep tariffs on steel and aluminum, in 2018, and proposed specific tariffs on Chinese goods in retaliation for China's theft of trade secrets and technology, it was met with swift retaliation, resulting in higher prices for consumers and businesses in the U.S., with negative consequences on the U.S. economy and industry.

3-1 Arguments for Protectionism

Sections 3-1a through 3-1f describe arguments most often advanced to justify the imposition of tariff and nontariff trade barriers.

gopixa/shutterstock.com

3-1a Protection of Markets with Excess Productive Capacity

Markets with excess productive capacity have committed significant resources to their production facilities. In the case of China and the former Eastern Bloc, most production during the central planning years under strict communist rule took place in factories employing tens of thousands of workers, each often charged with minuscule tasks under an elaborate division-of-labor program. The goal of such programs was both to ensure productivity and a place of work to every individual. Such factories had, in addition to workers, redundant oversight structures with multiple layers of directors, all served by several secretaries whose specializations varied from typing and answering telephones to running errands.

After the fall of communist rule in the Eastern Bloc, the new factory owners (often foreign) quickly realized they needed only a fraction of the workers for optimal production and proceeded to fire the rest, leading to local unrest. As in China, some of the remaining factories are protected from foreign investors and competing higher-performance products to maintain stable employment. Governments argue that such restrictions were instituted for the protection of markets with excess productive capacity.

3-1b   Employment Protection and Protection of Markets with Excess Labor

Under the scenario above, the markets of the former Eastern Bloc and China are now experiencing high levels of excess labor and underemployment, all of which could lead to social unrest. As a result, local politicians have actively lobbied against granting import licenses for products competing with locally produced goods. Arguments invoking employ-

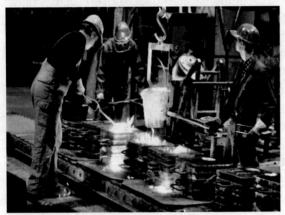

industryviews/shutterstock.com

ment protection are used to ensure that firms do not import products made elsewhere that might drive local manufacturers out of business, leading to local unemployment. The argument also is used against firms that might purchase local plants and fire most of the redundant workers to create acceptable levels of profitability.

A related argument, invoking the protection of markets with excess labor, is also used to prevent foreign businesses from taking over local businesses and streamlin-

ing operations. In France, Emmanuel Macron won the 2017 presidential election in part because of his pledge to fight the transfer of manufacturing jobs from France to Poland and Romania, members of the European Union where wages are considerably lower. Macron criticized French companies for taking advantage of the European Union laws that allow free movement of goods, persons, and services. Polish firms have become the back-office of French firms, performing customer-service and human-resource management tasks at wages well below those of French employees.

3-1c Infant Industry Arguments and Arguments Related to the Industrialization of Developing Countries

Infant industry arguments and arguments related to the industrialization of developing countries are valid under WTO rules; developing countries must protect their markets from large multinationals from countries with an established industrial base. Establishing a new industry is a costly investment and it takes time until the industry becomes competitive. Without protection, foreign competitors would be able to undercut it, offering established brands at competitive prices. Western countries have used this argument dating as far back as the late 1700s, up to the 1980s, until the emergence of globalization. Even Latin American governments introduced industry protection policies ("import substitution"), decades ago, promoting industrialization and increased wages in the manufacturing sector. However, these giant government-owned steel mills and manufacturing facilities were highly inefficient and costly to operate. Consumer goods actually became more expensive, and of lower quality. For example, a bicycle in Chile cost four times more than in the United States.[3]

3-1d Natural Resources Conservation and Protection of the Environment

The resource conservation and environmental protection arguments are valid under WTO rules, especially in light of the worldwide shortage of raw materials. The problem with these two arguments arises when they are used arbitrarily, with a clear bias against international firms, either imposing the standards only on foreign firms or requiring them to meet higher standards than local firms.

3-1e Protection of Consumers

Protection of consumers is an often-echoed argument that ultimately favors local, over international, business. Standards that are rigidly applied against foreign businesses, quality controls that necessitate layers of costly bureaucracy, and arbitrary product origin requirements, among others, are instituted invoking this argument. Politicians in the European Union have long argued that they are protecting consumers by imposing standards on imported beef: Listening to the unified voices of their constituencies and attempting to protect the local beef industry against the high-quality, cheap, corn-fed U.S. beef, the European Union has banned the import of all hormone-fed beef for two decades. Although there is little scientific evidence that supports the ban, the EU applies the precautionary principle when it comes to food safety; this means that, in case of scientific uncertainty, it could take measures to protect consumers. The United States, in turn, had banned the import of all European beef since the late 1990s, claiming it was protecting consumers from mad cow disease; it subsequently lifted the ban in 2015 by allowing imports of Irish grass-fed beef.

David Tadevosian/shutterstock.com

3-1f National Defense Interests

The national defense argument is often invoked in international trade forums. Publications that attempt to destabilize the government, armaments, and other similar products are legitimately under an import ban. More recently, the national defense argument has been advocated by countries that attempt to control their population and restrict access to Western influence. Such nations may perceive a threat in the unrestricted imports of information-based services through electronic channels; for instance, China, Singapore, and Saudi Arabia impose restrictions on, and even ban ownership of, satellite dishes, whereas other nations are attempting to control citizen access to the Internet.[4] Expatriate forums in the Middle East frequently lament the restrictions on the use of the free Skype, What's App, and other video services, forcing individuals to use costly telephone service instead.

3-2 Tools of Government Protectionism: Tariff and Nontariff Barriers

3-2a Tariffs

Tariffs are any type of tax imposed on goods entering a particular country. Tariffs are imposed to:

- Discourage imports of particular goods, such as consumer goods, which are not considered essential goods in developing countries.
- Protect local industry: For example, the United States imposed tariffs on Chinese solar panels to protect U.S. industry and to penalize China for subsidizing solar panel exports. In 2018, the U.S. imposed tariffs on steel and aluminum imports and threatened to impose tariffs on specific Chinese goods.

Ivan Marc/shutterstock.com

- Penalize countries that are not politically aligned with the importing country, or countries that are imposing tariffs or nontariff restrictions on goods from the importing country.
- Generate revenues for the importing country.

Tariffs assessed by the United States are relatively low, less than 15 percent. Some countries may set tariffs higher than 100 percent for products that compete with an infant industry.

3-2b Nontariff Barriers

Nontariff barriers include all measures, other than traditional tariffs, that are used to distort international trade flows. Such barriers raise prices of both imports and import-competing goods and favor domestic over foreign supply sources by causing importers to charge higher prices and to restrict import volumes. It is often said that international trade is no longer a game of tariffs, but a game of quality, standards, and compliance with the requirements of the global market. Exporters – from emerging markets, in particular – struggle extensively with nontariff barriers in their quest for international markets. [5]

In the past 20 years, in an attempt to keep markets closed without going against the General Agreement on Tariffs and Trade (GATT) and the WTO (see Chapter 4, "Regional Economic and Political Integration"), governments have created new nontariff barriers, such as orderly market arrangements, voluntary import expansion, and voluntary export restraints, which limit market access for foreign businesses. These nontariff barriers have been erected by many countries, but most are imposed by the United States, members of the European Union, and other industrialized countries on exporting countries such as Japan, South Korea, and developing countries.[6] But even local governments, such as the government of the state of New York, can erect such barriers, as the International Marketing Illustration 3-1 (next page) describes.

Other, more traditional, nontariff barriers include quotas, currency controls, and standards, such as environmental, quality, performance, and health standards, all of which are expensive to provide and evaluate. Boycotts, embargoes, and sanctions are the most severe barriers to trade that are imposed, usually to punish a company or a national government.

Nontariff barriers are constantly evolving: They are in a continuous process of refinement, aimed at avoiding scrutiny from the World Trade Organization or other trade organizations. Although the most frequently encountered nontariff barriers are described here, it is important to note that new variants of the barriers described are constantly emerging in the global trade arena.

Direct shipping laws provide an example of nontariff barriers to trade. Such laws enacted locally, by states, restrict international trade. For example, New York State law denies all firms outside the state the ability to sell directly to New York consumers. These laws restrict consumer choice, and consumers have to pay higher prices because fewer competitors are available in the market. New York consumers could order wine from a company in Alsace, France, at a lower cost than buying the same wine from a New York retailer. However, the ability of New York consumers to purchase wine from abroad or from other states in the United States should increase competition and lead to lower prices and more wine choices for consumers.

New York law states that only New York distributors can dispense any case of wine entering the state from foreign suppliers. In effect, New York distributors have a monopoly over the market. Retailers are also affected by this law because they, too, have to purchase their wine from New York distributors. A comparison of wine prices reveals that states that allow direct shipping have a lower average price than states that do not allow it.

New York is currently considering permitting direct shipping – with limitations – and enacting related legislation.

Sources: Robert Eyler, "Direct Shipping Laws, Wine, and Societal Welfare," International Journal of Wine Marketing, Vol. 15, No. 2, 2003, pp. 25–34. Emma Balter, "Wine Legislation Roundup: A Consumer's Guide to 2018 State Politics," *Wine Spectator*, March 26, 2018, accessed at http://www.winespectator.com/webfeature/show/id/Wine-Consumer-Guide-2018-State-Politics on May 4, 2018.

Iakov Filimonov/shutterstock.com

Import Quotas, Orderly Market Arrangements, and Voluntary Export Restraints (VERs)

Quotas specify a maximum quantity (unit limit) or a value (usually specified in the national currency) of a product that may be imported during a specified period. Quotas are administered either on a global first-come, first-served basis or on a bilateral basis to restrict shipments from a specific supply source.[7] An example of a quota is Japan's restriction on imported rice. Each year Japan imports 770,000 tons of rice tariff-free, or about 10 percent of its annual consumption, under a 1995 World Trade Organization quota agreement. Beyond that import quota, Japan maintains a hefty levy on imported rice.[8]

The United States also makes active use of quotas to protect the U.S. sugar beet and sugar cane growers. The U.S. Department of Agriculture imposes a strict quota and tariff system on sugar imports. These market controls benefit the 5000 or so U.S. sugar beet and sugar cane growers. However, this means that consumers in the U.S. will pay higher prices for products with sugar content.[9]

Similar to quotas, but presented as negotiated and voluntary, are orderly market arrangements and voluntary export restraints. Orderly market arrangements or voluntary export restraints (VERs) are self-imposed export quotas by the importing country. The exporting country limits the quantity of products it exports, primarily because it attempts, by doing so, to avoid more severe mandatory import restrictions in the future. The United States, for example, has used VERs to protect local steel and automobile industries; for example, it sent automobile industry representatives to Japan in the 1980s to persuade the Japanese to limit their exports to the United States. VERS are still used today, even though they have been banned by the General Agreement on Tariffs and Trade since 1999, and are thus against WTO rules. In fact, after the U.S. imposed tariffs on steel and aluminum in 2018, the European Union was cautioned by experts not to give in to some kind of negotiated settlement, engaging in voluntary export restraints, which would violate WTO rules.[10]

Voluntary Import Expansion

Under a **voluntary import expansion** (VIE), a country agrees to open its markets to imports. Voluntary import expansions increase foreign access to a domestic market, while increasing competition and reducing prices. Voluntary import expansions are not voluntary at all. A country agrees to import products as a result of pressure from another country. An example of voluntary import expansion is Japan's decision to avert U.S.-imposed trade sanctions by importing U.S. semiconductors, automobiles, and medical equipment. VIEs have only rarely featured in international trade since the 1980s. However, in 2018 the United States called on the Chinese government to increase imports from the U.S. by some $200 billion per year in order to help close the annual $330 billion+ trade deficit in goods and services.

KPG_Payless/shutterstock.com

Non-Automatic Import Licenses

Non-Automatic import licenses are issued on a discretionary basis and are used to restrict imports of a given product. They are justified under WTO rules if they are used for security reasons, or for balance of payment reasons, and development. Countries often institute such licenses under conditions not covered by these exceptions, which is incompatible with WTO rules. The EU, for example, has previously challenged Argentina's noncompliance.[11] Indonesia has also been previously accused of applying non-automatic import licenses inconsistently.

Automatic Import Licenses

Automatic import licenses are granted freely to importing companies. Automatic licenses are used by the importing country's government for the purpose of import surveillance. The licenses have the potential to discourage import surges, to place additional administrative and financial burdens on the importer, and to raise costs by delaying product shipments.[12] Within most common markets, it is assumed that import licenses are automatic, if they exist at all; however, that is not always the case. For example, Brazil terminated automatic import licenses for several products, such as wheat, flour and some cheeses and wines, most imported from Argentina, another member country of MERCOSUR, the Southern Common Market.

Price Controls: Increasing Prices of Imports

Price controls have a direct effect on a product mix aimed at a particular market. Increasing the price of imports to match minimum prices of domestic offerings is one such strategy that is frequently used for both products and for retailers. For example, Japan uses such controls to ensure that locally produced rice is not at a disadvantage relative to rice imports from the United States, which are of equally high quality but are sold at much lower prices. In this instance, the prices of imports are held artificially high so that local consumers would not discriminate in favor of U.S. competitors. Similarly, Wal-Mart and other discounters and category specialists (see Chapter 12, "International Retailing") in the European Union are constantly scrutinized and often pressured by local authorities to raise prices. EU governments charge that these international retailers price products below cost to drive out smaller competitors.

Price Controls: Antidumping and Countervailing Duty Actions

Antidumping and countervailing duty actions were designed to counter unfair competition, such as predatory pricing. Dumping refers to selling below fair value to undermine competitors who are charging the market price or to get rid of excess inventory. When used as price controls, antidumping measures involve initiating investigations to determine whether imports are sold below fair value, imposing duties to offset dumping, as well as adopting other measures to counter the effects of dumping. Countervailing measures include investigations to determine whether imports are sold below fair prices as a result of subsidies. Such a determination is usually followed by duties imposed to offset the effects of subsidies. In one example, the United States initiated punitive duties on tires of passenger vehicles and trucks imported from China. The Commerce Department determined that the tires were sold at dumping prices, and that the producers and exporters had received subsidies ranging from 20 to 100 percent.[13] As of December, 2017, the United States has had active anti-dumping cases against China for products ranging from porcelain cooking ware, roller bearings and paper clips.[14]

To the detriment of international trade, antidumping and countervailing duty actions have become tools used to intimidate importers and restrict trade. The European Union has been accused in the past of the excessive use of antidumping investigations to deter imports.

Price Controls: Paratariff Measures

Paratariff measures are charges that increase the costs of imports in a manner similar to tariffs. Such measures include allowing an initial number of product units to enter the country duty-free and charging tariffs to subsequent shipments in excess of this quota. They also include advance import deposits, additional import charges, seasonal tariffs, and customs charges. The United States uses many of these paratariff measures to discourage shipment of certain agricultural products from developing countries.[15]

Ditty_about_summer/shutterstock.com

Standards

Standards as barriers to trade are frequently used to block imports. They are primarily imposed by high-income countries, and aimed at imports from emerging markets. Most challenging are standards that are especially strict, such as those imposed on safety grounds by the European Union against hormone-fed U.S. beef, bioengineered corn, and soybeans. Standards that discriminate against foreign firms in particular, or that simply create more bureaucratic hurdles for importing firms, act as nontariff barriers to trade.

On the positive side, standards often do help local and international industry by deterring gray markets. For example, the United States has strict environmental and manufacturing standards for automobiles. Importing an automobile that is not specifically designed according to U.S. standards is costly; one has to use expensive automobile conversion services and obtain the appropriate Department of Transportation authorization to use the vehicle.

Local Content Requirements and Foreign Ownership: Percentage Requirements

Governments of many emerging market economies require that a certain percentage of the products imported is produced locally, mandating a local content requirement. This requirement is typically met by manipulating and assembling the product in the importing country—usually in a foreign trade zone.

China has always presented a challenge to importing firms. Multinational firms often join with Chinese partners and agents to either package or manufacture enough of the product to have it qualify based on local content requirements; firms often do tricky calculations on local services and part values to meet such local content edicts.[16] In 2006, the United

xieyuliang/shutterstock.com

States and the European Union challenged China at the WTO, taking aim at Chinese regulations intended to encourage Chinese automobile makers to use domestic, rather than imported, automobile parts. According to the United States and the EU, this, in effect, creates local content rules enacted through a complex tariff system that raises tariffs from 10 percent to 25 percent if imported parts make up more than a certain proportion of the automobile.[17] Russia, during the 2015 economic crisis resulting from the sanctions imposed after its annexation of Crimea, enacted local content requirements and import substitution policies for products such as medical devices, textiles, machinery, vehicles, and software. [18] In 2017, the U.S., Canada, and Mexico engaged in negotiations over proposed modifications to the North American Free Trade Agreement (NAFTA). The U.S. called for an increased percentage of U.S. content in all automobiles manufactured in Canada and Mexico and sold in the U.S. [19]

In addition to local content requirements, there are other forms of favoring local contribution and labor. For example, governments often impose regulations to protect local carriers for passenger and freight transportation. Foreign ownership restrictions also are widely used – for example, requiring 51 percent or more of a joint venture to be owned by a national firm. Creative strategies are used to block entry of international service providers, or to place them at a disadvantage relative to local competitors.

Boycott

A boycott is usually initiated as the result of an action group or government calling for a ban on consumption of all goods associated with a particular company or country. Often, boycotts target a company that is representative, or even synonymous, with its country of origin. For example, French consumers boycotted McDonald's when the U.S. threatened to impose tariffs on French cheese imports. Boycotts sometimes have broader targets; for example, discontent with uneven economic globalization, Western-led modernization, and anti-U.S. and anti-Israel sentiments have created a phenomenon known as consumer jihad (holy war), where consumers declare war on Western products, boycotting them. [20]

Nestlé has been the target of a long-standing boycott because it was perceived to contribute to the death of infants from developing countries by aggressively marketing baby formula to consumers who cannot afford enough formula to ensure babies' healthy development. One organization, Baby Milk Action (www.babymilkaction.org), actively lobbies against Nestlé, and replaced the company's jingle "Good Food, Good Life" with "Nestlé, Good Grief."

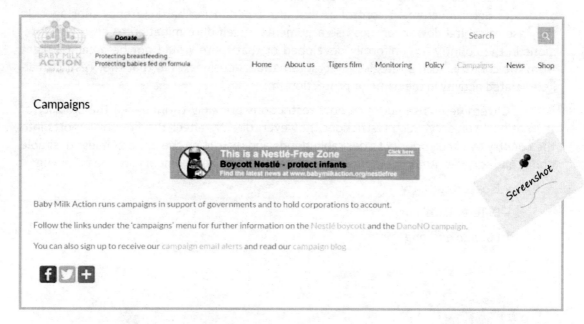

Embargoes and Sanctions

Embargoes and sanctions are imposed by a country (or a number of countries) against another country. An embargo prohibits all business deals with the country that is the target of the embargo, often affecting businesses from third countries that do business with both the country imposing the embargo and the country under embargo.

The United States has imposed, for decades, a full embargo against Cuba, which covers any commercial and noncommercial relationship with Cuba. As of now, the embargo is still in effect even though Cuba and the United States established diplomatic ties in 2015. There are exceptions to the embargo for certain U.S. agricultural exports to Cuba. In 2016, U.S. agricultural exports to Cuba were approximately $250 million.[21] Rules for US tourist visits and educational missions to Cuba have also been eased since 2015.

The Cuban embargo has been one of the most enduring trade embargoes in modern history. The U.S. embargo prohibits multinational companies from other countries doing business in the United States from engaging in any business deals with Cuba. Unfortunately for the United States, this strategy does not appear to reach its goal—punishing Cuba's leadership and its communist regime, by derailing its economy.

Economic sanctions involve penalties against a targeted country that could take various forms, such as trade barriers and restrictions on commerce, among others. Over the past four decades, the U.S. has led the international community in imposing sanctions on

Iran to punish it for its support of terrorism and for developing its nuclear capacity. The sanctions crippled Iran's economy and cut its oil exports in half. In 2015, Iran agreed to limit its nuclear program under international supervision in exchange for a reduction in economic sanctions. However, in 2018, the U.S. curtailed participation in the agreement and instituted new unilateral economic sanctions, to the chagrin of its allies, France and Germany. These sanctions target Iranian businesses, as well as any other businesses that engage in trade with Iran.

Currency and Capital Flow Controls

Strategies involving currency and capital flow controls are used in economies that are under tight government control or that are experiencing hard-currency shortages. In the case of capital flow, countries use arguments of self-determination to ensure that regions in the country are uniformly developed or that there would not be a capital flight from the country. Such strategies affect international businesses in that they restrict market-dictated activity in the name of protectionism.

Governments use currency flow restrictions primarily to influence the stability of the national currency. Such restrictions, however, directly affect the flow of imports into the country by giving priority to desirable goods and restricting the import of less desirable goods and services. Among the currency controls used by governments are the following:

- Blocked currency
- Differential exchange rates
- Foreign exchange permits

tony4urban/shutterstock.com

Blocked Currency

A country using a blocked currency strategy does not allow importers to exchange local currency for the seller's currency. This strategy can be used as a political weapon, to create obstacles for international businesses attempting to enter a country. More often, however, the strategy is used because the country is experiencing acute balance-of-payments difficulties. Larger, more sophisticated firms with international sales in multiple markets, fortunately, have at their disposal countertrade strategies to address this type of barrier.

Another method that firms can use to bypass blocked exchange rates entails using unofficial (and, from the perspective of the importing country, illegal) exchange offices. Such offices exist both abroad and in the importing country; however, they offer unfavorable exchange rates and expose the company to the risk of government action against it.

Differential Exchange Rates

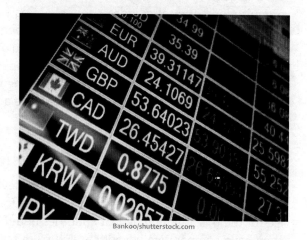

Bankoo/shutterstock.com

Two types of differential exchange rates can be used. The first, which is government imposed, refers to a strategy the government uses to promote imports of desirable and necessary goods, such as armaments and petrol, and to discourage imports of less desirable and necessary goods, such as consumer goods and services, entertainment, and the like. Offering a less favorable exchange rate for international products and services reflects a government strategy that ultimately increases the cost of this second category of products to the final consumer and discourages its purchase. For example, in Venezuela, the official exchange rate in 2018 was approximately 66,870 Venezuelan Bolivares to the U.S. dollar. This rate was available only for government-approved imports. Most other import transactions required the purchase of foreign currencies at the prevailing black market exchange rate, which was approximately 623,000 Venezuela Bolivares to the U.S. Dollar. [22]

A second type of differential exchange rate is favorable to the international firm importing products into this market. In this situation, a difference exists between the black market exchange rate and the official government exchange rate, with the black market rate being higher than the government rate. The rate difference is a reflection of economic distortion: A high black market exchange rate can signal a likely depreciation of the local currency, foreign exchange rationing by the government, or both. A large difference between the government and the free exchange rate can also be interpreted as a tax on exports and a subsidy on imports, stimulating the diversion of resources from the official to the black market sector. [23]

Foreign Exchange Permits

Countries attempting to control foreign exchange often require the use of foreign exchange permits. Such permits are typically provided by the central bank of the country. They also give priority to imports of goods that are in the national interest and delay access to foreign exchange for products that are not deemed essential. An exchange permit can also stipulate differential exchange rates. Most countries that experience a shortage of hard currency require foreign exchange permits. China, Ethiopia, the Czech Republic and many other countries require such permits for imports.

3-3 International Trade and Trade Facilitators

Several important international and local institutions play an active role in promoting international trade and have a considerable impact on the development of international trade and marketing operations. International trade and development organizations and governmental organizations alike are working individually and jointly to increase the flow of goods, open access to products and services, and minimize costs to companies and final consumers by limiting or eliminating the layers of bureaucratic interference in the firms' international operations. Sections 3-3a through 3-3d address Ricardo's theory of comparative advantage and discuss some of the most prominent international trade and development organizations. They also address the role of national governments in promoting the international involvement of local business and in opening local markets to foreign investment — particularly foreign direct investment. It should be mentioned, however, that equally important strides have been made to date by trade agreements; some agreements have led to the free movement of labor and capital, leading to open or nearly open access to previously restricted or closed markets. This topic will be addressed in Chapter 4, "Regional Economic and Political Integration."

3-3a The International Trade Imperative

Free trade is essential to economic development. One argument for free trade is based on economist David Ricardo's classical theory of comparative advantage. The premise for the this argument is that countries benefit from specialization in an industry in which they have comparative advantage and from trading with one another. For example, India specializes in the software industry, achieving economies of scale in training its workforce in the necessary skills for optimal production and in the production process itself. As it sells software on world markets, India acquires the income to import other goods that meet the needs of the population. At a worldwide scale, this improves overall productivity and output of goods, and increases the economic wealth of nations. Consider the example of two countries, East and West: In a year, an Eastern worker makes two bicycles or produces four bushels of wheat. A Westerner can produce only one bushel or one bike. Each country has 100 workers split evenly between producing bikes or wheat; thus, East produces 200 bushels and 100 bikes, and West produces 50 bushels and 50 bikes. East thus has absolute advantage in producing both; West has no absolute advantage, but it does have comparative advantage in producing bikes. According to the comparative advantage theory, the two countries are better off specializing in the industry in which they have comparative advantage. If East specializes in growing wheat, moving 10 workers from making bikes to wheat, it would produce 240 bushels and 80 bikes. If West moves 25 workers from wheat production to bike manufacturing, in which it has comparative advantage, it will produce 75 bikes and 25 bushels. Subsequently, consumers in both countries can enjoy more bikes and wheat if they trade at terms at which both gain—at one and a half bushels (sold by East) per bike (sold by West).[24]

Other arguments for free trade suggest that opening up the home market increases competition, lowering prices for local consumers. Also, the presence of efficient multinationals will encourage efficiency in local manufacturing and services as well — leading to lower prices and thus yet another benefit to the final consumer. Free trade also means that firms no longer have to limit themselves to the local or national market. These companies can increase production, achieve economies of scale, and offer competitively priced products to world markets.[29] In other words, free trade also means economic growth. Table 3-1 offers figures on international trade (imports and exports) in different countries of the world.

Table 3-1 Trade in Goods and Services ($ millions)

Country	Import 2016	Import 2013	Export 2016	Export 2013
Albania	5,449.94	4,414,121	3,439.97	2,418,420
Algeria	60,193.85	51,405,915	32,786.72	64,526,125
Argentina	74,496.23	66,948,163	70,731.68	73,784,740
Australia	257,930.51	199,129,552	248,403.90	253,962,376
Botswana	6,670.47	7,590,848	7,770.37	6,663,317
Denmark	145,452.11	91,059,667	164,447.72	95,509,783
Ecuador	19,052.39	22,307,787	19,565.23	27,261,244
Hungary	99,971.81	91,800,159	112,693.96	97,332,160
Indonesia	159,351.43	180,152,836	167,772.63	201,172,141
Kenya	16,452.16	16,289,151	10,275.44	5,185,370
Mexico	420,918.01	339,748,285	398,892.84	393,272,653
Saudi Arabia	198,110.22	142,235,884	200,860.08	352,464,074
United Kingdom	804,206.15	620,636,797	749,113.42	418,892,276
United States	2,712,865.00	1,964,475,472	2,208,071.00	1,396,565,654

3-3b International Trade and Economic Development Organizations

This section provides an overview of the most important trade and economic development organizations worldwide in terms of their overall impact on companies and markets. It must be noted, however, that, in addition to these organizations, other entities provide similar, but typically more targeted, input into the international trade process. They do so directly, by facilitating trade, or indirectly, by developing national infrastructures essential to the flow of goods and communication. For example, the Belgian government and the Dutch government have specific structures that operate individually and jointly with other international development organizations to offer aid to their respective former colonies in East Africa and Asia. The French Ministry of Cooperation has a similar mission for France's former colonies.

This section centers primarily on the WTO and the organizations that have made significant inroads with regard to the liberalization of trade in the past two decades, facilitating the marketing of goods and services in markets previously deemed inaccessible and reducing barriers to trade worldwide. It also focuses on the two Bretton Woods organizations, which have provided support for development and trade in the free world since 1944 — the World Bank and the International Monetary Fund.

The World Trade Organization and the General Agreement on Tariffs and Trade

The General Agreement on Tariffs and Trade (GATT) was signed by 123 nations agreeing to promote trade and eliminate trade barriers. Under the agreement, the signatory countries committed to open their markets to international business and to use the GATT forum to resolve trade disputes. In practice, however, trade disputes took too long to be resolved, and GATT had no enforcement power. GATT's Uruguay Round, which took place between 1986 and 1994 and was subsequently finalized at Marrakech in 1995, substantially changed international trade regulation, replacing the original GATT regulations with a newly empowered World Trade Organization (WTO), which has 164 member countries, with Afghanistan the most recent member to join in 2016. The WTO is forever changing the way countries regulate international business on their own territory and beyond. The organization's most important trait is that membership is predicated on full implementation and adherence to all GATT agreements.

WTO candidate countries often must radically change trade practices and, implicitly, their internal economic structures, to gain membership. For example, China attempted for 15 years to gain membership in the World Trade Organization, before being accepted in 2001. Its impediments to access were attributed primarily to its trade restrictions (attributed to concerns about the impact of open markets on its economy) and its demands to be allowed to subsidize agricultural output at the rate

catastrophe_OL/shutterstock.com

of developing countries. To gain access to the WTO, China had to lower tariffs on imports such as automobiles and new technologies and make it easier for foreign companies to establish certain types of businesses in the country.[25]

The WTO is run by member governments, and its decisions are made either by governments' trade ministers (the organization's highest authority), who meet every two years, or by official representatives, who meet regularly in Geneva, Switzerland, the organization's headquarters. Ministerial meetings have met with protests, with opposition groups viewing globalization as the promotion of corporate interests to the detriment of the individual, developing countries, and the environment. More recently, however, the opposition to the WTO has lost some of its attraction because the organization has made important inroads in improving health and education in previously underserved areas, such as the African continent.

The WTO's main functions are:

  • Providing assistance to developing and transition economies.

  • Offering specialized help for export promotion, through the International Trade Center.

  • Promoting regional trade agreements.

  • Promoting cooperation in global economic policy making.

  • Reviewing members' trade policies.

  • Engaging in routine notification when members introduce new trade measures or alter old ones.[26]

WTO agreements cover goods, services, and intellectual property and address issues such as:[27]

• Reducing tariff and nontariff trade barriers on specific categories of goods and services. In this regard, the WTO has made important strides in the area of manufactured goods, as well as in the area of information technology. It is still working on eliminating barriers in the area of agriculture, where GATT allowed, until recently, government subsidies and import quotas.

• Opening service markets to international business. The General Agreement on Trade in Services (GATS) has established rules for specific sectors, outlining principles that require countries to offer access to their markets. GATS initially covered banking, securities, and insurance.

• Regulating the protection and enforcement of intellectual property rights for trademarks, patents, and copyrights—under the Agreement on Trade-Related Aspects of Intellectual Property Rights (TRIPS).

• Dealing with antidumping activities.

• Addressing subsidies and trade restrictions designed to safeguard domestic industries such as technical regulations and standards, import licensing, rules of origin, and other measures that impede international trade.

• Reviewing regularly individual countries' trade policies to ensure compliance with the WTO, and transparency.

• Settling disputes. Member states cannot ignore any of the dispute resolution decisions handled by the Dispute Settlement Body (DSB) — as they previously did, under GATT.

Examples of disputes handled by the DSB are Venezuela's complaint against the United States over discrimination in gasoline imports (requiring higher standards for imports than for locally produced gasoline).

The WTO has been a fruitful forum, where countries have kept each other in check, ensuring that they follow WTO rules. In 2018, for example, the WTO ruled that the European Union failed to remove support for the Airbus A380, resulting in losses for Boeing. The WTO was also a venue for the U.S. to air its concern over China's subsidies of steel production and its coercion of foreign firms to transfer technology to their Chinese partners, and for China to fight the U.S. imposition of tariffs on steel and aluminum, and for threatening China with the imposition of a separate $50 billion in tariffs.

Alexey Struyskiy/shutterstock.com

Group of Seven (G7)

Members of the Group of Seven (G7) are Canada, France, Germany, Italy, Japan, the United Kingdom, and the United States. The Group of Seven (G7), comprising the world's most industrialized countries, was formed during the 1970s economic crisis as a forum for addressing economic and financial issues. Russia started to regularly participate in G7 meetings in 1994, and in 2006, it became officially the eighth member of the group (G8, at the time), even though its economy was only the size of Denmark's. Subsequently, after the Russian Federation annexed part of the Ukraine, it was no longer invited to the meetings.[28]

The organization's yearly meetings involve heads of state, government ministers, and directors of central banks. The G7 currently addresses issues such as biotechnology and food safety, economic development, disarmament, arms control and nonproliferation, organized crime, drug trafficking, terrorism, environmental issues, digital opportunities issues, microeconomic issues, and trade.

The G7 has proved to be an important forum for addressing crises, by creating the European Bank for Reconstruction and Development to aid with the transition of Eastern Europe to a market economy, by addressing the financial crisis of 2008 and the Greek debt crisis in 2010, among others. However, its influence over the years has waned. Nevertheless, its summits have been important venues to address issues such as the environment, global health, empowerment of women, and poverty, among others.

Group of Twenty (G20)

Members of the Group of Twenty (G20) are Argentina, Australia, Brazil, Canada, China, France, Germany, India, Indonesia, Italy, Japan, Republic of Korea, Mexico, Russia, Saudi Arabia, South Africa, Turkey, the United Kingdom, the United States, and the European Union. This group has made important inroads for the past two decades, addressing issues such as trade, climate, and the refugee crisis. At the 2017 summit in Hamburg, the priority agenda centered on financial regulation, fighting transnational crime, and ties with Africa. [29]

G20 countries flags

Australia Argentina Turkey Japan Canada
Germany Brazil UK South Africa France
Italy Saudi Arabia India Indonesia China
Mexico Russia EU South Korea USA

Viktorija Reuta/shutterstock.com

The International Monetary Fund and the World Bank

The International Monetary Fund (IMF) and the World Bank were created at the United Nations Monetary and Financial Conference, as a result of the Bretton Woods Agreement in 1944, to address the need for global economic development, stability, and rebuilding after World War II and the Great Depression of the 1930s. Both the IMF and the World Bank are specialized agencies of the United Nations; membership in the World Bank requires membership in the IMF.

The goal of the IMF was to establish an innovative monetary system and an institution charged with monitoring it. The IMF is based on the proposals put forth by Harry Dexter White in the United States and John Maynard Keynes in the United Kingdom. At its foundation lies a system that would encourage the unrestricted conversion of one currency to another by establishing a clear and unequivocal value for each currency.[30] Currently, the organization, whose mission has significantly expanded since its debut, is located in Washington, D.C. The IMF comprises 189 member countries who are free to join the organization — as such, they are obligated to adhere to its charter of rights and obligations — or to leave the organization (as Cuba, Indonesia, and Poland have done in the past).[31]

The IMF directly links members' voting power to the amount they contribute to the institution; as such, the United States has more than 16 percent of total votes.[32] The organization's civil servants are international experts and nationals of the different member countries and operate under a managing director, who is typically a European.

Traditionally, the IMF has played the role of lender of last resort. More recently, however, it has also assumed the position of mediator between debtors and creditors. Through its stabilization programs, the IMF imposes debt reduction guidelines; ceilings for bank credit, budget deficit, borrowing, and international reserves; and particular development programs that the borrowing countries have to follow. Among others, the IMF offered countries in Central and Eastern Europe loans for restructuring their economies; it bailed out Brazil and Turkey to the tune of billions of dollars; and Argentina was a bailout recipient in the early 2000s, and, in 2018, it was seeking again a substantial loan. After the 2008 recession, Ireland received a €78 billion bailout package from the IMF-EU and from the United Kingdom, Denmark and Sweden in 2010; Portugal received a €78 billion IMF-EU bailout package in 2011; and Greece received from the IMF, the European Central Bank, and the European Commission $375 billion worth of public credit. Greece's bailout, however, failed to revitalize the Greek economy, and Greece was the first high-income country to ever miss a payment. Greece received an additional bailout package of just under $100 billion subsequently.[33]

In addition to it lender role, the IMF also offers training and technical assistance for monetary and financial strategists from borrowing countries through its field offices and publishes statistical information based on accurate data that member countries provide as a requirement for membership. The World Bank is the largest international bank that sponsors economic development projects. The World Bank, headquartered in Washington, D.C., employs international specialists in economics, finance, and sectoral development. In addition, it has field offices in developing countries, overseeing projects in the area of industry, health, poultry and dairy production, among others. [34] In 2018, the World Bank increased its annual lending by over 25 percent (at about $80 billion), in a change of focus from developing countries across to economic spectrum – with over $2 billion going to China, an upper-middle-income country – to primarily providing support to low-middle-income countries. [35]

The accomplishments of the World Bank and the IMF and their impact on economic development and trade cannot be ignored. They have been instrumental in fostering economic and political stability in developing countries. They have protected banks from developed countries by preventing firms in volatile regions from defaulting on their debt. They

have helped create viable industrial, agricultural, and infrastructure projects. In
Poland, the World Bank financed the modernization of several important ports (see
Figure 3-1). Also, they have contributed
substantially to the training and development of local expertise in different sectors. Furthermore, the two agencies provide reliable statistics in areas related to
finance, economic development, trade,
population trends, and national policies,
among others.

Artur Bogacki/shutterstock.com

Figure 3-1: The World Bank Szczecin-Swinoujscie Seaway
and Port Modernization Project had as its main charge improving the aging facilities of the port and the access
infrastructure in order to promote trade with Poland.

Other Multilateral Development Banks

A number of development banks
with a regional focus also are instrumental
in advancing economic development and in providing support for business and trade.
Among the development banks are the following:

The African Development Bank (www.afdb.org), headquartered in Abidjan, Ivory
Coast, has as a primary goal poverty reduction. It provides support and expertise in areas
such as agriculture, human resources, and health services, and small businesses are its primary target recipients.

The Asian Development Bank (www.adb.org), headquartered in Manila, the Philippines, focuses on the private sector. The bank sponsors projects aimed at increasing access
to technology and improving the functioning of government. Together with the World Bank
and the IMF, the Asian Development Bank was instrumental in Asia's recovery from the financial crisis of the 1990s.

The European Bank for Reconstruction and Development (www.ebrd.com) headquartered in London, United Kingdom, has as main goals reforming and strengthening markets in the transition economies of Central and Eastern Europe. Among others, it has played
an important role in the development of legal and institutional frameworks, reducing barriers to foreign investment, and strengthening the countries' financial markets and their private sector.

The Inter-American Development Bank (www.iadb.org), headquartered in Washington, D.C.), has as primary clients companies that do not ordinarily deal with the large development banks. Like the other banks, the IADB funds private sector projects, but it also has
as priorities modernizing the government, strengthening institutions, and overcoming the
"digital divide."

United Nations Organizations

A number of United Nations (www.un.org) bodies promote the economic and financial welfare of developing countries. In particular, these organizations focus on developing
the industrial, communication, and transportation infrastructure of developing countries.
The impact of such development on fostering trade and foreign direct investment in these
markets is substantial. Among the United Nations agencies involved in economic development are the United Nations Development Program (UNDP), headquartered in New York.

Drop of Light/shutterstock.com

The UNDP assists, coordinates, finances, and supervises various projects, ranging from institutional strengthening and support to building factories, to developing methane gas extraction facilities, to financing the building of bridges and highways or telecommunications networks. In its efforts, the UNDP, primarily a human development organization, is assisted by other specialized United Nations Organizations — about 16 in number. Among those that directly involved in economic development and the development of international trade are:

The United Nations Industrial Development Organization (UNIDO), headquartered in Vienna, Austria. UNIDO offers or subcontracts expertise in industrial project design and implementation, often, with additional bilateral and multilateral aid, providing turn-key factories to countries in need.

The United Nations Conference on Trade and Development (UNCTAD), headquartered in Geneva, Switzerland. UNCTAD assists developing countries in increasing international trade relations and promotes the integration of trade, environment, and development.

The Regional Economic Commission for Africa; for Asia and the Pacific; for Europe, North America, and the Commonwealth of Independent States (CIS); for Latin America and the Caribbean; and for Western Asia. This regional arm of the United Nations offers support for the economic and social development of its member states, fosters regional integration, and promotes international cooperation for regional development.

The Food and Agriculture Organization (FAO), headquartered in Rome, Italy. The FAO offers expertise in agricultural projects.

The United Nations agencies also provide statistical data on developing countries, with a focus on different industry sectors, health, and agriculture.

3-3c Government Organizations

Promoting international trade constitutes one of the more important tasks of the national and local governments of most countries. Most of the international marketing literature explores the different strategies used by government to protect local industry, trade, and service providers from international competition; such publications often ignore efforts of local and national government bodies in increasing exports and in promoting foreign direct investment locally. This discussion details the involvement of the United States' federal, state, and local governments in promoting international trade. Most high-income countries have similar institutions to those described herein and offer similar support to local businesses attempting to market their products internationally and to international businesses entering the local market.

Regardless of the level of country economic development, most international trade issues are addressed by a national Department of Commerce, known as the Ministry of Trade or, more specifically, the Ministry of Foreign Trade. Frequently, the Ministry of Trade works in tandem with the State Department, known as the Ministry of Foreign Affairs, promoting a country's foreign policy.

United States Agencies: Federal and State Government

Many United States federal, state, and local government agencies promote the interests of U.S. businesses abroad, encouraging their international involvement in the form of export promotion or by providing foreign direct investment support. They also actively encourage foreign direct investment in the United States. Among the U.S. agencies supporting activities of international business are the United States Agency for International Development and the United States Department of Commerce.

United States Agency for International Development (USAID)

The United States Agency for International Development (USAID) is an independent agency of the federal government. Like the UNDP and other development organizations, USAID engages in economic development–related operations. Unlike the development organizations previously discussed, USAID is an arm of the United States Department of State, supporting the economic development of and trade with developing countries aligned politically with the United States. USAID's origins are traced to the Marshall Plan of reconstruction in Europe after World War II. USAID was created to advance U.S. foreign policy in developing countries by supporting economic growth and agricultural development, global health, conflict prevention, and developmental relief. In doing so, USAID gives priority to U.S. contracting firms; it has working relationships with more than 3,500 U.S. companies. [36]

Yet, in spite of USAID's success, and that of other aid organizations, not all the contributions to development are appropriately used. A case in point is the example from the Kyrgyz Republic, illustrated in International Marketing Illustration 3-2.

International Marketing Illustration 3-2 International Aid in Private Pockets

The newly independent Kyrgyz Republic is one of the five countries of central Asia that have emerged from the former Soviet Union and one of the few in the former Union that is making important strides toward adopting a market economy. Firms are eager to profit from consumers who are positively predisposed toward Western goods.

The international aid community rapidly embraced the Kyrgyz Republic as well: Germany, Japan, the Netherlands, Switzerland, Turkey, the United States, the EBRD, the EQ, the IMF, and the World Bank have invested substantially in this country.

As aid continues to pour into the country, however, it is evident that much of it is squandered. For example, USAID sent large quantities of vegetable oil to help meet the needs of Kyrgyz consumers. However, the oil, labeled "not for sale," is sold at prices few can afford on the open market – not surprising for a country ranked 136 out of 170 on Transparency International's Corruption Perception Index.

This example is not an aberration, but rather the norm in many developing countries. Agricultural automobiles are often used for personal purposes by rural mayors, aid products for flood victims often appear on local store shelves in areas of a country not affected by the floods, and government officials hire their relatives to ensure a distribution of aid products that most effectively serves their families rather than the broader target community of the aid effort. Nevertheless, with adequate monitoring, international aid efforts ultimately raise the standard of living and the ability of countries to become attractive trade partners.

Sources: Leo Paul Dana, "Change and Circumstance in Kyrgyz Markets," Qualitative Market Research, Vol. 3, No. 2, 2000, p. 62. Transparency International Corruption Perception Index 2016, accessed at: https://www.transparency.org/news/feature/corruption_perceptions_index_2016 on May 10, 2018.

United States Department of Commerce and United States Department of Agriculture

The **United States Department of Commerce International Trade Administration (ITA)** (www.trade.gov) offers extensive assistance to U.S. exporters of goods and services. The ITA has a network of more than 100 U.S. Export Assistance Centers throughout the United States that provide export counseling services to new as well as established exporters. Via these local offices, exporters can also gain direct access to industry specialists in Washington, D.C., as well as Department of Commerce export-promotion officers at U.S. embassies around the world. The in-country Department of Commerce personnel can assist with introductions to prospective agents, distributors, and end users. They can also advocate on behalf of U.S. exporters with foreign governments in order to assure fair access for U.S. firms. Most of these services are free or carry a nominal charge. The agency's website is a treasure trove of country analysis information, best market opportunities, and other important resources for businesses pursuing international opportunities.

U.S. services exporters can include technology consultants, major law firms, financial services companies, etc. In recent years, the ITA has also actively promoted the recruitment of international students to attend U.S. colleges and universities. The tuition paid by international students is counted as U.S. exports, just the same as, for example, an export of machinery to an international buyer. Both activities result in U.S. dollars paid to a U.S. supplier. The Department of Commerce has also become much more proactive in supporting foreign direct investment (FDI) in the United States by international firms.

The Department of Agriculture provides similar counseling and export promotion assistance to U.S. businesses exporting agricultural products. The Foreign Agricultural Service (www.fas.usda.gov/exporting) also has representatives located at U.S. embassies in key export markets.

Gil C/shutterstock.com

Export-Import Bank of the United States

The **Export-Import Bank of the United States (EXIM)** (www.exim.gov) is the official export credit agency of the United States. Established in 1934, EXIM is an independent, self-sustaining executive branch agency. Notwithstanding the somewhat confusing name, EXIM's sole focus is on promoting U.S. exports by offering a range of short and medium-term financing programs. Examples of the EXIM Bank's financial assistance are export credit insurance, guaranteed loans, pre-export financing to small and medium-sized exporters, grants for feasibility studies and project planning for projects in developing countries, and technical assistance grants, among others. The EXIM Bank also made loans to foreign purchasers who purchased U.S. goods and services. [37]

Exports of big-ticket items such as aircraft often require medium-term financing packages for millions of dollars, including loans directly to foreign buyers. The largest U.S. beneficiary of these programs is Boeing. This has created controversy, with the EXIM Bank dubbed as "Boeing's Bank." The loans to support Boeing's export sales have also come under fire as a form of corporate welfare and an unfair subsidy for the company's export sales. [38]

Congressional authorization for the bank lapsed in July 1, 2015, but it later reauthorized the bank until 2019. However, the Bank cannot extend loans beyond $10 million.

U.S. Trade and Development Agency

The U.S. Trade and Development Agency (USTDA) (www.ustda.gov) is a small federal government agency that provides grants for feasibility studies on major international infrastructure projects like airports, sewer systems, etc. The grant funds enable the international project developer to hire a U.S. consulting firm for project design and technical assistance. In turn, this can facilitate the selection of U.S. contractors and product suppliers for the final project.

State and Local Government Agencies

Examples of government agencies actively supporting international trade are the state economic development offices. Most of the 50 U.S. states have a department whose goal is to provide local firms with export promotion assistance; this is typically the Department of Economic Development. A number of U.S. states further international trade interests of local companies by setting up representative offices abroad, in key markets such as the European Union and Japan. They often also target big emerging markets, such as those of China, Brazil, and India — countries with a large and increasingly prosperous middle class. In addition, many large U.S. cities, counties and regional economic development groups have in-country representatives in key international markets.

Among the trade services that state governments provide — often free of charge — are export counseling, full or partial sponsoring of trade promotion (primarily trade shows), and dissemination of market information. State trade promotion agencies typically work closely with local and regional U.S. Department of Commerce Export Assistance Centers to provide services to local firms. Local firms may also include international firms that use a manufacturing presence in a state for exports. For example, STIHL, the large German-owned manufacturer of chain saws has a factory in Virginia Beach, Virginia, with almost 2000 employees. STIHL exports products made in Virginia to Latin America, which is much more cost-effective than shipping products from Germany.

State and local governments also aggressively compete with each other to recruit international businesses to set up operations in the United States. In fact, domestic and international business recruitment has become the dominant activity of state economic development offices.

For example, the state of South Carolina was able to recruit substantial investments from international firms such as BMW and Michelin. Michelin, which employs 22,000 workers in 19 plants across Alabama, Indiana, Ohio, North Carolina, and South Carolina, and whose U.S. headquarters are in Greenville, South Carolina, was just named by *Forbes* as No. 1 for "America's Best Employers."[39]

3-3d Other Institutions and Procedures Facilitating International Trade

Foreign Trade Zones

A foreign trade zone (FTZ), also called free trade zone or special economic zone (SEZ), is a tax-free area in a country that is not considered part of that country in terms of import regulations and restrictions. Products can be shipped to an FTZ, undergo additional manufacturing processes, and then be shipped further to the target market. Such products are not assessed any duties and cannot be subjected to tariffs or quotas unless they enter the territory of the host country of the FTZ. An FTZ is a site within a particular country that is considered to be an international area. Merchandise in the FTZ, both foreign and domestic, is outside the jurisdiction of the host country's customs services.[40]

Initiated by governments, FTZs stimulate domestic and international commerce. In the United States, FTZs are created for the purpose of stimulating U.S. domestic and international commerce. They allow businesses to lower their tariffs through operations that

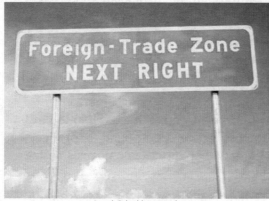

Joseph Sohm/shutterstock.com

take place within the FTZs. FTZs are usually located in or near a port of entry, and are usually operated as by a public entity such as the Port of Baltimore, Port of Houston, Port of Savannah, or the Front Royal, Virginia, FTZ, operated by the Virginia Port Authority. As of April 2018, there were more than 225 foreign trade zones in the United States. [41]

Foreign trade zones offer advantages to both the host country and to international firms operating in these zones. In the host country, the foreign trade zone benefits:

• Domestic manufacturers, distributors, and suppliers by creating demand for their services, products, and raw materials. FTZ activities may involve manipulation, such as product inspecting, labeling, repairing, and sorting; small- and large-scale manufacturing, including manufacturing, assembling, and processing; warehousing; exhibiting; and distributing to domestic and foreign markets.[42] Such operations also create jobs in the FTZ country.

• The country's trade balance. Re-exports from the country where the FTZ is located add to the total number of exports from that country, thereby increasing its trade balance.

The international firm operating in the FTZ benefits from the following:

• Foreign goods that enter the foreign trade zone are exempt from the usual customs duties, tariffs, and other import controls, as long as the goods do not enter the country.

• For firms that ultimately export to the country where the FTZ is located, the FTZ lowers or defers tariffs for goods that are subject to tariffs. There are no time limitations for the foreign goods' presence in the FTZ. Thus, goods that are assessed tariffs on the imported components are placed in storage in the FTZ and are imported into the country only when demand for the product is high or when import quota opportunities open up.

• Rather than bringing the equipment directly into the country and paying duties immediately, equipment could be brought into the FTZ, shown to customers, and the payment of duties delayed until the goods are sold.[43]

•An FTZ is also used to break bulk. Components from a foreign supplier can be shipped into the FTZ in bulk to optimize quantity discounts and shipping costs. In the FTZ, they are repackaged into smaller quantities for shipment, helping the company postpone payment of duties until items are shipped rather than when they arrive in the country. [44]

• An FTZ lowers prices for goods sold in the importing country; unassembled goods are cheaper to transport, and duties are assessed at lower rates for unassembled, than for assembled, goods. Furthermore, duties can be avoided for goods that have been damaged in transportation.

• An FTZ also helps when an importing country imposes local content regulations on products from abroad; local content is provided through the manipulation processes taking place in the FTZ.

• FTZs are usually bonded and must be secured and enclosed, which makes them safer than most ports of entry, thus decreasing insurance costs for companies using them. In the United States, for example, unauthorized removal of goods from an FTZ is a federal offense.[45]

• Products that are manipulated in a FTZ may be labeled as manufactured in the FTZ host country. A favorable attitude toward the respective country and its products (that is, a favorable country-of-origin effect) greatly benefits the companies selling the product.

• Manufacturers assembling products in a FTZ may realize important savings on duties. For example, a bicycle assembled in a FTZ would consist of various different parts: frame, tires, chains, handlebars, etc. Many of these components may be imported. The combined duties on the individual components may be more than the duty on the finished bicycle that ultimately leaves the FTZ and enters the stream of commerce in the importing country.

FTZs can range from no more than an assigned building close to a river port or a floor in a building adjacent to the local airport, to a gigantic operation with fully integrated multimodal access. An example of a large FTZ operation in the United States is FTZ 20, operated by the Port of Virginia in Norfolk. (http://www.portofvirginia.com/stewardship/economic-development/foreign-trade-zone-20/) at several sites in the Norfolk-Virginia Beach area. To receive benefits from FTZ 20, companies must be located within 90 miles or 60 minutes from the Customs Port of Entry in Norfolk. Companies, notably manufacturers, can apply to have a portion or all of their facility declared as a subzone under FTZ 20. Typically, the subzone includes the manufacturing area and imported components used in the assembly process. This subzone must be physically separated by a wall, fence, etc. from the rest of a company's facility that is not part of the subzone. [46]

Other Types of Customs-Privileged Facilities

Worldwide, there are variations on the FTZ. They are similar to the FTZ in that they have some type of customs-privileged facilities that may be restricted to a region, to a plant (when such a plant is used for product assembly purposes, it is known as an offshore assembly plant), or to a bonded warehouse. Special economic zones (SEZs) in China (see below) and maquiladoras in Mexico are examples of customs-privileged facilities that typically exist in countries with low-cost labor. Under most arrangements, products are brought into an in-bond area, manipulated (processed, repackaged, assembled), and then re-exported to the country where the products originated. Low import tariffs are only assessed at this point and only on the value-added processing that took place in the SEZ. Some limits are typically placed on products that are imported into the SEZ country to encourage re-exporting.

The Chinese Foreign Trade Zone Model: Special Economic Zones

China only has eleven FTZs, with seven more on the way. However, its FTZs are enormous, spread over 50 square miles, capable of handling millions of tons of cargo, with thousands of miles of roads and expressways. To provide some sense of the magnitude of China's FTZ operations, Marketing Illustration 3-3 offers some insights into the Waigaoqiao FTZ.

International Marketing Illustration 3-3 The Shanghai Pudong WaiGaoQiao FTZ

The Shanghai Pudong Waigaoqiao Free Trade Zone is the oldest and the largest of the fifteen free trade zones in China – it was approved by the State Council in 1990. It is located northeast of Shanghai, close to the Yangtze River and the eastern coast of China. This is a perfect location considering the main functions of the FTZ include free trade, export processing, logistic warehousing and bonded commodities. It is 20 km away from Shanghai's downtown, 40 km from Shanghai's Pudong International Airport (the largest cargo airport in mainland China), and it ajoins the Waigaoqiao Port of Shanghai.

The facilities available at the FTZ provide road, sea, rail, and air access. The FTZ's main road, Yanggao road, is a 50 m wide and 24.5 km long highway that connects to the Shanghai beltway and other cities through suspension bridges. The FTZ is serviced by a full light rail transport system. For air travel, it is served by Hongqiao International Airport and Shanghai's Pudong International Airport. The main industries at the FTZ are semiconductors, automobile production and assembly, electronics assembly and manufacturing, research and development, shipping, ware-

housing, logistics, and distribution.

The FTZ has access to a workforce of over 16 million people, and it has attracted over 9300 companies; among them, there are 135 Top Fortune 500 companies. A total of $6.561 billion is invested into this FTZ, and investors come from 127 countries and regions around the world.

Sources: Why SHFTZ/WaiGaoQiao Zone? Accessed at http://www.ftz-shanghai.com/ WaiGaoQiao_Free_Trade_Zone on July 21, 2015; RightSide Asia, "Shanghai Waigaoqiao Free Trade Zone, accessed at http:// rightsite.asia/ en/industrial-zone/shanghai- waigaoqiao-free-trade-zone on July 21, 2015.

glen photo/shutterstock.com

Since 2000, China has also allowed the creation of 25 export-processing zones (EPZs)—geographic areas offering special incentives to business. Among them are Chengdu (Sichuan Province); Dalian (Liaoning Province); Guangzhou and Shenzhen (Guangdong Province). EPZs are established only within existing economic and technological development zones.

The main difference between FTZs and EPZs is that goods delivered from Chinese companies outside the EPZs to companies inside them are treated as if they were exports, meaning that the selling company outside the EPZ is eligible for export refunds, and the buying company inside the EPZ is exempt from paying value-added tax (VAT) for the purchases. EPZs can be established only inside existing economic, industrial, and technological development zones and must obtain prior approval from the State Council (see Figures 3-2a and b on next page).[47]

Although many of the new economic zones are exploding in the Shanghai region, Fujian Province found a niche that has attracted much government attention — and investment. Xiamen, in Fujian Province, is across the strait from Taiwan, and is known as the Economic Zone on the West Coast of the Strait, implicitly associating it with the larger zone on

Figure 3-2a Export processing zones in China can only be established inside existing economic, industrial, and technological development zones. This sign above is for the Shanghai Qingpu Export Processing Zone.

Figure 3-2b The Shangai Qingpu Export Processing Zone was established in the Shanghai Qingpu Industrial Zone, pictured here; the Industrial Zone is thirty minutes outside of the city of Shanghai.

the east side of the strait that includes Taiwan. In this manner, Fujian Province is playing into China's strategy of using economic integration to entice Taiwan into unification with the mainland. With this strategy in mind, the Chinese government is increasing its infrastructure investment there, increasing railway lines by more than 50 percent, cargo-handling capacity by 80 percent, and passenger capacity by 100 percent. The Chinese government expects 60 percent of the investment in the zone to come from Taiwan – in fact, in 2018, China upped the incentives to lure Taiwanese business and companies by allowing them to compete in the local market on an equal footing with locals.[48]

Trade Bills

In most other countries, new laws dealing with trade are enacted after repealing previous statutes; U.S. trade law, on the other hand, was created using amendments to the existing statutes, some dating back to the eighteenth century. These amendments were enacted as omnibus bills that include provisions dealing with trade-related issues. To provide a brief history, in the 1970s, the U.S. balance of trade, the difference between its exports and its imports, changed from a slight surplus to a massive deficit. The U.S. government attributed this deficit to the fact that, while the U.S. imposed minimal tariffs on imports, trade partners imposed high tariffs on U.S. products imported in their countries. This led to the enactment of important omnibus bills, such as the Trade Expansion Act of 1962, the Trade Act of 1974, the Trade and Tariff Act of 1984, the Omnibus Trade and Competitiveness Act of 1988, and the Trade and Development Act of 2000. Of these, the Trade Act of 1975 revised many aspects of U.S. trade law, including authorizing the Generalized System of Preferences, instituted in 1976 and renewed periodically, most recently in 2018.The Generalized System of Preferences, also an outcome of the Trade Act of 1975, allows 129 developing countries to export 4,800 specified duty-free goods to the United States.[49]

Summary

Identify different trade barriers imposed on international trade and arguments used by governments to erect and maintain these barriers. Governments impose barriers to international trade to protect national industries and nationals (consumers, employees). Arguments for protectionism include protection of markets with excess productive capacity, employment protection, protection of infant industries, protection of national resources and the environment, protection of consumers, and national defense. Governments can impose tariffs on foreign business or nontariff barriers, such as import quotas, required import licenses, voluntary imports, or voluntary export restraints. They also can impose price controls, such as simply increasing the prices of imports, filing antidumping and countervailing duty actions to delay imports, or imposing additional tariffs (paratariffs) to shipments that exceed quotas. Alternatively, they can impose currency and capital flow controls by blocking local currency exchange, charging differential exchange rates, and restricting the number of foreign exchange permits issued. Standards are also used to restrict imports, as are local content requirements. Finally, boycotts, embargoes, and sanctions restrict international trade by blocking all trade to the targeted areas.

Provide an overview of key international organizations facilitating international trade directly or by promoting economic development. Among the organizations that are most active in, and have the greatest impact on, promoting international trade are the World Trade Organization, which provides trade assistance and development assistance to developing countries, promotes trade agreements, and reviews member countries' trade policies to ensure that they conform to the organization's trade requirements; the Group of Seven, which is a forum of the most developed countries in the world that addresses economic and financial issues, with trade as a main focus; the International Monetary Fund and the World Bank, two specialized United Nations agencies that address the need of global economic development, imposing restructuring standards on aid recipients; other development banks; and the different United Nations organizations that promote the economic and financial welfare of developing countries, as well as their participation in international trade.

Identify government efforts involved in promoting economic development and trade. National and local governments are active in promoting international trade and development through a number of agencies and departments. Among them are the United States Agency for International Development, which supports the economic development of and trade with developing countries that are politically aligned with the United States; the Department of Commerce, which engages in activities from promoting export assistance, to organizing trade shows and events, to providing financial assistance to international business; and various state and local government agencies whose primary mission is to promote international trade involvement of local business.

   Describe other trade facilitators, such as foreign trade zones, offshore assembly plants, and special economic zones, and the Normal-Trade-Relations Status. Foreign trade zones are tax-free areas in a country that are not considered part of that country from the import regulations' perspective and where products undergo additional manufacturing and are further shipped to other destination countries. They create employment in the host country and lower or defer import duties for the manufacturing firm. Offshore assembly plants and special economic zones are customs-privileged facilities in countries with low-cost labor where products are manipulated and then re-exported.

Key Terms

African Development Bank

antidumping

Asian Development Bank

automatic import license

blocked currency

boycott

comparative advantage

countervailing duty actions

currency and capital flow controls

differential exchange rate

embargo

employment protection

European Bank for Reconstruction and Development

foreign exchange permit

foreign trade zone

General Agreement on Tariffs and Trade (GATT)

Group of Seven (G7)

import quota

infant industry argument

Inter-American Development Bank

International Monetary Fund (IMF)

local content requirement

maquiladora

Ministry of Foreign Affairs

Ministry of Trade

non-automatic import license

nontariff barriers

offshore assembly plants

orderly market arrangements

paratariff measures

price controls

protectionism

protection of markets with excess labor

protection of markets with excess productive capacity

sanctions

special economic zones

standards as barriers to trade

tariffs

United Nations organizations

United States Agency for International Development (USAID)

United States Department of Commerce

United States Department of State

voluntary export restraints(VER)

voluntary import expansion

World Bank

World Trade Organization (WTO)

Discussion Questions

1. Discuss the different arguments used by countries invoking the protection of national industry and consumers.

2. Look up recent articles regarding China's trade restrictions. Which of these arguments does it appear to advocate?

3. What are the different financial controls imposed on international trade (i.e., price controls and currency controls)?

4. Describe the mission and accomplishments of the World Trade Organization.

5. How do international organizations overlap in their efforts to promote trade and economic development?

6. What are the U.S. equivalents of the Ministry of Foreign Trade and the Ministry of Foreign Affairs? How do they promote trade?

Chapter Quiz

True/False

1. The infant industry argument used against international firms is related to the protection of local employment in the respective country.

True

Rationale: The employment protection argument used against international firms refers to the protection of local employment. The infant industry argument is used to protect industries in their infancy.

2. The local content requirement requires that a certain percentage of a particular product be produced in a second country.

False

Rationale: The local content requirement mandates that a certain percentage of a particular product be produced locally, in the country of the company's target consumers. Section 3-2b, "Nontariff Barriers"

3. The premise for the comparative advantage argument is that countries benefit from specialization.

True

Rationale: The premise for the comparative advantage argument is that countries benefit from specialization in an industry in which they have comparative advantage and from trading with one another. At a worldwide scale, taking advantage of countries' comparative advantage improves overall productivity and output of goods and increases the economic wealth of nations. Section 3-3a, "The International Trade Imperative"

4. The United States Agency for International Development (USAID) has as a primary mission the promotion of trade.

False

Rationale: The U.S. *Department of Commerce* has as a primary mission the promotion of trade. Section 3-3c, "Government Organizations"

Multiple Choice

1. Tariffs are meant to
    a. discourage imports of particular goods.
    b. generate revenue.
    c. penalize countries imposing tariffs on goods from the importing country.
    d. all of the above

Answer d is correct.

Rationale: Tariffs have as goals discouraging imports, penalizing countries that are not politically aligned with the country, and generating revenues.
Section 3-2a, "Tariffs"

2. Restrictions imposed by the United States on Japan to protect the U.S. automobile industry are known as

        a. voluntary import expansion.

        b. voluntary export restraints.

        c. nonautomatic import licenses.

        d. automatic import licenses.

Answer b is correct.

Rationale: Voluntary export restraints were imposed on Japan in the 1980s to ensure that Japanese automobiles did not handicap the U.S. automotive industry.
Section 3-2b, "Nontariff Barriers"

3. Which organizations were created as a result of the Bretton Woods Agreement in 1944 to address the needs of global economic development, stability, and rebuilding?

        a. GATT and WTO

        b. IMF and World Bank

        c. G7

        d. UNDP and FAO

Answer b is correct.

Rationale: The International Monetary Fund (IMF) and World Bank were created with the purpose of addressing global economic development and creating political stability.
Section 3-3b, "International Trade and Economic Development Organizations"

4. Which United Nations organization assists developing countries in creating international trade relations and promotes the integration of trade, environment, and development?

        a. UNCTAD

        b. UNIDO

        c. FAO

        d. CIS

Answer a is correct.

Rationale: The United Nations Conference on Trade and Development assists developing countries in creating international trade relations and promotes the integration of trade, environment, and development.
Section 3-3b, "International Trade and Economic Development Organizations"

5. Foreign trade zones benefit international firms in all the following ways EXCEPT

        a. FTZs lower prices for goods sold in the importing country.

        b. FTZs are enclosed and safer than most ports.

        c. Just-in-time inventory can be shipped in bulk to FTZs.

        d. Labeling, repairing, and sorting create jobs in the FTZ country.

Answer d is correct.

Rationale: The creation of jobs benefits the country, not the international firms.
Section 3-3d, "Other Institutions and Procedures Facilitating International Trade"

Notes

1. Victor V. Cordell and Erin Breland, "Conflicting Competition Policies in a Globalized Business Environment: Prospects for Cooperation and Convergence," *Competitiveness Review*, Vol. 10, No. 1, 2000, pp. 104–122.Taos Turner and Paul Kiernan, "How Latin America Pays the Price of Protectionism," *The Wall Street Journal*, November 25, 2016. Accessed at https://www.wsj.com/articles/how-latin-america-pays-the-price-of-protectionism-1480089781 on April 30, 2018.

2. "Leaders: Storm Over Globalization," *The Economist*, Vol. 353, No. 8147, November 27, 1999, pp. 15–16.

3. Sebastian Edwards, *Left Behind. Latin America and the False Promise of Populism.* pp. 47-48 2012. Accessed on April 30, 2018.

4. Poonam Mohun, "Beyond Tariff Walls: Non-Tariff Hurdles in Sub-Saharan Africa," *Bridges Africa*, December 1, 2014, accessed at http://www.ictsd.org/bridges-news/bridges-africa/news/beyond-tariff-walls-non-tariff-hurdles-in-sub-saharan-africa on March 20, 2018; Don P. Clark, "Are Poorer Developing Countries the Targets of U.S. Protectionist Actions?" *Economic Development and Cultural Change*, Vol. 47, No. 1, October 1998, pp. 193–207.

5. Washington Trade Report, accessed at http://www.washingtontradereport.com/dictionarys.htm#_Voluntary_Export_Restraint on August 5, 2015; Cordell and Breland, "Conflicting Competition Policies in a Globalized Business Environment," pp. 104–122.

6. Clark, 1998; Mohun, 2014.

7. Ibid.

8. Mitsuru Obe and Yuka Hayashi, "Rice Is Sticky Issue for Japan in Trans-Pacific Trade Talks," *The Wall Street Journal*, May 19, 2015, accessed at http://www.wsj.com/articles/rice-is-sticky-issue-for-japan-in-trans-pacific-trade-talks-1432025782 on May 2, 2018.

9. U.S. Dept. of Agriculture Economic Research Service, "Sugar-Sweetners Policy," November 1, 2016. Accessed at https://www.ers.usda.gov/topics/crops/sugar-sweeteners/policy.aspx on April 30, 2018.

10. Alan Beattie, "How the EU Could Outflank Trump and His Tariffs," *Financial Times*, April 30, 2018, accessed at https://www.ft.com/content/13ba7260-4c65-11e8-8a8e-22951a2d8493 on May 4, 2018.

11. The European Commission, "Q&A: EU's Challenge to Argentina's Import Restrictions at the WTO," May 25, 2012, accessed at http://europa.eu/rapid/press-release_MEMO-12-376_en.htm?locale=en on May 5, 2018.

12. Clark, 1998.

13. Shanghai Daily, "U.S. to impose punitive duties on Chinese tires despite China's strong objections," July 15, 2015, accessed at http://www.shanghaidaily.com/article/article_xinhua.aspx?id=292694 on May 4, 2018.

14. The Government of the Hong Kong Special Administrative Region "Trade Relations," Accessed at https://www.tid.gov.hk/english/trade_relations/ad/ad_cic_mainland.html on April 30, 2018.

15. Clark, 1998.

16. Jack Robertson, "Foreign Exporters Learn to Deal with China's Local-Content Rules," *Ebn*, Issue 1258, April 16, 2001, p. 43.

17. James Mackintosh, Raphael Minder, and Christopher Swann, "Challenge to Beijing at WTO," *Financial Times*, March 31, 2006, 5.

18. Sandler, Travis & Rosenberg Trade Report, "WTO Reviews Local Content Requirements Favoring Domestic over Imported Goods," April 25, 2015, accessed at http://www.strtrade.com/news-publications-local-content-requirements-WTO-042215.html on July 21, 2015; Lovelock and Yip, "Developing Global Strategies for Service Businesses," pp. 64–86.

19. Eric Martin, Josh Wingrove, and Justin Sink, "Trump Threatens Endless Nafta Talks After Walk-Back on Autos," *Bloomberg Politics*, April 12, 2018. Accessed at https://www.bloomberg.com/news/articles/2018-04-12/trump-is-said-to-further-soften-demand-on-nafta-car-content on April 30, 2018.

20. Elif Izberk-Bilgin, "Infidel Brands: Unveiling Alternative Meanings of Global Brands at the Nexus of Globalization, Consumer Culture, and Islamism," *Journal of Consumer Research*, Vol. 39, No. 4 (December 2012), pp. 663-687

21. Office of the U.S. Trade Representative, "Cuba," accessed at https://ustr.gov/countries-regions/americas/cuba on April 30, 2018.

22. *Bloomberg Markets* https://www.bloomberg.com/quote/USDVEF:CUR, April 27, 2018. *Dollar Today*, https://dolartoday.com/indicadores/, April 30, 2018.

23. Martha de Melo, Cevdet Denizer, Alan Gelb, and Stoyan Tenev, "Circumstance and Choice: The Role of Initial Conditions and Policies in Transition Economies," *The World Bank Economic Review*, Vol. 15, No. 1, 2001, pp. 1–31.

24. Discussion adapted from Patrick Lane, "World Trade Survey: Why Trade Is Good for You," *The Economist*, Vol. 349, October 3, 1998, pp. S4–S6.

25. Elizabeth Olson, "Beijing Clears Major WTO Obstacles," *International Herald Tribune*, July 4, 2001, p. 9.

26. www.wto.org

27. Ibid.

28. *Pravda*, "Putin Russia Sanctions," accessed at http://english.pravda.ru/russia/politics/22-06-2015/131049-putn_russia_sanctions-0, on July 12, 2015.

29. Council on Foreign Relations, "What's at Stake at the G20 Summit?" July 5, 2017, accessed at https://www.cfr.org/expert-roundup/whats-stake-g20-summit on May 8, 2018.

30. www.imf.org

31. Ibid.

32. Ibid.

33. Hans-Werner Sinn, "Why Greece Should Leave the Eurozone," *The New York* Times, July 24, 2015, accessed at http://www.nytimes.com/2015/07/25/opinion/why-greece-should-leave-the-eurozone.html?_r=0 on July 25, 2015.

34. World Bank, "Who We Are," accessed at http://www.worldbank.org/en/who-we-are on May 8, 2018.

35. Andrew Mayeda and Jess Shankleman, "World Bank Edges Near Capital Boost as U.S. Drops Objection," Bloomberg, April 25, 2018, accessed at https://www.bloomberg.com/news/articles/2018-04-21/world-bank-moves-closer-to-capital-boost-as-u-s-drops-objection on May 10, 2018.

36. www.usaid.gov

37. See www.exim.gov for information about the Ex-Im Bank.

38. Timothy P. Carney, "Boeing Loves the Export-Import Bank but Boeing Doesn't Need the Export Import Bank," *Washington Examiner,* February 17, 2017. Accessed at https://www.washingtonexaminer.com/boeing-loves-the-export-import-bank-but-boeing-doesnt-need-the-export-import-bank on April 30, 2018.

39. *Forbes,* "America's Best Employers -2018," accessed at https://www.forbes.com/companies/michelin-group/ on May 10, 2018.

40. George F. Hanks and Lucinda Van Alst, " Foreign Trade Zones," *Management Accounting,* Vol. 80, No. 7, January 1999, pp. 20–23.

41. U.S. Dept. of Commerce, "List of Foreign-Trade Zones in the United States," April 24, 2018. Accessed at https://enforcement.trade.gov/ftzpage/letters/ftzlist-map.html on May 1, 2018.

42. Lynette Knowles Mathur and Ike Mathur, "The Effectiveness of the Foreign-Trade Zone as an Export Promotion Program: Policy Issues and Alternatives," *Journal of Macromarketing,* Vol. 17, No. 2, Fall 1997, pp. 20–31.

43. Ibid.

44. Ibid.

45. Ibid.

46. Foreign Trade Resource Center. Accessed at https://www.foreign-trade-zone.com/ps_appprocess.htm on May 1, 2018

47. *EIU ViewsWire,* "China: Trade Regulations," February 16, 2007.

48. *The Economist,* "Asia: Digging for Victory – Fujian," Vol. 381, No. 8505, November 25, 2006, p. 73. *Taipei Times,* "Xiamen Unveils Its Own Incentives for Taiwanese," April 12, 2018, accessed at http://www.taipeitimes.com/News/biz/archives/2018/04/12/2003691128 on May 9, 2018.

49. US Customs and Borders Protection, "Generalized System of Preferences," accessed at https://www.cbp.gov/trade/priority-issues/trade-agreements/special-trade-legislation/generalized-system-preferences on May 10, 2018.

Case 3-1 Transshipments: An International Trade Challenge

James Crane, a customs broker at Ship-Modal Transportation in the Port of Norfolk, was about to call a customs officer. Something about a household shipment from Germany was odd: it contained just toys, too many toys. Box after box revealed Thomas the Tank Engine, Barbie dolls, and Ninja Turtles. No beds, sofas, and other items listed in the bill of lading. They were shipped in new, large boxes, with prominent "Made in China" labels. The port agent called in a customs officer to look over the paperwork. Together, they looked over the bill of lading from a managing agent in Hamburg, Germany. The shipper was a reputable firm with offices worldwide and headquartered in the Czech Republic. The shipment was consigned to the order of a private individual living in the Norfolk, Virginia, area. The ocean carrier was Eastern Arabia, and the port of loading, Bremerhaven, Germany (the port of receipt, Hamburg, CFS). The goods were in one crate, and the description of goods stated: "Used Household Goods, HS CODE: 99909999." All seemed to be in order, except for the contents: new toys, in original boxes, rather than used household goods.

The customs officer contacted the consignee, the private individual who was supposed to pick up the shipment. He arrived at the port, filled out the paperwork, and had the shipment picked up for delivery to a warehouse. The Department of Homeland Security followed the trail of the shipment and identified a distributor who eventually delivered the goods to distributors of counterfeit goods. On debriefing, they found that they were dealing with a transshipment from China. The Chinese manufacturer had used this distribution venue to hide the products' origin, to avoid high tariffs and quotas imposed on Chinese products and to suspicion that the goods might be counterfeit.

Transshipments—also known as laundering trade—are not unusual. When Cambodia started shipping large quantities of garlic to the European Union, analysts at Europe's Olaf antifraud office questioned it. The garlic was Chinese, shipped through Cambodia to hide its origin and avoid high EU tariffs and strict quotas. Chinese garlic production has tripled since 1995 to 13 million tons a year, but its EU export quota is only 37,480 tons. Once the quota is used up, the tariff paid climbs to 209.6 percent, up from 9.6 percent. The EU agent dispatched to Cambodia found no increase in local produc-

MOLPIX/shutterstock.com

tion; soon thereafter, Italian and U.K. customs found that a Taiwan trading company had shipped 3,000 tons of garlic from Qingdao, China, to Sihanoukville, Cambodia, and after spending two days in port, the garlic was re-exported to Naples, Italy, and Felixstowe, in the U.K. The scheme cost the EU roughly $5 million in lost tariff fees. U.K. and Italian authorities charged the importers with fraud.

Subsequently, EU officials discovered 43 operations transshipping garlic from China, with countries used as conduits including Jordan, Russia, Serbia, Turkey, the Dominican Republic, and the Philippines. The EU estimates transshipment of garlic alone has cost $80 million in lost tariff fees in the past five years. At stake are also jobs in domestic industries—from shoes to food—under threat from low-cost competition from Asia.

In another example, the United States enacted a stiff tariff on Chinese honey after U.S. producers complained that the Chinese were dumping honey (selling it below cost) on the U.S. market. Remarkably, honey imports from other countries not known for their bee populations spiked after these tariffs were imposed. For example, Malaysian beekeepers have the capacity to make 45,000 pounds of honey a year, but they exported 37 million pounds a year to the United States. Laboratories established that, without a doubt, this honey originated in China.

Chinese products are particularly scrutinized by the United States and the EU, which have imposed increasing numbers of quotas and punitive tariffs to combat Chinese dumping (i.e., pricing of goods below cost to secure market share). Another reason the goods are scrutinized is safety: China manufactured every one of the 24 types of toys recalled for safety reasons in the United States. Examples of safety violations of products made in China abound: A fake eyeball toy was recalled after it was found to be filled with kerosene; toy drums and a toy bear were recalled because of lead paint, and an infant rattle was recalled because it was a safety hazard.

China has a network of brokers that bypass Western tariffs by shipping goods through other countries. Their websites boast of sending steel, aluminum, solar panels, and event stainless steel sinks to Europe and the United States while evading tariffs. Their activity is particularly intense now, after the U.S. imposed stiff tariffs on steel and aluminum in 2018.

Transshipments are not just a Chinese phenomenon. In the EU, authorities found evidence of transshipment for 90 percent of the 91 products subject to the bloc's antidumping tariffs. In fact, customs agents in both the United States and the EU found that transshipment rings sell everything from shoes to cigarette lighters, to energy-saving light bulbs. The most sensitive of all is food. Last year, the EU reported 84 instances of food transshipped from China, including duck, chicken, beef, and milk. The agents are concerned that these transshipped goods could allow unsafe or contaminated foods to leak into food chains.

Even though transshipment is illegal, it poses a major challenge for law enforcement; as in the case of the Norfolk shipment, the goods tend to carry documentation that looks legitimate.

Sources: The case is fictitious; sources used are: Keith Brandsher, "Tariff Dodgers Stand to Profit Off U.S.-China Trade Dispute," *The New York Times*, April 22, 2018, accessed at https://www.nytimes.com/2018/04/22/business/china-trade-tariffs-transshipment.html on May 17, 2018. Peter Andrey Smith, "Food Detectives on a Tough Case, *The New York Times*, January 19, 2015, accessed at http://www.nytimes.com/2015/01/20/science/a-lab-is-trying-to-keep-china-from-dodging-us-tariffs-on-honey.html?_r=0 on May 8, 2018; John Miller, "Why Some China Exports Are Taking Illegal Detours," *The Wall Street Journal*, May 25, 2007, Section B, p. 1; Eric S. Lipton and David Barboza, "As More Toys Are Recalled, Train Ends in China," *The New York Times*, June 19, 2007, A1.

Analysis Suggestions:

1. What are the reasons behind transshipments? Address them from the perspective of U.S. law-enforcement officers and from the perspectives of Chinese manufacturers.

2. What types of barriers to trade are transshipments attempting to bypass?

3. Are punitive damages the right approach to addressing transshipments? Explain.

Case 3-2 The Damocles' Sword of Trade Wars

The lights are on at Klue Automotive Specialty Tools, in DeKalb, Illinois, and the assembly line is buzzing around the clock. Since 1977, the family-owned business has manufactured high-quality tools used to repair automotive engines, ignition, and brake systems. Jonathan Klue, the company's CEO, has relied on high-quality imported German steel to manufacture tools – his pitch for his company, founded by his father, has been "German-quality tools made in the USA." The business has experienced its ups and downs over the years. The last time the U.S. imposed tariffs on steel, in 2002, the company was forced to cut one fourth of its workforce. The tariffs were imposed for only six months (they were intended for two years), but their impact on the U.S. economy was substantial, leading to a loss of millions of the total GDP.

Jonathan Klue learned in early 2018 that the U.S. was planning to impose new tariffs. The United States caused shockwaves when it unveiled 25 percent tariffs on imported steel and 10 percent tariffs on aluminum, but then quickly granted temporary exemptions for countries responsible for furnishing those metals to the U.S., including the European Union. The goal pursued by the U.S. was to get the E.U. to agree on "voluntary" quotas on exports to the U.S. In order to implement this "voluntary" strategy, the U.S. was maintaining the threat, periodically postponing the deadline when the tariffs would be instituted. Klue believed that this was going to be a Damocles' sword, ready to drop at any time. It would be prudent, he thought, if Klue Automotive Specialty Tools were to negotiate a price increase with their main accounts, and streamline production to serve only those accounts that would remain the most profitable.

Klue Automotive Specialty Tools would not be the only company to rethink its strategy while the U.S. government figured out how to deal with the potential tariffs. JE Grote Company, a family-run business manufacturing pizza preparation machines, bacon slicers, and sandwich makers, was in a similar position: about half of its $60 million in annual sales came from overseas and the company purchased specialty steel from Europe. It too had to grapple with the possibility of having to increase prices and streamline operations.

Threatening to impose tariffs has harmed the U.S. reputation as a reliable supplier. According to Devry Boughner Worwerk, of Cargill, a top U.S. grain-trading multinational, "it is not a good idea to insult your best customers. Businesses that use steel and aluminum are forced to pay higher prices. In fact, U.S. fabricators of metal products have already eliminated some offerings because of the difficulty and cost of acquiring steel and aluminum. And executives at large U.S. industrial firms stated that, if tariffs were to increase the cost of manufacturing plants in the U.S., they would simply shift production to plants in Europe or Asia.

In fact, many companies that used to import raw metals and process them in the U.S. — bending or forging steel or aluminum into complex shapes – are preparing to move this value-added work to other countries.

Sources: The case is fictitious; sources used are: *The Economist*, "Trade Wars Threaten to Disrupt American Firms' Global Supply Chains," May 3, 2018, accessed at https://www.economist.com/business/2018/05/03/trade-wars-threaten-to-disrupt-american-firms-global-supply-chains on May 20, 2018. United States International Trade Commission (September 2003). "Volume III: Executive Summaries and Investigation No. 332-452 (Report and Appendices)." *Monitoring Developments in the Domestic Industry (Investigation No. TA-204-9) and Steel-Consuming Industries: Competitive Conditions with Respect to Steel Safeguard Measures (Investigation No. 332-452).* (Publication 3632). Washington D.C., accessed on May 15, 2018.

Analysis Suggestions:

1. The U.S. is attempting to get the E.U. to agree on "voluntary" quotas on exports to the U.S. In order to implement this "voluntary" strategy, the U.S. was maintaining the threat, periodically postponing the deadline when the tariffs would be instituted. What type of barrier to trade does this strategy suggest?

2. Is this barrier to trade legal under WTO rules?

3. What are some of the dangers that are likely to affect businesses when tariffs are imposed?

This page is intentionally blank.

Chapter 4

Regional Economic and Political Integration

Chapter Outline

Not long ago, shipping goods throughout Europe was a complicated process: Waiting in long lines at the border, filling out paperwork, going through customs, and paying duties were all part of the border-crossing process. Today, much of Europe has customs offices only at airports or ports, and in these locations, no companies from the European Union are subjected to customs processing and duties. Removal of restrictions in the European Union is not limited to the movement of goods; it covers movement of all capital and labor.

European countries that are not members of the European Union, such as Georgia, Ukraine and Macedonia, aspire to become members and to benefit from the many advantages of integration. Countries in the rest of the world are actively building similar integrated markets, gradually removing all trade and other barriers. Multinational companies are eagerly endorsing economic and political integration because it reduces their costs, allowing them to offer their products to customers at lower prices and to increase shareholder equity. Take, for example, IKEA, the Swedish company whose core business is functional home furnishing products at low prices.

IKEA in the European Union

IKEA has a complex product mix, consisting of its core business (functional home furnishings) and products for everyday life, such as bath and kitchen products, and even Scandinavian food products. Standardization of the product mix is one of the factors that ensure that IKEA can keep prices low. In the United States, standardization is relatively easy to accomplish because the company is, in fact, marketing to consumers in a single country. In the European Union, on the other hand, IKEA has to market to consumers in different countries — and it has done so successfully for decades. As of May 2018, IKEA had approximately 265 stores around the world. In Germany alone, the company has more than 40 stores, more than 30 in France, and 20 in Sweden, among others; in comparison, IKEA has only about 50 stores in the United States, which has proportionately a much larger market.

European Union retailing regulations are gradually becoming uniform, and companies such as IKEA no longer have to navigate the legal complexities of each individual European Union country.

In terms of packaging, important content information must be translated in every single language of the countries where IKEA's products are sold. Taking one item, the Indira brand bed cover has picture signs suggesting that the product be washed in water at 40 degrees Celsius, that it should be ironed, that the dimensions are 150 by 250 centimeters, among others. It also has content information—100% cotton, 6% shrinkage—in the following languages: English, German, French, Dutch, Italian, Spanish, Portuguese, Swedish, Danish, Norwegian, Finnish, Polish, Czech, Slovene, Hungarian, Russian — as well as Chinese and Japanese (see Figure 4-1). In the entire European Union, the price of the twin bed cover is €14.99.

hadran/shutterstock.com

Figure 4-1 IKEA's Indira bed cover is marketed in
this package throughout the European Union.

IKEA and its consumers are benefiting from unification; it spends less to conform to variable local legal requirements, and it can afford to charge less for its products. This level of standardization was unthinkable as recently as twenty years ago. Today, companies like IKEA are more likely to benefit from regional economic and political integration.

This chapter describes the determinants of integration, the different forms of integration, and, for each type of regional integration, it offers examples of successful agreements in all regions of the world.

4-1 Determinants of Economic and Political Integration

Numerous factors prompt countries to favor trade with other countries (neighboring countries in particular). Sharing a culture, a common language, a common history, or even common borders may lead countries to join forces in an effort to eliminate barriers to trade. The factors described in Sections 4-1a through 4-1e compel countries to lower barriers and expand trade with each other for mutual benefit.

4-1a A Common Culture

Regardless of whether a common culture was fostered by a former colonial power, people in neighboring countries often share a language, as well as other cultural elements, such as traditions, norms, and religion. As will be addressed in Chapter 5, many areas in the world are characterized by cultural similarity. For example, in North Africa and the Middle East, the preponderant language is Arabic, and the environment of business, as well as everyday life, is structured in accordance with Islamic law (see Figure 4-2). Similarly, countries in Latin America share Spanish as the dominant language (with the notable exception of Portuguese-speaking Brazil) and the Catholic religion, and consumers in this region share rituals, traditions, and values.

The commonality of language and other elements of culture facilitate interaction between neighboring countries and promote cooperation. In an economic relationship in which culture does not constitute a barrier to communication, individuals are more likely to understand their counterparts and their position. In addition, a common language facilitates commerce and marketing communication in particular. For example, Holland's Appelsientje, a Friesland Campina Foods apple juice, is also marketed to Belgian consumers nearby, who speak the same language and would understand the product information on the packaging.

Figure 4-2 In Islamic countries, towers known as minarets provide a visual and auditory cue, calling the faithful to prayer. The call to prayer, five times each day – at dawn, noon, mid-afternoon, sunset, and at night – comes from the prayer hall in the mosque via a speaker located in the minaret.

4-1b A History of Common Economic and Political Dominance

A history of dominance by one nation in a region often leads to shared cultural elements among the different peoples in that region, as well as to similar economic and political structures. Russia's economic, political, and cultural dominance in the former Soviet Union has resulted, for example, in the use of the Russian language from the Baltics (Estonia, Lithuania, and Latvia) and Ukraine, to the Asian republics of the former federation, such as Turkmenistan, and Tajikistan. The countries also shared economic and marketing structures, many of which continue to survive, such as state-owned enterprises and large, nationwide distributors. In other examples, countries in East Africa formerly colonized by Belgium share a common second language (French), as well as extensive economic and political ties with the former colonist. And former colonies of the British Empire form the Commonwealth of Nations, a body that meets periodically to address issues of common concern and that recognizes the British monarchy as its symbolic leader. These former colonies continue to use English as a secondary national language and share many cultural elements with the former colonial power.

From a marketer's point of view, such similarities facilitate a standardized approach to the market, allowing the company to communicate with the target consumers in the region using the shared language and appeal to them using shared cultural elements.

4-1c Regional Proximity

Regional proximity is an important facilitator of economic cooperation. Although countries do not need to have a common border to engage in cooperative agreements, access that is facilitated by direct and effective transportation and communication systems greatly increases the likelihood that the economic relationship will survive over time. In the case of the **European Union (EU)** (www.europa.eu.int), the member countries are quite dissimilar culturally; however-

Ivan Marc/shutterstock.com

er, their regional proximity and the highly developed transportation infrastructure within the region, as well as economic similarity among the different countries, have all greatly contributed to the success of regional economic and political integration.

4-1d Economic Considerations

It has been amply demonstrated that countries characterized by a similar level of economic development are more likely to be successful in establishing and maintaining regional economic integration mechanisms than countries of different levels of economic development. In the latter case, it is typical that the larger, more developed economies are likely to further their interests at the expense of countries that lag behind in economic development. In effect, countries of similar development levels are more likely to create a successful common market that assures preferential treatment for goods manufactured in the region, while also securing a substantial local consumer market. As countries prosper as a result of this proven mechanism, the regional market then opens to firms from outside its boundaries, benefiting international enterprise regardless of national origin.

As mentioned above, the EU is not characterized by a shared regional culture. The EU is successful primarily due to economic commonalities shared by member countries. Among these commonalities are:

• A highly developed industrial base and overall productivity, translating into a high gross domestic product (GDP) per capita

• An extensive transportation and telecommunications infrastructure, which is indispensable in trading relationships

• Prosperous consumers who can afford to purchase the goods and services of local firms

It should be emphasized, however, that member countries have developed at different levels, and, often, constituents and government representatives of the wealthier countries (such as Germany and the Netherlands) have deplored having to adopt policies that would benefit the less economically advanced countries in the EU. Factions in the German government, even the finance minister himself, advocated the exit of Greece from the Eurozone when Greece no longer met the requirements of membership due to its economic hardships after the 2015 Greek Depression.

Furthermore, the member countries of the EU and of other forms of regional economic integration often differ with regard to the economic and trade policies they advocate. For example, Germany and the Netherlands stress the importance of market mechanisms and interfere only minimally in the regulation of business, whereas France is more likely to intervene. France stresses social welfare at the expense of market development and is often plagued by union activity that paralyzes different sectors of the economy. (The post office and the national airline industry constitute just two examples.) Similarly, in the case of the Southern Cone Common Market (Mercosur), the member countries disagree with associate members on the common external tariffs they should impose on international business entering the region.

It should be noted that, in the EU, the economic disparity between the old members and the new members is leading to substantial controversy, as discussed in International Marketing Illustration 4-1 (on next page).

The economic recession that started in 2008 created yet another important, and, most likely, lasting division, this time among the long-time members of the EU and some members of the Eurozone, creating a pejorative name for the countries that have had high economic instability, huge national sovereign debts which were impossible to refinance without the assistance of the EU and/or the IMF: the PIIGS countries, Portugal, Italy, Ireland, Greece and Spain. Greece was perceived as particularly problematic after falsifying its public financial debt information – a debt that was created by public sector wages and pension commitments that were difficult to sustain.

As mentioned in Chapter 3, Portugal, Ireland and Greece have received substantial rescue packages from the EU, IMF, and from other countries, ultimately leading EU finance ministers to approve a rescue package of almost a trillion U.S. Dollars to ensure financial stability.

4-1e Political Considerations

One of the more important obstacles to regional economic and political integration is the threat of losing national identity and sovereignty as part of the larger regional structure. Countries have many icons of national identity that generations have fought to maintain; such icons range from the form of government (republic, monarchy, or loose federation) to currency, language, and traditions. In the process of engaging in regional political and economic integration, member countries must choose, to a certain extent, to relinquish

International Marketing Illustration 4-1
Creating a Level Playing Field in the New European Union

Meeting the new guidelines for the European Union (EU) is a challenge for the new members, the former Eastern Bloc countries that are the largest body of countries to join the EU in history. These countries are facing new EU duties on imports from Asian markets and high expenses to meet EU safety, health, and other standards. For example, small farmers have to house pigs and cows in different buildings and build expensive septic tanks to conform to regulations, greatly increasing their expenses. The added hurdles and their often-negative consequences force many small and medium-sized enterprises in the new member countries to fold, leading to calls for secession and renationalization.

Adding to the frustration of the joining nations are attitudes of the long-time members of the EU, who are clearly not receiving the new members with open arms. Germany, for example, intends to keep citizens of the new member countries from working there for many years. And Denmark will not offer unemployment benefits to the workers from the Eastern Bloc who lose their jobs. Moreover, Germany and Sweden repeatedly rebuke the new members for maintaining low tax rates that help to bring more jobs to the area, while at the same time benefiting from a generous aid package from the EU.

However, the tax controversy is likely to disappear; according to the European Commission's plans, companies will pay a common consolidated corporate tax on their business activities in the future. They would adopt a tax base for their EU-wide activities, rather than face the complexity of their different tax regimes.[1] To illustrate, the corporate tax rates for the old EU members are much higher than those charged by the newcomers (see table).

The United States enacted a sweeping federal corporate tax rate reduction in 2017, with changes effective in 2018 – the average combined federal and local corporate tax rate fell from 40% to 27%. In response, several European countries lowered their corporate tax rates to remain competitive: the average corporate tax rate in Europe fell from 20.24% in 2015 to 19.48% in 2018. While the difference is small, it does suggest that Europeans are rethinking policies of regular tax increases to fund government programs.

EU Member	Percentage (%) Tax Rate
Austria	25
Belgium	29
Cyprus	12.5
Czech Republic	19
Denmark	22
Estonia	20
Finland	20
France	33
Germany	30
Greece	29
Hungary	9
Ireland	12.5
Italy	24
Latvia	20
Luxembourg	26.01
Malta	35
Netherlands	25
Poland	19
Portugal	21
Slovakia	21
Slovenia	19
Spain	25
Sweden	22
Europe Average Corporate Tax Rate	19.48

Source: KPMG's Corporate Tax Rate Survey, 2018, accessed on May 01, 2018 at:

https://home.kpmg.com/xx/en/home/services/tax/tax-tools-and-resources/tax-rates-online/corporate-tax-rates-table.html

important aspects of their sovereignty and identity. For members of the EU, such decisions ranged from minor issues, such as the number of hours that civil servants have for a lunch break (in Spain, it was argued it was the individual's right to have more than one hour — but, in 2005, they abolished the long siesta), to completely doing away with the French franc, the German Deutsche Mark, the Italian lira, and the other currencies in favor of the common currency, the euro.

A principal consideration in accepting the need to relinquish part of the national identity is the importance of the regional group as a whole to the advancement of national priorities. A successful regional economic and political integration is one that promises a more substantial and more rapid economic development for member countries than they would otherwise experience in isolation from the country group, and one that equitably addresses and protects regional, as well as national, economic and political interests. In the case of the EU, considerations of national sovereignty and national priorities take second place to joint interests in the creation of a viable, large market that provides a credible balance to large economic and political powers, such as those of the United States, Japan, China, and Russia, among others. Mercosur accomplishes similar goals for its large and small South American member countries.

4-2 Levels of Regional Economic and Political Integration and Examples of Integration Successes

Typically, member countries go through different stages of regional economic and political integration. Although most member countries start at the industry-specific bilateral or multilateral agreement level, theoretically at least, more complex regional agreements could jump to a more advanced stage, such as a common market, while simultaneously setting up a framework for a free trade agreement and customs union. Most commonly, however, member countries could target a more advanced framework, as their name might indicate (e.g., Common Market), but go through the different steps nevertheless. Sections 4-2a through 4-2f present the different levels of economic and political integration agreements, from the more basic to the more advanced, along with current and some past examples within each category.

4-2a Bilateral Agreements and Multilateral Forums and Agreements

Numerous examples of bilateral and multilateral agreements exist. Some are industry specific, others involve some or all products exchanged between countries. In fact, most member countries of the more complex regional economic and political forms of integration engaged, as a first step, in some type of regional cooperation. Governments could enter into agreements that are limited to a particular industry. Such agreements could involve the development of an industry sector, such as participating in the development of a hydroelectric plant in an area that would serve neighboring countries, or it could entail lowering or eliminating tariffs on certain goods that are traded between the member countries, such as coal and steel. The EU had its earliest attempts at economic integration in the form of the European Coal and Steel Community, established in the late 1950s, and the subsequent structure, the European Atomic Energy Community.

What differentiates these agreements from the formal regional integration formats is that they are either limited to two countries (bilateral agreements), or, if they involve multiple countries (multilateral forums and agreements). These agreements do not aim at regional integration. Examples of bilateral agreements are infinite, and they are often the foundation for the more formal regional integration attempts. Multilateral agreements that primarily provide a forum for regional cooperation endeavors are numerous. Some are industry specific, such as the Organization for Petroleum Exporting Countries (OPEC). Some are military in nature, such as the North Atlantic Treaty Organization (NATO). Others have an economic focus—for example, the Organization for Economic Co-operation and Development (OECD).

GrAI/shutterstock.com

One noteworthy economic organization is the Asia-Pacific Economic Cooperation, or APEC (www.apecsec.org.sg). APEC was established to mitigate the economic block and trade protection trend prevailing in the 1970s and 1980s; it was established in 1989 at a ministerial meeting in Canberra, Australia, with the mission to create an open economic alliance in the Asia-Pacific region.[2] This trade group includes all the major economies of the region (the United States and Canada are member countries), accounting for 42 percent of global trade.[3] APEC provides a forum for economic cooperation and the gradual reduction of barriers to trade and investment between member countries. Although the group does not attempt to forge an institutional integration that would be required under a free trade association or a more advanced regional economic and political integration format, APEC has nevertheless been instrumental in fostering free trade. APEC members agreed on a moratorium on customs duties over the Internet, on safeguards against software piracy, and on eliminating tariffs on computers and semiconductors. APEC also represents a forum for member countries to address issues critical to trade. For example, before its ascension to the World Trade Organization (WTO), China used the APEC forum to announce a number of important reductions in protectionism.[4]

Since its inception, APEC has become one of the world's most important regional groupings, with a total of 21 member countries, a population greater than 2.6 billion people, accounting for approximately 56 percent of world GDP and 49 percent of world trade. A number of countries are candidates to membership, among them India, Pakistan, Bangladesh and Ecuador. One of its main goals is to radically reduce trade transaction costs and lower all tariffs, and, ultimately, to create the Free Trade Area of the Asia-Pacific (FTAAP). [5]

An example of a political agreement — which we place in this category because of its failure to achieve a substantial level of regional integration — is the Commonwealth of Independent States (CIS) or the Russian Commonwealth. The nine non-Baltic successors of the former Soviet Union formed the Commonwealth of Independent States. This organization has never had a noteworthy economic element; and, even politically, the CIS became fractured in the second half of the 1990s with the GUUAM grouping (Georgia, Ukraine, Uzbekistan, Azerbaijan, and Moldova) operating explicitly as a counter to Russian hegemony.[6] The Union of Four (Russia, Belarus, Kazakhstan, and the Kyrgyz Republic) considered creating a customs union, with Russia's tariff as the putative common external tariff, but, apart from steps toward a bilateral agreement between Belarus and Russia aimed at creating an economic union, nothing has come to fruition.[7]

bibiphoto/shutterstock.com

Finally, the Central Asian states of the former Soviet Union have drawn up numerous plans for regional cooperation. They must cooperate on nontrade matters such as the desiccation of the Aral Sea. But the establishment of a Central Asian Economic Community has had little impact to date.[8]

The current official members of the CIS are Armenia, Azerbaijan, Belarus, Kazakhstan, Kyrgyzstan, Moldova, Russia, Tajikistan, and Uzbekistan, with Turkmenistan as an unofficial associate member. Georgia exited the CIS in 2009, after the 2008 military conflict with Russia. Ukraine, although a founding member, never ratified the treaty and formally pulled out of the CIS after Russia's annexation of Crimea in 2014; however, Ukraine maintains agreements with CIS member states outside of the formal organization.

4-2b Free Trade Agreements

A free trade agreement takes place between two or more countries and involves a reduction in, or even elimination of, customs duties and other trade barriers on all goods and services traded between the member countries. Countries are free to charge their own tariffs to all entities external to the free trade market. The following are existing or proposed examples of free trade agreements:

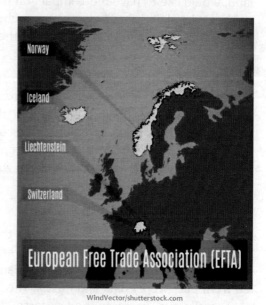

WindVector/shutterstock.com

Figure 4-3 EFTA Member countries.

- European Free Trade Association
- Association of Southeast Asian Nations
- ASEAN Free Trade Area
- North American Free Trade Agreement
- Free Trade Area of the Americas
- Southern African Development Community

The European Free Trade Association

The current member countries of the European Free Trade Association (EFTA) (www.efta.int) are Iceland, Liechtenstein, Norway, and Switzerland (see Figure 4-3). Previously, Sweden, Austria, and Finland were also members but have since joined the EU. For decades, EFTA has constituted another example of successful regional economic integration in Europe, in addition to the EU. Iceland, Liechtenstein, and Norway entered into the Agreement on the European Economic Area (EEA) in the early 1990s. The parties of the EEA are Iceland, Liechtenstein, and Norway, and the European Union members. Switzerland is maintaining its independence in this relationship but has a bilateral free trade agreement with the European Union.

In 1993, EU and EFTA created the European Economic Area, representing the world's largest single market with 380 million consumers. Since then, the EU has created new regulations with the Maastricht, Amsterdam, and Nice treaties and has created new powers of authority in areas such as environmental and labor market policies. EFTA countries are part of the Schengen agreement on the elimination of border controls in the EU. None of the EFTA countries have joined the European Monetary Union. [9]

At present, politicians in the EFTA countries want to be at least unofficially part of the EU but believe that public opinion at home is against further EU integration. The EU, on the other hand, does not appear to be interested in new negotiations that would offer EFTA members a greater involvement in the EU. The focus of the EU is eastern expansion, and the members are faced with a variety of constraints.[10]

Numerous complexities related to the different stages and phases of eastward enlargement:

- Possibilities of looser associated memberships
- Special rights of nonmembers
- Periods of transition to membership and special arrangements

In general, the perception of EU members is that EFTA, especially Norway and Iceland, would like to have more impact on the decision-making process within the EU, in particular on legal decisions (where nonmembers have no influence at all), and share in the benefits of the single European market, but they are not prepared to share in the costs and other obligations of membership.[11]

In spite of the national vote against joining the EU, Switzerland is engaging in bilateral negotiations, securing agreements that would help it join the EU eventually. It has negotiated issues in the area of the collection of statistics, the environment, agricultural production and customs fraud, cross-border security, youth, and education, among others.[12] EFTA continues to pursue free trade negotiations with countries outside of the EEA, such as Turkey, Georgia, and Canada, and, in Latin America, with Mercosur and the Central America Free Trade Area.

The Trans-Pacific Partnership

In 2016, a new trade agreement, the Trans-Pacific Partnership (TPP), was signed by the United States and countries in the Pacific region, specifically, Australia, Brunei, Canada, Chile, Japan, Malaysia, Mexico, New Zealand, Peru, Singapore, and Vietnam. Notably excluded from pact were China and Russia. The goal of the TPP was to lower trade barriers, protect intellectual property, and enforce standards for labor and environmental law. The agreement was also intended to serve as a major economic and political counterweight to growing Chinese influence in the region. However, the TPP proposal encountered many objections from member countries on issues such as intellectual property protection and Japan's reluctance to open its agricultural markets.[13] Subsequently, in 2017, the United States announced that it would pull out of the agreement, citing concerns that the TPP would be harmful to U.S. interests. The remaining member countries moved forward with negotiations, and the agreement, formally known as the Comprehensive and Progressive Agreement for Trans-Pacific Partnership, was signed in 2018. The pact covers some 500 million people on both sides of the Pacific Ocean. Several other Asian nations including Indonesia, Thailand, and South Korea are considering joining. It is still possible that the U.S. may ultimately join the TPP. [14]

The Association of Southeast Asian Nations (and the ASEAN Free Trade Area) (www.asean.org)

The Association of Southeast Asian Nations (ASEAN) is the leading example of regional economic integration in Asia. Member countries are attempting to reduce tariffs and create an environment that promotes mutual involvement in industrial development in the region. The goal of ASEAN is ultimately to create a free trade area where tariff and nontariff barriers are eliminated and to provide a substantial market of more than 330 million consumers. Members of ASEAN are Brunei Darussalam, Cambodia, Indonesia, Laos, Malaysia, Myanmar, the Philippines, Singapore, Thailand, and Vietnam; they have signed the ASEAN Free Trade Area (AFTA) agreement (see Figure 4-4).

The goals of the Association are to accelerate economic growth, social progress, and cultural development and to promote regional peace and stability in the, while adhering to the principles of the United Nations Charter. ASEAN leaders identified three pillars of the association as the ASEAN Security Community, the

WindVector/shutterstock.com

Figure 4-4 Member countries of the Association of Southeast Asian Nations.

ASEAN Economic Community, and the ASEAN Socio-Cultural Community. The ASEAN Vision 2020 is one of a partnership within a community of caring societies.[15]

ASEAN is pursuing free trade agreements with different partners. With the European Union, it committed in 2015 to a Strategic Partnership covering economic, political, and security cooperation; it established partnerships with countries such as Japan,[16] even laying the groundwork for the formalization of currency swap agreements with Japan, South Korea, and China, whereby countries agree to give each other money to bolster foreign exchange reserves in the event of a currency crisis.

An important development for ASEAN is the plan to create the Regional Comprehensive Economic Partnership (RCEP), composed of the 10 member states of the ASEAN and six states with which ASEAN has prior free trade agreements, Australia, China, India, Japan, New Zealand, South Korea. The Partnership does not include the U.S., but it includes Japan and Australia, both TPP signatories. RCEP would be one of the world's largest free-trade areas – RCEP countries make up 46 percent of the global population and have 24 percent of global GDP.[17] China plays a leading role in RCEP and considers it a national priority – RCEP has, in fact, become a regional priority after the U.S. pulled out of the TPP in 2018.

The North American Free Trade Agreement (www.nafta-sec-alena.org)

Signatory countries of the North American Free Trade Agreement (NAFTA) are the United States, Canada, and Mexico (see Figure 4-5). The goal of the 1994 treaty was to eliminate all tariff and nontariff barriers, such as import licenses and quotas, between the member countries and to offer free access to companies from member countries to a single market of almost 400 million consumers. As with other free trade agreements, member countries charge their own duties and other tariffs to companies from nonmember countries entering the respective markets. One of the more important decisions for NAFTA involves the rules of origin; to benefit from a duty-free status, goods must have a 60 percent North American content.

NAFTA initially generated great fears in the United States. It was described by a former presidential candidate and NAFTA opponent as the "giant sucking sound" that would move all jobs south of the U.S. border. Indeed, U.S. workers have experienced some level of job loss that can be directly attributed to NAFTA, in the lumber and textile industries, for

WindVector/shutterstock.com

Figure 4-5 Member countries of the North American Free Trade Agreement.

instance. However, it also can be argued that NAFTA created jobs in the United States. For example, in terms of trade flow, NAFTA has fared very well: U.S. merchandise exports to Mexico grew fourfold, and the United States exports to Canada more than doubled.[18] NAFTA has brought substantial foreign direct investment to Mexico,[19] creating stability in the country and lessening its dependence on the United States.

In spite of its free-market rhetoric, however, the United States has engaged in protectionist activity that hampers free trade, for example, keeping Mexican trucks out of the U.S. In fact, by 2017, the U.S. ran a large trade deficit with Mexico – $64 billion, with exports of U.S. goods and services at $276 billion, while imports from Mexico totaled $340 billion. However, these figures include goods shipped from Mexico to U.S. that are then re-exported to a third country. This causes some distortion in the U.S. trade import figures. In spite of these issues on trade with Mexico, the country remains the third largest goods trading partner for the United States.[20]

Central American Free Trade Agreement— Dominican Republic

Central American Free Trade Agreement—Dominican Republic (CAFTA-DR) was signed in 2004 with final implementation on January 1, 2009. The members are the United States, the five countries of Central America — Costa Rica, El Salvador, Guatemala, Honduras, and Nicaragua — and the Dominican Republic (DR). It was designed to eliminate tariffs and barriers to trade and to expand regional opportunities for workers, manufacturers, consumers, farmers, and service providers of the member countries. CAFTA-DR immediately eliminated tariffs on more than 80 percent of U.S. exports, phasing out the rest over 10 years. CAFTA-DR countries provide reciprocal access for U.S. products.[21]

While CAFTA-DR has had considerable success, with increasing trade flows between the countries, it has not been without bumps along the way. For example, the United States and Guatemala have been at odds since 2014 regarding labor reforms: Guatemala has failed to facilitate labor inspector access to worksites and to verify employer compliance with labor court orders. As for agriculture, with the elimination of most tariffs on agricultural products, exports of U.S. grain and food products to CAFTA-DR countries increased quickly. Local growers with small plots of land could not compete with large U.S. multinational agribusiness firms, with the latter gaining a large market share – as had previously happened after NAFTA's implementation.[22]

The Southern African Development Community

The Southern African Development Community (SADC) is a free trade organization that promotes economic cooperation among a coalition of 15 of Africa's more affluent and developed nations. The organization is designed to foster increased economic and governmental stability through the use of collective peacekeeping forces and should be credited for the recent relative stability of the region. SADC is a free trade area since 2008, aiming to reduce tariffs throughout the region. Its goal is to create a common market, but it has yet to deal with the challenges involved in creating a customs union.[23] Among its many projects aimed at improving the economy is the development of a renewable-energy research center that will help member countries battle chronic blackouts.[24]

Its member countries are Angola, Botswana, the Democratic Republic of Congo (DRC), Lesotho, Madagascar, Malawi, Mauritius, Mozambique, Namibia, Seychelles, South Africa, Swaziland, United Republic of Tanzania, Zambia, and Zimbabwe (see Figure 4-6).

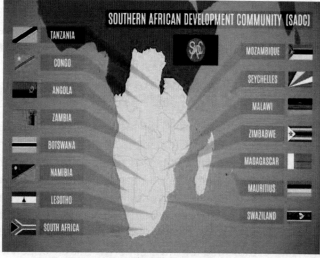

WindVector/shutterstock.com

Figure 4-6 Member countries of the Southern African Development Community.

4-2c Customs Unions

A customs union is a free trade association that may have either eliminated or greatly reduced all tariffs and other trade restrictions for member countries and that has adopted common external tariffs on products imported from outside the free trade area.

Member countries of the South African Customs Union (SACU) are Botswana, Swaziland, Lesotho, South Africa, and Namibia. The group's main trading partner is South Africa, and member countries have either partially or entirely tied their currencies to the South African rand. The states form a single customs territory, with a common external tariff that applies to nonmembers of the organization. The organization aims to create a common market, and has created a number of bodies, such as the Council of Ministers, a Commission, and Tribunal, marking the incipient stages of a potential political union.

4-2d Common Markets

Member countries to a common market agreement eliminate all tariff and nontariff barriers to trade, adopt common external tariffs, and allow for the free movement of capital and labor within the common market. The European Union has all the characteristics and institutions necessary to form a common market, and it has gone beyond this stage to form a monetary and political union. Mercosur follows closely, but it has yet to achieve full agreement with regard to fully unified customs.

In Europe, member countries agreed at the Treaty of Rome to establish the European Economic Community (EEC), the predecessor of the European Union, eliminating all internal tariffs and duties, establishing common external tariffs, and allowing for the free movement of capital and labor within its territory. At this point, member countries also set in place regulations and bodies that would ultimately form the basis for a monetary and political union — an event that was to take place in 1992 on the occasion of the Maastricht Treaty, commonly known as the eagerly anticipated "Europe 1992."

An example of common monetary policies and a precursor to a monetary union is provided by the European Monetary System. In 1971, the United States decided to no longer link the dollar to the price of gold — which initially secured monetary stability after World

War II ending the system of fixed exchange rates. The EU decided to prevent fluctuations of more than 2.5 percent between the European currencies by intervening in the currency markets, thus setting up the European Monetary System (EMS) in 1979. The EMS consisted of a credit mechanism, whereby each currency transferred 20 percent of its currency and gold reserves to a common fund; a reference currency known as the ecu, consisting of a basket of all the currencies; and a float.[26]

The float was known as the European Exchange Rate Mechanism (ERM), also known as the "snake" because it changed its shape based on the fluctuation of the different currencies. According to the ERM, a currency could fluctuate only up to 2.5 percent of its value in either direction, as mentioned earlier. When this value fluctuated consistently, the mechanism would adjust the currency upward or downward, respectively, creating a snakelike structure. A float that performed well was an important prerequisite to the success of a monetary union; this, as we will see in Section 4-2e, "Monetary Unions," was not the case in 1992, the date established for the creation of the European Monetary Union.

Other examples of regional economic integration aiming to establish a common market are as follows:
- Latin American Integration Association
- Andean Community
- Southern Cone Common Market
- Central American Common Market
- Common Market for Eastern and Southern Africa

Ulrike Stein/shutterstock.com

The Latin American Integration Association

The Latin American Integration Association (LAIA) was created in 1980 to replace the Latin American Free Trade Association (LAFTA). LAFTA was an attempt by member countries to establish a free trade association. Its demise was attributed to the disparity in the level of development of member countries and to the protectionist policies of countries with enormous foreign debt experiencing high inflation, currency devaluation, and economic crises. LAFTA is important in that it constituted a first step in an ambitious plan to create a common market that comprises all of Latin America, under the umbrella of the LAIA.

The LAIA member countries are Argentina, Bolivia, Brazil, Chile, Colombia, Cuba, Ecuador, Mexico, Panama, Paraguay, Peru, Uruguay, and Venezuela. Under LAIA, member countries are encouraged to establish bilateral and multilateral agreements aimed at reducing tariff and nontariff barriers. LAIA offers differential treatment to countries of different levels of development to avoid preferential treatment of the larger countries (blamed for the failure of LAFTA). Some member countries are at present also members of two successful common markets, the Andean Community and the Mercosur.

The Andean Community

The Andean Community, known previously as the Andean Pact, was established in the 1970s and renamed as the Andean Community in 1996. In addition to eliminating trade restrictions (tariff and nontariff) within the Andean region, the Andean Community also provides for uniform external tariffs and rules for foreign investment. Its member countries are Bolivia, Colombia, Ecuador, and Peru. After the cooperation agreement with Mercosur, the Andean Community gained four associate members, Argentina, Brazil, Uruguay, and Paraguay. Similarly, Mercosur granted associate membership to all the Andean Community nations. Chile, initially a founding member, withdrew from the pact, but now has come back as another associate member. Venezuela withdrew in 2006, after joining Mercosur.

Andean Community's accomplishments include a sizable increase in economic and commercial links among member countries, the development of community institutions and legal provisions, the consolidation of the common market (which also entailed progress with establishing a common external tariff) and substantially increasing trade with other countries and country groups. One of its primary trading partners is Mercosur. [27]

Roney Lucio/shutterstock.com

The Southern Cone Common Market

The Southern Cone Common Market (Mercosur, or Mercosul) initially started as a bilateral agreement between Brazil and Argentina aimed at eliminating trade restrictions between the two countries. Mercosur now comprises additional member countries: since 1991, Paraguay and Uruguay, Venezuela, and, since 2015, Bolivia. Chile, Colombia, Ecuador, and Peru have associate status. The countries with associate status disagree with the other members on the common tariffs (Chile insists on a much lower external tariff than the agreement provides for) to be charged to companies from nonmember countries. New Zealand and Mexico have observer status.

Venezuela had yet to comply with all the conditions for membership, such as bringing import duties in line with the group's common external tariffs; however, its former president, Hugo Chavez, led the charge of the group, seeking a region-wide organization that endorsed his ideological, anti-U.S. vision. In 2016, Venezuela was indefinitely suspended from Mercosur for violating its rules on democracy. Bolivia, however, was invited to apply for full membership, but, as of 2018, the four current members have not signed off on Bolivia's move to full membership. [28]

Initially, Mercosur was expected to look north, to NAFTA, for trade and cooperation accords. Surprisingly, it has opted in 1999 to approach the EU in an ambitious agreement to reduce trade barriers. Almost two decades later, in 2018, negotiations started with four Mercosur members, Argentina, Brazil, Paraguay, and Uruguay as a part of a broader agreement between the two regions. The trade deal aims to remove barriers to increase exports, to encourage companies to act responsibly and uphold high food safety, labor, and environmental standards, and to grow jobs on both sides. [29]

The Central American Common Market

The customs union includes five Central American countries: Costa Rica, El Salvador,

Guatemala, Honduras, and Nicaragua, known as the Central American Common Market (CACM), includes plans for forming a regional economic union similar to the EU and to advance regional and international trade. The plan also encompasses political, cultural, and environmental measures.[30] However, a number of countries in the common market have had adversarial relationships, and the permanence of the pact is often questioned.

The Common Market for Eastern and Southern Africa

Naruedom Yaempongsa/shutterstock.com

The Common Market for Eastern and Southern Africa (COMESA) plans full economic integration. It's goals are: the free movement of labor and capital, the free movement of people, and a currency union by 2025. It is clear, however, that the organization faces substantial political and economic obstacles given the political and economic instability in the region.[31] Specifically, the difficulties facing member countries include a poor compliance with tariff reductions and concerns over customs revenue losses; further complicating the matter is the fact that, despite diplomatic pressure, South Africa is not a member.[32] COMESA has 19 member countries: Burundi, Comoros, Democratic Republic of Congo, Djibouti, Egypt, Eritrea, Ethiopia, Kenya, Libya, Madagascar, Malawi, Mauritius, Rwanda, Seychelles, Sudan, Swaziland, Uganda, Zambia, and Zimbabwe.

4-2e Monetary Unions

The establishment of a monetary union involves the creation of a unified central bank and the use of a single currency. The following are examples of successful monetary unions:

- European Monetary Union
- West African Economic and Monetary Union
- Economic Community of West African States

It should be noted, however, that successful monetary unions do not necessarily mean successful economic integration and the elimination of all trade restrictions.

The Eurozone

The 1992 Maastricht Treaty had as a purpose to provide for the European Monetary Union (EMU) (www.europa.eu.int) and to create the European Central Bank, a single currency, and fixed exchange rates. The creation of the monetary union was, however, hindered in 1992 by an exceptionally strong German mark, boosted particularly by the financing of reconstruction for East Germany (the former German Democratic Republic, part of the Soviet Bloc) and the high interest rates it offered to foreign investors. This, coupled with a recession taking place in Europe, led to a crisis that caused the other currencies, in particular, the British pound and the Spanish peseta, to lose their value overnight and to float out of the European ERM; they also left the EMA. To member countries at the time it appeared that the German Central Bank was likely to dominate the European body, and, for a while, the euro lost popular support, especially in Britain.

The EMU had three stages. The first (which ended in 1994), involved the free movement of all capital in the EU, the abolition of all exchange controls, the creation of structural funds to remove inequalities between countries, and convergence of economic policies. The second stage began in 1994, and it involved establishing the European Monetary Institute (EMI), made up of governors of central banks, assuring the independence of national central banks, and establishing rules to curb budget deficits. In the third stage, starting in 1999, Austria, Belgium, Finland, France, Germany, Ireland, Italy, Luxembourg, the Netherlands, Portugal and Spain adopted the euro, with Greece (joining in 2001), Slovenia (2007), Cyprus and Malta (2008), Slovakia (2009), Estonia in (2011), Latvia (2014), Lithuania (2015). These 19 countries make up the Eurozone (see Figure 4-7).

Pyty/shutterstock.com

Figure 4-7 Member countries of the European Union and the Eurozone countries.

The European Central Bank took charge of monetary policy from the EMI, defined and implemented in euros. Euro notes and coins were issued in 2002 in the 12 euro-area countries, and national currencies were withdrawn from circulation. To be admitted to the third stage, each EU country must meet the following criteria: price stability, with inflation in check; interest rates varying no more than two percent from average interest rates, budget deficits below three percent of GDP, public debt not exceeding 60 percent of GDP, and exchange rate stability.[33]

The new EU members are all due to adopt the euro, when they are able to meet the criteria. Three EU members, the United Kingdom, Denmark and Sweden, have not entered the third stage and still use their own currency today.

The West African Economic and Monetary Union

The West African Economic and Monetary Union (UEMOA) is one of the first attempts at economic integration in Africa. Although successful as a monetary union that has adopted a single currency (the CFA franc) trade is quite modest within the UEMOA.[34] UEMOA member countries are Benin, Burkina Faso, Ivory Coast, Guinea-Bissau, Mali, Niger, Senegal, and Togo.

The Economic Community of West African States

The purpose of the Economic Community of West African States (ECOWAS) is to achieve complete economic integration. At present, ECOWAS member countries are also attempting to address impediments to the integration process that are attributed to civil unrest, regional conflict, a lag in economic development compared with other market groups in the world, and the domination of the group by Nigeria.

ECOWAS's plans, however, are ambitious. Six of the 15 members (Gambia, Ghana, Guinea, Liberia, Nigeria, and Sierra Leone) have set up a monetary union and have committed to adopting a common currency and to merge with the UEMOA. In this regard, they have pledged to meet stringent convergence criteria, such as five percent inflation, a maximum budget deficit-to-GDP ratio of four percent, and central bank financing of the budget deficit limited to 10 percent of the previous year's tax revenue, among others.[35] ECOWAS member countries are Benin, Burkina Faso, Cape Verde, Ivory Coast, Gambia, Ghana, Guinea, Guinea-Bissau, Liberia, Mali, Niger, Nigeria, Senegal, Sierra Leone, and Togo.

4-2f Political Unions

A political union represents the highest level of integration. It assumes a viable economic integration and involves the establishment of viable common governing bodies, legislative bodies, and enforcement powers. Although there are many examples of political unions, the European Union (www.europa.eu.int) is the only example to date of successful voluntary political integration. In a noteworthy past example, the countries of the Soviet Bloc were members of the Council of Mutual Economic Assistance (CMEA), an economic body similar to a free trade area, as well as members of the Warsaw Pact, a political and military body aimed at countering NATO. The countries formed a political union dominated by the Soviet Union, but the structures did not survive after the fall of communism. Another example of political semi-voluntary integration is the Commonwealth of Independent States, discussed in Section 4-2a, "Bilateral Agreements and Multilateral Forums and Agreements."

The EU, composed of 28 member states, is an established political union. The member states are Austria, Belgium, Bulgaria, Croatia, Cyprus, the Czech Republic, Denmark, Estonia, Finland, France, Germany, Greece, Hungary, Ireland, Italy, Latvia, Lithuania, Luxemburg, Malta, the Netherlands, Poland, Portugal, Romania, Slovakia, Slovenia, Spain, Sweden, and the United Kingdom – until 2019. Albania, Macedonia, Montenegro, Serbia, and Turkey are candidate countries.

In the 2016 referendum, The United Kingdom voted to leave the European Union in 2019 (the departure is referred to as Brexit), which means that the U.K. would no longer be part of the European single market, or the EU customs union, and it would no longer adhere to EU law. Since the referendum, the U.K. per-capita income has declined dramatically, and the banking and other industries are moving their headquarters and/or operations to large cities elsewhere in the European Union. It is still difficult to predict all the repercussions of this divorce.

Ivan Marc/shutterstock.com

Governmental Bodies of the European Union

As a political union, the EU agreed on a common foreign policy and a common security policy that includes defense agreements, a common legal system, and a common enforcement system that works across borders for mutual purposes. As such, it has set in place a number of governmental bodies.

The European Council, in which heads of government meet, is the highest policy-making body of the European Union.

The European Parliament, located in Strasbourg, France, is a body of 751 members (as of 2018) elected every five years by direct universal suffrage. Seats are allocated among member states based on their population.

The Parliament debates the policies and legislation in the EU. In the past, it was mainly a consultative body that passed on most of the proposed legislation with a simple majority voting. More recently, however, it has experienced extensive debates and lobbying from member countries on key international business issues. In one example, the Parliament killed a measure that would have made it easier to mount corporate takeovers. The vote is attributed to a string of hostile takeovers, such as Vodafone, the British mobile telephone company taking over its German rival, Mannesmann.[36]

The Parliament is consulted in many important matters, including those related directly to marketing in the EU. The European Commission is often consulted extensively on changes to e-commerce laws, in favor of consumers.

The Council of Nations consists of representatives from parliaments of member states, and it acts as a constitutional council. It has the power to overrule the Court of Justice.

The Council of Ministers, the decision-making body (the legislature) of the EU, is composed of one minister from each member country. The Council of Ministers passes laws based on proposals of the European Commission. Different ministers from each country, depending on the issue debated, meet at various locations to vote on directives advanced by the Commission. For example, EU energy ministers met in Stockholm to vote on EU electricity and natural gas directives to allow businesses and households to choose their electricity and natural gas suppliers.[37]

skyfish/shutterstock.com

The European Commission is subordinate to the Council, as a civil service. The Commission consists of a president and commissioners who are appointed for a four-year term and are in charge of initiating and supervising the execution of laws and policies. This executive body of the EU is located in Brussels, Belgium. It is important to note that the European Commission acts only on behalf and in the interest of the EU, and not that of individual member states. It answers to the European Parliament.

Many of the European Commission rulings affect international business worldwide: A company that wants to do business in Europe must abide by the Commission's ruling.[38] For example, the European Commission blocked General Electric's $42 billion takeover of Honeywell International, due to the danger that General Electric could use Honeywell's strength in avionics equipment to expand its competitive strength in aircraft engines.[39] It approved, however, the merger of two huge corporations, the U.S. seed company Monsanto and the German crop-chemical conglomerate Monstanto.[40]

The European Commission also enacted an important directive aimed at unfair commercial practices. Its Directive on Unfair Commercial Practices addresses the tangle of national bans, limits, and other restrictions that impede small and medium-sized enterprises from taking full advantage of the EU market and provides consumers anywhere in the EU the same opportunities and protection as elsewhere in the market. The primary areas covered are misleading practices, aggressive practices, and facilitation of cross-border shopping.

Misleading practices are targeted in particular; for example, the directive would be used to outlaw the use of sports stars in food advertising directed at children. The directive bans "bait advertising" scams, whereby a product is advertised as a special offer without the retailer carrying it in stock in sufficient amounts. It also bans use of liquidation sales when in fact the retailer is not going out of business, and use of pyramid schemes. Aggressive practices are also banned. For example, harassment, coercion, and undue influence in sales are banned, as is excessive solicitation. Consumers will also be able to confidently engage in cross-border shopping. Before this directive was enacted, consumers were worried that their rights would not be guaranteed to the same extent as in their home country and did not willingly purchase products over the Internet. This aspect of the directive also evens the playing field for companies in the EU. For example, companies that were unwilling to sell their products to consumers in untested areas because they were not familiar with national laws are now assured of the same protection anywhere in the European Union.[41]

In other examples, EU Commissioner for Consumer Affairs decided on an overhaul of online marketing to consumers, so that e-shopping becomes a more trusted marketplace, and it was the EU Justice Commissioner and European Commission vice-president who initially proposed – in 2012 – the General Data Protection Regulation (GDPR) of 2018. The GDPR ensures data protection and privacy to all individuals, changing how businesses and organizations handle the information of their customers in the EU – and, ultimately, elsewhere in the world.

The European Central Bank is charged with enacting monetary policy for the countries that share a common currency, the euro. Its goal is to maintain price stability within the European Monetary Union. The members of the European Central Bank board are appointed by the European Council by a simple majority vote. The equivalent of the Federal Reserve Bank for the United States, the European Central Bank tends to be more conservative and does not typically yield to individual countries' demands to reduce interest rates in an attempt to boost the economy during a downturn.

The European Court of Justice is the EU's equivalent of the U.S. Supreme Court. The Court's decisions are final, binding to member countries, and cannot be appealed in national courts. Also, European Court judgments overrule those of national courts.

In addition to these bodies, the European Union has adopted other common policies; among them are commercial policies, foreign and defense policies, and policies concerning immigration and the granting of asylum.

Other Parastatal Institutions in Europe

In Europe, there are parastatal institutions that have no affiliation to the EU, and yet they are significant players in the life of this region. One such is the Council of Europe, composed of 47 European states, which is involved in such areas as human rights, legal cooperation, cultural heritage, social, economic, and environmental planning, and local democracy. Two of its institutions are the Palais de l'Europe and the European Court and Commission for Human Rights.

Elenarts/shutterstock.com

Summary

Provide an overview of the determinants of regional economic and political integration. A number of factors prompt countries to favor trade with other countries. They are sharing a common culture, language, traditions, a history of common economic and political dominance, regional proximity, a similar level of economic development, and the desire to relinquish part of a nation's national identity in favor of advancing other national priorities.

Examine the different levels of economic and political integration and identify, within each world region, economic and political agreements that have met with success. The first level of integration involves establishing bilateral and multilateral agreements; these agreements involve, to some extent, opening of markets and elimination of trade barriers. At the next level, a free trade agreement involves a reduction in, or even elimination of, customs duties and other trade barriers between member countries. Examples of free trade agreements are the European Free Trade Association, the Association of Southeast Asian Nations Free Trade Agreement, the North American Free Trade Agreement, and the Southern African Development Community. The Trans-Pacific Partnership and the Regional Comprehensive Economic Partnership offer great promise for lower trade barriers.

At the next level, a customs union is a free trade area that has eliminated or greatly reduced internal tariffs and that imposes common external tariffs. An example is the South African Customs Union. A common market is an agreement to eliminate all barriers to trade, to adopt external tariffs, and to allow for the free movement of capital and labor in the region. Examples of common markets are the Latin American Integration Association, the Andean Community, the Southern Cone Common Market (Mercosur), the Central American Common Market, and the Common Market for Eastern and Southern Africa. The establishment of a monetary union involves the creation of a common central bank and the use of a single currency. Examples of monetary unions are the Eurozone, the West African Economic and Monetary Union, and the Economic Community of West African States. The only viable political unions that have survived to date are the European Union and the Commonwealth of Independent States.

Examine the functions of the different policy and governance bodies of the European Union. The different bodies of the European Union are the European Council, which is the highest policy-making body of the European Union, made up of heads of governments; the European Parliament, which debates policies and legislation of the European Union; the Council of Nations, which consists of representatives from parliaments of member states and acts as a constitutional council; the Council of Ministers, which is the decision-making body (the legislature) of the European Union that passes laws based on proposals of the European Commission; the European Commission, which is subordinate to the Council and initiates and supervises the execution of laws and policies; the European Central Bank, which is charged with enacting monetary policy for the countries that share a common currency; and the European Court of Justice, an equivalent to the U.S. Supreme Court.

Key Terms

Andean Common Market

ASEAN Free Trade Area (AFTA)

Asia-Pacific Economic Cooperation (APEC)

Association of Southeast Asian Nations (ASEAN)

bilateral agreement

Brexit

Central American Common Market (CACM)

common market

Common Market for Eastern and Southern Africa (COMESA)

Key Terms

Commonwealth of Independent States (CIS)
Council of Ministers
Council of Mutual Economic Assistance (CMEA)
Council of Nations
customs union
Economic Community of West African States
(ECOWAS)
European Atomic Energy Community
European Central Bank
European Coal and Steel Community
European Commission
European Council
European Court of Justice
European Exchange Rate Mechanism (ERM)
European Free Trade Association (EFTA)
European Economic and Monetary Union (EMU)
European Parliament European Union (EU)
free trade agreement
Latin American Free Trade Association (LAFTA)

Latin American Integration Association (LAIA)
Maastricht Treaty
monetary union
multilateral forums and agreements
North American Free Trade Agreement (NAFTA)
North Atlantic Treaty Organization (NATO)
Organization for Economic Cooperation and Development (OECD)
Organization for Petroleum Exporting Countries (OPEC)
political union
Regional Comprehensive Economic Partnership (RCEP)
South African Customs Union (SACU)
Southern African Development Community (SADC)
Southern Cone Common Market (Mercosur)
Trans-Pacific Partnership (TPP)
West African Economic and Monetary Union (UEMOA)

Discussion Questions

1. Identify the determinants of regional economic and political integration.

2. Describe the different stages of regional economic and political integration. What is the difference between a free trade association and a common market?

3. There are arguments that much of the groundwork for the Free Trade Area of the Americas already has been done by other free trade agreements in the region targeted for economic integration. Which free trade agreements are operating within this area?

4. Identify the different bodies of the European Union and describe their main function.

Chapter Quiz

True/False

1. Determinants of successful economic and political integration include a common culture, a common history, and regional proximity.

                                                                                                    True

Rationale: Neighboring countries with a common culture and history have been successful at creating a single market. Section 4-1, "Determinants of Economic and Political Integration"

2. Bilateral agreements and multilateral forums and agreements are different from formal regional political and economic integration.

                                                                                                    True

Rationale: The goal of these agreements tends to be less comprehensive, focused on one industry or natural resources, for example. Section 4-2a, "Bilateral Agreements and Multilateral Forums and Agreements"

3. The goal of NAFTA is to eliminate all tariff and nontariff barriers between the United States, Canada, and Mexico.

True

Rationale: The North American Free Trade Agreement was created to reduce and, ultimately, eliminate all tariffs and other barriers between the three countries. Section 4-2b, "Free Trade Agreements"

4. A common market is characterized by limited movement of goods, labor, and capital.

False

Rationale: Key to the definition of a common market is the free movement of goods, labor, and capital within the respective market. Section 4-2d, "Common Markets"

5. The European Parliament debates policies and legislation of the European Union.

True

Rationale: The European Parliament used to be a consultative body that passed on most of the proposed legislation with a simple majority voting; it now actively debates policies and legislation in the European Union. Section 4-2f, "Political Union"

6. The European Council is the highest policy-making body of the European Union.

True

Rationale: The European Council, which is the highest policy-making body of the EU, is made up of heads of government of the member states. Section 4-2f, "Political Union"

Multiple Choice

1. All the following are examples of free trade agreements EXCEPT the
   a. Association of Southeast Asian Nations.
   b. North American Free Trade Agreement.
   c. Southern African Development Community.
   d. World Trade Organization.

Answer d is correct.

Rationale: The World Trade Organization is an organization that actively promotes trade by offering help for export promotion and promoting regional trade agreements and cooperation in global economic policy making. Section 4-2b, "Free Trade Agreements"

2. Current members of the European Free Trade Association include all the following EXCEPT
   a. Norway.
   b. Liechtenstein.
   c. Sweden.
   d. Ireland.

Answer c is correct.

Rationale: Sweden is not a member of EFTA. Section 4-2b, "Free Trade Agreements"

3. Which agreement is credited with eliminating all internal tariffs and creating the European Economic Community?
   a. The Southern Cone Common Market
   b. The Treaty of Rome
   c. The Andean Economic Agreement
   d. The Maastricht Treaty

Answer b is correct.

Rationale: The Treaty of Rome is credited with eliminating tariffs, establishing common external tariffs, allowing for the free movement of capital and labor within what is today the EU, and setting in place regulations and bodies that would ultimately form the basis for a monetary and political union. Section 4-2d, "Common Markets"

Notes

1. "Finance and Economics: A Common EU Tax Base," *The Economist*, Vol. 383, No. 8527, May 5, 2007, p. 84.

2. "The History of APEC," *Business Korea*, Vol. 17, No. 4, April 2000, pp. 54–55.

3. Ibid.

4. Laura D'andrea Tyson, "The Message from Asia: Trade Locally, Think Globally," *BusinessWeek*, Issue 3710, December 4, 2000, p. 28. APEC at a Glance, accessed at http://publications.apec.org/publication-detail.php?pub_id=1610 on July 22, 2015. Deutsche Welle, "China's President Xi Touts 'Asia-Pacific Dream' Ahead of APEC Summit," November 9, 2014, accessed at http://www.dw.com/en/top-stories/s-9097 on May 17, 2018.

5. Ibid

6. Richard Pomfret, "Reintegration of Formerly Centrally Planned Economies into the Global Trading System," *ASEAN Economic Bulletin*, Vol. 18, No. 1, April 2001, pp. 35–47.

7. Ibid.

8. Ibid.

9. Robert von Lucius, "Nordic Neighbors Feel Snubbed," *Frankfurter Allgemeine Zeitung*, No. 154, July 6, 2001, p. 3.

10. Ibid.

11. For a discussion of the current conflict between the EU and EFTA, see Lucius, "Nordic Neighbors Feel Snubbed," p. 3.

12. Edward Taylor, "EU and Switzerland Resume Talks on Bilateral Accords," *The Wall Street Journal Europe*, July 6–7, 2001, p. 2.

13. Ernesto Londona and Motoko Rich, "U.S. Allies Sign Sweeping Trade Deal in Challenge to Trump," *The New York Times*, March 8, 2018, accessed at https://www.nytimes.com/2018/03/08/world/asia/us-trump-tpp-signed.html on May 2, 2108.

14. Ibid.

15. www.aseansec.org/64.htm

16. ASEAN.org, "ASEAN-EU Discuss Future Direction of Partnership, " accessed at http://www.asean.org/news/item/asean-eu-discuss-future-direction-of-partnership# on July 28, 2015; "Asia/Pacific Rim: Japan, ASEAN Set Up Free Trade Agreement Study Group," *World Trade*, Vol. 14, No. 7, July 2001, p. 18.

17. Chris Schnabel, "ASEAN Opens Up Half the World to PH Trade," accessed at http://www.rappler.com/business/economy-watch/97380-asean-aec-free-trade-agreements on July 28, 2015; Neil Saker, "The Foundations of Stability," *Far Eastern Economic Review*, Vol. 164, No. 20, May 24, 2001, p. 55. Emiko Jokuza, "RECEP vs. TPP: Trade Deals Explained, CNN, January 24, 2017, accessed at https://www.cnn.com/2017/01/24/asia/tpp-rcep-nafta-explained/index.html on May 17, 2018.

18. Alan M. Field, "A New Vision for NAFTA," *Journal of Commerce*, June 28, 2004, p. 1.

19. Ibid.

20. Office of the United States Trade Representative, "U.S.-Mexico Trade Facts," accessed at https://ustr.gov/countries-regions/americas/mexico on May 2, 2018.

21. www.ustr.gov/Trade_Agreements/Bilateral/CAFTA/CAFTA-DR_Final_Texts/Section_Index.html, June 15, 2007; Joint Statement from 2012 NAFTA Commission Meeting, 3 April, 2012, http://canada.usembassy.gov/news-events/2012-news-and-events.

22. *Sourcing* Journal, "U.S., Guatemala Fail to Resolve CAFTA-DR Labor Dispute," April 30, 2014, accessed at https://www.sourcingjournalonline.com/u-s-guatemala-fail-resolve-cafta-dr-labor-dispute-ik on July 28, 2015. Kimberly Amadeo, "CAFTA Explained, with Its Pros and Cons," *The Balance*, March 29, 2018, accessed at https://www.thebalance.com/what-is-cafta-3305580, on May 2, 2018.

23. Southern African Development Community, "Integration Milestones," accessed at http://www.sadc.int/about-sadc/integration-milestones/common-market on July 28, 2015; Ryan Fahey, "Congo Tensions: The SADC's Shortcomings," *Harvard International Review*, Vol. 21, No. 2, Spring 1999, pp. 14–16.

24. Paul Burkhardt, "Southern Africa Energy Ministers to Mull Renewables Research Hub," *Moneyweb*, July 21, 2015, accessed at http://www.moneyweb.co.za/news/south-africa/southern-africa-energy-ministers-to-mull-renewables-research-hub on July 28, 2015.

25. http://europa.eu/index_en.htm

26. www.sice.oas.org

27. *EIU ViewsWire*, "Venezuela Politics: Hijacking Mercosur," January 22, 2007.

28. *Pravda*," What prevents an EU-Mercosur agreement?," July 23, 2015, accessed at http://english.pravda.ru/business/companies/23-07-2015/131449-eu_mercosul-0/#sthash.kSpjJroo.dpuf on July 28, 2015; Benedict Mander, "Uruguay Threatens to Downgrade Mercosur Role," *FT.com*, March 8, 2007, 1. Claire Felter and Danielle Renwick, "Mercosur, South America's Fractious Trade Bloc," *Council on Foreign Relations*, December 26, 2017. Accessed at https://www.cfr.org/backgrounder/mercosur-south-americas-fractious-trade-bloc on May 2, 2018.

29. European Commission, "In Focus: EU-Mercosur," accessed at http://ec.europa.eu/trade/policy/in-focus/eu-mercosur-association-agreement/ on May 18, 2018.

30. Elizabeth Gonzales, "Weekly Chart of Free Trade in the Americas, *Americas Society/Council of the Americas*, December 1, 2016, accessed at http://www.as-coa.org/articles/weekly-chart-free-trade-americas on May 28, 2018.

31. *Country Monitor*, "Comesa's Free-Trade Area," Vol. 8, No. 43, November 6, 2000, p. 4. , and http://www.comesa.int/, accessed on May 18, 2018.

32. "International Economy," *Barclays Economic Review*, pp. 29–31.

33. http://europa.eu/abc/12lessons/lesson_7/index_en.htm, June 15, 2007.

34. Jacqueline Irving, "Point/Counterpoint: The Pros and Cons of Expanded Monetary Union in West Africa," *Finance & Development*, Vol. 38, No. 1, March 2001, pp. 24–28.

35. Ibid.

36. Paul Meller, "EU Parliament Rejects Bill to Ease Takeovers," *International Herald Tribune*, July 5, 2001, pp. 1, 10.

37. "EU Energy Chief Expects Power Deal by the End of the Year," *The Wall Street Journal Europe*, July 6–7, 2001, p. 3.

38. Brian M. Carney, "Mario Monti, Central Planner: Does the European Union's Competition Commissioner Really Believe in Competition?" *The Wall Street Journal Europe*, July 6–7, 2001, p. 6.

39. European Commission, "Commission Blocks Proposed Acquisition of TNT Express by UPS," January 7, 2013, accessed at http://europa.eu/rapid/press-release_IP-13-68_en.htm on July 28, 2015; Edmund L. Andrews and Paul Meller, "EU Vetoes GE's Plan to Acquire Honeywell," *International Herald* Tribune, July 4, 2001, pp. 1, 5.

40. Arthur Nelsen, "Monsanto and Bayer Are Set to Merge," *Huffington Post*, May 25, 2018, accessed at https://www.huffingtonpost.com/entry/monsanto-bayer-merge_us_5afeef96e4b07309e0578b5e on May 28, 2018.

41. http://europa.eu.int/comm/consumers/; and Lucy Alcock, Paul Chen, Hui Min Ch'ng, Sarah Hodson, et al., "New European Union Directive to Curb Unfair and Misleading Commercial Practices," *Journal of Brand Management*, Vol. 11, No. 2, 2003, p. 125.

42. *New Media Age*, "U.K. Firms Should Get Involved in the EU Etail Consultation, February 22, 2007, 16.

43. http://europa.eu.int/comm/enlargement, accessed on July 30, 2015.

44. http://ec.europa.eu/growth/index_en.htm accessed on July 30, 2015

45. http://ec.europa.eu/growth/index_en.htm accessed on July 30, 2015.

46. http://ec.europa.eu/environment/chemicals/reach/reach_intro.htm, accessed on July 30, 2015.

Case 4-1 Damianov Press

Damian Damianov, a retired director of a formerly communist metallurgic factory in the capital city of Sofia, Bulgaria, bought an abandoned printing press with quality equipment in the outskirts of Sofia. His goal is to produce books for art publishers in the European Union (EU). The press, privatized in the early 1990s, after the fall of communism in Bulgaria, was recently abandoned by its previous owner because it was considered an environmental hazard by the state. The previous owner did not want to invest in new equipment needed to meet environmental requirements of the EU, which Bulgaria joined in 2007.

The fall of communism in Bulgaria created numerous opportunities for newly privatized larger companies, as well as small and medium-sized enterprises. However, many businesses were greatly challenged by the 1996 crisis, and it took years for the economic recovery to bring back entrepreneurial enthusiasm. Since the 1996 crisis, Bulgaria has achieved macroeconomic stability, it has a stable currency, and its real growth is accelerating significantly. It was considered the most attractive of the 2007 candidates for membership in the EU. It is fertile ground for aggressive expansion of multinational business, especially business from the EU. The government encourages the establishment of new small and medium-sized enterprises, in line with the EU requirements, which specify that Bulgaria should focus on resolving uncertainties in the legislative and taxation areas and reinforcing delivery mechanisms for promoting entrepreneurship. As such, Bulgaria had to implement the European Charter for Small Enterprises,[43] which would create a strong competitive position for Damianov's new enterprise.

Damianov is working with Bulgarian venture capitalists to establish a new enterprise, the Damianov Press. His goal is to produce quality art books at much lower prices than Western European presses. This would serve the publishing clients well, as the industry is characterized by strong price competition. At present, much of the art book production in the EU takes place in Spain, where costs are somewhat lower than in the rest of the EU. Damianov has just returned from the Frankfurt Book Fair, where he met with a few of the German art book publishers: Prestel, Hatje Cantz, and DuMont. The Prestel representative appeared interested in the possibility of producing lower-cost, high-quality art books. With the high costs of development, translation, and production, exhibition catalogues and art books in general are becoming quite expensive. If costs can be reduced on the production side, these books can have greater appeal to the art public in the German-speaking world and elsewhere—as art books published in Germany frequently have side-by-side English translations. Damianov Press could produce those same high-quality, contemporary art books at a fraction of the cost.

Venture capitalists are gathering at the company's primary warehouse next week for a meeting. Each representative has individually assured Damian Damianov of contributions that would assure the financial viability of the company. They understand that their charge is to finance the refurbishing of old equipment and to invest in new equipment. Damianov needs to share information on the types of equipment needed and on issues related to compliance with European Union equipment requirements.

In reviewing the EU requirements for equipment, Damianov found that the European Commission offered a package of measures aimed at boosting community-wide trade that benefits primarily small and medium-sized enterprises (SMEs.) For Damianov Press, these measures make it easier to obtain high-quality, safe machinery: The EU market surveillance structures were reinforced to catch unsafe products and remove them from the market. Also, the testing, certification, and inspection bodies have greater oversight than in the past, thus assuring the safe performance of equipment. [44]

Damianov Press can also be assured that it will have access to energy-efficient equipment. The European Commission's Integrated Product Policy has accelerated, for industry, the move toward improving the efficiency of products, in terms of energy and water consumption, waste generation, and extension of lifetime. Damianov Press will be able to purchase equipment awarded the Eco-label, which guarantees its environmental efficiency. [45]

European Union regulations also require that new businesses conduct a study of environmental impact assessment, nature protection, and industrial pollution to ensure that the new company conforms to EU requirements. The study is mandated by the Bulgarian government for all new businesses. The new company also needs to conform to EU requirements in areas of antidiscrimination, equal opportunities, labor law, and occupational safety and health. As a company that deals regularly with chemical printing components, Damianov Press must comply with the REACH Regulation. The regulation entered into force in 2007, and is under the oversight of the European Chemicals Agency. The Agency's goal is to improve health and environmental protection through better and earlier identification of the properties of chemical substances. It imposes responsibility on the business to manage risks from chemicals and provide safety information, which means that Damianov will have to pay particular attention to the processes involving the chemicals, as well as to chemical waste disposal. [46]

Analysis Suggestions

1. What are some of the challenges that Damianov Press is facing in its new business?

2. What are some of the advantages that Damianov Press derives from Bulgaria's membership in the European Union?

3. What are the costs that Damianov will incur directly due to Bulgaria's membership in the European Union?

Case 4-2 Navigating Brexit: Majestic Interior Design Company

Ian Spiderson is the owner and general manager of Majestic Interior Design Co., a U.K. manufacturer and retailer of upscale home décor furnishings. Located in the famous university town of Cambridge, Majestic has a prominent clientele in London, as well as a flourishing business with owners of country manor houses throughout England and Scotland. The firm's classical styles and impeccable quality have also attracted a wide following in Western Europe. The company has also expanded into new international markets in Asia and North America – in fact, about one-third of Majestic's 2017 sales were outside the U.K. The year 2017 was a banner year for Majestic. Annual turnover (sales) reached 20 million Pounds ($26.7 million), with excellent margins and record profits.

Majestic provides complete fee-based interior design services along with their exceptional line of products. Many of the company's furniture items are produced at a contract manufacturing facility in Cambridge, with local artisans who have worked with Majestic for years. In addition to the furniture line, Spiderson and his team have developed attractive offerings of specialty rugs, lighting fixtures, and accessories. While many of these items are sourced in the U.K., others are imported from EU-member countries, as well as China and India. Imports of components, including specialty woods from forests in Romania, along with finished goods represented approximately twenty per cent of Majestic's 2017 costs.

Spiderson is keen on retiring, and hopes to turn over the daily management of the business to his son, John. However, Ian's plans are currently very much in the air. Like many in the U.K., and around the world, Ian was shocked at the results of the special referendum on June 23, 2016: a majority of British voters favored leaving the European Union! In early 2016, Prime Minister David Cameron concluded negotiations with the EU to grant the U.K. somewhat more autonomy from EU policies on immigration and other matters of administrative control by Brussels. However, U.K. "Eurosceptics," including some members of Cameron's own Conservative party, felt that the U.K. was still giving up too much. PM Cameron called the special referendum to ask British voters if the U.K. should continue in the EU under the revised terms or leave. Following the "No" vote, Cameron quickly resigned.

The new Conservative government led by Prime Minister Teresa May, invoked Article 50 of the EU Treaty in March 2017, setting in motion the formal two-year process of withdrawal. The United Kingdom was to leave the EU on March 29, 2019. The U.K. has been attempting to strike an acceptable balance between preserving some benefits of preferential access to the large EU market, versus accepting the EU policies on immigration and other laws that impact U.K. sovereignty. The full outcomes of Brexit are still to be determined. One estimate is that a "hard Brexit" – meaning that it would give up full access to the single market and customs union along with the European Union – would cost Britain over 70,000 jobs and over $13 billion in tax revenue. However, others have suggested that Brexit represents an opportunity for U.K. businesses to tap into new international markets. The U.K. Inward Processing Relief may enable companies to avoid some tariffs on imported items that are ultimately destined for re-export.

Like many British business owners, Ian is concerned over the future of his company. He is confronting numerous issues starting with lost sales in the U.K. as well as in international markets. In addition, he must now confront new issues with his supply chains for both imported components for manufacturing, as well as for the finished goods that Majestic sells. He is worried about manufacturing costs and margins. It seems evident that Ian will be delaying retirement and his planned move to a beachfront flat in the Canary Islands.

Analysis Suggestions

1. Describe the marketing challenges that Majestic faces. What steps could Majestic take regarding its product/services mix? What about new target markets? Are there any opportunities to expand international sales via existing U.K. trade treaties with other nations?

2. What are some of Majestic's new challenges on the supply side of the business? How will Brexit affect his supply chains, costs, and profit margins? What steps could he consider to remain competitive on pricing while still retaining quality?

3. It may be assumed that Majestic will no longer have preferential access to EU markets after March 29,

2019. Determine what Majestic's new potential tariffs might be for exports of home furniture, rugs, and lamps to the EU zone.

        Sources: Alice Foster, "EU Referendum 2016 Aftermath: All the Key Dates. When will Britain Leave the EU," The Daily Express, June 23, 2017, accessed at https://www.express.co.U.K./news/politics/644178/EU-referendum-dates-European-Union-Brexit-David-Cameron-Brussels on May 28, 2018; "Business Update," University of Pittsburgh School of Business, October 7, 2016, accessed at https://business.pitt.edu/faculty/blog/brexit-a-fasinating-case-study-in-strategy on May 28, 2018; Daniel Waldron, "International Trade in a Post-Brexit World; How to Adapt," Armagard Export Worldwide, January 18, 2018, accessed at https://www.linkedin.com/pulse/international-trade-post-brexit-world-how-adapt-daniel-waldron on May 28, 2018; "Inward Processing Relief," Langdon Systems, accessed at http://www.langdonsystems.com/ipr_overview.asp on May 28, 2018. "Brexit Preparations: Supply Chain Mapping," Linklaters, May 2017, accessed at file:///C:/Users/ghiller/Downloads/Brexit-preparations-Supply-chain-mapping-toolkit%20(1).pdf on May 28, 2018.

Chapter 5

Cultural Influences on International Marketing

Learning Objectives

After studying
this chapter,
you should be able to:

- Identify the elements of culture and examine how they affect marketing practices around the world.

- Describe national and regional character based on dimensions such as time orientation, business practices, gift giving, socializing, gender roles, and materialism.

- Discuss cultural variability in terms of the Hofstede dimensions with appropriate examples and address cultural change in a marketing context.

- Address the self-reference criterion and ethnocentrism and describe how they impede mutual understanding and cooperation, with direct negative effects on marketing practices.

- Describe the global consumer culture as it manifests itself around the world.

Chapter Outline

The Turkish Client

You are in the middle of negotiations with a potential Turkish client in Istanbul, over lunch, at the Conrad Hilton Hotel. You go to the self-service buffet and pile on your plate some tasty pork chops from a serving dish clearly marked "pork." You ask the waiter to bring a bottle of wine and offer some to your potential Turkish client; he declines. Your products are known for their quality in Turkey and elsewhere in the world, and your client seems receptive to your price quote. After lunch, the potential client invites you to his home for coffee; you decline and state that you need to stay at the hotel to get some work done and bid him goodbye. You come back to the United States and find that you cannot reach your Turkish client. His secretary always claims he is not in, and he does not return your calls. What went wrong?

Koraysa/shutterstock.com

You subsequently learn that, in Turkey, the dominant religion is Islam, and Islam bans the consumption of pork and alcohol. Could your lunch have offended your client? Probably not too much because he still seemed receptive to your offer as you were eating the "dirty animal" in front of him. Could he have been offended by your refusal to go to his house for Turkish coffee? Even though you refused, you did not tell him that you really hate the stuff and you were dreading spending even a few hours in 90-degree weather in a home that most likely was not air-conditioned. You were, after all, showing how dedicated you were to your job by staying at the hotel to work. Could the hotel staff have told him that you spent the evening next door, at another air-conditioned hotel, a former palace, having yet another bottle of wine? It is very possible – in many cultures, you are never alone, and the strangers at the next table might be paid to observe you and report to local clients, company management, or the competition.

This chapter examines in depth the effect of different cultural influences on consumer behavior and on a company's international operations. It examines national character and provides illustrations of behaviors in line with national character.

A full understanding of local culture in markets where one's firm is operating constitutes a minimal condition for successful global marketing operations. Although cultural understanding alone cannot guarantee a firm's success in a new international market, not fully understanding the local culture and engaging in marketing practices that may be discordant with the culture guarantees failure.

Walmart (in Germany)

The wrong strategies will quickly backfire for companies that do not fully research their target market. In Germany, Walmart banked on matching low prices with friendly service, only to find out that German shoppers just want to be left alone to shop, without the friendly chat, which they thought was imposing, fake, and, possibly, adding to their prices.

Coca-Cola (in India)

Hindustan Coca-Cola Beverages incurred great losses in India. It was thought the partnership with Parle, the leading local soft-drink manufacturer, was a coup. But Indians were not happy about it, thinking that it would lead to the destruction of local beverage brands . . . and they were right: Coke was focusing its promotional efforts on building its international brands, phasing out Parle's Thums Up, which was the leading soft drink in India. Eventually, however, Coke figured out that it was better to continue selling the Indian brand, which, with Coke, has 62 percent of the Indian cola market. In the

end, the Thums Up brand was so successful that Coca-Cola decided to take it international. The brand had some international presence: it was sold in the Middle East to the Indian diaspora and it was successful in neighboring Bangladesh. However, in 2018, Coca-Cola launched Thums Up in markets across South Asia, as a first step in what is believed to be a global rollout of the brand.[1]

Microsoft

In its long history of internationalization, Microsoft has made a few costly mistakes. In the Spanish version of Windows XP, destined for Latin America, it asked users to select their gender between "not specified," "male," and "bitch" — all due to an unfortunate error in translation. When coloring in 800,000 pixels on a map of India, the company colored eight areas in a different shade of green, representing the disputed Kashmiri territory. Thus, Kashmir was shown as non-Indian, and the product was promptly banned in India. Microsoft had to immediately withdraw 200,000 versions of the program. Similar errors with maps brought Microsoft employees to face the government of China and apologize. In another example, Microsoft developed a fighting game called Kakuto Chojin, in which the fighting takes place to a background chanting of the Koran. Microsoft decided, nevertheless, to issue the game in the United States, believing that it would not be noticed. But the Saudi government protested and Microsoft withdrew the game a year later.[2]

Culture is difficult to navigate in international marketing. The right product, coupled with the right local marketing decisions, can, potentially, create great customer franchise, and, implicitly, high profits. But making the right decisions is not always easy, as the previous examples illustrate. Walmart brought its low-price, consumer-friendly culture to Germany and customers responded with a shrug. Walmart's prices were low, but not that low compared with other similar long-entrenched businesses, such as Netto, Pennymarkt, and Aldi. And a high customer focus means higher prices to German shoppers, who are not used to being fussed over even when they pay higher prices. Coca-Cola, as mentioned, proceeded in India as it did everywhere else: It bought its competitor and tried to put it on ice — to phase it out — and it priced Coke too high. Coca-Cola executives did not anticipate the adverse reaction of consumers who were angry about the disappearance of a successful Indian brand and unhappy with the high price of soft drinks. Coca-Cola lost millions before it was able to appease the Indian public. And Microsoft lost millions as well, withdrawing products after creating ill will in their many target markets.

When armed with knowledge about the local culture, companies such as Walmart, Coca-Cola, and Microsoft are in a better position to communicate effectively with the target consumer and avoid the blunders described earlier. Culture is recognized as having a strong influence on all aspects of consumption; it is expressed in the consumption of numerous products and services, in homes, offices, stores and marketplace sites, with differences noted across various subcultures and nations.[3] Cultural factors also exert a profound influence on a firm's other stakeholders, such as government representatives, national and international consumer groups and interest groups, service providers, suppliers, channel members, and shareholders, among others. Culture is the key determinant of the manner in which individuals do business or respond to a company's marketing strategy.

5-1 Culture Defined

Culture—a society's personality—is defined as a continuously changing totality of learned and shared meanings, rituals, norms, and traditions among the members of an organization or society.

It should be noted that the notion of culture is relatively ambiguous and controversial among both practitioners and academics.[4] Some elements of culture, however, are thought to affect important aspects of marketing, and they are addressed in this chapter.

The pivotal constituents of culture are as follows:

• Ecology — The manner in which society adapts to its habitat (i.e., the distribution of resources within an industrialized country versus a developing country; the desire for efficiency, space-saving devices, or green products).

• Social structure — The organization of society.

• Ideology — The manner in which individuals relate to the environment and to others; this includes attitudes toward time, space, possessions, and referent others (peers).

These areas are complexly interrelated.[5]

Rawpixel/shutterstock.com

Subcultures are components of the broad culture. Subcultures are groups of individuals with shared value systems based on ethnicity or common background. Subcultures could be based on regional differences. Southern Italian consumers have different lifestyles than Italians in the north, for example. Northern Germans have a different worldview from Germans in the southern state of Bavaria. Turkish Germans maintain many of their home-country traditions and strong ties to the old country. They have larger, extended families living under one roof or nearby; they purchase products in Turkish shops, which pepper the retailing landscape in larger German cities; and they maintain their Muslim religious traditions. German and Italian immigrants are important groups in southern Brazil, where the cultural climate is more conservative than the more freewheeling beach-oriented culture of Rio de Janeiro.

Subcultures can be based on religion, an important element of culture. Muslims make up a large minority in cities in Britain, and they retain their religious customs, as the following paragraphs illustrate.

Muslim Women in the United Kingdom

London parks have many Muslim women watching their children play. The women take children to school and run errands covered from head to toe in flowing black gowns that permit only a slit for their eyes. The women say that they are targets of abuse by non-Muslims; Britons, on the other hand, often state that their limit of tolerance is being tested.

In fact, there are efforts underway to place legal curbs on the full-face veil. A lawyer wearing the veil was not allowed to represent an immigration client because the judge could not hear her; a teacher wearing the veil was dismissed from school; a student barred from wearing the veil to school sued and lost. And British education authorities are proposing a ban

Ayoub kayor/shutterstock.com

of the veil in school. The British interpret the veil as a statement that men are such brutes that if exposed to normally clothed women, they cannot be trusted to behave, and that women who do not wear a veil are indecent. People in England think the women wearing the veil are oppressed and do not speak English. However, the veil is worn by many second-generation Britons, who are even told by Britons to go home, although they were born in Britain and their accent bears no hint of their heritage — Britain is home for these women. Among the younger women who wear the veil, many have taken it up recently as an expression of Islamic identity and as a form of rebellion against the policies of the British government overseas and at home. And many more Muslim women wear the head scarf, covering all or some of their hair, rather than the full veil. France bans the full-face Islamic veil in public places, and the European Court of Justice ruled that private employers may ban wearing head scarves on the job. In Britain, however, Muslim women can wear the headscarf, and even the full veil, almost anywhere.[6]

In other European examples, the Netherlands have large Indonesian and Surinamese subcultures; Austria has large Bosnian and Croatian subcultures; and Sweden has a large Ethiopian subculture. Historically, the Jewish subculture used to be the largest in such countries as Poland, the Baltics, and Germany, but that ended in the 1930s and 1940s, when many were forced to emigrate or were deported to death camps. In some European cities, such as Berlin, there is a revival of Jewish life; Jews from the former Soviet Union account for the growth in the Jewish population, but, in many places, a Jewish presence is just a memory (see Figure 5-1 on next page).

Subcultures can also be defined based on sexual preference. Gay and lesbian consumers constitute an important market, avidly courted by businesses, especially for high-end consumer goods, vacation travel, etc. The companies that actively target gay and lesbian consumers have been able to reap substantial rewards: Gay and lesbian consumers have a fierce loyalty to a brand they identify as supportive.

In Section 5-2, "Elements of Culture," we describe the elements of culture that are most relevant to international marketing managers.

Figure 5-1 In the Tiergarten district of Berlin, the presence of the Jewish subculture is only a memory. Jewish temples and schools were eradicated in the 1940s. This memorial stands at the entrance of a playground, commemorating the transport of area Jews from the Levetzowstraße Synagogue to the death camps.

5-2 Elements of Culture

5-2a Language

Language has a prominent role as an element of culture: The language one learns in the community where one is born and raised shapes and structures one's worldview. Some languages, such as the Bantu languages, are broad and do not differentiate, for instance, between the "here" and the "now."[7] Other languages are precise, some in domains such as agriculture; they may have several terms for an object or a body part, depending on the current function of the object or body part. For example, for the word "tail," Batwa languages have a term that refers to its use by cattle as protection against flies, another term as an illustration of joy, yet another as an indicator of attention, and so on. The key to communicating in a particular culture is understanding all the nuances and complexities of the language of the target market.

Language consists of the spoken/written language and the nonverbal language, and fully understanding both is essential for fully understanding communication.

Spoken/Written Language

The spoken/written language poses a number of concerns to marketers. First, in terms of translation, the diversity of languages creates difficulties for marketers operating internationally. Even if the same language is shared by different countries, marketers should be aware of differences in meaning: Procter & Gamble sells "nappies" in the United Kingdom, as opposed to "diapers"; the "boot" of the Ford automobile is actually its "trunk"; and housewives or house-husbands who are "hoovering" in the United Kingdom may actually be "vacuuming" using an Electrolux vacuum cleaner.

Problems could arise in the process of translation: Firms have placed in jeopardy the viability of their brands by relying on primary translations and not ensuring that either the product name is appropriate in a given culture or that the communication actually conveys the intended message. Using procedures described in Chapter 6, back translation

(translation back into the original language) and parallel translation (translation by another translator for comparison purposes) diminishes the likelihood that a company will commit blunders when communicating with the target market. Many companies have made translation blunders, and the marketing literature is replete with examples. Using translation software increases the possibility of creating such blunders.

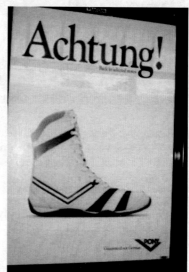

Good translation is expensive, especially in markets where multiple languages are spoken. For example, in India, there are more than 300 minor languages and 3,000 dialects. Only 15 distinct languages are widely spoken, however; Hindi, the official language, is spoken by 30 percent of the population, and English is widely used in administrative, commercial, and political life. To effectively communicate with this promising multicultural market of approximately one billion, a firm's decisions on which language to use are crucial.

Marketing practitioners using the same marketing strategy in a unified market experience similar dilemmas: deciding which language to use and whether to use multiple languages. The European Union presents an interesting case. When companies target this market, product information is typically provided in, at minimum, two or three languages. An Evian bottle that has French, Dutch, and German labeling is probably sold in France, Belgium (where both French and Dutch – Flemish – are spoken), the Netherlands, Germany, Austria, Luxembourg, Liechtenstein, and in the German and French regions in Switzerland.

It is important to communicate in the appropriate language with the target market in areas where multiple languages are used. Marketers selling their products in the United Arab Emirates will find that a significant proportion of consumers there do not speak the national language, Arabic. The Emirates have a large population of guest workers from India, Pakistan, and Southeast Asia. For example, in Ajman, one of the emirates east of Dubai, only about 20 percent of the population is Emirati. In targeting these markets, firms would benefit from using English, which is widely understood, and the main language used in business, rather than Arabic.

Other aspects of the written language convey meanings as well. For example, calligraphy in China is perceived as an art, and the calligraphy itself conveys information about the writer's erudition and talent. It is said that the Chinese fine arts and Chinese calligraphy share the same origin. Chinese characters are the only pictographic symbols among the modern languages. Writing, in fact, is perceived as an art form higher than painting in that it is more abstract. To appreciate the beauty of the calligraphy, "it takes deep Chinese cultural nourishment and higher intellect."[8]

Calligraphy is often performed in public parks, with a water brush that leaves no permanent marks. A calligrapher is usually surrounded by a crowd interested in the message and in the art. Sensitivity to and an understanding of this type of communication are essential to understanding the Chinese (see Figure 5-2 on next page).

Nonverbal Communication

Nonverbal communication includes body language, gestures, facial expressions, eye contact, and even silence. Silent communications, especially gestures, have different mean-

Figure 5-2: Understanding Chinese calligraphy takes deep
Chinese cultural nourishment and higher intellect.

toonman/shutterstock.com

ings across cultures, and marketing managers must be aware of them to avoid embarrassing or costly mistakes. Examples of nonverbal communication are provided in the next paragraphs.

Proxemics refer to the relationship between physical space and the process of communication. One of the peculiarities of American culture that most foreigners find intriguing is the "bubble," the personal space around the individual, which, if one violates, one must apologize. This "bubble" is unheard of in countries where standing in line means that the person behind another will periodically engage in a "poking exercise," pushing the person in front lightly, hoping that he or she might advance. In these countries, even in polite society, apologizing for maneuvering too closely or cutting off another is not necessary.

In general, Greeks, Central and Eastern Europeans, Japanese, and South Americans feel more comfortable standing or sitting closer to strangers than those of other nationalities.[9]

Similarly, in the Middle East, even in the business world, men prefer standing close to people with whom they are conversing and take great offense if someone backs away from them. Latin Americans also have a much smaller sense of personal space than their English-speaking counterparts. In addition to close proximity, while conversing, a Latin American may touch his conversation partner's elbow. Moreover, with many women in Latin America, both in and out of business, personal courtesies are often expected; these include opening doors, holding the chair for seating, etc. Failure to observe those nonverbal cues may lead a Latin American to assume that a prospective international business partner is uncouth and not trustworthy. [10]

Postures, orientations, and oculesics refer to individuals' positioning relative to their counterpart and avoiding eye contact during communication. Individuals' approaches to greeting, for example, differ in different parts of the world. In the United States, when shaking hands, one is supposed to look his or her counterpart in the eye; this should make an impression of being forth-right, as well as having a take-charge attitude. The handshake should be firm and brief. This same handshake, however, would be perceived as arrogant and aggressive by one's Asian counterpart. In Asia, a soft hand-shake, a humble posture, and avoidance of eye contact convey an attitude of respect. In Eastern Europe, a woman may expect to have her hand kissed (this also conveys respect for her as a representative of her gender), and men typically kiss each other on the cheeks. A kiss on the cheek in Central and South American countries, France, and Mexico is proper and perhaps even necessary (to avoid insult). But in countries such as Korea and Japan, a slight bow is a better choice; placing the hands together and bowing slightly would offer a nice

aslysun/shutterstock.com

welcome in India and Thailand.[11] With an extensive Western presence in the countries mentioned, however, the expectation that foreigners should adhere to these patterns of behavior has diminished.

When contemplating shaking hands, it is important to be aware that touching, in many countries, especially in the Middle East, is taboo, whether through a handshake or otherwise: In Muslim and Jewish orthodox communities, it is improper for men and women to touch members of the opposite sex other than spouses or close family. Also, tipping or removing a hat may be respectable in many countries but inappropriate in Jewish and Muslim cultures, which require head coverings. [12]

Certain sitting positions may even get one in trouble. For example, a person should not cross his or her legs or show the sole of his or her shoe to another person in the Middle East and Thailand because the gesture implies that the person is "worthy of being stepped on," or, according to other interpretations, "likened to a shoe sole." And, in many countries, it is appropriate to remove shoes and socks when entering a home or a religious area. Finally, pointing with a finger is not appropriate in Asian countries, although offering direction with the full hand is acceptable.

Chronemics refer to the timing of verbal exchanges. Americans expect prompt responses and are uncomfortable with a slow response or silence. They attempt to fill in the silence and further probe into the issue at hand to ensure that their counterparts understand them. Other nationalities, such as the Japanese, prefer to use this "quiet time" as contemplation time in which they evaluate the message. Often, translation comes in handy in this situation, especially if the negotiating parties understand each others' languages. Consecutive translation often provides the time necessary to digest and interpret messages, thus eliminating the need for the additional contemplation time. Often, the translator familiar with the Americans' discomfort with silence will intervene and explain that the time is being used for contemplating the deal.

Haptics refer to the use of touch while conversing. Again, this nonverbal communication is rarely used by Anglo-Americans, who prefer to keep others at the periphery of their "bubble." Latinate cultures tend to make extensive use of touch in order to convey their messages.

Kinesics refer to the movement of part of the body in order to communicate. Compared with many cultures, Americans gesture very little while communicating. Yet the French and Italians use hand gestures frequently to express themselves. It is important to understand the meanings of these gestures to function efficiently in these cultures. At the same time, it is wise not to assume that the gestures used in one's home country are identical with those used in other countries. It is possible, for example, that those gestures may have no meaning in other cultures, or, worse yet, they may have meanings other than those one would like to convey. For example, the sign of "OK" commonly used in the United States signifies "zero" in France, is a symbol for money in Japan, and is a vulgar gesture in parts of South America, as a company that had this sign printed quickly found out.[13]

Jeanette Dietl/shutterstock.com

Movements of the head are the most difficult to interpret. Western gestures such as shaking the head up and down to signify "yes" and from side to side to signify "no" have different equivalents in other cultures. In the Middle East, people raise their head in a haughty manner to say "no," while sometimes accompanying the gesture with a click of the tongue. "No" is conveyed with a wave of the hand in front of the face in parts of Asia, and with a shake of the finger from side to side in Ethiopia. On the other hand, the U.S. gesture to slit one's throat means "I love you" in Swaziland, folding one's arms conveys respect in Fiji and arrogance in Finland. In Mexico, the gesture of tapping the palm of one hand with opposite elbow (codo, in Spanish) refers to someone who is very thrifty or perhaps even cheap. [14]

Paralinguistics refer to nonverbal aspects of speech that include emotional intonation, accents, and quality of voice. Again, a louder, more aggressive intonation denoting self-assurance and strength in some cultures, such as that of the United States, may be perceived as threatening or insulting by other cultures, where softness is equated with politeness and respect. In the cultures of West Africa, laughter indicates embarrassment, discomfort, or surprise, whereas in some other cultures, laughter is discouraged altogether.[15]

Although many people view North Americans as fairly loud and aggressive, the Spanish speak even louder, often shouting at each other to express enthusiasm.[16]

Nestor Rizhniak/shutterstock.com

Appearances refer to one's physical attire and overall grooming. Each culture has its own expectations and norms with regard to what is appropriate in different circumstances. For example, Western business attire for men consists of a well-tailored dark suit, complemented by a conservative shirt and tie and elegant shoes. Western business attire for women may also consist of a well-tailored suit or a conservative dress and high heels. European dress codes allow for a more casual look or a more personal style than North American dress codes. In the Middle East, depending on the country, men's business attire may consist of a gallabeya (a long, typically white garment) and a head cover, whereas women in business may have their hair covered and wear an equally long, conservative dress, known as the abaya or the hijab.[17]

In South Asia (India, Pakistan, Bangladesh, Nepal, and others), appropriate business attire for women may be the traditional sari, typically an exquisitely embroidered or designed material that is wrapped using a specific pattern. In Africa, women wear a similarly colorful outfit, but taking the form of a gown with country-specific prints—a bou-bou (pronounced "boo-boo"); men wear a short-sleeve shirt with a political party pin attached and a pair of slacks, with the exception of the most formal circumstances, when a coat and tie are worn.

Olfactions refer to the use of odors to convey messages. Typically, such messages have a religious meaning: Incense is frequently used to purify the air of evil presence in both temples and churches, as well as in private homes. Finally, odors are evaluated differently in different cultures. For example, U.S. culture finds body odors and garlic breath as offensive, whereas East Asian cultures avoid consumption of dairy products believed to cause intolerably bad breath.

The Nonverbal Language and High-versus Low-Context Cultures

The high-low context continuum defines the extent to which a spoken statement conveys a full message.[18] In **low-context cultures**, what is said is precisely what is meant. For example, in the United States, Canada, Germany, and Switzerland, a verbal message carries the full meaning of the sentence. In this environment, business is typically done at arm's length and change is readily accepted.

In high-context cultures, such as those of East Asia, the Middle East, and North Africa, the entire context of the message — the message source, his or her standing in society or in the negotiating group, level of expertise, tone of voice, and body language — is meaningful. Marketing managers must evaluate the nonverbal communication accompanying a message and interpret the full message accordingly. In low-context cultures, business is conducted via e-mail or on paper, in contract form, whereas in high-context cultures like Latin America, it is more important to establish solid personal relationships and trust in the process of conducting business. In general, relationships are highly valued in high-context cultures, and on the social side of commerce, trust is crucial; a handshake in the Middle East is as important and reliable as a paper contract.

5-2b Religion

Religion defines a society's relationship to the supernatural and, as a result, determines dominant values and attitudes. Religious beliefs are important determinants of consumer behavior: Purchase motivation; consumption preferences and patterns; customs and business practices; attitudes toward authority, family, peers, and foreigners; as well as attitudes toward material possessions, cultural values, and norms, among others, can all be traced to religion (see Figure 5-3).

IRIT/shutterstock.com

Figure 5-3 Woman holding prayer beads and wheel. Tibetan Buddhist temple. Tibetan Buddhists are spiritual, as well as industrious and energetic.

It is also erroneous to assume that Islamic law affects negatively all credit-granting activity or that, because of the restrictions imposed by gender isolation, marketing to women is impossible in Islamic societies—quite the contrary: The restrictions merely require the use of different strategies and adaptation to local practices. For example, instead of selling on credit, businesses typically offer price discounts to individuals paying the full cash value, and no discount for those paying in installments. With regard to gender, women can use creative ways to interact (though not directly) with their male counterparts. The use of e-mail and the Internet has greatly facilitated the interaction between genders at work, even in the most conservative societies.

Similarly, the restrictions on consumption do not mean that the respective products are prohibited in a particular country. For example, alcohol is available at diplomatic and other expatriate shops even in one of the most strict Islamic countries, Saudi Arabia. It is also readily available at regular supermarkets in expatriate enclaves. In the United Arab Emirates, alcohol can be readily purchased for home consumption in Ajman, but not in Dubai, where one has to have a license. And driving with alcohol from Ajman to Dubai could potentially get you in trouble, as you would have to drive through the more conservative emirate of Sharjah, where it is illegal to possess alcohol.

Pork and pork products are readily available in Islamic countries and in Israel, targeted to the non-Muslim and non-Jewish population, respectively, and beef is available in India for consumption by non-Hindu consumers. But even in India, fast-food chains having to choose between offending Hindu consumers by offering beef, or Muslim consumers by offering pork, have elected to offer chicken, lamb burgers, or vegetarian burgers instead.

Discussions of religions and their relationship to overall consumer/market behavior and, specifically, consumption are offered in the sections "Religion and Business Days," "Religion and Gender Roles," "Religion and Gift Giving," and "Religion and Marketing Practices."

Religion and Business Days

In countries where Christianity predominates, it is customary to work full days Monday through Friday and a half-day on Saturday. In Islamic countries, businesses are closed on Friday, the holy day of Islam. And, in Israel, the Shabbos (Saturday) is the day of worship when all businesses close.

In addition to noting business days, individuals doing business abroad must also note national holidays, when businesses are usually closed, and religious events/ holidays. One religious observance that can substantially affect business operations is the month of Ramadan in countries where Islam is the national or a dominant religion. During Ramadan, observers are not allowed to drink or eat until sundown. This is typically not a very productive time in the Near East and North Africa. In Israel, no business is conducted during the High Holidays (Rosh Hashanah and Yom Kippur). Throughout Latin America, businesses, government offices, and schools are normally closed during the week between Palm Sunday and Easter Sunday; this is referred to as Holy Week, or Semana Santa in Spanish. Russia closes down from about December 29 until sometime close to mid-January, as Russians celebrate New Year's with champagne, fireworks, and Christmas trees, and, later, the Orthodox Christmas, on January 7. Since the long-vacation tradition started in 2005, sociologists and economists found that the extended holiday resulted in disturbing consequences: economic slowdown, seasonal spikes in fires, domestic abuse, and alcohol poisoning. Cities in Russia offer people little to do inexpensively and in bad weather. After so many days of holidays, consumers run out of money and problems are likely to start. For this reason, Putin cancelled the long holiday for government officials in 2014. Other countries also experience long holidays, unofficially: Europe slows down in July and August.[19]

During the regular work week, one should not be surprised if a Muslim with whom one is talking business abruptly ends the conversation by gathering his rug, kneeling, and praying; Muslims are required to pray five times a day at specific times. In this situation, the non-Muslim business partner should just find a seat and wait quietly until the man is finished.[20]

Religion and Gender Roles

In the most traditional Islamic countries, women's business activities are channeled toward interaction in a women-only environment. As such, a salesman cannot engage in door-to-door selling in Saudi Arabia, for instance, in an effort to appeal to the woman of the house. In this country, women depend on men in the family for simple activities, such as driving them to and from a destination; while the law now permits women to drive cars, they cannot walk alone, unaccompanied by a male relative. Afghan women educated before the Taliban rule know that banning girls from school is forbidden in Islam; this encourages Afghan women to seek knowledge from cradle to grave, from every source possible.[21]

Maximum Exposure PR/shutterstock.com

In the more traditional Islamic societies, personal services can be performed only by individuals of the same gender. For example, women bank only at women's banks, have their hair done only by other women, and so on. The genders usually do not interact in traditional Islamic countries except within the family. Even in the secular Islamic countries, women are often seated separately from men, in a separate dining room or area.

Although business is male-dominated in Islamic countries, it should, nevertheless, be noted that women have historically held prominent government positions in countries such as Turkey and Pakistan. Notwithstanding its reputation as a male-dominated (macho) society, in recent years women have served as Presidents of Argentina, Brazil, and Chile.

A more in-depth discussion of gift giving is offered in Section 5-2e, "National/ Regional Character." This section will address religious holidays as important opportunities for sales. In countries where Christianity is predominant, holidays such as Christmas and Easter constitute important dates for product sales. In addition to these holidays, Saint Nicholas is celebrated on December 6 in Holland and Belgium and gifts are offered to children, usually placed in their shoes, which are nicely lined up under a window. During the time predating these holidays, promotional activity (advertising and sales promotion) is intense. In Eastern Orthodox countries, such as Greece, Bulgaria, Serbia, Romania, Russia, and the other European countries of the Commonwealth of Independent States, name days (feast days of the saints after whom one was named) are celebrated, and gift giving is a must.

Diwali is an important Hindu holiday, when the believers engage in a Puja (prayer) and typically wear new clothing. This day also is an important marketing event. The Jewish holiday of Chanukah is an eight-day-long celebration and an occasion for daily gift giving.

Religion and Marketing Practices

Firms often must adapt their offering to the local culture to address consumers' religious concerns. Fast-food restaurants operating in Israel find that they can better serve their Jewish consumers by offering ample choices of vegetarian food, which does not compromise consumer kosher requirements. Keeping kosher requires the separation of milk products and meat products and of the implements used to serve or process them; vegetarian products are pareve or neutral, with regard to kosher requirements.

With advertising, substantial censoring occurs in many countries. In Saudi Arabia, women should not be portrayed in advertisements; however, it is appropriate to show the covered arms and wrists of a woman demonstrating product use. For magazines of Western provenance, censorship is enforced. For example, when such magazines are brought into the country by individuals or delivered by mail, any area of a woman's uncovered body and her face in photographs are blackened with a marker. In other Islamic countries, such as Malaysia, women should not be portrayed sleeveless, whereas in the streets of Turkey, Wonderbra billboards were common before the election of a more conservative government in 2003.

5-2c Cultural Values

Values are enduring beliefs about a specific mode of conduct or desirable end-state; they guide the selection or evaluation of behavior and are ordered by importance in relation to one another to form a system of value priorities.[22]

Values guide individuals' actions, attitudes, and judgments, which are derived from and continuously modified through personal, social, and cultural learning, ultimately affecting their perception of products and product preferences. Cultures are set apart by their value systems— the relative importance or ranking of values.

Western cultures (U.S., Canadian, and Western European) place more stress on success, achievement, and competitiveness, whereas Eastern cultures are more likely to be concerned with social welfare.[23] Examples of universally held values are provided by Rokeach [24] (see Figure 5-4). According to this classification, values can be related to goals (terminal values) and to the processes whereby one can attain those goals (instrumental values).

Members of a culture share a system of meaning, a set of beliefs about what is right or wrong. Values are learned

Instrumental Values (the means by which terminal values are achieved)	Terminal Values (goals reached by means of instrumental values)
Ambitious	A Comfortable Life
Broadminded	An Exciting Life
Capable	A Sense of Accomplishment
Cheerful	A World of Peace
Clean	A World of Beauty
Courageous	Equality
Forgiving	Family Security
Helpful	Freedom
Imaginative	Inner Harmony
Independent	Mature Love
Intellectual	National Security
Logical	Pleasure
Loving	Salvation
Obedient	Self-Respect
Polite	Social Recognition
Responsible	True Friendship
Self-Controlled	Wisdom

Figure 5-4 Instrumental and Terminal Values
(Rokeach).

from those with whom individuals are in contact: family, friends, teachers, clergy, politicians, and the media. The process by which individuals learn the beliefs and behaviors endorsed by one's own culture is known as enculturation. Learning a new culture, which most managers must when doing business abroad, is known as acculturation. Acculturation encompasses intercultural interaction and adaptation, and it includes the assimilation of a new culture, maintenance of the new culture, and resistance to both the new and old cultures.

Consumer acculturation refers to contact with a new culture and the resulting change for consumers in terms of their approach to consumption in the new environment, whereas marketer acculturation refers to contact with a new culture and the resulting change for the marketer.[25]

Acculturation does not necessarily mean abandoning all home-country traditions; it does not mean complete assimilation of the new culture. For example, recent Asian Indian immigrants to the United States are less likely to be assimilated in this culture because they maintain their original religious practices, language, food consumption, housing, and friendship patterns, as well as contact with India. Although Indian Americans are not easily assimilated, they are, nevertheless, acculturated in the U.S. culture. They consume fast food, shop at supermarkets, root for their favorite baseball or basketball team, and, overall, successfully integrate in the U.S. culture, without necessarily being assimilated. On the other hand, descendants of Japanese Americans tend to quickly acculturate to the U.S. culture, and typically, by the third generation they are likely to be fully assimilated. Similarly, there are different degrees of acculturation and assimilation for Latinos and Hispanics in the United States, who now represent 18 percent of the U.S. population (approximately 58 million people). Latinos and Hispanics represent many countries and a very wide variety of immigration experiences, ranging from Hispanic families who have lived in the state of New Mexico in for hundreds of years to newly-arrived immigrants who may be undocumented and speak very little English.[26] For the marketing practitioner, acculturation means adaptation to the new culture in a manner that would render him or her more readily capable of addressing the needs of the target market in that culture.

The United States is an avid exporter of its own culture, and one can argue that the rest of the world is acculturating to American trends. According to Tommy Hilfiger management, "America is an aspirational brand that has an enduring appeal despite what is happening in the news. People in many countries... respond to some of the core values that American culture and this brand have in common—diversity and optimism, being inclusive and youthful. They still see the U.S. as fun, authentic and free-spirited."[27]

Figures 5-5a and b illustrate trends exported from the United States to the rest of the world.

Figure 5-5a (left) Exporting culture: Trends are quickly transferred from the United States. European and Asian stores carry a vast array of inline skates, basketballs, and running shoes. Running has become a trendy activity among young professionals in the larger cities in China. Figure 5-5b (right) Western brand-name sports clothing and equipment are in high demand in China.

5-2d -Cultural Norms: Imperatives, Exclusives, and Adiaphoras

Norms are derived from values and are defined as rules that dictate what is right or wrong, acceptable or unacceptable. To be successful in the markets where the firm is currently operating or where it is planning a presence, marketers need to be capable of discerning between the following:

• What an outsider must or must not do (cultural imperative)

- What locals may do but an outsider cannot (cultural exclusive)
- What an outsider may or may not do (cultural adiaphora) [28]

Familiarity with the first two constitutes a minimum requirement for survival in a new country environment. Although most local employees are willing to accept that their foreign counterpart is not fully familiar with local practices, working for a firm that is planning a strong commitment to the respective market may render local representatives and clients less tolerant of ignorance of local customs.

Imperatives

Imperatives refer to what one must or must not do in a certain culture. Respecting rank and position, especially in more formal societies, is crucial in developing a lasting relationship. In Germany, for example, individuals in a close business relationships would address each other by their last names for decades. In Latin America, it is imperative to use the correct title to note one's educational, professional status, or social status. For example, in Mexico and Central America, the word *Licenciado* or *Licenciada* would be used in front of a person's name to indicate that he or she holds an undergraduate college degree. A representative of a U.S. firm working in this environment would need to be aware of this expectation – but he or she might be afforded some lenience as a foreigner for addressing his or her counterpart by the first name.

Rehan Qureshi/shutterstock.com

Obtaining government formal or informal approvals before engaging in transactions is essential: A company must become acquainted with local officials at all levels of government and to seek their input as part of a close working relationship. If a company does not, any operation of the firm in the country could come under scrutiny and subjected to complications and higher costs. Obtaining the appropriate permissions before building on company-owned grounds, conducting marketing research, or approaching potential distributors is an imperative in many countries.

Other examples of imperatives involve women working in Islamic countries. Take Saudi Arabia: Until 2017, it was the only country where women were not allowed to drive motor vehicles. Females there have to cover their wrists, ankles, hair, and face. In business, males do not interact with females – female accountants communicate with male colleagues by e-mail and exchange papers through a tray moving through a wall that divides the genders.

Another cultural imperative is the presentation of business cards: in Asia, a business card represents the person, and thus it should be handled with respect. When business cards are presented, typically at the beginning of a meeting, one should stand up for the occasion. The cards should be received with both hands, acknowledged, and handled carefully during the meeting, rather than promptly placed in one's purse, or worse, in one's pants' pocket. When doing business in Asia, it is helpful to have the card printed in English on one side and in the local language – Chinese, Japanese, Korean, and so on – on the other side. Business cards should also prominently display one's title in the company. The card presented should be in impeccable shape, presenting your best face to your client.

Exclusives

Exclusives refer to activities that are appropriate only for locals and from which an individual from a foreign country is excluded. For example, whereas a citizen of Kenya is likely to show allegiance to the government of Uhuru Kenyata by wearing a pin in his party's colors bearing his picture, a foreigner wearing such a pin would not only raise eyebrows, but he or she also may be perceived as attempting to interfere in the country's internal affairs.

Nataly Reinch/shutterstock.com

Adiaphoras

Adiaphoras refer to customs that a foreign representative may engage in, but conformity in this respect is not required. Eating with chopsticks in East Asia, drinking banana beer in East Africa, and greeting a woman by kissing her hand in Hungary, Poland, or Romania are all examples of adiaphoras.

5-2e National/Regional Character

Each country is thought to have a distinct set of behavior and personality characteristics, characteristics that may be shared by a number of countries in a certain geographic region.[29] This section discusses some of the national and regional characters that are likely to influence international marketing operations.

Time Orientation

An aspect of time relevant to marketers is related to the manner in which tasks are approached. **Monochronic time (m-time)** is attributed to individuals who usually do one thing at a time in sequence. These individuals tend to be prompt and to adhere strictly to agendas; countries where individuals typically operate on monochronic time are Germany, Switzerland, Austria, Scandinavian countries, the countries of Benelux, the United States, and Canada. **Polychronic time (p-time)** is attributed to individuals who tend to perform multiple tasks at once; for these individuals, time is not linear but fluid. They are less likely to adhere to schedules, and they consider business as an opportunity for socializing. Countries where individuals operate on polychronic time are Italy, France, Spain, the countries of North Africa, the Middle East, and Latin America. This aspect of time orientation explains some of the examples provided in this section, describing attitudes toward time in different parts of the world.

North Americans like to plan their activities or to expedite matters by setting deadlines. Arabs facing deadlines, on the other hand, may feel threatened and would back into a corner.[30] A saying translated as "God-willing tomorrow" means, loosely, "It will happen soon." At times, businesspeople in the Middle East arrive late for a meeting or do not arrive at all; they believe that Allah (God) controls time, so punctuality is unimportant. One should not be surprised if a Middle Eastern businessperson is not ready for an appointment. It is imperative that one does not criticize this lateness or absenteeism because the individual would most likely become offended and resentful.[31] It should be noted, however, that this behavior cannot be generalized to all business conducted, especially in many of the larger cities or in international joint ventures operating in the region, where punctuality is mandatory and expected.

This behavior is not limited to the Middle Eastern context. In many countries in sub-Saharan Africa, Southern and Eastern Europe, and Latin America, delays are common.

Greeks feel that setting time limits is not only constraining, but also insulting. Latinate cultures, such as those of Latin America and Southern Europe, do not put much premium on punctuality. When one is invited to a dinner party, arriving at the specified time indicates poor manners, suggesting that the person may be very hungry. Arriving half an hour after the indicated time is considered being on time, while arriving one hour late is still no reason to apologize, especially if one is socially prominent, or, in the United Arab Emirates, if one has wasta (high connections or social standing). In these same countries, however, for business meetings, it is safer to arrive within 15 minutes of the agreed-on time.

Business Hours and Business Days

The hours of doing business differ from country to country. The nine-to-five schedule prevalent in the United States is unusual in many countries. In countries where the climate is too hot to permit work at midday, businesses open early, at seven, and close for two to three hours at noon, to re-open again at two or three in the afternoon. Traditionally, this was also the case for businesses in Latin America and in many countries in Europe, where

D. Bond/shutterstock.com

lunchtime was spent at home having a large meal with the family, followed frequently by a nap. Nowadays, however, lunchtime is restricted to an hour. Even the staunchest supporters of siesta time in Spain abandoned hope for a long lunch break.

In much of Europe, it is not particularly common to find someone at the office on Friday afternoons. In many European countries, there is a move toward shortening the workweek. You can have a small flood in your apartment at noon on Friday, and your management company — or landlord, if you are renting — will not be bothered until Monday morning. For a fire, however, it is very possible that things are different.

As mentioned in Section 5-2b, "Religion," working days differ, depending on the dominant religion in the different countries. Where Christianity is dominant, Sunday is a rest day; in Islamic countries, businesses are closed on Fridays; and, in Israel, businesses are closed on Saturdays. In Islamic countries, during the month of Ramadan, observers are not allowed to eat until sundown, and during the regular work week, Muslims are required to pray five times a day. The best time to be in school in Europe is the spring semester, where, in addition to a two-week-long Easter vacation, students in several countries may have a nice break in February and also several saints' days in much of March and May. Needless to say, business is not very active during those long breaks.

Finally, vacation time, designated in Europe as the latter part of July, the entire month of August, and the last two weeks in December, tends to be slow and not very productive for most business activity, with some exceptions.

Gift Giving

Knowing what gifts are appropriate to give to one's hosts is important. Some gifts are considered inappropriate in certain cultures, whereas others may be appropriate on certain occasions and inappropriate on others. In the United States, bringing a bottle of wine to one's host is perfectly appropriate; the same gesture would not be appropriate for a similar occasion in the Middle East, where Islamic religion prohibits alcohol. This rule holds true for any other gifts that may contain alcohol, such as chocolates. In Southeastern United States, when invited for dinner, one is expected to politely ask "What can we bring?" Often, the host will think of something that would go well with the planned meal, such as bread or a salad. However, in the Middle East, bringing food or drink to the home of one's host could be an insult, implying that the host's food is inadequate.[32]

Other inappropriate gifts are cutlery in Latin America, signifying cutting off a relationship,[33] or handkerchiefs in Latin America and in southern and eastern Europe, signifying a final, imposed separation, usually death; handkerchiefs and small hand towels are typically given as gifts at funerals of the Eastern Orthodox faith.

Although an even number of flowers (e.g., a dozen roses) constitutes the norm for gift giving in the United States, in Eastern Europe, odd numbers are expected because even numbers of flowers such as calla lilies are offered only at funerals or religious commemorations. Giving one's host an even number of flowers or calla lilies could even trigger superstitious fears.

In developing countries, gifts of Western provenance such as good-quality pens or t-shirts with (preferably) English writing on them for children would probably meet with appreciation. So would some products that might be unimaginable as gifts in the United States, such as cigarettes, pantyhose, and hairspray. In fact, for more than two decades before the fall of communism, Kent cigarettes constituted the gift of choice in Romania, where they had the added value as commodity money.[34]

everything possible/shutterstock.com

Even the manner in which gifts are given is important. For example, in the Middle East, gifts should be presented publicly to avoid the appearance of bribery, whereas, in Asia, gifts of significance should be given privately to avoid embarrassment.[35] Nevertheless, gifts such as pens with a company logo or insignia will be graciously accepted, regardless of timing. The Chinese may refuse a gift multiple times before finally accepting it. Make it known to your client that the gift is from your company. It is advisable to express appreciation when the gift is received.[36]

Some rituals related to the giving and acceptance of gifts also should be noted. For instance, in many cultures, it is customary for the recipient to refuse the gift so vigorously that the gift giver may be tempted to withdraw it. Such a gesture, however, will meet with a noted disappointment; it is merely appropriate for the recipient to refuse the gift and then accept it reluctantly, but humbly and kindly. The ready, eager acceptance of a gift may be considered as a sign of bad manners or a confirmation of gift expectations.

In the Middle East, the mere admiration of any object in an individual's home may obligate the host to yield that object to the admirer. Although it may be appropriate to decline, such a gesture may be perceived, to a degree, as a rejection of the host's hospitality. The example on the next page addresses the ethics of gift giving in many parts of the world.

Socializing

If a marketing manager is planning on a working breakfast or a working lunch or on discussing business over dinner, as is often done in the United States, it may be useful to first inquire about the extent to which such a practice is appropriate in the country where business is being conducted. Although many business partners may have been schooled in

Gift Giving or Bribe?

Bribery is a way of life in many countries. You cannot park your car without having to bribe the policeman wandering nearby. You cannot see a doctor without paying a bribe in addition to the doctor's fee. You cannot pass your medical boards, your entrance exam into college, or obtain an exit visa without bribing the appropriate authorities. Leaving the country as a tourist may mean bribing the baggage officer to put your luggage first in line to make sure you go through customs on time; bribing the customs officer to make sure that your luggage will not be turned inside out in the process of seeking that elusive illegal gizmo, and bribing the health officer who will permit your exit from the country for a destination that may require immunizations. Does this sound outrageous? In this author's experience, it can take one case of Johnny Walker Red and a case of Kent cartons to pass the

ismed_photgraphy_SS/shutterstock.com

university entrance exam; the alternative is working in a factory as an unskilled worker. Does that sound attractive to the average high-school graduate? It could take a pack of Kent or Marlboro cigarettes to have access to quality meat — meat for which you must also pay. Or it could take tens of thousands of euros to get a good job after graduation. Bribing is the price one pays for survival in many countries. You need to bribe to live a decent life, and firms need to bribe to make reasonable profits.

Companies attempt to institute a code of conduct worldwide. They have the same expectations for their operations in the United States and Singapore, where there is relatively strict adherence to norms that shun corruption, as they do for operations in countries where they must offer substantial gifts to government officials, such as expensive watches, or even automobiles, depending on the importance of the contract. Caterpillar states in its code of conduct that, "in dealing with public officials, other corporations, and private citizens, we firmly adhere to ethical business practices. We will not seek to influence others, either directly or indirectly, by paying bribes or kick-backs, or by any other measure that is unethical or will tarnish our reputation for honesty and integrity. Even the appearance of such conduct must be avoided."

The U.S. Foreign Corrupt Practices Act (FCPA) allows small payments to foreign government officials to expedite the processing of paperwork and documentation where this is part of their normal duties. These are known as "grease payments." While infrequent small sums may be permissible , a regular pattern of such payments could lead to a formal investigation by the U.S. government. It remains a challenge for U.S. companies as well as foreign companies operating in the United States to work successfully within the guidelines of the US. Foreign Corrupt Practices Act. [37]

the United States and will, consequently, readily acquiesce to these types of working circumstances, other parties involved may feel uneasy if business is conducted during a meal.

In the countries of South America and in many countries in Europe, a meal is widely seen as an important occasion to personally get to know one's business counterpart; hence, the suggestion of a working lunch or dinner may indicate to the local representative a lack of interest in establishing a friendly basis for the future working relationship. For example, it is very important to not immediately "get down to business" at an initial meeting with a Mexican business manager. He/she would usually prefer to first develop a personal relationship and trust before discussing specific business matters. An initial meeting could also include a breakfast or lunch. Business dinner meetings with a new prospect would not be typical in Mexico. [38]

Much like in Latin America, when first meeting a businessperson in the Middle East, one should not get down to the business at hand; instead, one should initiate "positive small talk." The purpose of the first meeting is to start developing a friendly relationship, not secure business.[39] Similarly, in China, knowing one's business partner socially is imperative because the relationship is seen as a long-term engagement, rather than a short-term transaction.

Gender Roles

When one engages in business internationally, it is important to understand the role that women are expected to hold in the respective society. In the countries of East Africa and in parts of West Africa (Nigeria, for example), the role of women in business, particularly in running a business and sales, is crucial and more important than the role of men. Men still hold an important decision-making role, however, when it comes to major sales or purchase decisions. In India and Pakistan, women share responsibility with men in business. It is noteworthy, however, that women play a more limited role politically, where only a few hold notable positions, despite the famous women leaders who have left important legacies in these countries.

It is important to understand the family structure and authority patterns. Addressing the wrong person in the family may jeopardize transactions. In South Korea and Japan, it may be extremely difficult to undertake business transactions with women, because they are not readily accepted in certain business settings. In Latin America, the number of women in management is expanding and women receive a majority of college degrees; however, it is important to be cognizant of the challenges confronting women in management and especially in executive positions. [40] In Islamic societies, it is inappropriate for genders to mix, due to religious restrictions.

A discussion of gender roles in Islamic societies, as well as their impact on marketing activity and consumer behavior, was provided in Section 5-2b, "Religion."

Status Concern and Materialism

Related to one's background is one's concern with status, or status concern— maintaining it or acquiring it — and with material possessions, or materialism. Individuals' concern with status is related to the values placed on symbols of status and on the attainment of high status. Often, the products consumed convey messages about the consumer in the same way that language does.[41] Status, like social class, to which it is related, is easier to transcend in highly-developed countries. In the United States, the Protestant ethic of hard work has led to centuries of individual prosperity and, at the individual level, to status advancement; in the United States, it is not shameful for prominent politicians and business-people to refer back to their humble beginnings. In other countries, including Great Britain, Spain, and many developing countries, one's social class is rigid, and consequently, one's status remains stable. Expatriates from these countries who have transcended their social class in the United States typically hide their lower-class origins. Those from developing countries might state, for instance, that they came from the capital city when, in fact, they did not, because of the high likelihood of low-class provenance associated with a village origin.

Due to the influence of 800 years of Moorish control, Spain still has a rigid class structure described as feudal and autocratic.[42] However, countries that historically have had a polarized class structure (for example, Mexico) are developing a middle class or merchant class in response to expanding capitalism and international trade.[43]

Within the context of highly hierarchical Asian societies, individuals are always conscious of their place in a group, institution, or society and of the appropriate behavior, dress, and speech corresponding to status. They also are extremely aware of the need to maintain their own dignity and that of others. Careful attention is given to purchasing products whose price, brand, and packaging match one's social standing. In terms of personal appearance, the color, material, and style of clothing should match an individual's status, which is defined by age, gender, occupation, and so on. In Japan, for example, a married woman's kimono is much more subdued in color than a single woman's.

One region of the world where status has undergone great changes and individuals have lost "status security" is Central and Eastern Europe. A study on status changes in Romania [44] notes that status, guaranteed during the communist regime by one's standing in the communist party and one's position in the government, has undergone significant changes with the advent of democracy. In the past, nomenklatura members (top communist leaders) enjoyed the highest status and living standard, despite the communists' goal to abolish differences between social classes. In Russia, this same privileged class, before the fall of communism, could rent 100 square meters of living space for a ridiculous price; had the free use of a country home (dacha) in a prime vacation spot; and conspicuously consumed caviar, sturgeon, salmon, and other goods not available at regular shops — things that the average person could not aspire to. They drove foreign cars with low-numbered license plate numbers (indicative of high governmental position) at high speeds and without concern for traffic laws, dressed extravagantly, and conspicuously flaunted their Western possessions.[45]

Ekaterina Losevskaya/shutterstock.com

With the transition to a market economy, former party members and intellectuals found that, to survive, they had to accept jobs below their former status, as taxi drivers, sales clerks, and street vendors. At the same time, individuals who had previously held a low status, such as blue-collar workers who started lucrative businesses, prospered and, as a consequence, engaged in consumption behavior beyond anything imagined during the days of communism. Take, for example, Romanian George (Gigi) Becali, a former member of the European Parliament from 2009 until 2012. Becali made his fortune by trading land on the outskirts of Bucharest that he did not initially own, with prime land owned by the Romanian Army. Becali was the majority owner of the Steaua Bucuresti soccer team, one of Romania's top teams, for several years, and, in 2008, he tried to open the Becali Bank by investing 30 million euros (the Romanian government did not give him permission to do so). Becali maintains a high profile by endorsing nationalist causes, making derogatory anti-Semitic, xenophobic and homophobic statements, and getting into trouble that has landed him in prison. Nevertheless, he is one of the important faces of Romanian post-communist elite.

Other Cultural and Behavioral Differences

Many other national and regional character differences require companies to adapt their marketing practices. For example, as Figures 5-6 and 5-7 illustrate, people use different means of transportation to purchase products and get about in their daily lives. In the U.S., marketing strategies address a driving public, the shopper parking at the supermarket and loading the contents of the shopping cart into the family van. Europeans might take the bus or their bicycles to the supermarket and use automobiles only for out-of-town destinations. In Central Asia and sub-Saharan Africa, buses with crowded upper-level decks or trucks with protective grids of bars are used for local and long-distance transportation. These consumers are likely to transport goods in crowded environments where they must also keep their balance. A fast-food drive-through is not likely to serve the needs of these consumers. In other differences, Mexicans prefer to go to malls anchored by large department stores, whereas, in the U.S., consumers are less inclined to shop at such malls, favoring online shopping instead.

Figure 5-6 (upper left): For visits to the local supermarkets, consumers will either walk or take the bus or local train everywhere except in the United States, where most marketing strategies address a driving public. In China, at rush hour, you can count on buses to come one after the other to pick up their passengers.

Figure 5-7 In China (upper right), bicycles are essential for transportation as well, whereas, in Taiwan, motorized scooters are omnipresent. (left)

5-3 Cultural Variability

Cultural variability is the term used to identify differences between cultures using the Hofstede dimensions. All cultures can be classified based on a number of dimensions. Each dimension should be thought of as a continuum. Section 5-3a presents the Hofstede dimensions: power distance, uncertainty avoidance, masculinity, and individualism.[46] This cultural analysis system is based on the research and theories advanced by Geert Hofstede, a Dutch social psychologist and former IBM executive, as described on his consulting platform, Hofstede Insights (https://www.hofstede-insights.com/models/national-culture).

5-3a The Hofstede Dimensions

Power Distance

Power distance refers to the manner in which interpersonal relationships are formed when differences in power are perceived. In some cultures, a vertical relationship is typical, whereas, in others, relationships are based on equality and informality. In the United

Odua Images/shutterstock.com

States, for instance, individuals customarily address each other on a first-name basis, regardless of rank. Top managers often illustrate their solidarity with the lower ranks by engaging in work activities that they do, going to the plant floor or eating in the workers' cafeteria. Similarly, in Ireland, professional titles are not prevalent in business culture; in fact, they are perceived as arrogant. In the Czech Republic and Mexico, however, titles are extremely important distinctions and are essential when conducting business.[47]

Similarly, in Latin America, Eastern Europe, the Middle East, it is unacceptable to address a superior informally or for a superior to mingle with underlings. There, decisions are determined by the upper-level executives and only later shared with those in lower positions. It is important to address senior management first, before addressing other individuals in the company.[48] When doing business in a hierarchical system, find a counterpart in the partner firm or government responsible for the activities of the firm before even approaching the business in question.

Uncertainty Avoidance

Uncertainty avoidance is the extent to which individuals feel threatened by uncertainty, risk, and ambiguity and thus adopt beliefs, behaviors, and institutions that help them avoid uncertainty. In countries where uncertainty avoidance is high, there is a feeling that what is different is dangerous; consumers resist change and focus on risk avoidance and reduction. In cultures low in uncertainty avoidance, there is a feeling that what is different is interesting and worth exploring.[49] In this regard, China and Central and Eastern Europe were high in uncertainty avoidance, primarily due to the communist system's assurances of work, a home, and a standard of living. During the transition period, however, attitudes toward risk manifested themselves strongly, with some (especially the older generations) holding on to the status quo and rejecting privatization and change, and with other, younger individuals taking unwarranted risks. Overall, most in this region continue to manifest symptoms of high uncertainty avoidance, electing (or supporting, in the case of China) conservative, welfare-oriented governments. Despite this trait, however, with regard to consumption, consumers here are eager to experience new products from different parts of the world and are open to new market offerings, such as food establishments and other services.

In another example, Belgian consumers, who are higher in uncertainty avoidance, prefer insurance that costs more but that does not have variable fees, whereas the Dutch, who are low on uncertainty avoidance, prefer cheaper insurance with variable fees.[50]

Masculinity

Masculinity is the degree to which a national culture is characterized by assertiveness rather than nurturing. Femininity is the degree to which a national culture is characterized by nurturing rather than by assertiveness. Masculine societies emphasize values such as wealth, material success, ambition, and achievement, whereas, in feminine societies, benevolence, equality, caring for the weak, and preserving the environment are emphasized.[51] Another key distinction that characterizes these types of societies is that masculine societies "live to work," whereas feminine societies "work to live."

In masculine societies, such as those in Australia, Canada, Great Britain, and the United States, successful marketing strategies focus on consumers' achievement motivation. Marketing communications should stress personal accomplishment and have ego appeal. In feminine societies, such as in Asian cultures, marketing strategies should steer away from a materialist, acquisitive focus and, instead, appeal to consumers' sense of good will.

Individualism versus Collectivism

Individualism refers to the degree to which people in a country prefer to act as individuals, in their self-interest, rather than as members of a group, which is a characteristic of collectivist societies. In individualist cultures, such as those of the United States, Great Britain, and Australia, the social fabric and group norms are much looser. People tend not to follow social norms but, rather, make decisions and initiate behaviors independently.[52] Such cultures stress the individuals' ability to achieve personal goals and make their way in life on their own and, in the process, seek self-fulfillment and excitement. Collectivist cultures, such as those of Latin America, Asia, and the Middle East, stress subordination to the collective (group, business, family) and require acting in the interest of the group rather than in one's self-interest. Cultures tend to evolve from collectivist to individualistic as countries become more industrialized,[53] and as individuals become less conformist.

Although Asia, with 50 percent of the world's population, is culturally more heterogeneous than, for example, Europe, the emphasis on social harmony is an overriding and unifying belief across all Asian societies – which are fundamentally collectivist. This is considered necessary in order not to disturb social harmony. Such thinking grounded in Confucianism, Buddhism, and Islam contrasts sharply with Western individualism. The difference is profound and has major implications for consumer behavior. Whereas Asians tend to identify themselves in terms of their social frame or relationships, Westerners define themselves in terms of personal attributes or achievements. Despite the fact that individualism has come to be considered a natural component of "modern" society, Asian cultures are now challenging this assumption. Japan, a "modern," industrialized nation by any standard, is still strongly collectivist. South Korea, Singapore, and Taiwan combine features of modern societies with a firmly entrenched collectivism orientation.[54] See Table 5-1 for the cultural positioning of countries on the Hofstede dimensions.

	Uncertainty Avoidance	Power Distance	Masculinity	Individualism
100				
	Japan	China	United States	United States
				Australia
	Eastern Europe	Eastern Europe	Argentina	United Kingdom
50				
	United States	Germany, United States	China	China
1				

Table 5-1 Expected Country Dimension Scores (0 = Low; 100 = High)

Hofstede Insights, the consulting platform Geert Hofstede created (https://www.hofstede-insights.com/models/national-culture), presents two additional dimensions, aside from the original four. They are: long-term pragmatic orientation vs. short-term normative orientation, and indulgence vs. restraint. These two dimensions have not been applied to all of the countries included in the original set of dimensions. As described by Hofstede, countries with low scores on long-term orientation would be more inclined to preserve time-honored traditions while being suspicious of new trends and procedures. On the other hand, countries with high scores in this dimension would be expected to take a more pragmatic approach to change. Such countries would be more future-oriented and focused on education as a way to prepare for change. Germany has a high score of 83, whereas, the U.S. is a low 26. On the indulgence/restraint dimension, countries with high scores would be expected to seek more immediate gratification and enjoyment, whereas, countries with low scores have strong social norms focused on delayed gratification in order to better plan and prepare for the future. For example, Mexico has a score of 97 on this dimension, compared to 68 for the United States.

Free sources for national culture information are the Country Reports of the Economist Intelligence Unit (www.eiu.com); the U.S. Department of Commerce Country Commercial Guides (https://www.export.gov/ccg); and the Business Culture and Etiquette reports from the International Business Center: (www.internationalbusinesscenter.org). The International Business Center reports also include analyses of how to do business in countries based on the Hofstede cultural dimensions.

5-4 Cultural Change and Marketing

Being aware of the particulars of any culture may not be enough to succeed. Culture is under-going continual change all over the world as a result of external influences. For example, a manager obtains textbook training in business practices in a certain country. That textbook will probably not fully prepare the manager for all the changes in the cultural environment of the respective country that he or she can expect. Cultural training should involve immersion in the culture of the country, an understanding that goes beyond the world of business. Companies that are aware of the importance of such training go to great lengths to offer it. Consider, for instance, the case of Samsung, which spends $80,000 a year per person for employees to go abroad and literally goof off (go to malls, watch people, etc.), convinced that cultural immersion is likely to better help them understand what the customers of that country want.[55]

To appeal efficiently to a new market, marketers need to identify the symbolic elements and cultural meanings that are important to a market segment and use them effectively in creating the marketing mix. For example, a fast-food joint in the U.S. has a very different appeal than one in other cultures. McDonald's and Pizza Hut are perceived in some cultures as trendy, fashionable places (see Figure 5-8).

Figure 5-8 The cultural meanings of McDonald's and Pizza Hut vary from country to country. In emerging and developing countries, they are not just fast-food joints; they are the hip place to take a girlfriend out on a date, the location where business is transacted, or where lifetime commitments are celebrated. The McDonald's in this photograph is in the center of Tallinn, Estonia.

Marketers can use the following checklist [56] to integrate culture when designing a marketing strategy:

• Research the present and possible symbolic elements and cultural meanings in consumers' lives.

• Identify cultural meanings and physical properties of the product.

• Design the product and packaging accordingly.

• Design the marketing campaign using symbolic elements that carry cultural meanings.

5-5 The Self-Reference Criterion and Ethnocentrism

As mentioned in Chapter 1, when interpreting cultural phenomena in other countries, marketers must avoid the unconscious reference to their own value systems, to their own way of doing things; that is, they should refrain from resorting to the self-reference criterion, as defined by Lee.[57] Instead, they should assess each culture as objectively as possible. Lee suggests a four-step correction mechanism to address individuals' tendency to resort to the self-reference criterion, which is herein adapted to a marketing context:

• Define the marketing problem or goal in terms of one's home-country's cultural traits, norms, and values.

• Define the marketing problem or goal in terms of the host-country's cultural traits, norms, and values.

• Isolate the self-reference criterion influence and evaluate it to understand how it affects the marketing problem.

• Redefine the marketing problem and, in the process, eliminate the self-reference criterion influence. Solve the marketing problem based solely on the unique conditions of the host country.

Negative outcomes of using the self-reference criterion are inflamed nationalist feelings or antiforeigner feelings targeting a particular company — even if the foreign company relies extensively on local suppliers and locally manufactures most products. The French often perceive Americans as imposing their way of life and their culture on the rest of the world without any sensitivity to the local culture. For the French, symbolizing these views are, among others, McDonald's, Coca-Cola, and Disneyland Resort Paris; Disney has often been referred to as an attempt to "McDonaldize" France. Americans are successfully selling their fast food in a country where food preparation and serving constitute an art form. They are successfully selling

Alexandros Michailidis/shutterstock.com

mindless Hollywood action movies in a country that prizes high culture and art films. More recently, Americans have been arm-wrestling Europe, where natural foods are prized, into permitting the imports of hormone-treated beef. As expected, Gallic resentment and retaliation are omnipresent: A few years ago, 150 farmers in southwestern France (in Auch) occupied a McDonald's restaurant and slapped posters that said "No to the American dictatorship" and "No hormones in foie gras country." Similarly, one restaurant, Creperie Domino, charged $8 per Coca-Cola bottle, instead of a little more than $1 (its regular price).[58]

Mainstream publications, the blogosphere, and social media are full of anti-Coke and anti-McDonald's rhetoric. Examining the Belgian site for radio and television, RTBF (Radio Télévision Belge Francophone), brings up several articles, such as "The effects of a soda can on your body in one hour" with a photo of Coke bottles, and "Mexico: Coca-Cola and Nestlé guilty of encouraging obesity," with repeated mentions of cancer causing chemicals in the product, and its ability to "work" on your stomach in a manner similar to WD40, a product used to prevent corrosion, and on and on.

Worldwide, there is a decline in the number of people who like and use, or desire to use, American brands: NOP World, a global research firm, found that McDonald's, Coca-Cola, Microsoft, and Nike were among the brands that suffered a decline in popularity and international consumer trust. A survey of 30,000 consumers in 30 countries outside North America found that the total number of consumers who use U.S. brands fell from 30 percent to 27 percent, whereas non-American brands remained stable. Blame can be attributed to U.S. military actions in the world, and a general disaffection with U.S. culture and policies.[59]

Ethnocentrism is described in Chapter 1 as a belief related to the self-reference criterion, that a particular culture is superior to another and that strategies used in the home country (presumably a developed country) will work just as well abroad. Many examples illustrate the fallacy of this strategy in situations. Attempting to sell clothes dryers in rapidly developing markets where the cost of electricity continues to remain high relative to a family's monthly income has resulted in failure, as have television advertisements, aired in a conservative country, depicting a woman describing in detail the use of a female hygiene product.

A related concept is consumer ethnocentrism, the belief that purchasing foreign products is wrong because it hurts the domestic economy, causes loss of jobs, and is unpatriotic.[60] Although ethnocentric attitudes are, to a degree, related to the standard of living and economic performance in a country at a particular point in time, it is important to note that consumer ethnocentrist tendencies frequently affect foreign firms. The North American Free Trade Agreement, presented in the previous chapter, was, to a certain extent, diminished by ethnocentric feelings in all three of the member countries.

5-6 The Global Consumer Culture

Global consumer segments — consumers who associate similar meanings with certain places, people, and things — have developed worldwide and, with them, a global consumer culture. The global consumer culture is defined in terms of shared sets of consumption-related symbols, such as brands, and consumption activities that are meaningful to segment members. A global consumer culture is often attributed to the diffusion of entertainment from the United States to the rest of the world and to the dominance of English in both business and entertainment.[61] For example, the Internet reaches viewers everywhere in the world, and, among teens, eight out of their top 10 activities are media related. The direct outcome of this is a "global mall,"

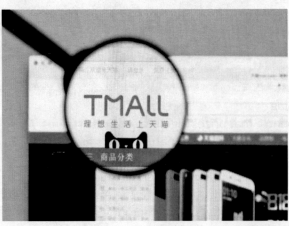
Casimiro PT/shutterstock.com

whereby teens display the signs of this global culture by buying music, hamburgers, jeans, and running shoes —veritable emblems of the teen global culture.[62] In Africa, this distinctly American video channel, MTV, now beams a line-up of local pan-African stars and several U.S. stars to audiences in 48 of the 53 African nations using both satellite and terrestrial television stations. MTV Base Africa is changing the continent, and it has an impact on the 680 million people living in sub-Saharan Africa. Wireless service and deregulation in the industry have connected Africa more than ever before, affording even poor Africans access to the Internet. Even the most remote slums boast a few Internet cafés in mud homes or in converted shipping containers.[63]

The global consumer culture has been identified as involving one or more of these trends:

• The proliferation of transnational firms and their brands worldwide and the related globalized capitalism
• Globalized consumerism and the desire for material possessions (the desire for fashionable or novel goods used to gain status and social acceptance)
• Global consumption homogenization, wherein consumers worldwide eat similar foods, desire similar brand names, and are exposed to the same entertainment

In addition to the described consumption behavior, certain gift-giving occasions have been adopted in many parts of the world where both traditions and religion are different from those in the industrialized Western world. Examples of such occasions are Christmas in Muslim countries where gifts are exchanged on New Year's Day, Valentine's Day in many countries of the world (including most of Western Europe) where it was not previously celebrated, and, increasingly, Halloween. Santa Claus (even in Buddhist, Muslim, and animist cultures), much like products such as Coca-Cola, represents the symbol of a consumer paradise widely imagined to exist in the United States.[64]

In response to an increasingly global consumer culture, marketers have devised marketing programs that appeal to individuals who would like to feel one with this culture. Among such messages are "United Colors of Benetton," "ADM, Supermarket to the World," and Philips' "Let's Make Things Better," which feature individuals and synopses from different countries. Such strategies are examples of global consumer culture positioning and identify a particular brand as a symbol of a given global culture.[65] Such positioning is typically accompanied by the extensive use of English in environments where English is not widely spoken. As the primary language of international business, the mass media, and the Internet, English currently represents modernism and internationalism to many consumers. It is also accompanied by aesthetic styles, which increasingly belong to the global consumer culture, such as the use of widely known spokespeople in advertising.[66] Examples of such endorsers are Neil Patrick Harris for Heineken Light, Rihanna for Puma, or, a few years ago, Harrison Ford for Kirin Beer and Jodie Foster for different Japanese soft drinks.

People Image Studio/shutterstock.com

According to Alden et al., this strategy is different from local consumer culture positioning, which associates the brand with local cultural meanings, reflects the local culture, is portrayed as consumed by locals, and is depicted as locally produced for local people. For instance, Chevy trucks and Dr. Pepper have been positioned as part of the "American" way of life.

The strategy also differs from foreign consumer culture positioning, whereby the brand is positioned as symbolic of a foreign culture. For example, Hermès in the United States is positioned as a desirable French product. Yoplait yogurt also emphasizes its French origin with the slogan "C'est si bon"— "it's so good"—(whereas, in France, its slogan is "La petite fleur"—"the little flower"). And men in lederhosen sing into the Alphorn with the Matterhorn mountain as the backdrop for the Swiss Ricola cough drops, while Juan Valdez stresses the quality of pure Colombian coffee. In Japan, Coca-Cola advertising shows young Japanese driving on American desert roads, stopping for a drink at a remote truck stop, and instantly gaining locals' acceptance by consuming Coke. All these examples illustrate successful foreign consumer culture positioning strategies, focusing on desirable countries of origin for the different product categories.

Summary

Identify the elements of culture and examine how they affect marketing practices around the world. Culture, a society's personality, represents a totality of shared meanings, rituals, norms, and traditions shared by members of society. Its elements are language (verbal, written, and nonverbal), religion, values, and norms. They have a significant impact on consumer behavior and marketing practices in general, delineating gender roles, rules for gift giving, and appropriate behaviors in a business setting; they also create rules for individual interaction. International marketing managers must be familiar with local culture, practices, and expectations and behave in accordance with those rules.

Describe national and regional character based on dimensions such as time orientation, business practices, gift giving, socializing, gender roles, and materialism. For someone to be able to perform optimally in a country's environment, traits such as time orientation, degree of status concern, and materialism at the societal level; rules for socializing; and gender roles are important to master. Such knowledge should be used in determining the appropriate settings for transactions, the appropriate messages that should be used in advertising, and, in general, all interactions with local society.

Discuss cultural variability in terms of the Hofstede dimensions with appropriate examples and address cultural change in a marketing context. Hofstede suggested four dimensions for classifying cultures that could benefit the marketing manager in deciding on the appropriate behavior. Those dimensions are power distance, which refers to interpersonal relationships when there are differences in power between the respective individuals; uncertainty avoidance, which refers to the extent to which individuals take risk in the respective culture; masculinity, which is the degree to which a culture is characterized by assertiveness; and individualism, the degree to which people prefer to act as individuals in their own self-interest, and collectivism, the degree to which people prefer to act as members of a group; long-term orientation, the degree to which individuals are more inclined to preserve time-honored traditions and take a more pragmatic approach to change; and indulgence, the degree to which individuals are likely to seek more immediate gratification and enjoyment.

Address the self-reference criterion and ethnocentrism and describe how they impede mutual understanding and cooperation, with direct negative effects on marketing practices. Two impediments to cross-cultural relationships are the self-reference criterion, which is the unconscious reference to one's own values and way of doing things, and ethnocentrism, the belief that one's culture is superior to others. Marketing managers must refrain from using self-reference or from adopting ethnocentric attitudes in the process of making decisions related to local operations.

Describe the global consumer culture as it manifests itself around the world. The advent of a global consumer culture has created important opportunities for multinational firms: similar segments of consumers who share brand preferences; share a taste for similar consumer goods and services, such as fast food and entertainment; and respond similarly to a company's marketing strategies. Marketers are using three strategies to target consumers: global consumer culture positioning, which identifies brands as symbols of a particular global consumer culture; local consumer culture positioning, which targets the local consumer culture and portrays products as consumed by local consumers; and foreign consumer culture positioning, whereby the brand is positioned as symbolic of a foreign culture.

Key Terms

acculturation

adiaphoras

appearances

assimilation

chronemics

collectivism

cultural variability

culture

ecology

enculturation

ethnocentrism

exclusives

femininity

foreign consumer culture positioning

gender roles

gift giving

global consumer culture positioning

haptics

high-context cultures

ideology

imperatives

individualism

kinesics

language

local consumer culture positioning

low-context cultures

masculinity

materialism

monochronic time

national and regional character

nonverbal communication

norms

oculesics

olfactions

orientations

paralinguistics

polychronic time

postures

power distance

proxemics

religion

self-reference criterion

social structure

spoken/written language

status concern

subcultures

time orientation

uncertainty avoidance

values

Discussion Questions

1. How does religion affect international marketing and international business operations in a target market?

2. What are the different cultural norms and values, and how do they differ around the world?

3. Margaret Hogan is an international marketing manager planning to accept an assignment representing her company interests in Saudi Arabia. What are some of the cultural elements that will have an impact on her performance? How can she best prepare for this assignment?

4. Many messages aimed at consumers in Central and Eastern Europe have a status compo-

nent. Why? If you were assigned to work in this environment, would you, as a manager, show solidarity with the workers and symbolically work alongside them in the factory? Explain.

5. How do managers use the global consumer culture to position their goods in the local market?

Chapter Quiz
True/False

1. A sari is considered appropriate business attire for women in South Asia.

True

Rationale: The sari is appropriate business attire for Indian women. Section 5-2a, "Language"

2. In high-context cultures, what is said is precisely what is meant.

False

Rationale: In low-context cultures, what is said is precisely what is meant. In high-context cultures, the context of the message, including the characteristics and role of the sender, is equally meaningful. Section 5-2a, "Language"

3. Little attention to business is paid during the High Holidays month in the Islamic religion, when observers are not allowed to eat until sundown.

False

Rationale: The month of Ramadan in the Islamic religion is demanding of observers, who are not allowed to eat or drink until sundown. The High Holidays, Rosh Hashanah and Yom Kippur, are Jewish holidays. Section. 5-2b, "Religion"

4. Acculturation is the learning of beliefs and behaviors endorsed by one's own culture.

False

Rationale: Enculturation is defined as the learning of beliefs and behaviors endorsed by one's own culture. Section 5-2c, "Cultural Values"

5. Learning a new culture is known as assimilation.

False

Rationale: Acculturation is defined as learning a new culture. International managers need to acculturate to new cultures when they are posted abroad. Section 5-2c, "Cultural Values"

6. In Japan, Coca-Cola advertising that includes a Japanese man driving through American desert roads is an example of foreign consumer culture positioning.

True

Rationale: The brand is positioned as symbolic of a foreign culture in foreign consumer culture positioning. Section 5-6, "The Global Consumer Culture"

Multiple Choice

1. Which of the following is a terminal value?

    a. Ambition
    b. Cleanliness
    c. Freedom
    d. Joy

Answer c is correct.

Rationale: Freedom is an important terminal value—a value that can be related to the goal of freedom. Section 5-2c, "Cultural Values"

2. The process by which individuals learn the beliefs and behaviors endorsed by their own culture is
   a. acculturation.
   b. enculturation.
   c. assimilation.
   d. none of the above.

Answer b is correct.

Rationale: Enculturation refers to learning one's own culture better and further probing into its different cultural elements. Section 5-2c, "Cultural Values"

3. The norms referring to what individuals must or must not do in certain cultures are
   a. adiaphoras.
   b. exclusives.
   c. imperatives.
   d. none of the above.

Answer c is correct.

Rationale: A cultural exclusive refers to what locals may do but an outsider cannot, whereas adiaphora refers to what an outsider may or may not do. Imperatives refer to what one must or must not do in a culture. Section 5-2d, "Cultural Norms: Imperatives, Exclusives, and Adiaphoras"

Notes

1. *EIU ViewsWire*, "India Company: Coca-Cola's Long Road to Profit," March 12, 2003. Ravi Balakrishnan, "Coca-Cola to Take Thums Up Globally," *The Economic Times*, February 2, 2018, accessed at // economictimes.indiatimes.com/articleshow/62754626.cms? utm_source=contentofinterest&utm_medium=text&utm_campaign=cppst on May 28, 2018.

2. http://news.com.com/How+eight+pixels+cost+Microsoft+millions/2100-1014_3-5316664.html

3. Lisa Penaloza and Mary C. Gilly, "Marketer Acculturation: The Changer and the Changed," *Journal of Marketing*, Vol. 63, No. 3, July 1999, pp. 84–104.

4. Raj Mehta and Russell W. Belk, "Artifacts, Identity and Transition: Favorite Possessions of Indians and Indian Immigrants to the United States," *Journal of Consumer Research*, Vol. 17, March 1991, pp. 398–411.

5. Michael R. Solomon, *Consumer Behavior: Buying, Having, and Being,* Eleventh Edition, Upper Saddle River, NJ: Prentice Hall, 2014.

6. Jane Perlez, "Muslim's Veils Test Limits of Britain's Tolerance," *The New York Times*, Online Edition, June 22, 2007. Dan Bilefsky, "Ban on Head Scarves at Work is Legal, E.U. Court Rules." *The New York Times,* March 14, 2017, accessed at https://www.nytimes.com/2017/03/14/world/europe/headscarves-ban-european-court.html on May 15, 2018. BBC News, "The Islamic Veil across Europe," May 31, 2018, accessed at http://www.bbc.com/news/world-europe-13038095 on June 2, 2018.

7. Jean-Claude Usunier and Julie Anne Lee, *Marketing Across Cultures,* New York, NY: Pearson, 2013.

8. Lecture on Chinese Calligraphy, Prof. Tang Yi-Ming, National Chengchi University, Taiwan, May 18, 2007.

9. For this and many other examples of blunders of translation, see David A. Ricks, *Blunders in International Business,* Fourth Edition, Hoboken, NJ.: Wiley-Blackwell 2006.

10. Sami Abbasi and Kenneth W. Holman, "Business Success in the Middle East," *Management Decision*, Vol. 31, No. 1, 1993, pp. 55–59. Megan Stewart, "Business Culture and Etiquette in Latin America," *University of Texas Global Biznet"*, February 17, 2017, accessed at http://sites.utexas.edu/longhornglobalbiznet/business-culture-and-etiquette-in-latin-america/ on May 15, 2018

11. Mark Lee Levine, "The Impact of Cultural Mistakes on International Real Estate Negotiations, *Real Estate Issues*, Vol. 31, No. 2, Fall 2006, pp. 25–30.

12. Ibid.

13. David A. Ricks, *Blunders in International Business,* Fourth Edition, Hoboken, NJ.: Wiley-Blackwell 2006.

14. "Six Common Mexican Gestures," *Speaking Latino.com.* Accessed at https://www.speakinglatino.com/ mexican-gestures on May 15, 2018. David A. Ricks, *Blunders in International Business,* Fourth Edition, Hoboken, NJ.: Wiley-Blackwell 2006.

15. David A. Ricks, *Blunders in International Business,* Fourth Edition, Hoboken, NJ.: Wiley-Blackwell 2006.

16. Roger Colles, "Spain—A Hot Prospect," *Resident Abroad,* November 1993, pp. 16–20.

17. In countries where this type of dress is expected of women, those same women will be encountered only in a business environment that excludes the presence of males.

18. E. T. Hall, *Beyond Culture,* Garden City, NY: Anchor Press, 1976.

19. Szu Ping Chan, "Putin Cancels Christmas for MPs as Finance Minister Warns Over Growth and Deficit," *The Telegraph,* July 29, 2015, accessed at http://www.telegraph.co.uk/finance/economics/11313690/Putin-cancels-Chrismas-for-MPs-as-finance-minister-warns-over-deficit.html on July 29, 2015; Steven Lee Myers, "Russia's Extended Winter Holidays: A Binge of Drinking and Spending," *The New York Times,* January 8, 2007, A4.

20. Abbasi and Holman, "Business Success in the Middle East," pp. 55–59.

21. http://www.islamfortoday.com/ruqaiyyah09.htm

22. See Milton J. Rokeach, *The Nature of Human Values,* New York: The Free Press, 1973; and Jan-Benedict E. M. Steenkamp, Frenkel ter Hofstede, and Michel Wedel, "A Cross-Cultural Investigation into the Individual and National Cultural Antecedents of Consumer Innovativeness," *Journal of Consumer Research,* Vol. 63, April 1999, pp. 55–69.

23. Solomon, *Consumer Behavior,* 2014.

24. Rokeach, *The Nature of Human Values,* 1973.

25. Penaloza and Gilly, "Marketer Acculturation," pp. 84–104. Antonio Flores, "How the U.S. Hispanic Population is Changing," *Pew Research Center,* September 17, 2017, accessed at http://www.pewresearch.org/fact-tank/2017/09/18/how-the-u-s-hispanic-population-is-changing on May 16, 2018. Maria Fernanda Bayona Arevolo, "Enculturation, Assimilation, and Acculturation," *Hispanicad.com,* March 16, 2016, accessed at http:// hispanicad.com/agency/research/enculturation-assimilation-and-acculturation on May 16, 2018.

26. Mehta and Belk, "Artifacts, Identity and Transition," pp. 398–411; Darrell Montero, "The Japanese Americans: Changing Patterns of Assimilation over Three Generations," *American Sociological Review,* Vol. 46, December 1981, pp. 829–839; and Mehta and Belk, "Artifacts, Identity and Transition," pp. 398–411.

27. Joan Voight, "How Hilfiger Exports the Culture of Cool," *Adweek,* February 17, 2015, accessed at http:// www.adweek.com/news/advertising-branding/how-hilfiger-exports-culture-cool-162971 on August 5, 2015.

28. Ricks, *Blunders in International Business,* 2006.

29. Jan-Erik Lönnqvist, Kenn Konstabel, Nellystiina Lönnqvist and Markku Verkasalo, "Accuracy, Consensus, In-Group Bias, and Cultural Frame Shifting in the Context of National Character Stereotypes," *Journal of Social Psychology,* Vol. 154, No. 1, pp. 40-58; Terry Clark, "International Marketing and National Character: A Review and Proposal for Integrative Theory," *Journal of Marketing,* No. 54, October 1990, pp. 66–79.

30. Ricks, *Blunders in International Business,* 2006.

31. Abbasi and Holman, "Business Success in the Middle East," pp. 55–59.

32. Ricks, *Blunders in International Business,* 2006.

33. Ibid.

34. Guliz Ger, Russell W. Belk, and Dana-Nicoleta Lascu, "The Development of Consumer Desire in Marketizing and Developing Economies: The Case of Romania and Turkey," in L. McAllister (ed.), *Advances in Consumer Research.* Association for Consumer Research, Vol. 20, 1993, pp. 102–107.

35. Ricks, *Blunders in International Business,* 2006.

36. http://www.buyusa.gov/iowa/etiquette.html and "When Does a Grease Payment Become a Bribe Under the FCPA," *FCPA Compliance and Ethics,* February 2, 2011, accessed at http://fcpacompliancereport.com/2011/02/when-does-a-grease-payment-become-a-bribe-under-the-fcpa/ on May 16, 2018.

37. www.cat.com

38. Perry A. Trunick, "Culture and Custom Combine with Logistics," *Transportation and Distribution,* Vol. 35, No. 1, January 1994, p. 38.

39. Abbasi and Holman, "Business Success in the Middle East," pp. 55–59. "More Women Business Leaders in Latin America and the Caribbean, but Still Room for Progress at the Top," *International Labour Organization News,* May 23, 2017, accessed at http://www.ilo.org/global/about-the-ilo/newsroom/news/WCMS_554702/lang--en/index.htm on May 16, 2018.

40. Mark Lee Levine, "The Impact of Cultural Mistakes on International Real Estate Negotiations, *Real Estate Issues*, Vol. 31, No. 2, Fall 2006, pp. 25–30.

41. David K. Tse, Russell W. Belk, and Nan Zhou, "Becoming a Consumer Society: A Longitudinal and Cross-Cultural Content Analysis of Print Ads from Hong Kong, the People's Republic of China, and Taiwan," *Journal of Consumer Research*, Vol. 15, March 1989, pp. 457–472.

42. Cyndee Miller, "Going Overseas Requires Marketers to Learn More than a New Language," *Marketing News*, Vol. 28, No. 7, March 28, 1994, pp. 8–10.

43. Trunick, "Culture and Custom Combine with Logistics," p. 38.

44. Dana-Nicoleta Lascu, Lalita A. Manrai, and Ajay K. Manrai, "Interpersonal Influences on Shopping Behavior: A Cross-Cultural Analysis of Polish and Romanian Consumers," in J. Bloemer, J. Lemmink, and H. Kasper (eds.), *European Marketing Academy Proceedings*, Vol. 3, 1994, pp. 1369–1371.

45. Ibid.

46. Geert Hofstede, *Culture's Consequences: International Differences in Work-Related Values*, London: Sage, 1984.

47. http://www.buyusa.gov/iowa/etiquette.html

48. Abbasi and Holman, "Business Success in the Middle East," pp. 55–59.

49. Steenkamp, Hofstede, and Wedel, "A Cross-Cultural Investigation," pp. 55–69.

50. Ibid.

51. See Hofstede, *Culture's Consequences*, 1984; and Steenkamp, Hofstede, and Wedel, "A Cross-Cultural Investigation," pp. 55–69.

52. Steenkamp, Hofstede, and Wedel, "A Cross-Cultural Investigation," pp. 55–69.

53. Harry C. Triandis, "The Self and Social Behavior in Differing Cultural Contexts," *Psychological Review*, Vol. 96, July 1989, pp. 506–520; and John A. McCarty and Patricia M. Hattwick, "Cultural Value Orientations: A Comparison of Magazine Advertisements from the United States and Mexico," *Advances in Consumer Research*, Vol. 19, 1992, pp. 34–38.

54. Hellmut Schutte, "Asian Culture and the Global Consumer," *Financial Times*, November 1998, Mastering Marketing, Part Two: Understanding Consumers, pp. 2–3.

55. "Korea's Biggest Firm Teaches Junior Execs Strange Foreign Ways," *The Wall Street Journal*, December 31, 1991, 1.

56. Adapted from Grant McCracken, "Culture and Consumer Behavior: An Anthropological Perspective," *Journal of the Market Research Society*, Vol. 32, No. 1, January 1990, pp. 3–11.

57. James A. Lee, "Cultural Analysis in Overseas Operations," *Harvard Business Review*, March–April 1966, pp. 106–114.

58. Craig R. Whitney, "Food Fight: French Impose Own Tariffs," *The International Herald Tribune*, July 31–August 1, 1999, p. 9.

59. "How the American Dream Became a Global Nightmare," *Marketing Week*, June 3, 2004, p. 32.

60. Terence A. Shimp and Subhash Sharma, "Consumer Ethnocentrism: Construction and Validation of the CETSCALE," *Journal of Marketing Research*, Vol. 24, No. 3, August 1987, pp. 280–289.

61. See Dana L. Alden, Jan-Benedict E. M. Steenkamp, and Rajeev Batra, "Brand Positioning through Advertising in Asia, North America and Europe: The Role of Global Consumer Culture," *Journal of Marketing*, Vol. 63, No. 1, January 1999, pp. 75–87; and Guliz Ger and Russell W. Belk, "I'd Like to Buy the World a Coke: Consumption-scapes of the 'Less Affluent World,'" *Journal of Consumer Policy*, Vol. 19, No. 3, September 1996, pp. 371–404.

62. Chip Walker, "Can TV Save the Planet?" *American Demographics*, Vol. 18, May 1996, pp. 42–49; and Alden, Steenkamp, and Batra, "Brand Positioning through Advertising," pp. 75–87; and Edna Gundersen, "MTV, at 20, Rocks on Its Own," *USA Today*, August 1, 2001, http://www.usatoday.com/life/television/2001-08-01-mtv-at-20.htm. MTV Base Africa, accessed at https://outlook.office.com/owa/?realm=richmondo.onmicrosoft.com&path=/mail/inbox on June 5, 2018

63. Quentin Hardy, "Hope & Profit in Africa," *Forbes*, Vol. 179, No. 13, June 18, 2007, p. 92.

64. See Ger and Belk, "I'd Like to Buy the World a Coke," pp. 371–404.

65. Alden, Steenkamp, and Batra, "Brand Positioning through Advertising," pp. 75–87.

66. Ibid.

Case 5-1 When Companies Fail to Understand the Local Market:
Walmart in Germany

When the retail giant Walmart entered the German market, it made every conceivable mistake, looking past the country's restrictive policies on store hours and new development, difficult economic conditions, unfavorable demographics, and intense price competition. Walmart entered the country with great confidence stemming from its past success in the United States. First, it bought 21 profitable, large-format Wertkauf stores in 1997, followed by 74 Interspar stores that were smaller and unprofitable, and it had a difficult time coordinating business with the two chains. Walmart's greatest challenge was that it did not understand the German market, the consumer culture, and the employee culture.

The Retailing Market and Competition

When Walmart entered Germany in 1997, success was nearly impossible: Retail sales growth was stagnant, and profit margins in German retailing, especially in the food businesses, were lower compared with other European countries; Walmart's net margins were less than one percent. Walmart encountered fierce competition. Frugal Germans already had a number of well-established alternatives. Among competitors were Aldi and Lidl, the privately owned discounters; Globus; Real (Metro), the country's largest listed retailer; Kaufland, Lidl's sister operation, which competed directly with Walmart's hypermarkets; and Toon (Rewe Group).

All of these competitors had efficient if drab out-of-town sites and offered economies of scale. Furthermore, these competitors had greater geographic penetration in Germany, which enabled them to adopt "zone pricing" tactics to match Walmart prices in areas where it was a key competitor. In the ensuing battle over prices, all the retailers suffered. At the end of the day, price pressure was so intense that Walmart's formula of clear price leadership did not work.

Regulations

The German regulatory environment was demanding. Until 1996, closing hours were restricted to 6 P.M. on weekdays and 2 P.M. on one Saturday each month. (These restrictions have been lifted since then to allow an additional 10 hours per week, including Saturday opening until 4 P.M.) Other regulations prohibited loss leader pricing — that is, pricing a product under cost to draw traffic into the store. More important, German law dealt a blow to Walmart's signature pricing strategy, everyday low pricing (EDLP). Under German law, an item must be sold at the same reduced level for two months to be classified as EDLP.

The Customer

Walmart believed that the German market was similar to that of its home state in the United States, Arkansas, and the German consumer would, similarly, desire low prices but excellent customer service. Walmart's strategy for Germany was to improve in-store appearance and ambience and emulate its U.S. and Canadian success by achieving price leadership through cost leadership. It would also deliver high quality customer service and act as a "market spoiler" on the service attribute. Walmart offered free shopping bags in a market where consumers were used to paying for bags, bag packing service, maximum allowed opening hours, credit card acceptance, baby trolleys and hospitality, especially greeters at the store entrance. The retailer was attempting to break customer perceptions in Germany away from their narrow focus on price as the main attribute for store choice—all the while advertising low pricing.

Walmart fully misunderstood Germans, who like to bargain hunt on their own, without cheerful assistants to hover around. Moreover, customers also failed to see what all the fuss was about because Walmart's low-price message played in a very low-price marketplace. To illustrate, most German discounters make Walmart look downright luxurious. Germany's so-called "hard discounters" tear open shipping cartons, set them on the floor and let consumers pick out the products. Discounting means no-frills open boxes and just bare fluorescent bulbs. And consumers in Germany like a bargain and are used to hunting for one.

They also have not taken kindly to the smiley face logo or traditional greeters, as homey charm does not work well in a country that leans more toward staunch traditionalism. In general, Germans are not quick adopters, as they tend to have set habits. It is difficult to get them to switch retailers if they do not consider themselves to be underserved. The typical German consumer is also loyal to national manufacturers' brands, buys on price, and pays cash. A retailer accepting credit cards is not particularly attractive to Germans, who do not have the benefit of the loyalty programs that credit cards offer in the United States.

It should be mentioned, however, that some of Walmart's efforts elicited positive response from German consumers. The retailer adapted to local tastes, adding fresh carp at Easter, and consumers responded well. Walmart also launched singles shopping events on Friday nights. Walmart workers greeted customers with a glass of sparkling wine and freshly shucked oysters, took their photo, and tacked it on a singles bulletin board, along with their age, interests, and the qualities sought in a prospective partner. Walmart stated that about 30 couples found each other at a singles shopping night, and its employees were fighting to work Friday evening shifts.

Employees

From the beginning, German employees were somewhat antagonistic toward Walmart's practices. First, when Wertkauf's Karlsruhe headquarters closed in favor of Interspar's, some talented people resigned. And Walmart bought the Interspar chain after committing to retain 200 hand-picked employees, many of whom were poorly trained, prompting consumers to complain about inferior service. In general, the employees resisted the company's customer-service culture and stood stone-faced as exuberant U.S. managers did the company cheer.

Even more problematic was that Walmart managed its international operations from its home office in the United States, rather than delegating decision-making and buying functions to the local Walmart team. In fact, Walmart's person in charge in Germany spoke no German and insisted that his managers work in English. The next in charge, an Englishman, ran the show from England.

Employees were in uproar when they learned that Walmart ethics code included a ban on relationships at work and a hotline for employees to report on colleagues' violations of the rules. The clause infuriated workers' councils in Germany and prompted a lawsuit.. A German labor court ruled that parts of the U.S. retailer's ethics code contravened German law.

Walmart also encountered other cultural problems, clashing with Ver.di, Germany's service workers' union on other issues and refusing to participate in national wage negotiations.

The End of Walmart's German Venture

Walmart conceded failure after nearly a decade of courting Germany, leaving the German market in 2006. It was an expensive lesson for the retail giant, who sold its stores to Metro. The end result for Walmart was a $1 billion pretax loss. German retailer Metro Group AG said its acquisition of Walmart Stores Inc.'s stores helped almost double the company's net profit in 2006. Metro operates about 2,400 stores in 30 countries in a mix of department stores, wholesale stores that sell to other businesses, consumer electronics stores, and supercenters under its Real and Extra brands. It closed 15 of Walmart's stores and converted 22 into Real stores, which are Walmart-style supercenters.

Walmart may be right to forget about Europe – in fact, it appears that it is divesting from other markets where it is not performing well. In 2018, it sold an 80 percent stake in its Brazilian operations to a private equity firm. The company is doing better than ever in its North American markets, United States, Canada, and Mexico, and focusing all its efforts on expanding in China and India.

Sources: Nandita Bose and Tatiana Bautzer, "Walmart Sells Majority of Brazil Unit, Takes $4.5 Billion Charge," *Reuters*, accessed at https://www.reuters.com/article/us-walmart-brazil/walmart-sells-majority-of-brazil-unit-takes-4-5-billion-charge-idUSKCN1J01L0 on June 1, 2018; Cecilie Rohwedder, "Metro's Walmart Deal Helps Boost Profit," *Wall Street Journal*, online edition, March 22, 2007; Mike Troy, "Walmart Bids Auf Wiedersehen, Ends Nine-Year Grind in Germany, *Retailing Today*, Vol. 45, No. 14, August 7, 2006,pp. 1–2; *The Economist*, "Business: Heading for the Exit; Retailing, Vol. 380, No. 8489, August 5, 2006, p. 54; Gerrit Wiesemann and Jonathan Birchall, "Why Walmart Decided to Pack Its Bags in Germany," *FT.com*, July 29, 2006, p. 1; Betina Wassener, "German Blow to Walmart Ethics Code," *Financial Times*, June 17, 2005, 23; Laura Heller, "Cracking the German Code Not So Easy This Time Around," *DNS Retailing Today*, Vol. 23, December 13, 2004, pp. 55–56; Ann Zimmerman and Almut Schoenfeld, "Walmarts in Germany Redefine the Term 'Checkout Aisle,'" *The Wall Street Journal*, November 9, 2004, B1; John Fernie and Stephen J. Arnold, "Walmart in Europe: Prospects for Germany, the UK, and France," *International Journal of Retail & Distribution Management*, Vol. 30, No. 2/3, 2002, pp. 92–102.

Analysis Suggestions

1. Do an analysis of the German food retail consumer. How do consumers in Germany differ (or do they?) from consumers in the United States?

2. What assumptions did Walmart make regarding German consumers that were incorrect? Why did the company make erroneous assumptions?

3. How did Walmart's employee culture clash with Germany's employee culture?

Case 5-2 Disney Post-Paris Taking on China: Reflections on the Past, Plans for the Future

Disneyland Resort Paris started out as an epic failure, as Euro Disney, in its first incarnation on the European continent. After its launch in April 1992, many name changes were made with the purpose of distancing the company from the bad publicity. The company learned many important lessons, and then pursued an Eastward expansion.

The Paris Experience

The idea of expanding the Disney magic to Europe proved to be a project that involved more attention to marketing than even this advertising giant could handle. Many Europeans did not want the American dreamland to distract their children, economy, and countries from their own homegrown successful entertainment. David Koenig, author of *Mouse Tales: A Behind-the-Ears Look at Disneyland*, commented, "To the Parisian intellectuals, Disneyland was a symbol of everything contemptible about America: artificial, unstimulating, crass, crude, for the masses. Yet here was a 5,000 acre Disneyland springing up half an hour from the Louvre."

Disney believed that locating the theme park in close proximity to Paris, France, would both ensure growth for Disney and offer an opportunity for it to incorporate different European cultures. It envisioned a Discoveryland that incorporated the histories of European countries through its fairy tales: Italy for Pinocchio, England for Alice in Wonderland, and France for Sleeping Beauty's chateau.

In its first incarnation as Euro Disney, the company failed in many aspects of its marketing strategy:

• Euro Disney failed to target the many different tastes and preferences of visitors from dissimilar countries, such as Norway, Denmark, and Germany, on one hand, and Spain, Italy, and France, on the other.

• Disney's admission costs were 30 percent higher than a DisneyWorld ticket in the United States, and the company refused to offer discounts for winter admissions.

• Euro Disney ignored travel lifestyles of Europeans, who are accustomed to taking a few long vacations, rather than several short trips, which fit with the Disney model. The company also neglected to consider national holidays and traditional breaks when Europeans are more likely to travel.

• Its restaurants did not appeal to visitors. A Rhode Island firm designed classic American-style restaurants, which most Europeans consider exotic and unusual – and the Europeans did not respond well to this format.

• Euro Disney assumed that all Europeans wanted gourmet meals, which is not the case. Although French consumers tend to live a more lavish lifestyle and spend more for gourmet meals, many other consumers in Europe do not. Meal scheduling was also problematic: The

French, for example, are accustomed to having all businesses close down at 12:30 for meal time, but the park's restaurants were not made to accommodate such large influxes for meals, leading to long lines and frustrated visitors. Finally, Euro Disney initially had an alcohol-free policy, which did not fit with local traditions, where wine is an important part of the culture.

Disney's failed marketing strategy for Euro Disney led to below-average attendance levels and product sales and the park was on the edge of bankruptcy in 1994, with a loss per year of more than a billion dollars. Changing strategies — as well as its name, to Disneyland Resort Paris — eventually led to increased revenues. With a full-scale change in the company's marketing direction, Disneyland Resort Paris has been successful in attracting visitors from many countries. Access was a priority for Disney. The company worked on access to the park via the fast train, the TGV. It also worked deals with the EuroStar and Le Shuttle train companies. Disney negotiated deals with trains and airlines to reduce prices, a move that ultimately benefited all. New Disney offices were established in London, Frankfurt, Milan, Brussels, Amsterdam, and Madrid and were given the task of tailoring package deals to the vacation life-styles of the different European segments. Disney also offered discounts for the winter months and half-price discounts for individuals going to the park after 5:00 P.M.

The resort hotels also lowered their room rates and offered less expensive menu choices in their restaurants. The restaurants created more suitable food options, catering to different regional European tastes, but continued to offer large American-size portions. Crepes and waffles are on the menu of almost every street stand in the park.

Mickey Mouse and Donald Duck have French accents, and many rides were renamed to appeal to French visitors: In Adventureland, one can find Le Ventre de la Terre (Galleries under the tree), l'Ile au Tresor (Treasure Island), La Cabane des Robinson (Robinsons' Cabin); in Fantasyland, Sleeping Beauty's Castle, rather than Cinderella's Castle at Disney World, United States, and in Discoveryland, L'Arcade des Visionnaires, Le Visionarium (a time-travel adventure with Jules Verne), among others.

Disney capitalized on its European success by offering yet another grand theme park adjacent to Disneyland, the Walt Disney Studios. Disney promoted Walt Disney Studios in a manner that did not cannibalize attendance at Disneyland Resort Paris. Among its attractions are a Rock'N'Roller Coaster Starring Aerosmith, capitalizing on the U.S. band's success in Europe; Animagique; and Cinemagique. The park is dedicated to the art of cinema, animation, and television, and it focuses on the efforts of many Europeans who made it possible to bring fantasy to reality.

The Shanghai Disney Resort

In 2011, Walt Disney Company broke ground on a $5.5 billion theme park in Shanghai, in an effort to attract many of China's 1.3 billion consumers. Like the Paris Disney venture, its first theme park in China, opened in Hong Kong in 2005, ran into trouble, once again because the company did not understand the local culture. Disney expected consumers to linger no more than 20 minutes at its restaurants, as is the case for the other Disney resorts, but, in Hong Kong, the average amount of time was 40 minutes. This resulted in many consumer complaints. In addition, the government and some consumers, much like in France, disliked that Disney was exporting American culture.

A. Aleksandravicius/shutterstock.com

The Shanghai theme park, opened in 2016, has a 225-acre Magic Kingdom-type $3.7 billion park with various themed areas and the largest Disney castle, the Enchanted Storybook Castle, which sits at the center of the park and celebrates all of Disney's princesses, rather than just one (as in the other parks). The Disney experience includes two hotels, a lake, and a shopping area, eventually stretching for over 1,730 acres, and the longest parade route.

Sources: Ben Fritz, "Disney Unveils Shanghai Disneyland Details," *The Wall Street Journal*, July 14, 2015, accessed at http://blogs.wsj.com/speakeasy/2015/07/14/shanghai-disneyland-attractions/ on July 28, 2015; David Barboza, "Disney Plans Lavish Park in Shanghai," *The New York Times*, April 7, 2011 (www.nytimes.com); "Disney Parks and Resorts Plan New Attractions, Expansion in 2007, Both Land and Sea," *Financial Wire*, January 5, 2007, 1; "Euro Disney SCA: Revenue Increases by 13% on Back of Solid Attendance," *Wall Street Journal*, July 27, 2006, B8; "Business: Trouble in the Royaume Magique: Euro Disney," *The Economist*, Vol. 372, No. 8387, August 7, 2004, p. 57; Juliana Koranteng, "Taking It to the Tube: Parc Asterix to Unleash National TV Campaign," *Amusement Business*, February 11, 2002, p. 6; Juliana Koranteng, "Euro Disney Revenues Rise," *Amusement Business*, August 6, 2001, p. 38; Juliana Koranteng, "Future May Be Bright for Euro Disney," *Amusement Business*, May 21, 2001, p. 19; "Euro Disneyland SCA," *International Directory of Company Histories*, Vol. 20, December 1997, pp. 209–212; Harriet Marsh, "Variations on a Theme Park," *Marketing*, London, May 2, 1996, p. 14; "The Kingdom inside a Republic," *The Economist*, April 13, 1996, Vol. 339, No. 7961, p. 66; David Koenig, *Mouse Tales: A Behind-the-Ears Look at Disneyland*, Irvine: Bonaventure Press, 1994; Gail Ghetia, "As American as French Fries: Euro Disneyland, When It Opens, Will Feature Typically American Restaurants," *Restaurant Hospitality*, August 1990, p. 20; Barbara J. Mays, "French Park Still Negotiating for Airline Partnership," *Travel Weekly*, April 20, 1992; Barbara Rudolph, "Monsieur Mickey: Euro Disneyland Is on Schedule, but with a Distinct French Accent," *Time*, March 25, 1991, pp. 48–49.

Analysis Suggestions

1. How do the values and lifestyles of European and Chinese consumers differ from those of consumers in the United States? Discuss the Disney failure to address European and Chinese (Hong Kong) consumers' preferences based on values and lifestyles.

2. How did Disneyland Resort Paris manage a turnaround? What did it do to convince consumers to come back? What lessons were there to learn in Hong Kong? How the Shanghai venture different?

3. Is there a world amusement-park consumer segment that is similar across different cultures? Discuss.

Case 5-3 Target's Departure from Canadian Market

Barely two years after its grand entrance into the Canadian market, Target closed all 133 stores and 107 pharmacy franchises in Canada on January 15, 2015. How did this happen? The Canadian market is very similar to the market in the United States, and strategies for one country tend to work well when targeting consumers in the other country. In fact, many multinationals have adopted regional standardized strategies for the two countries with great success. Where did Target go wrong? Target was not the first store to leave Canada; it followed in the footsteps of Best Buy and Big Lots, which left years earlier. Sears too, although it has had a long tenure in Canada, has been doing poorly as of late, surviving by selling off leases at its high-profile locations.

But Target is a favorite retail brand of consumers in the U.S., a treasure trove of trendy but affordable fashion and higher-quality merchandise. It is the quintessential middle-class store, where top designers occasionally offer their brands, creating a shopping frenzy. So why was Target not successful in Canada?

In 2011, Target arrived in Canada with great fanfare and great hopes, predicting that it would be profitable by 2013. It undertook a radical remodeling of 124 former Zeller stores into the recognizable red and white Target big-box stores. But the transformation of the old Zeller stores was much more costly than expected, and Target did not seem to be quite prepared for the challenge, with understocked shelves and few reasons for Canadian consumers to give it an enthusiastic reception. By 2015, Target had a $2 billion net loss in its two years of operation in Canada. When the closing was announced, company CEO Brian Cornell shared their analyses, which predicted that Target Canada would not be profitable until 2021. In the end, it cost a half a billion dollars to close down all the operations in Canada, as the company had to create an employee trust to give its 17,600 workers a minimum of 16 weeks of compensation, with wages and benefits included.

Dissecting the Lack of Appeal to Canadian Consumers

Canadians have a way of life similar to Americans, but the shopping habits of Canada's 36 million consumers are different enough to make it a potential minefield for U.S. retailers. Certainly understocked shelves would not appeal to Canadians – they would not appeal to American shoppers either. But Target's problems were compounded by their purchase of Zellers stores. They were dumpy, low-end stores, poorly configured for Target's big-box layout, and they were located in desolate areas that were not frequented by the middle class. Experts described those locations as "awful."

Consumers in Canada are used to paying low prices for their products. Costco has had substantial success in Canada, and Wal-Mart has done well in this market since 1994. Once Target entered the market, Wal-Mart started a price war to protect its hard-earned Canadian market share. Target did not respond promptly, creating a perception that their products were unnecessarily expensive. In fact, consumers were particularly unhappy that Target's Canadian prices were higher than their prices in the U.S.

In Canada, incomes at the high end have been growing twice as fast as incomes at the low end. This means that the wealthy have money to shop and the middle class is increasingly searching for bargains. The losers in the equation are those retailers and brands that focus on middle-income earners, such as Target and Sears. The winners at the low end are dollar stores, such as Dollarama, and various other discounters. The winners at the high end are luxury department and specialty stores – Nordstrom and Saks Fifth Avenue are actively and successfully pursuing Canadian shoppers.

Paul McKinnon/shutterstock.com

The United States experienced similar developments in terms of a growth in the high-income consumer segment. However, the market is much larger, with the U.S. population at 319 million. As such, there are still sufficient middle-class consumers who can afford the slightly higher prices at Target and who respond well to its appeal.

In May 2015, Target began to return its leases back to the landlords and started auctioning off properties and leases in Canada, and today it continues to divest. In 2018, luxury store Saks Fifth Avenue opened its Calgary store at the CF Chinook Center mall – a former Target location.

Sources: Phil Wahba, "Why Target Failed in Canada," *Fortune,* January 15, 2015, accessed at http://fortune.com/2015/01/15/target-canada-fail on November 4, 2015; Daniel Tancer, "Growing Wage Gap Makes Dollarama, Luxury Stores Winners, *Huffington Post Canada,* March 3, 2014, accessed at http://www.huffingtonpost.ca/2014/03/15/canada-wage-gap-retail-cibc_n_4965273.html on November 4, 2015; Banjo, Shelly, and Rita Trichur. "How Target Missed the Mark in Canada." *Wall Street Journal,* May 08, 2014, accessed at http://www.wsj.com/articles/SB10001424052702304655304579548321031549910 on November 4, 2015; Talsma, Julia. "Target to Shut 133 Stores in Canada, Open 15 in U.S." Drug Topics 159.2 (2015): 14. ProQuest. 6 Nov. 2015; "Target Bids Good-Bye to Canada." *Progressive Digital Media Retail News,* Jan 16 2015 ProQuest. 6 Nov. 2015; Ziobro, Paul, and Rita Trichur. "Target Bails Out of Canada." *Wall Street Journal,* Jan 16 2015, Eastern edition ed. ProQuest. 6 Nov. 2015. *Retail Insider,* "Saks Fifth Avenue Announces Calgary Opening Details," October 26, 2017, accessed at https://www.retail-insider.com/retail-insider/2017/10/saks-calgary on June 1, 2018.

Analysis Suggestions

1. Discuss the impact of social class and income on the purchase patterns of U.S. and Canadian consumers. How is Target's target market in Canada different from the target market in the U.S.?

2. What types of retailers appear to be more successful in Canada? Explain.

3. What competitive challenges did Target encounter in Canada? Explain.

Part 3

International Marketing
Strategy Decisions

Chapter 6

International Marketing Research: Practices and Challenges

Learning Objectives

After studying
this chapter,
you should be able to:

- Define international marketing research and provide a description of its immense scope; offer examples of each type of research conducted in international marketing.

- Describe the steps involved in the international marketing research process while addressing the international constraints involved for each step.

- Introduce the concept of decision support systems for international marketing and describe the sales forecasting process.

Chapter Outline

International marketing managers in unfamiliar environments need a thorough understanding of their target market if their marketing efforts are to be successful. Numerous marketing plans fail due to an incomplete understanding of the market. Companies selling consumer products are especially prone to challenges in foreign markets. Many such examples exist: European and U.S. multinationals have entered many low- and medium-income markets with large and expensive bottles of cleaning products and tubes of toothpaste, only to find that consumers will not purchase them, in spite of the fact that they prefer Western brands. As soon as those products were packaged in cheap, small sachets, consumers started purchasing large volumes. In another example, sales of Coke packaged in 200 ml recyclable bottles took off instantly in India. In the United States, 24-packs of any drink fly off the shelves, but internationally, products sell better when they come in smaller packages. In fact, smaller-sized products often do better, especially where space is at a premium, as in Berlin (see the story below).

Living in an Apartment in Berlin

It is not unusual for a European family of four to live in a one-bedroom apartment. That apartment may be on the fourth floor in a five-story building with no elevator. Try to sell this family a package of 12 giant Bounty-brand rolls of paper towels, and they will ignore your product. Sell them just one giant Bounty roll of paper towels and they will wonder if they really need the paper roll when they can use their kitchen towel? Environmentally conscious Europeans think twice before creating waste because waste is expensive and difficult to unload. Figure 6-1 shows a typical garbage disposal site shared by three homes. It is kept under lock and key to prevent access by nonresidents.

Containers can fill up quickly, one often has to hold on to waste until the garbage trucks come around the following week. And where would they store this giant Bounty? Kitchens are tiny, so hanging a roll above the sink will impede access to the sink, and the few inches of countertop has to be free to allow for food preparation (see Figure 6-2).

Figure 6-1 (left): Guarded garbage, only available with key access. The garbage must be separated into paper, plastic, organic waste, bottles, metal, and . . . garbage. Figure 6-2 (right) A typical kitchen sink in an apartment barely contains a plate. Woks are popular, but they must be cleaned in the bathtub.

Western European apartments are not unique. In Japan, many apartments are small, with just 500 square feet and paper-thin walls. Storage space is limited and products are best sold in small quantities. In Japan, as in Europe, products for the consumer market should be smaller in size. Procter & Gamble did not take into consideration women's needs for a thinner diaper due to high frequency of changes and limited storage space, and their market share was quickly eroded by a local competitor that provided thinner diapers that were in line with market demands.[1]

An understanding of the market also means active monitoring of the international market and the local market for new entrants. Leading multinationals can, in a heartbeat, lose their grip of the global or local market. In 2018, two major German discount grocery store chains, Aldi and Lidl, aggressively opened new stores across the U.S., taking on Publix, Costco, and Walmart. They took away customers with their smaller stores packed with goods still in shipping boxes, but with quality private label goods, a large selection of organics, and specialty goods, like a marzipan-laden stolen at Christmas (unlike any available at four times the price in U.S. specialty stores), and the real bratwurst, not the U.S.-imagined version, along with sweet Bavarian mustard. Belgian chocolate, cheap wine, eggs cheaper than anywhere else, U.S. supermarket chains should worry...

Amazon, the giant e-commerce retailer has disrupted the U.S. grocery business in late 2017 through their purchase of Whole Foods Market, but, it, too, is looking over its shoulder at the potential competitive threat that Alibaba's entry in the U.S. market might present. Alibaba is the leading Chinese e-commerce company providing consumer-to-consumer, business-to-consumer, and business-to-business sales service via the Internet. Its Taobao consumer-to-consumer and business-to consumer arm has already entered Australia with its payment system, Alipay (similar to PayPal). In late 2017, Alipay made its initial entry into the U.S. market with its mobile payments platform, taking on the established U.S. credit and debit card markets.

Further roiling the retail sector was Walmart's announcement in May, 2018 of plans to buy a controlling stake in Flipkart, a major Indian e-commerce retailer. Flipkart has been struggling in the large Indian market to compete with Amazon. Although investors initially questioned the price Walmart paid, it is clear that Indian consumers stand to benefit from the increased competition in the market.[2]

Rawpixel/shutterstock.com

Companies must conduct research in their local markets to understand consumers, their needs and wants, and consumption patterns. This chapter defines marketing research and examines its broad scope across all components of the marketing mix (product, place, price, and promotion). The chapter addresses the international marketing research process and the complexities of the process in an international setting.

6-1 The Need for International Marketing Research

Marketing managers must constantly monitor the different forces affecting their international operations. Marketing information, the basis for all executive action, must be taken into consideration to improve the chances of success in a complex environment. Such information needs to be carefully evaluated and viewed in light of the purpose for which it was collected. In some countries, data may not be available at all, and if available, it may be questionable. For example, production and sales data reported may be tainted by pressures of governments on factories to exceed unrealistic plans or production quotas.

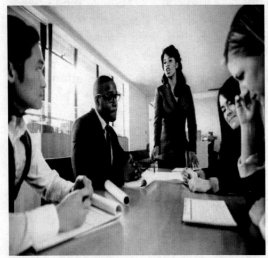

El Nariz/shutterstock.com

International marketing research is especially complex. International managers are likely to encounter not only the obstacles they have learned to master when conducting research in their own countries, but also obstacles laden with the specifics of the international market where they are conducting the research, specifics that may differ substantially from those of their national market. Consider a male researcher working for a hair care firm interested in launching its lines in the beauty salons of the Middle East.

In the United States, it is perfectly appropriate for this individual to assess interest in the company's product line by collecting data in beauty salons. In most countries in the Middle East, however, women's beauty parlors cater exclusively to women (men's barber shops cater exclusively to men), and the presence of males in this environment would constitute a breach of Islamic law, which forbids males from seeing a woman's hair if they are not closely related.

Another aspect of the difficulty of engaging in research internationally is readily observable in Eastern Europe, where consumers remain suspicious of attempts by foreigners and locals to investigate local markets and related consumer behavior. Consumers prefer not to participate in opinion polls and regard such attempts as an intrusion or as suspect. And, since instituting a market economy over 20 years ago, prospective respondents feel that they understand business and they will promptly demand payment for any time and effort required by the investigation.

These and many other environmental factors encountered in international marketing research complicate the task of marketing researchers, who should have not only an expertise in the most advanced techniques of scientific inquiry, but also a profound understanding of the markets under investigation.

6-2 Defining International Marketing Research

We define *international marketing research* as follows:

International marketing research is the systematic design, collection, recording, analysis, interpretation, and reporting of information pertinent to a particular marketing decision facing a company operating internationally.

This definition of international marketing research contains a caveat also present in the general definition of marketing research: an acquired understanding of the market environment. In an international setting, the environment is particularly complex, and it displays obvious and important subtle differences in culture, religion, customs and business practices, and general market characteristics from the environment of the company's home country.

6-3 The Scope of International Marketing Research

International marketing research has a broader scope than domestic research: Managers need additional information to compensate for lack of familiarity with the foreign environment. Initially, marketers must determine if the target country is an acceptable place to do business. There must be a reasonable level of confidence in the political, governmental, and economic structures in the target country, and whether such risks are manageable. If these country factors are negative, this may preclude the need for any subsequent research. For example, Argentina has a population of forty million, a large middle class, abundant natural resources, and high literacy. However, in recent years, mismanagement by the country's populist governments led to default on Argentina's debt. Notwithstanding the large consumer market, international companies are reluctant to consider new investments in Argentina. [3]

Sections 6-3a through 6-3f describe some general research categories (see Figure 6-3). [4]

Figure 6-3 The scope of international marketing research.

6-3a Research of Industry, Market Characteristics, and Market Trends

Studies of industry, market characteristics, and market trends, often in the form of acquisition, diversification, and market-share analyses, are conducted regularly by marketing research suppliers and shared with subscribers. This topic will be further addressed in this chapter.

Dmitry Kalinovsky/shutterstock.com

6-3b Buyer Behavior Research

Examining brand preferences and brand attitudes falls into the category of *buyer behavior research*. To the uninformed, China is an emerging market that cannot afford many luxuries. However, buyer behavior research found that the Chinese luxury market is growing, and this market is demanding. Researchers at General Motors (GM) know that well.

Consumers in China tend to go for established luxury brands, such as Rolls Royce, BMW, Audi, and Cadillac. In fact, in most Asian countries, as well as in Latin America, uncertainty is strongly avoided, resulting in high brand consciousness, brand loyalty, greater insistence on quality, and consumers' active reliance on reference groups and opinion leaders. People tend to shop in groups, and they are slower to accept new products. Whereas consumers worldwide are concerned about monetary, functional, physical, psychological, and social risks, Asians tend to be more sensitive to social risk than Westerners.[5]

Cadillac in China

General Motors conducted extensive buyer behavior research in China to find that luxury consumers responded well to special treatment. Its Chinese dealerships greet visitors with cigars and Napa Valley wines on black marble bars, VIP rooms with leather sofas, and movie shots of the brand. GM has done well with Buick and Chevrolet, and now it is ready for a sales offensive that will ensure that Cadillac succeeds in this market. Cadillac is expensive because the Chinese government adds a 25 percent import tax. Models sold in China are four inches longer than the U.S. model, in deference to Chinese customers who tend to have chauffeurs.

Buyer behavior research found that luxury automobile brands are the fastest growing segment in the Chinese market and that consumers desire luxury-brand automobiles and related accessories (see Figure 6-4).

Figure 6-4 Large cities in China boast several showrooms for luxury automobiles.

Brand awareness research and purchase behavior studies are often conducted by companies to assess their position in the market. Hilton hotels, in an attempt to change the way customers perceive them, engaged in a worldwide study of brand awareness of the Hilton brands, including its limited-service offerings.

Other useful studies that belong to this category are consumer segmentation studies, which are conducted to identify market segments. Such studies are also used to identify profiles of heavy product consumers and occasions for consumption. Cosmetics companies, for example, have conducted research looking at emerging market cosmetics consumers in Eastern Europe and China. The segments behave differently when it comes to cosmetics, as the following examples illustrate; cosmetics companies need to devise marketing strategies accordingly.

Hilton Hotels

Hilton Hotels Corp. aims to create a truly global company and expand the Hilton brand in Asia, Europe, and the Middle East. In China and India, it is partnering with companies to convert underutilized office buildings and retail space into limited-service, home-away-from-home type hotels, such as the Hilton Garden Inn, Hampton Inn, and Double Tree hotel. In Europe, it is also focusing on the limited-service sector, where comparable, lower-service hotels are nonexistent.

Helen89/shutterstock.com

Hilton studied consumer hotel perceptions and brand awareness of its brand. In Europe, it found that, except for resorts, consumers perceive them as expensive and snooty, with hired doormen to keep out riff-raff. Based on the studies, Hilton believes that limited-service hotels could change perceptions and create brand loyalty among travelers. The company is working to change consumer awareness of the broader Hilton brand, and to position their limited-service offerings as an extension of the home, without an imposing exterior and without the grand entrance – offering fourteen full and limited-service brands, including the new Tru limited service brand launched in 2016. Tru targets millennials in their 20s and 30s who prefer sleek, modern hotels with large public spaces for working and socializing.[6]

Eastern European and Chinese Cosmetics Consumer Segments

Russians want to impress at any price. Russian women focus primarily on outward appearance and strive to make a bold personal statement. They spend heavily on cosmetics: Many twenty-something professionals spend $300 a month on cosmetics, and even students manage to spend $150 in spite of little or no income. In fact, Russia spends 1.3 percent of GDP on cosmetics and toiletries, double what Western Europeans spend. Russian women have high awareness of and receptivity to Western brands. They desire opulence and are drawn to audacious retail environments. In line with these research findings, brands such as Olay are marketed as prestige brands, rather than products for the mass market — a strategy used in Western Europe and the United States.

In comparison, Polish women are more concerned with products that make a difference from the inside out. They desire heavily advertised Western cosmetics, but they are also price conscious and prefer high-quality Polish brands. They expect retailers to be knowledgeable about the cosmetics they sell. Chinese consumers, on the other hand, are receptive to different strategies. They prefer less color and simple graphics and typography. White is the preferred color for skin products because it projects luminescence and clarity of skin. Black is an indicator of quality and brand status. Consumers enjoy going through skin care regimens and rituals, unlike Western women, who have less patience for rituals, and respond well to prestige messages. [7]

Vira Mylyan-Monastyrska/shutterstock.com

6-3c Product Research

Concept development and testing studies are usually performed in developed countries by the firms' research and development departments. When going international, multinational firms usually already have a successful product to bring to the marketplace; nevertheless, it is still important that they evaluate the product/service they offer and the related marketing mix in light of the different regional and local target markets. And, although the initial concept development and testing studies are performed in high-income countries, increasingly, they are being performed in important emerging target markets, such as China.

Chapter 6   -192-   International Marketing Research:
                                                                       Practices and Challenges

For example, the Honda Concept C was first tested in China, and only later the automobile was introduced in different countries in Asia.

Brand name generation and testing is used not only in the consumer goods industry, where its importance is obvious, but also in companies that have traditionally marketed their products regionally, such as agricultural goods companies. These companies need to test brand names when they market their products internationally. The annals of marketing are replete with examples illustrating the importance of testing a brand name in different countries. International Marketing Illustration 6-1 addresses challenges that marketing managers have faced in the process of deciding on brand names.

International Marketing Illustration 6-1 Naming the Brand

Marketers, historically, rushed to international markets with proven brands, and immediately proceeded to market them. However, brand names have hurt companies' efforts in many markets; name-related blunders are amply documented in the history of international marketing. As a result, companies have changed strategies accordingly, researching the appropriateness of a brand name for their target markets, and changing it, if necessary. Examples of U.S. brands in China with extensively researched local names are: Coca-Cola, which means "tastes good and makes you happy," Keebler, which means "rare treasure," Ford, which means "happy and unique or special," and Marlboro, which means "a road with 10,000 treasures." Choosing an appropriate brand name is more than simply a translation exercise; the translation should consider the local culture, norms, tradition, and history to ensure an optimal appeal.

In the case of global products, it is important to research their meanings in different languages. Kodak, Exxon, Xerox, and Ajax are examples of product names selected only after extensive testing. Frequently, companies have to come up with different names for products to ensure their acceptance in each region or country. As a result of brand name testing research, Maxwell House introduced its product under the name Maxwell Kaffee in Germany, Legal in France, and Monky in Spain. In other examples, KFC is known as PFK in Quebec –Poulet Frit Kentucky – to ensure that it conforms with the requirement of using French in communication in the region; Mr. Clean is known as Monsieur Propre in France and Don Limpio in Spain; Dannon yogurt is known as Danone everywhere outside of the United States; Burger King is known as Hungry Jack's in Australia, because the name was already trademarked in the country before Burger King entered the market; and Axe deodorant is known as Lynx in the U.K., Ireland, Australia, and New Zealand. It is, however, important to note that brand names that were selected because of their effectiveness in the languages of key target countries are not necessarily particularly resonant in other countries. For example, the name "Accenture" was created by combining the words accomplishment, enthusiasm and future. In an English or French business setting, these connotations have value; however, in other languages, the meaning is lost.

ArliftArto22205/shutterstock.com

Sources: Sources: Laura O'Rielly, "12 Huge Brands That Are Called Something Completely Different Outside the U.S.," *Business Insider*, August 13, 2015, accessed at http://www.businessinsider.com/brand-names-outside-the-us-2015-8 on August 15, 2015; Lily C. Dong, "Brand Name Translation Model: A Case Analysis of U.S. Brands in China," *Journal of Brand Management*, Vol. 9, No. 2, 2001, pp. 99–115; Charlotte Clarke, "Language Classes," *Marketing Week*, Vol. 20, No. 17, July 24, 1997, pp. 35–39; and David Ricks, *Big Business Blunders*, Homewood, IL: Dow Jones, 1983.

Product testing identifies the extent to which the product conforms to local tastes. For example, PepsiCo Foods International decided to undertake extensive product testing in China before introducing its Cheetos snack food brand. The outcome was not favorable, with respondents indicating that they did not like the cheesy taste of the snack. As a result, PepsiCo's local joint venture, Guangzhou Frito-Lay, got rid of the cheese and replaced it with cream and steak flavors. Sales increased dramatically. Similarly, when Duke's Mayonnaise, a major southern and southwestern U.S. brand, conducted research in Latin America in 2016 (with the assistance of researchers at the University of Richmond and a partner university in Mexico), it became clear that Duke's needed to offer a lime-flavored product for the Mexican market. How much lime flavor was needed? Like Frito-Lay in China, Duke's had to test market a number of revisions in order to successfully develop lime-flavored mayonnaise for the Mexican market.[8]

mis-tery/shutterstock.com

Other examples are competitive product studies, which determine the product strategy, the price the market will bear, the promotion appropriate in light of the competition, and so on.

As for product packaging design studies, firms must consider consumers' reaction to the package, the extent to which it communicates information, and the distribution implications of packaging decisions. Packaging may distinguish between local and international products. In the Czech Republic, Poland, and Romania, local dairy products are available in recyclable glass jars, have no brand name, and may contain only the dairy's address information. International products, on the other hand, come in colorful, sophisticated, disposable packaging. To the local consumers, however, simple packaging represents freshness, a local origin, and a lack of additives. After researching this phenomenon, Tesco Extra, the U.K. hypermarket, is selling its Tesco brand packaged in the same no-frills packaging.

In Latin America, Duke's Mayonnaise needed to develop a pouch for the local consumer market, as opposed to the traditional glass jar it uses in the U.S. market in order to better serve local preferences.

The choice of package color is another important dimension that necessitates researching. One color could have different meanings in different countries: Green signifies abundance in North Africa and the Middle East, disease in the Amazon region, and healthful contents in North America and Western Europe. In Western Europe, bio (organic-type) foods are most often presented in green packaging.

In another example, Primus, a Belgian beer manufactured under license in Rwanda, is sold in one-liter bottles, rather than in the 33 cl bottles that most other Western beers use in this market. In researching the Rwandan market, Primus found that the Rwandan consumer typically drinks beer at night, sharing with family and friends. Research also showed that beer is usually purchased and transported on foot for distances of one or two kilometers. Consequently, the bottles are typically sold in crates of 12 fitted such that they could be easily transported on one's head, allowing the individual to also carry other goods.

Test marketing is another important research procedure belonging to the product research category. Procter & Gamble test marketed Swiffer, a disposable mop, in Cedar Rapids, Iowa, and Sens, France, among other international markets. The company hoped to craft an international new-product success with the goal of evaluating whether a consistent brand image could be achieved in a number of major markets.[9] This research was the first step in the company's strategy to introduce the product worldwide in 18 months, rather than in the traditional four to five years.[10]

6-3d Distribution Research

The distribution function is particularly important in international marketing, where special attention should be given to import/export regulations and practices, and where companies are well advised to engage in comprehensive analyses. For example, import/export analyses aid companies in identifying the logistics companies most capable of handling the paperwork and getting products through customs in a timely and cost-effective manner. Federal and state governments in the United States are often instrumental in helping with this type of research.

Virojt Changyenchan/shutterstock.com

In the United States, many importing companies will hire a licensed customs broker to clear their shipments through U.S. Customs. These individuals must pass a rigorous exam in order to be licensed by U.S. Customs and Border Protection. A licensed broker will determine any applicable tariffs and other import regulations, and then file all necessary paperwork and payments on behalf of the importer. While importers could handle this process on their own, it is typically much more cost-effective to hire a customs broker. These brokerage firms can also advise export clients on any regulations and required pre-approvals to export potentially sensitive products and technology. [11]

Researching individual exporter and importer expertise and the firm's local influence are crucial to the success of the firm in a particular market. In one example, a private shipper from the U.S. attempted to export older, high-quality Louis XV armchairs from Romania to the United States. In the process, the firm obtained the appropriate documentation from the State Patrimonium Commission, attesting to the fact that these armchairs were not antiques or important local historical artifacts. However, the large local export company (a vestige of the former communist firm ROMTRANS) encountered obstacles involving the local customs office that prevented it from exporting the armchairs. Only after contacting a different and much smaller firm, owned by a well-connected former government official, was it possible to export the armchairs. This same influential firm arranged for the chairs to be shipped via the Romanian airlines directly to New York at a fraction of the cost of the shipment quote from the initial top shipping firm, by ship. Had the U.S. shipper researched the local import/export service providers, it would have found that influence is crucial in facilitating shipments.

Trade with Turkmenistan serves as an example of the importance of researching specific requirements imposed on importers by the local government. The government of

Turkmenistan tightly monitors all foreign trade through the State Commodity and Raw Materials Exchange. All import and export contracts must be registered with the exchange at a 0.3 percent commission. According to foreign companies, connections with someone holding a seat on the exchange facilitate registration. Similarly, distributing in Kazakhstan, a small but growing market for U.S. consumer goods, is a challenge. Geography and the inexperience of local wholesale distributors require exporters of consumer products to pay close attention to developing and maintaining a distributor network in this region, a task that is not easy to implement. Most of the population is located in two areas: the southeast, around the city of Almaty, and the north and northeast, the republic's industrial and mining centers. Some existing infrastructure already supports distribution. An extensive railway network carries products within Kazakhstan, to other Commonwealth of Independent States countries, and to Europe. On the other hand, poor roads and bad telecommunications, when combined with geography, make it virtually impossible to rely on just one regionally based distributor. Smaller foreign companies may wish to start with a small, regionally located distributor and gradually build a countrywide network from there. Larger firms may consider a larger up-front investment to establish their own distribution in Kazakhstan.[12]

Another important type of study is that of channel performance and coverage studies, which may reveal either that channels need to be further developed at significant expense to the company, or that, in certain markets, particular channels dominate much of the activity in a particular area. In Japan, channel performance research reveals that the dominant firms that can offer the most efficient and broad distribution for the firms that can afford their high fees are the large trading companies, such as Mitsui and Mitsubishi. This research also finds that distribution in Japan is multilayered, with many distributors involved at each level. Much channel performance and coverage research has been conducted to date by U.S. multinationals in Asia to devise ways in which to adjust U.S. distribution practices to better fit with local market practices.

Finally, plant/warehouse location studies are important, as are evaluations of the transport infrastructure (roads, shipping, and warehousing infrastructure). In countries with an underdeveloped infrastructure or a mountainous terrain, warehousing is available only in the main cities. Distribution to remote locations is difficult, and firms may elect to avoid it. For example, in Ecuador, transportation between the capital Quito and Cuenca, a large city, is facilitated by a developed highway system between the cities, both at high altitude in a plateau region. Moving products from one location to another does not present problems because the transportation infra-

Salvador Aznar/shutterstock.com

structure is adequate and warehousing facilities exist in both cities. If, however, a firm is to transport goods to Guayaquil from the capital city, it is likely to encounter difficulties because the transportation infrastructure between these two locations is complicated by the terrain. Guayaquil is easily accessible by sea, the route taken by most imported goods and services aimed at the island's tourist market. Goods from Quito are more likely to be transported by air than by truck.

In the United States, location decisions for distribution facilities and manufacturing operations are also influenced by the proximity of foreign trade zone sites (see Chapter 3 for a discussion of foreign trade zones.) In Virginia, major retailers maintain large warehouse and distribution facilities near the Port of Virginia, in the Norfolk-Virginia Beach area. Shipping containers can be off-loaded at a Port facility and quickly delivered to the warehouse/foreign trade zone. In addition, manufacturers like STIHL, the German chainsaw company, take advantage of their proximity to the Port of Virginia to import components for use at its Virginia Beach plant. The Port of Savannah, Georgia, is another example of a region that has successfully recruited important distribution facilities linked to the Port and local foreign trade zone, with distribution facilities linked to the Port. [13]

6-3e Promotion Research

Rawpixel/shutterstock.com

Promotion research is crucial for companies doing business internationally. By doing such research, the firm evaluates the extent to which it effectively communicates with the market, it ensures that certain promotional strategies are appropriate for that particular market, and, finally, it evaluates the extent to which the local media are appropriate for developing the intended message.

First, in terms of studies of premiums, coupons, and deals, it is important to identify the practices in each country where the specific promotion will run. When an agency has developed an idea to run in a number of countries, it first needs to check on the legality of premiums and coupons across those markets. As individual European Union (EU) countries relaxed their limits on consumer promotions to align their retail policies with those of the EU, IKEA introduced the family promotion, offering cardholders a 25 percent discount on selected "family" products in the store, such as bath robes, backpacks, umbrellas, and so on. After testing the loyalty card, the company launched the promotion worldwide.

It is important to determine whether consumers are likely to respond to promotions as expected. According to sales promotions experts, the most difficult aspect about promoting in Eastern Europe is that consumers are just not accustomed to entering competitions and sending off coupons. In the EU, on the other hand, consumers are keen on in-store promotions, going shopping in droves to take part in competitions for free product giveaways and the like. In Latin America, research conducted by Nielsen in Argentina, Brazil, Chile, Colombia, and Mexico found that the diverse consumers had diverse reactions to consumer promotions, but that, in general, promotions clouded price perception accuracy for consumers, acting as a driving force for the increase in the bargain-hunting segments. Coupon use is highest in North America and Asia, especially in the U.S. and China. But, even in India, e-couponing sites are all the rage – Coupon Dunia, Groupon, and several others have seen their revenue rise as much as 500 percent. Many shoppers start their shopping journey at the couponing site, which gets commissions between two and 15 percent, depending on the merchandise. [14]

Advertising effectiveness research is often conducted to examine the effectiveness and appropriateness of advertisements aimed at individual markets. Frequently, ads initially developed for home-country markets and tested there are later used abroad; such ads are frequently dubbed and do not fit with the culture of the local environments where they are broadcast. Tailoring the ads to the local market will always pay off, but it is more expensive.

Advertising must appeal to the target customer to be considered effective. In one example, Switzerland's tourism authority launched an advertising campaign aimed at soccer widows (women temporarily abandoned by husband spectators). The ads showed beefy, waxed men in various states of undress performing uniquely Swiss tasks, forking hay at the farm, sawing logs, milking cows. In the ad, Switzerland invites women to visit because Swiss men would pay more attention to them. What the ad created was, in fact, a homegrown version of the Village People, and it ended up attracting more gay men as a result. The ad was effective in promoting tourism to Switzerland, but not in the way the tourism authority had intended.[15]

Media research also is important. It is important to determine the appropriate media for advertising a company's products. In many countries, television advertising is broadcast only in between programs, rather than at 10-minute intervals as in the U.S., and viewers often use the time to take a break from television. In some developing countries, the local

REDPIXEL PL/shutterstock.com

TV channel is government owned and might advertise programming and city events, but they might not offer commercial advertising opportunities. Alternatively, media access and use may be very similar in different countries. However, regulations and enforcement might differ, leading to very different use of the media outlets. For example, French food companies have many restrictions: Television advertising must recite the harmful effects of sugary foods and recommend five portions of fruit and vegetables; the ads cannot have a popular hero endorsing the product; and so on. In neighboring countries, there are no such restrictions. French food websites targeting children must emphasize nutrition, and restrict consumer-brand game interactions (advergaming); elsewhere, advertising to children may be less closely monitored. Similarly, Mexico, with the highest obesity rate in the world, instituted advertising restrictions and introduced a tax on sugary drinks that had an immediate effect in reducing their consumption.

Researchers do not always have access to information regarding programming and audiences. They can find out who are the formal cable subscribers or satellite dish users, but they may not necessarily identify all the viewers. In Germany, for example, many purchase a digital box to append to the television set (for about $30) and are able to receive numerous subscription programs. Thus, even though satellite dishes dominate the apartment landscape (see Figure 6-5), research cannot possibly identify the millions of users of digital boxes and fully understand their viewing behavior.

Finally, studies pertaining to personal selling activities, such as sales force compensation, quota, and territory studies, are crucial in helping to determine the appropriate strategies for different markets. Even the highly industrialized countries with a tradition of a well-trained sales force have deficits with regard to sales force compensation. For example, sales research in the electronic component supply industry shows great dissatisfaction among salespeople in Europe, as seen in the following discussion.

Figure 6-5 Many apartment dwellers in Germany have satellite dishes.

Sales Commissions for European Electronic Component Suppliers

Many electronic component suppliers are encountering disappointing sales results in Europe. First, there has been a mass exodus of production to China. Second, many are still using sales commission structures in place since the 1990s, adding to their costs and eroding the motivation of salespeople. European component suppliers must develop a worldwide structure and a more logical and consistent approach to determining and awarding sales commissions. Otherwise, Europe ould be squandering its last chance to remain a major player in high-tech industry. For example, design centers, where purchasing decisions often start, tend to be far from manufacturing centers, where parts orders are scheduled and shipments are received. Thus, it is difficult to determine which sales team should receive a commission and how much it should earn. To deal with this problem, the companies split the commission among different regions based on complex and arbitrary methods. As a result, sales staff motivation suffers.[16]

6-3f Pricing Research

Internationally, pricing research is much more problematic than when it is performed locally, in a developed country. In addition to studies projecting demand, such as international market potential studies, sales potential studies, sales forecasts, cost analyses, profit analyses studies, price elasticity studies, and competitive pricing analyses, which are typical of most pricing research studies conducted by U.S. firms in the United States, a firm also must look at issues regarding countertrade and currency issues, inflation rates, and a national tradition of bargaining for every transaction, all of which have implications for pricing decisions. These points will be further addressed in Section 6-4e, "Designing the Data Collection Instrument," as well as in Chapter 16, "International Pricing Strategy."

At the retail level, pricing decisions could make or break a product. In countries where salespeople typically keep the change, it is important to price the product a few pennies/centimes below the amount that can be paid using larger currency denominations. For example, for a product costing $10.00, pricing it at $9.50 will give the salesperson a $.50 "tip" because customers would not demand change — an important consideration, especially in markets where salespeople have a considerable latitude as to which product they make available to the consumer.

In industrial marketing, research in cost analysis would reveal that high product certification cost could significantly contribute to the price of a product and ultimately adversely affect its marketability. This is the case in Russia, where the lack of transparency connected with certifying products confronts both foreign and domestic companies. Although such companies are awaiting political solutions to these problems, marketers should be aware and plan ahead for certification. Often, the process may be cumbersome. Generally, there is some choice among the certification centers inside and outside Russia that are accredited to certify a given type of product or equipment. In some cases, however, the product itself may fall into several categories, and two certificates may be required.[17]

6-4 The International Marketing Research Process

Effective international research involves the steps shown in Sections 6-4a through 6-4g. Researchers attempting to obtain accurate and reliable information regarding a problem experienced in a firm's international operations are likely to encounter a number of difficulties, such as translation and cross-cultural comparison complications, which do not, as a rule, affect firms engaging only in domestic research. These difficulties will be addressed for each step in the subsections titled "International Constraints."

6-4a -Defining the Research Problem and Research Objectives

The first step in the international marketing research process requires the international marketing manager and marketing researcher defining the research problem and jointly agreeing on the research objectives. The complexity of the environment of international operations does not afford marketing researchers the opportunity to have a clear idea of the specifics that the research study should examine. Instead, they may need to engage in exploratory research of the problem to define the relevant dimensions of the problem. Exploratory investigations may help to further define the problem, suggest hypotheses, or even actually identify additional problems that need to be investigated. Descriptive research, on the other hand, portrays a situation. For instance, how frequently do shoppers in Cairo shop for food items; do they prefer to shop for meat products in state stores,

Rawpixel/shutterstock.com

which are cheaper but offer inferior-quality products, or in private stores, which are more expensive but offer a higher quality and assortment of meat products? Finally, causal research examines cause-and-effect relationships, such as the extent to which Sony's offer of financial incentives to electronics salespeople in Ahmedabad, India, is likely to increase sales of the Sony brand.

Managers must note that a fine line should be maintained between identifying the problem too broadly ("What are French consumers' entertainment needs?") or too narrowly ("Will enough French consumers pay an additional four euros to gain access to a specific American movie channel to make an investment in such a business worthwhile?") Better questions are: "What should be the price of this service in order to draw sufficient subscribers?" "What is the interest of French audiences in the movies carried by this channel?" "To what extent would anti-American sentiment affect subscriptions?"

At this point, the researcher, in conjunction with the marketing manager, sets specific research objectives identifying:

- What is the interest of French audiences in the types of movies offered by the American movie channel?
- How many subscribers will the company have if the subscription costs 4 euros? 3 euros? 2 euros?
- Will the channel gain customers in spite of the anti-American feelings in France?

6-4b Developing the Research Plan

The research plan is a blueprint for a study, indicating the decisions to be made with regard to information sources, research methods, data collection instruments, sampling procedures, data collection, data analysis, and, based on these decisions, the projected costs of the research.

6-4c Deciding on Information Sources

Next, the researcher must determine the extent to which available information may shed further light on the problem by identifying useful data collected either by the company itself (internal) or by some other firm or agency (external) — secondary data. The data may help the clearly define the problem and set better objectives. It helps the researcher pinpoint the information that needs to be gathered for the goals articulated in section 6-4a, "Defining the Research Problem and Research Objectives." The data collected to address the problem at hand is primary data.

International Constraints (for Both Secondary and Primary Data)

Conceptual Equivalence: Concepts that have different meanings in different cultural environments. A "household" in the U.S. is different from a household in developing countries. In the U.S., it consists of a nuclear family, although this is changing to include of single parents with children or households with roommates. In urban Europe, a household typically consists of roommates, or unmarried companions and their children, whereas the new immigrants tend to have a more traditional family consisting of married parents and their children, or even an extended family under one roof. In developing countries, the household may include an extended family with relatives and servants who have spent their lives as part of the household.

In high-income countries, rural areas have a solid infrastructure, whereas, elsewhere, rural areas may have no electricity, poor roads, and high poverty. In some formerly socialist countries, little distinction exists between urban and rural areas; there, local governments did away with villages, in favor of high-rise concentrated living. Today, those urban areas may be in a disrepair, such that the newly built villages look much more developed than these urban areas.

In the U.S., shopping is designed for car drivers going to the supermarket once a week. In most other countries, the population is largely "pedestrian." Consumers shop daily for food, as they are unlikely to have refrigerators, or, if they do, they are small, under the counter. And they may have to make special and costly plans to take a long trip — using public transportation rather than a personal car — to a larger city to shop for department-store-type items. How should researchers study these markets differently than they would the U.S. market? Practices such as mall-intercept interviewing will have a bias toward those motivated to go the distance to shop there, rather than simply reflect consumers in the general area. Imagine conducting a research study at the Khan El-Khalili bazaar in Cairo or at the "Russian markets" in Ukraine or Poland where Russians sell household goods. There, even a study based solely on observation is logistically complex, given the crowded, aggressive environment where consumers can barely keep their balance and get around, let alone respond to interviews.

Retailers and service providers differ greatly from one country to another. A drug store in much of the rest of the world outside the United States is known as a pharmacy or apothecary. A mall in the United States typically is one huge structure anchored by large department stores. In other countries, a mall could be a centrally located shopping avenue that may or may not be covered, or a pedestrian shopping zone. However, that is changing rapidly, as more and more countries adopt the U.S. covered-mall concept, even as U.S. consumers increasingly Figures 6-6 and 6-7 (on next page) show malls in Asia and Europe — not much different than those in the U.S.

Functional Equivalence: Products themselves might be used for different purposes in different country environments. Whereas, in many countries, jewelry advertises status and style, reflecting concern with appearance, in India and Pakistan, jewelry is used as a way to accumulate wealth. In other examples, refrigerators might be used in the U.S. to chill

Figure 6-6 (left) Taiwanese mall: Different country, same scene. In Taiwan, as in the United States, young consumers are avid shoppers and spend weekends at the mall with friends. Figure 6-7 (right) German malls are similar structures to malls in the United States and Taiwan; however, do not expect to find many premium brands at these malls — premium brands prefer a location in a prime downtown shopping district or inside a luxury department store.

soft drinks, whereas, elsewhere, soft drinks are consumed at room temperature or with just one ice cube. In the United States, ice is consumed in large quantities, so the refrigerators have ice makers. But in much of the rest of the world, ice is consumed in small amounts, and ice trays are common. Companies manufacturing plastic wrap also make plastic bags with small compartments that are filled with water and frozen. Then, the ice is squeezed out, as needed.

In another example, coffee, in southeastern Europe and the Middle East, is the quintessential drink for socializing. It is ground finely, boiled with water in a special container called the ibrik, and then poured into cups carefully, reserving the foam, which is added at the end. Close friends socializing over a cup of coffee might, when finished, turn the cup over to read each other's fortune in the grounds. In France, making coffee is perceived as an art, reflecting the ability and talent of the host. In Italy, people linger with friends in outdoor restaurants with a cup of coffee, and many cigarettes later, they may still continue to socialize. In Austria and Germany, coffee is also a tradition called the kaffeehaus tradition. Smoky, elegant coffee houses pride themselves on the coffee and cakes they serve. The instant coffee popular in Britain would not work in these markets. In Asia, tea replaces coffee, and the tea ceremony is central to many cultures there. With all these traditions, it is an impressive feat that Starbucks has done so well worldwide.

Problems also are encountered when companies assume that, if individuals have a certain purchasing power, the market is ripe for timesaving devices that appeal to Western consumers. Standard of living is not necessarily an indicator of such needs, particularly in countries where a wide gap exists between the haves and the have-nots. In many middle-class and upper-class families worldwide, household work is done by hired workers, and there is little likelihood that much thought would be given to facilitating their work. Moreover, servants themselves perceive timesaving devices as a threat to their job security.

In fact, the immense popularity of Western luxury goods among high-income earners and teenagers in Asia is not necessarily proof that they have joined the rest of the world's Western consumers. They may try some goods, but for different reasons. Brand name goods such as Louis Vuitton bags might be bought more for "face" reasons and the importance of the regard of others than from an individual preference for the product. Remy Martin cognac and Lafitte red wine might not be consumed because consumers really prefer them over local liquor or beer but because of peer pressure. Strong market position can therefore be built on foundations different from those in the West and require different marketing activities — in other words, an approach especially geared toward globalization but more efficient in terms of creating value for the consumers, and, as a result, earning higher returns.[18]

In yet another example, consumers shop differently worldwide. Marketing Illustration 6-2 compares shoppers in China and the United States. Clearly, shopping has different meanings in the two cultures.

International Marketing Illustration 6-2
A Comparison between Shoppers in China and the United States

Nielsen's annual reports on Chinese shoppers' habits suggest that foreign retailers have focused on the wrong things, assuming that consumers want a one-stop-shopping experience when, in fact, they do not. Mass retailers such as Carrefour SA and Wal-Mart Stores, Inc., have built hundreds of look-alike sprawling stores offering food, appliances, and housewares but met with declining sales per store and little consumer loyalty. What went wrong? These retailers built these stores around the Western one-stop, infrequent shopping concept. But consumers in China prefer to go daily to open-air markets selling fresh produce, meat, and dry goods (see Figure 6-8). In fact, these markets account for more than 80 percent of food expenditures.

Yet, when Chinese consumers do go to supermarkets, they take more than one hour, expect the experience to be relaxing and entertaining, and spend relatively little money, compared with consumers in Europe and the U.S. Indeed, U.S. consumers expect entertainment — hence the success of creative supermarket retailers such as Stew Leonard's, who have mooing cows and singing farmer puppets, and the fun product sampling experiences provided by many retailers. However, in the process of enjoying their shopping experience, U.S. consumers spend substantially more compared with their Chinese counterparts.

In other differences, U.S. supermarket consumers shop in bulk at supermarkets or warehouse clubs once a week, loading the family automobile with large packages of food, freezing the meat and some of the vegetables for later consumption, or purchasing these products frozen.

In contrast, Chinese consumers place little value on convenience. Chinese households spend 72 percent of their total food budget on fresh food, 9 percent on frozen food, 9 percent on convenience food and canned food, and the remaining 10 percent on basic necessity items (rice, oil, sauces, oranges, apples, Chinese cabbage, lettuce, bean curd, pork, pork spare ribs, mandarin fish, and big head fish.

What do consumers in the U.S. and China have most in common? They pursue good value over prices when it comes to retailer choice and they report the highest coupon use of all consumers.

Sources: *Shopping & Saving Strategies around the World: A Nielsen Report*, A.C. Nielsen, October 2011 (http://hk.nielsen.com); "World Watch," *The Wall Street Journal*, March 21, 2003, A12.

Figure 6-8 Market stall in Lhasa, Tibet. Consumers here purchase daily products such as grains, yak butter, and meat.

Secondary Data

Researchers first must determine whether information is available, and if so, how much. Doing so may aid in gaining insights into the problem at hand. Secondary data are defined as data collected for a problem other than the problem at hand. They are examined first, and offer the advantage of low cost and ready availability in many of the developed countries. Secondary data is internal, if collected by the company to address a different problem, or collected by the company to address the same problem but in a different country, or external, if collected by an entity not affiliated with the company.

Internal Secondary Data

Assuming that Reynolds aluminum foil is available in Saudi Arabia but not in Sudan and that the firm has no prior experience in Sudan, internal secondary data are useful only if the company has collected similar information from relevant respondents in a country with a similar environment. For example, after considerable research, Reynolds' advertising in Saudi Arabia portrays the hands (with the wrists covered) of a woman preparing a sandwich for storage. An male voice describes the use of the foil and endorses its use. Because, from a religious perspective, the two countries are similar (although Sudan is less conservative), transferring this advertisement to Sudan will likely work. In this case, an analogy approach is appropriate.

External Secondary Data

Marketing researchers in developed countries have ample access to different sources of external secondary data. They include government sources, provided by governments or government agencies—such as the Census Bureau, the World Bank, the various United Nations agencies, professional associations, various publications, and Internet sources.

Secondary Data Sources

Researchers must check established sources of information on countries, regions, markets, competitors, and consumers. As a first step, researchers can conduct online searches using search products such as EBSCO, Lexis-Nexis, and others, as well as Google, Yahoo, and other similar search engines or portals. As discussed in Chapter 5, there are many useful comparative research tools on culture including the Hofstede analyses and the U.S. Dept. of Commerce Commercial Guides. The comprehensive Global Edge website published by Michigan State University has a section devoted to cultural information resources for individual countries.

Researchers can access various publications and national and international marketing associations – see Table 6-1 on page 211.

Secondary data collected by different research suppliers are quite useful. In the past, U.S. research suppliers dominated the market; nowadays, there are more and more international players. The leading firms in all areas of market research are ranked in Table 6-2 on page 211.

Researchers searching secondary data internationally are likely to encounter a number of constraints, which are addressed in the next section.

International Constraints

In many international markets, information sources may be limited and inaccurate. Although information accuracy is usually closely linked to the level of country development, the data collected can have shortcomings attributed to factors other than development, such as translation, correspondence, and so forth. The following are some of the shortcomings of secondary data in international markets:

Availability: in many markets, very little useful data is available to help with marketing decisions. The data readily available in high-income countries may not elsewhere. Also, data on income and sales from tax returns can be inaccurate in countries where this information is not declared.[19] Finally, state-run research organizations may be reluctant to disclose the details of the data-collection method and process used; no information may be available on response rates, questionnaire development, and the nature of the sample.[20]

Reliability and validity: governments in developing countries often exaggerate poverty figures to solicit international aid. On the other hand, dictatorships that desire to tout the success of their policies may inflate figures to project prosperity. Errors may be unintentional, attributed to lack of education, or carelessness. Regardless, unless the researcher is convinced of the credentials of the research firm performing the study, the secondary data should be regarded with skepticism.

Overall, the accuracy of government-published secondary data is questionable. Published statistics contain high margins of error, beyond the tolerance range of reliability.[21] In addition, published data may be fragmented or aggregated in inconsistent formats by different research organizations. Researchers might obtain the data for estimation, but, in most instances, they are likely to view the data with skepticism.[22]

Some reliable data sources are the World Bank, the United Nations Development Program, and the Organization of Economic Co-operation and Development. Countries are slowly improving their data. For example, the Chinese government introduced important criteria for high-quality statistical service: accuracy, timeliness, relevance, diversity, and richness.[23] Overall, the State Statistics Bureau has expanded its role from data collection and compilation to a role similar to that of a business consultant.[24] The Latin American Network Information Center (LANIC) at the University of Texas (http://www1.lanic.utexas.edu/la/region/statistics/) publishes a list of statistics resources for Latin America as well as individual countries in the region.

Regardless of the source, secondary data must be carefully scrutinized and interpreted. Researchers might construct a checklist to determine the extent to which the data are usable. This list might contain items such as:

• Who collected the data and for what purpose? Was this actual research, or was it used to support a decision already taken (i.e., is it pseudo-research)?

• When was the data collected? What were the environmental country-conditions then?

• What stakes did the firm managers have in the study?

• What stakes did the researchers have in the study?

• Who else might have a stake in the findings of the study (government entities, businesses)?

• What methods were used?

• How consistently were the methods applied?

• Do the findings appear to be consistent with the findings of previous studies or with studies conducted in similar countries?

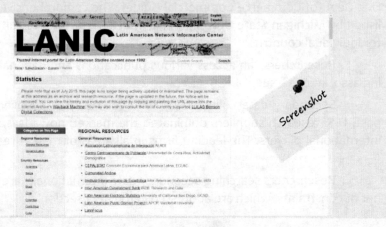

Table 6-1 Sources for Secondary Data: Publications and Professional Associations

Professional Organizations
Academy of International Business
Academy of Marketing (U.K.)
Academy of Marketing Science
Advertising Research Foundation
American Academy of Advertising
American Marketing Association
American Psychological Association
Asia Pacific Marketing Federation
Association Française du Marketing
Association for Consumer Research
Australia-New Zealand Marketing Academy
Center for Service Marketing
Chartered Institute of Marketing
Direct Marketing Association

European Direct Marketing Association
European Marketing Academy
Hong Kong Institute of Marketing
Institute for the Study of Business Markets
Institut fuer Qualitative Markt und Wirkungsanalysen, Germany
Interactive Marketing Institute
Japan Marketing Association
Market Research Society, U.K.
Marketing Research Association
Marketing Science Institute
Medical Marketing Association
Sales & Marketing Executives Association

Publications
Advertising Age
Adweek
Brand Marketing
Brandweek
Catalog Age
Chain Store Age
Discount Store News
Marketing
Marketing and Research Today
Marketing Management
Marketing News
Marketing Research
Mediaweek
Sales & Marketing Management
Target Marketing

Table 6-2 The Top 10 Market Research Organizations

Rank 2017	Organization (Country)	2016 Research Revenue (US$b)
1	Nielsen (U.K.)	6.309
2	Kantar (U.K.)	3.847
3	QuintilesIMS (U.S.)	3.301
4	Ipsos SA (France)	1.962
5	GfK SE (Germany)	1.677
6	IRI (U.S.)	1.027
7	Westat (US)	.5115
8	Wood MacKenzie (U.K.)	.4428
9	INTAGE Holdings (Japan)	.4416
10	dunnhumby (U.K.)	.4290

Source: Adapted from The AMA 2017 Gold Top 25 Report, American Marketing Association, October 1, 2017, accessed at https://www.ama.org/publications/MarketingNews/Pages/2017-ama-gold-global-report.aspx on May 23, 2018.

Primary Data

Primary research is used internationally far less than it should be. Cost-benefit analyses suggest that spending on research in remote markets of questionable value is unwise; consequently, the temptation is to use secondary data to serve all research functions.[25]

Even the largest firms often use a wide variety of quick, ad hoc research techniques and look at databases and online information to get their projects off the ground.

Yet many U.S. firms are interested in conducting research in the international markets where they operate. In an interview of 313 executives at major U.S. corporations who were responsible for conducting research and hiring outside research firms, 61 percent indicated that they would devote a larger percentage of their research budgets to international research over the following three years.[26]

Most international marketing research projects involve the collection of primary data, information collected for a specific purpose, to address the problem at hand. It requires substantial expertise in both instrument design and administration and, as a consequence, it is expensive and time consuming.

International Constraints

Lack of Marketing Infrastructure: the costs of collecting primary data in foreign markets are likely to be much higher, given the lack of a marketing infrastructure. Many markets do not have research firms or field-interviewing services. Consequently, the sponsoring firm has to invest in developing sampling frames and training interviewers.[27]

6-4d Determining Research Approaches

When collecting primary data, researchers might use qualitative and quantitative research. Qualitative research methods typically have some of the following characteristics:

- Fewer respondents belonging to a nonrandom sample
- Open-ended answer format
- Nonsystematic observation
- Researcher involvement as participant

Qualitative Research

Qualitative research has been particularly useful either as a first step in studying international marketing phenomena, when conducting exploratory research, or as one of the methods of exploring the problem at hand in a multiple-method approach. Focus group research and observation fit in this category. In certain countries, such as France and Italy, there is a preference for qualitative data as a complement to quantitative data, whereas in others, such as Germany, the United States, and Scandinavian countries, quantitative data are deemed as most valuable.

Qualitative Research: Focus Group Interviews and Depth Interviews

Focus group interviews typically involve six to twelve participants recruited to meet some previously decided characteristics — ethnic background, a certain age group, social class, tribal allegiance, and use of certain products — and a moderator who guides the discussion based on a certain discussion agenda. Often, representatives from the sponsor observe the group's deliberations through a one-way mirror or on closed-circuit television. A video camera or video chat systems may also be used to record the group's deliberations on a certain topic of interest to the sponsor. The participants are typically given a small financial reward for participating in the study or products such as free beer and food, product samples, and the like.

fizkes/shutterstock.com

Focus groups are used extensively in international marketing. When McDonald's Corp.'s Japanese unit posted its first operating loss in early 2015 due to negative press, McDonald's created the "Mom's Eye Project," a focus group for mothers, to discover ideas about how to communicate to consumers the company's focus on cleanliness and quality. One of the outcomes of these focus groups was McDonald's new concept of a one-day pop-up restaurant. On July 27, 2015, one of its Tokyo restaurants – renamed Restaurant M for the day – featured a new Fresh Mac LTO (lettuce, tomato, onions) line and Vichyssoise Mac Fries at a white-tablecloth sit-down meal for 20 people. The meal featured toothpicked wedges of beef, chicken, and fish patties, served with McDonald's dipping sauces, tea, and Oreo McFlurry with berries served in an elegant bowl.[28]

Depth interviews are one-on-one attempts to discover consumer motivations, feelings, and attitudes toward an issue of concern to the sponsor using a loose and unstructured question guide. They are typically used if the issue under study is a complex behavioral or decision-making consideration or an emotionally laden issue. Depth interviews are used frequently in international marketing by multinationals, as well as local firms. In the United Kingdom, for example, unlike the United States, most consumer data collection is dominated by face-to-face interviewing, which accounts for more than 50 percent of U.K. research.

International Constraints

Focus groups, consumer panels, and depth interviews are frequently problematic to appiy in international settings. In Eastern cultures, responses are likely to be affected by "acquiescence bias" or "good-subject role," whereby consumers agree to please the interviewer. When conducting international research using focus groups, researchers should be aware of the significance of culture in the dialogue because many societies do not condone open exchange and disagreement between individuals. Also, topics such as domestic and consumption habits are considered too private and embarrassing to discuss with strangers. In these environments, researchers would benefit more from using observational approaches.[29]

Qualitative Research: Observation

One type of observational research that is particularly useful in international research is naturalistic inquiry. Naturalistic inquiry requires the use of natural rather than contrived settings because behaviors take substantial meaning from their context.[30] The researcher is the data collection instrument and part of the behavior, verbal and nonverbal. The analysis performed by the researcher is inductive, rather than deductive; that is, unlike in conventional research methods, the researcher does not rely on previous theory in the process of developing hypotheses, but, rather, theories are developed from data. Ethnography, the study of cultures, is largely based on naturalistic inquiry. Both academic researchers and practitioners have used observation to better understand international consumers and consumer motivations. It is often used by researchers who attempt to increase the validity of their studies by acquiring an intimate knowledge of a culture's daily life through personal observation[31] (see Figure 6-9).

IR Stone/shutterstock.com

Figure 6-9 Observing consumers shopping collectively or on their own in the shopping districts reveals dynamics of the shopping experience (interpersonal influences, atmospheric influences, etc.) more readily than conducting an interview with the respective shoppers.

Other observational methods — such as the study of garbage (garbology); physiological measurement methods, which measure a respondent's nonvoluntary responses to stimuli; eye tracking, which is used in packaging research and in advertising; and response latency, which measures the time interval between the question and the response to that question — are used only to a limited extent in international research, usually in developed countries. They are costly because they require sending expensive experts to the research site abroad and obtaining data only on limited, usually nonrepresentative samples.

Information technology provides new sources for observation-based information, such as point-of-sale (POS) store scanner data, which can offer outlets high-quality, instant, as well as longitudinal, information on the movement of goods. Such resources are amply available in the United States, Canada, and the countries of the European Union. Increasingly, they are used in Asia and in the emerging markets of Latin America. This information is used for tracking, as well as for managerial decision making. This topic will be addressed in Section 6-5a, "Sales Forecasting." Other sources for observation-based information include people meters, used to identify television audience watching behavior. In the United States, Nielsen also links this type of data with self-reported purchase behavior of consumers.

International Constraints

Observation can have a number of shortcomings. Individuals in different cultures may react differently if they note that their behavior is being observed. Also, the observer may need to be familiar with all the different languages spoken at the study site.[32]

PKpix/shutterstock.com

Quantitative Research

Quantitative research methods are more structured, involving either descriptive research approaches, such as survey research, or causal research approaches, such as experiments.

Quantitative Research: Content Analysis

Content analysis, an example of descriptive research, is a quantitative analysis that entails counting the number of times preselected words, themes, symbols, or pictures appear in a given medium such as printed material or any medium with verbal or visual content. Content analysis is particularly useful in international marketing research, helping international marketing practitioners understand the complex multicultural environments in which they compete. At the same time, content analysis makes them aware of the subtle qualitative differences, such as taste, tradition, and symbolism, that are especially useful in market segmentation.[33]

One area where content analysis is used extensively is advertising research, in an attempt to discover themes that are more popular in certain countries, for particular product categories. One study examined differences in the portrayal of women in magazines of different countries.[34] Using U.S. and international male and female judges, the study found that, in general, North American and Western European magazines portrayed women displaying more positive emotions, compared with Latin American, East European, and African magazines. In addition, the women from Latin America appeared to be older, sexier, and more aggressive than their Western counterparts. Table 6-3 (next page) is a partial content analysis questionnaire used to gather this data.

Table 6-3 Partial Content Analysis Questionnaire

Women are frequently used in advertising. Advertisers portray them differently, depending on the mood/feeling they would like to convey. Please look at each ad and indicate to what extent you believe that THE WOMAN IN THE AD appears to have the following characteristics by circling the corresponding number, as follows:

1 = if the ad/woman DOES NOT AT ALL HAVE the respective characteristic
2 = if the ad/woman DOES NOT HAVE the respective characteristic
3 = if the ad/woman SEEMS TO HAVE the respective characteristic
4 = if the ad/woman HAS the respective characteristic
5 = if the ad/woman DEFINITELY HAS the respective characteristic

The woman in the ad appears to be:

Soft	5	4	3	2	1
Cool	5	4	3	2	1
Seductive	5	4	3	2	1
Scornful	5	4	3	2	1
Kitten-like	5	4	3	2	1
Optimistic	5	4	3	2	1
Maternal	5	4	3	2	1
Loving	5	4	3	2	1
Practical	5	4	3	2	1
Proud	5	4	3	2	1
Comic	5	4	3	2	1
Calm	5	4	3	2	1
Superior	5	4	3	2	1
Elegant	5	4	3	2	1
...					
Caucasian	5	4	3	2	1
Afro-American	5	4	3	2	1
Hispanic	5	4	3	2	1
East Asian	5	4	3	2	1
Asian Indian	5	4	3	2	1

The woman in the ad is looking at:

People	5	4	3	2	1
An object	5	4	3	2	1
Nothing	5	4	3	2	1
The reader	5	4	3	2	1
Herself	5	4	3	2	1

The woman's age is approximately ___ years.

Quantitative Research: Survey Research

Survey research, another example of descriptive research, involves the administration of personal, telephone, mail, or online questionnaires. This assumes that respondents are both capable and willing to respond to the questions. A cheap survey method involves the use of mail questionnaires; however, this method is fraught with obstacles in many developing countries, where there may be a low literacy level. Nevertheless, this method is popular in international marketing research, especially because it can be effectively used in cross-national comparisons.

International Constraints

Respondent Factors: in some countries, researchers may not have access to certain household members – a male researcher collecting data in Saudi Arabia will not have access to female respondents. Companies should hire local female interviewers for any study that involves women and male interviewers for studies involving men. Procter & Gamble conducted a study in Saudi Arabia examining women's consumption. The marketing department invited the husbands and brothers of Saudi women to participate in a focus group study. The study produced useful results that helped Proctor & Gamble develop appropriate strategies for this market.[35]

In Latin America, the top five percent of society controls fifty percent of disposable income, and they are reluctant to share information with researchers. Door-to-door inquiries are problematical in high-crime area in Latin America. There, employees would be unlikely to give candid answers to survey questions and would avoid responses or participation that might be construed as critical of an employer. Similarly, In Eastern Europe, there continues to be considerable suspicion of any attempts to gain personal information. In fact, the word used for "research" is a variant of the Slavic *ankieta*, meaning inquiry (of the same type as that conducted by the feared secret police).[36]

It is crucial that researchers have a good understanding of the culture and local practices to be able to obtain adequate response rates.

Infrastructure Factors: research using the telephone as the contact method has changed greatly in the past decade alone. It used to be that, in many countries, the use of telephones limited the data collection to a handful of individuals who had access to a landline. However, today, with cheap access to prepaid cell phones, pretty much anyone can be reached. Because most subscribers do not have to pay for phone calls they receive, telephone interviewing is much easier than in the past. Random digit dialing is probably the best method to use to ensure a representative sample of the population. Using the telephone book as the sampling frame is problematic because it restricts the sample to landline subscribers, and many today choose not to have a landline.

Using mail surveys is problematic in many international markets where mail is unreliable and slow. Even in India and Saudi Arabia, with efficient mail systems, mailing surveys to peoples' homes is not advised.[37] In low-income countries, the low literacy rate eliminates many respondents. There, a personal interview is the preferred data collection approach.

Online research has become a key approach to data collection worldwide; however, response rates can be a problem. Moreover, the sampling frames needed for data collection (Internet subscribers, mailing lists, telephone books, or other relevant databases) may not be available. In business-to-business research, sampling frames such as industry-association directories are often used – if they are at all available.

Quantitative Research: Experimental Research

Experimental research has the highest validity and reliability of all types of research. This research looks at cause-and-effect relationships, eliminating or controlling other extraneous factors that may be responsible for the results, and eliminating competing explanations for the observed findings. It requires the use of matched groups of subjects who are subjected to different treatments to ascertain whether the observed response differences are statistically significant.

Given the many constraints that this type of research imposes on the researcher, experimental research findings are difficult to transfer to other countries where the control factors behave differently. Given the fact that results are not easily generalizable to similar environments, and that this type of research can be costly, experimental research is rarely used in international research.

6-4e Designing the Data Collection Instrument

International marketing phenomena are particularly difficult to measure and require an intimate knowledge of the culture. Themes that are functionally and conceptually equivalent across nations, such as the universal concept of "affection," manifest themselves differently in different environments. For instance, hugging, a common manifestation in the West, is inappropriate in Eastern cultures and taboo in others.[38] Given these differences, phenomena specific to each culture are best measured by emic instruments, which are constructed for each nationality to measure the particular factor. The instrument employed must then conform to the specific characteristics of each culture.

In other examples, the type of store referred to as a "supermarket" in the United States is typically a large store belonging to a national or regional chain. It carries a wide assortment of competing brands in each product category, including its own brand, a couple of dealer brands, and numerous national brands. (However, as discussed in Chapter 5, the traditional supermarket concept in the U.S. is now being challenged by the two German giants, Aldi and Lidl, with their smaller, streamlined, low-service supermarkets.) Supermarkets in Europe, such as Migros in Switzerland, Edeka in Germany, and Albert Heijn in the Netherlands, carry a larger variety of products, but not as wide an assortment of competing brands as their U.S. equivalents. Alternatively, supermarkets in sub-Saharan Africa, such as Alirwanda and La Galette, in Kigali, Rwanda, are more similar to Western specialty shops, carrying primarily fresh meat and dairy products, and expensive brand name products

Bjoern Wylezich/shutterstock.com

such as confectionery items, alcoholic drinks, jams, and Belgian and French magazines and newspapers. In many Latin American countries, the super-center concept is very popular. Similar to Walmart in the U.S., these stores would carry everything from groceries to garden furniture. Studying the supermarket shopping experience should be done using market-specific measures. Comparing consumer choice behavior across the different environments is not possible because the choice variables are different for each market. Consequently, an emic measure is needed for each market.

International managers are frequently faced with problems related to the need for survey instruments that can be used across different cultures, especially for comparative evaluation of market characteristics such as response to an advertising campaign and other types of multi-country research. For this type of study, etic instruments, which are culture neutral and extremely difficult to develop, can be used to measure the same phenomenon in different cultures. Going back to the supermarket example, studying consumer behavior at the cash register can easily be measured with an etic measure. Some dimensions that such a study can capture are the payment method, the degree of yielding to store-aisle impulse purchases, as well as the emotion during the purchase transaction, among others. Then, these measures can be compared across the different countries.

When deciding on the data collection instrument, the researcher needs to come up with an appropriate format and to offer precise instructions. Frequently, respondents do not answer entire sections of the questionnaire, unless advised that full completion is essential for the integrity of the study. A typical semantic differential scale, anchored by words with opposite meanings (good . . . bad, important . . . not important) could be confusing to respondents as well. Clear instructions, preferably with examples, help respondents in filling out the questionnaire appropriately. A variant of the semantic differential scale follows (note the detailed explanation of the numbers to be circled). The typical Likert scale anchored by "strongly disagree" and "strongly agree" is unfamiliar to respondents in many cultures. Explaining the procedure in detail, as well as the meaning of circling a particular response, is essential. See the questionnaire in Table 6-4 for a variant of the Likert scale.

Table 6-4 Sample Partial Consumer Research Questionnaire
(Version Translated into Romanian, Bulgarian, and Hungarian)

Please indicate the extent to which you agree or disagree with the statements below by circling 5 if you strongly agree, 4 if you agree, 3 if you neither agree nor disagree, 2 if you disagree, or 1 if you strongly disagree with a statement. Please answer every question; the questionnaire cannot be used unless you do so.

	Strongly Agree				Strongly Disagree
1. I don't care to find out about what types of brand names of appliances and gadgets my friends have.	5	4	3	2	1
2. I often read advertisements just out of curiosity.	5	4	3	2	1
3. I rarely read advertisements that just seem to contain a lot of information.	5	4	3	2	1
4. When I hear about a new store or restaurant, I take advantage of the first opportunity to find out more about it.	5	4	3	2	1
5. Companies are usually out to make money even if it means violating ethics and taking advantage of consumers.	5	4	3	2	1
6. Most durable products could be made to last much longer but are made to wear out quickly to necessitate repurchase.	5	4	3	2	1
7. If people really knew what businesses do to deceive and take advantage of consumers, they would be up-in-arms.	5	4	3	2	1
8. Most Western products I buy are overpriced.	5	4	3	2	1
9. Most local products I buy are overpriced.	5	4	3	2	1
10. Businesses could charge lower prices and still be profitable.	5	4	3	2	1

Sources: Dana Lascu, working paper; Dana Lascu, Harold W. Babb, and Julie Bodine, "Western and Own-Country Product and Service Evaluations: Perspectives from Eastern Europe," *Journal of East-West Business*, Vol. 4, No. 4, 1999, pp. 49-67.

An easier approach (from the point of view of the respondent, and certainly not from the perspective of the individual coding and analyzing the data) is to use open-ended questions that elicit the appropriate answer from the respondent. This format allows the interviewer to probe in depth into the issue at hand and the respondent to fully address the points.

6-4f Deciding on the Sampling Plan

The sampling plan calls for the manager and researcher to jointly decide on the following issues:

- Sampling unit—Determining who will be included in the survey
- Sample size—Determining how many individuals will be surveyed (the larger the sample, the higher the study reliability)
- Sampling procedure—Determining how the sampling units will be selected (the most representative sample is a random probability sample)

Determining the sampling plan is likely to be affected by some of the same problems discussed previously. First, the sampling unit itself may have a different definition, depending on the country where the data are collected. In developed countries, for example, research examining family consumption patterns typically surveys a nuclear family, whereas in many developing countries, an extended family, including relatives living with the nuclear family, may be part of the sampling unit. Similarly, as already mentioned, the concept of household varies across different countries. This is certainly the case in Latin America, where the extended "family" may include several generations, in-laws, godparents, etc.

The sampling procedure also presents a problem, as previously discussed, especially the sampling frame (the list from which sample units are selected). Mailing lists are inadequate, and telephones are available to only a small percentage of the population in many countries of the world.

International Constraints

Instrument Translation: instruments developed in one country require translation into the language of the country where they will be administered. Many concepts, however, are likely to lose some of their meaning when translated into another language. Idioms are particularly problematic, and their literal translation has led to numerous marketing blunders.

In cross-cultural research, all steps should be performed by individuals fluent in both the original language of the questionnaire and in the language of the country where it will be administered. First, a questionnaire is translated from the language in which it was originally written into the language in which it will be administered. There are two possible alternatives to further ensure that the instrument has been translated as intended. One is back translation, whereby the translated questionnaire is again translated into its initial language by a different individual. Another possibility is parallel translation, whereby the questionnaire is translated from its original language by two different individuals and the two versions are compared. The successive translation (by different translators) of the instrument between the original language and the language of administration with the purpose of obtaining an instrument that is closest in meaning to the original questionnaire is known as decentering.

The consumer research questionnaire in Table 6-4 contains a number of scales developed in marketing in the United States, among which are attitudes toward business ethics, pricing practices, comparison shopping, dogmatism, fashion concern, dress conformity, and information search. The translated scales performed well and were considered highly reliable when used in the different countries.

6-4g Collecting, Analyzing, and Interpreting the Information

In the final stage of the marketing research process, the researcher or research team is ready to collect the primary data. This expensive undertaking can be eventful. Researchers are frequently faced with respondents who have never had any experience participating in surveys. Nonresponse (inability or, more frequently, refusal to participate in the study) can be a particularly serious problem, as previously seen. Even lateral processes that do not involve data collection per se, such as briefing the field force (training the interviewers) and evaluating the fieldwork quality, can be particularly difficult if the marketing researcher is not a national because communication may be encumbered by language and cultural differences. Ideally, local researchers should be in charge of implementing the data-collection process. They are aware of the particulars of the environment that may have an impact on the data collection.

The University of Richmond offers an experiential learning course in which teams of students spend the semester developing market entry strategies in Latin America for a Richmond-area firm. The instructor has worked with professors and students at partner universities in Latin America to develop and administer surveys and even do product testing. This has been a cost-effective and engaging way to gather market intelligence for the client projects.

Finally, it is important that marketing managers not base all their decisions on the data collected because even proper planning of the data collection effort does not exclude the possibility of shortcomings in the study. For example, after one market research firm indicated that there was a substantial market for a specific product, a Swiss pharmaceutical firm built an $8 million manufacturing firm in Southeast Asia. The researchers, however, over-looked an important aspect of that market: the black market controlled by government officials. The added competition of the black market led to lower earnings for the company.[40]

6-5 Global Marketing Decision Support Systems (MDSS)

A decision support system is "a coordinated collection of data, systems, tools, and techniques, complemented by supporting software and hardware designed for the gathering and interpretation of business and environmental data."[41] In a global environment, the environmental data take into account home-country and host-country developments, as well as developments in other global markets that may affect operations.

Ideally, a global marketing decision support system should be:[42]

• Computerized — Having a computerized support system is now possible in the case of most global markets, due to the increase in the capability of personal computers to perform more complex tasks.

• Interactive — Managers can use online instructions to generate reports, without assistance from a programmer, who now may only be needed periodically, for system updating and training, reducing the number of expatriates needed on site.

• Flexible — Managers can access and integrate data from a variety of sources and manipulate it in a variety of ways. The system allows managers to access information about firm operations in similar markets where the firm may be present and competitors' operations where such information is available.

• Discovery-oriented — Such systems should produce diagnostics that reveal trends and identify problems.

In a global environment, there are different, country-specific information systems. Integrating the different approaches may lead to operational difficulties, and managers must continually take into consideration such differences as they interface with the system.

A number of areas lend themselves well to marketing decision support systems (MDSS). In Section 6-5a, "Sales Forecasting," we discuss different possible applications for such systems.

6-5a Sales Forecasting

Different approaches to sales forecasting are discussed in this section. The more complex these techniques are, the more their efficiency can be improved in an MDSS environment. Nevertheless, input obtained from using the simpler methods (sales force composite estimates, jury of executive opinion, and the Delphi method) can be used to cross-validate the estimates given by the more sophisticated forecasting techniques (time series and econometric models).

fizkes/shutterstock.com

Sales Force Composite Estimate

Forecasts from sales force composite estimates are based on the personal observations and "hunches" of the local sales force. Salespeople are in the closest contact with the international consumer, and they are likely to find out about consumer desires and overall changing market trends. The sales force is likely to be constituted of locals who have a good understanding of the market. They, in turn, report to the manager, who may or may not be an expatriate sent abroad by the home office. Ideally, the individual occupying this position is schooled under both home- and host-country systems; if not, it is recommended that this individual undergo at least some training in host-or home-country approaches to doing business. This training is important because this individual is typically responsible for interpreting the predictions of the sales force.

Jury of Expert Opinion

Forecasts from the jury of expert opinion are based on the opinions of different experts about future demand. The experts' opinions are then combined, and an aggregate demand estimation is offered. Because experts could come from both home and host country, as well as countries where other companies, or the company in question, may face similar problems, obtaining a consensus perspective or aggregate forecast may be more difficult to achieve. At the same time, the awareness of the different possible outcomes or individual perspectives may prove invaluable in gaining insight on demand, particularly for a market new to the company.

The Delphi Method

The Delphi method entails asking a number of experts to estimate market performance, aggregating the results, and sharing this information with the experts. This process is repeated several times until a consensus is reached. Clearly, such an approach would be most cumbersome when dealing with a global company. First, in addition to impositions on executives' time, the company also must incur expenses related to the logistics of bringing together experts from different countries. Second, should the company attempt to use the Delphi method by mailing forecasting surveys, there is always the risk that international mail might impose, in addition to the high likelihood of noncompliance by executives, who could perceive such an exercise as an imposition on their time. Typically, these types of studies are performed at yearly or quarterly meetings of international managers.

The Delphi method has been used in within-country studies to identify the needs for professional training for life insurance sales representatives and to examine the competencies needed by those sales representatives in the United States and in Taiwan. Sales representatives of the same company receive the same training in both the United States and Taiwan, but the Taiwanese did not exhibit the same high performance levels as their U.S. counterparts. A study using the Delphi technique revealed that the life insurance companies studied needed to offer additional training to the Taiwanese salespeople especially in problem solving, communication, and information technology utilization.[43]

Time Series and Econometric Models

Time series models use data of past performance to predict future market demand. Typically, these models give more weight to recent developments. These methods assume that the future will be similar to the past. Econometric models, on the other hand, take into account different deterministic factors that affect market demand, factors that may or may not depend on past performance trends.[44]

An example of an application of econometric models to global marketing is provided by the application of an autoregressive moving average (ARMAX) to predict consumer demand for beer in the Netherlands. The variables used as predictors of the demand for beer were temperature, price, consumer expenditures, and company advertising expenditures. The study concluded that advertising expenditures are not good predictors for beer demand; the authors suspected that the reason is a saturated market where all competitors advertise extensively and where additional advertising efforts may go unnoticed.

Time series and econometric models are dependent on the availability of historical data, data that are mainly available in developed countries but not in developing countries. For these markets, then, it is appropriate to estimate demand by analogy, noting responses of markets with similar relevant characteristics, levels of economic development, cultural characteristics, and so forth.

Analogy Methods

The analogy method is an estimation method that relies on developments and findings in markets with similar levels of economic development, markets where the product is in the same development stage, or markets with similar cultural characteristics, or it may be based on sales of a related product in the key market of study. For example, to estimate anticipated adoption rate of cell phones in Latvia, it may be appropriate to identify the proportion of new adopters in a more advanced country in the Baltic region — Estonia, which is more developed — where cell phone service is widely available, but which shares a similar history and similar geopolitics with Latvia. This is an example of country performance analogy.

To estimate the adoption rate of Internet service in Sri Lanka, it may be appropriate to evaluate the adoption rate of computers in this country. This is an example of product performance analogy.

Typically, in the country performance analogy, adjustments are made based on development level, cultural differences, trade barriers, competition, and so on. In the product performance analogy, adjustments are made for consumer traits such as purchase power, consumer innovation rate, and competitive environment.

WathanyuSowong /shutterstock.com

Point-of-Sale Based Projections

Point-of-sale based projections are made with the help of store scanners, which are increasingly used by research suppliers, particularly in the United States (Nielsen and Information Resources, among others), to assess market share and other relevant market dimensions. Weekly or biweekly store audits reveal the movement of goods within the store and from warehouses. Internationally, although scanning technology is widely available, it is mainly used for inventory purposes, rather than for research purposes.

Summary

Define international marketing research and provide a description of its immense scope; offer examples of each type of research conducted in international marketing. International marketing research involves gathering information for international marketing decisions. It is wide in scope, covering industry research, market traits and trends, buyer behavior, and the marketing mix. Examples of product research are product testing, product package studies, and competitive product analysis. Distribution research covers areas such as import/ export analysis, international channel performance and coverage, as well as plant/warehouse location studies. Promotion research has the widest scope, with studies of premiums, coupons, and deals; advertising effectiveness; media research (which is especially important in highly industrialized countries); and sales force analyses. Pricing research involves studies projecting demand, as well as international market potential studies, sales potential studies, cost analyses, and profit analyses.

Describe the steps involved in the international marketing research process while addressing, for each step, the international constraints involved. The first step of the international research process involves defining the research problem and setting the research objectives. This is usually done in conjunction with a local team and international experts and consultants. The development of the research plan involves deciding on the information sources— primary and secondary (evaluating the validity and reliability of secondary data) — and determining the appropriate research approach. The research approach may involve collecting qualitative data, using focus groups or observation methods, or quantitative data, using descriptive (surveys, content analyses) or causal research methods (experimental research). They, in turn, determine the contact methods. The next step requires the researcher to design the data collection instrument and translate it into the local language(s). Next, the sampling plan must be determined: selecting the sampling procedure and sample size, frame, and unit. Finally, the researcher must collect, analyze, and interpret the information.

Introduce the concept of decision support systems for international marketing and describe the sales forecasting process. Decision support systems represent a coordinated approach to collecting and interpreting business and environmental data. International sales forecasting techniques can be improved in this environment. Methods used in international sales forecasting are international sales force composite estimates, jury of expert opinion, the Delphi method, time series and econometric models, the analogy method, and point-of-sale-based projections, all of which can be used in an international setting with various degrees of success.

Key Terms

advertising effectiveness research

analogy method

availability

back translation

brand awareness research

brand name generation and testing

buyer behavior research

causal research

channel performance and coverage studies

competitive pricing analyses

concept development and testing studies

conceptual equivalence

consumer segmentation studies

content analysis

cost analyses

data collection instrument

decentering

decision support system

Delphi method

depth interview

descriptive research

econometric model

emic instrument

etic instrument

experimental research

exploratory research

external secondary data

focus group interview

functional equivalence

import/export analyses

internal secondary data

international market potential studies

international marketing research

jury of expert opinion

media research

observational research

open-ended questions

parallel translation

plant/warehouse location studies

point-of-sale–based projections

premiums, coupons and deals

price elasticity studies

primary data

product packaging design studies

product testing

profit analyses studies

purchase behavior studies

qualitative research

quantitative research

reliability

research approach

sales forecast

sales potential studies

sales force compensation, quota, and territory studies

sales force composite estimates

sample size

sampling frame

sampling procedure

sampling unit

secondary data

studies of premiums, coupons, and deals

survey research

test marketing

time series model

validity

Discussion Questions

1. Describe the broad scope of marketing research with a focus on promotion-related research.

2. You have been hired to evaluate the purchase behavior of adolescents in Latvia. What types of research studies could you conduct?

3. What are some of the limitations of secondary data available to international marketing researchers?

4. Describe the challenges that researchers experience when designing and administering questionnaires in countries that are culturally dissimilar from their own.

5. Discuss the quantitative data collection methods that researchers can use in an international study and the problems they pose to the validity and reliability of the findings.

6. Describe the international sales forecasting methods that marketing managers can use to better monitor and more efficiently react to information in the local environment.

Chapter Quiz

True/False

1. Brand awareness research and purchase behavior studies are often conducted by companies to identify the profiles of heavy consumers of the product.

False

Rationale: Consumer segmentation studies are used to select profiles of heavy product consumers. Brand awareness research and purchase behavior studies are conducted by companies to assess their position in the market. Section 6-3b, "Buyer Behavior Research"

2. Advertising effectiveness research uses studies that evaluate media availability and the appropriateness of the medium.

False

Rationale: Advertising effectiveness research is conducted to examine the effectiveness and appropriateness of advertisements aimed at individual markets. Section 6-3e, "Promotion Research"

3. Research that examines cause-and-effect relationships is also known as causal research.

True

Rationale: Causal research examines cause-and-effect relationships using experimentation as a method of investigation. Section 6-4a, "Defining the Research Problem and Research Objectives"

Multiple Choice

1. Which product research method mainly deals with testing new-product performance in a limited area of a national or regional target?

        a. Test marketing

        b. Product testing

        c. Competitive product studies

        d. Brand name generation and testing

Answer a is correct.

Rationale: Test marketing is a product research procedure that attempts to evaluate new product performance in a particular region characterized by demographics that are representative of the international target audience. Section 6-3c, "Product Research"

2. Which product research method attempts to identify the extent to which the product conforms to local tastes?

        a. Test marketing

        b. Product testing

     c. Competitive product studies

     d. Brand name generation and testing

Answer b is correct.

Rationale: Product testing identifies the extent to which the product conforms to the tastes of the local target market. Section 6-3c, "Product Research"

3. Kraft Food's research on identifying the top distribution firm in Azerbaijan is an example of which distribution research method?

     a. Plant/warehouse location studies

     b. Channel performance and coverage

     c. Import/export analyses

     d. None of the above

Answer b is correct.

Rationale: Channel and performance coverage research is essential for firms planning to enter an international market. Firms are advised to identify the main distribution firms in the market and to partner with them to distribute the product locally. Section 6-3d, "Distribution Research"

4. Which of the following is a stage of the research plan?

     a. Deciding on the research methods

     b. Deciding on the information sources

     c. Deciding on the sampling procedure

     d. All of the above

Answer d is correct.

Rationale: When designing a research plan, the researcher, together with top local management, decides on the research methods, the information sources, and sampling procedures appropriate for the research. Section 6-4b, "Developing the Research Plan"

5. Data collected by a company on previous occasions to address a problem not directly related to the current research question is also known as

     a. first-tier data.

     b. primary data.

     c. internal secondary data.

     d. external secondary data.

Answer c is correct.

Rationale: Internal secondary data are collected from sources within the company. The data were collected previously to address similar issues in another market or in the present market. Section 6-4c, "Deciding on Information Sources"

6. Qualitative research methods include

     a. survey research.

     b. focus group research.

     c. experiments.

     d. all of the above

Answer b is correct.

Rationale: Focus group research typically involves 6 to 12 participants and a moderator who guides the discussion based on a certain discussion agenda. The outcome of focus group research is a qualitative analysis. Survey research and experiments, on the other hand, involve data and measurement; they are thus quantitative research methods. Section 6-4d, "Determining Research Approaches"

7. A sampling plan relies on specific decisions for a

        a. sampling unit.

        b. sample size.

        c. sampling procedure.

        d. all of the above

Answer d is correct.

Rationale: The sampling plan specifies the sampling unit, the sample size, and the sampling procedure. Section 6-4f, "Deciding on the Sampling Plan"

Notes

1. Alecia Swasy, *Soap Opera: The Inside Story of Procter & Gamble,* New York: Times Books, 1993.

2. Sadanand Dhume, "Walmart's Big Bet Could Pay Off For India," *The Wall Street Journal,* May 17, 2018 accessed at https://www.wsj.com/articles/walmarts-big-bet-could-pay-off-for-india-152659884 on May 21, 2018.

3. "The Tragedy of Argentina, a Century of Decline," *The Economist,* February 17, 2014, accessed at https://www.economist.com/briefing/2014/02/17/a-century-of-decline on May 21, 2018.

4. This section is organized based on a framework provided in a table in Thomas C. Kinnear and Ann R. Root, eds., *1988 Survey of Marketing Research: Organization, Functions, Budgeting, and Compensation,* Chicago: American Marketing Association, 1989, p. 43.

5. See Rolf F. H. Seringhaur, "Comparative Marketing Behaviour of Canadian and Austrian High Tech Firms," *Management International Review,* Vol. 33, No. 3, Third Quarter 1993, p. 247; and James D. Hlavacek and B. C. Ames, "Segmenting Industrial and High-Tech Markets," *Journal of Business Strategy,* Vol. 7, October 1986, pp. 39 –51. William L. Shanklin and John K. Ryans, Jr., "Organizing for High-Tech Marketing," *Harvard Business Review,* Vol. 62, 1984, pp. 164–171. Hellmut Schutte, "Asian Culture and the Global Consumer," *Financial Times,* November 1998, pp. 2–3.

6. Joe Gose, "Hilton Builds Brand Awareness Worldwide," *National Real Estate Investor Worldwide,* Vol. 48, No. 10, October 2006, p. 115. Nancy Trejos, "Hilton Announces New Affordable Hotel Brand, Tru," *USA Today,* January 25, 2016, accessed at https://www.usatoday.com/story/travel/hotels/2016/01/25/hilton-tru-new-hotel-brand/79185810/ on May 21, 2018.

7. Liz Grubow, "Branding Eastern European Shoppers," *Global Cosmetics Industry,* Vol. 173, No. 2, February 2005, pp. 30–32.

8. Helen Johnstone, "'Little Emperors Call the Shots," *Asian Business,* Vol. 32, No. 9, September 1996, pp. 67–68. Katie Demeria, "Duke's Mayonnaise From Richmond-Based C.F. Sauer To Be Sold in Colombia" *Richmond Times-Dispatch,* July 7, 2016, accessed at http://www.richmond.com/business/local/duke-s-mayonnaise-from-richmond-based-c-f-sauer-s/article_b8033218-f1d8-56f4-997f-ee4742c89d0b.html on May 21, 2018.

9. James I. Steinberg and Alan L. Klein, "Global Branding: Look Before You Leap," *Brandweek,* Vol. 39, No. 43, November 16, 1998, pp. 30–32.

10. "P&G Goes Local," *Country Monitor,* Vol. 47, No. 3, October 27, 1999, p. 9.

11. U.S. Customs and Border Protection, "Becoming a Customs Broker,", accessed at htwww.cbp.gov/trade/programs-administration/customs-brokers/becoming-customs-broker on May 23, 2018.

12. Irina Begjanova and Lisa Palluconi, "Trade with Turkmenistan," *BISNIS Bulletin,* September 1996, p. 5. Kevin Lyons, "Distribution in Kazakstan," *BISNIS Bulletin,* November 1996, pp. 1, 5. This article was adapted from the *Country Commercial Guide* for Kazakstan, produced by the U.S. Commercial Service in Almaty.

13. "Georgia Ports Authority Posts Record TEUs for 2017," *Georgia Foreign-Trade Zone News and Events*," January 23, 2018, accessed at http://www.georgiaftz.com/category/georgia-news/ on May 23, 2018.

14. Richard Cuthbertson, "Ikea's Card Is a Global Drive for Local People," *Promotions & Incentives*, March 2007, p. Payal Ganguly and Aditi Shrivastava, "E-retailer's Fight for Buyers Drives Sales at All Couponing Sites, *The Economic Times*, September 24, 2014, accessed at http://articles.economictimes.indiatimes.com/2014-09-24/news/54279514_1_couponing-amazon-india-myntra on August 14, 2015; Nielsen, "Shopping and Saving Strategies Around the World," October 2011, accessed at http://www.nielsen.com/content/dam/corporate/us/en/reports-downloads/2011-Reports/Nielsen-Global-Shopping-Saving-Report-October-2011.pdf on August 15, 2015; Guillermo D'andrea, Martin Schleicher, and Fernando Lunardini, "The Role of Promotions and Other Factors Affecting Overall Store Price Image in Latin America," *International Journal of Retail & Distribution Management*, Vol. 34, No. 9, 2006, p. 688.

15. Tyler Brule, "Good Summer Holiday Idea? Find a 'Badi' in Switzerland," *Financial Times*, August 5, 2006, 18.

16. Derek Lidow, "Global Industry, Global Approach," *Electronic Business*, Vol. 30, No. 4, April 2004, p. 72.

17. Judith Robinson, "Product Certification in Russia," *BISNIS Bulletin*, August 1996, p. 6.

18. Schutte, "Asian Culture and the Global Consumer," pp. 2–3.

19. Lalita A Manrai, Ajay K Manrai, Dana N Lascu, "Retailing in the Transition Economies of Poland and Romania: A Comparative Analysis," *Journal of Marketing Channels*, 2012, Vol. 19, No. 4, pp. 272-294.

20. T. K. Sherriff Luk, "The Use of Secondary Information Published by the PRC Government," *Journal of the Market Research Society*, Vol. 41, No. 3, July 1999, pp. 355–365.

21. Naresh Malhotra, *Essentials of Marketing Research*, 2015, Prentice Hall: Englewood Cliffs, NJ; Naresh Malhotra and J. Agarwal, "Methodological Issues in Crosscultural Marketing Research: A State of the Art Review," *International Marketing Review*, Vol. 13, No. 5, 1996, pp. 7–43.

22. Luk, "The Use of Secondary Information," pp. 355–365.

23. Ibid.

24. Ibid.

25. Michael R. Czinkota and Ilkka A. Ronkainen, "Market Research for Your Export Operations: Part II— Conducting Primary Market Research," *International Trade Forum*, Vol. 1, 1995, pp. 16–26.

26. Allison Lucas, "Market Researchers Study Abroad," *Sales and Marketing Management*, Vol. 148, No. 2, February 1996, p. 13.

27. Ibid.

28. Scott Hume, "McDonald's Goes Swanky with 'Restaurant M' in Tokyo," *The Christian Science Monitor*, July 15, 2015, accessed at http://www.csmonitor.com/Business/The-Bite/2015/0715/McDonald-s-goes-swanky-with-Restaurant-M-in-Tokyo on August 12, 2015.29. Czinkota and Ronkainen, "Market Research for Your Export Operations," pp. 16–26;Choudry, Y.A. 1986. "Pitfalls in International Marketing Research; Are you speaking French Like a Spanish Cow?" *Akron business and Economics Review* (Winter): 18-28.

30. See Yvonna S. Lincoln and Egon G. Guba, *Naturalistic Inquiry*, London: Sage Publications, 1985; Laura A. Hudson and Julie L. Ozanne, "Alternative Ways of Seeking Knowledge in Consumer Research," *Journal of Consumer Research*, March 14, 1988, pp. 508–521.

31. Jerome Kirk and Marc L. Miller, *Reliability and Validity in Qualitative Research*, London: Sage Publications, 1986.

32. Czinkota and Ronkainen, "Market Research for Your Export Operations," pp. 16–26.

33. David R. Wheeler, "Content Analysis: An Analytical Technique for International Marketing Research," *International Marketing Review*, Vol. 5, No. 4, Winter 1988, pp. 34–40.

34. Dana-Nicoleta Lascu, "Women in Advertising: A Cross-Cultural Study of Emotion," working paper.

35. Zafar U. Ahmed, Dana-Nicoleta Lascu, and D. Neil Ashworth, "International Management and Marketing Research in Developing Countries," in *Proceedings of the Sixth Annual Meeting of the American Society of Business and Behavioral Sciences*, Vol. 10, February 1999, pp. 9–14.

36. Dana-Nicoleta Lascu, Lalita Manrai, and Ajay K. Manrai, "Marketing in Romania: The Challenges of the Transition from a Centrally-Planned Economy to a Consumer-Oriented Economy," *European Journal of Marketing*, Vol. 27, No. 11–12, 1993, pp. 102–120. John Price, "Best Practices for Market Research in Latin America," *AMI-Americas Market Intelligence*, December 12, 2016, accessed at https://www.slideshare.net/AmericasMarketIntelligence/best-practices-for-market-research-in-latin-america-70061657International Constraints on May 23, 2018.

36. Ahmed, Lascu, and Ashworth, "International Management and Marketing Research in Developing Countries," pp. 9–14.

37. The material in this section is adapted from Choudhry, "Pitfalls in International Marketing Research," pp. 18–28.

38. Ravi Parameswaran and Attila Yaprak "A Cross-National Comparison of Consumer Research Measures," *Journal of International Business Studies*, Spring 1987, pp. 35–49.

39. William R. Dillon, Thomas J. Madden, and Neil Firtle, *Marketing Research in a Marketing Environment*, Burr Ridge, IL: Irwin, 1993.

40. Ibid.

41. Chiang Ku Fan and Chen-Liang Cheng, "A study to identify the training needs of life insurance sales representatives in Taiwan using the Delphi approach," *International Journal of Training & Development*, Vol. 10,No. 3, September 2006, p. 212.

42. Naresh Malhotra, *Essentials of Marketing Research*, 2015, Prentice Hall: Englewood Cliffs, NJ.

43. "British Retailer Goes Wireless," *Automatic I.D. News*, Vol. 14, No. 11, October 1998, p. 14.

44. Gerry Eskin, "POS Scanner Data: The State of the Art, in Europe and the World," *Marketing and Research Today*, Vol. 22, No. 2, May 1994, pp. 107–108.

Case 6-1 Hilton Sorrento Palace

Two hours south of Rome on the way to Naples by the Eurostar, the Italian high-speed train, and an additional hour west along the Bay of Naples via the Circumvesuviana regional railway is the town of Sorrento. The Hilton Sorrento Palace reigns high on the hills of Sorrento, overlooking Mount Vesuvius, the now-dormant volcano (since 1944) that buried the towns of Pompeii and Herculaneum in the year 79 CE.

Sorrento is a small resort town, known well throughout Europe, an ideal vacation destination for its picturesque location and mild weather. A favorite of British travelers, the town of Sorrento has 10,000 beds according to Mr. Ziad Tantawi, director of business development at the Hilton Sorrento Palace. The Hilton Sorrento Palace is the largest of all hotels in the small resort town, with 383 rooms. Owned by the Sorrento Palace Gruppo since its year of construction (1981), the hotel became part of the Hilton chain in May 2001, and is now under Hilton management. One of the few hotels open in the winter in Sorrento, the Sorrento Palace boasts an average occupancy rate of 60 percent, with an average occupancy of 30 percent from November to March and more than 85 percent from May to October.

The Hilton Sorrento Palace faces competition from three categories of competitors. Family-run lodging, such as a bed and breakfast, and Airbnb lodging are very popular. The bed and breakfasts are competitively priced at or below the room rates of leading hotels in the area. Most bed and breakfast accommodations are open year round.

Sorrento is also a popular destination for cruise lines during the summer months. For cruise ship passengers, Sorrento offers easy access to the ruins of Pompeii, Mount Vesuvius, and the Isle of Capri. Overall, prices for cruise ships are higher than those of hotels, but they include meals and entertainment, as well as airfare to Italy.

Other local hotels compete directly with the Sorrento Hilton. The historic Europa Palace Grand Hotel, for example, offers close views of the Bay of Naples and the cliffs of Sorrento.

The Hotel Offerings

The four-star Hilton Sorrento Palace is situated on a hill overlooking the town and the Bay of Naples, a short walk from downtown's busy tourist markets. Surrounded by residences and lemon and orange groves, the hotel is modern and elegant. Its restaurant, L'Argumento, is situated amidst blooming cannas and orange and lemon trees. Le Ginestre has frescoes and elegant columns and an indoor pool with a lush painted background. Its other four restaurants

BAHDANOVICH ALENA/shutterstock.com

abound in blooming bougainvillea and oleander and have a splendid view of the Bay of Naples and Mount Vesuvius.

The indoor lounge has excellent performers scheduled every evening and boasts a view of the city and the bay. The executive lounge is situated on the top floor of the hotel and has a splendid view of the gulf and town. It also boasts an infinity pool at the highest altitude in the region. The lounge serves complimentary food and drinks to executive guests and to gold- and diamond-level Hilton Honors members.

The hotel has a total of six outdoor swimming pools of different depths, flowing into each other, a tennis court, and a relatively well-equipped fitness center. Among the services offered at the hotel pool is the Hilton Kids Club: Every day, from 10 to 12 in the morning and from 2 to 4 in the afternoon, the children staying at the hotel can enjoy entertainment by the pool (uno spazio giochi per bambini).

Marketing Strategies

The hotel's targeting strategies focus primarily on meetings. Its meeting space is one of the largest in Europe.

The Centro Congressi (congress center) has a full range of rooms for conferences and conventions of any type or size, from the 1,500-seat auditorium to smaller rooms, a 37,140 square-foot exhibition space, 24 meeting rooms, a banquet facility that can accommodate 1,000 people, and a parking facility that can accommodate 300 automobiles. In addition, the Centro also offers conference interpreting systems (six conference interpreting booths) and audio-visual presentation equipment, including a megascreen, making it an ideal venue for international events. About 65 percent of all hotel guests are conference participants. Hilton's sales offices in Italy (Milan) and overseas (in Germany, the United Kingdom, France, Sweden, and the United Arab Emirates) are responsible for conference sales.

Tour operators constitute a second target group, accounting for 25 percent of the hotel's business. Their demand is highest in the months of July and August, when demand exceeds supply — Sorrento's location on the Bay and up a steep hill does not allow for space that could accommodate additional hotels. Only 10 percent of the hotel's business comes from individual bookings, the Internet, and telephone reservations.

The Hilton Sorrento Palace's main target market is Italy. In addition, the hotel also actively targets groups from the United Kingdom, Germany, Belgium, France, and Japan, in that order, according to Mr. Ziad Tantawi, director of business development at the Hilton Sorrento Palace. Visitors from the United States previously constituted a large proportion of guests at the hotel, particularly in the summer, in organized tours. However, the number of American guests decreased considerably in recent years, starting with the terrorist attacks of September 11, 2001. Today, the numbers are even lower, as tourists from the United States often restrict their visits to the main tourist attractions in Rome, Milan, Venice, and Florence.

However, as European economies tend to follow a similar economic cycle, it is preferable for the hotel to diversify and to attract more visitors from the United States. Recently, the hotel made extensive marketing attempts aimed at Japanese tour groups, with great success. The hotel's management would like to repeat those successes with U.S. visitors. They would like to find out how to best direct the hotel's marketing strategies to U.S. travelers visiting Italy and to persuade them to spend a weekend in a peaceful, semi-tropical paradise at the Hilton Sorrento Palace. The hotel is close to Rome, very close to Naples, and just a short flight from Milan, the primary airport for U.S. visitors. The hotel management would also like to increase conference attendance at the hotel in the off-season (November to March). Hilton managers are wondering how to attract professional groups from the United States using the organizations' counterparts in Italy. They had some initial discussions with an area business school about hosting an international management conference at the hotel. They would like to identify similar opportunities that would entail working with other local, regional, and national university groups, pharmaceutical companies, and medical organizations that would be able to bring U.S. guests to the Hilton Sorrento Palace.

Sources: Interview with Mr. Ziad Tantawi, director of business development at the Hilton Sorrento Palace; Hilton Sorrento Palace, Hilton Hotels, accessed at http://www3.hilton.com/en/hotels/italy/hilton-sorrento-palace-RROHIHI/index.html on May 31, 2018.

Analysis Suggestions:

1. Conduct a study for the hotel (provide the entire research design) to identify U.S. travelers who have already committed to visit popular destinations in Italy (not including Sorrento).

2. Your research has a second step: to persuade U.S. travelers who have already committed to visit popular destinations in Italy to spend a weekend at the Hilton Sorrento Palace.

3. Conduct a third study to identify area businesses and organizations that are planning to host conferences at the Hilton Sorrento Palace during the off season.

4. For each of the previous studies, provide a complete research design and provide sample questionnaires that will be used in the research conducted with each segment.

Case 6-2 Tom Ford: Euro-Luxury with an American Attitude

Tom Ford is an American high fashion designer who sells beauty products, high-fashion clothing, and accessories for men and women – he is also a film director, screenwriter, and producer. Ford took Europe by storm in the 1990s, re-energizing Gucci as its creative director, bringing it back from the brink of bankruptcy, and then working as creative director for Yves Saint Laurent, after Gucci acquired it in 1999. He had become an icon of European high fashion.

Tom Ford then established his American brand, launching a line of fragrances and cosmetics, in 2004. He then expanded to menswear in 2006, and launched his fashion collection for women in 2010. His high fashion brand started off pricy and exclusive, with a smaller customer base; he felt his clothing offered high-net-worth individuals membership to an even more exclusive club. Over the years, this exclusive consumer base broadened with Ford's underwear line, with prices that even the middle class could afford. This move – coupled with a return to the United States – most likely led him to consider appealing to the broader, affordable luxury market.

Ford has always been particularly enthusiastic about watches – he designed several while working for Gucci, and has acquired a large collection over the years, starting at a young age. His passion for watches led him to start selling watches and watch accessories along with Tom Ford branded jewelry. His line of watches are, in fact, an affordable luxury.

Across his product lines, Ford's strategy is to establish direct relationships with his customers in order maintain as much control as he can. When possible, sales are completed with one customer per sales person, even offering private appointments, to ensure high-quality service. In order to maintain an even greater control of the company, Ford owns 63.75 percent of the shares and controls the fragrance, beauty, and eyewear licenses, which allows him to have the final say on all matters.

For his watch collection, he partnered with Bedrock Manufacturing in order to create Swiss-made watches and to more effectively manage licensing. When the Tom Ford fashion brand was first launched, the majority of his consumers were of a similar age to Ford – today, they are in their forties and fifties. With his watch collection, Ford is attempting to bring in younger customers in order to modernize his brand and follow today's trends. By pricing his new watches as at lower price points, Ford can target a larger consumer market, who can afford the brand, and younger consumers – Millennials in particular. Millennials are less likely to buy expensive luxury goods, as they would rather avoid purchases of high-priced, unnecessary items. The watches are also unisex, with a broader appeal as well.

What makes Tom Ford watches unique – emphasized greatly by Ford himself – are the multitude of accessories for the watches. Instead of having to purchase multiple watches, buyers can purchase different wristbands to switch. Thus, the watch can have a completely different look, without burdening consumers to purchase a new watch. There are even multiple bands, varying in both texture and color, for different seasons. The costs range from about $170 to $480, depending on which band – certainly more affordable than purchasing a completely new watch for $2,000. The customer can still have a brand new look, without buying a new watch.

In order to appeal to younger consumers, Ford is creating simpler everyday "watch wear." When he struggled with his womenswear sales, he noted that, "women's daytime clothes have evaporated…They wear jeans, a t-shirt, a cool jacket, and a great pair of shoes. Evening, however… is mega…." (Sherman, 2017). Rather than dressing up for the day, young buyers tend to be more casual. Ford addresses this with the multiple band strategy; people can purchase different bands for varying occasions, rather than have to wear the same style watch every day.

There is substantial competition for watches in the current market, many technologically advanced, such as the Apple Watch and the Fitbit. Ford is not attempting to compete with these brands. Instead, he attempts to create an elegant watch that people can confidently wear. In his opinion, a watch is an essential accessory and can also be a status symbol. Thus, this watch is more a piece of jewelry than a sophisticated instrument.

Sorbis/shutterstock.com

Consumers are looking for affordable ways to show personality and status, with accessories as well as clothing that are versatile. Rather than having a watch, or clothing that they can only wear when they are dressing up, young buyers want something they can wear every day, comfortably. A sleek style with affordable prices will reach a broader consumer base than just the exclusive, high-fashion brands. The existing high-fashion companies have substantial brand equity, which allows them to have an exclusive consumer base. However, it is difficult to enter the market as a new fashion designer and immediately attract consumers with extremely expensive products. Customers spend on brands they trust, they need to be sure they are buying quality. Tom Ford, through his brand experience, as well as his extensive experience working with brands such as Gucci, can deliver coveted fashion successfully – at a lower price, and with greater versatility, thus growing the target market.

Sources: Ellison, Jo. (2018). Tom Ford interview: on watches, underwear, and putting the fun in fashion. How to Spend It. Retrieved from https://howtospendit.ft.com/mens-style/203127-tom-ford-interview-on-watches-underwear-and-putting-the-fun-in-fashion on June 1, 2018. Felder, R. (2018). Tom ford designs a watch. But the price isn't what you'd expect. *The New York Times.* Retrieved from https://www.nytimes.com/2018/05/10/fashion/tom-ford-bedrock-watches.html on June 11, 2018. "Millennials Infographic." *Goldman Sachs,* 2018, www.goldmansachs.com/our-thinking/pages/millennials/ on June 11, 201 Sherman, L. (2017). Tom ford: what's next. *Business of Fashion.* Retrieved from https://www.businessoffashion.com/articles/people/tom-ford-whats-next on June 11, 2018. Yotka, Steff. (2018). Tom ford's new timepiece collection is going to change the way you wear your watch. Retrieved from https://www.vogue.com/article/tom-ford-launches-watches on June 11, 2018.

Analysis Suggestions:

1. Examine the websites of Tom Ford in the United States and Europe. Develop a comparative research study on how Tom Ford is marketed differently in the United States than in Europe.

2. Design a research study that examines the likelihood of Millennials in Europe to purchase Tom Ford watches.

3. Design a comparative study that examines the likelihood of Millennials in the United States to purchase Tom Ford watches.

Chapter 7

International Strategic Planning

Learning Objectives

After studying this chapter, you should be able to:

- Develop a general understanding of international marketing strategy at the different levels of the international organization and provide some insights into the international marketing planning process of selected companies.

- Identify the rationale for adopting a target marketing strategy in international markets.

- Identify the requirements necessary for effective international market segmentation.

- Introduce the concept of country attractiveness analysis and offer a blueprint for conducting the analysis.

- Identify the bases for consumer segmentation and offer company application examples.

- Describe the three targeting strategies used by companies worldwide.

- Describe the six positioning strategies that international companies can use to position their brands in the minds of target consumers.

Chapter Outline

General Motors, the second largest automaker in the United States, has had a long history in India, where it had a number of partnerships. In 2012, it restructured operations and announced a $1 billion investment in India, shifting production to a single plant with a 220,000 vehicles capacity, expected to produce ten new Chevrolet models by 2018, a third for export. Ford was similarly betting on India, where it opened a new factory in 2015.[1] GM and Ford have a number of models that are well suited for emerging markets; they are affordable, small enough to access narrow streets in small villages, and well-built to take on the rough roads in low- and middle-income countries.

szefei/shutterstock.com

By 2015, GM had already experienced losses, some due to a large recall of its multi-purpose Tavera automobile, and it lost market share to local giants Tata Motors, Maruti Suzuki India, and Mahindra, as well as to international players Ford, Toyota, and Hyundai. At that point, all further investment was put on hold, and, on April 2017, GM shut down its Gujarat plant and announced that it would stop selling cars in India. It still has two other factories that will manufacture automobiles for export to South America. GM leadership concluded that its strategy for India did not work: it was unable to make any impact in the market.[2]

In the example above, GM did not accurately assess the fit between the company strengths and goals, and the dynamics of the Indian market. Certainly, India has a promising market, with buying power is increasing rapidly, and Indian consumers indeed have a strong preference for Western brands. However, GM did not properly consider the aggressiveness of its competitors and the quality of their offerings at a low, competitive price. This chapter offers an overview of international marketing strategies and insights into international marketing planning. The chapter is linked to the International Marketing Plan in Appendix A, which provides a detailed template on developing an international marketing plan; please refer to it for the steps in the development of the plan.

7-1 Developing an International Marketing Strategy

An international marketing strategy involves developing and maintaining a strategic fit between the international company's objectives, competencies, and resources and the challenges presented by its international market or markets. The international strategic plan forges a link between the company's resources and its international goals and objectives in a complex, continually changing international environment. Given the changing nature of the environment, the international company's strategic plan cannot afford a typical long-term focus (five or ten years); rather, the planning process must be systematic and continual, and it must reevaluate objectives in light of new opportunities and potential threats.

Another dimension of international marketing strategy is linked to the company's commitment to its international markets. In the past, some companies approached international markets just to "test the waters," often with no clear international strategy, or simply with the goal of unloading overproduction. However, in today's competitive global markets, companies both large and small are committed to international markets and recognize the strategic importance of customer relationships outside the home country. A long-term international commitment that entails substantial investment in terms of resources and personnel is likely to bring the company the greatest rewards. Such a strategy makes the company a stronger competitor in the world market, as well as at home.

International strategic planning takes place at different levels (see Figure 7-1).

Figure 7-1 Planning activities in the international firm.

At the *corporate level,* the strategic plan allocates resources and establishes objectives for the whole enterprise worldwide. The corporate plan has a long-term focus and involves the highest levels of management. For example, PepsiCo Beverages headquarters (including its international headquarters) are located in Purchase, New York. The company's corporate plan is developed there. Planning at this level involves international target market selection decisions, deciding which country or countries to target based on the screening criteria and processes described in this chapter.

At the *division level,* the strategic plan allocates funds to each business unit based on division goals and objectives. In the PepsiCo example, its divisions are organized regionally— for example, in Eastern Europe, its regional division is located in Vienna, Austria. From there, the company coordinates all regional operations. At this point, PepsiCo may use various portfolio analysis tools to decide which brands to harvest, to invest in, or to divest, and plan its resources accordingly. PepsiCo's product portfolio for North America is the most comprehensive, with brands such as Pepsi, in a number of versions, such as Diet Pepsi, Pepsi

Max, and Pepsi Next, with Mountain Dew in several different versions, such as Diet Mountain Dew, Mountain Dew Dewshine, Sangrita Blast, Baja Blast, and Game Fuel, Mountain Dew Kickstart offerings such as Pineapple Orange Mango, Strawberry Kiwi, Black Cherry, Limeade, Orange Citrus, and Fruit Punch, and so on. For other drinks in the Pepsi portfolio, Sierra Mist comes in versions such as Sierra Mist regular, Diet Sierra Mist, Sierra Mist Cranberry Splash, and Diet Sierra Mist Cranberry Splash. Similarly, 7UP comes in versions such as 7UP, 7UP Ten, Diet 7UP, Cherry 7UP, and Diet Cherry 7UP. These are only a few of the company offerings in the U.S. market. Internationally, Pepsi's diet version is named Pepsi Light, since the word "diet" is usually in reference to a medical diet. In the international market, the company offers brands such as Mirinda, and Mirinda Light, Rockstar, Schwip Schwap, Punica, Kas, Bitterkas, Kasfruit, Matutano, Kero Coco, Yedigun, and others. [3]

hilalabdullah/shutterstock.com

At the *business unit level,* within each country, decisions are made regarding which consumer segments to target, using criteria described in this chapter. At this level, PepsiCo develops a strategic plan.

At the *product level* (line, brand), the actual international marketing plan is developed for achieving objectives. In the United Kingdom, Pepsi's marketing plan involves a heavy emphasis on advertising. Pepsi is the king of big budget, star-studded television commercials and sophisticated web art. Their intention has always been for viewers to talk about the ads as much as about the programming on which the ads appear. Pepsi stars have been the "who's who" of the pop world, starting with Michael Jackson in the 1980s, continuing with Madonna and Ray Charles in the 1990s, then with the Spice Girls, Robbie Williams, Britney Spears, Pink, Enrique Iglesias, and Mariah Carey, and, more recently, Beyoncé. It also signed up with U.K.'s ITV's series *Pop Idol* when it first started in 2002, and with its series *I'm a Celebrity* in 2004, and, subsequently, with David Bekham. As a consequence, Pepsi became one of United Kingdom's biggest brands. [4]

In other company examples, at division level, Kraft-Heinz has its North America Commercial division, its largest division with many offerings (beverages, dairy, grocery, snacks and cereals, foodservice, among others), and its much smaller Kraft International Commercial division, which is organized on the geographic region it serves, not on the products it sells. [5]

In this discussion, it is important to note again that the majority of U.S. exporters are small and medium-size (SMEs) businesses, companies with fewer than 500 employees, often privately owned. Many SMEs will only export to a handful of countries, notably Mexico, Canada, and in Western Europe. SMEs typically would not have the distinct layers of "division levels" and "business unit levels." Instead, a single international sales manager or small team would typically perform all of these functions. Another key development is the growing importance of services exports for the U.S. economy, as well as other nations. The United States is, by far, the largest services exporter in the world, with exports topping $700 billion per year. Of all U.S. exports, services exports are growing at a much faster pace than merchandise exports, and can present especially attractive market-entry opportunities for SME exporters. Developing the international marketing plan for services exports has some special challenges as contrasted with the marketing of tangible goods and commodities, starting with a lack of hard data on services exports. Note that the basic organizational template for the international marketing plan as discussed in this chapter also applies to services firms. [6]

7-1a Developing an International Marketing Plan

At this stage of the planning process, the international company develops marketing strategies for the target market, deciding on the product mix for the local target market, as well as on the other components of the marketing mix (distribution, promotion, and pricing); plans the international marketing programs; and manages (organizes, implements, and controls) the marketing effort.

The decision on which elements of the marketing mix to use in a particular target market is closely linked to the product's life cycle and to the market entry strategy selected. A product in the early stages of its life cycle, such as the newest version of a smart phone, will most likely be sold to consumers in highly industrialized countries for a high price, accompanied by heavy promotion. Such a product will most likely be manufactured in a developed country and exported to the rest of the world. Alternatively, a product in the later stages of its life cycle, such as a CD player, will be sold to consumers worldwide, regardless of country development level. The company selling the product will heavily compete on price and, thus, most likely manufacture the product in a developing country, where labor is inexpensive, to sell all over the world. Most likely, the company will have at least one subsidiary located in the country of product manufacture.

Rawpixel/shutterstock.com

As in the example on the top of the next page, companies entering new countries, buying local products, and bringing their own international brands to these markets, have to make important decisions regarding their local and regional portfolios. And, in the process, they must monitor not only the constantly changing marketing environment, but also changes in competitive intensity, competitor product/service quality strategies, supply chains, and consumer expectations. This will then help them to carefully target international market segments and appropriately position their products relative to those of the international and local competition.

7-2 The Rationale for Target Marketing

With the exception of narrow markets, one single company, however large its resources and capacity, could not possibly serve all customers. Consumers worldwide are too numerous, and their needs and wants are too diverse. Companies must focus on those segments that they can serve most effectively and design products and services with these segments in mind; that is, they must engage in international target marketing.

International target marketing is used by companies to:

Kraft Foods and Mondelēz International

Insights into the marketing strategies that companies use to target international markets reveal that marketing mix decisions are complex and based on extensive research. Kraft Foods (www.kraftfoods.com), a company based in the United States, has made interesting product portfolio management decisions. Kraft was one of the largest international consumer foods and beverage companies in the world, boasting some of the best-known international brands. Until 2012, Kraft Foods had pursued a successful strategy expanding internationally. In October 2012, the company spun off its North American grocery business, as Kraft Foods Group. The parent company marched on with a new identity, as Mondelēz International, headquartered in Deerfield, Illinois, with a global snacks business and with all the Kraft grocery brands outside of the U.S. Kraft Foods Group then soon merged with Heinz in 2015, creating a new company, Kraft Heinz, a primarily North American company that gets 98 percent of its sales from North America. [6]

SSokolov/shutterstock.com

Mondelēz International comprises many brands resulting from the internationalization efforts of parent – or parent of parent – companies Kraft, Philip Morris, and Nabisco. These include famous household names such as Oreos, Wheat Thins, Fig Newtons, and Ritz crackers made by the former Nabisco Company. Its Toblerone chocolates are available all over the world, its Suchard and Milka chocolate brands are available in most of Europe. Its Côte d'Or brand, available in Belgium, Netherlands, France, and Italy; Marabou and Daim, available in the Nordic countries; Freia in Norway; Sonho De Valsa and Laka in Brazil are among its international offerings. Kraft experienced negative consumer sentiment, often in the form of consumer boycotts, and has been the target of anti-globalization activism. A new identity for its global brands, one not immediately recognized as Western, would neutralize negative attitudes toward its offerings in countries where there is a pronounced activism against global brands. Its new name, Mondelēz, is derived from the Latin *mundus*, meaning "world" and delez, a proxy for the word delicious. It is a word that is more readily associated with Latin America, rather than with the United States.

The resulting companies, Kraft Heinz and Mondelēz, were created after a careful evaluation of the consumer segments and their preferences, and of the companies' own capabilities and internationalization goals: Kraft Heinz has a North-American focus, whereas, Mondelēz has a global focus. Mondelēz, however, has seen only limited success due to consumers shifting preferences from snacks to healthy food.

Sources: David Gelles, "A Big Deal in Big Food, Irene Rosenfeld Retires From Mondelēz," *The New York Times*, November 14, 2017, accessed at https://www.nytimes.com/2017/11/14/business/food-irene-rosenfeld-retires-mondelez.html on May 29, 2018. Justin Fox, "Kraft was global, and then it wasn't," *Bloomberg View*, March 27, 2015, accessed at http:// www.bloombergview.com/articles/2015-03-27/kraft-was-global-then-it-wasn-t-and-now-will-try-again on June 13, 2018.

- Identify countries and segments of international consumers that are similar with regard to key traits, who would respond well to a product and related marketing mix (international market segmentation).
- Select the countries and segments that the company can serve most efficiently and develop products tailored to each (international market targeting).
- Offer the products to the market, communicating, through the marketing mix, product traits and benefits that differentiate it in the consumer's mind (market positioning).

7-3 International Market Segmentation

International market segmentation involves identifying countries and consumers that are similar with regard to key traits, such as product-related needs and wants, and that would respond well to a product and related marketing mix. International segmentation, thus, must be performed at the country level (macro-segmentation) and at the consumer level (micro-segmentation).

At the country level, segmentation analysis identifies countries that are similar in aspects relevant to the company. If a company produces luxury goods, for example, economic variables can help determine whether a sufficient number of consumers can afford to purchase the company products. At the consumer level, segmentation analysis identifies consumers who are looking for the same benefits in the product. Although all consumers seek an efficient mode of transportation when they purchase an automobile, they also fulfill other desires. Consumers in rural Scotland may seek a small, versatile vehicle that can maneuver through tight single-lane roads, whereas executives in Dubai or Abu Dhabi of the United Arab Emirates may want a luxury automobile that exudes high status and elegance to navigate on impeccable roads.

7-3a Requirements for International Segmentation

Regardless of whether the segmentation analysis is performed at the country level or at the individual consumer level, several requirements must be met for market segmentation to be effective. The requirements, which apply equally to country and consumer segmentation, are shown in Figure 7-2.

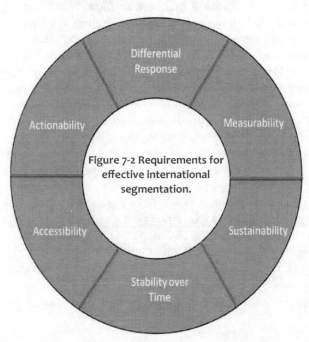

Figure 7-2 Requirements for effective international segmentation.

Differential Response

Actionability

Measurability

Accessibility

Sustainability

Stability over Time

Measurability

Individual market segments should be easy to identify and measure, thus ensuring measurability. International market segments pose numerous challenges in this regard. First, in many developing countries, reliable population statistics, including market size and economic development data, are difficult to come by. Even if the International Monetary Fund and other development organizations' data are reliable and valid, international companies still run into difficulties when evaluating culture-related dimensions, such as product preferences, especially food products, and benefits sought. Collecting data on such variables also presents many challenges.

For example, working backward, from product performance to segmentation, the Wonderbra has sold well in Islamic countries. What benefit could women seek when purchasing the Wonderbra in an environment where many women are fully covered in thick clothing in public? Research would find that women dress primarily to impress other women in many Islamic countries, in a friendly competitive way. To be able to reach such conclusions, the research study would have to explore motivations beyond basic product benefits. Furthermore, the subjects must be willing to share such information.

Substantiality

The segment should be large enough to warrant investment. Assuming that the segment can be measured, this step — determining substantiality — is relatively easy. Even if research determines that the local market segment is not large enough, it can be grouped together with an identical segment in another country and targeted jointly. Another dimension that must be evaluated is the segment's growth potential. Such data must be evaluated with surrogate statistics, such as economic development measures (i.e., as an increase in GDP per capita or income per capita), employment data, the level of foreign direct investment in the country, exports from the country, and trends in consumer spending. An important consideration here is also the intensity of competition directed at the same segment. All of these examples constitute important variables that must be evaluated to determine the market's viability in the future. A substantial and growing market is listeners of world beat music; see International Marketing Illustration 7-1.

International Marketing Illustration 7-1

The World Beat Consumer: A Substantial World Market

World beat, or world music, is a popular genre of music that has been around since the late 1980s. It is a mix of techno and Latin beats, hip-hop, and African or Arab beats, with a synthesized ethnic melodic touch. This music is marketed effectively to the world beat consumer segment world-wide. Some classify world beat as a catch-all that does not include the music genres popular in the United States, such as top 40, rock, country, classical, jazz, and so forth. World beat ranges from more traditional Europop groups to African hip-hop or reggae, Afropop, Bhangra,

 and Latin American jazz groups, such as Cuba's Buena Vista Social Club. Even heavy metal groups have dabbled in world beat, starting as early as the 1970s, with Led Zeppelin's album *Kashmir*, to current performers such as Neneh Cherry and Yassou N'Dour. National Public Radio is popularizing this format in the United States. However, worldwide, this genre has much broader appeal.

The market for world beat is the world beat consumer. This genre of music appeals across cultures and across age groups; in Europe, Asia, and Africa, listeners range from teenagers to forty-somethings. The opportunities that this segment presents to entertainment companies are immense. In North America, this type of music is especially popular in Canada. In one example, the International Jazz Festival in Montreal, attended by hundreds of thousands yearly, is in fact a world beat event, featuring contemporary world music artists such as Keith Jarrett, Anouar Brahem, Tord Gustavsen, Nik Bärtsch's Ronin, and Stefano Bollani.[7]

Stability over Time

In the past, stability of a segment over time was a primary consideration mainly for developed countries. Today, however, stability over time is an important consideration in a world environment where products are in different life-cycle stages and where preferences are continually changing with an increase in Internet use and online ordering across borders from countries of all development levels. In a rapidly changing environment, it is important to constantly reevaluate this segment.

Accessibility

The ability to communicate with the target market, determining the market's accessibility, is essential as well. Internationally, the differences in language in individual countries may pose obstacles, greatly increasing the cost of advertising and other promotions. Marketing in large emerging markets, such as India and China, could present challenges for different reasons: Communicating with Indian consumers outside of the large metropolitan areas necessitates expensive translation into the many local languages. Similarly, communicating with Chinese consumers in the countryside may be difficult because the large rural population has a more limited access to technology. The ability to serve the market is also essential. Companies should be able to freely access the market; the market must be open to international companies and reachable (i.e., topography, local governments, and local media should permit access to the target market.

sreetflash/shutterstock.com

Actionability

Actionability refers to the idea that the market should respond to the marketing strategies used, assuming that the company is targeting the market with the appropriate marketing mix. Consider, for example, the Colgate-Palmolive strategy for Latin America and the Balkans. In both markets, the company noted that its dishwashing liquid was not selling well. Research revealed, for this large market segment, a different approach to washing dishes — using soap slivers in a tub. As soon as the company developed a tub with dishwashing paste and promoted the product to the market, sales took off. The segment responded as intended to the strategy: The segment was actionable.

Differential Response

The segments should be easy to distinguish from each other and should respond differently from other market segments to marketing strategies; they should have a noticeable differential response. If consumers all over the world had similar or identical preferences — and this is hardly the case — there would be no need for international target marketing.

7-3b Macro-segmentation: Country Attractiveness Analysis

Companies have different criteria that they consider essential for committing to a particular market. PepsiCo International did not consider profit as the main criterion when it approached the former Soviet Union to establish a countertrade agreement; rather, market size and the ultimate potential of the market were the company's primary concerns. As a first step in the segmentation process, companies engage in macro-segmentation, grouping countries based on such criteria as economic performance, evaluating the potential of a particular market; political, legal, and financial environment; marketing support infrastructure;

the company brand's standing or potential standing relative to existing competition; and the degree of market fit with company resources, policies, and goals. These criteria, in turn, are used in the screening process to select and target the countries that present the highest potential to the company.

Firms could use the following criteria to group countries and, based on these criteria, select those countries that offer the most opportunity for the company and those countries that should be targeted:

- Market potential
- The political, legal, and financial environment of the country
- The marketing support infrastructure in the country
- Brand/company franchise relative to competing products/companies
- Degree of market fit with company policies, goals, and resources

Market Potential

Countries can be grouped based on market potential. The potential of a market can be evaluated based on the rate of economic development, as expressed through validated, reliable market indicators, such as:

- Gross domestic product (GDP) per capita
- Industrial and agricultural sectors statistics
- Market size and potential
- Consumer buying power
- International investment figures, such as foreign direct investment data and other trade statistics

Such indicators identify countries and markets where the company should invest important resources and engage in long-term commitment. Attractive big emerging markets, such as Brazil or China, have initially presented many challenges to international companies. Brazil in the 1970s and 1980s was plagued by runaway inflation and instability, whereas China was an unpredictable market closed to international scrutiny and influence.

With time, both countries have opened their markets to international investment, which has led to rapid economic development and market growth. With a population of more than 211 million, of which almost half are younger than 25 years old, and the 7th largest GDP in the world.[8]

Similar potential is now presented by the countries of the former Soviet Union. These countries, despite being plagued by inflation and instability, all have a literate, educated work-force and excess of highly qualified labor on one hand and a consuming public that is eager to experience new products on the other. Among attractive markets of the former Soviet Union are the Baltic states (Estonia, Latvia, and Lithuania), Russia, and Belarus, all actively targeted by multinationals; Estonia adopted the euro in 2011 and, since then, business is booming with cross-border shoppers. See Figure 7-3 (next page).

Of great potential are the Asian former Soviet republics, Armenia, Georgia, Azerbaijan, Kazakhstan, the Kyrgyz Republic, and Uzbekistan. Kazakhstan, and the Kyrgyz Republic are rapidly developing their banking systems and have adopted pro-market structural reforms, attracting substantial foreign direct investment.

Figure 7-3: Cross-border shoppers are abundant in Estonia. Full ships go back daily from Tallinn to Helsinki, carrying Finnish consumers loaded with primarily alcoholic drinks, taking advantage of lower prices in Estonia – and of the ability to pay in euros.

Latin America also offers competitive markets for international trade and investment. Chile is the most competitive market in Latin America, ahead of many European countries. Panama, Colombia, and Peru are all also recognized as attractive and growing international markets.[9]

The Political, Legal, and Financial Environment of the Country

Countries also can be grouped based on their political, legal, and financial environment. Some of the following criteria should be considered when evaluating a potential country for entry:

• Ethnic conflict in the region

• History of war engagement

• Populist anti-business governments and policies. Antiforeigner rhetoric.

• Recent nationalization activity

• Legal ambiguity—especially in business including non-recognition of contract law.

• Tariff and other trade barriers erected by government to protect local business

• Exchange rate controls

• Financial management of the country. Payments of international debts.

Companies are not likely to succeed in markets where there is high political risk. Sri Lanka, a small country located southeast of the Indian subcontinent, is no longer even a viable export market. Tensions between the Sinhalese majority and the Tamil minority have escalated out of control, with Tamil separatists targeting Sri Lanka's airport. Over two decades, the conflict has practically demolished the country economically, driving the once-booming tourism industry out of Sri Lanka.

Even oil-rich countries could present a risk for companies considering entering these markets. Sudan, for example, discovered substantial oil reserves. However, its initially modest exports have only further fueled an ethnic civil war that has been raging for more than two decades. As previously mentioned, Venezuela, one of the largest oil-producing countries in the world, has descended into political and economic chaos.

Ambiguities in the legal system create an environment that renders companies vulnerable to competitive theft, lack of intellectual property protection, bribery pressures, and employee theft. In such an environment, where everything is perceived as allowed unless expressly forbidden, even exporting could pose difficulties. For example, it could force firms to incur bribery costs, which in the case of a U.S. company could expose the firm to civil and criminal penalties under the U.S. Foreign Corrupt Practices Act. Unwary exporters who are not familiar with agent/distributor laws in international markets may discover they are liable for sizeable payments if an in-country agent or distributor is terminated. Finally, exchange rate controls could restrict the types of products that can be exported to the target market and impede the repatriation of profits.

One related issue is whether the country is a member of the World Trade Organization (WTO) or of a regional block, such as the European Union or the Southern Cone Common Market (MERCOSUR). Countries that adhere to regulations of the WTO and that have the supra-national controls of regional integration are more likely to have a stable environment that promotes trade and investment.

The Marketing Support Infrastructure in the Country

The marketing support infrastructure of the target country is an important determinant of country attractiveness. Important to international firms are the availability and reliability of distribution and logistics providers to ensure that the product is delivered in a timely fashion at locations convenient to consumers.

Countries also can be grouped based on the availability of competent partners for firms contemplating international partnerships. A firm entering a new market should have access to capable local firms. In many developing countries, only few such firms may be available, and all other competitors will attempt to approach them. For instance, for large multinationals attempting to enter the Turkish market, Sabanci Holdings is in great demand and already boasts joint-venture and distribution partners in companies as varied as Carrefour supermarkets, Danone dairy products, Dresdner Bank, DuPont, IBM, Mitsubishi, Philip Morris, and Toyota.

metamoreworks/shutterstock.com

The information technology available to members of the local distribution chain is an important consideration in that it maximizes supply chain efficiencies and minimizes ware-housing and logistics costs to the company. The level of local telecommunications development is also essential in ensuring adequate data flow and access to suppliers, clients, and company headquarters. Countries also should be evaluated on the availability of adequate local advertising support, such as local advertising talent and open access to media for advertising and other communication purposes. Finally, the availability of other service providers, such as marketing research firms, financial firms, and management consulting firms, is also essential for company performance in the market.

Brand/Company Franchise Relative to Competing Products/Companies

Markets where a brand or company name is already established with local consumers, either by reputation, through advertising, or experience (for consumers who have bought the product abroad or have heard of the company), offer greater potential to the company.

This situation is especially true if the company has only few viable direct competitors. Markets can thus be segmented based on the reputation of the product and company in the market and on the competitive density in the market for the company's products. Here, a related dimension is also useful: that of *lead country* (a country where products are first adopted) versus *lag country* (a country where products are last adopted). The lead/lag concept also is closely linked to the level of economic development and is particularly relevant to firms at the forefront of technology. Firms usually first introduce their products in lead countries.

Degree of Market Fit with Company Policies, Goals, and Resources

For companies that have the resources and the goal to saturate the world market, such as McDonald's and Coca-Cola, no market is too small. Other companies that have the resources but whose products cater only to the luxury market will most likely ignore countries with a limited number of elite consumers and focus on industrialized countries or countries with substantial revenues from national resources, such as oil and diamonds. Yet other companies have limited resources and can afford to target consumers in only one or a few countries. For these companies, it is essential to select those markets that are perceived as the most appropriate for their goals and that provide the lowest level of risk.

7-3c Micro-segmentation: Focusing on the Target Consumer

The purpose of micro-segmentation is to identify clusters of consumers that respond in a similar fashion to a company's marketing strategies. Identifying individual market segments enables the company to produce products that meet the precise needs of target consumers with a marketing mix that is appropriately tailored for those segments. The international company typically conducts extensive marketing research to identify such segments.

Bases for Segmentation

In the process of analyzing consumer demand and identifying clusters of consumers that respond similarly to marketing strategies, firms must identify bases for segmentation most relevant for its offerings. The bases for segmentation are described next.

Demographic and Psychographic Segmentation

Demographics are statistics that describe the population, such as age, gender, race, income, education, occupation, social class, life-cycle stage, and household size. Demographics are easy to measure and to compare across countries and are thus widely used. Consumers exhibit many differences with regard to demographic segmentation variables. The following examples demonstrate how these differences have important implications for marketing:

Age — Countries that have a rapidly aging population present different challenges and opportunities to international firms than countries with a young population (see International Marketing Illustration 7-2).

International Marketing Illustration 7-2 The Global Youth Consumer Segment

The global youth segment presents an important opportunity for U.S. corporations to leverage their investment. The global youth segment has a purchasing power of more than $100 billion; in the U.S., only 21 percent of the population is aged 14 or younger, but in many other countries, the youth market outnumbers that of the United States. In India, 35 percent of the population is younger than 14.

There are emerging similarities in the youth culture across the globe. Technology is a major focus of the youth market, and brands and styles preferred by young people around the world are surprisingly alike. The more exposure they have to common information, the more homogeneous young people appear to become. In South Korea, much like in the rest of Asia, imported luxury brands are all the rage. Youth in Asia aspire to have large apartments, expensive clothing, and to travel the world.[10]

Continued...

Global youth purchase Levi's and Diesel jeans, Nike shoes, and Ralph Lauren clothing. They see newly released movies, listen to popular musicians, and go to clubs. Marketers find this segment particularly attractive: Coca-Cola has successfully targeted global teenagers and preteens (see Figure 7-4) with messages that use local and international celebrities.

Coca-Cola recently targeted the youth segment with a global interactive marketing initiative called iCoke, aimed at connecting with youth through digital music and mobile and branded entertainment, offering promotions aimed at driving customers to the iCoke websites. It also partnered with mobile music company Shazam Entertainment for a joint ringtones and downloads promotion across 275 million Coke and Diet Coke cans.[11]

Figure 7-4 These representatives of the global youth segment listen to rap, and are increasingly fashion conscious.

Syda Productions/shutterstock.com

Urbanization and social class — Industrialized countries, such as the United States, Japan, and the countries of Western Europe, are primarily urban and have a large middle class with substantial buying power. (Interestingly, Latin America is the most urbanized region in the world.) China's rural consumers are poor and have limited buying power. Its urban consumers fall into four segments: "working poor" and "salaried class" — together accounting for 80 percent of the urban population; "the little rich," 15 percent of the urban population; and young urban professionals, or "yuppies," representing nearly five percent of the urban households.[12] Although multinationals such as Coca-Cola and Starbucks actively target middle-class consumers in the industrialized countries with their global brands, in China, they target their global brands primarily to yuppies; for the remaining 95 percent of the population, they have developed or acquired local brands in addition to their premium global brands.[13]

Education — Most developed countries, countries that were formerly communist, and countries that are under a communist rule (China, for example, where the literacy rate is close to 90 percent) have a high literacy rate and heavily emphasize education. In contrast, countries in sub-Saharan Africa have a lower literacy rate; here, education is a privilege. Companies that target low-literacy consumers have to adapt the marketing mix, describing product use pictorially in their communications. Countries where education is stressed present opportunities for educational institutions intending to expand globally, to firms selling training technology and software, and so on.

Demographics are related to psychographics, which include lifestyles, values, attitudes, interests, and opinions. Cultural variables such as religion, norms, and language also influence consumer product preferences. As such, these variables are as bases for segmentation. For example, Hofstede's dimensions, described in Chapter 5, "Cultural Influences on International Marketing," can be used to segment countries based on individualism, collectivism, masculinity, femininity, uncertainty/avoidance, and power/distance. A study found that Scandinavian consumers are more egalitarian, take more risks, are individualistic and rate low on competitiveness. They seek variety and prefer environmentally friendly products.[14]

Many management consulting firms have come up with systems for segmenting consumers, clustering them on different behavioral and psychological dimensions, or

psychographic segmentation. In the United States, a popular classification system is *ESRI's Tapestry*, which classifies individuals based on ZIP code. Another classification of lifestyles is provided by Strategic Business Insights, which offers the *VALS 2* psychographic consumer segmentation system (see screenshot below). Upon completing a questionnaire containing lifestyle and demographic questions, individual respondents are categorized based on resources and on the extent to which they are action oriented. VALS also has a survey that is especially designed for the Japanese market.

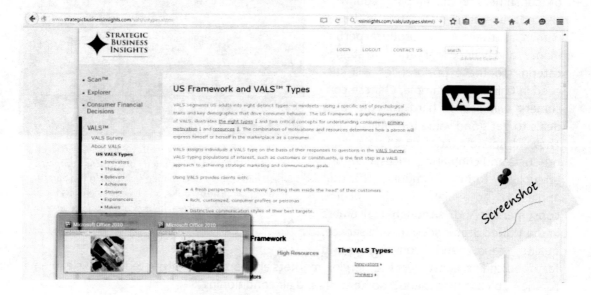

Global market segments present important opportunities for standardized marketing. Among the global psychodemographic (a combination of psychographic and demographic segments) segments that have emerged are the following:

Global youth segment—Psychographically, teenagers are described as astute consumers with precise desires for brand name clothing products and entertainment. They are described in International Marketing Illustration 7-2.

Global elite—The global elite have the highest income of all consumers. From a psychographic perspective, they travel the globe, often have homes in more than one country, and spend money on luxury brands, such as Rolex, Prada, and Mercedes (the E-Class models and beyond). The marketing mix typically used to target this group focuses on status: exclusive distribution, high price, and status-oriented advertising messages.

Global gay and lesbian segment—This psychographic segment has received much focus from marketing in recent years. The gay and lesbian segment has been identified as a loyal segment, purchasing brands that are positioned as gay-friendly. It has also been identified as a segment with a high percentage of disposable income — and with a willingness to spend it for travel, entertainment, and luxury items (see Figure 7-5 on next page).

Benefit Segmentation

Benefit segmentation also is a useful tool for identifying uniform consumer segments. Marketers who understand the motivation behind consumer purchases are able to send the appropriate message to the relevant market segments. Internationally, important differences exist between the benefits sought from purchasing a particular product. Consumers in the United States purchase soft drinks such as Coke and Pepsi to quench their thirst on a regular basis. In Eastern Europe, Southern Asia, and Africa, these brands are purchased primarily as special-occasion drinks.

In other examples, the majority of consumers in developing countries are not as much interested in brand names as they are in product performance and value. Marketing strategies catering to these preferences will succeed in China. For example, Chinese consumers will search hard for the best deals to get good value for their money. They will spend a lot of time researching products and comparing prices, and they are unlikely to buy on impulse. This trait applies to both high- and low-income consumers.[15] And, although consumers in the United States seek speedy service, quality food, and convenience in fast-food chains, consumers in emerging markets are particularly attracted to the clean environment, pleasant ambience, polite staff, and air conditioning.[16]

Figure 7-5 Christopher Street Day Parade: Gay-friendly brands in this parade included Ford Motor Company, which had its own automobile featured in the parade, Red Bull, Smirnoff Vodka, and Nivea, as well as local goods and services. Nivea, in its promotional giveaways (shampoo, hair gel, lotion), was positioning itself as "a man's thing."

Usage and User Status Segmentation

Usage rate indicates the extent to which individuals are:

- Nonusers
- Occasional users
- Medium users
- Heavy users

Consumers worldwide can be segmented based on these usage segmentation dimensions. Segments of consumers identified as heavy users of a product category would constitute prime target markets for new brands in the category. For example, French women are heavy users of perfume, have a refined understanding of scent, and use different brands (often of the same company) at different times of day and for different occasions. Similarly, German, Dutch, and Belgian consumers are heavy consumers of beer. In each country, hundreds of breweries carry specialty beers, and each country is also an exporter of global beer brands.

User status refers to the status as:

- Users of competitors' products (nonuser)
- Ex-users
- Potential users
- First-time users
- Regular users

cornfield/shutterstock.com

In terms of user status segmentation, the ideal consumer is the regular, heavy user. Companies introducing a product for the first time to a market of nonusers face enormous and costly challenges, in that they have to educate consumers about the product and convince them to buy, but these companies also can reap huge rewards, especially if they are first in the market. The paper towel offering in Europe was practically nonexistent before the introduction of the Procter & Gamble Bounty brand; consumers typically used cloth towels in the kitchen. Bounty introduced its quality, heavy-duty paper towels in the late 1990s, accompanied by heavy promotion, particularly direct mail samples. In the Netherlands, those samples consisted of just one towel, nicely folded, and mailed in a plastic bag. The brand quickly took off, and now many households have an accessory previously nonexistent in European households: a paper towel holder. It is, however, much smaller than its U.S. counterpart—about half the height, with the roll also half the width.

Geographic Segmentation

Geographic segmentation can be performed at the macro-segmentation level — country analysis, membership in international trade forums, regional blocks, and so on — as well as within the country. Consumers differ within countries with regard to demographics and psychographics, such as ethnicity, religion, and language spoken. Even in small countries such as Switzerland, the marketing mix needs to be adapted for German Swiss, French Swiss, and Italian Swiss consumers; they constitute segments that differ not only linguistically, but also with regard to other aspects of culture, and consequently are likely to respond differently to marketing strategies. Belgium also is a case in point: A Dutch-speaking Flemish culture thrives in the north; in the French-speaking south, people view themselves as Wallonians rather than Europeans or Belgians; and a small German-speaking community exists in the southeast.[18]

elenabsi/shutterstock.com

7-4 Targeting International Consumers

7-4a Target Market Decisions: Country Screening and Selection

· Companies engage in processes that involve extensive evaluation of countries' attractiveness for the purpose of market entry. In this evaluative process, a company must ensure that it does not overlook countries with potential and that it does not target markets in countries that do not provide sufficient potential or that present a high risk. To ensure that markets that present the most promise to the company — based on the company's goals and resources — are selected, countries are submitted to a screening process. Most often, screening of potential markets follows a variant of these three stages:

- Assigning an importance score to country screening criteria
- Evaluating country performance on each of the screening criteria
- Calculating the country attractiveness score

Assigning an Importance Score to Country Screening Criteria

An international company would typically aggregate a selection of criteria, discussed in Section 7-3b, "Macro-segmentation: Country Attractiveness Analysis," that the company deemed important. Among these criteria are market potential, determined using economic indicators; the degree of political and financial stability; the extent to which the legal system is transparent and predictable; the state of the marketing infrastructure in the country; the degree to which consumers have a preference for company brands; the extent of competitive intensity in the market; and the market fit with company goals, policies, and resources. The criteria deemed important are selected from suggestions by brand managers in different international markets, salespeople, industry country specialists working for management consulting firms, and international suppliers and distributors. Each criterion is then assigned an importance weight that denotes the extent to which the company considers a particular trait important in its decision to enter the market.

Evaluating Country Performance on Each of the Screening Criteria

In the second stage of country screening and selection, potential target countries are rated on each of the criteria enumerated. The rating process may involve the same evaluators as in the first stage.

Calculating the Country Attractiveness Score

In the third stage of country screening and selection, the importance score is multiplied by the performance score for each of the screening variables. The total score for each country is then calculated by adding the resulting scores. This is the country attractiveness score that can be used to compare potential target countries.

7-4b -Target Market Decisions: The Target Market Strategy

Companies that have ample resources can, and often do, address the needs of all segments of consumers. Procter & Gamble, Henkel, and Unilever attempt to target all consumers with the products they sell, filling the supermarket and discount store shelves with what seemingly are competing brands and saturating the media with their communication, meeting all related needs of the global consumer at a nice profit. Other companies with sufficient resources choose to focus on one well-established brand, improving it continually, offering alternatives under the same umbrella brand name. Boeing uses such a strategy and, to date, it has only one true direct competitor, Airbus Industries. Not all international companies have the resources of the companies mentioned here. Frequently, small and medium -sized businesses are quite successful internationally, as they are in the home-country market, by best addressing the needs of one segment, or a niche. One common trait of all these international companies is that they research closely their consumers and target and position their products accordingly.

Companies can use the three main strategies in Table 7-1 (next page) to target their intentional markets.

Table 7-1 International Targeting Strategies

Strategy	Purpose
Differentiated targeting strategy	Differentiated targeting strategies identify, or even create, market segments that want different benefits from a product and target them with different brands, using different marketing strategies.
Concentrated targeting strategy	Companies select only one market segment and target it with a single brand. Companies that cannot afford to compete in a mature market with an oligopoly may choose to pursue a small segment—a niche.
Undifferentiated targeting strategies	The product is aimed at all markets using a single strategy, regardless of the number of markets and countries targeted.

Differentiated Targeting Strategy

Companies that use a differentiated targeting strategy identify, or even create, market segments that want different benefits from a product and target them with different brands, using different marketing strategies. Some companies have the necessary resources to offer at least one product to every conceivable market segment. Procter & Gamble, for example, offers a variety of laundry detergents and fabric care products in North America: Bounce, Cheer, Downy, Dreft, Era, Febreze, Gain, Ivory, and Tide. To Western European consumers, the company offers Ace, Antikal Ariel, Bounce, Bonux, Dash, Daz, Dreft, Fairy, Febreze, Gama, Lenor, and Vizir.[18] Each of these laundry detergents appeals to a different market: consumers who want a detergent that has an excellent cleaning ability, consumers who need whitening, consumers who need fabric softening agents in the washing process, consumers who need a product for sensitive fabrics or for babies' sensitive skin, and consumers who may be allergic.

Of course, not all companies doing businesses internationally sell directly to consumers. Many companies, including a large number of U.S. exporters, target business customers. Here, too, targeted marketing strategies are employed. For example, Boeing Aircraft sells jet airliners around the world. The Boeing commercial aircraft product mix ranges from the smaller 737, aimed at smaller regional carriers or at leading global airlines for short-haul routes, to the 787 *Dreamliner*, or the 777 for long-haul routes.

Concentrated Targeting Strategy

Not all companies can afford to offer something for everyone, and not all companies want to meet the needs of all consumers. In fact, many companies select only one market, and segment and target it with one single brand, using a concentrated targeting strategy. Mont Blanc, originally a company manufacturing pens and fountain pens, used to offer a relatively limited product selection that it marketed using the same theme worldwide," the art of writing." This product is targeted at the professional class. From this concentrated targeting strategy, the company has engaged in some degree of diversification, and today it sells watches, perfumes, jewelry, leather goods and accessories, and eyewear.

There is a global market for industrial equipment, chemicals, and, as previously discussed, professional services. Major international law firms based in the United States and other countries would also employ a combination of targeted marketing strategies. Legal services would be typically marketed under the firm's name/brand. The firm would then target a small number of specialty market segments in which they have demonstrated expertise. These could include investment underwriting, regulatory compliance, mergers/acquisitions, etc.

Undifferentiated Targeting Strategies and Standardization

The existence of similar consumer needs worldwide presents opportunities for international firms. They can reap the benefits of standardization by achieving economies of scale in the manufacturing process and in distribution and promotion. Pure standardization can be described as an undifferentiated targeting strategy, in which the product is aimed at the market using a single strategy regardless of the number of countries targeted and regardless of the locations where it is marketed.

Yet even products that are created as pure global brands, such as Coke, are not marketed using a standardized, undifferentiated strategy. Coke is sold primarily in recyclable glass and plastic bottles requiring a high deposit in Africa and Europe, whereas, in the United States, it is sold in disposable cans and plastic bottles. Its taste differs depending on the market. Diet Coke is sold as Coca-Cola Light elsewhere in the world. Heineken, the Dutch beer that bills itself as the world's most international brewery, uses a global positioning strategy of premium pricing and high quality, whereas, in Holland, the beer is positioned as a product for the masses. It costs slightly more than a one-liter bottle of Coke. And in North America and Europe, Volkswagen's Passat has been offered under different brand names in the international market. Among these names are Santana, Dasher, Quantum, Mogotan, and Corsar. Santana has the highest name recognition of all the automobile brands in China and most taxicabs in Shanghai, for example, are Santana automobiles (see Figure 7-6).

Figure 7-6: Shanghai Volkswagen, a partnership between Shanghai Automotive and Volkswagen, sells the Santana automobile, the automobile that has the highest brand awareness among Chinese consumers.

7-5 Positioning the Brand

Positioning entails placing the brand in the consumer's mind in relation to other competing products, based on product traits and benefits that are relevant to the consumer. Such a process entails identifying the international and local competitors, determining how the competitors are perceived and evaluated by local consumers, determining the competitors' positions in the consumers' mind, analyzing the customers, selecting the position, and monitoring it.[19]

Brands are positioned using a theme— a unique selling proposition. This theme could be unique to each market, for companies that customize their offering to local markets, or uniform, throughout the world. A third approach also is common: a uniform positioning strategy that still allows local management freedom for adaptation, if necessary. Coca-Cola, for example, formulates its worldwide positioning at its Atlanta headquarters but enables its affiliates in different markets to alter the strategy as needed.

Bloomicon/shutterstock.com

The six international positioning strategies are illustrated in Sections 7-5a through 7-5f.[20]

7-5a Attribute/Benefit Positioning

Procter & Gamble focuses on product attributes and benefits to position its products. An attribute/benefit positioning strategy uses product or service attributes and benefits to position it in the consumers' mind relative to competitors' products and services. The following are examples of product positioning by the company:[21]

- Cheer, in powder or liquid, with or without bleach, is positioned as protecting against fading, color transfer, and fabric wear.

- Dreft is positioned as a detergent that removes tough baby stains and protects garment colors.

- Gain, as a liquid and powder detergent, is positioned as having exceptional cleaning and whitening.

- Procter & Gamble's premium product worldwide, Tide, in powder or liquid, with or without bleach, is positioned as a laundry detergent with exceptional cleaning, whitening, and stain removal.

Such precise positioning, which is reflected in the company's communication with its respective segments, clearly differentiates each brand from the other company brands and from those of competitors such as Unilever and Colgate-Palmolive.

7-5b Price/Quality Positioning

Products and services can be positioned as offering the best value for the money. The price/quality positioning strategy is especially useful for companies marketing in developing countries. Manufacturers such as Toyota, Daewoo, and Philips and retailers such as Walmart and Sears emphasize the value aspect of their offerings.

Alternatively, products and services can be positioned at the other end of the price/ quality continuum as the best product that money can buy. In addition to stressing high price and high quality, such positioning also entails an exclusive distribution or access, an expert sales force and service, and advertising in publications aimed at the global elite. Mercedes-Benz claims that, in a perfect world, everyone would drive a Mercedes. Kempinski Hotels and Resorts, an upscale German chain, "reflects the finest traditions of European hospitality, luxurious accommodation, superb cuisine and unrivalled facilities— complemented by impeccable service."[22]

7-5c Use or Applications Positioning

Uses or applications are often used to position products in the use positioning or applications positioning strategies, respectively. Procter & Gamble's Era is positioned as a high-technology detergent that pretreats and washes fabrics to suspend dirt. This precise application differentiates it in the consumers' minds from other laundry detergents that have a more general use.

Sometimes the uses or applications differ from one market to another: A bicycle manufacturer would most likely position its offerings in Asia and Europe as efficient transportation machines, whereas, in the United States, it would position them as high-performance recreation instruments.

lentamart/shutterstock.com

7-5d Product User Positioning

The product user positioning strategy focuses on the product user, rather than on the product. The marketing mix for the Mont Blanc pen is targeted at the business executive anywhere in the world. The pen is usually pictured along with a quality business letterhead, with a passport, and with an attaché case. In this case, the product is understood to be among the highest quality pens around, so it receives only associative emphasis.

7-5e Product Class Positioning

Disney sells magic, not just entertainment. Harley-Davidson sells excitement, not just motorcycles. And Parliament sells a glamorous, romantic America all over the world, not just cigarettes. Products using a product class positioning strategy differentiate themselves as leaders in a product category, as they define it.

7-5f Competitor Positioning

When a firm compares its brand with those of competitors, it uses a competitor positioning strategy. Some comparisons are direct, if the local legal environment allows it. Others are somewhat subtle. The Airbus 330neo claims to use 14 percent less fuel per seat, compared to its older 330 version – thus competing with Boeing's 787 Dreamliner, touted until 2018 as the most fuel-efficient plane on the market.

All positioning, ultimately, is relative to competition, only not always explicitly so. Even symbols hint at competition: Merrill Lynch is bullish on the market (it is embodied by the bull); all other competitors are probably wimps. Quick, a local competitor of McDonald's in France, advertises cheaper prices: Its restaurants are quick and they are cheaper than McDonald's — and they are right across the street.

Summary

Develop a general understanding of international marketing strategy at the different levels of the international organization and provide some insights into the international marketing planning process of selected companies. Planning takes place at different levels. At the corporate level, the strategic plan allocates resources and establishes objectives for the whole enterprise worldwide. At the division level, the strategic plan allocates funds to each business unit based on division goals and objectives, whereas, at the business unit level, within each country, decisions are made on selecting target consumer segments. At the product level (line, brand), a marketing plan is developed for achieving objectives. An important decision is which product mix to use in the different countries where the company is present.

Identify the rationale for adopting a target marketing strategy in international markets. International target marketing is used to identify countries and segments of international consumers that are similar with regard to key traits, who would respond to a particular marketing mix (i.e., segmenting the market); to select the countries and segments that the company can serve most efficiently and develop products tailored to each (i.e., targeting the market); and to offer the products to the market, communicating, through the marketing mix (i.e., positioning), product traits and benefits that differentiate it in the consumers' minds.

Identify the requirements necessary for effective international market segmentation. For segmentation to be effective, segments must be easy to measure, stable over time, accessible, actionable, and respond differentially from other segments to a company's marketing strategy.

Introduce the concept of country attractiveness analysis and offer a blueprint for conducting the analysis. Country attractiveness can be assessed by measuring market potential using indicators such as GDP per capita, industrial and agricultural sectors statistics, market size, and consumer buying power. It also can be assessed by evaluating international investment figures, such as foreign direct investment data and other trade statistics; the political, legal, and financial environment in the country; the existing marketing support infrastructure; the existing brand and/or company franchise for the product and/or company, and for competitors' products and/or companies; and the degree of market fit with company policies, objectives, and resources.

Identify the bases for consumer segmentation and offer company application examples. Consumers are segmented on demographics, psychographics, geography, usage and user status, and benefits sought from purchasing the product or service. International firms segment based on the criteria that are most appropriate for their product or service. The job of the international marketing manager is facilitated by the emergence of homogeneous demographic segments worldwide, such as global teenagers and the global elite.

Describe the three targeting strategies used by companies worldwide. These strategies are differentiated marketing, whereby companies address the needs of different segments by offering them different brands and using different marketing mix strategies; concentrated marketing, whereby companies address a single consumer segment that is large and stable enough to warrant the investment; and undifferentiated marketing, whereby a company can reap the benefits of standardization by using the same strategy to market to consumers worldwide.

Describe the six positioning strategies that international companies can use to position their brands in the minds of target consumers. International companies can position products by focusing on product attributes or benefits; by positioning the brand as a high-price/high-quality product or as the best value for the money; by positioning the brand based on use or applications; by positioning the brand based on product users; or by positioning it as the best product in its class.

Terms

accessibility	geographic segmentation	segmentation
actionability	global elite	stability over time
applications positioning	global youth segment	substantiality
attribute/benefit positioning	Lag country	target market
benefit segmentation	lead country	target marketing
competitor positioning	measurability	undifferentiated targeting
concentrated targeting	price/quality positioning	usage segmentation
demographic segmentation	product class positioning	use positioning
differential response	product user positioning	user status segmentation
differentiated targeting	psychographic segmentation	

Discussion Questions

1. International planning involves planning activities at different levels of an organization. Describe the planning processes that take place at each level of an international company.

2. International marketing managers use a number of criteria to ensure that segments are useful. Describe the effective types of segmentation and offer examples for each.

3. Macro-segmentation refers to country-level segmentation, and micro-segmentation refers to consumer-level segmentation. What bases and strategies do marketing managers use for segmenting their international markets using macro- and micro-segmentation?

4. Describe the principal targeting strategies. Go to the Mercedes-Benz USA home page (**www.mbusa.com**). What targeting strategy does the company use? Explain.

5. Go to the VALS 2 webpage (**www.strategicbusinessinsights.com/vals/ustypes.shtml**) and read the description of each population segment. What segments would you ascribe to Mercedes users based on VALS 2?

6. What are the six positioning strategies? What strategies does Mercedes-Benz USA use for its U.S. market? Does Mercedes use different strategies for its international market? (Go to the other English-language Mercedes sites to answer this question.)

Chapter Quiz

1. International positioning involves identifying countries and consumers that are similar with regard to key traits and would respond well to a product and related marketing mix.

False

Rationale: International segmentation involves identifying countries and consumers that are similar with regard to key traits and would respond well to a product and related marketing mix. Positioning entails placing the brand in the consumer's mind in relation to other competing products, based on product traits and benefits that are relevant to the consumer. Sections 7-3, "International Market Segmentation," and 7-4, "Targeting International Consumers"

2. Measurability refers to the requirement that the segment should be large enough to warrant investment.

False

Rationale: Substantiality refers to the requirement that the segment should be large enough to warrant investment. Measurability refers to the ability to measure the size of the segment. Section 7-3a, "Requirements for International Segmentation"

3. Actionability refers to the ability to communicate with the international target market.

False

Rationale: Accessibility refers to the ability to communicate with the market and to serve the respective market. Section 7-3a, "Requirements for International Segmentation"

4. Macro-segmentation involves grouping countries together based on their political, legal, and financial environments.

True

Rationale: Macro-segmentation involves grouping countries based on such criteria as economic performance, evaluating the potential of a particular market; on their political, legal, and financial environment; on their marketing support infrastructure; on the company brand's standing or potential standing relative to existing competition; and on the degree of market fit with company resources, policies, and goals, among others. Section 7-3b, "Macro-Segmentation: Country Attractiveness Analysis"

5. Identifying markets based on age and gender is an example of demographic segmentation.

True

Rationale: Demographics are defined as statistics that describe the population; gender and age statistics are examples of demographic variables. Section 7-3c, "Micro-segmentation: Focusing on the Target Consumer"

1. Target marketing involves:

a. market segmentation.
b. market targeting.
c. market positioning.
d. all of the above

Answer d is correct.

Rationale: International target marketing identifies countries and consumer segments similar with regard to key traits that would respond well to a product and related marketing mix (international market segmentation); selects the countries and segments that the company can serve most efficiently and develops products tailored to each (international market targeting); and offers the products to the market, communicating, through the marketing mix, differentiating product traits and benefits (market positioning). Section 7-2, "The Rationale for Target Marketing"

2. Which segmentation requirement refers to the ability to communicate with the international target market?
a. actionability
b. substantiality
c. accessibility
d. measurability

Answer c is correct.

Rationale: Accessibility refers to the ability to communicate with the market and to serve the respective market. Section 7-3a, "Requirements for International Segmentation"

3. Proctor & Gamble offers a variety of laundry detergent brands to European consumers, which appeal to different market segments. This is a good example of
a. undifferentiated targeting.
b. concentrated targeting.
c. differentiated targeting.
d. none of the above

Answer c is correct.

Rationale: Differentiated targeting refers to identifying, or even creating, market segments that want different benefits from a product and targeting them with different brands, using different marketing strategies.
Section 7-4b, "Target Market Decisions: The Target Market Strategy"

4. Which type of positioning focuses on offering the best value for the money?
a. applications
b. price/quality
c. product class
d. attribute/benefit

Answer b is correct.

Rationale: Companies using price/quality positioning present the products and services as offering the best value for the money. This strategy is especially useful when marketing to consumers in developing countries. Section 7-5b, "Price/Quality Positioning"

Notes

1. Santanu Choudhury, "General Motors to Build New Models in India, Some for Export," *The Wall Street Journal*, July 29, 2015, accessed at http://www.wsj.com/articles/gm-to-introduce-10-new-vehicles-in-india-1438178105 on August 16, 2015.

1. Murali Gopalan, "Why GM Never Found the Spark on India Beat," *The Hindu Business Line*, May 18, 2017, accessed at https://www.thehindubusinessline.com/companies/why-gm-never-found-the-spark-on-india-beat/article9707019.ece on June 10, 2018.

2. www.pepsico.com, www.pepsico.fr, www.pepsico.de, www.pepsico.com.tr,www.pepsico.com.br, www.pepsico.com.mx, all accessed on August 20, 2015.

3. Robert Klara, "Why Celebrities Want to Be in PepsiCo's Ads," *Adweek*, June 8, 2015, accessed at http://www.adweek.com/news/advertising-branding/why-celebrities-want-be-pepsicos-ads-165217 on August 17,2015; "Brandfame: Pepsi," *Marketing*, September 2005, p. 38.

4. www.kraft.com, accessed on August 17, 2015.

5. Natalie Soroka, "Small and Medium-Sized Enterprises Reaching New Markets," *U.S. Dept. of Commerce Newsletter*, December 19, 2017, accessed at https://www.commerce.gov/news/blog/2017/05/small-and-medium-sized-enterprises-reaching-new-markets on May 30, 2018. "Service Exports – High Growth," *U.S. Department of Commerce Newsletter*, October 20, 2016, accessed at https://www.export.gov/article?id=Service-Exports-with-High-Growth-Potential on May 30, 2018.

6.www.montrealjazzfest.com/questions-en/default.aspx, accessed on August 17,2015; www.montrealjazzfest.com /Fijm2007/splash.aspx, accessed on September 1,2007.

8."Brazil GDP-Gross Domestic Product 2017," *CountryEconomy.com*, accessed at https://countryeconomy.com/gdp/brazil on May 30, 2018.

9."Global Competitiveness Index 2017-2018," *World Economic Forum*, accessed at http://reports.weforum.org/global-competitiveness-index-2017-2018/competitiveness-rankings/, on May 30, 2018.

10. Agnieszka Kacprzak and Katarzyna Dziewanowska, "Does a Global Young Consumer Exist?" *Journal of Marketing and Consumer Behaviour in Emerging Markets*, Vol. 1, No. 1, 2015, pp. 47-61; Tim Stock and Marie Lena Tupot,"Common Denominators: What Unites Global Youth?" *Young Consumers*, Vol. 7, No. 2, 2006, pp. 36-43.

11. "Coca-Cola Prepares iCoke for Global Youth Marketing Drive," *New Media Age*, May 19, 2005, p.1.

12. Geng Cui and Qiming Liu, "Executive Insights: Emerging Market Segments in a Transitional Economy: A Study of Urban Consumers in China," *Journal of International Marketing*, Vol. 9, No. 1, Spring 2001, pp. 84–106.

13. Ibid.

14. Sudhir H. Kale, "Grouping Euroconsumers: A Culture-Based Clustering Approach," *Journal of International Marketing*, Vol. 3, No. 3, 1995, pp. 35–38.

15. Helen Wang, "Five New Trends of Chinese Consumers," *Forbes*, Dec. 17, 2012, accessed at http://www.forbes.com/sites/helenwang/2012/12/17/five-new-trends-of-chinese-consumers on August 18, 2015.

16. Geng Cui and Qiming Liu, "Executive Insights: Emerging Market Segments in a Transitional Economy: A Study of Urban Consumers in China," *Journal of International Marketing*, Vol. 9, No. 1, Spring 2001, pp. 84–106.

17. Art Weinstein, "A Primer for Global Marketers," *Marketing News*, Vol. 28, No. 13, June 20, 1994, p. 4.

18. www.pg.com

19. Adapted from David A. Aaker and Gary J. Shansby, "Positioning Your Product," *Business Horizons*, Vol. 25, No. 3, May/June 1982, pp. 56–62.

20. See Aaker and Shansby, "Positioning Your Product," pp. 56–62.

21. www.pg.com, accessed on June 10, 2018.

22. www.kempinski.com

Case 7-1 **Prosperity Painting Equipment**

James Vreeland is an international marketing manager with Prosperity Painting Equipment in Kunming, in the Yunnan Province in southwestern China. He was previously a manager for Baker Equipment, an equipment manufacturer on the East Coast of the United States, a former Peace Corps volunteer in Nepal, and an MBA graduate, with a marketing concentration, of the College of William and Mary in Virginia. He recently married a Chinese woman from Kunming and decided to settle there.

Prosperity Painting Equipment is a supplier of painting equipment for three small automobile manufacturing firms — three out of many in China's booming automobile industry — and is a medium-sized firm with reasonable potential for growth in a rapidly expanding market. Prosperity Painting Equipment's competitors are medium-sized and large state-owned enterprises, as well as smaller private firms. The firm's director, Zhang Chen, hired Vreeland for his excellent English and his polished presence, and to date, his primary task was to learn about China's automobile industry. Zhang Chen had important decisions to make regarding the future growth of the company and Vreeland was going to play an important part in his plan.

The Chinese Automobile Market

In 2017 China produced approximately 28 million vehicles (cars, trucks, and buses). Although percentage growth in 2017 was somewhat smaller as the industry entered a more mature phase, Chinese production grew in fourteen years from 2 million vehicles per year to 28 million. The revenue for the automobile manufacturing industry in China was over $600 billion, increasing at an annual rate of 10 percent since 2010. This growth is driven by rising domestic demand across urban and rural areas and increasing exports. For many automobile brands – especially luxury brands – China has been the highest growing market in recent years. For example, in 2017, BMW, with sales of almost 600,000 vehicles, is the top selling luxury brand in China.

xieyuliang/shutterstock.com

In all categories other than the luxury market, however, Chinese-made automobiles are ahead of competition. This is attributed to price, especially in the large-vehicle segment, where, for the price of one foreign heavy truck, one can purchase three Chinese ones. Automobile buyers are pickier, but a cheap automobile appeals to many Chinese consumers.

In 2017, the best-selling car in China (about 650,000 sold) was the Wuling Hongguang, a seven-seat SUV. Wuling is a joint venture with General Motors China, Shanghai Automotive Industry Corp, and Linzhou Wuling Motors Co., Ltd. The GM joint venture was formed in 2002, and is situated about 1,200 miles west of Shanghai. Many of the other Wuling brands are tiny, with the best-selling Sunshine van at a third the size of GM's Chevrolet Tahoe SUV. The starting price of a Wuling Sunshine van with a one-liter engine is $3,700, about the same price of a low-end Chevy Spark. Wuling's sales were over three million in 2015. Wuling's target customers earn $200 to $600 a month, do not own a car, and travel on bicycles, scooters, or motorized three-wheel vehicles. Wuling's automobiles — the Sunshine, and the more upscale Hongtu — are not designed for mature markets, such as the United States; the engine and wheels are small, and air bags are optional. At the Wuling factory, workers do the jobs that are performed by robots at Western GM plants, taking advantage of low wages. Wuling is a model closely studied by GM operations in other locations, such as India.

In other examples, the Changan Automobile Group Co. is an important newcomer to the automobile industry, with BenBen, a microvan that has been on the market since 2007. BenBen quickly became the number two seller in China's booming microvan segment.. Its target market is Chinese farmers and small business owners in smaller provincial towns. Shanghai Automotive, in turn, acquired design rights for U.K.'s Rover and is planning to offer an automobile with a higher sticker price, positioned upmarket. By 2018, Changan was one of the "Big Four" Chinese automobile manufacturing companies, along with SAIC, Dongfeng, and FAW. These companies have joint ventures and other manufacturing agreements with major international automobile manufacturers such as Ford, General Motors, Mazda, and so on.

For Chinese consumers, automobile brands with the highest brand recognition are Santana, Red Flag, Mercedes, Beijing Jeep, Shanghai VW, BMW, Honda, Volkswagen, Toyota, and Buick, according to the Gallup Research Co. LTD. Today, these brands include many more local makes, including the Chery.

Chinese Automobile Exports

Vreeland reviewed the state of Chinese automobile exports: Chinese automobile manufacturers exported 891,000 personal and commercial vehicles in 2017, up almost 26 per cent from 2016. However, the export market had been flat for years, as the market was coming out of a recession. In 2014, China exported 530,000 vehicles. Chinese automotive exports were bound primarily for developing countries in the Middle East, Russia, and Southeast Asia.

Earlier predictions of Europe and the United States being flooded with cheap and popular Chinese cars may be premature, as Chinese manufacturers must first build cars that meet European and U.S. safety and environmental standards, and, equally important, consumers' standards for quality. Jiangling Motors' Landwind, a copy of Opel's Frontera, spectacularly failed European crash tests. International joint ventures in China, with the exception of Honda, have little interest in selling automobiles outside of China, because they would face political and economic disadvantages. Instead, they are focusing on tapping the growing Chinese market. However, in 2018, GAC, a Chinese-government controlled automobile manufacturer announced plans to introduce a new SUV in the U.S. market in 2019. But, even if only few of China's automobiles are available in the West (Chrysler has signed a letter of intent with Chery to build a small car in China for Chrysler to sell in North America), they are likely to heighten competition for U.S. automobile manufacturers worldwide. In the face of growing political pressure in the U.S. and Europe to address China's large trade surplus, this may spell trouble for Chinese exports in general in the future.

The Task

Zhang Chen set up a meeting with James Vreeland. They started their conversation casually exploring Vreeland's take on the Chinese automobile industry. Zhang Chen informed him that the supplier of painting equipment for the SAIC GM Wuling Automobile Co., the GM joint venture, has just been contracted to supply General Motors' operations worldwide. Zhang Chen would like Prosperity Painting Equipment to enter into a similar relationship, supplying the worldwide operations of a large automobile manufacturer with painting equipment.

James Vreeland's task is to create a presentation for the company's investing partners that will segment the automobile market in China based on dimensions such as degree of focus on the Chinese market, joint-venture partnership, export orientation, and brand recognition. Then, Vreeland is to present a targeting strategy that is appropriate for his firm. The strategy proposed must convince investors to provide the necessary funding for Prosperity Painting Equipment's growth.

Sources: Statista, "Statistics and Facts About the Number of Automobile Import and Export Industry in China," accessed at http://www.statista.com/topics/1013/car-imports-and-exports-in-china/ on December 30, 2015. Ibis World, http://www.ibisworld.com/industry/china/automobile-manufacturing.html http://media.gm.com/media/us/en/gm/ news.detail.html/content/Pages/news/cn/en/2014/Dec/1203_sales.html.Jack Perkowski, "What's in Store for China's Auto Industry This Year? 2017 Provided Some Clues," Forbes, February 2, 2018, accessed at https://www.forbes.com/sites/jackperkowski/2018/02/07/china-autos-a-2017-wrap-up-and-2018-preview/#37731e8d3bce on June 1, 2018. "BMW Poised to Become China's No. 1 Luxury Brand," Automotive News China, December 15, 2017, accessed at http://europe.autonews.com/article/20171215/ANE/171219809/bmw-poised-to-become-chinas-no.-1-luxury-brand on June 2, 2018 Sami Haj-Assaad, "Top Ten Best-Selling Cars in China," Auto Guide.com, March 3, 2017, accessed at http://www.autoguide.com/auto-news/2017/03/top-10-best-selling-cars-in-china.html on June 2, 2018. "Changan Automobile," Wikipedia, accessed at https://en.wikipedia.org/wiki/Changan_Automobile on June 2, 2018. "China's Auto Export Up 25.8% Year On Year In 2017, China Automotive News, January 24, 2018 accessed at http://autonews.gasgoo.com/china_news/70013287.html on June 3, 2018. Russ Mitchell, " China Wants to Enter the US Car Market, but a Rough Ride Lies Ahead," Los Angeles Times, February 5, 2018, accessed at http://www.latimes.com/business/autos/la-fi-hy-china-auto-export-20180205-story.html on June 3, 2018.

Analysis Suggestions:

1. Provide a competitive analysis for Prosperity Painting Equipment.

2. What are the bases for segmentation appropriate for Prosperity Painting Equipment's industry? Refer to the automobile industry in your analysis.

3. Identify the different automobile-manufacturing segments based on the degree of focus on the Chinese market, joint-venture partnership, and export orientation.

4. Present a targeting strategy that is appropriate for Prosperity Painting Equipment.

Case 7-2 Volkswagen Phideon in China

Volkswagen's new Phideon, announced in 2018, with plans for release in China, will compete with its sister brand, Audi, a luxury brand. The Phideon is less flashy, launched in response Chinese President Xi Jinping's call to cut down on extravagant lifestyles and the purchasing of products that display one's wealth.

Audi is one of the most successful premium car manufacturers in the market. Audis are flashy, sporty, and sophisticated. Consumers buy Audi because it is a reliable brand, one that gives a good first impression to others, and is a symbol of status. The Audi A6, specifically, highlights these characteristics. This luxury car portrays status, "from the widened single frame, to the side air intakes with the sporty chrome trims, to the narrow headlights," and it "gives a great impression at first sight...the exterior mirrors have a sporty location by the armrest," ("Der Audi A6", 2018). Audi strives to continually market the sports car look of its automobiles and offer a sophisticated first impression.

Another one of the company's main concerns is driver safety. It highlights all the ways that the company takes customer safety seriously, in order to create a sense of trust and reliability. Additionally, the driver assistant aspect in Volkswagen cars is meant to create a more comfortable and enjoyable driving experience for consumers. The company also places a strong emphasis on digitalization as one of the company's main goals for the future. Consumers want to connect all aspects of their lives, including their cars, with advanced technology. Audi believes that it can create a more comfortable and efficient experience for its customers.

The Volkswagen Group, the parent company, stresses comfort and sustainability, rather than luxury and status with its cars. After facing a scandal in 2015, with engines emitting nitrogen oxide pollutants, the company has been working on creating an image of sustainability and concern for consumer health and safety in order to regain the market trust.

In order to rebuild its reputation, Volkswagen has to prove to consumers that it is working towards innovative cars, ones that are environmentally friendly. The Phideon is one of Volkswagen's concept cars, which means that the company believes it is at the center of innovation, with much future potential. This car has a hybrid, plug-in system, which can be charged both while driving or when the car is parked. It is a very wide vehicle, with substantial interior space, so it is classified as a saloon. Furthermore, there are low-profile windows, which allows the car to portray exclusivity and privacy. This is a high-quality automobile, but rather than being flashy, it offers a sense of comfort and presents confidence. With its hybrid technology, this car is innovative and progressive.

xujun/shutterstock.com

Rather than launching this car internationally, Volkswagen will only sell it in China, the world's leading market for automobiles. The Phideon's features and structure hold great appeal to China and its consumers. The Chinese government is a strong proponent of hybrid and electric cars: "...propelled by vast amounts of government money and visions of dominating next-generation technologies, China has become the world's biggest supporter of electric cars," (Bradsher, 2107). Sustainable cars are at the center of the automobile industry in China as 300,000 of these automobiles are expected to be sold this year, which is, "three times the number expected to be sold in the United States and more than the rest of the world combined," (Bradsher, 2107). Thus, the Phideon is ideal for the Chinese market, as it has an innovative hybrid system and will be manufactured by Volkswagen, which emphasizes electric cars as a focal point of the company.

Instead of opting for flashy sports cars that will indulge an extravagant lifestyle, Chinese consumers prefer comfortable, luxuriously modest automobiles that do not display their wealth. The Phideon saloon style gives customers the large interior space they are seeking and allows people the option of using a chauffeur. While the Audi A6 and the Phideon are very similar in style, Volkswagen is able to launch the Phideon without risking cannibalization because of the cars' different market segments. The Audi A6 targets a market that advertises its wealth with flashy products and sports cars, while the Phideon will appeal to consumers that are searching for high quality without advertising wealth.

Sources: "Audi at a glance." (2018), accessed at https://www.audi.com/corporate/en/company/audi-at-a-glance.html on June 16, 2018. Bradsher, K. (2017), "China hastens the world toward an electric-car future," *New York Times*, accessed at https://www.nytimes.com/2017/10/09/business/china-hastens-the-world-toward-an-electric-car-future.html on June 8, 2018. Bradsher, K. (2018). China is opening its car market. But not enough, say auto companies. *New York Times*. Retrieved from https://www.nytimes.com/2018/04/25/business/china-auto-trade.html. Corporate strategy (2018), accessed at https://www.audi.com/corporate/en/company/corporate-strategy.html on June 16, 2018. K. Culmer (2017), "The bewildering saloon range of Volkswagen China explained," *Autocar*, accessed at https://www.autocar.co.uk/opinion/industry/bewildering-saloon-range-volkswagen-china-explained. Der Audi A6. (2018, June 06). Retrieved June 09, 2018, from https://www.audi.com/en/models/a6.html. Hotton, R. (2015). Volkswagen: the scandal explained. *BBC*. Retrieved from https://www.bbc.com/news/business-34324772. Spring, J. (2016). VW challenges sister brand Audi with new China-only model. *Reuters*. Retrieved from https://de.reuters.com/article/volkswagen-china/vw-challenges-sister-brand-audi-with-new-china-only-model-idUKL4N1CN22U. Volkswagen Phideon. (n.d.). Retrieved June 09, 2018, from http://www.volkswagen.co.uk/about-us/concept-cars/phideon. VW Technology | Car Technology. (2018). Retrieved June 08, 2018, from http://www.volkswagen.co.uk/technology.

Analysis Suggestions:

1. Describe the Chinese target market for the Phideon in terms of demographics – age, gender, race, income, education, occupation, social class, life-cycle stage, and household size.

2. How are luxury automobile consumers in China different from consumers elsewhere in the world?

2. The case illustrates clearly the segment of Chinese consumers likely to buy the Phideon. What market segments would Phideon appeal to in the United States, were it to be sold in this market?

This page is intentionally blank…

Chapter 8

Expansion Strategies and Entry Mode Selection

Learning Objectives

After studying
this chapter,
you should be able to:

- Understand company expansion strategies, entry mode selection, and the risks involved at each level.

- Describe different types of strategic alliances involving international companies

Chapter Outline

SpeedKingz/shutterstock.com

Dial your airline, your credit card company or your Internet service provider, and you will likely have someone in Bangalore, India, or San Jose, Costa Rica, make your reservations or help you with questions about your account. You may be dealing with Delta or United Airlines, Capital One, Citibank, Microsoft, and many other service providers, and you will hear at the other end of the line an English speaker with a precise Indian or Spanish accent. And, if you make a joke, your customer representative may quickly steer you on to business, without letting on that he or she does not quite understand your joke. Ask your service rep where he or she is located, and the response may be even another country like China, the Philippines, Mexico, or Poland. Then look around you in your community, and you will find individuals recently laid off by service companies, such as credit card businesses, software companies, and customer service providers. The chances are high that their jobs were outsourced.

Companies join forces to broaden their market access and appeal and to take advantage of economies of scale. National airlines become instant worldwide carriers by establishing strategic alliances. For example, Delta Airlines started the SkyMiles partnership with Air France, Aeromexico, Aeroflot, China Southern, Czech Airlines, Korean Air, Saudia, and Virgin Atlantic, to name a few. These partnerships involve, in addition to code sharing and mutual partner booking in areas not serviced by the airline, other types of advantages that ultimately benefit consumers, such as a frequent-flyer miles exchange. In addition to helping airlines cut costs and increase their customer base, the alliances may even help individual carriers weather temporary financial challenges. Other airlines actually share routes, with a flight bearing numbers of two airlines. Such sharing enables firms to have multiple flight options to a destination; it also lowers airport access fees. Examples of airlines sharing routes are United Airlines with German company Lufthansa, Delta with Air France and Aeromexico, and British Airways with American Airlines.

This chapter examines international expansion of firms, exploring issues such as outsourcing and entry mode selection and evaluating the control and risks associated with each entry mode option.

8-1 Going International: Evaluating Opportunities

Managers of small and medium-sized enterprises (SMEs) and multinational firm managers alike must evaluate the costs of delivering their products and services to their target markets. They need to take into consideration a number of important factors in their decisions related to the manufacturing and distribution of their goods. In Chapter 1, "Scope, Concepts, and Drivers of International Marketing," we examined the drivers of international expansion in the environment, such as competition, regional economic and political integration, economic growth, technology and converging consumer needs, and the firm international expansion drivers, such as product life-cycle considerations, new product development costs, experience transfers, and labor costs. Many firms cross borders in search of lower factor costs, such as low-cost labor, capital, and land. As Table 8-1 illustrates, hourly compensation costs for production workers in manufacturing in the United States are quite high, averaging around $39.03. However, in Taiwan and Hungary, average hourly costs are $9.82 and $8.60, respectively; considering the high productivity of these countries' highly educated workforce, Taiwan and Hungary may be attractive labor markets for skilled manufacturing work. Moving manufacturing to the Philippines would further lower labor costs to less than $3.00 per hour. (It should be noted that Table 8-1 is expressed in U.S. Dollars. The U.S. Dollar has been very strong in recent years. Therefore, even though wages in local currencies may have increased, when converted to U.S. Dollars, end-of-year 2016 average hourly production costs in some countries may actually be less than in previous years.)

However, wages are only part of the cost of production. Other costs are equally important — capital equipment, components, and land, for example. Firms must examine all costs and opportunities when deciding which markets to enter. An international manufacturing presence could mean greater access to those markets facilitated by local governments that favor firms engaging in foreign direct investment. Companies need to examine the fit between the costs of international involvement (and the opportunity costs that they would incur if they ignore the international market), company resources, and market potential. They should also evaluate exactly how much risk they are willing to take in the process of going international and how much control they desire to maintain over the marketing mix.

8-2 Control versus Risk in International Expansion

Companies must decide whether to use middlemen when taking their products internationally or to market directly to the market. Using middlemen requires a company to relinquish control because the distributors or agents handle most of the selling of the product. However, distributors and agents have different legal status and different sales responsibilities. Middlemen allow the company to become involved in international business, while minimizing the typical risks involved in international marketing. On the other hand, direct international involvement exposes the company to substantial risk, but it also affords the company significant control of the marketing mix. Figure 8-1 (next page) illustrates the control and risk trade-off facing international firms in the process of selecting the international entry mode.

Table 8-1 Hourly Compensation Costs in U.S. Dollars for Production Workers in Manufacturing

Country	Compensation (in US$)
Switzerland	60.36
Norway	48.62
Belgium	47.26
Denmark	45.32
Germany	43.18
Sweden	41.68
United States	39.03
Finland	38.72
Australia	38.19
France	37.72
Ireland	36.23
Netherlands	34.60
Italy	32.49
Canada	30.08
United Kingdom	28.41
Japan	26.46
New Zealand	23.67
Spain	23.44
South Korea	22.98
Israel	22.63
Argentina	16.77
Greece	15.70
Estonia	11.60
Slovakia	11.57
Portugal	10.96
Taiwan	9.82
Hungary	8.60
Mexico	3.91
The Philippines	2.06

Source: Adapted from The Conference Board, International Labor Comparisons, December 2016, accessed at https://www.conference-board.org/ilcprogram/ on June 3, 2018.

Figure 8-1 Control and risk for entry mode alternatives.

International expansion using middlemen is a first step in direct participation in local markets. Note that the majority of U.S. firms directly engaged in business internationally are exporters utilizing agents and/or distributors to market their goods. Some firms seeking higher profits and greater market share in a target international market may eventually opt for direct international involvement, often via a "brick and mortar" investment in the country. Section 8-3 addresses the different international entry mode selection and expansion strategies for international markets.

8-3 Deciding on the International Entry Mode

The entry mode classifications offered in Sections 8-3a to 8-3i follow a general model of low to high control and risk, respectively. That is, company control over operations and overall risk increases from the export mode to the wholly owned subsidiary entry mode. In general, companies tend to use the export mode in their first attempt to expand internationally. There are, however, many exceptions; companies that have been present for decades in international target markets, such as Airbus Industries and Boeing, continue to export to those markets, rather than manufacture abroad. For example, Airbus has a strong market in Asia, where it is fulfilling many orders for the A320 and A330 aircraft. However, despite many years of profitable business in Asia, Airbus has only recently engaged in manufacturing on this continent, creating a wholly-owned subsidiary in India in 2013, Airbus India Operations, partnering with prominent firms such as Tata in India or buying Satair in Singapore. In 2018, Boeing announced plans to open an assembly plant in China in partnership with Commercial Aircraft Corp. of China, Ltd., a state-controlled company. The new facility will complete assembly of some 737 models for the Chinese market. China represents about 20 percent of Boeing's global market.[1]

8-3a Indirect Exporting

Indirect exporting means that the company sells its products to intermediaries in the company's home country who, in turn, sell the product overseas. A company engaging in indirect exporting can use middlemen such as export management companies or trading companies. Typically, these types of trading companies will buy and take title to the goods from the home country manufacturer (described in Chapter 11, "Managing International Dis-

tribution Operations and Logistics")
to distribute its products overseas.
Alternatively, the company can use
cooperative exporting, — also referred to as "piggybacking" or
"mother henning." With cooperative exporting, companies use the
distribution system of exporters
with established systems of selling
abroad who agree to handle the
export function of a noncompeting
(but not necessarily unrelated)

Avigator Thailand/shutterstock.com

company on a contractual basis. Such companies are paid on commission or are charged a
discount price for the product. They are larger companies with extensive experience in and
knowledge of the target international market. The companies facilitating indirect exporting
may have different names in different countries. The primary indirect exporters in the United Kingdom are known as export houses. They cover a variety of different organizations.
For example, export houses might buy goods for export, acting on their own behalf, or act
on behalf of an overseas principal wishing to purchase U.K. goods. As such, the export
house is similar to wholesalers selling goods internationally.[2]

Using indirect exporting does not require market expertise or a long-term commitment to the international market. The company essentially sells its product to a distributor
with little investment and without having to learn about the international market. The company's risk also is minimal; at most, it can lose a product shipment. Among disadvantages
are lack of control over the marketing of its products, which could ultimately lead to lost
sales and a loss of goodwill that might ultimately affect the perception of the company and
its brands in other markets where it has a greater commitment.

In the United States, it was often assumed that only very large firms had the ability
to become successful exporters. However, the vast majority of U.S. exporters are now
smaller and medium-size companies (SMEs.) These successful SME exporters recognize
they must actively cultivate their international relationships just as they do with their domestic customers. As a result, there are a growing number of U.S.-based SMEs where exports present an important percentage of the firm's annual sales. The largely-discarded notion of being able to simply unload domestic overproduction on unsophisticated importers
abroad is, simply put, a failed idea from another era.

Some companies use indirect exporting as a first step toward a greater degree of
involvement. After a sufficient consumer response is secured and the market is tested with
the initial shipment, a company might commit resources for additional investment in the
market. It should be mentioned, however, that indirect exporting in the long term does not
necessarily mean that the company is not committed to the market; it simply means either
that the company does not have the resources for greater involvement or that other markets are performing better and need more company resources.

One of Europe's leading car makers, Volkswagen, operates through independent
importers and distributors in Belgium, the Netherlands, Switzerland, and Austria, whereas in
France, Germany, Italy, and Spain, which together account for the largest percentage of European sales, it controls its wholesale operations directly.[3]

8-3b Direct Exporting

Companies engaging in direct exporting have their own in-house exporting expertise, usually in the form of an international sales manager or team. With a distributor relationship, the exporter is typically selling the goods to a local in-country distributor, as an arms-length transaction. Such exporting companies may retain some control over the marketing mix in the target market. They can require that their international distributors, wholesalers and retailers, observe the company's marketing policies, charging the suggested sale price, offering the appropriate promotions, and handling customer requests promptly and satisfactorily. This kind of exporting relationship with an international distributor is more common for mass-market consumer goods and other lower-cost items.

For export sales of expensive custom-made equipment, such as mining equipment, medical technology equipment, etc., the manufacturer would typically not seek an in-country stocking distributor, except perhaps for spare parts and repairs. Instead, the manufacturer may engage the services of an in-country commission sales agent to represent the foreign manufacturer. The agent would be responsible for developing sales to in-country buyers. Depending on the relationship with the manufacturer, the in-country agent may be able to sign sales contracts on behalf of the company. For these types of high-value export sales, the exporter is selling directly to the international end-user. Exporters must also be consider in-country laws and regulations, especially in the case of any disputes between the export manufacturer and a local agent or distributor.

More control, however, is expensive. Companies carry the cost of their export department staff and the costs involved in selecting and monitoring the different middlemen involved in the distribution process — agents, distributors, freight forwarders, shipping lines — as well as other marketing service providers, such as consultants, marketing researchers, and advertising companies.

One venue that offers many opportunities for direct exporting is the Internet. With a well-developed website, companies now can reach directly to customers overseas and process sales online. Catalog retailers, such as Lands' End, long ago made their first international incursions through their catalog business, exporting their products to consumers abroad and successfully expanding their international operations. Today, many small and medium-sized enterprises in emerging markets are able to penetrate international markets if they have an online presence and good online marketing skills. Amazon, the top U.S. online retailer, is also a leading retailer worldwide, with numerous in-country distribution centers. Its Chinese counterpart, Alibaba, with its consumer-to-consumer retail arm Taobao,

BigTunaOnline/shutterstock.com

is fighting Amazon for market share worldwide. Amazon and Alibaba are also moving quickly to capture market share in the expanding global e-payments sector. In 2018, Amazon upended the e-payments and banking sectors in Mexico with their introduction of a new pre-paid debit Master-Card, targeting a large number of Mexican citizens who do not have checking accounts or credit cards. They can use the new "Amazon Rechargeable" card for online purchases at Amazon, at ATMs, etc. The card can be re-loaded at convenience stores across the country, with no checking account required.[4]

The primary export destinations for U.S. products are listed in Table 8-2. Note that our neighbors to the north and south, Canada and Mexico, are the primary purchasers of U.S. exports.

8-3c Licensing

A popular international entry mode, licensing presents more risks to the company but also offers more control than exporting. Licensing also offers substantial flexibility to the company, allowing for rapid international expansion and high brand awareness worldwide. Licensing often does not require knowledge of the local market, and it may not even require any capital investment, allowing for a low-cost market penetration. Licensing involves a licensor and a licensee. The licensor offers know-how, shares technology, and often shares a brand name with the licensee. The licensee, in turn, pays royalties. The licensor might license the product without the name, or it might license the product allowing the use of the brand name. A licensor is selective when choosing a licensee, ensuring that products manufactured under license are of the highest quality. When quality cannot be guaranteed, either because the licensee does not allow the licensor sufficient control and scrutiny or because the licensee's products tend to be inferior, it is preferable for the products produced under license not to carry the licensor's brand name.

Table 8-2 Top Purchasers of U.S. Exports Ranked by U.S. Total Export Value for Goods, in millions of U.S. dollars

Country	2016	2017
1 Canada	$226,797	$282,392
2 Mexico	$229,702	$242,989
3 China	$115,602	$130,370
4 Japan	$63,236	$67,696
5 UK	$55,289	$56,329
6 Germany	$49,363	$53,493
7 South Korea	$42,309	$48,277
8 Netherlands	$39,690	$42,230
9 Hong Kong	$34,895	$40,024
10 Brazil	$30,107	$37,077
11 France	$31,132	$33,582
12 Belgium	$32,097	$29,911
13 Singapore	$26,725	$29,753
14 Taiwan	$26,037	$25,754
15 India	$21,652	$25,700
16 Australia	$22,160	$24,601
17 Switzerland	$22,777	$21,694
18 UAE	$22,401	$20,005
19 Italy	$16,707	$18,323
20 Saudi Arabia	$17,972	$16,261

Source: Adapted from U.S. Department of Commerce, Census Bureau, Economic Indicators Division. Accessed at https://www.trade.gov/mas/ian/build/groups/public/@tg_ian/documents/webcontent/tg_ian_003364.pdf on June 4, 2018

In the early 1970s, Italy's Fiat granted a license to AvtoVAZ, Russia's largest automobile manufacturer, to manufacture Lada, Russia's most popular automobile and an important export to neighboring and other developing countries. Under a similar arrangement, France's Renault granted a license to build Dacia brand automobiles in Romania in the 1960s. Dacia is a Renault subsidiary today. Note that Italy's Fiat did not allow AvtoVAZ to use the Fiat name for its automobiles and that Renault did not allow the Romanian licensee to use the Renault name for its automobiles; Fiat and Renault created some distance between the established brands and the automobiles created under license. Thus, if Lada or Dacia automobiles were not up to par – and they were not – this would not reflect poorly on Fiat or Renault.

Licensing is a lower-risk entry mode that allows a company to sell a product all over the world and offers the brand a global distribution. Beverly Hills Polo Club (www.bhpoloclub.com), for example, conducts business in more than 100 countries around the globe, producing apparel licensed under its own name, all licensed apparel for Harvard

University, as well as "Kulanui" (Hawaiian handbags), Beverly Hills Athletic Club, and Kinloch Anderson, a line that sells kilts, tartans and Highland dress. In fact, companies may choose to engage in trademark licensing, whereby brand names appear on merchandise without any design input from the parent company. For example, Eskimo Pie ice cream, a Nestlé brand, is sold around the world, but the product is not manufactured according to its original recipe. The only constant for this brand, in international sales, is its name.

Licensing permits the company access to markets that may be closed or that may have high entry barriers. In the earlier example, Lada and Dacia were sold in the countries of manufacture, the Soviet Union at that time, and Romania, at low prices, while automobile imports were charged tariffs at rates ranging from 50 to 100 percent.

Companies that engage in licensing agreements also limit their exposure to economic, financial, and political instability. In the event of a national disaster or a government takeover, the licensor licensing without the name incurs only the loss of royalties. The licensor that permits the use of the name may suffer a loss of reputation in the short term if the products are manufactured without licensor supervision and if they do not uphold the licensor's standard. In the latter case, the licensor has some control, at least in international markets. For example, it can bring to the attention of international trade bodies the sale of products that are illegally using its brand name, assuming the company has international trademark protection. In most markets, it also can sue the former licensee.

A downside of licensing is that it can produce a viable competitor in the licensee, who is well equipped to competently compete with the licensor. Training locals in company operations, particularly technology, can lead to the development of skills for future competitors.

8-3d Franchising

Franchising is a principal entry mode for the service industry, and it is the service industry's equivalent to licensing. The franchisor gives the franchisee the right to use its brand name and all related trademarks and its business know-how, such as secret recipes and customer interfacing techniques; the franchisor also may provide the franchisee with advertising and sales promotion support — all in return for royalties.

Alexander Gatsenko/shutterstock.com

Figure 8-2 There are few European city centers without a McDonald's.

The popularity of U.S. franchises worldwide is undisputed: McDonald's Golden Arches decorate the picturesque Scottish countryside, elegant buildings in centuries-old European cities (see Figure 8-2), and are centrally located at train stations and in malls. They border suks (bazaars) in the Middle East and anchor strategic corners of Shanghai streets (see Figure 8-3 on next page). Among other fast-food franchises present all over the world are Pizza Hut, KFC, and Burger King. Many of these franchises adapt to local markets, serving

Victor Jiang/shutterstock.com

Figure 8-3 A busy KFC in downtown Shanghai, with a McDonald's around the corner.

spicy vegetarian dishes (and no beef) in India and Sri Lanka and beer and wine in Europe. Although some products differ, as do portion sizes (huge in the United States, meager elsewhere), the franchises look similar. They also offer the same courteous service, air conditioning, clean toilets, and they run similar promotions.

Surprisingly, franchises succeed even if the service's primary offering (hamburgers) runs counter to the local culture (religious ban on eating beef). When companies set up franchises, it is important to evaluate the market's acceptance of the offering and to envision how the company can fit in the life of the local consumers. For example, in a bold move, a few years ago, Starbucks decided to compete with Austria's coffee houses. Although coffee consumption is high in Austria, at 56.8 gallons per person annually, Starbucks encountered some challenges. The company's concept runs counter to an environment that perceives American coffee and the pace of life associated with American cafés as different from the Austrian café business perfected over the course of 200 year: the kaffeehaus tradition. Nevertheless, the company has done well, positioned as a place to relax. Its signs inside read "Aroma protection through smoke-free spaces," and the company thanks customers for their understanding.[5]

A franchise is often associated in the consumer's mind with the franchise's country of origin. For consumers the franchise may, in fact, be representative of its country of origin, which may be high on the target list for individuals who do not agree with the politics of the franchise home country, as exemplified in International Marketing Illustration 8-1 (on next page).

The advantages and disadvantages of a franchise system are similar to those of licensing. The franchisor experiences less risk and a higher level of control over operations and offerings to the target market. Franchising also is a method that allows for rapid market penetration, which is important especially when new markets open their doors to foreign

International Marketing Illustration 8-1: Successful U.S. Franchises in a Hostile World

Franchises are often scapegoats for action groups protesting U.S. politics and trade, or globalization in general. In their use of English, with the corollary loss of stature of other languages, franchises are perceived as an imperialist enemy, driving out local traditional operations and imposing U.S. culture and traditions. KFC in India was closed by the government on grounds of compromised hygiene. A McDonald's franchise was vandalized in France and access to McDonald's was blocked in France and Belgium. A McDonald's was bombed in Xian, China, and another in Istanbul was a target of a pipe bomb. Franchises were bombed in Moscow, Beirut, Riyadh, and in an eastern Indonesian town. Even governments have targeted McDonald's. In Russia, in response to U.S. sanctions, the company was targeted for supposed health violations and its key locations were forced to shut down temporarily.

In yet another example, in Islamabad, Pakistan, angry crowds protesting against derogatory cartoons published in European newspapers, attacked and damaged two McDonald's restaurants and a Pizza Hut, before pelting a Holiday Inn hotel with stones. Still, U.S. franchises continue to do well abroad, even in hotbeds of anti-U.S. sentiment.

Franchises stress the local origin of the products they sell, the local labor they employ, and their stature as local citizens. They even make fun of their U.S. origins: in France, McDonald's ads feature cowboys who boast that the McDonald's franchises refuse to import American beef as a health guarantee. To position themselves as local, U.S. franchises also support nationalist and local ethnic causes of broad appeal. For instance, in Serbia, McDonald's hands out free burgers at rallies and has added a Serbian nationalist cap to the golden arches, using the slogan "McDonald's is yours." In Saudi Arabia, for every Big Mac purchased during Ramadan, it offers a 30 cent contribution to the Red Crescent Society. In Russia, McDonald's started an advertising campaign emphasizing its local ties and its 25-year history in Russia, playing down the Golden Arches' global significance as a bright beacon of America. In 2015, one McDonald's billboard in the heart of Moscow read: "Made in Russia, for Russians."

Sources: Adapted from Michael Birnbaum, "Russia's anti-American fever goes beyond the Soviet era's," *Washington Post*, March 8, 2015, accessed at https://www.washingtonpost.com/world europe/russias-anti-us-sentiment-now-is-even-worse-than-it-was-in-soviet-union/2015/03/08/ b7d534c4-c357-11e4-a188-8e4971d37a8d_story.html on August 28, 2015; B. Muralidhar Reddy, "Protests Turn Violent in Pakistan" *The Hindu*, February 15, 2006, 1; Philip F. Zeidman, "The Global Brand: Asset or Liability?" *Franchising World*, Vol. 35, No. 4, 2003, p. 52.

Sorbis/shutterstock.com

firms. On the downside, franchising can create future competitors who know the ins and outs of the franchise's operations. In fact, one hears many stories of former employees from fast-food restaurants who offer a precise replica of the original franchise, while offering lower prices. Ideas of franchises can also be copied (see Figure 8-4 on next page). As soon as Esso (Exxon) stations in Europe started offering a Tiger Mart (a convenience store affiliated with the Esso franchise), local competitors immediately set up their own version that was even better adapted to local demands, selling, for example, potted flowers at discounted prices in affiliation with local growers. Aral, a pan-European gas station franchise, has its own shopping mart. In addition to products serving each market with convenience items, the mart also accepts recycling goods, offering cash back for plastic and glass bottles.

Takashi Images/shutterstock.com

Figure 8-4 Franchises often find that their concept is easily copied. This Burger King in Germany has to compete with a similar burger joint a few feet away.

It should be mentioned that franchisors are often also exporters. For example, U.S. fast food franchisors companies will often require their local franchisees in the U.S. and abroad to buy store fixtures and other business items from the parent company.

8-3e Joint Ventures

Joint ventures involve a foreign company joining with a local company, sharing capital, equity, and labor, among others, to set up a new corporate entity. Joint ventures are a preferred international entry mode for emerging markets. In developing countries, they often involve an international firm and a local state-owned enterprise, that is, the local government. The company is thus assured instant local access and preferential treatment. Setting up a local joint venture with majority ownership by a state-owned or local private sector company may be the required mode of entry for an international firm in many developing markets.

Developing countries welcome this type of investment as a way to encourage the development of local expertise, of the market, and the country's balance of trade — assuming the production is exported abroad. In developing countries, the international firm typically provides expertise, know-how, most of the capital, the brand name reputation, and a protected trademark. The local partner contributes labor, the physical infrastructure (factory), local market expertise and relationships, as well as connections to government decision makers.

It is typical for the local government of the developing country to limit the joint-venture ownership of international firms to less than 50 percent. It is also typical for the local government to encourage the reinvestment of profits into the firm, rather than the repatriation of profits by the international firm. As such, the government, in effect, leads the international firm to engage in transfer pricing, a method whereby the parent company of the international joint-venture partner charges the joint venture for equipment and expertise, for instance, above cost.

Joint ventures could constitute a successful approach to a greater involvement in the market, which is likely to result in higher control, better performance, and higher profits for the company. Successful joint ventures abound. In one example, British Petroleum PLC established a joint venture in Russia, under the name Petrol Complex, with ST, a powerful local partner with close ties to the Moscow city government. The company owns 30 BP gas stations, each of which sells an average of 3.5 million gallons of gasoline a year, four times the average of a gas station in Europe.[11] BP offers Russian drivers good service (a rare commodity in this market), as well as minimarkets with espresso bars and a wide selection of wines. This is in stark contrast to the Russian gasoline stations where customers pay for gasoline by stuffing cash through a tinted window and where they communicate with the salesperson through a microphone.[6]

The joint-venture entry mode is not limited to developing countries. Numerous joint ventures are operating throughout Europe, and they are increasingly coming under the scrutiny of the European Commission, which assesses their impact on competition.[7] Typically, the Commission appoints a task force to investigate the impact of the joint venture on competition and then issues a statement of objections within six to eight weeks, giving the companies involved a chance to respond and request a hearing before the Commission makes its final decision with regard to the joint venture.[8] Whenever no such statement is issued, the deal is assumed to be on its way for approval.[9] One joint venture that the European Commission scrutinized the diamond giant De Beers Centenary AG (the world's largest diamond-mining company) and the French luxury goods company LVMH Moët Hennessy Louis Vuitton SA (which owns Christian Dior, Moët & Chandon, Louis Vuitton, and Donna Karan). The company produced De Beers-branded jewelry and opened a network of exclusive shops all over the world. In the end, De Beers bought the 50 percent stake held by LVMH, taking full ownership of the retail operation.[10]

In another example, Polo Ralph Lauren Corp., the fashion giant, entered a joint venture with Geneva-based watch and jewelry concern Compagnie Financiere Richemont AG to design and market luxury watches and fine jewelry. The venture is named Polo Ralph Lauren Watch and Jewelry Co. Polo and Richemont, and each partner owns 50 percent of the new company. Set up in 2008, the joint venture develops and distributes the products through Ralph Lauren boutiques and through independent jewelry and upscale watch retailers around the world. This is Polo's first venture into the fine jewelry and luxury watch business, and it is Richemont's first joint venture with a fashion designer.[11]

Companies can improve the chances for success of the joint venture by carefully selecting the partner. Factors leading to success are the firm's previous internationalization experience and the proximity between the culture of the international firm and that of the host country; a greater distance erodes the applicability of the parent's competencies.[12]

A major issue with many joint ventures in the value-added manufacturing, pharmaceuticals, and technology sectors is requiring the transfer of technology and patents to the in-country joint venture. This has become an especially contentious matter in ongoing trade negotiations between the United States and China. U.S. companies complain that they are forced to share such technology with Chinese partners, and are subsequently losing control over their intellectual property in the Chinese market. However, in 2018, the Chinese government vowed to end such forced technology transfers. [13]

However, even with careful planning, multinational firms have little recourse when local governments take actions favoring the local partner. The local government may step in to control energy sources, offering an advantage to local competitors, who are then in a position to take over. A joint venture recently started by BP in Russia offers an example.

BP in Russia

In 2003, BP announced, with great pomp, a landmark investment of $6.15 billion in Russia, in the form of a joint venture, the TNK-BP. The joint venture is the second largest private oil company in Russia, after Lukoil, and the only Russian energy company with partial foreign control.

However, four years later, the Russian government stepped up its control over its natural resources. State-controlled energy companies Gasprom and Rosneft quickly responded by showing interest in purchasing additional shares in TNK-BP, moving rapidly in a direction that would leave BP at a disadvantage. TNK-BP has been a very successful investment for BP, accounting for almost a third of the company's production, 27 percent of its reserves, returning $19 billion in dividends. Nevertheless, the obstacles posed by the government are such that BP has actively attempted to sell its shares in the company – without much success, as the Russian joint venture partners are blocking the sale.[14]

Like licensing and franchising, joint-venture partners can turn into viable competitors that know the firm's operations and competitive strategies. In this case, the local partner will undoubtedly become a formidable competitor in the region, where the firm will be protected by the government. Internationally, however, the international firm has some capability to combat the new competitors through controls and agreements with the supply chain and distributors that will prevent access to equipment or to markets, for example.

klevo/shutterstock.com

8-3f Consortia

Consortia involve three or more companies. An example of a successful company that started out as a consortium is Airbus. Airbus Industries began as an international consortium involving France (Aerospatiale with a 37.9 percent ownership), the United Kingdom (British Aerospace, with a 20 percent ownership), Germany (the former DaimlerChrysler DASA subsidiary, with a 37.9 percent ownership), and Spain (Construcciones Aeronauticas, with a 4.2 percent ownership).[15] Today, it is a joint stock company.

Governments and trade organizations are concerned with the monopoly effect of consortiums. In the case of Airbus, it was successfully argued that a single European country would not have the resources to provide a challenge to Boeing, the U.S. manufacturer. In general, companies are allowed to set up consortia in the area of research and development, where they can share the cost of developing products that are at the forefront of technology.

Interestingly, consortia can have international subsidiaries. For example, the Airbus consortium had subsidiaries in the United States, Japan, and China. In the United States, the newest Airbus engineering facility — and largest as well — in Wichita, Kansas, started its operations in 2015. It is the first design and engineering venture of the company in North America, and its engineers worked on the largest Airbus aircraft, the A380, the company's twenty-first century flagship airplane. Airbus has six main centers of operations in the United States, and it employs more than 3200 employees. Airbus also imports billions of dollars' worth of components from U.S. aerospace manufacturers.[16]

8-3g Wholly Owned Subsidiaries

Companies can avoid some of the disadvantages posed by partnering with other firms by setting up wholly owned subsidiaries in the target markets. The assumptions behind a wholly owned subsidiary are that:

- The company can afford the costs involved in setting up a wholly owned subsidiary.
- The company is willing to commit to the market in the long term.
- The local government allows foreign companies to set up wholly owned subsidiaries on its territory.

The company can develop its own subsidiary, referred to as greenfielding, which represents a costly proposition, or it can purchase an existing company through acquisitions or mergers. Many opportunities for acquisitions have recently emerged in emerging and developed markets alike: Governments have been desocializing services and industries, rapidly privatizing industries that were formerly government owned or operated. Opportunities have emerged in the area of telecommunications, health care, energy, and even the national mail service.

The most important advantage that a wholly owned subsidiary can provide is relative control of all company operations in the target market. In particular, a subsidiary offers the company control over how to handle revenue and profits. Wholly owned subsidiaries also carry the greatest level of risk. A nationalization attempt on the part of the local government could leave the company with just a tax write-off.

Additional difficulties could arise when a company decides to acquire or merge with another. In the case of the joint venture between Daimler, the maker of the Mercedes automobile, and Chrysler, known at the time as DaimlerChrysler, Daimler quickly found out that

Chrysler was not performing up to par and quickly proceeded to restructure, weeding out former Chrysler employees. Daimler ultimately sold Chrysler in 2007.

In general, the company acquiring another or building its wholly owned subsidiary is not able to share risks with a local partner, nor will it benefit from a partner's connections; it must build its own. Yet, even selling the subsidiary can eventually haunt the company years later. Harrods Buenos Aires was originally set up as a subsidiary of Harrods London but became an independent company in 1913 and changed hands several times. Today, Harrods Buenos Aires operates in Argentina and has no relationship whatsoever with Harrods London — which cannot address this issue successfully in the local courts in Argentina.

8-3h Branch Offices

The primary difference between subsidiaries and branch offices is that subsidiaries are separate entities, whereas branch offices are part of the international company. Companies that set up branch offices abroad often must engage in substantial investments. For example, Stihl, a German multinational manufacturer of chain saws, has a branch office in Bucharest, Romania, that handles all company operations in the country. In addition to overseeing product sales, Stihl also ensures that servicing contracts are appropriately honored and that the representatives have adequate training. In low-income countries in sub-Saharan Africa, where Mercedes-Benz is a standard of luxury, but where only a few locals and a handful of expatriates can afford to purchase the brand, Mercedes must still incur substantial investment costs. At the minimum, it must invest in a sales office that has substantial staffing requirements and in a showroom that displays a few models. The company also is likely to engage in the distribution of parts to service stations and in the training of mechanics in handling Mercedes parts.

dotshock/shutterstock.com

Branch offices of service providers typically engage in a full spectrum of activity in the domain of their specialization. For example, the Chase branch offices in different European capitals handle the banking needs and credit to corporate and individual clients, in effect serving these markets the same way they serve the home markets.

Branch offices, like subsidiaries, also offer companies a high level of control over operations and profits in international markets. In terms of risk, however, the company invests much less in the market that can be lost in a government takeover attempt, compared with a subsidiary.

Companies also can have a presence in international markets in other formats that could be informal or more formalized. For example, the company could have a sales office (low risk, especially if the company does not carry any inventory in the country; some control). Alternatively, the company could be part of a strategic alliance, which varies in the level of control it provides the international company, as well as in the level of risk to the company, depending on the type of alliance and resource commitments. Strategic alliances are described on the next page.

8-3i Strategic Alliances

All joint ventures and licensing and franchising agreements are occasionally loosely referred to as strategic alliances between companies attempting to reach joint corporate and market-related goals. This textbook, however, adheres to the mainstream thought that strategic alliances are formats that tend to be more short term in nature and that do not entail the same level of commitment as the previously described categories. Such alliances crop up frequently and have various forms and degrees of "alliance." They vary from a contract manufacturing agreement that requires the contracting firm to provide raw material and training to the contracting factory in return for production that could last for two years, to an exchange of loyalty points (hotel, frequent flyer) between companies. The following are some examples of alliances:

- Manufacturing alliances
- Marketing alliances
- Distribution alliances
- Outsourcing

Manufacturing Alliances

The category of manufacturing alliances covers many types of alliances, from contract manufacturing to technological, engineering, and research and development

wavebreakmedia/shutterstock.com

alliances. A typical example of a manufacturing alliance is that between the Google-owned U.S. company Motorola, Inc., and Singapore's Flextronics International, Ltd., whereby the Singapore-based electronics manufacturer made billions of dollars' worth of Motorola products.[17] Subsequently, Flextronics took over Motorola's plants.[18] In another example, Porsche has engaged in different types of technical alliances with Harley-Davidson, the U.S. motorcycle icon, primarily helping it develop low-noise, low-emissions motorcycles; most recently, Porsche helped Harley-Davidson develop its water-cooled Revolution engine.[19]

Marketing Alliances

Some marketing alliances focus on all aspects of marketing. Historically, marketing alliances have taken on a variety of formats. Many marketing alliances focus on sales. For example, U.S.-based Delta Airlines is in charge of all sales in the United States for the KLM Royal Dutch Airlines and Air France. These two major European carriers are also part of Delta's SkyMiles program for frequent-flyer awards. One of many examples of marketing alliances is one between AOL Deutschland (Germany) and eBay; together with Google, it has a marketing alliance with several travel websites – www.spartours.de, www.ReisepreisVergleich.de, and www.lastminute-express.com.

Distribution Alliances

Distribution alliances are common as well. Mitsui and Mitsubishi have set up distribution alliances with Coca-Cola in Japan, bottling and distributing all Coke products in this market. Numerous distribution alliances exist under various formats and in countries of all levels of development. Emerging markets are well served by such alliances. In an example, Carrier Air-con distributes Toshiba's high-end air conditioners in India. The Toshiba air conditioners are positioned as a super premium product catering to a wealthy niche market. Carrier set up a separate exclusive distribution network for them.[20]

Outsourcing: A Rapidly Growing International Expansion Mode

   Outsourcing is defined as the strategic use of outside resources to perform activities that are usually handled by internal staff and resources.[21] Outsourcing has established itself as an effective cost-cutting technique for companies around the world. It involves transferring service-sector and manufacturing jobs to overseas locations where labor is competent and cheap; hence, outsourcing is also known as **offshoring.** Millions of jobs have gone from high-income countries to low- and medium-income countries, such as India and China.[22]

   Outsourcing has been around for a long time, but, until the late 1990s, much of the out-sourcing was in the technology industry. Today, it is present in many domains and prominent in providing activities usually handled by internal staff, such as customer service and billing. Outsourcing offers opportunities for strategic alliances for the service industry, and even for manufacturing businesses using outside resources to perform activities normally handled by internal staff. The growth of the global outsourcing market has been phenomenal, and all indications suggest that this trend will continue, with the outsourcing market pegged at US$100 billion and growing. More than half of low-skill jobs and 25 percent of all U.S. jobs are at risk of being offshored in the years ahead.[23]

   Asia has emerged as the outsourcing hub and back-office of the Western world, and India, China, the Philippines, and Singapore are competing for the business. India has initially received the lion's share of outsourcing opportunities, starting with information technology: A software developer in India costs US$6 per hour, compared with one in the United States, who costs US$60 per hour.[24] Subsequently, many other businesses turned to India for outsourcing, taking advantage of the low-cost, educated, and English-speaking labor force of about

ProStockStudio/shutterstock.com

150 million. As seen in the introductory section, Delta Airlines, as well as many other airlines, financial services companies, etc. outsource many customer service functions to India. Tata Consultancy Services, the largest outsourcing firm in India, became the first information technology company in India to make more than $10 billion in revenues – in March 2012.[25]

   China had initially focused on providing back-office support for financial services, telecom, software, and retailers in neighboring Asian countries because its operators can easily talk to people in Taiwan, Japan, and Korea in their native languages — China has plenty of Japanese and Korean speakers. However, China is rapidly making inroads as an outsourcing base for English-speaking nations, a business initially dominated by India.[26] Nevertheless, workers in the United States and in other English-speaking countries should be less concerned about a challenge from China, which comes largely in manufacturing, and more concerned about the challenge from India, which comes in the area of services. Moreover, information-service jobs are the easiest to outsource because of the efficiency with which they can be performed electronically. Another industry that has outsourced jobs is the mortgage industry. It was recently reported that "the total annual value of such outsourcing contracts around the world is over $1 billion."[27]

Although outsourcing offers benefits, it requires careful implementation. Nearly half of all outsourcing deals fail, with 60 percent of the problems due to errors in communication — new employees are capable and understand the technology, but not the goals of the company.[28]

The success of outsourcing strategic alliances is contingent on the use of the right strategy, as seen in the following:[29]

• Outsourcing must have clear objectives and expectations.

• Outsourcing partners must be selected based on their expertise in the outsourcing activity and based on their cultural fit with the firm.

• The outsourcing firm must provide its partner with adequate training and skills that will help the partner adapt to other cultures.

• The outsourcing plan should have clear expectations, requirements, and benefits.

Outsourcing has been challenged in the United States; government and labor union representatives, urged on by their constituencies who are directly affected by the job losses attributed to outsourcing, are attempting to ban outsourcing, especially business process outsourcing. Some experts in the United States, the United Kingdom, and other European countries worry that this trend will spell the end of their economic domination. Moreover, consumers are not keen on outsourcing, as they feel that their personal information is not well protected when handled by employees in countries where U.S. consumer protection laws may not be enforced.[30] In fact, outsourcing is not necessarily an ideal method for cost cutting; JetBlue, for instance, found that U.S. call-center operators cost about the same as Indian call-center operators, especially after communications and start-up costs are factored in. The offshoring of manufacturing jobs to China and especially to Mexico continues to be a major economic and political issue in the U.S.

Other experts argue that radical changes have occurred in the past, with Western nations benefiting most. They suggest that, for every dollar going offshore, the U.S. economy gets back more than $1.12 in income, whereas the countries doing the work gain 33 cents.[31]

It is important, however, that policies on trade, education, and social welfare, for instance, be modified to accommodate the radical societal changes linked to outsourcing. With time, different geographic locations and economies will develop different comparative advantages. According to this argument, outsourcing will not cause massive unemployment in the United States; rather, it will require job creation in other industries.[32]

Summary

Understand a company expansion strategies, entry mode selection, and the risks involved at each level. A company can use different entry modes to enter a new market. They range from the lowest-risk mode and the mode that provides the least control to the highest-risk/highest-control mode. Exporting is at the lowest level of control and risk. Indirect exporting requires minimal internationalization and involves selling the product to distributors, such as export management companies, trading companies, or export agents in the company's home country, who then distribute the product internationally. Direct exporting requires in-house exporting expertise, usually in the form of an exporting department. Such companies have more control over the marketing mix in the target market than indirect exporters. Licensing and franchising are popular entry modes that allow flexibility and allow for rapid international expansion and high brand awareness. Joint ventures, consortia, and wholly owned subsidiaries are examples of foreign direct investment; wholly owned subsidiaries offer the greatest commitment to a particular market but also present the highest risk to investors.

Describe different types of strategic alliances involving international companies. A company can use various forms of strategic alliances (manufacturing, marketing, distribution, and outsourcing alliances) to enter a new market. Such alliances are industry-specific, ... have various degrees of stability over time.

	franchisor	marketing alliance
...nufacturing	greenfielding	mother henning
... exporting	indirect exporting	offshoring
...orting	joint venture	outsourcing
...n alliance	licensee	piggybacking
entry mode	licensing licensor	strategic alliance
franchisee franchising	manufacturing alliance	wholly owned subsidiary

Discussion Questions

1. What is the difference between international franchising and international licensing? Explain.

2. Briefly describe each type of international entry mode, from exporting to wholly owned subsidiary, and address the risks and controls characterizing each entry mode.

3. There are many types of international alliances. Go to the home page of American Airlines (http://www.aa.com/homePage.) and identify the company's alliances.

Chapter Quiz

True/False

1. Companies need to examine the fit between the costs of international involvement, company resources, and market potential.

True

Rationale: Companies need to examine the fit between the costs of international involvement (and the opportunity costs that they would incur if they ignore the international market), company resources, and market potential. Section 8-1, "Going International: Evaluating Opportunities"

2. Licensing is an international entry mode that presents less risk to the company but offers more control than exporting.

False

Rationale: Licensing is higher risk than exporting, but it also offers more control. Section 8-3c, "Licensing"

3. One of the benefits of franchising is that it keeps out new competitors.

False

Rationale: Franchising has the potential of creating competitors among local employees who can learn the business and transfer the know-how to a local competitor. Section 8-3d, "Franchising"

4. Competing companies are allowed to work in consortia in industry sectors where the government can control their monopolistic activity.

True

Rationale: Competing companies are allowed to form consortia and work in domains where the government can scrutinize their activities. Section 8-3f, "Consortia"

5. Outsourcing involves the strategic use of outside resources to perform activities that are usually handled by internal staff and resources.

True

Rationale: Outsourcing is defined as the strategic use of outside resources to perform activities that are usually handled by internal staff and resources. Section 8-3i, "Strategic Alliances"

Multiple Choice

1. Which of the following is correct about using international middlemen?
   a. They increase company control over marketing strategy.
   b. They subject the company to less risk than direct international involvement.
   c. They maximize control for the company in the target market.
   d. All of the above

Answer b is correct.

Rationale: Using international middlemen subjects the company to less risk than direct international involvement. Section 8-2, "Control versus Risk in International Expansion"

2. Direct international involvement has as a result which of the following?
   a. The company is exposed to less risk than if it used middlemen.
   b. The company has greater control over marketing strategies.
   c. The company faces greater risk in the market.
   d. b and c only

Answer d is correct.

Rationale: The company has greater control but also faces greater risk if it opts for direct international involvement. Section 8-2, "Control versus Risk in International Expansion"

3. Companies may choose direct exporting because it allows them to
   a. monitor retailers.
   b. control suggested sale prices.
   c. observe the handling of customer complaints.
   d. all of the above

Answer d is correct.

Rationale: Advantages of direct exporting are the ability to monitor retailers, control prices, and address customer concerns. Section 8-3b, "Direct Exporting"

4. Franchising constitutes a primary entry mode for the_____industry.
   a. automobile
   b. technology
   c. service

d. machine-tools

Answer c is correct.

Rationale: The preferred entry mode for services is franchising—the process whereby the franchisor gives the franchisee the right to use its brand name, related trademarks, and its business know-how, such as secret recipes and customer interfacing techniques, in return for royalties. Section 8-3d, "Franchising"

5. Which of the following is a reason for the failure of joint ventures?

    a. Natural disasters
    b. Poor performance by a partner
    c. Partners becoming competitors
    d. All of the above

Answer d is correct.

Rationale: Many joint ventures fail; the primary reason for failure is usually attributed to one partner—although reasons outside the partners' control, such as the economy or natural disasters, can lead to the demise of the joint venture. Section 8-3e, "Joint Ventures"

6. Porsche helping Harley-Davidson to produce its water-cooled Revolution engine is an example of which type of strategic alliance?

    a. Distribution
    b. Marketing
    c. Manufacturing
    d. None of the above

Answer c is correct.

Rationale: The Porsche–Harley-Davidson alliance, in this situation, involves only manufacturing processes, not distribution or marketing. Section 8-3i, "Strategic Alliances"

Notes

1. Raghu Krishnan, "Airbus looks at MRO in India with IndiGo bonanza," *Business Standard*, September 1, 2015, accessed at http://www.business-standard.com/article/companies/airbus-looks-at-mro-in-india-with-indigo-bonanza-115083100865_1.html on September 1, 2015. Doug Cameron, "Boeing to Open Plant in China This Year," *Market Watch*, April 25, 2018, accessed at https://www.marketwatch.com/story/boeing-to-open-china-plant-this-year-2018-04-25 on June 3, 2018.

2. Jacqui Bishop, "Entry Strategies," *Supply Management*, Vol. 11, No. 3, February 2, 2006, p. 37.

3. Frank Bradley and Michael Gannon, "Does the Firm's Technology and Marketing Profile Affect Foreign Market Entry?" *Journal of International Marketing*, Vol. 8, No. 4, 2000, pp. 12–36.

4. Daina Beth Soloman, "Amazon Launches First Debit Card Mexico E-Commerce Push," *Reuters*, March 13, 2018, accessed at https://www.reuters.com/article/us-amazon-com-mexico/amazon-launches-first-debit-card-in-mexico-e-commerce-push-idUSKCN1GP35A on June 4, 2018.

5. "Starbucks Targeting Austria's Coffeehouses," *International Herald Tribune*, Frankfurt Edition, July 5, 2001, 12. "Starbucks Company Invades Austria," *Austria Information*, Vol. 55, November/December 2002, http://www.austria.org/nov02.

6. Sabrina Tavernise, "In Russia, BP Profits at the Pump," *International Herald Tribune*, Frankfurt Edition, July 5, 2001, 12.

7. European Commission, accessed at https://ec.europa.eu/commission/index_en on June 13, 2018.

8. Ibid.

9. Brandon Mitchener and Deborah Ball, "EU Clears De Beers-LVMH Venture," *Wall Street Journal Europe*, July 6–7, 2001, 3.

10. Reuters, "Diamond Group De Beers Buys Out Retail Partner LVMH, March 23, 2017, accessed at https://www.reuters.com/article/us-diamonds-debeers-lvmh-idUSKBN16U157 on June 19, 2018.

11. Terry Agins, "Polo, Richemont Team Up in Watch and Jewelry Venture," *Wall Street Journal* online edition, March 5, 2007.

12. Harry G. Barkema, Oded Shenkar, Freek Vermeulen, and John H. J. Bell, "Working Abroad, Working with Others: How Firms Learn to Operate International Joint Ventures," *Academy of Management Journal*, Vol. 40, No. 2, April 1997, pp. 426–442.

13. Wendy Wu, "China Vows to End Forced Tech Transfers in Manufacturing Sector," *South China Morning Post*, March 20, 2018, accessed at http://www.scmp.com/news/china/diplomacy-defence/article/2138087/china-vows-end-forced-tech-transfers-manufacturing on June 4, 2018.

14. Catherine Belton and Guy Chazan, "Oligarchs threaten BP's Russia sale plans," *Financial Times*, June 4, 2012, p. 1; Andrew Kramer and HeatherTimmons, "After Setbacks, BP May Be Forced to Give Up Some Control of Joint Venture in Russia," *New York Times*, January 16, 2007, C3.

15. www.airbus.com (accessed June 20, 2012).

16. Airbus, "Airbus in the U.S.," http://www.airbus.com/company/worldwide-presence/united-states.html accessed on June 19, 2018.

17. "Motorola Scales Back Flextronics Outsourcing Deal," *International Herald Tribune*, Frankfurt Edition, July 4, 2001, 11.

18. Reuters, "Flextronics Takes Over Motorola's Plants," December 20, 2012, accessed at https://www.reuters.com/article/us-flextronics-motorola/flextronics-takes-over-motorola-assembly-plants-idUSBRE8BA01H20121211 on June 19, 2018.

19. Tim Burt, "Porsche Fires Revolution at Harley," *Financial Times*, July 14–15, 2001, p. 8.

20. "Friendly Rivals," *Country Monitor*, Vol. 11, No. 16, 2003, p. 5.

21. Dean Elmuti, "The Perceived Impact of Outsourcing on Organizational Performance," *Mid-American Journal of Business*, Vol. 18, No. 20, 2003, pp. 33–36.

22. Tom Holman, "A Passage to India," *Bookseller*, Vol. 5246, 2006, pp. 6-7.

23. Alan S. Blinder, "Offshoring: The Next Industrial Revolution?" *Foreign Affairs*, Vol. 85, No. 2,   March – April 2006, p. 113.

24. Pankaj Mishra, "US Proposes Ban on Outsourcing," *Asia ComputerWeekly*, February 16, 2004, p. 1. Andrew Soergel, "Study: 1 in 4 U.S. Jobs at Risk of Offshoring," *U.S. News & World Report*, July 17, 2017, accessed at https://www.usnews.com/news/economy/articles/2017-07-17/study-1-in-4-us-jobs-at-risk-of-offshoring on June 4, 2018.

25. Business Standard, "TCS beats $10-bn revenue mark in FY12 Posts 23% growth in net profit," April 24, 2012 (http://www.business-standard.com/india/news/tcs-beats-10-bn-revenue-mark-in-fy12/472437; accessed May 14, 2012).

26. Bruce Einhorn and Manjeet Kirpalani, "Move Over India, China Is Rising Fast as a Services OutsourcingHub," *BusinessWeek*, August 11, 2003, p. 42.

27. "Home and Away," *The Economist*, July 10, 2006, Vol. 381, No. 8499, p. 82.

28. "Outsourcing Success Is All about the Relationship," *eWeek*, October 18, 2006, p. 1.

29. Dean Elmuti, "The Perceived Impact of Outsourcing on Organizational Performance," *Mid-American Journal of Business*, Vol. 18, No. 20, 2003, pp. 33–36.

30. "Home and Away," p. 82.

31. Pankaj Mishra, "US Proposes Ban on Outsourcing," *Asia ComputerWeekly*, February 16, 2004, p. 1.

32. Alan S. Blinder, "Offshoring: The Next Industrial Revolution?" *Foreign Affairs* Vol. 85, No. 2, March-April 2006, p. 113.

Case 8-1 Danone's Ups and Downs in China

For Danone, the French dairy multinational corporation, China is one of the most attractive markets. In 2017, it reported a 17 percent growth internationally, despite a weak dairy business in Europe. Its growth is largely attributed to a strong Chinese demand for Danone's high-end baby formulas Aptamil and Nutrilon, with a more than 50 percent growth in demand – the demand is helped by a sharp rise in births as China is ending its one-child policy, by urbanization, and an affluent middle class. Danone Waters China, a subsidiary whose brands include Evian and Danone, are also rapidly increasing sales and distribution all over the country, in particular in southwestern China.

But things did not always look rosy for this company's China operations. In 1996, the company was China's largest bottled water maker, with 39 percent of the market, and the largest seller of soft drinks, with an 18 percent share. Danone created the Wahaha joint venture with Hangzhou

Wahaha, its local partner. Danone owned 51 percent of the joint venture, which brought in $1.4 billion in sales in 2006 alone. The relationship between the joint venture partners was smooth at first. However, in 2007, Groupe Danone SA of France filed suit against the joint venture partner, accusing it of creating a parallel manufacturing and distribution structure for the Wahaha brand, against the terms of the joint venture agreement.

Anyone traveling to China has had at least one bottle of Wahaha water or some of the company's other drinks. ("Wahaha" in Chinese mimics the sound of a baby laughing.) The Hangzhou Wahaha Group Co., Ltd., is China's leading *domestic* beverage producer. Its predecessor, the Hangzhou Shangcheng District School-Run Enterprise Sales Department, funded its start-up operations in 1987 with a government loan. Zong Qinghou; the company's founder, and two retired schoolteachers initially sold milk products and popsicles at the local school store. With the support of the Hangzhou government, the company bought a large, old state-owned enterprise and changed its name to the Hangzhou Wahaha Group Co.

After joining with Danone, in 1996, Hangzhou Wahaha's production increased dramatically. The state owned a majority share of Danone's joint-venture partner, Hangzhou Wahaha, and the company had foreign investment, as well as Chinese investment. Zong, its founder and chair, has played such an active role in the company that, in the Chinese marketplace, Hangzhou Wahaha is regarded as a private enterprise. Its products are sold in France, Germany, Japan, Malaysia, the Netherlands, Spain, Taiwan, Thailand, and the United States, among others. Its product mix includes milk and yogurt drinks, purified and mineral water, carbonated soft drinks, fruit and vegetable juice, sports drinks, tea, as well as rice porridge, canned food, and health products, such as children's vitamins. The company expanded into children's clothing in 2002, and is planning to diversify into personal care products, including shampoo and toothpaste. One of its brands, Future Cola, is positioned as a challenger to Coke and Pepsi. The company emphasizes its Chinese origins, encouraging consumers

to support their country by selecting the Wahaha brand. In 2007, Groupe Danone SA of France filed suit against the joint venture partner, Zong Qinghou, and his daughter. It filed for arbitration with a body in Sweden specializing in commercial disputes involving China. Danone accused Zong of producing and selling Wahaha products outside of the joint venture structure established in 1996. Danone found evidence of the existing parallel business in 2005. Danone, which owned 51 percent of the 39 joint ventures with Wahaha, accused Wahaha of setting up independent companies to sell products identical to those sold by the joint ventures. In the lawsuit, Danone demanded a 51 percent stake in the Wahaha companies that are not part of the joint venture. The Wahaha group rejected the demand. In response, Zong Qinghou, Hangzhou Wahaha's founder and chairman, used nationalistic imagery, accusing Danone of trying to control subsidiaries that were not part of the partnership. He claimed that the terms of the joint venture were not fair.

Danone also decided to use Western courts to challenge its joint venture partner, filing a lawsuit in the United States against one of Wahaha's subsidiaries and two of Zong's relatives owning an offshore company. It claimed that a Wahaha company registered in the British Virgin Islands has been illegally selling the joint venture's drinks. In response to this action, the joint venture partner accused Danone of utilizing global pressure to force Wahaha to concede. Chinese customs, in response, seized 118,000 liters of Evian mineral water, a Danone brand, which officials claimed had unacceptable levels of bacteria. Danone claimed that this seizure was directly related to its actions against Hangzhou Wahaha.

The founder and chairman of the joint venture, Zong Qinghou, resigned in June 2007. Since then, Zong and Hangzhou Wahaha have actively battered Danone in public, posting venomous letters on the Internet and vowing to punish Danone for its evil deeds and destroy the company. Wahaha employees even showed up at Danone's Shanghai headquarters protesting against the company. By 2009, Danone gave up the fight and Wahaha agreed to pay cash to acquire Danone's 51 percent, ending the joint venture. The two companies also agreed to drop all legal proceedings. In an unrelated story, in December 2011, Danone also closed a yogurt factory in China.

At that point, the future of Danone in China did not look as promising as once thought, and analysts feared that this event marked the end of Danone in China. Not so. Danone persevered, and, today, its waters, Evian and Danone, are perceived as high-quality, exclusive offerings, and its baby formula brands' sales are soaring. Danone's presence in China continues to rely on partnerships, such as joint ventures with Chinese firms, but, for water, it now operates a subsidiary of the Danone Group, Danone Waters China.

Sources: Greg Knowler, "Danone Links with JD to Grow West China Business," *JOC*, November 23, 2017, accessed at https://www.joc.com/international-logistics/danone-links-jd-grow-west-china-business_20171123.html on June 10, 2018; *Food Business Africa*, "Danone Reports a 16.6% Increase in Sales, Driven by China," October 19, 2017, accessed at https://www.foodbusinessafrica.com/2017/10/19/danone-reports-a-16-6-increase-in-sales-driven-by-china/ on June 10, 2018; Chloe Rigby, "Brands from Feelunique and Danone Waters Update for the Chinese Market," *Internet Retailing*, November 27, 2017, accessed at https://internetretailing.net/themes/themes/brands-from-feelunique-and-danone-waters-update-for-the-chinese-market-15886 on June 10, 2018. Tyler Rooker, "Foreign Investors Face Challenges," *China Daily*, July 27, 2015, accessed at http://europe.chinadaily.com.cn/business/2015-07/27/content_21416877.htm on September 6, 2015; David Barboza, "Danone Exits China Venture After Years of Legal Dispute," *The New York Times*, September 30, 2009 (www.nytimes.com); James T. Areddy, "Danone Seeks Ways to Fix China Venture; Vow Not to Walk Away Follows Resignation of Partner Amid Tussle," *Wall Street Journal*, June 13, 2007, A8; David Barboza, "Wahaha Executives Threaten to Quit Danone," *International Herald Tribune*, Online Edition, June 13, 2007; Geoff Dyer, "Danone Files US Lawsuit Against Wahaha," *Financial Times*, June 6, 2007, 28; Adam Jones, "Chinese Seize Cases of Danone Water," *Financial Times*, May 31, 2007, 27; Paula M. Miller, "The Chinese Beverage Company's Expansion Is No Laughing Matter," *China Business Daily Online*, September – October 2004.

Analyses Suggestions:

1. Describe the joint venture between Danone and Hangzhou Wahaha. What were some of the important ownership characteristics? Who contributed what to this relationship?

2. What were the advantages to Danone and to Hangzhou Wahaha in setting up the joint venture?

3. What were the disadvantages to Danone and to Hangzhou Wahaha in this joint venture relationship?

Case 8-2 sweetFrog's Expansion to Egypt and the Dominican Republic

Founded in Richmond, Virginia, in 2009, the sweetFrog franchise serves high-quality frozen yogurt to customers in a family-friendly environment. The company has over 350 frozen yogurt parlors in the United States and abroad, and this number is expected to continue to increase. The company has expanded to traditional, non-traditional, and mobile locations in order to prove to its consumers that it wants to embrace innovative marketing strategies so it can reach families on the go. Non-traditional locations include amusement parks, universities, airports, and stadiums.

The company strives to emphasize its commitment to local communities in every community it serves. It is a self -declared Christian company, with F.R.O.G. in sweetFrog standing for "Fully Rely On God." The company uses local partnerships and fundraisers to become embedded in the community. One of sweetFrog's largest franchisees is the nation's military; the company provides special treats and programs for them throughout the year. This frozen yogurt store has proven its flexibility to exist in different locations and continually adjusts to fit in, all while maintaining its core values of being a wholesome company, one that offers a family-friendly and inclusive environment. Patrick Galleher, CEO of sweetFrog, commented on the Veteran and mobile franchises stating that "the fantastic franchise partners operating these mobile and non-traditional locations will create success stories we can replicate in national and international markets."

Kristi Blokhin/shutterstock.com

sweetFrog first expanded to the Dominican Republic in 2013, when it opened two locations there. In 2017, the company opened its seventh store in the country. In the Dominican Republic, sweetFrog has used the strategy of co-location with Bravo supermarkets, allowing each location consistent access to fresh ingredients, as employees can quickly buy any products at the supermarkets when supplies run low. sweetFrog is a symbol of joy, freedom, and sharing to people in the Dominican Republic, continuously coming up with new product options that cater to Dominicans' tastes and preferences. While the overall concept and environment stays consistent from location to location, sweetFrog attempts to consider customers' preferences in its different stores. Galleher states that sweetFrog has been so successful in its international expansion because the concept of this brand translates internationally well. It also helps that the Dominican Republic has a high frozen dessert consumption per capita.

More recently, sweetFrog opened new stores in Egypt. In 2014, it signed a development agreement with Vantage Egypt for Tourism & Entertainment, the Food and Beverage division of the Halawa Group, allowing sweetFrog to open locations in Cairo. Through combining efforts with Vantage Egypt, sweetFrog was able to further penetrate the market and create family-friendly environments in Egypt.

The international expansion strategy, whereby sweetFrog partners with franchisees overseas, has proven to be successful for the company, creating more brand equity for the company. The family-friendly, comfortable, and uplifting environment of sweetFrog is now familiar to many different consumers beyond the borders of the United States.

Sources: About sweetFrog. (2018). Retrieved June 11, 2018, from https://sweetfrog.com/about. Hallman, R. (2015, April 11). Sweet Frog hops to a new beat. Richmond Times-Dispatch. Retrieved from http://www.richmond.com/business/local/sweet-frog-hops-to-a-new-beat/article_a8e60f75-884f-520b-8a39-35c74476275b.html. Hoppe-Spiers, J. (2017, January 30). Sweetfrog. Franchising Today. Retrieved from http://www.franchising-today.com/sections/profiles/182-sweetfrog. Michaels, L. (2018, January 24). Corripio group puts 'an experience' first in DR. Franchise Times. Retrieved from http://www.franchisetimes.com/February-2018/Corripio-Group-puts-an-experience-first-in-DR. Slack, E. (2016, August 05). SweetFrog. Food and Drink. Retrieved from http://www.fooddrink-magazine.com/sections/restaurants/2042-sweetfrog. SweetFrog frozen yogurt franchise costs & fees. (2018). Retrieved June 12, 2018, from https://www.franchisedirect.com/foodfranchises/sweetfrog-premiere-frozen-yogurt-franchise-12635/ufoc. SweetFrog opens seventh Dominican Republic location. (2017, April 7). QRS. Retrieved from https://www.qsrmagazine.com/news/sweetfrog-opens-seventh-dominican-republic-location. SweetFrog reports robust franchise growth in 2017. (2018, February 8). QRS. Retrieved from https://www.qsrmagazine.com/news/sweetfrog-reports-robust-franchise-growth-2017. Tosta, A. (2014, July 16). SweetFrog premium frozen yogurt is going to Egypt. Retrieved from http://www.prweb.com/releases/2014/07/prweb12017468.htm.

Analyses Suggestions:

1. Why did sweetFrog go international?

2. Interestingly, sweetFrog is only present internationally in the Dominican Republic and Egypt. Why would a company prefer to limit its international presence to these countries? Why did they not go to neighboring countries, Canada and Mexico, taking advantage of greater proximity and trade facilitations through NAFTA?

3. sweetFrog's entry mode in the Dominican Republic was through franchising. Could it have simply exported frozen yogurt to this market, instead of selecting the higher-risk entry mode of franchising?

Part 4

Managing the International Marketing Mix

Chapter 9

Products and Services: Branding Decisions in International Markets

Learning Objectives

After studying
this chapter,
you should be able to:

- Describe drivers for international standardization and offer an overview of the international standardization– local adaptation continuum and respective company strategies.

- Examine country-of-origin effects on brand evaluations in relation to product stereotypes and consumer ethnocentrism.

- Examine challenges faced by service providers in international markets.

- Address issues related to brand name protection and the reasons behind widespread international counterfeiting.

- Address the marketing of industrial products and services and related product and service standards

Chapter Outline

Adapting to Local Preferences

The world has been gradually moving toward one large, global marketplace. As Chapter 4, "Regional Economic and Political Integration," illustrated, a fragmented Europe merged into one large, unified market. Asia and North America are also gradually removing barriers and allowing more access to multinationals, and to regional and local brands from high-income and middle-income countries. Mature products in many industries are addressing the needs of consumers worldwide with the same brands and only minimal, market-specific modifications. Established brands such as Braun and Krups (Germany) sell kitchen appliances using the same marketing mix across continents with only minor mandatory adaptations (voltage, cycles, television systems). Similarly, franchises such as KFC, Pizza Hut, McDonald's, and Burger King offer the global market unified brands, adapting their offerings to local preferences, offering wine and beer in most European countries, vegetarian burgers in India, offering the more demanding U.S. consumers free refills on their drinks, free ketchup and mayonnaise, lower prices and much larger portions. A "small" soft drink in the U.S. is a "giant" elsewhere in the world, and a "supersize" is simply unimaginable elsewhere. Ask for a large Coke at McDonald's in Amsterdam and you get a drink in something the size of a vial. Moreover, you still need to negotiate for one of those hard-to-come-by ice cubes to cool it off.

Keith Homan/shutterstock.com

Mineral water distributors, such as Gerolsteiner (Germany), Evian and Volvic (France), and confectionery manufacturers, such as Ferrero Rocher are modifying only their labels to conform to local labeling requirements when selling their products across different continents. Mondelez's Toblerone bars look the same in Seattle, Cairo, Quito, Paris, Addis Ababa, Budapest, and Beijing, and they taste exactly the same.

Yet, for certain product categories that appeal to local preferences, multinational firms have to adapt their offerings to effectively compete with local manufacturers and service providers and to more directly cater to the individual needs of local markets. Advertising agencies and numerous financial and legal service providers typically partner with local firms to create successful campaigns and strategies aimed at individual markets. This chapter examines the driving forces behind a company's decision to standardize, or to partially or fully adapt its offerings to individual international markets. It also addresses barriers faced by brands from private-label offerings and by service providers from local government. The chapter also addresses brand name protection issues and the reasons behind the proliferation of counterfeiting activity worldwide.

9-1 Standardization versus Adaptation

The topic of standardization versus adaptation, to a certain extent, parallels the concepts introduced in Chapter 1, "Scope, Concepts, and Drivers of International Marketing," addressing geocentric, regiocentric, and polycentric orientations. Global standardization reflects a geocentric company orientation, regional standardization reflects a regiocentric orientation, and local adaptation reflects a polycentric orientation, respectively (see

Figure 9-1 The Global Standardization:
Local Adaptation Continuum

Figure 9-1). It must be noted, however, that multinational companies may adopt a combination strategy, depending on the particulars of individual markets. For instance, PepsiCo is a global company with, most likely, a geocentric orientation; however, it has progressively moved from a localized strategy to a regional strategy for of its distribution and purchasing.

9-1a Global Standardization

Global standardization, frequently used interchangeably with the term "glocalization," refers first to standardization of products across markets and, ultimately, to the standardization of the marketing mix worldwide. The main reason why firms favor global standardization is obvious: It is cheaper to have the same product and the same integrated marketing communication and distribution strategy worldwide. And standardization is possible because consumers increasingly have the same product preferences.

The primary reason for uniform preferences is the media, the instant penetration of Internet, cellular telephones and television in homes everywhere in the world. In the most remote areas in developing countries, technology makes it possible to have Internet cafés, cell phones and television. In many countries worldwide, in addition to premium international channels, such as CNN, access to neighboring countries' television programs is commonplace. Serbian television is preferred by many viewers in western Romania, as the following example illustrates.

Serbian Television: Who Would've Thought?

In the city of Timisoara, in western Romania, one has access to all the national Romanian programming and regional Transylvanian programming. One also has access to Hungarian and Serbian television programs and to Italy's Rai Uno, as well as MTV and CNN and other cable channels for those who have subscriptions. Serbian television, in particular, has had a long tradition in this part of Romania, and further inland in Southern Romania.

Before the fall of communism, Serbian television programs carried much more Western programming than Romanian TV, whose main focus was building socialism and mocking capitalism. The Belgrade television stations presented film marathons from Friday evening until Sunday evening, offering adventure-type films and comedies during the day and horror and more risqué films at night. Serbian television stations had great reception in Timisoara, the Romanian city closest to the Serbian border. Elsewhere in Romania, individuals built elaborate antennas that could receive sufficient reception from the much-coveted Belgrade stations. As a result, there are generations of Romanians who learned Serbian to understand the programming. Today, those same viewers continue to have a preference for Serbian television programs and to watch them regularly online today.

Exposure to overlapping media increases exposure to brand advertising: Companies are able to build brand awareness beyond the borders intended for the diffusion of the respective media. In the previous example, advertising on Serbian television and Serbian online advertising for Apple's iPad will reach Romanian viewers, who are also exposed to Apple iPad advertising on Romanian television channels and online. In addition, blogs and online publications all over the world provide individuals with endless opportunities to compare notes on Apple or other brands and product styles with others with similar interests. Another reason for uniform consumer preferences is international travel. Intracontinental travel is cheap and common. Round trip flights from Moscow to London with discount airlines such as Easy Jet and Air Baltic airlines can cost as little as $150. Crossing the Atlantic can cost as little as $600 now that discount carriers such as Norwegian Air, Wow, etc. have entered the market. As more consumers cross borders, they are exposed to more brands, more branded services and experiences, and more brand advertisements.

As a result of this exposure, the interests and product/service-related needs of consumers are becoming more and more homogeneous worldwide. Consequently, products and, indeed, brand preferences are gaining a common definition across continents, leading to the emergence of global consumers. Penny Skateboards are in great favor with teens in New York, Warsaw, Rio de Janeiro, and Copenhagen. Teens ride them wearing wide, baggy trousers in traffic-safe colors, and then party the night away at clubs known for their electronic dance or hip-hop music.[1] Blonde, svelte Barbie dolls and Barbie-doll look-alikes are on the wish lists of little girls in developed countries and developing countries. Nike sneakers, Coke, Levi's jeans, and Timberland shoes are in with the preteen to college segment. Business people watch CNN, and everyone watches American sitcoms.

The strategy used to address these increasingly homogeneous consumer needs is global branding. A global brand has the same name, logo, image, and positioning everywhere in the world. Main streets in most world capitals and malls worldwide advertise and sell brands such as Ralph Lauren, Escada, and Michael Kors, while logos of Pepsi, Coca-Cola, and Marlboro cigarettes adorn umbrellas in many central squares and beach resorts (see Figure 9-2). These are global brands, enjoying worldwide reputation and

recognition, demanded by consumers in Shanghai, Antananarivo, and Paris alike. These brands have a high awareness among world consumers and are perceived to be of high quality.

Standardization is particularly important for product research and development. Economies of scale can be achieved if there is a concentration in research and development, and coordination also gives a firm flexibility in responding to competitors' R&D efforts.[2] Such coordination is

Figure 9-2 Pepsi umbrellas at a Polish resort on the Baltic Sea warm up the landscape.

expensive. Moreover, governments may restrain the flow of information and people, which are required to coordinate research and development activities.[3]

With regard to the other components of the marketing mix, advertising savings can be achieved by having a uniform advertising strategy in each country. PepsiCo, for example, saves millions as a result of using the same film for television advertising in different international markets, and Levi Strauss typically uses one series of TV commercials around the globe.[4] These companies are lowering their media expenditure costs while benefiting from advertising consistency and from the brand image consistency they have created.

Similarly, the standardization of supply chains has resulted in cost reductions in transportation and distribution, with significant cost reductions and overall shorter transportation times. In addition, research and development, purchasing, packaging, and customer service, among others, have also benefited from standardization.[5] The standardization of point-of-sale (POS) systems is creating efficiency within the supply chain. McDonald's has standardized its point-of-sale system worldwide, using the NewPOS, produced by Savista Corp. The new system replaced the decentralized system McDonald's used in the past, which made it difficult for the chain to mandate technology standards. Almost 65 percent of all McDonald's restaurants worldwide are operated by franchisees, and as recently as 2001, McDonald's operations featured "800 combinations" of POS hardware and software and back-office applications. Today, McDonald's views POS not just as a commodity, but as yet another strategic asset that helps in the process of standardizing McDonald's processes of supply-chain management and customer interface.[6]

Sorbis/shutterstock.com

Issues related to the standardization of distribution and promotion will be further examined in Chapter 11, "Managing International Distribution Operations and Logistics," and Chapter 13, "The International Promotional Mix and Advertising Strategies."

9-1b Regional Standardization

A variation of global standardization, a regional standardization strategy refers to the use of a uniform marketing strategy within a particular region. This strategy is becoming more appealing to companies as regional market integration is gaining strength worldwide, notably with the European Union and NAFTA. Pan-European brands are becoming common, even for U.S. multinationals, such as Procter & Gamble (whose Ariel detergent was its first Pan-European product; today, the brand is available in most markets, with the exception of North America).

In addition to regional branding strategies, companies also benefit from economies of scale by concentrating certain marketing activities regionally. We mentioned the Levi Strauss attempts to standardize its communication as much as possible—even having one TV commercial worldwide, whenever possible. However, with a large corporation and with consumers perceiving it as a premium brand in some parts of the world and as an everyday, basic brand in its home country of the United States, Levi Strauss is forced to engage in some level of adaptation, as the example below illustrates.

Standards Redefined

Levi Strauss is reconciling its efforts to standardize its offering through regional standardization, organizing its operations into three regional divisions: Levi Strauss, the Americas, based in San Francisco; Levi Strauss Europe, Middle East, and Africa, based in Brussels, Belgium; and the Asia Pacific Division, based in Singapore.[7] For the United States, Levi Strauss' strategy has always been one of offering a quality brand at lower prices, whereas, internationally, the company has been charging premium prices. However, with consumers worldwide learning of the lower jeans prices in the U.S., and demanding cheaper brand-name jeans, Levi Strauss has had to adapt and offer a "value range of clothing," distributed through discount hypermarkets Tesco and Asda.[8]

In other examples, PepsiCo centralized purchasing across all of its European businesses, thus achieving volume savings from sugar, cooking oil, flour, and packaging materials, for a total savings of $100 million per year.[9] Nike has streamlined its European distribution by replacing more than 20 national warehouses in Europe with one single distribution center located in Belgium.[10] Similarly, Mercedes-Benz (www.mercedes.com) engages in regional standardization, centralizing its operations under the Mercedes-USA umbrella. One of the reasons behind the regional standardization is that Mercedes' premium positioning in the United States market was undercut by gray marketing channels in the 1970s, when many lower-priced Mercedes automobiles were shipped from Europe and sold to customers in the United States at prices lower than those of U.S. dealers. As a result of the regional standardization, the European[11] offerings are different from those in the United States. For passenger cars, the Mercedes A-Class, a lower-priced series (see Figure 9-3), is available everywhere except in the United States, where it was introduced in 2019.[12] Mercedes also offers the B-Class, with the B-150 to B-200, which comes in a turbo model as well. For the B-Class, only the more expensive Electric Drive version is available in the U.S., at over $40,000. For the United States, Mercedes insists on being only a luxury automobile, at least for the time being.

TonyV3112/shutterstock.com

Figure 9-3 The A-Class Mercedes is about as large as a Ford Focus; it even looks like one.

A product often must be adapted to the demands of the local market because consumers might have specific preferences. Alternatively, adaptation might be dictated by the political and legal environment, by the technological environment, or by other particulars of the market (trade relationships, climate, etc.). The degree of economic development in a market also is a factor that determines the degree of product adaptation needed. The lower the level of economic and market development, the more the product needs to be changed to serve the needs and demands of the market.[13]

Host governments affect the globalization of products by imposing local content requirements, standards (technical, emission, etc.), and ownership restrictions and requirements on technology transfer. In the case of services, consumer participation in production may be affected by government barriers to global strategy.[14] Banking in the Middle East is gender-based: Women's banks are separate from banks used by men, and cross-access is restricted.

Government restrictions affect not only banking; China, Singapore, and Saudi Arabia ban private satellite dishes, and China is restricting citizen access to the web (see the example below).

9-1c Global Localization

In the Levi Strauss example, one size of jeans does not fit all. First, culture can limit the types of jeans for a particular market. For example, in Islamic countries females are discouraged from wearing tight-fitting attire, whereas Japanese consumers prefer tighter fitting jeans than their American counterparts. Secondly, average height can dictate product specifications. Jeans for the East Asian market, where the average height of individuals is less than in the West, require shorter inside leg measurements than for Western countries.[16]

Kdonmuang/shutterstock.com

Few products and services can succeed with a purely global strategy, where the product undergoes no changes, and where the promotional mix, distribution, and pricing remain the same. A degree of adaptation to local conditions is frequently imperative for company success. According to marketing experts, the idea of marketing a standardized product with a uniform marketing plan around the world remains purely theoretical. Although a product concept may be universal, it must still be adapted to differences in local culture, legislation, and even production capabilities.[17] The term global localization, or glocalization, is frequently used to describe the practice of global branding and localized marketing adaptation.

Product managers must decide on which aspects of a product they want to standardize across markets and which aspects of the product to localize. In this decision, they resort to two approaches: One involves offering parts (modules) that can be assembled worldwide in different configurations, depending on the needs of the market — modular adaptation; the other, standardizing the core product/service, but allowing for easy modification from market to market, is core product strategy. In an instance of the latter, the core product is identical from one country to another, but certain aspects of the offering differ from market to market.

To illustrate this concept, marketers with brands heralded as global icons often act using a local strategy; McDonald's Golden Arches are omnipresent throughout the world. Its offerings, however, are adapted to the local culture. At its restaurants in New Delhi, where most Indian consumers consider cows sacred and do not eat beef, McDonald's offers the Maharaja Mac (two all-mutton patties, special sauce, lettuce, cheese, pickles, onions on a sesame-seed bun). Similarly, Volvo, unlike Mercedes (as mentioned in Section 9-1b, "Regional Standardization"), has a similar core product in every market. However, it offers air conditioning as a standard feature only for the U.S. market.

EQRoy/shutterstock.com

Figure 9-4: Starbucks "You Are Here" Mugs representing Chinese landmarks. They are collectible souvenir coffee mugs available in Starbucks stores throughout the world.

Similarly, other fast-food restaurants have adapted their offerings in different markets (see Figure 9-4). Yum! Brands companies (Pizza Hut and KFC, in particular), Burger King, and McDonald's offer beer and wine in Europe. In the Netherlands, McDonald's offers a large Coca-Cola Light (Diet Coke)[18] in containers slightly smaller than medium-drink containers in the United States. Pizza Hut in Germany sells Pepsi at take-home windows outside a café-restaurant on Munich's Leopoldstrasse, a café-lined street. KFC had to change its product size in Japan because consumers prefer morsel-sized food.

In another example, Disney, as a global company, decided to allow its regional organizations to create their own programming. The company first decided to localize production for its shows in India. Disney's first television show in India, *Vicky Aur Vetall,* was based on an Indian myth about a prince and a genie-like figure. After this successful venture, it decided to offer the Indian market a show called *Dhoom Machaoo Dhoom* (Hindi for "let's have a blast"), aimed at teenagers. The show is about two teenage girls and is popular with Indian audiences of all ages. *Dhoom* is a breakthrough because it is one of the few programs produced for teenagers — specifically, for girls — in this market. This is similar to family serials because it is real and close to the lives of teenagers. After its success in India, Disney decided to expand its localization efforts in Britain and Japan as well. Disney's competitors are quickly following suit. Time Warner is offering an Indian version of *Sesame Street* called *Galli Galli Sim Sim,* using some material from the popular U.S. show, but set on Indian streetscapes and anchored by local Muppets. Big Bird is replaced with a big lion called Boombah.[19]

9-1d Mandatory Adaptation

To render products usable, manufacturers of appliances adapt their products to local requirements. Such mandatory adaptations involve electricity—220 volts and 50 cycles for Europe, whereas, in the United States, the standard is 110 and 60 cycles. Other such adaptations involve telephone jacks and television systems (NTSC in the United States, PAL and SECAM I and SECAM II in the rest of the world).

In other examples, automobiles must be adapted to driving on the left side of the road in the United Kingdom, Ireland, and Australia. The United States requires a conversion to local specifications (emissions and other standards) for any imported automobiles that were not manufactured according to U.S. standards. Subsequent to conversion, the U.S. Department of Transportation must approve the conversion for the vehicle to be registered locally, which makes this, overall, a costly undertaking.

Other types of mandatory adaptation abound. For example, a number of Middle Eastern countries continue to restrict the import of products that have components manufactured in Israel. Food products, in particular, must be scrutinized: Alcohol content is prohibited from distribution without special and limited authorization in many countries in North Africa and the Middle East, and food products containing pork have limited appeal and face inspections and other restrictions there. Magazine censors used to black out with a marker faces or bodies of women in Saudi Arabia. After women were given the right to drive (in 2017), there was outrage when *Vogue Arabia* portrayed a Saudi princess driving on the cover page.

▲ Princess Hayfa bint Abdullah Al Saud on the controversial front cover. Photograph: Tasneem Al Sultan/Vogue

9-1e Local, Nonmandatory Adaptation

Many global companies adapt their offerings to better meet the needs of the local market, thus performing a local, nonmandatory adaptation. Examples of multinational companies offering products aimed at local markets abound. In most instances, the products result from a buyout. Unilever and Procter & Gamble bought numerous brands in Central and Eastern Europe; for instance, Unilever bought Romania's Dero, a detergent that is now part of the company's product mix in that country. It is also one of the few Romanian communist brands that survived post-communism, inspiring artists to use the name in titling works dealing with Romanian society. In other examples, Unilever also has a Bulgarian dressing, Kaliakra, in its mix, as well as a Serbian margarine, *Sunce*. In 2017, Unilever acquired Qualas, a Latin American personal care product line. Multinational companies have also developed new brands for individual local markets. Häagen-Dazs Japan offers its customers Royal Milk Tea ice cream, a full-bodied, creamy green ice tea; Weight Watchers offers consumers in France Mousse Legeres (light mousse) in two different four-pack combinations; and Nestlé offers to U.K. consumers a drinkable fruit yogurt named Squizzos, which sports Disney characters on its packaging.[20]

9-2 Private-Label (Retailer) Brands

Private-label (retailer) brands pose an increasing challenge to manufacturers' global or local brands. European food retailers, such as Sainsbury in the United Kingdom and Albert Heijn in the Netherlands, as well as North American retailers, offer quality products with the "Sainsbury" and "ah" brands, respectively, packaged impeccably and positioned on the shelves side-by-side with popular multinational/national brands.

A well-known private label is the Tesco brand, very popular in the Czech Republic, Hungary, and in its home country, the United Kingdom. Among other European private labels with broad appeal are Marks & Spencer, from the U.K. and Dallmayr, a specialty store offering gourmet food from Munich, Germany, whose specialty goods are now available in many supermarkets in Europe, and in specialty stores in the U.S.

Linda Bestwick/shutterstock.com

It used to be that private labels appealed to consumers primarily during downturns in the economy, when they were more likely to make their brand selection based on price. However, this is no longer the case. Consumers worldwide have become more price conscious, demanding higher quality at lower prices. Walmart, Aldi, Metro, and Costco private labels are highly rated by consumers and independent organizations, such as *Consumer Reports*; they increase price competition, to the benefit of consumers.

9-3 Global Branding and Country-of-Origin Information

Country of origin is defined as the country with which a particular product or service is associated. The country could be the country of manufacture, in the case of products, or the country where the company headquarters are located, for both products and services. The key to determining a product's perceived country of origin depends on which of the two (country of manufacture or home country of the company) elicits the stronger association. For example, many of the appliances Philips sells are manufactured in Asia; however, the Philips' headquarters are in the Netherlands. The country of origin for Philips appliances, then, is not the particular country in Asia where they are manufactured, but the Netherlands. A new, unknown brand, however, will be associated more strongly with the country of manufacture.

In the absence of other product information, the country of origin of a product or service affects consumers' evaluations of that product or service. Country-of-origin information constitutes a product trait that is external to the product itself, acting as a surrogate for product quality, performance, reliability, prestige, and other product characteristics that cannot be directly evaluated. Products manufactured in highly industrialized countries are perceived as being of higher quality and having greater prestige than those manufactured in developing countries. Consumers from highly developed countries tend, in general, to evaluate home-country products more favorably than products from other countries. The opposite is true for consumers in developing countries and newly marketizing economies[21] who evaluate home-country products as inferior to products from developed countries.

When consumers have additional product information, such as brand name, or if they purchase the product at a store with a good reputation, country-of-origin information is no longer a primary source consumers use for product quality evaluation. Increasingly, with products manufactured with components made in various countries, determining the "true" product country of origin is difficult. For example, BMWs for the U.S. market are manufactured in South Carolina, rather than in Germany, Michelin tires are made in South Carolina, the Mercedes M-class in made in Alabama, and software used by many U.S. businesses is made in India. The automobile assembly industry in North America is now highly integrated throughout NAFTA-member countries Canada, Mexico and the U.S. A Ford automobile assembled in Mexico and sold in the U.S. will contain a large percentage of parts manufactured in the U.S. U.S. buyers do not typically focus on whether the final assembly point is in Michigan or Mexico.[22]

In developing countries, local brands have difficulty competing with global brands, and when they do well, they are often quickly bought by global competitors. Marketing Illustration 9-1, however, suggests that Chinese consumers are starting to appreciate Chinese brands.

Marketing Illustration 9-1 Multinational versus Chinese Brands

One of the most noteworthy developments in the Chinese marketplace is the coming battle and shrinking disparity between multinational and local brands: Can Chinese brands compete at home against Western, Japanese, and Korean brands preferred by China's 1.3 billion consumers? Chinese brands have differentiated themselves primarily on price and distribution, rather than quality or brand attributes, which are known to create consumer loyalty and high profit margins. On the other hand, multinational brands are ubiquitous and heavily advertised; on the way to Shanghai from Pudong International Airport, one of the first billboards is for the Hooters chain of restaurants. Michael Jordan smiles from a Hanes ad in taxis, and iPods are everywhere. According to Gavin Heron, managing director of TBWA/Shanghai, China is a story of international brands, not local ones, and as soon as a local brand has traction, it is quickly bought out by a multinational.

J. Alfonso A. De Dios, Procter & Gamble director, suggests that China should innovate and move from "made in China" to "created in China."

Keith Homan/shutterstock.com

Xiaoguang Fang, consultant with Gallup Research, suggests that Chinese brands have come a long way. In 1994, brand recognition rate was highest for non-Chinese brands, whereas today, there is high brand recognition for Chinese brands, such as Wahaha (bottled water), Bank of China, Tsingtao beer, China Telecom, and Haier.

When asked who makes the best products, Chinese responded, in the following order: Japan, United States, Germany, France (especially for luxury goods), Britain, South Korea, Taiwan, and China.

Sources: Xiaoguang Fang, Vice Chairman/ Senior Strategic Consultant, Gallup Research Co. LTD, lecture on consumer trends in China, May 23, 2007, University of Richmond Faculty Seminar, Beijing, China; Scott Donaton, "Chinese Challenge: Local Brand More Copycats than Creators," *Advertising Age*, Vol. 76, No. 49, December 5, 2005, p. 21.

9-3a Product-Country and Service-Country Stereotypes

Kenyan or Colombian coffee, Chinese silk (see Figure 9-5), German beer and electronics, French perfume, Italian fashion, Swiss chocolate, and Russian caviar are examples of strong product-country stereotypes of quality held by consumers in the United States. Among such stereotypes shared elsewhere in the world are Iranian pistachios and rugs, Polish vegetables, Israeli oranges, and Czech and Italian crystal, to name a few. Such stereotypes are product specific and do not apply usually to other products from that particular country.

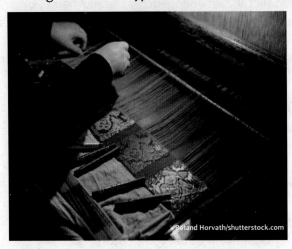

Figure 9-5 *Chinese silk is perceived by consumers worldwide as a high-quality silk.*

Services too have their own stereotypes. Eastern European cosmeticians, for example, are popular in the West. Names such as Ilona of Hungary, Frederic Fekkai, and Erno Laszlo cosmetics are prominent on Madison and Fifth Avenues in New York. Tourists going to Eastern Europe often use the services of local beauticians or even go for extended stays to spas specializing in mud baths and life-renewal therapies.

Unfortunate negative stereotypes also exist. French waiters have an unfair reputation of arrogance in the United States. U.S. consumers believe that French waiters have a deep dislike of Americans, but that is absolutely not the case, as American consumers tip about 20 percent (at least until they live in France long enough to learn about the local norms), whereas French and European consumers tip less than 10 percent. Consumers from the United States are, in fact, preferred worldwide as they tend to tip substantially more than locals or to tip where the tradition is not to tip at all if the service charge is included in the bill. In general, customer service tends to be less enthusiastic in most other countries. Employees do their job and expect a set salary in return; there is rarely a premium for service that is above and beyond expectations.

9-3b Country Branding

The analysis above suggests that products develop an image that is closely associated with the their respective countries. Country branding refers to a combination of elements that provide the country with a brand identity that differentiates it from other countries. In a broader sense, that identity, and hence the country brand, is defined culturally; it is also closely linked to the products produced in the country and its services – including the tourism sector – and the reputation and relevance of those offerings for target consumers. The country brand is in continuous flux, as it is shaped by its products' reputations and its broader environment, the local economic, cultural, political, technological, and natural environment. For example, Hungary is primarily known for its high-quality food – Hungarian salami, goulash, and paprika – and for its wine. It has had a positive country brand, as home to erudite thinkers and composers, with people who have fought valiantly to maintain their national identity.

The Hungarian Tourist Board has attempted to reposition Hungary in the mind of

world tourists as a country of palatial hotels that echo a grand Austro-Hungarian
history, of magical medicinal baths, of fu-
turistic bridges, and of quirky inventions,
such as the Rubik's Cube and the Prezi,
and important innovations such as light-
transmitting concrete. However, in 2015,
Hungary, besieged by hundreds of thousands of refugees fleeing Syria, Iraq, and
Afghanistan, appeared callous as the
world community witnessed police wearing surgical masks tossing food to caged

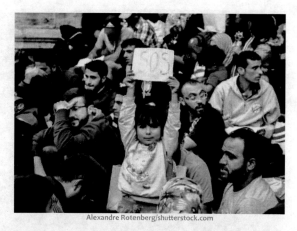
Alexandre Rotenberg/shutterstock.com

migrants at a holding center, after a camerawoman for an extreme right publication was
filmed tripping migrants holding children in their arms. The crisis also brought the world attention to the country's right-leaning, xenophobic leadership. The events have tarnished the
country brand, which will need years to recover. They have partially undone the country's
marketing efforts, since a country brand must match the identity promoted.

In other examples, France's brand is one of elegance and luxury. France is the home
of established luxury fashion designers and perfumes. The country brand for Italy is one of
skilled craftsmanship. Italian fashion designers rival those of France, and their craft in the
area of ultra-luxury sports automobile manufacturing is unparalleled. The country brand for
Germany is one of exact engineering, boasting leading electronics and automobile brands,
and so on.

Latin America has been slow to adopt proactive country branding initiatives, with
the possible exception of tourism promotion in Mexico. However, recently, Colombia, Costa
Rica, and Peru were recognized for their innovative country brand recognition strategies.
Many of these new country promotional efforts in Latin America focus on brand recognition
to attract prospective international manufacturers and other business investors. [23]

Countries must maintain and support their country brand, which ultimately com-
mands high prices for its products and generates high sales on world markets.

9-3c Country of Origin and Ethnocentrism

We have learned about ethnocentrism as a company philosophy, an approach to
international marketing as an extension of domestic marketing with minimal adaptation to
the needs of the international consumers and the peculiarities of the local market. This second definition of ethnocentrism, used in relation to country of origin, is related to consumers' beliefs that purchasing foreign products is morally wrong. Ethnocentric consumers believe that purchasing imported products hurts the economy, causes loss of jobs, and is unpatriotic, and consumers purchasing foreign products are worthy of contempt. [24] This concept then translates into a preference for products from one's own country (i.e., "buy
American") and a rejection of products with a foreign country of origin. This attitude can
exist at the individual consumer level or at the aggregate societal level.

Companies often try to circumvent any ethnocentric tendencies of local consumers
by marketing their products as local, trying to persuade locals that the brand is their own,
or, at least that a part of the product is locally produced. The ad in Figure 9-6 (next page)
illustrates a Swiss McDonald's ad stressing that the bread used in its buns is local.

Figure 9-6: *In Italian-speaking Switzerland, McDonald's is advertising hamburger buns as being of Swiss origin.*

Governments also frequently engage in practices in which they favor locally produced products and local service providers for government-sponsored work. For example, federal employees and recipients of U.S. government grants are required to use U.S. carriers for travel pursuant to the Fly America Act.

9-3d The Brand Name

A brand is what comes to the mind of the consumer when he or she hears or sees the brand name. If there is an exchange – a sale – the brand creates value for both the consumer and the company. When a consumer thinks of Toblerone chocolate, she thinks of the yellow package, of the triangles neatly cut so they could be easily detached, of the creamy chocolate and the crunchy caramel. The consumer could also think of it emotionally, as a surprise that she can put in her son's lunchbox, so he would think of his mommy when he has lunch at school with his little friends; the son would know his mother loves him because it is one of his favorite chocolates.

The brand name is central to communicating the product's personality and its position to the competition. Toblerone sounds a little Italian or maybe French; Tobler sounds German... Clearly, Toblerone is European. The mountain on the package, the Matterhorn, in the Swiss Alps, confirms the brand's European origin, and, since "Swiss chocolate" or "European chocolate" is a desirable product association worldwide, the brand is well positioned in the consumer's mind.

Global marketing managers should make sure that brand names are easy to pronounce in most languages, and memorable, and that they do not have a negative or an undesirable meaning in languages of markets where the products are sold. Using the same brand name in all international markets is valuable to the company, because it means greater brand recognition with consumers traveling overseas, and lower marketing costs. Over time, a brand name used worldwide will increase in value as the brand attracts more consumers. Table 9-1 (next page) ranks the top global brands. Those with the highest brand value have been around over decades, such as McDonald's, IBM, and Coca-Cola, or they are technology brands, such as Apple, Google, and Amazon. Facebook ranked eigth in the most recent ranking, moving up from 29 the previous year. Interestingly, luxury brands such as Louis Vuitton, Hermès, and Gucci, all with a much lower market share, have a high brand value.

dennizn/shutterstock.com

Table 9-1 The Top Global Brands

Name	Domain	Brand Value	Country
		(millions, in USD)	
1 Apple	Technology	$184,154	United States
2 Google	Technology	$141,703	United States
3 Microsoft	Technology	$79,999	United States
4 Coca-Cola	Beverages	$69,733	United States
5 Amazon	Retail	$64,796	United States
6 Samsung	Technology	$56,249	South Korea
7 Toyota	Automotive	$50,291	Japan
8 Facebook	Social Media	$48,188	United States
9 Mercedes-Benz	Automotive	$47,829	Germany
10 IBM	Business Tech.	$46,829	United States
11 General Electric	Manufacturing	$44,208	United States
12 McDonald's	Restaurants	$41,533	United States
13 BMW	Automotive	$41,521	Germany
14 Disney	Media, Tourism	$40,772	United States
15 Intel	Technology	$39,459	United States
16 Cisco	Technology	$31,930	United States
17 Oracle	Technology	$27,466	United States
18 Nike	Sportswear	$27,021	United States
19 Louis Vuitton	Luxury	$22,919	France
20 Honda	Automotive	$22,696	Japan

Sources: Interbrand, *Best Global Brands,* 2017 accessed at
http://interbrand.com/best-brands/best-global-brands/2017/ranking/ on June 6, 2018.

9-4 The Service Side: Tariff and Nontariff Barriers to Entry

This section examines challenges that service providers face in their international involvement. These challenges, or service barriers, in one form or another, represent a manifestation of ethnocentrism at the firm level, government level, or consumer level. Among such challenges are:[25]

• The requirement to use national services. This requirement is a form of protectionism: Company or government policies provide implicit or explicit preference for a domestic supplier, which makes it difficult for international service providers to survive.

• The prohibition against the employment of foreign nationals or other barriers; for example, demanding a local certification such as certified public accountant (CPA), which requires a degree in accounting from a U.S. institution as well as passing the CPA exam.

• Direct competition from government providers, such as a local government monopoly over natural gas and electricity.

• Restrictions on movement; for example, limiting access for tourists in a particular region or the number of flights allowed into the country.

• Tariffs imposed on international service providers.

Frequently, the challenges posed to international service providers can be attributed to the close cultural link between a society and services.[26] Section 9-5 addresses the relationship between products, services, and culture.

9-5 Products, Services, and Culture

Service encounters are primarily social encounters, and rules and expectations related to services vary from culture to culture.[27] Studies in marketing reveal that it is important for international service providers to understand the factors that affect customer considerations in service evaluations and to emphasize the various dimensions of service quality accordingly.[28] To illustrate, Japanese consumers do not expect special treatment in a medical environment. Medicine is perceived as a public good, and it would be selfish of anyone to expect special attention. Similarly, the Japanese also hold doctors in high esteem, and customers expect and accept rudeness from doctors.[29] They also expect to be treated with a greater degree of formality by all service providers compared with consumers in the United States, whereas consumers in the United States prefer a greater degree of service personalization.[30]

Daniel M Ernst/shutterstock.com

Culture also influences the perception and evaluation of a brand in a particular country. Pepsi and Coca-Cola continue to market their diet brands as Pepsi Light and Coca-Cola Light outside of the U.S., where the word "diet" refers to a medically restricted diet. In Rwanda, Fanta Citron is a preferred mixer for hard liquor. Housewives in the United Kingdom are "hoovering" when they are vacuuming (regardless of the brand of vacuum cleaner they are using), and they buy Jell-O in a semi-gelled, rather than powder, format. Culture also determines the degree of brand loyalty. Consumers from collectivist cultures, such as Latin America and Asia, prefer established brands and purchase them in the maturity stage. Europeans tend to be brand name conscious; in urban areas, high-priced designers such as Prada and Hermès sell well to middle- and upper-middle-class consumers who may otherwise live in small rental apartments.

9-6 Protecting Brand Names

Brand names are valuable assets to a company. Companies pay millions to protect their brand names from dilution by registering them anywhere they are present and defending them in court, primarily because counterfeit merchandise harms the brand's reputation as well as company profits. The Uruguay round of the General Agreement on Tariffs and Trade (GATT) addressed standardizing global trademark legislation that is now incorporated under the World Trade Organization (WTO) umbrella. The question that remains is whether individual governments can and will enact this legislation. To illustrate, Yiwu, a city five hours from Shanghai, is one of the largest wholesale centers of China, where 200,000 distributors purchase up to 2,000 tons of goods daily. It also is China's counterfeit capital, where counterfeit products bearing established brand names — such as Procter & Gamble's Safeguard soap and Rejoice shampoo, Philip Morris cigarettes, Prada clothing, all sold at a fraction of their genuine counterparts' cost.[31] Counterfeiters range from small shampoo and soap manufacturers to large state-owned enterprises selling car batteries and motorcycle knockoffs. These products are distributed all over the world, including in the United States.[32]

9-6a Identifying Types of Counterfeiting

Examples of counterfeiting are design counterfeiting and brand name counterfeiting:

Design Counterfeiting

Copying designs or scents, known as design counterfeiting, is quite common and risk free. The Ralph Lauren Polo-style shirt is replicated by many companies, with a design that approximates the logo of the polo rider. The design of women's Peugeot watches is close to that of the Rolex Oyster Perpetual. Unknown perfume manufacturers suggest that their brand is similar in scent to a particular brand of perfume, which they name in their product packaging and advertising.

At some point, though, color and design cease to be distinctive if broadly adopted; then, it is no longer appropriate to refer to them as design counterfeits. The traditional Hermès orange leather handbag with its distinctive color and pronounced leather grain maintained its clear identity until about 2012, when many designers, luxury or not, started to use the color with a similar grain in their own handbag designs. The purse in Figure 9-7 is by a competing luxury designer. Here, it is elegantly displayed on sale, with another object of status consumption, Veuve Cliquot champagne. There are, however, many other handbags in the marketplace that are not particularly faithful copies of the very expensive Hermès Birkin bag that is distributed only in limited quantities to the company's boutiques.

Figure 9-7 *The bag portrayed in this display is a distinctive orange color, much like that of Hermès handbags. However, it is not a design counterfeit – the orange color of Hermès is now omnipresent in window displays*

These design counterfeits have similar saddle stitching and an identical color, with the distinctive locks in a clochette and the top flaps closing with the two buckles.

Brand Name Counterfeiting

At the next level is brand name counterfeiting. In Cairo, for about a dollar one can purchase simple, cotton shirts with the Christian Dior name on the label. Purses with names such as Prada, Fendi, and Louis Vuitton are sold practically on the steps of the actual retailers, in many capital cities, as are fake Rolex watches. Bazaars in Istanbul and Cairo are known for their "quality" fakes. Hong Kong markets where counterfeit products are sold are popular with tourists. Counterfeit products even make it to flea markets in the United States. In different countries, Pizza Hut and Domino's Pizza restaurants are quite different from the originals, and are not legitimate franchises. In the city of Shanghai, even stores carry names that invite scrutiny (see Figure 9-8).

Multinational businesses need to address several factors that contribute to the counterfeiters' success:

- Consumer factors
- Technology factors
- Distribution factors
- Local government factors

Consumer Factors

On the consumer side, there is a high willingness to purchase counterfeit goods. Studies have shown, for example, that a large proportion of consumers are

Figure 9-8 *This shoe store in central Shanghai is called Nibe, and its symbol is a version of the Nike swoosh.*

likely to select a counterfeit apparel item over a genuine product when there is a price advantage, primarily because function risks are low for apparel, whereas prestige gains are high.[33] In this sense, products that are visible and consumed publicly are more likely to be in demand than products that are less visible and not consumed publicly.

To consumers in both emerging markets and high-income countries, the difference between a brand and its counterfeit is often not obvious. However, consumers in high-income countries can rely on the guarantees from the legitimate retailers with exclusive brand distributorships, whereas consumers in many emerging markets have to rely on guarantees from retailers who themselves do not have guarantees that they are selling the real thing.

Technology Factors

The spread of advanced production technology (affordable, quality, color-copying machines), as well as production lines supplied by pirates or know-how stolen from joint-venture multinationals required to transfer technology to local partners, has made it possible for counterfeiters to make perfect replicas of the original products. Frequently, neither the manufacturer nor the consumers can tell fakes from the real product.[34] Especially problematic is the fact that advanced technologies allow for the marketing of fake car parts, as described in International Marketing Illustration 9-3.

International Marketing Illustration 9-3 Taking Counterfeiting to New Heights

Global counterfeiting is at an all-time high, accounting for seven percent of world trade, or US$500 billion a year. Counterfeiters from China, Taiwan, India, and South Korea have created knockoffs not just for clothing, but also for car parts, which now account for $12 billion a year in sales. Fake car brake pads, fan belts, oil and fuel filters, spark plugs, batteries, and windshields, all packaged with fake logos sell well in North America, but the largest market for these products is the Middle East.

The problem facing large automobile manufacturers, however, is not just the loss of sales. If someone purchases a fake part, which causes injury to the passengers, these leading automakers have to prove that the parts are not theirs. Even more deadly are counterfeit medications. The World Health Organization (WHO) estimates that as many as one million people die every year from ingesting counterfeit medications. Fake drugs seized by U.S. customs have traces of pesticides, rat poison, brick dust, and paint. Counterfeiters don't intend to poison people – they are merely using the cheap binding agents to maximize profits.

In Latin America, the counterfeit drug threat is large and increasingly dangerous! Ten percent of total drug sales in Mexico are counterfeit.

In Venezuela, which is experiencing hyperinflation and a virtual shutdown of the economy, the estimate is that one in four pharmaceuticals is counterfeit or fails to meet regulatory standards.

Counterfeiters are using advanced technology to manufacture the different counterfeit goods. They are investing in scanners to duplicate trademark labels that they can then attach to these knockoffs.

Sources: Gena Somra, "Patients Fooled by Fake Drugs Made with Poison and Brick Dust," CNN, August 30, 2015, accessed on June 24, 2018, at http://www.cnn.com/2015/08/30asia/pakistan-fake-drugs; Murray Hiebert, "Chinese Counterfeiters Turn Out Fake Car Parts," Wall Street Journal, March 3, 2004, A14; "Latin America Battles Counterfeit Drug Threat," FDA News, accessed on June 24, 2018 at https://www.fdanews.com/articles/84857-latin-america-battles-counterfeit-drug-threat.

designtools/shutterstock.com

Distribution Factors

Supply chains are not adequately controlled. Traders use Internet chat rooms and unauthorized dealership networks to sell the products and mix counterfeit products with legitimate products sold on the secondary gray market.[35]

Local Government Factors

Governments in many developing countries are reluctant to crack down on counterfeiting, especially when state-owned enterprises are involved in the operations. In the case of China, for instance, local governments hesitate to crack down on product pirates because they create thousands of jobs and keep the local economy going. And, even when local authorities take action against counterfeiters (most of whom evade taxes), persuading them to close down the state-owned factories engaging in illegal production is impossible.[36]

Counterfeit products are openly available in many developing countries. Here consumers, as well as customs representatives inspecting the counterfeit product shipments, are not familiar with many international brand names. Further, customs officials in many developing countries often are not sufficiently trained in identifying illegal trade in mass-market products. And, as mentioned, counterfeit products are also widely available in developed countries. The prevailing reason is that in the industrialized countries, customs officers inspect the contents of only a small fraction of the goods that go through customs.

9-6b Combating Counterfeiting

Multinational companies have used a number of strategies to combat counterfeiting. Lobbying the U.S. government, as well as the governments involved, is a first step. This process involves filing appeals to the World Trade Organization and lobbying other governmental organizations in the United States and abroad regulating trade. The outcome is uncertain, however. For example, even though member countries of the World Trade Organization are expected to abide by the organization's antipiracy provisions, they are not entirely successful in combating the sales of counterfeit products. Another multilateral effort is the Anti-Counterfeit Trade Agreement (ACTA) negotiated and signed by the United States and several other countries. Although the treaty was completed in 2011, it has not yet been ratified by the required number of countries to come into force. It was rejected by the European Parliament in 2012, which means ACTA can never come into force in the EU.[37]

Alternatives involve concerted action by companies to combat counterfeiting by changing a product's appearance to differentiate authentic products from fakes, using images that are difficult to replicate. The most successful anti-counterfeiting attacks were launched with local governments' cooperation. In China, a raid was launched by battery makers, including Gillette, Energizer, and Panasonic, with the help of 200 government agents, on 21 factories in a southwestern city. As a result of the raid, 150 pieces of manufacturing equipment and three million counterfeit batteries (with Russia as their destination) were confiscated.[38]

9-7 International Perspectives of Industrial Products and Services

Marketing industrial products and services across borders has certain similarities to the marketing of consumer goods. However, there are also important differences. For example, in the marketing of consumer products, culture plays a key role, and firms must be aware of norms, values, and traditions in the target country. However, cultural differences are not readily relevant in the production process, in the types of products that businesses purchase, such as major equipment, buildings, land, accessory equipment, fabricated and component parts, process material, maintenance and repair parts, operating supplies, raw materials, goods for resale, and business services. Culture is relevant when it comes to the selection of suppliers. Typically, the decision to purchase industrial products rests with management — and often with top management at the company's headquarters in the home country for the most expensive products — and the purchase process often takes several months.

In many countries, the national government in the country of operation has substantial input in the supplier deci-

GaudiLab/shutterstock.com

sion, favoring national suppliers over foreign businesses. National government input can be even more restrictive when it comes to the purchase of business services. For professional services, which include legal services, auditing and consulting services, and medical services, the national government can directly restrict the company to local service suppliers, or it can require that the respective service providers have local licenses and other credentials, which could essentially mean hiring local businesses. For operating services, which include Internet services, telephone service, shipping, and insurance, which are typically contracted out for a fixed period of time, the national government can require the business to hire local providers. If not, the business can handle those services using the most cost-effective approach, which could still mean resorting to local services, or even outsourcing them to a third country where labor costs are lower. Many companies launch a request for bids for these types of services on an annual basis, and the national government could require that, all things being equal, the national company must be selected.

The U.S. Department of Commerce Advocacy Center advocates on behalf of U.S. exporters of goods and services bidding on international contracts. The Advocacy Center works with overseas governments to ensure U.S. firms have the best possible chance when participating in competitive bids for contracts with foreign governments and government agencies. The Advocacy Center works closely with U.S. Dept. of Commerce export-promotion offices located at US. diplomatic missions around the world (https://2016.export.gov/advocacy).

SreetVJ/shutterstock.com

Industrial consumers are manufacturers, wholesalers, retailers, government agencies, and nonprofit organizations. Unlike consumer markets, business-to-business markets are characterized by fewer buyers and a larger purchase volume. In addition, the business-to-business market has important geographic concentrations. The world banking centers and advertising centers are concentrated in New York, London, and Tokyo. The world insurance centers are Geneva, London, and Munich. And demand for industrial products is derived from demand for consumer products and thus is much more volatile: Small changes in demand for consumer products can lead to substantial changes in demand for industrial products. Fluctuations in one market readily affect industries elsewhere. For example, the surplus of steel in China and elsewhere has dealt a blow to the steel industry in the industrialized countries, to the point that some have imposed protectionist measures. In 2018, the United States imposed tariffs on steel and aluminum imports. In designing industrial products and services for international markets, firms must consider the formal buying process, starting with the identification of needs, establishment of specifications, identification of product solutions and vendors, evaluation and selection of vendors, and negotiation of purchase terms. The decision to purchase a particular product is contingent on the entire package offering — the product, the service contract and availability of replacement parts, and the product price. For example, in the process of identifying product solutions and vendors, a firm needs to evaluate whether the product comes with installation, training, and other after-sales service. Even the local availability of after-

market replacement parts may constitute an important factor in the purchase decision. Replacement parts are often expensive, but, if they are readily available locally at a significantly lower cost than having to ship them to Thailand from New Jersey, the respective brand
becomes much more attractive.

9-7a Product Standards

The discussion in Section 9-1, "Standardization versus Adaptation," is less relevant in
industrial marketing because common industrial consumer needs have led to a high degree
of standardization of industrial products and services. In addition, the world industrial community is attempting to create standards for each industry. And, with quality taking an important place in the competition for global markets, businesses are adhering to the international quality standards set by the International Organization for Standardization (ISO),
which was established in 1946 as a nongovernmental federation of national standards bodies.

The organization issues the ISO 9000 certification, which addresses quality management,
whereby quality refers to all product or service features that are required by the customer. In ISO
terms, quality management implies that the organization ensures that the products or services it sells
satisfy customer requirements and comply with any
regulations applicable to those products or services.
In broad terms, ISO 9000 specifies that the organization must meet customer and regulatory requirements and follow its policies and procedures while

mushan/shutterstock.com

advancing quality through continuous improvement. It addresses issues such as the phases
of product development from the initial design phase to the delivery phase. It also requires
performance measurement throughout the process through performing internal audits,
monitoring customer satisfaction, and taking corrective action.[39]

In 1992, the United Nations Conference on Environment and Development (UNCED)
requested that the ISO introduce the ISO 14001 four years later. ISO 14001 is the first of the
ISO 14000 family of environmental management system standards designed to help businesses reduce their impact on the environment and to facilitate sustainable development
and foster international trade by providing an international system of standards. ISO 14001
certification guidelines discourage multinational firms from engaging in hazardous environmental practices, such as locating plants that generate hazardous emissions in poor countries with weak environmental regulations, and ensure that corporate policies promoting
environmentally sound, efficiency-embracing, innovative technologies and processes will
contribute to establishing twenty-first century production and distribution systems that are
far less environmentally degrading and wasteful. To receive the ISO 14001 certification, multinational companies have to develop environmental management systems (EMS) similar to
the ISO 9000 standards for total quality management and a policy that stresses a commitment to continual improvement and prevention of pollution, assurances that the company
will comply with relevant laws and regulations, and a framework for setting and regularly
reviewing environmental objectives and targets. The respective policy must be documented, communicated to all employees, and made available to the public. The current ISO
14001 guidelines were issued in 2015. [40]

It is very important to note that both ISO 9000 and ISO 14000 address the production process, rather than the product. However, it is implied that the process affects the product. In the context of both, certification refers to the issuing of a certificate by an independent external body that has audited the organization's management system and verified that it conforms to the requirements of the standards. The auditing body then registers the certification in the client's register.[41]

Summary

Describe drivers for international standardization and offer an overview of the international standardization–local adaptation continuum and respective company strategies. The emergence of uniform market segments, such as global consumers (global teenagers, the global elite), increased international travel, and a general consumer preference for products of higher quality at a lower price, led to opportunities for global standardization strategies. Such strategies offer numerous benefits, primarily the capability for a firm to market its goods at lower costs and higher profits. A purely global strategy, however, will invariably result in ignoring specific segment preferences and in targeting strategies that have a higher likelihood of failure. Some adaptation can be attempted using a global localization strategy, where the main module of the strategy is maintained, while making minor modifications from market to market. Sometimes, however, adaptation may be required (mandatory), or the adaptation is necessary to better meet the needs of the local market.

Examine country-of-origin effects on brand evaluations in relation to product stereotypes and consumer ethnocentrism. Country-of-origin information is used in making product evaluation inferences in situations in which little other information (brand name, for instance) is available to evaluate the product. Country information also can be used to exclude products from the consideration set. For example, ethnocentric consumers, who believe that purchasing foreign products is morally wrong, will refuse to purchase products unless they are made in their home country.

Examine challenges faced by service providers in international markets. Service providers face numerous barriers to entry in international markets. In addition to tariffs, international service providers may be prohibited from hiring international employees, or they may be required to have certain certifications that are difficult to obtain and can be obtained only locally. They might also face direct competition from government providers, such as a local government monopoly, or they could face restrictions on movement.

Address issues related to brand name protection and the reasons behind widespread international counterfeiting. Counterfeiting, ranging from direct copying to design counterfeiting, is flourishing due to improved technology, inadequate channel control, lax enforcement locally and worldwide (despite World Trade Organization involvement), and consumer demand.

Address the marketing of industrial products and services and related product and service standards. Industrial products and services are marketed differently than consumer products and services: They are not as culture dependent and are more standardized. To create quality standards for products worldwide, the ISO 9000 certification addresses quality management standards, and the ISO 14000 certification addresses environmental management standards.

Key Terms

adaptation

brand name counterfeiting

core product strategy

country of manufacture

country of origin

design counterfeiting

ethnocentrism

global consumers

global localization

global standardization

glocalization

gray marketing

ISO 9000 certification

ISO 14000 certification

mandatory adaptation

modular adaptation

nonmandatory adaptation

private labels

product-country stereotypes

regional standardization

service barriers

Discussion Questions

1. Describe the global standardization–local adaptation debate. What are the drivers for globalization and for adaptation? Explain.

2. Give examples of mandatory and nonmandatory adaptations.

3. How do private-label (retailer) brands compete with international and local brands? Give examples.

4. Discuss the different barriers to entry that international service providers face worldwide.

5. What are the reasons behind counterfeiting, and what efforts are taking place to combat it? Are they successful?

Chapter Quiz

True/False

1. Overlapping media among countries makes it easier to create awareness of a product.

Answer: True

Rationale: Consumers are exposed to the message frequently and in different environments, thus increasing product awareness. Section 9-1a, "Global Standardization"

2. Global branding creates different images for the product in the different regions where the product is sold.

Answer: False

Rationale: A global brand has the same name, logo, image, and positioning everywhere in the world. Section 9-1a, "Global Standardization"

3. A product's country of origin is always the country where the product was manufactured.

Answer: False

Rationale: Country of origin is defined as the country with which a particular product or service is associated. That country may be different from the country where the product is manufactured; the company may have moved production in the country of manufacture to take advantage of lower labor costs. Section 9-3a, "Product-Country and Service-Country Stereotypes"

4. Multinational companies often try to combat counterfeiting by differentiating their products with signature traits.

Answer: True

Rationale: Along with lobbying governments, firms can combat counterfeiting by changing a product's appearance and features to differentiate authentic products from fakes. Section 9-6b," Combating Counterfeiting"

5. Wal-Mart and Tesco products sold under the respective company's umbrella name are known as private-label brands.

Answer: True

Rationale: Products sold under a retailer's brand name are also known as private-label brands. Section 9-2, "Private-Label (Retailer) Brands"

6. Culture is essential in the marketing of industrial products.

Answer: False

Rationale: In the marketing of consumer products, culture plays a key role, and firms must be aware of norms, values, and traditions in the target country. However, culture does not play as important a role in the production process or in the types of products that business-es purchase. Section 9-7, "International Perspectives of Industrial Products and Services"

Multiple Choice

1. Girls around the world participating in similar pastimes such as inline skating or playing with Barbie dolls are an illustration of:

      a. differentiated consumer preferences.

      b. global consumers.

      c. international production.

      d. none of the above

Answer: b is correct.

Rationale: Global consumers want the same products worldwide—and share the same pastimes and interests. Section 9-1a, "Global Standardization"

2. Ford's success in promoting "world cars" like the Ford Focus is a successful example of:

      a. international positioning.

      b. international travel.

      c. satisfying consumer preferences.

      d. all of the above

Answer: c is correct.

Rationale: Consumers worldwide are willing to sacrifice product-related features, function, and design to obtain higher quality at a lower price; with the Ford Focus, the company was able to address uniform consumer preferences worldwide. Section 9-1a, "Global Standardi-zation"

3. Promoting its products globally and altering parts of their promotion based on specific areas is common of a company focused on:

      a. nonmandatory adaptation.

      b. global standards.

      c. glocalization or global localization.

      d. none of the above

Answer: c is correct.

Rationale: The practice of global branding and localized marketing adaptation is known as global localization, or glocalization. Section 9-1c, "Global Localization"

4.   The following is an example of mandatory adaptation for the United States market:

      a. U.S. automobile emission standards

b. 110 volts

c. NTSC television

d. all of the above

Answer: d is correct.

Rationale: All of the above are requirements for the U.S. market. The U.S. Department of Transportation enforces emission standards for imports. Most appliances in the U.S. work only on 110 volts, and televisions are all on NTSC. Section 9-1d, "Mandatory Adaptation"

5. Philips is headquartered in the Netherlands, but many of its appliances are manufactured in Asia. The country of origin of Philips:

a. is the Netherlands.

b. is the country in Asia where the product is manufactured.

c. depends on the perception of the consumer.

d. none of the above

Answer: a is correct.

Rationale: The country of origin of Philips products is, in the minds of most consumers, the Netherlands. Section 9-3, "Global Branding and Country-of-Origin Information"

6. Which of the following are examples of products that businesses purchase?

a.   Major equipment, buildings, land

b.   Accessory equipment and fabricated and component parts

c.   Process material and maintenance and repair parts

d.   All of the above

Answer: d is correct.

Among the products that businesses purchase are major equipment, buildings, land, accessory equipment, fabricated and component parts, process material, maintenance and repair parts, operating supplies, raw materials, goods for resale, and business services. Section 9-7, "International Perspectives of Industrial Products and Services"

Notes

1. Dannie Kjeldgaard and Søren Askegaard, "The Glocalization of Youth Culture: The Global Youth Segment as Structures of Common Difference," *Journal of Consumer Research*, Vol. 33, No. 3, 2006, pp. 231–247; Dannie Kjeldgaard and Søren Askegaard, "Consuming Modernities: The Global Youth Segment as a Site of Consumption, Barbara E. Kahn and Mary Frances Luce (eds.), *Advances in Consumer Research*, 2004, p. 31.

2. Shaoming Zou and Aysegul Ozsomer, "Global Product R&D and the Firm's Strategic Position," *Journal of International Marketing*, Vol. 7, No. 1, 1999, pp. 57–76.

3. Ibid.

4. Demetris Vronitis and Peri Vronitis, "Levi Strauss: An International Marketing Investigation," *Journal of Fashion Marketing and Management*, Vol. 8, No. 4, 2004, p. 389.

5. Susan Segal-Horn, "The Limits of Global Strategy," *Strategy & Leadership*, Vol. 24, No. 6, November –December 1996, pp. 12–17.

6. Alan J. Liddle, "McD's Global Standardization Strategy Enhanced by Vendor Sale," *Nation's Restaurant*, Vol. 40, No. 19, May 8, 2006, p. 22.

7. Demetris Vronitis and Peri Vronitis, "Levi Strauss: An International Marketing Investigation," *Journal of Fashion Marketing and Management*, Vol. 8, No. 4, 2004, p. 389.

8. Ibid.

9. Segal-Horn, "The Limits of Global Strategy," pp. 12–17.

10. Ibid.

11. http://www.mercedes-benz.de/content/germany/mpc/mpc_germany_website/de/home_mpc/ passengercars/ home/new_cars/models/a-class/w176.flash.html, accessed on September 10, 2015.

12. www.mbusa.com accessed on June 20, 2018; Jens Meiners, "2019 Mercedes-Benz A-class Debuts, Will Spawn at Least three Models for US.," *Car and Driver,* February 2, 2018, accessed at https:// www.caranddriver.com/news/2019-mercedes-benz-a-class-debuts-will-spawn-at-least-three-models-for-u-s on June 5, 2018.

13. John S. Hill and Richard R. Still, "Adapting Products to LDC Tastes," *Harvard Business Review,* March–April 1984, pp. 92–101.

14. Christopher Lovelock and George S. Yip, "Developing Global Strategies for Service Businesses," *California Management Review,* Vol. 38, No. 2, 1996, pp. 64–87.

15. Charlotte Gao, "Google Stumbles Back to China, *The Diplomat,* January 16, 2018, accessed at https://thediplomat.com/2018/01/google-stumbles-back-to-china on June 5, 2018.

16. Vronitis and Vronitis, "Levi Strauss," p. 389.

17. Cyndee Miller, "Chasing the Global Dream," *Marketing News,* Vol. 30, No. 25, December 2, 1996, pp. 1–2.

18. This is yet another example of adaptation, this time by Coca-Cola, for consumers in Europe, to whom the term "diet" signifies medically imposed eating restrictions.

19. Vikas Bajaj, "In India, the Golden Age of Television Is Now," *New York Times,* February 11, 2007, Sunday Business section, 1, 4.

20. Donna Gorski Berry, "Global Dairy Food Trends," *Dairy Foods,* Vol. 99, No. 10, October 1998, pp. 32–37. Unilever, "Unilever Completes Acquisition of Qualas Personal and Home Care Brands," January 3, 2018, accessed at https://www.unilever.com/news/Press-releases/2018/unilever-completes-acquisition-of-qualas-personal-and-home-care-brands.html on June 20, 2018.

21. For a review of the country-of-origin effects literature, see Dalton Wilcox, "Country-Of-Origin Bias: A Literature Review and Prescription for the Global World," in *Marketing, Technology and Customer Commitment in the New Economy,* Developments in Marketing Science: Proceedings of the Academy of Marketing Science, Springer, pp 86-96; Lalita A. Manrai, Dana-Nicoleta Lascu, and Ajay K. Manrai, "Interactive Effects of Country of Origin and Product Category on Product Evaluations," *International Business Review,* Vol. 7, 1998, pp. 591–615.

22. Thomas Klier, "The Auto Industry and NAFTA-Links Between the U.S. and Mexico," Federal Reserve Bank of Chicago Newsletter, May 12, 2017, accessed on June 6, 2018, at www.dallasfed.org/~/ media/documents/research/events/2017/17tiesin21stcentury-Thomas.pdf.

23. "Current State of Place Branding Practice in Latin America," *The Place Brand Observer,* March 12, 2017, accessed at https://placebrandobserver.com/place-branding-practice-latin-america on June 23, 2018.

24. Saeed Samiee, Terry Shimp, Subhash Sharma, "Brand Origin Recognition Accuracy: Its Antecedents and Consumers' Cognitive Limitations, *Journal of International Business Studies* Vol. 36, No. 5, 2005, pp. 379–397.

25. For an in-depth description of these and additional restrictions, see Lee D. Dahringer, "Marketing Services Internationally: Barriers and Management Strategies," *Journal of Services Marketing,* Vol. 5, No. 3, Summer 1991, pp. 5–17.

26. P. B. Kenen, *The International Economy,* Englewood Cliffs, NJ: Prentice Hall, 1989; and Ikechi Ekeledo and K. Sivakumar, "Foreign Market Entry Mode Choice of Service Firms: A Contingency Perspective," *Journal of the Academy of Marketing Science,* Vol. 26, No. 4, 1998, pp. 274–292.

27. John A. Czepiel, "Service Encounters and Service Relationships: Implications and Research," *Journal of Business Research,* Vol. 20, 1990, pp. 13–21; and Kathryn Frazier Winsted, "Evaluating Service Encounters: A Cross-Cultural and Cross-Industry Exploration," *Journal of Marketing Theory and Practice,* Vol. 7, No. 2, Spring 1999, pp. 106–123.

28. Naresh K. Malhotra, Francis M. Ulgado, J. Agrawal, and I. B. Baalbaki, "International Services Marketing: A Comparative Evaluation of the Dimensions of Service Quality Between Developed and Developing Countries," *International Marketing Review,* Vol. 11, No. 2, 1994, p. 515.

29. Frazier Winsted, "Evaluating Service Encounters," pp. 106–123.

30. Ibid.

31. Dexter Roberts, Frederik Balfour, Paul Magnuson, Pete Engardio, and Jennifer Lee, "China's Pirates: It's Not Just Little Guys—State-Owned Factories Add to the Plague of Fakes," *BusinessWeek*, No. 3684, June 5, 2000, pp. 26, 44.

32. Ibid.

33. Peter H. Bloch, Ronald F. Bush, and Leland Campbell, "Consumer 'Accomplices' in Product Counterfeiting," *Journal of Consumer Marketing*, Vol. 10, No. 4, 1993, pp. 27–36.

34. Roberts, Balfour, Magnuson, Engardio, and Lee, "China's Pirates," pp. 26, 44.

35. Ibid.

36. Ibid.

37. David Meyer, "ACTA Rejected by Europe, Leaving Copyright Treaty Near Dead," *ZD Net*, July 4, 2012, accessed at https://www.zdnet.com/article/acta-rejected-by-europe-leaving-copyright-treaty-near-dead/ on June 6, 2018.

38. www.iso.cf, accessed on June 24, 2018.

39. Dennis Rondinelli and Gyula Vastag, "International Environmental Standards and Corporate Policies: An Integrative Framework," *California Management Review*, Vol. 39, No. 1, 1996, pp. 106–122.

40. www.iso.ch

41. Ibid.

Case 9-1 *Can the smart Make a Comeback in the U.S. Market?*

Mercedes-Benz would be a consistently profitable business, had it not been trying to fix its small car business. The smart, its iconic, but troubled brand, has been in the red ever since its launch in 1998. In 2005, the smart cost the company more than $2 billion in charges for job losses and cutbacks. In the process of restructuring to reduce Smart's fixed costs, the company had to cut hundreds of jobs.

Initially designed as a cute cobblestone negotiator in crowded European alleys, the little car has made valiant attempts to help U.S. consumers better negotiate their sometimes shrinking gasoline purchasing power in the land of SUVs . This is a story of market adaptation. Sort of.

The Story of Smart

In the world of joint ventures, the smart has a distinguished history. The smart was propelled to stardom in the mini-automobile category in the early 1990s, as a joint venture between Mercedes-Benz and Swatch. Daimler is the luxury automobile manufacturer that has created the Mercedes automobile, the worldwide standard for luxury on the road. Swatch is a creative and quirky company that makes Swatches, watches with colorful designs. The *smart fortwo* joint venture was created with the purpose of enhancing the Mercedes portfolio with an "ultra-urban" automobile that negotiates well narrow European alleys, fits neatly on the sidewalk if the parking spaces are all taken, and otherwise makes the driver look good (see Figure 9-9).

Though small,   the *smart fortwo* protects its passengers well. It has a tridion safety shell, a hard shell that protects occupants in case of impact. It is also equipped with electronic stability control, which prevents it from flipping over, and antilock brakes. It has a high driving position to ensure the greatest visibility on the road. The design team focused on creating an energy efficient automobile using recyclable materials. Compared with the luxury Mercedes line, the *smart fortwo* is affordable: A two-seat, nine-foot-long *smart fortwo* costs about $13,000 for the bare model, reaching about $20,000 for convertibles. Its gas consumption is 40 miles per gallon, and it reaches 90 miles per hour on the highway. It seats two and is so small that two cars can fit in a traditional parking spot.

The smart's problem, however, is that its market performance has been poor. Although Smart's global sales have grown steadily since its launch thanks to the introduction of new models, it

Figure 9-9 The smart fortwo is present everywhere in Berlin. On a city walk, there was a smart fortwo every eight cars or so, in your average-middle-class neighborhood – this yellow smart fortwo demanded a double-take.

has consistently missed its targets. The company launched the *forfour* model to compete in the saturated, highly competitive compact-car segment, but it was quickly discovered that the new model hurt the brand, ultimately resulting in its withdrawal from the market. In a parallel development, the company also intended to build the *formore*, designed for the U.S. SUV market. However, after steep losses, coupled with additional problems, — Mercedes had to recall 1.3 million vehicles.

The Turnaround

At first, Mercedes-Benz had considered eliminating the smart, but quickly determined that it had too much brand franchise. Its recovery plans included having Mercedes take over purchasing, sales, and service operations, and creating a better fit with the needs of European consumers. Smart has been testing several prototype models using alternative fuels, including an electric-powered smart, a compressed natural gas version, and a hybrid model. Smart's proposition of being the "ultimate urban solution" will be even more relevant now that more cities in Europe are looking to introduce congestion charging.

The U.S. Launch

The new *fortwo* model, launched in Europe in 2007, was introduced in the U.S. in 2008. The company first decided to use Roger Penske's United Automotive Group Inc., to distribute the product to the United States, serving as the interface between dealers and Daimler, ordering cars for the U.S. market and distributing them to about 60 dealers affiliated and nonaffiliated with the chain.

In the United States, *smart fortwo* was targeted at younger buyers, urban residents, baby boomers, and retirees. In order to target younger buyers, Penske followed the example of Toyota Motor Corp. and BMW AG, both of which successfully launched new small cars, the Scion and the Mini, respectively. Penske used a largely Internet-based advertising model that targeted niche buyers, which included younger buyers and other trendsetting groups. The company staged a 50-city road tour, so people could drive the car, and attracted 10,000 test drivers.

After a rip-roaring start, sales went down precipitously, to the point that Penske threw in the towel as the automobile's distributor in 2011. A redesign for the 2013 model provided some reassurance, with a stronger front bumper. U.S. sales increased to 10,500 units in 2014, of which 25 percent were electric.

However, by 2016 sales plunged to only 6,200 cars in the U.S. In 2017, Daimler announced they would discontinue offering the gasoline-powered smart in the U.S. market, focusing exclusively on the electric version. Following the announcement, about two-thirds of the Mercedes-Benz USA dealers decided to drop smart, leaving fewer than 30 dealers in the U.S. market. Could the smart be doomed on this side of the pond?

Sources: Paul Eisenstein, "Smart Car Pins Hopes on New Pint-Size Model," CNN, August 28, 2015, accessed at http://www.cnbc.com/2015/08/28/smart-car-pins-hopes-on-new-pint-size-model.html on September 13, 2015; Doron Levin, "U.S. sales of Smart cars hit a wall," CNN Money, February 19, 2011, http:// money.cnn.com/2011/02/18/autos/smart-car-penske-mercedes.fortune/index.htm; John D. Stoll, "Smart Car a Shrewd Move?" *Wall Street Journal*, June 27, 2007, A8; Gina Chon and Stephen Power, "Can an Itsy-Bitsy Auto Survive in the Land of the SUV? *Wall Street Journal*, January 9, 2007, B1; "Smart Car: Engineering a Recovery," *Marketing*

Week, May 11, 2006, p. 28; Paul Eisenstein, "Smart Struggles to Survive," *Professional Engineering*, April 13, 2005, Vol. 18, No. 7, p. 28; www.smartusa.com/company.html. Paul A. Eisenstein. "Daimler's Smart Cars are Going All-Electric in the U.S. Market," *NBCNews.com*, February 14, 2017, accessed at https://www.nbcnews.com/business/autos/smart-going-all-electric-u-s-market-n720781 on June 7, 2018. Fred Lambert, "Smart Brand's Move to All-Electric Results in Losing 2/3 of US Dealerships," *Electrek*, August 14, 2017, accessed at https://electrek.co/2017/08/14/smart-car-all-electric-us-dealerships/ on June 7, 2018.

Analysis Suggestions:

1. What strategies does smart use in the European market? Is the automobile adapted to consumers' driving needs in Europe?

2. Why is the smart not changing to adapt to the U.S. market, dominated by large trucks and sports utility vehicles? Has a lack of adaptation hurt sales in the United States? What strategies might smart employ to try and increase sales in the United States?

Case 9-2 The Landwind X7: Counterfeiting Design for the Home Market

The Landwind X7, introduced in 2015, is a Chinese sport utility vehicle that bears an uncanny resemblance to the Range Rover Evoque, and it costs less than a third of the price. Before the Landwind X7 appeared on the Chinese market, more than 5,500 people put down deposits for the vehicle, which is available at a starting price of less than $22,000. The Range Rover Evoque, which is Jaguar Land Rover's best-selling model worldwide, retails at over $72,000.

Aesthetically, the X7 is virtually indistinguishable from the Evoque. (see Figure 9-10 on next page.) Both models feature similar broad fenders, recessed door panels, a sloping roof, and an identical wheelbase. The X7, paraded at the 2015 Shanghai International Automobile Industry Exhibition, created great apprehension for the managers of Jaguar Land Rover China. This cheap lookalike would certainly make it difficult for Jaguar Land Rover to command a premium price for its model; it has already cut prices and its sales have fallen by 27 percent after the X7 introduction.

The British premium carmaker Jaguar Land Rover (JLR) is owned by India's Tata Motors Ltd. The CEO of Jaguar Land Rover China, Ralf Speth, angrily denounced the copycat: "I really regret that all of a sudden copy-paste is coming up again," he told the press at the Shanghai Auto Show. "That will not help the reputation of China, of Chinese industry at all." But he conceded that there are no laws to protect design counterfeiting in China so the company will not have any legal recourse – in Europe and elsewhere, protection can be ensured in the design language, in the features, as well as in the technology.

Landwind, a joint venture between China's Changan Auto and Jiangling Motors, produces a series of SUVs sold primarily on the Chinese market. Landwind did make history in 2005, however, when it became the first Chinese automaker to export its vehicles to Europe, but it quickly moved out after failing crash tests. The company denies that the X7 could take away market share since individuals in the market for a $90,000 Range Rover will not purchase a much cheaper Landwind X7. They also suggest that the Landwind X7 may even turn out to help Evoque sales.

The market conflict between Range Rover Evoque and Landwind X7 continues. At the 2017 Guangzhou Motor Show, Landwind introduced the new X7; the 2017 model has design changes that make it look a bit less like the Evoque. It is an open question whether the changes were a result of global pressure and bad publicity about the inaugural 2015 model or rather a planned refresh of the style.

JLR is well aware that companies have no recourse in China for design counterfeiting. The Chery QQ successfully copied the Chevy Spark with no negative consequences – the cars are perfectly identical and parts from one automobile can be used for the other. And Jia Yueting, the billionaire behind China's top-selling smart TV and a phone that sold 200,000 units in the first few seconds of its release, is planning on presenting Le* Car, a Tesla clone at the 2016 Beijing Auto Show. Le* Car looks very similar to the Tesla Model S and it is being developed with top talent poached from companies such as Tesla and BMW.

One of the challenges that well-established brands face in worldwide is design counterfeiting. The law regarding copying designs has been relatively lax, and fashion designers at the lower price points have been copying designs with impunity. An affordable Peugeot woman's watch looks very much like the Ladies' Rolex Oyster Perpetual Datejust watch, which retails for over $3,500. You easily pay a random unauthorized online distributor just $400 for a table that is identical to the Saarinen tulip table that normally retails for well over $3,000 at Knoll, the authorized distributor.

Figure 9-10 *Landwind X7 01 -- Auto Shanghai -- 2015-04-22"
by Navigator84 - Own work. Licensed under CC BY-SA 4.0
via Commons - https://commons.wikimedia.org/wiki/
File:Landwind_X7_01_--_Auto_Shanghai_--_2015-04-22.jpg#/
media/File:Landwind_X7_01_--_Auto_Shanghai_--_2015-04-
22.jpg*

More recently, however, various organizations of furniture designers pressed local and national governments to take action against design counterfeiting. The 2014 United Kingdom Intellectual Property Bill extends criminal penalties for the deliberate copying, importing or marketing of designs that have been registered with U.S. and EU intellectual property regulators. The new law brings penalties for violation of design rights into parity with existing protections for trademarks and copyrights. The law is designed to provide designers of manufactured goods like cars and smartphones the same protection as those afforded to book publishers, and infringers of designs may face up to 10 years in prison. The European Union is also scrutinizing design counterfeiting developments and planning to craft more stringent regulations.

The previously open door of design counterfeiting might be closing soon. The question that remains is: Will China abide by international regulations once that happens?

Sources: Brian Mahoney, "UK Floats Criminal Penalties for Design Counterfeiting," *Law 360*, May 10, 2013, accessed at http://www.law360.com/articles/440592/uk-floats-criminal-penalties-for-design-counterfeiting on November 12, 2015; *Bloomberg News*, "This $21,700 Land Rover Lookalike to Go on Sale in China," August 4, 2015, accessed at http://www.bloomberg.com/news/articles/2015-08-04/this-21-700-land-rover-lookalike-to-go-on-sale-in-china on November 12, 2015; Benjamin Zhang, "China Has Knocked Off a Range Rover and Is Selling It at a Third of the Price of the Real Thing," *Business Insider*, August 10, 2015, accessed at http://www.businessinsider.com/china-has-knocked-off-a-range-rover-and-is-selling-it-at-a-third-of-the-price-of-the-real-thing-2015-8 on November 10, 2015; Rene Chun, "Attack of the Chinese Tesla Clones," *Wired*, October 13, 2015, accessed at http:// www.wired.com/2015/10/attack-of-the-tesla-clones-from-china/ on November 10, 2015. Mark Tisshaw. "Range Rover Evoque Copycat Landwind x7 Updated With a New Look," *Autocar UK*, November 17, 2017, accessed at https://www.autocar.co.uk/car-news/motor-shows-guangzhou-motor-show/range-rover-evoque-copycat-landwind-x7-updated-new-look on June 7, 2018 Guy Wilmot, "The Intellectual Property Act 2014: What It Means For Small Businesses," *The Guardian*, October 2, 2014, accessed at https://www.theguardian.com/small-business-network/2014/oct/02/intellectual-property-act-what-means-small-businesseson June 7, 2018.

Analysis Suggestions

1. Discuss design counterfeiting from the perspective of the Chinese counterfeiter, the joint venture between China's Changan Auto and Jiangling Motors manufacturing the Landwind X7, and JLR.

2. How will a cheaper version of the Range Rover Evoque hurt its sales? Explain.

3. Should design counterfeiting be illegal? Why or why not?

This page is intentionally blank...

Chapter 10

International Product and Service Strategies

Energy Drinks

Red Bull, an Austrian energy drink, has systematically taken over energy drink marketing around the world. The drink, adopted by most of Europe in the early 1990s, took the U.S. by storm in 1997. By 2000, it created and propelled the energy drink category to $75 million in sales; today, energy drinks are a $50 billion industry. It is estimated that sales of energy drinks will reach $85 billion by 2025. In 2001, a California company introduced a successful challenger: Monster. Five years later, the company had $500 million in sales and claimed second place behind Red Bull. Annual sales for Monster in 2017 were an astounding $3.4 billion![1]

Copycats continue to battle for shelf space, where they are joined by newcomers from Coca-Cola (Full Throttle and RockStar, privately held but distributed by Coke's top bottler), and PepsiCo. While Red Bull sponsors NASCAR and professional soccer, Monster prefers to claim visibility at the fringes, selecting up-and-coming athletes in obscure sports, such as freestyle motocross

Dilok Klaisataporn/shutterstock.com

But it is well possible that those numbers might go down due to a potential backlash against energy drinks. In Canada, the product comes with a long warning label. In the United States, the Food and Drug Administration does not regulate energy drinks, but the caffeine content ranges from 80 milligrams for an eight-ounce Red Bull to over 350 milligrams in 16 ounces of the no-calorie energy drink Bang. The sugar content of energy drinks is on par with that of soda. With increased consumer focus on sugar content, the future of this product category is by no means certain.[2]

The international marketing environment creates complex challenges for products and services. For example, during the product life cycle, firms must coordinate their marketing activities with international trade and investment decisions to remain price competitive in the face of increased competition from manufacturers in developing and developed countries alike. New product development decisions involve consumers in target markets that differ from home-country consumers in their attitudes, interests, and opinions. The challenges of new product/service launches are amplified by the complexities of the marketplace and the competition from both local and multinational firms. And managing the product mix and the product portfolio in line with company strategy and the demands of different consumers offers many dilemmas to brand managers. This chapter attempts to shed light on some of these challenges.

10-1 The International Product Life Cycle

Products pass through distinct stages, during which profits can rise and fall. As a consequence, products require different marketing strategies in each stage. The international product life cycle (IPLC) involves a complex relationship between the product life cycle stage and international trade and investment. At a basic level, the premise of the IPLC is as follows: Firms from developed, industrialized countries produce products for domestic consumption in the early stage of the product life cycle primarily because product specifications and the manufacturing process are not yet stable. As the product advances to the maturity stage, product specifications and the manufacturing process stabilize. At this point, price competition becomes intense, and international markets emerge, prompting firms to move production abroad to benefit from lower manufacturing costs.[3]

Figure 10-1 describes the international trade and investment activity of an international corporation and of local competition during each stage of the international product life cycle (from the perspective of the international corporation). During the introduction and growth stages, production takes place in the home country or in another industrialized country, and the company exports the products to developing countries. At maturity, manufacturing moves overseas, and the product is imported to the home country and other industrialized countries. Local competitors then emerge; they compete with the international corporation in its home country or in other industrialized countries. During the decline stage, international sales keep the company afloat.

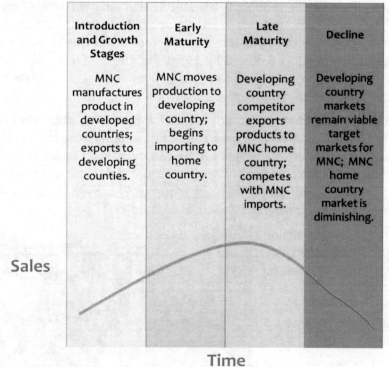

Introduction and Growth Stages	Early Maturity	Late Maturity	Decline
MNC manufactures product in developed countries; exports to developing counties.	MNC moves production to developing country; begins importing to home country.	Developing country competitor exports products to MNC home country; competes with MNC imports.	Developing country markets remain viable target markets for MNC; MNC home country market is diminishing.

Figure 10-1
The International Product
Life Cycle (IPLC)
and The
Multinational Corporation
(MNC).

Sales

Time

10-1a The Product Introduction Stage

During the introduction stage, products are developed in industrialized countries and supported by firms' substantial research and development budgets and by highly skilled product research teams. To quickly recover the high costs of product development and launching, a firm markets products in industrialized countries to consumers who can afford the high prices charged to recover the high costs, while it still has control of the market (the firm is the only manufacturer or one of the few manufacturers of the product). According to the initial IPLC theory (see Section 10-1, "The International Product Life Cycle"), these products are first marketed in the products' country of origin. Assuming a reasonable adoption rate in highly industrialized countries, the product also becomes available in developing countries, where it is exported by the firm.

Tesla's Model 3, its more affordable electric sports sedan, is a hot item, with hundreds of thousands of consumers in the U.S. and Canada on the waiting list for the automobile. Tesla only started international deliveries of Model 3 in 2019. Currently, thus, the Model 3 is in the introduction stage.[4]

10-1b The Growth Stage

The growth stage is characterized by increasing competition, with new product variants offered to the market, as well as rapid product adoption by the target market. Toward the end of this stage, the focus is on developing economies of scale in the manufacturing process. Price competition increases at this point and a standard is reached. An example of a product in the growth stage is the Apple iPhone, which is experiencing rapid adoption in high- and middle-income countries.

The iPhone is continuously innovating, introducing smart phones with must-have features, creating high demand. After the product is introduced, its demand remains high for a long period of time, so much so that Apple often finds it hard to keep up. The iPhone is in the growth stage in high-income countries and emerging markets.[5] For many consumers in emerging markets, however, the product is not easily affordable. Thus, while it takes the average worker in Toronto, Canada, one work week to afford an iPhone, it takes a worker in Nairobi, Kenya, 470 hours, and, in Kiev, Ukraine, 627 hours of work.[6]

Clearly, new products are not adopted instantly across the board. Adoption of new technology is uneven at best in each market, with urban areas first adopting the brand, followed, possibly decades later, by rural areas. In high-income countries, such as Japan (see Figure 10-2), the United States and the countries of Western Europe, consumer electronics typically pass quickly through the growth stage and reach maturity. There will always be a new offering that will attract the attention and the wallets of consumers.

During the growth stage, production continues to take place in industrialized countries, and manufacturers in industrialized countries continue to export their products in developing countries. At the end of the growth stage, the product is standardized – a particular standard is reached, such as a flat screen for television sets.

It should be noted that fast growth does not necessarily mean vast recovery of company investments in the market. For example, India is the fastest growth market for cell phones, but phone companies are not bringing in great profits. Rather, cell phone companies are investing in this market on the premise that, in the future, consumers will afford to pay for the phone services. For now, even those who make only $3 a day can afford

Figure 10-2 *In Japan, consumer electronics quickly pass through the growth stage and reach maturity, as consumers are keen on the new models with new capabilities.*

cell phones. How? They pay only for the calls they dial, hang up, and wait to be called back. A cellular service provider, in many instances, has to practically offer the service for free. Western callers pay more than $1000 a year for their cellular service; Indian callers pay only

$110. Nevertheless, phone companies compete for the Indian consumer. Among competitors are the Vodafone Group of Britain, the world's largest cellphone operator, Japan's NTT DoCoMo, and Teléfonos de Mexico. Multinational giants, including General Motors, Unilever, Coca-Cola, and many others have learned to make money with cheaper offerings, as India makes up for cheap prices with volume and breakneck growth.[7]

10-1c The Maturity Stage

Usually the longest stage in the product life cycle, the maturity stage is characterized by a slowdown in sales growth as the product is adopted by most target consumers and by a leveling or decline in profits primarily due to intense price competition. At this point, manufacturing moves to emerging markets to save on labor costs. For example, the U.S. electronics company Motorola selected Krakow, Poland, as its first European software center and the location of a chip plant, while Siemens AG, Macronix, and Intel Corp. are engaging in semiconductor manufacturing in Thailand, in a consortium with a local company.[8] Products manufactured abroad are then imported in the home country and other industrialized countries, competing on price in the respective developed countries. But this pattern — the product manufactured in a high-income country, and, with maturity setting in, moving manufacturing to emerging markets to take advantage of cheap labor — is slowly changing. For example, the initial and the new versions of the iPhone are produced in Taiwan and China. The new versions are now available in high- and middle-income countries simultaneously. Nevertheless, for most products, the initial pattern of production and diffusion is still dominant, with companies going to cheap labor markets to manufacture the product at low cost during maturity. Examples of products in maturity are television sets, sound systems, and cameras. In the United States, mobile phones belong in this category as well, and smartphones appear to be close to the maturity stage worldwide.

The Mobile Phone Carrier Oligopoly

A sign of maturity is an established oligopoly — and that is precisely what characterizes the wireless business in the United States, much like television networks in the 1980s. The mobile phone carrier business is dominated by Verizon, Sprint, AT&T, and T-Mobile, which control nearly 90 percent of the market. Wireless providers have used their oligopoly power to control the networks. When a client signs up for the service, he or she can only use the services the carrier provides. For those consumers who would like to purchase services such as ringtones from other companies, the wireless providers respond (fight back) by restricting the features available on the cell phones (e.g., by controlling the billing for add-ons).

locrifa/shutterstock.com

In other high-income countries, however, consumers have reasonable alternatives to the established wireless service carriers. In fact, developments in the industry are creating new competitive turbulence in the market, with new technologies that are keeping the mobile-phone industry in what has been a prolonged growth stage. Governments are encouraging new entrants in the business as well. In one example, the German government keeps auctioning additional UMTS-spectrum radio frequencies for mobile phones, allowing operators to meet rising demand for data-intensive services. This is likely to lure new operators into the German mobile-phone market. This auction creates a burden for the established provider, market leader Deutsche Telekom, which now faces more competition, while at same time losing market share in its fixed-line business.[9]

During maturity, international companies experience tremendous pressure to cut costs in order to lower product prices, so they establish strategic alliances with firms from emerging markets. Alternatively, they engage in contract manufacturing, or develop a wholly owned subsidiary. As they do so they train local talent to deliver an excellent product or service. In the process of investing in new local talent, international companies are likely to create highly skilled local competitors. These competitors from emerging markets then sell products to consumers or businesses in industrialized countries, competing directly with the international firm in its home market and in other high-income countries.

AlexLMX/shutterstock.com

Examples of successful companies from emerging markets exporting their products to high-income countries abound. "Made in India" is a sign of high-quality for software; in this market, top software companies include subsidiaries of U.S. companies, such as Motorola India Electronics Ltd. and IBM Global Services India, as well as local companies such as Infosys, Satyam Computer Services Ltd., Tata Consultancy Services, and Wipro Infotech. Brazil boasts successful banks, such as Banco do Brasil and Banco Bradesco, and Embraer, a Brazilian aerospace conglomerate that manufactures commercial, military, executive, and agricultural aircraft. [10]

10-1d The Decline Stage

Products in the decline stage are rapidly losing ground to new technologies or product alternatives. Sales and, consequently, profits are declining at this stage, and a firm might consider whether its presence in the market is warranted. However, having an international presence during the decline stage, particularly in developing countries, could be an advantage. One of the main benefits of going international and engaging in international marketing is the ability of a firm to extend the product life cycle. A product may be in the decline stage in the lead country, where it was developed, as well as in other industrial economies, and, at the same time, in a stable maturity stage in most developing countries.

Conceptually, the international product life cycle makes sense. Products are produced in developed countries where they are first adopted; then they are later made available in developing countries. However, consumers in emerging markets no longer conform to the international product life cycle, they buy products when they first come out. For example, wireless telephone service has made tremendous advances in transition economies because landline-based systems often have reception problems. Some countries have vaulted over traditional landline wired systems and moved directly into wireless telephone service.

10-2 Managing the International Product and Service Mix

The product portfolio of a firm is usually diversified into products that are in different stages of the product life cycle, such that profits from successful mature products can be used to invest in new products and products that have a lower market share. Most multinational corporations tend to have both local and global brands that they nurture through their life cycle. The international product mix is the complete assortment of the products that a company offers to its target international consumers, and it has a number of important dimensions. One important dimension of the product mix is the product line, a number of related brands in the same product category. Companies use different line strategies to reach market share and profitability goals. They use line extensions to target consumers who otherwise cannot afford a particular product. In the fashion realm, for example, numerous top designers target the masses with bridge offerings (secondary, more affordable lines): Escada with Laurel, Anne Klein with Anne Klein II, Donna Karan with DKNY, Armani with Emporio Armani, and so forth.

To illustrate the remaining product dimensions, we will use the example of Unilever (www.unilever.com), one of the largest consumer product companies in the world. Unilever is composed of two companies, Unilever NV and Unilever PLC, operating as one company linked by a series of agreements and common shareholders, and headquartered in London, United Kingdom, and Rotterdam, the Netherlands, respectively.[11] Although Unilever is organized primarily into two divisions, the foods division and the personal care division, the company has a number of product lines that are addressed as separate strategic business units.

Another important dimension of the product mix is product consistency. This term refers to the extent to which the different product lines are related, use the same distribution channels, and have the same final consumers. The Unilever brands are consistent within each of the company divisions. The Corporate Venture Activities is the only venture that might break this pattern of consistency.

The other dimensions of the product mix are product length, width, and depth. Table 10-1 presents a partial list of Unilever brands. For the purpose of this analysis, let us assume that it is a complete list of the offerings in the Unilever portfolio.

Division	Culinary/Frozen Brands	Spread Type	Spread Brands	Beverage/Care Type	Tea/Care Brands	Frozen/Care Type	Ice Cream Brands	Care Type	Household/Detergent Brands	Personal Care	Personal Care Brands
Culinary Products	Ragú Spaghetti Sauces		I Can't Believe It's Not Butter		Lipton		Magmum	Household Care	Domestos		Lux
	Calvé Whisky Cocktail Sauce		Rama Margarine	Tea	Bovril (UK)		Cote D'Or		Cif		Lynx
	Hellmann's Mayonnaise		Becel Spreads		PG Tips (UK)		Cornetto		Omo	Personal Care	Dove
	Knorr Soups	Margarine	Flora Spreads		Scottish Blend (UK)	Ice cream	Klondike Bars		Ala		Vaseline Intensive Care
	Bertolli Pastas		Blue Band		Rexona/Sure		Solero		Surf		Pond's
	Amora Vinaigrettes		Country Crock		Axe		Bryers	Detergents	Radiant		Lifebuoy
	Wishbone Salad Dressing		Doriana Light Spread	Deodorants	Dove		Ben & Jerry's		Snuggle	Corporate Venture Activities	Unilever Technology Ventures
	Colman's Mustard		Stork		Degree		Viennetta		Comfort		Unilever Ventures
	Pepperami	Cream Alternative	Elmlea		Impulse		Wall's		Persil		Langholm Capital
	Pot Noodle	Spread	Marmite		SunSilk		Signal				
Frozen Foods	Findus 4 Salti in Padella	Cheese	Boursin	Shampoos	ThermaSilk	Oral Care	Close-Up				
Fruit Drinks	Adez	Diet	Slim Fast		Organics						

Table 10-1 Unilever Products

10-2a Length

The product length is the total number of brands in the product mix — all the brands sold by the company. Counting the Unilever brands listed in Table 10-1, the total product length, as presented in this table, is 65.

10-2b Width

The product width is the total number of product lines the company offers. Counting the different select product lines in Table 10-1 (culinary products, frozen foods, ice cream, margarine, cream alternative, spread, cheese, fruit drinks, tea, diet, household care, detergents, deodorants, shampoos, personal care, oral care, and corporate venture activities), the total product width in Table 10-1 is 17.

10-2c Depth

The product depth refers to the number of different offerings for a product category. For example, in the detergent category, Unilever offers Omo, Ala, Surf, Radiant, Snuggle, Comfort, and Persil (Figure 10-3). Unilever's product depth for the detergent line, as presented in Table 10-1, is seven. Product depth for the detergent line is calculated by adding all the brands in the detergent category. In another example, Unilever has only one brand in its diet category: Slim Fast. The product depth for the diet line as illustrated in Table 10-1 is one.

Figure 10-3 In Europe, Unilever brands dominate the shelves in the laundry detergent category—in the United States, the dominant company is Procter & Gamble. Unilever's Persil is a major presence, from supermarket to supermarket, while Procter & Gamble's Ariel is often in a secondary position.

Companies alter their product mix by purchasing existing international or local brands. For example, Unilever purchased the Ben & Jerry's Ice Cream brand. In 2017, Unilever purchased a group of personal and home care brands in Latin America from Qualas. This included three haircare brands (not shown in Table 10-1).

10-3 New Product Development

To maintain their competitive advantage and to ensure survival and growth locally, regionally, or globally, companies must develop and introduce new products and services that meet the needs of their markets. International new product development is a costly process that involves the firm at all levels. If successful, product/ service development is the key to a company's success and future.

In general, new product development involves substantial risks and costs. The complex environment of the international marketplace adds considerably to both the risks and costs. Consider, for example, the case of Freeplay Energy, a company that started in Cape Town, South Africa (on next page).

These examples of Freeplay's innovations illustrate some of the complexities involved in developing new products internationally. The following are examples of risks and difficulties companies face when developing new products:

• International and local competitors could appropriate the product or service idea and deliver the final product or service to the market more swiftly, economically, and with stronger company backing (reputation, financial support) than the initial developer.

Freeplay Energy

Freeplay Energy started in Cape Town, South Africa (its headquarters are now in London, United Kingdom), developing electrical or electronic products such as lights and radios that are powered by hand-cranked generators that charge rechargeable batteries. Currently, they are rapidly expanding into the outdoor leisure and emergency preparedness markets. Freeplay Energy started out by manufacturing self-powered radios for the African market. The product initially failed in Africa, where consumers preferred to purchase batteries, rather than incur a one-time expenditure of about $50 for such a radio. The company, however, remained in business primarily due to its success in the United States and Europe.[12] After refocusing on markets in high-income countries, Freeplay developed its products with a sophisticated, Western consumer in mind. With the initial product, the radio had to be wound 20 seconds to produce 30 minutes of radio time; a lighter, smaller version produced one hour of playing time. Subsequent to its success in Europe, the product started selling in middle- and in low-income countries as well. The product is marketed using different strategies worldwide. In Japan and the United States, the product is marketed as part of earthquake and tornado survival kits; in Germany, interest in the product is fueled by environmental concern; whereas in the United Kingdom, consumers take pride in owning such an invention.

Interestingly, the company made a second attempt to fulfill the needs of the African market: Freeplay developed a self-powered generator intended to enable consumers in developing countries to charge their satellite telephones. The entrepreneurs developing this product believed that most of the growth in cell phones was going to be in the developing world. However, most African countries cannot afford the infrastructure needed, leaving satellite communication fueled by either expensive disposable batteries or self-powered technology as the only options.

Currently, Freeplay markets itself as a leading brand of clean, dependable energy products that harness human, solar, and rechargeable energy and convert it into electricity, replacing battery-operated systems. Their product range consists of radios, torches, lanterns, mobile phone chargers, and standalone foot-powered generators. Its affordable Companion Radio, for example, has a compact AM-FM radio, which doubles as a flashlight and a mobile phone charger, and it is self-charging, using solar power.[13] Freeplay is a global company today, manufacturing its products in emerging markets — some of its wind-up electronic products are made on production lines in Guangdong, China. Freeplay has signed a deal for 1.1 million wind-up mobile-phone chargers for sub-Saharan Africa and the Caribbean, worth $13 million a year. Freeplay is also developing rechargers for the U.S. Agency for International Development's One-Laptop-per-Child program. Its nonprofit arm, Lifeline Energy, has distributed more than 500,000 self-powering radios for group listening, reaching over 20 million listeners; and, among many other endeavors, it brought renewable energy to Rwanda, replacing old, polluting and dangerous kerosene lights with their durable lanterns that are able to light up a larger areas for longer periods of time. [14]

• International target consumers might not respond as anticipated to the offering (as in the case of Freeplay's wind-up radio) because it does not meet their needs, because they cannot afford it, or because they prefer to adopt a product at a later stage in the product life cycle.

• Local governments or the home-country government might impose restrictions on product testing procedures (in the case of pharmaceuticals, for example).

• The technological infrastructure of the market is substandard and cannot support the new product.

The steps that companies typically follow in the product development process are essentially the same as those involved in domestic product development. Figure 10-4 (next page) illustrates the international product development process. At each step, the process can be either terminated or restarted for each individual product idea; consequently, a product must go through each stage to reach the international product launching stage.

Figure 10-4 *Steps in the new product development process.*

10-3a Generating New Product Ideas

The first step in the new product development process is generating new product ideas. Depending on the products provided and company philosophy, ideas are sought using different strategies. Most product and service firms are driven by the marketing concept, and their product development decisions are based on identifying the needs, wants, and desires of consumers. For technology-driven firms, the focus is more likely to be on the product itself, and thus the research and development division is likely to be responsible for developing product ideas. Even in this second instance, however, products are developed with the needs of the consumer in mind. Freeplay Energy, with its wind-up radio, is an example of a product-focused company. An inventor created the radio independent of the market, and a marketer identified a market for the product — consumers in Africa who do not have electricity, use batteries for their radios, and could benefit from using wind-up radios.

Companies use multiple sources for ideas. Among the most common are consumers, competitive analyses, and some additional sources such as channel members, company employees, and so on.

Consumers

The most obvious sources for ideas are consumers in the home-country market of the firm. Other sources of product ideas are consumers in the company's international markets. Although, traditionally, products of U.S. multinational firms were driven entirely by consumers in the United States, these companies are now increasingly drawing on consumers around the world for new product or service ideas. A growing number of companies are developing products for one market and successfully marketing them in markets that are substantially different. Häagen-Dazs developed a caramel-flavored ice cream called Dulce de

Leche for Argentina. The company eventually brought this flavor to the United States, where it is second only to vanilla in sales, and to Europe, where it is moving from seasonal-flavor to year-round-flavor status.[15] In other examples, Nike found that a soccer cleat de-

kivni/shutterstock.com

signed and worn by Ronaldo, a player on the Brazilian soccer team, was popular with consumers in the United States. Similarly, Levi Strauss, the quintessential all-American jeans manufacturer, offered a dark version of denim jeans that was very popular with consumers in Japan, to U.S. consumers, who responded favorably to it.[16]

Competitive Analyses

Competition represents an obvious source for product and service ideas. Products that are in the test market phase or that are just being launched are always vulnerable to having their ideas copied. For example, Kao, a Japanese detergent manufacturer, developed a super-absorbent diaper, causing Procter & Gamble's Pampers to lose their lead in the Japanese market. However, Procter & Gamble promptly developed its own super-absorbent version of Pampers, selling it aggressively worldwide. This effort did not materialize in increased sales in China, however, so, a few years later, in 2015, Procter & Gamble rolled out a line of premium diapers in China with a new claim: "Made in Japan." The diapers have gold designs and elastic waistbands, and they are aimed at the high-end market, but well-heeled Chinese buyers are not convinced. Chinese consumers have embraced imported Japanese diapers at the expense of Pampers. P&G executives initially targeted China's frugal middle class with cheaper diapers; Chinese consumers, however, have been increasingly willing to splurge on luxuries, such as better diapers for their children. Merries, made by Kao, cost about $30 for a pack of 50 diapers, and consumers perceive that their absorbency and quality are superior than those of most other brands. These consumers had never considered Pampers for their children. Another problem is that P&G emphasized diapers whose sides are fastened together with tape, which requires babies to lie down during diaper changes, whereas, in China and other emerging markets, parents prefer diapers that look like underpants and can be slipped on while the children are standing up.[17]

P&G's new marketing strategy in China is now aligned with that of its Japanese competitor, Kao, copying its entire playbook, including the look, with gold designs, and with Japanese origins. With such a huge target market at stake, P&G decided to give its customers exactly what the more successful competitor offered.

Additional Sources

Other sources of ideas are channel members, who are closer to consumers than the manufacturer; company employees, such as sales personnel, engineers, or even top management; inventors; consultants; nonprofit research laboratories; universities; and research firms, among others. Research conducted by the firm in the form of brainstorming sessions and qualitative research also can be used in the process of generating product ideas.[18]

10-3b Screening New Product Ideas

In the process of screening new product ideas, it is best to consider both the extent to which the product fits with the target consumers, as well as with the overall mission of the organization. At this stage, a checklist is usually developed to screen for product ideas that do not meet these criteria. In a study of European, North American, East Asia, and Australian consumer packaged-goods firms,[19] researchers identified screening factors that appear to draw the line between new product adoption or rejection in a detailed screening:

- The support and endorsement of senior management
- Superior consumer fit — does the product satisfy and respond to changes in customer needs and values?
- Lucrative market potential
- Clearly defined promotional plan and clearly identified brand strategy
- Alignment with product-led strategy and technological advantage
- Demonstrating strengths in both market attack strategy and product-led strategy
- Likely trade adoption (retailers, supermarket chains)
- Resistance to brand switching

10-3c Developing and Evaluating Concepts

The next stage, developing and evaluating concepts, is very important for firms developing products for international markets. Key activities at this stage are to determine how the product will be viewed by consumers and how it will be used. Typically, the process

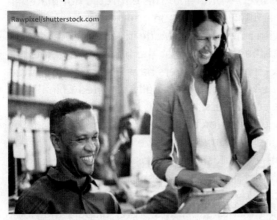
Rawpixel/shutterstock.com

involves developing a detailed description of the product and asking prospective consumers to evaluate it and to indicate their willingness to purchase the hypothetical product. Most often, this is done using a focus group of representative target consumers.

Even in cases in which firms are exporting products initially developed for the home-country market, it is essential that they engage in market research in the international target market. The shortening of the product life cycle and the intensity of international competition increase pressure on exporters to evaluate and reevaluate their international target market in light of rapid technological change and to conduct concept-testing research that ranges from formal methods, such as focus groups, to ad hoc information gathering.[20]

One method that is frequently used at this stage is conjoint analysis. In this method, respondents receive descriptions of different hypothetical products with varying levels of the same attributes, which they are then asked to rank. Analysts can determine the ideal combination of attributes, ascertain the importance of each attribute, and, assuming the data were collected from a sufficiently large sample of the target population, estimate market share.

10-3d Performing a Product Business Analysis

Performing a product business analysis should include calculating projected project costs, return on investment, and cash flow and determining the fixed and variable costs for the long term.[21] However enthusiastic the target consumers queried, if these figures do not fit the company budget, the project will be high risk. For many product categories, product price is a critical characteristic; at this stage, it is important to identify the price level at which revenue or profit best fit the manufacturer's goals.[22]

10-3e Designing and Developing the Product

At the next stage, designing and developing the product, product prototypes are developed. It is important that product prototypes precisely match the concept description developed in the concept development and evaluation stage. If the company strays from the initial description, testing the revised product description is crucial.[23]

The product now acquires a name, a brand identity, and the marketing mix is developed. The cross-functional team developing the product — research and development, engineering, operations, marketing, finance — must come together for this process.[24] This team must be focused on the project in such a way that a large percentage of team members' time is devoted to the project, rather than to other projects. It also is important that the team acts as a unit, focusing on project, rather than departmental, interests.[25]

For multinational companies, coordination takes place across subsidiaries, or in conjunction with international partners. Companies such as Boeing and Motorola coordinate research and development activities globally by establishing worldwide information systems to coordinate product and design development. For example, in developing the Boeing 777, the company used real-time computer-aided technology to design components jointly with Japanese partners.[26] Companies also tend to encourage communication among research and development facilities in different countries. Procter & Gamble, for example, requires extensive communication and information sharing among units to develop new offerings, such as single-dose laundry tablets, which they introduced in 2012.[27]

Products must fit client needs and specifications, so coordinating with clients is essential. In one example, the Airbus A380 was designed to hold more people and handle more cargo, creating efficiencies for the airlines. The issue that had to subsequently be resolved was where to land and park the enormous aircraft, and how to handle passenger processing (see International Marketing Illustration 10-1).

International Marketing Illustration 10-1 Airbus 380: The Superjumbo Double-Decker

The Airbus 380 is touted as the world's largest airplane, the world's only twin-deck air-liner, with a dedicated three-deck, 150-ton, long-range freighter. This giant is more fuel efficient than the average person's car. Its modern technology and economies of scale provide 15 percent lower seat-mile costs than today's most efficient aircraft. Thus, it is capable of offering passengers luxury travel at much more affordable prices — a cruise ship for the skies, the company claims.

The plane, which seats 555 passengers comfortably in a three-class interior layout, a superjumbo double-decker aircraft, advertises itself as 50 percent larger than the Boeing 747, with plenty of extra space that would allow passengers to lounge about in cozy confer-

ence rooms and attend chic in-flight gatherings. In reality, however, airlines could choose to pack 880 passengers in the A380; in all likelihood, airlines might do so if they are going to opt for running a highly profitable operation. It should be noted that a stretch version that can accommodate 1,000 passengers is in the works. At present, the lowest seat count is on board of Korean Airlines aircraft at 407 seats, and the highest is on Air France with 538 seats – with a comfortable layout, in this author's opinion. (continued...)

When such an aircraft is in use, it requires an entirely new infrastructure to support it. For example, airports had to increase their baggage handling capacity and increase the number of customs and immigration personnel to handle customs at one time. Taxiways and gates needed to be modified to accommodate an airplane that has 12 doors and four aisles. In 2015, there were 50 airports in the world with the capacity to handle the aircraft.

After entering service in 2007, the A380 has quickly claimed ground lost as a result of early production problems that delayed production by two years. The company slashed profit forecasts as it had to pay out compensation for delays to its customers. Moreover, because jets trade in dollars, the dollar weakness relative to the euro also eroded the company's profits.

Nevertheless, it is expected that the jet giant will account for a large proportion of the Airbus revenue, even if it is a small fraction of the aircraft sold by the company. At a price of more than $300 million, this jet is supposed to rake in the profits. However, Airbus occasionally faced serious challenges: UPS cancelled its order for 10 A380 freighters after Airbus said it was unable to deliver the planes until 2014. More recently, the jumbo Airbus' future has been in question, as many airlines refuse to commit to future orders – the greatest challenge the airlines have is flying the airplane with a full load.

Not least of the company's challenges is Boeing's 787 Dreamliner, the only other large commercial aircraft on the market. The Dreamliner is made primarily of carbon fiber, rather than aluminum, and it is touted as the most environmentally-friendly airplane ever built, more fuel efficient, and producing 20 percent less carbon dioxide than competitors. The Dreamliner is not a direct competitor for the A380, which is much larger; nevertheless, it is an important challenger to Airbus, as both the A380 and the Dreamliner are positioned as large commercial aircraft.

Sources: Phil Han, "Airbus A380 faces uncertain future as airlines ask for changes," CNBC,16 June 2015, accessed at http://www.cnbc.com/2015/06/16/on September 15, 2015; Airbus, "Where Is the A380 Flying?" accessed at http:// www.airbus.comaircraftfamilies/passengeraircraft/a380family/a380-routes/ on September 15, 2015; International Airport Review, "Continued Handling of the A380," 6 June, 2012 (http:/www.internationalairportreview.comtag/a380/); Rebecca Christie, "Airbus's Leahy Expects Few '07 A380 Orders, Surge in '08-'09," Dow Jones Newswires, March 26, 2007, 5:46 p.m.; Steve McGrath, "Airbus Puts A380 Freighter on Ice to Focus on Passenger Version," Wall Street Journal, March 2, 2007, p. 1; Joe Sharkey, "Where Do You Park a 747 on Steroids?" The New York Times, May 4, 2004, C7; www.airbus.com; Ham Granlund, "Are Airports Ready for A380?" Aviation Week & Space Technology, Vol. 160, No. 16, April 19, 2004, p. 6.

It should be mentioned that product development activities increasingly take place in emerging markets. India is one country where there is intense work performed in the area of new product development, as the example on the top of the next page illustrates.

10-3f Test Marketing

Test marketing a product can provide a good indication of how the product will be received when it is in the market, but this stage can also be expensive, time consuming, and open to competitive sabotage. The following are test marketing options firms can choose to evaluate the reaction of the market to their product. At the lower involvement level is simulated test marketing, which is not as costly and does not give competitors much information about the product. Controlled test marketing is limited to a few stores, is thus also less costly, and gives only limited exposure of the product to competitors. Actual test marketing necessitates important strategic decisions and commitments that involve channel members, intensive promotion, and high promotional expenses; test marketing could create conditions that make the product vulnerable to competitive reactions.

New Product Development—in India[28]

Dragon Images/shutterstock.com

Yokagawa's J-Team (standing for H.B. Jayanthi), is a group of 60 Indian engineers working for Yokagawa, the Japanese industrial control systems manufacturer, in Bangalore. The Team was trained to speak Japanese so they can communicate effectively with colleagues in Japan while collaborating on product development. Of Yokogawa's development engineers, 350 are based in India — and the number is increasing — while 1,000 are based in Japan. This is an example of offshored product development taking place in India. Revenues from these types of activities are about $500 million annually and growing at 25 percent a year. And India is not alone in this regard. The Czech Republic, China, and Russia are closely following in its footsteps.

Among other companies offshoring new product development to India are Johnson Controls, the U.S. vehicle parts maker and a big producer of seats and vehicle interiors, which employs 50 engineers in product development focused on the Indian market; Quest, another U.S. company with 650 engineers working on product development outsourcing contracts on behalf of customers such as U.K.-based aerospace company Rolls-Royce and General Electric; and Philips, the Dutch electronics manufacturer, which has just fewer than 1,000 employees developing new products, from projects such as low-power lighting systems for houses that work off rechargeable batteries to developing transportable health screening equipment, connected by satellite to hospitals.

Simulated Test Marketing

Because eight out of ten products fail, simulated test markets are often used to reduce the risks a company would incur in terms of marketing, sales, and capital expenses; cannibalization of the parent brand through line extension; and competitive reaction to the new product.[29] A top simulated test marketing research system employed today is ASSESSOR, whereby respondents are exposed to advertising and given the opportunity to purchase in a simulated store. Subsequently, laboratory purchase rates are combined with estimates of availability and awareness to predict initial market adoption, while repeat purchase is estimated based on mail order repurchase. Another widely used simulated test marketing tool is Nielsen's BASES II, a validated sales estimating system that also offers insights into how to improve the odds of consumer adoption.[30]

Other simulated test marketing research systems might recruit representative consumers who participate in a research study in a central facility in a number of markets.[31] After responding to questions about their product-related attitudes and purchase behavior, they view advertising of the new brand and of competitive brands that are embedded in a television program. The respondents then comment on the television program and advertising and then proceed to a simulated store stocking test brands and competitive brands where they can buy the products at a substantial discount. The proportion of individuals purchasing the test brand is then used to estimate product trialability.[31]

Controlled Test Marketing

Usually conducted by a research firm in industrialized countries, controlled test marketing involves offering a new product to a group of stores and evaluating the market reaction to it (consumer reaction as well as competitive reaction). In the process, different aspects of the marketing mix are varied — price, in-store promotion, placement in the store, and so on. A more informal controlled test marketing involves simply asking a number of stores to carry the product for a fee. Depending on the outcome, the manufacturing firm may decide to produce the product on a larger scale.

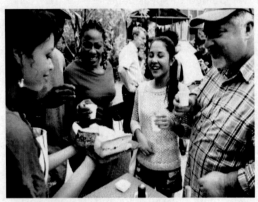
Rawpixel/shutterstock.com

Actual Test Marketing

A number of important decisions are involved in full-blown test marketing. Companies at this stage must decide on the cities that are most appropriate for testing the product, based on the availability of retailers and other necessary distribution and logistics service providers, and on availability of the infrastructure needed to conduct the test market, such as the necessary media, research firms, direct mail providers, and so forth. Multinational companies do not limit test marketing or product launching to their home countries. For example, MasterCard continually tests new products in the Netherlands and Germany by using direct mail. This strategy also appeals to service providers from developing countries. For example, Mexican exporters often use direct mail to test a market in the United States or Canada. However, this approach is problematic because the national mail service can be unreliable, ZIP codes are missing from database lists, and so on.[32] Test marketing exclusively using direct mail works well when it is aimed at a narrow, well-defined target market. Although this approach is possible in Europe, Canada, and the United States, where segmentation is a precise science, based on refined methods of demographic and psychographic assessment, in developing countries, such well-defined databases are not always available.[33]

Although test marketing can provide valuable information for the manufacturer, anticipating product performance in the short run, its usefulness is often questioned given the high expense it necessitates. In a rapidly changing competitive environment, being first in the market constitutes an important competitive advantage, the first-mover advantage. As such, the company is the first to attract consumers and to commit channel members for its new product. A company is also vulnerable to competitive reaction during the test marketing stage. On one hand, competitors could appropriate the product idea and be the first to offer the product to the market; on the other, the competition could sabotage the new brand, cutting prices for all competitive offerings.

Test marketing, nevertheless, can be a reliable predictor of national market share, costs, and profitability, and it can be a tool to assess and compare alternative product strategies. Yet, surprisingly, this tool is frequently overlooked in international marketing.[34] According to international marketing experts, some of the errors to avoid in international test marketing are incorrect forecasts, unrealistic market conditions, incorrect media translations, and choice of the wrong test market.[35]

10-3g Launching the Product Internationally

Strategies for launching the product internationally have an impact on later product performance. Products launched using a successful strategy have a higher rate of success and score high ratings on profitability, technical success, and positive impact on the company. "Goodness of launch" is characterized by the following, in order of impact: high service quality, on-time shipment and adequate product availability, quality sales force and enough sales effort and support, quality of promotion, and sufficient promotional effort.[36]

Product Launch Decisions: Consumers and Countries

In international marketing, an important decision at the launching stage is in which countries to launch the product. Whereas, in the recent past, most launching was aimed at consumers in the manufacturers' home countries, increasingly, multinationals launch products in countries that have the best consumer-product fit. Coca-Cola, for instance, launched coffee-flavored Coke Blak in the U.S. and France, attempting to appeal to consumers' preference for coffee-flavored drinks. The brand did not perform well and it was pulled from the market.

Timing of Launch

Another important decision is the timing of the new product launch. Companies often attempt to gain the first-mover advantage by being the first to launch the new product. In 2018, Amazon launched its first-ever branded prepaid debit MasterCard – in Mexico. The launch of the "Amazon Rechargeable" card had two key goals: capturing a larger share of the growing e-commerce market in Mexico while targeting the large number of Mexicans who do not have bank accounts, debit cards, or credit cards. The timing of this launch was ideal, with Amazon offering the card when no other businesses offered to serve their credit needs.[37]

Marketing Mix Decisions

Other important decisions at the product-launching stage involve setting the price that the target consumer is willing to pay for the product. Prices might be higher if the product is launched in industrialized countries with a wealthy consumer base. For consumers in emerging markets, the product is launched at a lower price, in order to initiate trial.

Firms typically choose to vary their product mix from one market to another. For example, in the United States, Colgate-Palmolive's Ajax offering is limited to a few cleaning products, compared to the company's Ajax offering in Europe (see Figure 10-5). Promotion, in the form of sales promotion, personal selling, and advertising, is crucial during the launching process. The introduction of Coca-Cola Zero in 2007 in Europe was accompanied by heavy advertising in metro stations, on busy street corners, anywhere one could imagine it. The message the ad sported in large print against a dark background was "As it should be: real taste and zero sugar."

Zull Must/shutterstock.com

Figure 10-5 In the United States, Ajax' offering is limited to just a few products, compared to most European markets, where the company offers a multitude of cleaning products in different scents, as those available in this Estonian supermarket.

Channel members constitute an important element of the marketing mix during the launching stage. Decisions such as shelf positioning, often contingent on the payment of slotting fees to retailers, as well as questions on inventory, trade allowances, and financing, are addressed at this stage. There are significant variations in distribution channels for individual product categories, with fragmented channels in markets such as Japan, concentrated channels in planned economies, and so on. This factor adds to the complexity and expense of the product-launching effort.

10-4 Degree of Product or Service Newness

Innovation is thought of as the creation of a better product or process and may range from the substitution of a cheaper material in an existing product to a better way of marketing, distributing, or supporting a product or service.[38] Degree of product or service newness refers to the extent to which a product or service is new to the market. Organizations that have a good record of innovation pursue innovation systematically, actively searching for change and supporting creative individuals who are internally driven.[39] Amazon's above-noted recent entry into the banking and e-payments sector in Mexico is an example of this kind of innovative corporate thinking and management.

Innovation takes on many forms, and there are different classifications for innovations. At the basic level, new products and services can be classified in one of five categories:[40]

- New product to existing market, new product to existing company — 33.7 percent of products.
- New line — This category represents a new product or product line to a company, but for a company already operating in that market. It accounts for 16.8 percent of products.
- New item in an existing product line for the company — This category accounts for 11.9 percent of products; these products are likely to have the highest success rate (83 percent) and the greatest impact on company sales and profit.
- Modification of an existing company product — 18.8 percent of products.
- Innovation, new product to the world — 18.8 percent of products.

Another classification organizes innovation into the radical, dynamically continuous, and continuous categories. Radical innovations (*discontinuous innovations*) create new industries or new standards of management, manufacturing, and service, and represent fundamental changes for consumers, entailing departures from established consumption.[41] Examples of radical innovations are the Internet and endoscopy, the innovations brought about by what is referred to as the Fourth Economic Revolution (a term originating with the 2016 World Economic Forum, referring to the effects of artificial intelligence on the economy and jobs).

Dynamically continuous innovations do not alter consumer behavior significantly, but they represent a change in the consumption pattern; the iPad is an example of such innovation. Continuous innovations produce no disruption of consumption patterns and involve only product alterations, such as new flavors, or just an improvement over the old offering. They usually are congruous, in the sense that they can be used alongside the existing systems. For example, Tide detergent and Cascade dishwashing powder are available in single-use packs that offer consumers precise measurement and, if needed, easier portability. Geox shoes, described in International Marketing Illustration 10-2, are a continuous innovation.

International Marketing Illustration 10-2
An Innovation That Could Relaunch the Italian Economy

Mario Moretti Polegato, a former wine-maker in Italy, was attending a wine convention in Nevada and went on a hiking trip. Hot and uncomfortable, he poked holes in his sneakers to cool off. This led him to go into the shoe business with a new product idea: a patented membrane on the soles of Geox shoes. The Geox membrane has dozens of tiny openings allowing sweat to evaporate while blocking water entry, thus making them more breathable than other shoes, a claim that is difficult to prove. Polegato claims the material is superior to leather, which aspirates water and keeps feet wet.

The success of this company is based on marketing: get all potential clients to believe that they perspire profusely and will be infinitely better off with shoes that have little holes. Of course, the shoes are made of the highest quality materials, including calfskin and other valuable and malleable skins. Engineers at the Geox laboratories in Venice test different prototypes. The shoes are submerged in a fast water current and have to "walk" for a hundred laboratory kilometers to be considered viable.

The company has been growing by leaps and bounds. It is Italy's largest shoe company, present in over 70 countries, and is planning to open several stores in the U.S. and more than 100 in China. Polegato claims that his is an innovation that could relaunch the Italian economy – after two years of losses, Geox returned to solid profitability in 2015. In 2017, annual sales surpassed $1 billion, with record net income reported. While Polegato remains Chairman of Geox, a new CEO, formerly with luxury-brand retailer Gucci, was appointed in early 2018. Using an image-based marketing strategy in a market where image is essential, he may further enhance the brand's

Sources: Nicole Vuiser, "Geox ou L'étonnante Envolée de la « Chaussure Qui Respire »" *Le Monde*, September 9, 2015, accessed at http://www.lemonde.fr/economie/portfolio/2015/09/11 geox-ou-l-etonnante-envolee-de-la-chaussure-qui-respire_4752771_3234.html#MKIJd7hd5uFmOphS.99 on September 20, 2015; 2017 Annual Financials for Geox, Sp.A., *MarketWatch*, accessed at www.marketwatch.com/investing/stock/gxsbf/financials on June 9, 2018. "Geox to Keep Up the Pace in 2018 After Return to Profit Growth." *Reuters*, February 23, 2018, accessed on June 9, 2018 at www.reuters.com/article/geox-results/update-1-geox-to-keep-up-the-pace-in-2018-after-return-to-profit-growth-idUSL8N1QD5OM.

Most of the innovation taking place today is continuous. However, a radical innovation, the Internet, has revolutionized all aspects of the marketing mix, with important implications for international marketing. As a distribution tool, it renders products accessible instantly worldwide, regardless of the firm's experience and size. It is an equal-opportunity distribution tool for companies from industrialized and developing countries alike, allowing for creative and innovative market penetration.

In one example demonstrating how the Internet can be used successfully in promoting developing country exports, the International Trade Center organized the world's first online coffee auction, selling Brazilian specialty coffee to bidders around the world via the Internet. The auction drew buyers around the world and generated high prices for Brazilian growers. [42]

In another example, Pavex Parquet, a medium-sized business in one of the most picturesque old towns in Transylvania, Sebes, in Romania, used the Internet to research custom-made hardwood borders, a product used in elaborate, high-end parquet flooring, and to sell the product, and to sell the product locally and internationally.

Pavex Parquet

Pavex Parquet is a Romanian company that specializes in the manufacture of hardwood borders for affordable parquet flooring of the highest quality. Their borders are used to enhance the esthetics of parquet and other hardwood flooring. What is especially noteworthy about this company is that it relied on the Internet to evaluate the market for hardwood borders and to sell its products to consumers and businesses around the world.

The company first conducted research on the Internet, to identify designs, and improved on them to create a portfolio of well-designed, well-structured borders. The hardwood borders include well-known patterns, such as the Greek key, lesser-used patterns, such as weaver lines and Victorian patterns; and truly unique patterns, such as the chain, the grill, and infinity. The company also used the Internet to research the market. It studied its competitors, the wood they used, and the specifications of their parquet flooring. Finally, the company conducted research to identify appropriate outlets for its Pavex Parquet brand.

In its promotional mix, Pavex Parquet relied heavily on the Internet as well, using its website, www.pavexparquet.com, to educate prospective consumers about hardwood borders and how they can integrate the elegant borders into their home-improvement or new-home-building efforts.

Pavex engaged in additional communication with prospective customers by publishing articles about parquet in different flooring, home-improvement, and remodeling forums.

10-5 Product Diffusion

Product diffusion refers to the manner in which a product is adopted by consumers worldwide — the speed of adoption by various groups. (The consumer adoption process is addressed in Section 10-5c, "Consumer Adopters.") A number of factors influence the speed of product adoption in different countries; they are discussed in Sections 10-5a through 10-5c.

10-5a Product Factors

In general, a number of attributes of an innovation are likely to accelerate the rate of adoption of a product or service.[43] First, the new product or service must offer a *relative advantage* compared with the other offerings available on the market and must be *compatible with the needs of consumers*. In addition, the product or service use must be *observable* (or communicable to others) and have a high trialability (for example, consumers can try the product on a limited basis, by renting it, for instance). Both product and country determinants of adoption rates are illustrated on Figure 10-7.

Figure 10-7 *Determinants of new product/service adoption.*

10-5b Country (Market) Factors

New products tend to be adopted at different rates in different international markets. Countries where the product or service is first introduced and adopted are referred to as lead countries, and countries where the product or service is adopted at a later stage are known as lag countries. This process is similar to the traditional two-step diffusion process, whereby products are first offered to wealthy consumers and, subsequently, to the mass market. By analogy, consumers in high-income, industrialized countries (lead countries) adopt the product first, whereas consumers in low-income countries (lag countries) adopt the product later.

Generally, the diffusion rate tends to be faster in lag countries, as consumers learn from the experiences of adopters in lead countries. Moreover, the later in the product life cycle the product or service is introduced in a lag country, the faster the adoption rate.

In the past, geographic proximity was also an important factor in rapid diffusion. However, today that is no longer the case. The various media have contributed to the instant adoption of styles and innovations worldwide for products that do not need a specialized technology infrastructure (see Figure 10-8 on next page). A more important factor affecting adoption is the country's cultural similarity to the country where the product was invented (the innovation center). Also, a country's wealth is a good indicator of the possibility of rapid new product adoption.[44]

10-5c Consumer Adopters

Target consumers — national, regional, or worldwide — can be segmented based on the manner in which they adopt new products throughout the respective products' life cycle. The segments are:

Figure 10-8 *Music rapidly diffuses from the U.S.A. to Germany. What is interesting is the age of consumers – adopters are often older consumers, as the ones portrayed here listening to a new group on tour, playing New-Orleans-style blues.*

- Innovators—These few (2.5 percent of the total market) risk takers can afford to pay the higher purchase price charged by companies during the introduction stage of the product (to recoup investment costs). See Figure 10-9. In developing countries, these consumers are the well-to-do business owners and leading government ministers and their families.

- Early adopters—The next consumers to purchase the product tend to be opinion leaders in their communities who take risks, but with greater discernment than innovators. They constitute about 13.5 percent of the total population.

TungCheung/shutterstock.com

Figure 10-9 *Top designers use creative fashion displays to attract fashion innovators who are able and willing to purchase the latest and most innovative designs.*

- Early majority—These consumers, who account for 34 percent of the total market, are more risk averse than individuals in the first categories but enjoy the status of being among the first in their peer group to buy what will be a popular product.

- Late majority—These consumers, who account for 34 percent of the total market, are individuals of more limited means who are likely to adopt products only if the products are widely popular and the risk associated with buying them is minimal. The products themselves are much more affordable at this stage.

- Laggards—These consumers, who account for 16 percent of the total market, are the last to adopt new products and do so only in late maturity. In general, laggards are risk averse and conservative in their spending.

The categories of adopters vary greatly in markets of different development levels. For example, all categories of consumers have significantly higher means in highly industrialized countries, compared with consumers in developing countries. Nevertheless, the segments are similar in terms of their risk propensity, their status in society, and their wealth relative to the rest of the consumers in the country where they live.

Chapter Summary

Evaluate the stages of the international product life cycle and identify the locus of operations and target markets at each stage. Most products are introduced in developed countries, where consumers can afford the high costs charged by manufacturers to recoup product development costs. During growth, the international company faces increasing competition worldwide from products also produced in the developed country. At maturity, standardized products compete primarily on price; manufacturing moves overseas to take advantage of cheaper labor. The company has a sales focus on emerging markets. In a product's middle and late maturity stages, competitors from developing countries enter the company's world markets and compete for consumers. In the product's decline stage, the company seeks new markets in countries of lower development levels.

Identify the different dimensions of the international product mix with company illustrations. Companies use different product mix strategies for different markets. The product mix refers to the totality of brands the company offers to its target markets. A company such as Unilever offers products in many categories — for example, coffee, ice cream, detergent, and others — but does not offer many varieties of each. Unilever, thus, has low depth but high product width, and its product offering is not consistent because it includes products for different uses. Other companies may offer high depth in certain markets and have a very limited offering in yet other markets.

Examine the new product development process and the activities involved at each stage in international markets. The new product development process starts with idea generation, in and outside the company. The next step involves idea screening using predetermined criteria, followed by concept development and evaluation. Product business analysis determines the extent to which the product is likely to be viable. In the next stage, product design and development, product prototypes are developed and evaluated by target consumers. Test marketing involves great expense on the part of the company, but it also leaves the company vulnerable to competitive idea theft. Often, companies use international markets as testing grounds for new products. The final stage, launching, requires significant commitment to the product and to the target market.

Examine degrees of product newness and address international diffusion processes. There are different types of new products: products that are new to an existing market or new to an existing company; new lines (i.e., new products or product lines to a company but for a company already operating in that market); new items in an existing product line for a company; modifications to an existing company product; and innovations (i.e., products that are new to the world). New products are first diffused in lead countries, typically industrialized countries where consumers can afford the products; here, the diffusion rate is slow. The countries where the product is adopted last are known as lag countries. In these countries, the diffusion rate is faster because consumers learn from the adoption experiences of consumers in lead countries.

Key Terms

continuous innovation
controlled test marketing
decline stage
degree of product/service newness
designing and developing the product

developing and evaluating concepts
diffusion process
dynamically continuous innovation
early adopters
early majority
generating new product ideas

growth stage
innovation
innovators
international product life cycle (IPLC)
introduction stage

Discussion Questions

1. Describe the international product life cycle and the activities involved in developed and developing countries.

2. What are the activities involved at each stage of the new product development process? Where are most new products developed?

3. Many products are advertised in the United States as "new and improved." What does this description mean in terms of new product classifications?

4. Describe the differences between lead and lag countries in terms of adoption status and adoption rate.

Chapter Quiz

True/False

1. A product line is defined as the complete assortment of products that a company offers to its target international consumers.

Answer: False

Rationale: The product line is defined as all the related brands a company offers in the same product category. Section 10-2, "Managing the International Product and Service Mix"

2. Product length is defined as the total number of product lines that a company offers.

Answer: False

Rationale: Product length is defined as the total number of brands in the product mix — all the brands sold by the company worldwide. Section 10-2a, "Length"

3. Test marketing has a number of disadvantages: It is expensive, time consuming, and subjects the company to competitive sabotage.

Answer: True

Rationale: Although test marketing provides a good indication of how the product will be received when it is in the market, it can be expensive and time consuming; plus, it exposes the company to competitive sabotage. Section 10-3f, "Test Marketing"

4. Product trialability interferes with the diffusion process.

Answer: False

Rationale: Trialability is an important attribute of an innovation: It tends to accelerate the rate of adoption of a product or service. Section 10-5a, "Product Factors"

Multiple Choice

1. The iPhone is relatively expensive. Companies are presently selling them to consumers in industrialized countries. In which stage of the international product life cycle is the iPhone?
    a. Product introduction
    b. Growth stage

c. Maturity stage

d. Decline stage

Answer: b is correct.

Rationale: Innovations and inventions are targeted at first to consumers in developed countries; during the introduction stage, these products are targeted primarily to innovators. Today, as this technology becomes more popular, they are targeted to the early adopters; thus, the iPhone is in the early growth stage. Section 10-1a, "The Product Introduction Stage"

2. DVD players are most likely in which stage of the international product life cycle?

a. Growth stage

b. Maturity stage

c. Competitive turbulence stage

d. Introduction stage

Answer: b is correct.

Rationale: DVD players are widely adopted and thus are in the maturity stage of the product life cycle. Section 10-1b, "The Growth Stage"

3. Anne Klein II is an example of a

a. line extension.

b. product mix.

c. product length.

d. none of the above

Answer: a is correct.

Rationale: A company is likely to increase the number of lines (related brands in the same product category) it offers to capture more loyal consumers. Anne Klein offers the Anne Klein II line extension to consumers who could otherwise not afford its expensive main product line. Section 10-2, "Managing the International Product and Service Mix"

4. The many different flavors of Unilever's Ben & Jerry's ice cream illustrate Ben & Jerry's

a. product length.

b. product width.

c. product depth.

d. all of the above

Answer: c is correct.

Rationale: Product depth refers to the number of different offerings in a particular product category. Section 10-2c, "Depth"

5. New product ideas can be found through

a. competitive analyses.

b. international employees.

c. international customers.

d. all of the above

Answer: d is correct.

Rationale: Sources of new product ideas are, among others, competitors and company employees and consumers. Section 10-3a, "Generating New Product Ideas"

6. When a company screens new product ideas, what are the most important factors to consider?

a. unique benefits to users

b. product requirements versus resources

c. narrowly specified target markets

d. a and b

Answer: d is correct.

Rationale: It is important for the company to match its resources with the new product requirements and to identify the benefits the products will have for new users. Section 10-3b, "Screening New Product Ideas"

Notes

1. Amy Fontinelle, "The Energy Drinks Industry," *Investopedia,* accessed at http://www.investopedia.com/articles/investing/022315/energy-drinks-industry.asp on September 15, 2015; Kenneth Hein, "Bull's Market," *Brandweek,* Vol. 42, No. 22, May 28, 2001, pp. 21, 23. "Energy Drinks Market Size Worth $84.80 Billion by 2025," *Grand View Research,* July 2017, accessed at https://www.grandviewresearch.com/press-release/global-energy-drinks-market on June 8, 2018. "Monster Beverage Reports 2017 Fourth Quarter and Full Year 2017 Financial Results," *CNBC,* February 28, 2018, accessed at https://www.cnbc.com/2018/02/28/globe-newswire-monster-beverage-reports-2017-fourth-quarter-and-full-year-financial-results.html on June 8, 2018.

2. Ana Medaris Miller, "Are Energy Drinks Really All That Bad?, *US News,* January 16, 2015, accessed at http://health.usnews.com/health-news/health-wellness/articles/2015/01/16/are-energy-drinks-really-that-bad on September 15, 2015; Amy Fontinelle, "The Energy Drinks Industry," *Investopedia* 2015; Alex Planes, "A Leap of Faith: Monster Beverage," *Daily Finance,* February 29, 2012 (http://www.dailyfinance.com/2012/02/29/a-leap-of-faith-monster-beverage/); Matthew Boyle and Dana Vazquez Castillo, "Fueled by Its Energy Drink, Hansen Natural's Stock Has Been on a Rocket Ride," *Fortune,* Vol. 154, No. 13, December 25, 2006, pp. 116—122.

3. See Raymond Vernon, "International Investment and International Trade in the Product Cycle," *Quarterly Journal of Economics,* Vol. 80, No. 2, 1966, pp. 190–207; Raymond Vernon, "The Product Cycle Hypothesis in a New International Environment," *Oxford Bulletin of Economics and Statistics,* Vol. 41, 1979, pp. 255–267.

4. Tesla, "Model 3 Reservations FAQ, accessed at https://www.tesla.com/support/model-3-reservations-faq on June 25, 2018.

5. Richard Goodwin, "Apple Has BIG Plans For The iPhone 7," *Know Your Mobile,* September 15, 2015, accessed at http://www.knowyourmobile.com/mobile-phones/apple-iphone-6c/23153/iphone-7-iphone-7-plus-and-iphone-6c-release-date-specs-features-rumours on September 19, 2015; Jeremy Caplan,"The iPhone Kick-Starts the Competition," *Time,* Vol. 169, No. 27, July 2, 2007, p. 36.

6. *The Globe and Mail,* "Here's how many hours you worked to afford that new iPhone,"Sep. 18, 2015, accessed at http://www.theglobeandmail.com/report-on-business/economy/the-amount-of-work-it-takes-to-afford-an-iphone/ article26422224/ on September 19, 2015.

7. Andand Giridharadas, "Big Names Competing for India's 2-Cents-a-Minute Caller," *The New York Times,* January 10, 2007, C9.

8. Milton Keynes, "Motorola Chooses Poland for New Site," Corporate Location, European Edition, May/June 1998, p. 7 and Faith Hung, "Consortium Looks to Build Thailand Fab—Siemens, Intel and Macronix Want to Jumpstart Country's Semi Industry," Electronic Buyers' News, June 5, 2000, Issue 1214, p. 4.

8. Tim Wu, "The Oligopoly Problem," *The New Yorker,* April 15, 2013, accessed at http://www.newyorker.com/tech/elements/the-oligopoly-problem on September 17, 2015.

9. Gerrit Wiesmann, "Berlin Plans Frequency Auction," *Financial Times,* February 7, 2007, p. 19.

10. FDC, "2014 Ranking of Brazilian Multinationals," accessed at http://acervo.ci.fdc.org.br/AcervoDigital/Relat%C3%B3rios%20de%20Pesquisa/Relat%C3%B3rios%20de%20Pesquisa%202014/2014%20FDC%20Ranking%20of%20Brazilian%20Multinationals.pdf on September 17, 2015; Michael Cusumano, "'Made in India' a New Sign of Software Quality," *Computerworld,* Vol. 34, No. 9, February 28, 2000, p. 36.

11. Unilever is described in detail at www.Unilever.com, a source for some of the material in this section.

12. These examples are detailed in Harriet Marsh, "Adapting to Africa," *Marketing,* March 30, 2000, p. 39.

13. http://www.freeplayenergy.com (accessed September 18, 2015).

14. Rahim Kanani, "Kristine Pearson on the Founding and Future of Lifeline Energy," *Forbes,* November 1, 2011, accessed at http://www.forbes.com/sites/rahimkanani/2011/11/01/kristine-pearson-on-the-founding-and-future-of-lifeline-energy/ on September 16, 2015; Eric Leech, "Freeplay Foundation Brings Light to Rwanda," Treehugger.com, December 9, 2008, accessed at http://www.treehugger.com/corporate-responsibility/freeplay-foundation-brings-light-to-rwanda.html on September 16, 2015; "Freeplay Energy," *Investors Chronicle,* October 6, 2006, p. 1.

15. David Leonhardt, "It Was a Hit in Buenos Aires—So Why Not Boise?" *BusinessWeek*, Vol. 3594, September 7, 1998, pp. 56–57.

16. Ibid.

17. Serena Ng and Laurie Burkitt, "P&G Tripped Up by Its Assumptions About Diapers in China," *The Wall Street Journal*, August 13, 2015, accessed at http://www.wsj.com/articles/p-g-tripped-up-by-its-assumptions-about-diapers-in-china-1439445897 on September 19, 2015; C. Samuel Craig and Susan P. Douglas, "Configural Advantage in Global Markets," *Journal of International Marketing*, Vol. 8, No. 1, 2000, pp. 6–26.

18. Gordon A. Wyner, "Product Testing: Benefits and Risks," *Marketing Research*, Vol. 9, No. 1, Spring 1997, pp. 46– 48.

18. Lisa Susanne Willsey, "Taking These 7 Steps Will Help You Launch a New Product," *Marketing News*, Vol. 33, No. 7, March 29, 1999, p. 17.

19. John Saunders, Veronica Wong, Chris Stagg, Mariadel Mar Souza Fontan, "How Screening Criteria Change During Brand Development," *Journal of Product and Brand Management*, Vol. 14, No. 4/5, 2005, pp. 239–250.

20. F. H. Rolf Seringhaus, "Comparative Marketing Behaviour of Canadian and Austrian High Tech Firms," *Management International Review*, Vol. 33, No. 3, 1993, pp. 247–270.

21. Willsey, "Taking These 7 Steps," p. 17.

22. Wyner, "Product Testing," pp. 46–48.

23. Robert S. Doscher, "How to Create New Products," *Target Marketing*, Vol. 17, No. 1, 1994, pp. 40–41.

24. Willsey, "Taking These 7 Steps," p. 17.

25. Robert G. Cooper, "How to Launch a New Product Successfully," *CMA*, Vol. 69, No. 8, 1995, pp. 20–23.

26. Shaoming Zou and Aysegul Ozsomer, "Global Product R&D and the Firm's Strategic Position," *Journal of International Marketing*, Vol. 7, No. 1, 1999, pp. 57–76.

27. Melanie Healy, North America and Global Hyper-Super-Mass Channel Group President, University of Richmond lecture, February 15, 2012.

28. Peter March, "Feast of a Movable Workforce: India's Revolution Part II," *Financial Times*, May 17, 2006, 12.

29. Kevin J. Clancy and Robert S. Shulman, "It's Better to Fly a New Product Simulator than Crash the Real Thing," *Planning Review*, Vol. 20, No. 4, July/August 1992, pp. 10–16.

30. Eric Anderson, Song Lin, Duncan Simester, and Catherine Tucker, "Harbinger of Failure," working paper, accessed at https://marketing.wharton.upenn.edu/mktg/assets/File/Anderson-Eric%202015_02_05_Harbingers.pdf on September 20, 2015; BASES II, accessed at http://www.nielsen.com/content/dam/nielsen/en_us/documents/pdf/Fact%20Sheets/Nielsen%20BASES%20II.pdf on September 19, 2015.

31. Stacey Ramirez, "Hand Outs," *Business Mexico*, Vol. 6, No. 5, May 1996, pp. 12–16.

32. Ibid.

33. Tamer S. Cavusgil and Ugur Yavas, "Test Marketing: An Exposition," *Marketing Intelligence and Planning*, Vol. 5, No. 3, 1987, pp. 16–20.

34. Ibid.

35. Robert G. Cooper, "Debunking the Myths of New Product Development," *Research Technology Management*, Vol. 37, No. 4, July/August 1994, pp. 40–50.

36. Nicholas Valery, "Survey: Innovation in Industry: Industry Gets Religion," *The Economist*, Vol. 350, No. 8107, February 20, 1999, pp. S5–S6.

37. Daina Beth Solomon, "Amazon Launches First Debit in Mexico E-Commerce Push," *Reuters*, March 13, 2018, accessed at https://www.reuters.com/article/us-amazon-com-mexico/amazon-launches-first-debit-card-in-mexico-e-commerce-push-idUSKCN1GP35A on June 9, 2018.

38. Cooper, "Debunking the Myths," pp. 40–50.

39. Michael-Jorg Oesterle, "Time-Span Until Internationalization: Foreign Market Entry as a Built-in-Mechanism of Innovations," *Management International Review*, Vol. 37, No. 2, 1997, pp. 125–149.

40. "World's First Internet Coffee Auction a Success," *International Trade Forum*, No. 1, 2000, pp. 37–38.

41. Everett M. Rogers, *Diffusion of Innovations, 3rd Edition*, New York: Free Press, 1983.

42. Sanna Sundqvist, Lauri Frank, and Kaisu Puumalainen, "The Effects of Country Characteristics, Cultural Similarity and Adoption Timing on the Diffusion of Wireless Communications, *Journal of Business Research*, Vol. 58, No. 1, 2005, pp. 107–110.

Case 10-1 *FrieslandCampina*

Royal FrieslandCampina is the world's sixth-largest dairy company, with sales over 11.3 billion euros, with 22,000 employees in 35 countries, and with millions of consumers. A European company that remains close to its Dutch roots, FrieslandCampina's image evokes picturesque Dutch cow pastures and healthy   lifestyles. The company is owned by dairy producers in the Netherlands, Belgium, and Germany. Its history can be traced to southern Holland, in the Eindhoven area. A dairy cooperative with the name "De Kempen" was created in 1947 and used the brand name "Campina." In 1964, the cooperative merged with another cooperative in the Weert region in Holland and formed Campina (named after a regional moor — its meaning is "from the land").

After several consecutive mergers, including, in 2008, with another Dutch dairy behemoth, Friesland Foods, the resulting company, FrieslandCampina, became one of the largest dairy cooperatives in the world, active from London to Moscow and from the United States to Japan. The company's products are milk, desserts, yogurt, dairy drinks, butter, cheese, condensed milk, powdered milk, and caseinate, and it has a large brand portfolio. It is also a company that takes corporate social responsibility seriously, and, as a result, it is well positioned in the industry, especially when it comes to relationships with consumers and public authorities.

FrieslandCampina must buy all the milk the farmers produce, while the farmers must finance the cooperative, and, in return, they obtain a yield of the products sold. FrieslandCampina itself is a nonprofit organization. Member farmers receive all the company profits. They have voting rights in the company that are proportional to the amount of milk they deliver, and they are represented by the Members' Council, which is the highest managerial body of the cooperative.

Industry Trends

The European Union remains the world's top dairy producer, manufacturer, and trader of dairy products. Because the EU is a mature dairy market, the emphasis is on value growth and processing milk into products with high added value. Among the trends in the industry is consolidation. Another important trend is the focus on convenience (a packaging issue) and on value-added nutrition for functional foods (a product ingredient issue). Changes include creating new packaging and unique containers for innovative products.

Marcin Niemiec/shutterstock.com

FrieslandCampina is a creative innovator when it comes to convenience, giving a new twist to dairy desserts. The company's new strudel is two product layers swirled into a single portion pack. It gives consumers a dessert that looks striking and offers a surprising combination of flavors, according to the company. FrieslandCampina was the first company to apply the swirl effect in desserts, thereby setting a trend. The two layers remain stable and do not run into each other.

Functional ingredients (health foods or ingredients that enhance the nutritional value of products) represent yet another important trend in the dairy industry. In this category are a number of health foods and other milk-based nutritional supplements sold to consumers. Examples are input products for pharmaceutical products, food ingredients, and ingredients used to enhance nutrition.

Finally, another industry trend is internationalization. FrieslandCampina is a veritable international company, present in Belgium, Denmark, Germany, Spain, Greece, the Netherlands, Poland, Russia, Thailand, Vietnam, India, China, Japan, Argentina, and the United States, among others.

Meeting Competitive Challenges at FrieslandCampina: Adopting a Market Orientation

Historically, milk production was supply driven, and excess milk was used to produce cheese and powdered milk. This strategy led to excess cheese and commodities on the market and the need for subsidies. FrieslandCampina initiated a change in this practice. Since the late 1980s, the company has been demand driven: Farmers are assigned production quotas that they are not allowed to exceed.

According to R. J. Steetskamp, Director of Business Development Worldwide, the company examines consumer behavior to determine where to fit products in consumers' lives. As such, the company offers four categories of products:

1. **Indulgence products.** This category constitutes an important growth area for the company. FrieslandCampina produces numerous milk-based desserts, with the exception of ice cream.

2. **Daily essentials.** This category includes FrieslandCampina products that shoppers purchase routinely, such as milk, buttermilk, yogurt, coffee cream, butter, cheese, and others. FrieslandCampina, using a strategy employed by all its competitors, also sells daily essentials under private-label (store) brands, rather than under its own brand name. For example, in Holland, it sells milk, plain yogurt, butter, Gouda cheese, and vla (chocolate or vanilla custard) under the Albert Heijn supermarket brand name.

3. **Functional products.** According to Mr. Steetskamp, this product category needs to be further explored and defined by the company. In this category are health foods and other milk-based nutritional supplements sold to consumers, such as proteins and powders.

4. **Ingredients** (food and pharmaceutical ingredients). This product category is targeted at other food product manufacturers, rather than at the individual consumers. The primary purpose of the food and pharmaceutical ingredients is to enhance the quality, taste, texture, and nutritive content of the products manufactured by FrieslandCampina's clients. With this category, FrieslandCampina becomes a supplier to other manufacturers, rather than a product manufacturer distributing to supermarkets.

International Expansion at FrieslandCampina

One of the most important undertakings at FrieslandCampina in the past two decades was to expand beyond the Netherlands. In its first expansion effort, the company bought Belgium's Comelco, another dairy cooperative. In Belgium, the company boasts the Joyvalle dairy products and milk brand and the Passendale, Père Joseph, and Wynendale cheese brands, all marketed under the FrieslandCampina umbrella brand.

FrieslandCampina expanded into Germany, purchasing a number of cooperatives: Sudmilch (southern Germany), Tuffi (western Germany), and Emzett (Berlin). In Germany, its primary brand is Landliebe; here, the company sells Landliebe milk, cream, yogurts (seasonal, fruit, and plain, in different types of containers); different types of puddings, including rice pudding, ice cream, cheese, and qwark (a uniquely flavored creamy cheese) plain or with fruit; yogurt drinks (with fruit flavors such as banana, cherry, lemon, peach, and orange); and different milk drinks with flavors such as vanilla and chocolate. The company also offers products such as coffee machines, cups, and spoons, for purchase online at its site, www.landliebe-online.de.

As a result of these acquisitions and mergers, FrieslandCampina is the market leader in the Netherlands, Germany, and Belgium – the latest acquisition in Belgium, of Belgian mozzarella producer Fabrelac, took place in 2015. The company is further expanding in the European Union and in other international markets, including a large acquisition in Pakistan in 2016. Currently, it produces, among others, liquid milk and drinks in Belgium, Germany, the Netherlands, Russia, Thailand, and Vietnam; yogurt and desserts in Germany, the Netherlands, and Russia; cheese and butter in Belgium, Germany, and the Netherlands; ingredients for the international food and pharmaceutical industries in Belgium, Germany, the Netherlands, and the United States; cream liqueurs in the Netherlands; and baby-animal feed in the Netherlands. It has sales organizations for consumer products in Belgium, Germany, the Netherlands, Russia, the United Kingdom, Spain, Greece, Thailand, and Vietnam. Its sales organizations for industrial products are in the Netherlands, Denmark, Poland, the United Kingdom, Spain, United States, Argentina, India, China, and Japan.

Sources: www.FrieslandCampina.com (accessed on September 20, 2015); Mark Astley, "FrieslandCampina completes acquisition of Belgian mozzarella producer," September 10, 2014, accessed at http://www.dairyreporter.com/Manufacturers/FrieslandCampina-completes-acquisition-of-Belgian-mozzarella-producer on September 20, 2015; www.prnewswire.co.uk/cgi/news/release?id=197343, May 2006; "An Overview of the World's Largest Functional Foods Companies," *Just Food*, July 2006, pp. 6–22; Arno Mathis, "Corporate

Social Responsibility and Policy Making: What Role Does Communication Play?" *Business Strategy and the Environment*, Vol. 16, No. 5, July 2007, p. 366; Sarah McRitchie, "Europe Shrinks to Expand," *Dairy Foods*, Vol. 100, No. 1, January 1999, pp. 75–79; Donna Berry, "Global Market Basket," *Dairy Foods*, September 2005, Vol. 106, No. 9, September 2005, pp. 32–36. Jim Cornall, "FrieslandCampina Completes Engro Foods Deal," *Dairy Reporter*, January 5, 2017, accessed at https://www.dairyreporter.com/Article/2017/01/05/FrieslandCampina-completes-Engro-Foods-deal on June 9, 2018.

Analysis Suggestions:

1. Perform a broad product mix analysis for FrieslandCampina. Calculate product width by examining *only* the product categories that the company carries.

2. Comment on the product consistency across the different product lines. Is product consistency important for a dairy company? What do all the lines have in common — in addition to FrieslandCampina ownership?

3. Look at the main Dutch brands on the Campina website. Click on some of them and look at their history. Click also on Napolact, a Transylvanian dairy in Romania. How is it different from the rest of the FrieslandCampina portfolio, and how is it similar?

Case 10-2 The Gigafactory:

A Partnership between Tesla and Panasonic

Tesla is a U.S. automotive and energy storage company that designs and manufactures luxury electric automobiles, components, and battery products. It sells its lithium-ion battery packs to a number of automobile manufacturers, including Toyota and Daimler. The Tesla Roadster, introduced in 2006, was its first automobile, an all-electric sports car and the first to use lithium-ion battery cells. It was also the first mass-produced electric automobile to travel more than 200 miles per charge. Tesla subsequently introduced Model S, a luxury sedan with a sales price starting at $71,000, and Model X, a crossover SUV with falcon wings, starting at $132,000. There is no electric car today on the market that is even remotely close in performance to Tesla: Its range is 300 miles, it goes from 0 to 60 miles per hour in 2.8 seconds and it has the industry-leading autopilot. Tesla offered its first affordable model, the Model 3, in 2016, which retails for about $50,000. Its new Model X has a waiting list that stretches out for almost a year. The company plans to go from 50,000 in sales in 2015 to 500,000 in 2020.

Aleksei Potov/shutterstock.com

However, by 2018, Tesla was experiencing major production issues with the Model 3: deliveries were less than one-half of the planned 5,000 units per week. The company called a temporary halt to production for the Model 3. Compounding Tesla's problems was the recall of some 123,000 Model S cars. These issues have raised major concerns among investors about Tesla's ability to be a viable auto manufacturer, resulting in a significant drop in the share price.

The Tesla batteries constitute one of the most innovative components of its automobiles. They are made up of thousands of cells wired together and guided by software to power the motor. Currently, Japan's Panasonic produces the batteries for Tesla in the Osaka Prefecture. Tesla Motors and Panasonic are also building a large-scale battery manufacturing plant – known as the Gigafactory – in Nevada, and it is expected that the $5 billion facility will be completed by 2020, with a part of the plant operational in 2016. The Gigafactory is being built to advance the mass market of electric vehicles. The enormous factory will create a dramatic reduction in costs, as it will substantially eliminate packaging, transportation, and storage costs, taking advantage of economies of scale in battery cell production that has never been seen before. Within the partnership, Tesla provides all the utilities for manufacturing, and Panasonic manufactures and supplies the lithium-ion battery cells.

Tesla's partnership with Panasonic to produce the first Gigafactory in Nevada has been fruitful, and Tesla is hoping to extend it to building another Gigafactory in Japan. Panasonic is the leader in automotive lithium-ion batteries, with half of the world market share, followed by Japan's Automotive Energy Supply, a joint venture of Nissan Motor and NEC, with a 17 percent market share, and by Korea's LG Chem, with an 11 percent market share. Tesla sources more parts from Japan than anywhere else, with the exception of the U.S. Japan also has one of the largest electric car markets in the world and boasts some of the most advanced technology.

Tesla executives are working closely with Japanese partners to pitch the idea. However, there are some reservations about Japan. Contrary to Tesla's aggressive and oftentimes risky expansion plans, Japan is much more risk-adverse and is slower at decision making and production. A director at Tesla, Kurt Kelty, has spoken about times where Tesla pushed for increased production and was met with opposition from the Japanese suppliers. In fact, a Japanese supplier suggested that the automaker slow down its expansion plans.

The reaction of Japanese suppliers and partners to Tesla's aggressive expansion strategy is not surprising. According to Harvard sociologist Mary Brinton, Japan suffers from a play-it-safe mentality that's become ever-present in daily life, as there is a general tendency to focus more on potential downsides rather than on opportunities. This may explain, for example, why 844 trillion yen, almost twice the country's yearly economic output, sits idle in cash at home and in savings accounts earning 0.02 percent and why fewer than four percent of working-age Japanese intend to be entrepreneurs. In fact, 73 percent describe themselves as risk-averse.

Tesla, however, is advancing its expansion plans undeterred, negotiating with South Korea's LG Chem to supply its lithium-ion batteries. (Tesla, until recently, has sourced this key component almost exclusively from Panasonic.) While Japan continues as a targeted location for the next Gigafactory due to the expected cost cuts and performance from the current partnership, Tesla CEO Elon Musk suggests that there will likely be many Gigafactories, maybe hundreds, in the future and not just for Tesla Motors, Inc., but for many other companies as well. However, as the Tesla Gigafactory comes on line in 2018, the company is also facing the prospect of stiff competition. Chinese battery producers may be able to produce three times as many batteries as the Nevada Gigafactory by 2021.

Sources: Tom Randall, "There's One Thing Volkswagen Can Do to Stop the Bleeding: Beat Tesla," *Bloomberg*, November 6, 2015, accessed at http://www.bloomberg.com/news/articles/2015-11-06/volkswagen-can-only-save-itsel-by-beating-tesla on November 9, 2015; "Panasonic and Tesla Sign Agreement for the Gigafactory," *News Bites – Automotive* Aug 01 2014. ProQuest, accessed on November 5, 2015; Craig Trudell and Horie Masatsugu, "Tesla Pushes Japanese Suppliers as It Seeks Battery Partners," *Bloomberg*, March 27, 2015, accessed at http://www.bloomberg.com/news/articles/2015-03-27/tesla-pushes-japanese-suppliers-as-it-seeks-battery-partners on November 8, 2015; Masaaki Iwamoto, Satoshi Kawano, and Jason Clenfield, "Japan's Fear of Risk is Getting Dangerous," *Bloomberg*, December 06, 2012, accessed at http://www.bloomberg.com/bw/articles/2012-12-06/japans-fear-of-risk-is-getting-dangerous on November 9, 2015; Kentaro Ogura, "LG Chem Tesla Tie-Up Could Jolt Panasonic," *Nikkei Asian Review*, October 28, 2015, accessed at http://asia.nikkei.com/Business/Deals/LG-Chem-Tesla-ti-up-could-jolt-Panasonic on November 9, 2015. Leon Poultney, "Hey Tesla, How Hard Can It Be to Actually Make a Car," *Wired UK*, April 22, 2018, accessed at http://www.wired.co.uk/article/tesla-model-3-production-stock-problems-engineering on June 9, 2018. Steven Loveday, "Battery Arms Race heats Up, Tesla Gigafactory to Face Stiff Competition," *InsideEVs*, August 19, 2017, accessed at https://insideevs.com/tesla-gigafactory-face-stiff-competition on June 20, 2018.

Analysis Suggestions

1. Is Tesla an innovator? Explain.

2. The Gigafactory is a giant enterprise. What are some of the advantages of building the Gigafactory?

3. Compare the attitudes toward expansion of Tesla management and those of Japanese suppliers. Explain the cross-cultural differences.

This page is intentionally blank...

Chapter 11

Managing International Marketing Channels

Chapter Outline

International distribution channels link manufacturers and final international consumers. Internationally, distribution channels vary greatly from one region to another and from one market to another. For most markets, consumer product channels of distribution tend to be longer than industrial product channels. Beyond this general trait, however, channel characteristics differ worldwide. The following are examples of such differences:

AlexLMX/shutterstock.com

• In Japan, there are many more levels of distributors for consumer products than in most other countries, whereas, for most industrial goods, the large trading companies deal directly with retailers.

• In economies where the state plays an important role in business, state-owned enterprises may act as massive distributors that frequently carry unrelated products. In these countries, China and Russia included, the state continues to keep close oversight of distribution activities.

• In emerging markets and low-income countries, network marketing is an established channel of distribution.

This chapter addresses all the aspects of managing international distribution, offering an overview of the different intermediaries involved in the international distribution process, the facilitators involved in distribution and logistics, and the challenges facing the distribution process.

Navigating Blocked Channels

In its heyday, when Kraft was a large multinational company, it used to team up only with the biggest logistics company in each region. However, in Hong Kong, in the mid-1990s, the leading distributors charged an exorbitant amount to distribute Kraft products. At first, the company refused to pay the price, and the distribution structure at the time blocked their access into the market. Years later, Kraft yielded, deciding to use the same over-priced distributors to sell its Kraft brand in Hong Kong and then China — for a few years longer, according to Bill Campbell, former Philip Morris chief executive officer (Kraft was a Philip Morris company at the time).

Kraft entered mainland China in the mid-1990s by setting up two joint ventures: Kraft Tianmei Foods in the northern city of Tianjin, which makes Tang, a fruit-flavored instant drink mix, and Sugus fruit-flavored chews; and Kraft Guangtong Food in the southern province of Guangdong, producing Maxwell House coffee. When entering these markets, Kraft, as usual, teamed up with the largest logistics companies, but changed its strategy after sometimes experiencing delays in its orders. In 2005, under its pledge to the World Trade Organization, China opened its logistics sector to foreign competition, bur Kraft continued to use its Chinese joint ventures to handle the logistics. Kraft has since created a new company, Mondelēz, to handle its international grocery and snack business. Continuing the practice established by Kraft, Mondelēz' current distribution operations in China continue to be handled by joint ventures.[1]

11-1 Issues Related to International Distribution

Some international markets have an underdeveloped distribution system for many industrial sectors and, to a lesser extent, for consumer goods. Distribution to these markets may be opportunistic and not adequately organized, or distribution channels may not exist at all. Alternatively, the complex structure of certain international channels may serve as a barrier to multinational company entry in an international market new to the company. The company first must determine whether it can use established channels or build its own.

11-1a Using Established Channels

Entering a new consumer goods market can be problematic for companies. In most cases, competitors already have a hold on existing channels and are thus likely to *block* them for new entrants. In addition to competitors, there are other obstacles to using established channels. For example, the amount charged by distributors could be so high that a company may be unwilling to use them. This was the case for Kraft Foods in its attempt to enter the Hong Kong market with its products.

The initial channel selection decision is important. Once in a channel relationship, a company may be bound to that relationship and may not legally be allowed to change distributors.

11-1b Building Own Channels

Although building channels is expensive, this strategy is especially necessary in situations in which no channels exist at all or no channels conform to the needs of the company. The example of Coca-Cola in Eastern Europe after the fall of communism is a case in point.

Although Pepsi had been present in the region since the late 1960s, Coke did not enter most of the countries until the 1990s. When Coca-Cola decided to enter this market, it found old state-enterprise-owned channels selling beverages and operating with low efficiency. Consequently, it decided to create its own channels of distribution that fit well with the market structure by working with independent truck drivers who had some experience working with soft-drink retailers.

In the case of new manufacturing operations in a target country, distribution channels must be established for the supply of needed components in manufacturing. With just-in-time inventory practices, manufacturers of automobiles and other industrial products often expect components to arrive on the day the final assembly is to take place. In addition, manufacturers must then develop distribution channels for the finished products. The foreign-owned automobile plants in the United States are an example of building channels for the manufacturing process *and* subsequent distribution of finished products in the marketplace.

11-2 Intermediaries Involved in International Distribution

Depending on company involvement in a particular market, a company can use home-country intermediaries or host-country intermediaries. A company that uses intermediaries in its own home country is likely not to be as involved in managing the marketing mix in the country where the target market is located. Home-country intermediaries typically provide all marketing services for firms that do not wish to enter the foreign market or do not have the capability to do so. Companies relying on home-country intermediaries relinquish their control of the marketing mix to their distributors in the international target-market.

A company using intermediaries in the host country is likely to have a presence there, in the form of a sales office, at the lowest level of direct international involvement, or in the form of a wholly owned manufacturing and distribution subsidiary, at the highest level of direct international involvement. The company, by using host-country intermediaries, also seeks to have a greater degree of control of the marketing mix in the foreign country.

11-2a Home-Country Intermediaries

Export Management Companies

Export management companies are highly specialized in certain industries, such as endoscopic surgery instruments or networking products, and typically represent smaller companies in a region of the country. Some of their activities include researching the international market, representing a company at trade shows and exhibitions, screening and selecting international distributors, shipping the company's product, and handling all the necessary export documentation, such as customs forms and export licensing.

Trading Companies: The Japanese Model

28 Nov. Foto/shutterstock.com

Japanese trading companies (also known as sogo-shoshas) existed for more than four centuries when the House of Mitsui was created, soon followed by Mitsubishi and Sumitomo. Because Japan was short on natural resources, it was heavily dependent on foreign markets for necessities and had no foreign exchange to pay for them. As a result, the trading companies specialized in the movement of goods. Currently, Japanese general trading companies account for about 10 percent of world export trade, and their operations range across finance, distribution, technology, mining, oil and gas exploration, and information. Over time, they have changed from pure traders to more financially sophisticated investment holding companies. Their basic functions are to serve as an intermediary for all marketing and import and export transactions and to perform financial intermediary activities and information gathering. Today, they also perform logistical and warehousing services and are involved in trading and distribution, management consulting, manufacturing, risk-hedging to deal with exchange rate and price fluctuations, domestic and overseas importing and exporting of technology, and joint ventures to develop foreign industrial markets. They act as intermediaries for half of Japan's exports and two-thirds of its imports.[2]

The biggest and the best of the traders are members of keiretsus, which are families of firms with interlocking stakes in one another. Here, the trading companies' role is to act as the eyes and ears of the whole group, spotting business trends, market gaps, and investment opportunities. The top sogo-shoshas, or general trading companies, are Itochu Corp., Sumitomo, Marubeni, Mitsui, and Mitsubishi. Mitsubishi, for example, consists of the Bank of Tokyo Mitsubishi, the largest bank in Japan, Mitsubishi Motors, Mitsubishi Trust and Banking, Meiji Mutual Life Insurance Company, which provides insurance for all the members of the keiretsu, and Mitsubishi Shoji, the trading company for the keiretsu, whose purpose is strictly limited to the distribution of goods around the world.[3]

Japanese export trading companies, that is, the companies tasked with distribution all over the world, are presently facing competition from companies in every domain of their activity. They are also increasingly facing competition from manufacturers, who are setting up their own distribution networks. As a result, they are gradually going to handle a smaller proportion of Japan's exports. On the other hand, their other domains of activity help them maintain a prominent profile across industries.

Trading Companies: The U.S. Model

In 1982, the U.S. Congress passed the Export Trading Company (ETC) Act to encourage the formation of export trading companies to promote U.S. exports and to facilitate the formation of export intermediaries. It is another tool of the U.S. government that can help companies identify the appropriate export trading or export management company for the company's target country as is shown in International Marketing Illustration 11-1 (next page).

The U.S. Export Trading Company Act [4]

The Act expected small and medium-sized firms to join an export trading company with a bank to provide major financing. The Act relieved some of the restrictions placed on U.S. companies by the antitrust laws.

In response to the ETC Act, in 1982, Sears formed its Sears World Trade Organization, intending to export and import trade with low-income countries, and General Electric also established a trading company. Both failed and agreed that it was due to the lack of expertise and qualified managers in trading. Moreover, the Act limited U.S. trading companies to exports, which

Travel mania/shutterstock.com

limited in turn their viability, and the administrative burdens of obtaining certification created too many hurdles for the firms to follow.

The ETC Act also created the Export-Import Bank (ExIm Bank), an independent government agency whose purpose is to guarantee loans to exporting companies. The main beneficiaries of the ExIm Bank, over the years, have been Boeing and General Electric (GE). When ExIm Bank's authorization expired on July 1, 2015, both companies threatened to move important operations overseas. In early 2015, some members of the U.S. Congress contended that ExIm Bank was merely a mechanism for government capitalism, and they fought to block its authorization. This meant that the bank could no longer extend any new loans or guarantees. There is still some hope that Congress would reconsider the funding in the near future. The Office of Trade and Economic Analysis in the U.S. Department of Commerce administers the Export Trading Company Act.[5]

International Marketing Illustration 11-1: Aiding Export Joint Ventures

For companies interested in partnering with competitors to export internationally, the U.S. government can provide help. Under Title III of the Export Trading Company Act, any U.S. resident, business association, group of firms, or state or local government entity may apply to the Office of Trade and Economic Analysis of the Department of Trade for a Certificate of Review. The certificate provides antitrust preclearance for the export activities of the certificate holder, essentially minimizing the application of U.S. antitrust laws to export activities and the related risk of expensive antitrust litigation. The Certificate of Review provides exporters with immunity from both government antitrust suits and with procedural advantages in private antitrust suits. The Export Trade Certificate of Review application is a free and quick process: The Department of Commerce determines whether the Certificate meets the certification standards contained in the Export Trading Company Act, obtains the concurrence of the Department of Justice, and then issues the final Certificate within 90 days.

Aquir/shutterstock.com

Some of the activities that could receive the Export Trade Certificates of Review are joint establishment of export prices; exclusive agreements with domestic suppliers and foreign representatives; joint export marketing/selling arrangements among domestic competitors; allocation of export markets, territories, or customers; refusals to deal; exchanges of business information; and the joint licensing of technology. Among the competitive advantages offered by export joint ventures are economies of scale and spreading of risk among the participating firms, which benefits most small and medium-sized enterprises that may be new to exporting or may have limited exporting experience.

Partnerships might take place in the areas of:

• Market research

• Market development, reducing the individual costs of attending trade shows or trade missions, and sharing the cost of generic advertising

• Overseas joint bidding

• Transportation and shipping, thus negotiating volume discounts and guaranteeing carriers sufficient cargo

• Establishment of uniform minimum export prices to avoid price rivalry

• Service and promotional activities

In one example, an Export Trade Certificate of Review was awarded to Florida Citrus Exports of Vero Beach, Florida. Florida Citrus Exports operates as an export service umbrella for its nine members (including grower-owned cooperatives and packing houses) sharing transportation and market development costs, engaging in joint promotion, preparing joint bids, assisting each other in maintaining quality standards, and spreading the risk of international involvement. In another example, the Export Trade Certificate of Review allows the American Film Export Association of Los Angeles, California, to engage in international licensing agreements and create financing documents that are the standard for the independent film and TV industry. It permits the organization to produce a membership sales survey to measure the licensing of motion picture and television products in 33 territories. It also facilitates the sharing of credit data on more than 500 film and television buyers from 56 countries.

In an example of facilitation, the American Film Export Association ran a Regional Market in Bangkok, Thailand, which opened opportunities for U.S. film companies to enter Vietnam, where cinema representatives were eager for the companies' business and were especially interested in learning how best to fight piracy. In another example, the American Film Export Association performed a study that found that countries such as Australia, France, Germany, Italy, Japan, Taiwan, Spain, and the United Kingdom can each provide revenues of $50,000 to $200,000 in theater, video, television, cable, and satellite markets.

Sources: www.filmfestivals.com/afm/afnewb4.htm www.mothermuse.com/markets.htm; www.ita.doc.gov/tdsif/office_of_export_trading_company.htm (accessed on May 16, 2012).

Antonio Guillem/shutterstock.com

Home-Country Brokers and Agents

Home-country brokers and agents bring international buyers and sellers together in the company's home country and do not carry title to the product. They can handle different export functions and specialize in certain product categories. Alternatively, they might represent a certain manufacturer on a commission basis for a particular deal; they are known as manufacturer's export agents. Or they might be buyers located in the firm's home country, representing different firms located abroad; in this case, they are known as buying offices.

Cooperative Export Arrangements

Cooperative export arrangements, also referred to as piggybacking or mother henning, involve exporters agreeing to handle export functions for unrelated companies on a contractual basis. Cooperative exporters are large multinationals with in-house know-how and resources, and extensive knowledge of international markets. The piggybacked products are noncompetitive with the cooperative exporter's own products but may be similar; an example is an auto manufacturer in the U.S. selling tires or seat covers for a much smaller company that is new to international marketing.[6]

Two types of firms are generally involved in cooperative export arrangements: complementary export agents and complementary export merchants. Complementary export agents export complementary products. This category includes individual firms exporting other firms' products that are complementary to their offerings (along with their own products). If these firms carry the other firms' products for a fee or commission, they act as complementary export agents. If, instead of operating on a fee or commission, the firms actually take title to the complementary products distributed and are compensated in the form of a discount in a buy-sell arrangement,[7] they act as complementary export merchants.

Webb-Pomerene Associations of Exporters

Webb-Pomerene Associations, established under the Webb-Pomerene Act and managed by the Federal Trade Commission, also are involved in cooperative exporting. Webb-Pomerene Associations are composed of competing companies that join resources and efforts to export internationally. The companies are granted immunity from antitrust prosecution under the Webb-Pomerene Act so that they can export products manufactured in the United States to compete effectively internationally, especially in world markets in which cartels are active. Examples of Webb-Pomerene Associations under Webb-Pomerene Act filings with the Federal Trade Commission are the American Cotton Exporters Association, American Natural Soda Ash Corporation, American-European Soda Ash Shipping Association, Inc., Phosphate Chemicals Export Association, Inc., Overseas Distribution Solutions, LLC, and Specialty Crop Trade Council, among others.[8]

Export Merchants

Export merchants are intermediaries who take title to and possession of the products they carry. They are responsible for shipping and marketing the products to the target market. In this sense, they have full control over the products' international marketing mix. Generally, they can carry competing brands. One type is the *export jobber*, who carries primarily commodity goods but does not take physical possession of the products. Another type is the Norazi agent, who deals in illegal and gray market products. Norazis might deal in legitimate exporting, but, among the exported goods, the agent will also deal in arms, untaxed liquor, or contraband. The Norazi agent will also export legitimate merchandise to countries where governments prohibit exports. (See also Section 11-4b, "Parallel Imports," later in this chapter.)

11-2b Foreign-Country Intermediaries

Foreign-country intermediaries can be merchant middlemen, who take title to and possession of the products they carry, and agents and brokers, who bring buyers and sellers together but do not carry title to and take possession of the products they deal with.

Merchant Middlemen

Merchant middlemen are intermediaries who carry the manufacturer's product line in a particular country. They carry title to, and have physical possession of, the products they distribute in the foreign country. Companies have close relationships with their intermediaries, allowing them to control their products strategy. Selecting them carefully is important because the relationship with a distributor might be difficult or impossible to dissolve without paying substantial compensation. One type of merchant middleman in a foreign country is an import jobber, who purchases commodity goods from the manufacturer to sell to the trade (wholesaler, retailer, business-to-business client). Also, wholesalers, retailers, and industrial consumers may import products directly for resale. As such, they act as merchant middlemen.

bluedog studio/shutterstock.com

Agents and Brokers

A company can select from many different types of agents and brokers. Agents can represent the manufacturer exclusively in a market, acting as a manufacturer's representative. This agent works practically as the company's sales representative and is paid on commission. The managing agent, also called the comprador, has an exclusive arrangement with the company, representing its operations in a particular country. This individual does not take title to the goods and is usually paid as a percentage of sales of the company he or she manages.

As with a merchant middlemen, many foreign countries do not allow the termination of a local sales agent or representative without defined cause. Moreover, in the event of any contract termination with a local agent, the foreign company may be liable for substantial damages and the payment of prospective lost commissions to the former sales agent. A related issue for the foreign firm can arise if a local court deems that the company is exercising too much control over the agent. In that situation, a court may conclude that an agent is actually an employee of the company, and is therefore entitled to even more protections and severance payments under local laws. These are potentially serious traps for unwary novice exporters, especially from the United States, who are more accustomed to sales agents as independent contractors with relatively fewer legal rights, allowing for simplified termination arrangements. Companies considering entering a new country should consult with an experienced international attorney to prepare distribution and/or sales agency agreements to safeguard the company's interests in the target market. Simply using the company's existing domestic distribution/sales agency agreements may expose the company to litigation and considerable expenses in a foreign market. [9]

11-2c Alternative International Distribution Structures

One type of alternative distribution structure is network marketing, a mode of distributing goods using acquaintance networks. Network marketing companies are gaining access to emerging markets all over the world, and many continue to find potential in developed countries. Because network marketing serves primarily a retailing function — all distributorships engage in selling to the final consumer — this topic is addressed later in this chapter.

11-3 International Logistics

The international distribution function is supported by a number of service providers. Among them are distribution centers, transportation firms, home-country freight forwarders and customs brokers, ocean ports and international airports, government agencies, nongovernmental organizations, logistics alliances, and other firms. They are described in Sections 11-3a through 11-3c.

Logistics costs account for a large percentage of a company's gross revenues (between 10 and 30 percent) and for a large percentage of GDP (almost 10 percent in the United States), and as high as 26 percent for emerging markets, such as those in Latin America. Overall, logistics constitute the single highest operating cost.[10] The largest percentage of multinationals' logistics costs is spent on transportation. Thus, money saved in this area is likely to lead to lower prices for the end consumers.

The primary functions of international logistics are transportation, warehousing, inventory control, and order processing. As previously discussed, transportation logistics refers to the movement of consumer goods as well as components for manufacturing.

MNBB Studio/shutterstock.com

11-3a International Transportation

Transportation is important in international marketing. The choice of transportation determines whether products arrive at the international destination on time and in good condition. The cost of transportation is also essential because transportation costs can increase the product price in the target country. Important for transportation is the transportation infrastructure of the country where the company is doing business. Transportation networks are excellent in industrialized countries, with the countries easily accessible by rail, air, and water. Highly industrialized countries with water access have numerous sea and inland waterway ports that can handle cargo shipments efficiently. Emerging markets are also quickly developing their port facilities to handle the brisk traffic of cargo and passengers. International cargo and passenger traffic services are highly competitive sectors and represent important sources of fees, taxes, etc. for local and national governments. In addition, highly-developed ports and inland distribution systems are major factors in a company's decision regarding where to open a warehouse distribution center, or even a manufacturing facility in a foreign country. See International Marketing Illustration 11-2.

International Marketing Illustration 11-2 Ports Facilitating Trade

The Port of Sète in southern France is one of many ports that offer international access to the French market, promoting international commerce. The port handles container vessels, conventional vessels, ferries, heavy lift ships, ocean-going barges and tugs, floating pontoons, livestock carriers, navy vessels, and military cargoes. It handles over three million metric tons of goods and hundreds of thousands of passengers, offering easy access to the rest of France via rail and truck. It also serves various local industries, among them seafood processing, wine and spirits, chemicals, building, and aquaculture. The port is served by shipping agents, freight forwarders, terminal operators, shipyard operators, naval services, and other logistics facilitators. The port also handles cruise vessels along the Mediterranean coast and from Bayonne to Dunkirk on the Atlantic, Channel, and North Sea range, to and from Morocco, and from Monaco to Sète, the latter a less-traveled destination that has much to offer.

Emerging markets are also developing their cargo and passenger facilities. There are still some complex geopolitical issues that affect transportation. For example, Kaliningrad Oblast is a Russian Federation enclave located between Lith-

uania and Poland where many Western companies manufacture products for tax-free shipping to Russia. Cadillac has manufactured luxury sedans there since 2011 and BMW has made its Series 3 and Series 5 models there since 2007. The Russian government plans to turn the area into the Russian Hong Kong.

In other examples, the Port of St. Petersburg, in the Russian Federation, is the largest port in the northwest of Russia and one of the oldest – it is the famous Port of Leningrad of the communist era, shipping dry goods to the rest of the European continent, and welcoming tours from the West for a rare glimpse of majestic art beyond its formerly rigid iron curtain.

The Port of Kaliningrad on the Baltic Sea is huge and of strategic importance when it comes to trade with the Russian Federation. LukOil, Russia's main petrol company, even has its own terminal in the port, loading tankers going to different international destinations. However, there is one factor that could potentially be problematic if there is any regional discord: shipments to and from mainland Russia have to pass through Lithuania and Belarus (see Figure 11-1 on next page).

Sources: www.sete.port.fr,accessed on September 30, 2015; www.agenatramp.fr,accessed on September 30,2015; www.portoftallinn.com,accessed on September 30, 2015.

Figure 11-1 *This cargo, photographed 10 miles from Vilnius, Lithuania, is traveling from Kaliningrad to mainland Russia. Good relations between Lithuania and the Russian Federation are important to be able to maintain cheap rail access as a transportation venue for products made in the enclave of Kaliningrad.*

Transportation firms are key players in international distribution, especially firms that can handle intermodal transportation, using two or more different transportation modes (truck, rail, ship – inland and sea or ocean shipping). Intermodal transportation has been greatly facilitated by containerization. For example, goods can be placed into containers at the factory, taken by truck to a train-loading facility, transported to a port, and loaded aboard a ship. After crossing the ocean, the containers are loaded on a truck and transported to their final destination.

In a variation on the above pattern, the Port of Virginia also utilizes several forms of intermodal transportation. For example, containers are now transported by barge to and from the Port of Virginia ocean terminals in Norfolk and Portsmouth, Virginia, and the new Port-owned Richmond Marine Terminal in Richmond, Virginia, approximately 120 miles from the ocean ports. The Marine Terminal has increased distribution efficiency while cutting down on truck traffic on the busy interstate highway corridor between Richmond and the Virginia Port Authority terminals. The Port of Virginia was an early leader in using an inland port facility to clear U.S. Customs and distribute goods. In partnership with the Norfolk Southern Railroad, double-stack container trains move daily between the Norfolk International Terminal and the Virginia Inland Port in Front Royal, Virginia. Front Royal is located sixty miles west of Washington, D.C. Major U.S. retailers such as Kohl's and Home Depot have established distribution centers in Front Royal to receive imported goods and distribute the merchandise to their retail stores in the mid-Atlantic region of the U.S. There are also a number of retail distribution centers in the Norfolk area as well near other major U.S. ports such as Savannah, Long Angeles/Long Beach, etc.[11]

All these maneuvers can be accomplished using the initial containers — thus providing a greater protection for the products, which do not have to be shifted individually from one vessel to another — at lower cost because loading the individual products from or into vehicles is more expensive than using containers. Table 11-1 (on next page) lists the top global transportation providers. The top global transportation company, DHL, now a division of the German logistics company Deutsche Post DHL, has an interesting history. It was founded in the 1960s in the United States to deliver documents between San Francisco and Hawaii. Subsequently, it decided to expand internationally, even in markets that were underserved by any other transportation provider, such as the Soviet Union and the Eastern Bloc countries. The company was subsequently acquired by Deutsche Post in 2002.

Rank	Company	Country	Revenue (in million U.S.$)
1	UPS	USA	$60,906
2	FedEx	USA	$55,227
3	DHL	Germany	$46,182
4	China Railway Corp.	China	$32,445
5	A.P. Moller Maersk	Denmark	$29,303
6	Russian Railways	Russia	$25,565
7	DB Schenker	Germany	$21,792
8	Kuehne+Nagel	Germany	$20,290
9	Union Pacific	USA	$19,941
10	Burlington No. SF	USA	$19,278

Table 11-1 Top Ten Global Transportation Providers

Source: *Top 50 Global Transportation Providers, Journal of Commerce*, 2016.https://www.joc.com/international-logistics/logistics-providers/parcel-carriers-fare-best-top-50-revenue-growth_20171029.html on June 28, 2018.

The different transportation modes offer advantages and disadvantages in terms of flexibility, cost, and speed. Table 11-2 summarizes the flexibility, cost, and speed characteristics of each mode of transportation.

Mode	Flexibility (in Terms of Area Coverage)	Cost	Speed	Product Examples
Truck	High	Higher	Higher	Consumer goods, perishables, automobiles
Rail	Medium	Medium	Lower	Coal, gasoline, forestry products, grains, automobiles
Air	High	High	Highest	Jewelry, electronics, expensive low-volume products
Water	Low	Low	Low	Grains, gasoline, forestry products, cement and fertilizers
Pipeline	Low	Lower	Low	Oil and gasoline, chemicals, semi-liquid coal, refined products

Table 11-2 Flexibility, Cost, and Speed Characteristics of Each Mode of Transportation

Tankers, barges, and other freighters in the sea and inland waterways account for a substantial proportion of international traffic. Waterways are used for transporting over long distances high-weight, high-volume products that have a low per-pound value, such as grains, gasoline, forestry products, cement, and fertilizers. Table 11-3 (next page) ranks the top ten container ports worldwide. Note that Asian ports have fully replaced all European and North American ports, which had spent decades ranked among the top ten; among these ports are Rotterdam, Hamburg, Antwerp, and Los Angeles.

Railways remain the primary mode for intracontinental freight transportation. Cargo that has a high-weight, high-volume, and low per pound value are transported by rail, with some exceptions. Examples of rail cargo are coal, gasoline, forestry products, and grains. Higher value products, such as equipment and automobiles, may also be transported by train. Railways are a low-cost, low-speed mode of transportation, and mobility is restricted to designated areas for freight handling.

Rank	Port	Country	Million Metric Tons
1	Shanghai	China	37.13
2	Singapore	Singapore	30.90
3	Shenzhen	China	23.97
4	Ningbo-Zhoushan	China	21.60
5	Hong Kong	China	19.60
6	Busan	South Korea	19.45
7	Guangzhou	China	18.90
8	Qingdao	China	18.00
9	Jebel Ali, Dubai	United Arab Emirates	15.73
10	Tianjin	China	14.49

Table 11-3 Top Ten World Container Ports

Source: *Top 50 World Container Ports 2016, Journal of Commerce 2016*, accessed at: https://www.joc.com/port-news/top-50-container-ports-2016-shanghai-tightens-grip-crown_20170810.html?destination=node/3338521 on June 28, 2018.

Truck transportation handles smaller shipments over shorter distances. Much of the local transportation, such as within cities, is handled by trucks, which offer high flexibility at competitive rates. Often, trucks transport products carried by ship and rail to the final product destination. Trucks may have refrigeration and processing capabilities, which allow them to carry a variety of products, such as consumer goods, perishables, and automobiles. Trucks offer high flexibility and competitive rates in Europe. However, a company should not expect delivery over the weekend even to key clients. In many countries, trucks are not allowed to drive on highways on Sundays (see Figure 11-3).

Figure 11-3 In Europe, trucks are found in rest areas on the highways, or parked outside of the city centers on the weekends, as they are not allowed on the highways.

Air freight is used for products that are low volume and low weight but high value, such as jewelry and electronics. Air freight is also used in situations in which handling documents or materials expeditiously is essential.

Pipelines provide a low-cost mode of transporting liquid or semi-liquid products from the source to the target market in a continuous manner, where there are no interruptions (unless interruptions are voluntary), and where intermediate storage is not necessary. Examples of pipelines are Basin, Bonito, and Capline for offshore and onshore crude oil; Harbor System and Wolverine Line for refined products; and the large, remote, and technically difficult pipeline, the Trans-Alaska Pipeline, a feat of engineering running from northern to southern Alaska across rough terrains and performing well in extreme weather conditions, transporting more than 1.4 million barrels of crude oil daily. Pipelines are typically owned by the producer or by joint ventures, and they are expensive to maintain.[12]

Pipelines encounter many challenges. Brazil needs more energy sources to meet its energy needs, and the Amazon jungle has huge oil and gas reserves. Petrobras, Brazil's state-controlled oil company, invested more than $7 billion in Amazon exploration, finding important resources there in 1986. But only now, after overcoming geographic, logistic, environmental, and political challenges, is it able to build the pipelines. The first pipeline carries gas more than 400 miles, from the Amazon jungle to the city of Manaus, a large port city at the junction of Brazil's largest two rivers. Petrobras worked extensively to make this possible, but even now it faces challenges. Its reputation tarnished after oil pipeline leaks and the collapse of an offshore drilling platform elsewhere in the country, the company still managed to woo its fellow citizens. It offered promises of economic benefits and it consulted scientists and environmentalists on how to minimize damage to the jungle, which alone covers a territory as large as Britain, France, Germany, and Italy put together. A second pipeline, going in a southern direction for more than 300 miles, to Porto Velho, faces challenges not only from environmentalists, but also from indigenous people, as it crosses Indian lands. It is also competing for government money with two large dams. The difficulties faced by Petrobras do not bode well for Venezuela's ambition to build a 5,000 mile north-south pipeline from Caracas, Venezuela, to Buenos Aires, Argentina, a plan also conceived with the intention to bring South America together.[13]

In the United States, there continues to be considerable controversy over the expansion of pipelines to carry oil and natural gas. In 2017, the U.S. Government approved the Keystone XL and Dakota Access pipelines to carry crude oil from Canada and the State of North Dakota to refining facilities on the U.S. gulf coast. This reversed the policy of the previous administration that refused to approve the pipelines, citing environmental concerns. Today, there continues to be major resistance from environmental groups and others to proposed new pipelines to transport fossil fuels such as natural gas and crude oil.[14]

11-3b Logistics Facilitators

Moving goods from the place of origin, normally a manufacturer, to the place of sale, normally the retailer, requires some type of facilitation. The two most common logistics facilitators are distribution centers and freight forwarders, but governmental and non-governmental organizations handle similar functions as well.

Distribution centers are designed to speed up warehousing and delivery by channeling operations to one center (hub) that is particularly well equipped to handle the distribution of products to their destination. This function is becoming a popular choice of multinational firms that have to efficiently warehouse and distribute their goods in target markets situated thousands of miles from their home country. Certain locations have become important players as hubs to a number of multinational firms. For example, Singapore is a leading regional and international logistics hub and host to virtually every major logistics player; logistics account for about seven percent of Singapore's gross domestic product.[15]

As previously mentioned in this chapter, major U.S. retailers such as Amazon, Home Depot, Target, etc. have regional distribution centers, often located close to ocean ports. These centers facilitate the timely arrival and clearance of imported consumer goods and the quick distribution to individual retail stores. In the case of online retailers, highly-efficient distribution center operations are especially critical, given the absence of brick-and-mortar retail locations. Some companies will also locate distribution centers within a Foreign Trade Zone in order to defer payments of duties until goods are actually shipped to the stores. U.S. state economic development agencies, including Virginia, are in heated competition with other states to land these distribution center projects and the jobs that go with them.[16]

Freight forwarders arrange for international ocean and air freight and other forms of transportation for their clients, acting as a travel agent for shippers. An export freight forwarder may also handle the completion and submission of required shipping documents for their client to commercial banks for payments under bank letters of credit. There is no federal licensing exam in the United States to become a freight forwarder. A U.S. customs broker represents import clients in the clearance of goods and payment of any required duties to U.S. Customs and Border Protection (CBP). A customs broker must be licensed by the CBP, and pass a comprehensive licensing exam. The entire licensing process can take a year or more. [17]

iam_Anupong/shutterstock.com

Many large transportation services firms offer commercial clients both freight forwarding and licensed customs brokerage services. A larger freight forwarder may specialize in geographic locations or other areas of expertise, such as commodities — flowers, seafood, and other types of perishable products. Many freight forwarders are adapting to fit the needs of their corporate consumers, pursuing different value-added techniques, such as developing distinctive competencies in terms of geography, type of business, or specific commodities. For example, Kuehne + Nagel (http://www.kn-portal.com) is well respected for its ability to expertly handle museum art and valuable exhibition material. The company has also developed expertise with respect to arranging trade fairs and art exhibits, as well as aid and relief for developing countries. Another freight forwarder, DHL, (www.dhl.com) specializes in health care, fashion, electronics, and live animals shipping.

In many countries, governments are directly involved in the international distribution process. Often, private distributors are not permitted by law to engage in any type of direct international transaction. This is the case for many developing countries and countries where national currencies are under strict control. But government involvement in distribution and logistics processes is not limited to low-income countries. In many high-income countries, governments are involved in the following processes:

• As promoters of national security interests and national regulations

• As promoters of international involvement of firms, particularly of small and medium-sized businesses

• As financing and insurance providers for higher-risk international ventures.

•In the United States, international distribution and logistics involvement are shared by a number of different government agencies, most of which are affiliated with the U.S. Department of Commerce (www.commerce.gov).

• The International Trade Administration (ITA) in the U.S. Department of Commerce offers export assistance to U.S. multinationals and to small and medium-sized businesses. The ITA's U.S. Commercial Service promotes and protects U.S. business inter-ests via offices at U.S. embassies in all key international markets. The Commercial Ser-vice also operates the network of Export Assistance Centers throughout the U.S., offering companies a range of export assistance services. These include trade educa-tion, access to a market research database, country analysis information, and eco-nomic data, as well as export and international business counseling from the Com-mercial Service's trade specialists. It also helps firms with export documentation (applications, licenses, declarations, etc.).

• The Bureau of Export Administration in the U.S. Department of Commerce ad-vances U.S. national security, foreign policy, and economic interests by regulating ex-ports of products and technologies that could affect them. The agency regulates ex-ports of products such as high-platform computers and weapons, and imposes sanc-tions against countries such as North Korea, Russia, and Iran; it enforces compliance with regulations and cooperates with other nations in monitoring the trade of sensi-tive goods.

Marc Van Scyoc/shutterstock.com

• The Export-Import Bank of the United States (ExIm Bank), should it be funded again, aids the financing of international sales of U.S. products and services; guaranteed loans and made loans to inter-national buyers of U.S. goods; it also insured many business ventures that international or local banks would not insure due to their high risk. Should the ExIm Bank be re instituted, it would not compete with commercial lenders and insurance firms.

• The United States Trade and Development Agency creates jobs for Americans by helping U.S. companies pursue overseas business opportunities. Although not directly involved in distribution and logistics, this agency funds feasibility studies, training, business workshops, and technical assistance aimed at infrastructure and industrial projects in developing countries.

Equivalent structures exist in most other countries, typically housed under the Min-istry of Foreign Trade, the equivalent of the Department of Commerce in the United States.

In addition to country-specific agencies, international bodies could facilitate distribu-tion and logistics. One example is the International Chamber of Commerce (ICC), a business organization that represents enterprises from all sectors in every part of the world engag-ing in international business. The ICC makes voluntary rules that govern the conduct of busi-ness and commercial payments across borders, and it provides important services, such as the ICC International Court of Arbitration, the world's leading arbitral institution.

Among other service providers are banks and insurance agencies financing and in-suring international distribution transactions, marketing research firms providing infor-mation on the target markets and trade, international trade lawyers, and various types of consultants that specialize in facilitating international distribution and logistics activities.

In the process of setting up a firm's distribution activity in the target market, the firm needs to set up successful logistics relationships. Many logistics alliances in Europe have been successful and are characterized by an atmosphere of openness between the customer and the provider, mutual trust, and a clear line of communication. Successful lo-gistics alliances typically are formed using the following steps:[18]

1. Establish objectives and selection criteria. Because choosing a logistics provider is a long-term decision, it is important to choose a partner that is likely to be a good match.

2. Identify qualified providers, with the help of consultants.

3. Express needs and wants. Here, issues such as integrating computer systems with that of the partner and other information-sharing needs should be expressed.

4. Evaluate bidders and select the partner, preferably after a site visit and interview.

5. Develop an integration plan. Because logistics involves many players, it is important to engage in system-wide integration.

6. Create a win-win relationship, based on continuous communication.

7. Measure and analyze performance.

8. Redefine goals and objectives.

11-3c Warehousing and Inventory Control

In international marketing, warehousing is of great importance. One of the critical decisions involves determining the number of warehouses and distribution centers needed to optimally implement the logistics function. In some countries, private warehouses, owned or leased by the company and operated by firms storing their own products, may be easy to come by and might provide more control and safety for the shipping firm than public warehouses. In other countries, public warehouses, used by firms that cannot afford to have their own facilities or that do not have a need for storage on a regular basis, represent a viable option: They are safe, have the necessary capacity, and are dependable in terms of other capabilities, such as refrigeration.

In most industrialized countries, distribution centers are an option for the international firm. They receive goods from different producers, take orders from buyers, and distribute them promptly. Warehouses located in free trade zones or those warehouses that are themselves customs-privileged facilities are typically also facilities where product assembly and packaging may be conducted.

Worldwide, companies are attempting to address customer demand while reducing inventory costs. Multinational manufacturing firms adopt a just-in-time inventory system

Golden Sikorka/shutterstock.com

where this is possible, reducing inventory by ordering products often and in lower quantity, creating product flow rather than holding a large inventory of manufacturing components in stock and on the manufacturing company's books. Where possible, all intermediaries use the Universal Product Code (UPC), which links suppliers' and customers' inventory systems through electronic data interchange, facilitating the flow of products. Both of these approaches aimed at reducing storage and inventory costs are widely adopted in developed countries. In developing countries, multinationals tend to adopt them, spending large sums to link suppliers to their own systems.

11-4 Challenges to International Distribution and Logistics

Firms selling across borders encounter numerous challenges. General challenges and parallel imports are discussed next.

11-4a General Distribution Challenges

One challenge firms face as they distribute their products overseas is the transportation infrastructure. Dirt roads are impassable when wet, and, in tropical climates, cool temperatures must be maintained for perishables such as pharmaceuticals. Containerization also poses problems; some ports have shallow drafts and cannot handle larger vessels. In the United States, an emerging issue is whether or not a particular port can accommodate the new class of deep-draft Super Panamax vessels. Ports that cannot may find themselves relegated to second-tier status with fewer port calls by ocean transportation companies. To meet this competitive challenge, several U.S. ports are spending hundreds of millions on dredging.[19]

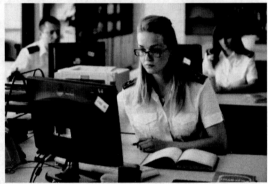

Furthermore, unloading the container can take weeks because of manpower restrictions. Custom inspections can also take long, may require cumbersome paperwork, or even paying off the inspector (bribing) to simply come and do his or her job! Shipments can be subjected to manual customs processes with inspections that often lack transparency or consistency; often, customs requirements are unnecessarily stringent, cumbersome, and unpredictable.[20]

Oleksil Chumachenko/shutterstock.com

Challenges sometimes crop up unexpectedly. In the U.S., there was a marked disruption to established supply chains in 2018 from new tariffs on aluminum and steel imposed by the U.S. on China and other countries, affecting supply and prices for products ranging from automobiles, to household appliances, to building materials.

11-4b Parallel Imports

Parallel imports are products purchased in a low-price market and diverted to other markets by means of a distribution system not authorized by the manufacturer; this is also known as a *gray market*. A low-price market is one where the products can be purchased for a lower price either because the company must lower prices to meet competitors' strategies, or because local taxes are lower. The Netherlands, for example, is a low-price market for Similac, an infant formula manufactured by Abbott Laboratories. There, a 900-gram can of Similac sold for about $10 at the Etos, Kruidvat, and DA Drogist drug stores in 2018. A can of Similac weighing 658 grams sold in the United States for $28 at Walmart in the United States. The reasons Abbott Laboratories engages in the differential pricing of Similac may be numerous. First, it might be attempting to further penetrate the market; although the product is well known in the United States, it is not popular in Europe. Second, it is priced just less than the other, local, competing products, so the company might be using a penetration-pricing strategy – although fifteen years, as noted by this author, is too long for such as strategy. Third, the Dutch government might have required the company to sell at a lower price (unlikely, but possible). Consequently, the Netherlands constitutes a low-price market for Similac. If an entrepreneur decided to bring Similac from the Netherlands to sell it in the United States, he or she would be engaging in parallel imports. He or she would be selling the product on a gray market that is not authorized by the manufacturer – but would be doing something entirely legal. When such products are available for sale in the unintended market, parallel imports then compete with the manufacturer's products intended specifically for this market, cutting into profits.

Examples of gray markets abound, and "gray" businesses take advantage of price differences between different markets, buying products from low-tax areas and selling them in high-tax areas, for instance. Purchasing cigarettes from Virginia, where cigarette taxes are low, and selling them in the European Union, where they are high, would create a nice profit. It would also be unauthorized cross-border trade, penalized by EU authorities. Products with a long history of parallel imports are automobiles (Mercedes-Benz until the mid-1980s, when they adopted stringent regional standardization), pharmaceuticals, and cigarettes.

Multinational corporations can choose from a number of alternative actions in the process of combating parallel imports (see Figure 11-4):[21]

· **Charge similar prices worldwide** — Gray markets exist only if there are high price differences.

· **Create products for low markets that are not as attractive or are not a perfect fit with an up-market** — Mercedes-Benz, after establishing its U.S. subsidiary Mercedes USA, attempted to create different automobiles for the European and the U.S. market. For example, to European consumers, Mercedes offers the B-Class, which is not available in the United States, and lower-number models that are too small to meet U.S. consumers' demands for comfort, such as the M160, are not available; the smallest crossover SUV available in the U.S. market is the ML350, a giant by comparison.

· **Complicate the repair and servicing process for the gray market goods** — Purchasers of gray market Mercedes-Benz automobiles in the United States will find that, often, replacement parts must be ordered from Germany, making maintenance costs high.

· **Inform consumers about the perils of buying gray market products** — Products may be new but technically outdated or might not benefit from manufacturer warranties.

· **Litigate** — Unlike in the case of counterfeit products, litigating is often not possible in many of the integrated markets, such as the European Union, where the free movement of goods is guaranteed by law.

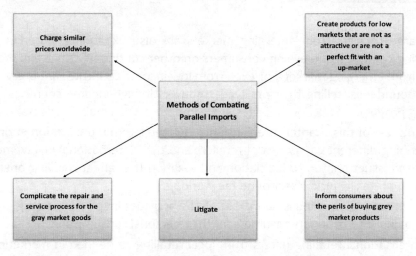

Figure 11-4 *Methods of Combating Parallel Imports*

11-5 International Retailing

Retailing is facing a revolution. Markets, technology, and consumers are changing, and retailers face challenges in every aspect of their operations. On the other hand, opportunities abound for retailers with astute, responsive market approaches. International retailing conglomerates are using creative strategies in their mature home markets to retain profitable consumers, and expanding rapidly into emerging markets, fighting equally aggressive international and local competition, navigating government restrictions and regulations, and courting the ever-increasing and appealing local middle class. Take, for example, the world's leading retailer, Walmart.

Walmart in China

Walmart had $485.9 billion in retail sales in 2017, with more than 260 million customers visiting the store weekly in one of its 11,500 stores in 28 countries, and via its e-commerce sites in 11 countries. In spite of its exit from Germany and South Korea, and a presence in India where, in 2018, it purchased the largest e-commerce retailer Flipkart, the chain keeps growing, surpassing all competitors. The retailing titan has been active in China since early 1996, with over 500 stores, employing more than 30,000 people. Similar to the U.S., the company has supercenters, Sam's Clubs, and Neighborhood Markets. With its Global Procurement Center in Shenzhen, Walmart is also a major exporter from China. Its direct and indirect purchases from China have steadily increased, with over $18 billion in exports annually. To date, it has relationships with more than 20,000 suppliers in China.[22]

In the city of Kunming, China, there are six Walmarts serving a population of six million. Their location is convenient, but not obvious. The location shown in Figure 11-5 is barely visible from a spaghetti junction at the edge of town. However, consumers know well its location, and local guides proudly announce the chain's presence in the city, as an indicator of the city's cosmopolitan nature.

Figure 11-5: *A Walmart store in Kunming, in the province of Yunnan, southwestern China, which is not as obvious and as dominant in the landscape as the stores are in the United States.*

Large retailers from emerging markets are also expanding, entering markets in neighboring countries, and eyeing consumers on other continents. Small and medium-sized retailers from emerging markets, or even from low-income countries, are breaking through national boundaries, selling their products to buyers in high-income countries. Consumers are selling products on auction websites and competing with established retailers.

The rest of this chapter offers insights into the internationalization efforts of retailers, describing different categories of retailers and their international involvement and expansion, and issues related to legislation and taxation that affect retailing operations. We also illustrate retailing practices around the world.

International retailing is defined as all the activities involved in selling products and services to final international consumers for their personal consumption.

International retailing differs from local retailing as defined in marketing management in that it addresses operations of international retailers beyond home-country borders, as well as operations of local retailers in different countries worldwide — in general and in response to the presence or entry of international retailers aiming for their target market. As such, an examination of international retail operations must include an evaluation of global and local retailing formats, retail practices, and an overview of local retailing environments. The next section provides an overview of developments in the process of the international expansion of retailing.

Retailers are rapidly expanding internationally to gain competitive advantage and to increase sales, profits, and overall firm performance. As they expand beyond their home-country borders, retailers also can take advantage of cost savings and learn from experiences in ways that can further enhance home-country operations. The 10 largest retailers, five U.S. companies (Walmart, Costco, Kroger, Home Depot, and Target), and five European companies (Carrefour, Schwartz, Tesco, Metro, and Aldi), dominate the market (see Table 11-4). In general, diversified retailers, operating across the food, apparel, and hard goods sectors enjoy the highest growth.[23]

French and German retailers have been, by far, the most globally active in the past decade, with 90 companies in the Global Powers of Retailing top 250 list. However, North American retailers boast the largest share of revenues in the group, at over $22 billion. Of the top 250 global retailers, French companies are the most international, expanding beyond France, in an average of over 30 countries. Of this same group, fashion retailers are the most global of all product groups. North American retailers are the largest, with an average size in excess of $19 billion, and with more than half of the top 250 retailers operating only within their own country's borders. Finally, in many of the slowing economies, retailers targeting upscale consumers have done well.[24]

International retail chains are creatively fighting to stay in business. European retailers, for example, are teaming up to be able to compete with U.S. internet giant Amazon. For example, French Carrefour and British Tesco decided to form a global long-term purchasing alliance to be able to cut their costs.[26] To understand international retailing changes, one needs to gain some insight into the many categories of retailers in different parts of the world. It is also important to understand how international retailing differs from retailing as defined in marketing management texts. Both of these topics are addressed in Sections 11-5 and 11-6.

Table 11-4 Top 10 Global Retailers FY 2016

Top 250 rank	Change in rank	Name of company	Country of origin	FY2016 Retail revenue (US$M)	FY2016 Retail revenue growth	FY2016 Net profit margin	FY2016 Return on assets	FY2011-2016 Retail revenue CAGR*	# Countries of operation	% Retail revenue from foreign operations
1	⟷	Wal-Mart Stores, Inc.	US	485,873	0.8%	2.9%	7.2%	1.7%	29	24.3%
2	⟷	Costco Wholesale Corporation	US	118,719	2.2%	2.0%	7.2%	6.0%	10	27.1%
3	⟷	The Kroger Co.	US	115,337	5.0%	1.7%	5.4%	5.0%	1	0.0%
4	⟷	Schwarz Group	Germany	99,256	5.3%	n/a	n/a	7.3%	27	61.7%
5	⟷	Walgreens Boots Alliance, Inc.	US	97,058	8.3%	3.6%	5.8%	6.1%	10	13.7%
6	↑ +4	Amazon.com, Inc.	US	94,665	19.4%	1.7%	2.8%	17.6%	14	36.8%
7	↓ -1	The Home Depot, Inc.	US	94,595	6.9%	8.4%	18.5%	6.1%	4	8.5%
8	⟷	Aldi Group	Germany	84,923 e	4.8%	n/a	n/a	7.7%	17	67.0%
9	↓ -2	Carrefour S.A.	France	84,131	-0.4%	1.1%	1.8%	-1.1%	34	53.2%
10	↑ +2	CVS Health Corporation	US	81,100	12.6%	3.0%	5.6%	6.4%	3	0.8%
Top 10¹				1,355,656	4.5%	3.0%	6.4%	4.5%	14.9²	27.3%
Top 250¹				4,410,828	4.1%	3.2%	3.3%	4.8%	10.0²	22.5%
Top 10 share of Top 250 retail revenue				30.7%						

*Compound annual growth rate   e = estimate
¹ Sales-weighted, currency-adjusted composites   n/a = not available
² Average

Source: Deloitte Touche Tohmatsu Limited. Global Powers of Retailing 2018. Analysis of financial performance and operations for fiscal years ended through June 2017 using company annual reports, Planet Retail database and other public sources.

11-6 Retail Formats: Variations in Different Markets

There are three main retail formats: general merchandise retailing, food retailing, and nonstore retailing. Sections 11-6a through 11-6c describe the retailers in each category and address the different international variations for each retail format, with a focus on local markets. It should first be noted that traditional department stores, grocery stores, and big box retailers are facing tremendous competition from online retailers like Amazon, as well as discount specialty chains. Nowhere are these trends more evident than in the United States. By 2018, traditional department store retailers like Sears and J.C. Penney were in a steep decline. Amazon's recent purchase of the Whole Foods Grocery chain is upending the traditional markets for Kroger and other major grocery retailers. The celebrated specialty retailer Toys R Us filed for bankruptcy and liquidated operations in 2018. These trends are not unique to the U.S. Retailers around the world are faced with similar competitive pressures to develop business models to retain traditional customers and to attract new ones. [27]

11-6a General Merchandise Retailing

Specialty Stores

Specialty stores offer a narrow product line and wide assortment. In this category are clothing stores (usually further specialized into women's, men's, or children's clothing stores), bookstores, toy stores, office supply stores, and consumer electronics stores.

In many markets, specialty stores, chains in particular, are expanding at the expense of all forms of nonfood retailing. For example, specialty store chains are taking market share away from traditional department stores worldwide. U.K. specialty retailers have made great strides in international expansion: Marks & Spencer is rapidly expanding in France, and retailers such as Virgin Megastores have already made substantial inroads into the U.S. market. They are also present in Ireland, France, Greece, and Germany (see Figure 11-6),

Figure 11-6: *The Virgin Megastore left Germany in 1994, complaining that the laws governing store opening hours were too restrictive, but they returned to Germany and opened a new store in Berlin's ultra-modern central train station in 2006.*

in Europe, as well as in Japan, Australia, and throughout North Africa and the Middle East, in the Kingdom of Bahrain, Egypt, Qatar, Kuwait, Lebanon, and the United Arab Emirates (Abu Dhabi and Dubai).

For apparel retailing, many European companies are rapidly entering new markets: Mango, the Spanish retailer specializing in youth fashion, has 2415 shops in 107 countries. [28] Rival Spanish chain Zara, with its distinctive brushed-steel staircases, and Swedish chain H&M are competing for these same consumers and are proving to be successful in mature markets worldwide. Esprit, a German apparel company, sells its international youthful lifestyle clothing brand worldwide: It offers 12 product lines of women's wear, men's wear, kids' wear, youth wear, as well as shoes and accessories through more than 900 directly managed retail stores (see Figure 11-7 on next page) and more than 7,800 wholesale point-of-sales, including franchise stores and sales spaces in department stores. The company is present in more than 40 countries. [29]

Figure 11-7: *Esprit stores are popular worldwide: Esprit has*
more than 770 stores in more than 40 countries.

In most developing countries, specialty stores represent the main retail format. Although Western and local specialty chain stores are quite popular and have done well for decades, developing country markets are dominated by independent (usually family-owned) specialty stores, such as apparel stores, cosmetics stores, and local arts and crafts stores aimed at the tourist market (see Figure 11-8), as well as other traditional retail systems as exemplified by specialized markets.

Specialized Markets

Specialized markets contain specialty stores focusing on a particular product category. Examples of such markets exist worldwide, in both developed and developing countries. Examples of specialized markets are the Cairo Gold Market in the Khan El Khalili bazaar, the Jade Market in Hong Kong, and the Gold Market and the Spice Market in the Covered Bazaar in Istanbul, Turkey (see Figure 11-9). Specialized markets may even cover entire cities. For example, the town of Otavalo, Ecuador, houses large and small retailers of leather goods.

Figure 11-8: *Tibetan shopping street*   Figure 11-9: *The Covered Bazaar in Istanbul, Turkey, is the prime*
where vendors sell local arts and crafts.   *destination for Turkish food and spices.*

In addition to these markets, local specialty stores affiliated with a project sponsored by governmental or nongovernmental organizations also are prevalent in many developing countries. Examples may be a poultry shop partially owned by local investors selling poultry raised in a project funded by the World Bank and the United Nations Development Program aimed at helping a developing country become self-sufficient with regard to meat production, or a folk art outlet selling handmade embroidery produced by young girls in a convent. In other examples, the Chinese government heavily promotes what are known as Government Friendship Stores (see Figure 11-10). The stores are owned by the government and Chinese tour guides are advised to take their busloads of foreign tourists to these destination retailers to unload their foreign currency. The stores specialize in the local crafts; in Shanghai, they sell silk and jade, and in Beijing, they sell cloisonné, for example. The stores advertise that prices are reasonable and there should be no bargaining — but one has yet to find a government store in China where bargaining is not going to result in a better deal.

Figure 11-10: *This Government Friendship Store is situated in the proximity of Beijing, adjacent to a cloisonné "factory"—a little shop where a handful of workers decorate cloisonné vases. The retailing operation adjacent to the "factory" is massive, selling thousands of dollars' worth of jade pieces, in addition to large, medium, small, and miniature cloisonné vases.*

Department Stores

Department stores offer a broad variety of goods and wide assortments. Among the products they carry are clothing for men, women, and children; household appliances and electronics; kitchenware; china; home furnishings; and toys and games. Outside the United States, department stores typically also have large supermarket sections, and some may even carry fresh produce; the more elegant the department store, the more upscale the supermarket section. See the Supermarket vignette on the next page.

In Europe, department stores typically tend to address the needs of home markets, with some efforts to expand mainly in the European Union. In the United Kingdom, Harrods department store in London (Knightsbridge), established in 1849, attracts an exclusive clientele to its 300 departments, covering a million square feet of selling space, and to its 21 restaurants.[30] In the Netherlands, three department stores dominate: Vendex (Vroom & Drees-

The Supermarket in the Department Store

One would not normally link a department store with a supermarket. Bloomingdale's, in its Manhattan store, has a handful of gourmet products, and plenty of chocolate, especially at holiday time. And your local Macy's might carry some Cellar-brand products such as nuts, cookies, dog chews. But your European department store comes with a full-scale supermarket. No, it is not your average Kroger-in-the-basement variety; rather, it is as comprehensive and fancy as the store itself.

Take, for instance, the German Kaufhaus des Westens (KaDeWe) or the French Galeries Lafayette, or Printemps. All three have huge spaces dedicated to lively displays of fresh exotic fish, posing as predators or as filets, smoked, fried, toasted, elaborately decorated and in ample quantities. Next to the fish displays, vegetables and fruit color the retail space and lure visitors toward a labyrinth of ethnic foods that includes a display of American goodies, including Oreo cookies, Swiss Miss hot chocolate, marshmallows, and French's mustard. The cold cuts are from every imaginable European source, in multiple displays that suggest endless ways to roast, smoke, preserve, and slice that ham. The cheese and the wine sections are immense, with every country of origin represented.

Figure 11-11:

German retailer Kaufhaus des Westens—KaDeWe, or the Department Store of the West—was founded in 1905 by Adolf Jandorf. It was destroyed in the 1940s and rebuilt in 1950. It is the largest store in continental Western Europe.

man), HEMA, and Bijenkorf. A similar concentration is encountered in Germany, with department stores, such as Karstadt, KaDeWe (see Figure 11-11), Wertheim, Alsterhaus, and others. French department stores are surviving despite the dominance of specialty shops and the increasing popularity of category killers and discount shops. Leading French department stores are Bon Marché, and Galeries Lafayette, and Printemps (see Figure 11-12). Galeries Lafayette made an unsuccessful attempt to enter the U.S., locating in midtown Manhattan. It opened a store in the former East Berlin — an architectural landmark, by architect Jean Nouvel. In Spain, the leading department store is El Corte Inglés, which dominates the Madrid retail scene.[31]

Figure 11-12: *Printemps is much like your typical U.S. department store, but more edgy and much more expensive. On the roof of its Paris store, there is a surprisingly affordable restaurant selling decent crêpes.*

In Eastern Europe department stores abound – the former communist regimes found them to be economical. With names such as Centrum or the Central Store in Eastern Europe and the Central Universal Store (TSUM) and its rival GUM in Russia, or bearing the name of the capital city or of socialist and nationalist symbols ("Victory," "Liberty," "Unity," etc.), these stores continue to thrive in different formats. In addition to their merchandise, they also have a substantial presence of leased departments. The leased departments are noteworthy in that they carry merchandise that directly competes with the store's offerings and with that of other leased departments.

In Latin America, department stores continue to expand. This includes Mexican leading chains Palacio de Hierro and Liverpool. Chile is home to two of the largest retail chains in South America, Cencosud and Falabella. Cencosud, with numerous department stores, specialty retailing, and grocery store operations throughout South America, is a major developer of shopping centers. Falabella, the largest department store chain in South America, has over 100 stores in Chile, Argentina, Peru, and Colombia. In 2018, Falabella announced a new franchise agreement with IKEA, the Swedish furniture retail giant, to open the first IKEA stores in South America. This is indicative of the strength of higher-end retailing in South America, as well as the continued push by global retailers into new high-growth markets. Shopping centers with department store anchors continue to be a significant part of the retailing scene in Mexico and other key markets in Latin America. This is a major departure from the retailing scene in the United States where enclosed regional malls anchored by middle-market department store retailers are under intense competitive pressure from Amazon and other online retailers. Finally, notwithstanding the continued growth of major retail chains in Latin America, it should be remembered that upwards of 50% of the economy (and jobs) are in the informal sector. This includes large numbers of small retail stores, street vendors, and other off-the-books retailers.[32]

In Asia, department stores have different histories. Japanese department stores started out as kimono shops that originally sold textiles. At present, Japan's department store groups (Mitsukoshi, Daimaru, ADO, the Seibu stores and affiliates, and Takashimaya) are designed to be cradle-to-grave providers of goods and services. Japanese department stores have also expanded in China and Hong Kong, where they control 50 percent of the market. In Taiwan, most department stores either come from Japan, or have sought affiliation with foreign — especially Japanese — department stores. Examples of department stores there are Shin-Kong Mitsukoshi, Tayeh Takashima, Pacific Sogo (see Figure 11-13), and Evergreen.[33]

Figure 11-13: *The Sogo department store in Taipei, Taiwan, is located on one of the busiest streets of a busy city, receiving high consumer traffic.*

asiastock/shutterstock.com

Although department stores remain a dominant retail outlet in Asia, they have been displaying symptoms of decline for some time, such as oversupply, over-duplication of merchandise, fierce competition, and declining profits. Shanghai alone witnessed the demise of five department stores. Existing department stores in this city have done well when changing their format, for example, specializing in European-style clothing and furnishings, or emulating the hypermarket environment by offering lower prices and maintaining a customer-friendly environment.

General Merchandise Discount Stores

General merchandise discount stores sell high volumes of merchandise, offer limited service, and charge lower prices. Discount stores are divided into two categories: all-purpose discount stores, which offer a wide variety of merchandise and limited depth, and category specialists (category killers), which carry a narrow variety of merchandise and offer a wide assortment.

jiawangkun/shutterstock.com

The all-purpose category is dominated by stores such as Walmart, Sears, and Target in the United States. Internationally, this retailer category tends to draw a substantial portion of profits from its supermarket section; consequently, it will be addressed in Section 11-6b, "Food Retailers." In the all-purpose category, Walmart has more than 6,200 stores in 27 countries (many of the international stores are hypermarkets). The company is present in Canada, Mexico, Puerto Rico, Costa Rica, Nicaragua, El Salvador, Guatemala, Honduras, Argentina, Brazil, China, Japan and the United Kingdom, among others. It serves more than 200 million international customers weekly in these markets, and it has a total of 2.2 million employees.[34]

Category specialists, also known as category killers or stores with category dominance, are large specialty stores that carry a narrow variety of merchandise and a wide assortment. Among examples of category specialists that are successful internationally are office supply stores, such as Staples, and Office Depot; home improvement centers, such as Home Depot and Baumax; bookstores such as Thalia; and furniture stores, such as IKEA, which dominates the modern, basic furniture market.

Many of the established international specialty retailers and numerous newcomers are attracting consumers with innovative approaches to merchandising. In the furniture business, IKEA has redefined furniture retailing for more than three decades with its impressive merchandising core competencies, its sourcing economies of scale, and the savings it passes on to consumers. As referred to in the previous section, IKEA's same-store sales growth has slowed. The retailer is now looking for growth by expanding into new markets in South America and elsewhere.

However, category specialists (category killers) are at risk of being killed off themselves. The specialty toy retailer, Toys R Us, announced in early 2018 that they would liquidate, closing all 735 stores in the US and Puerto Rico. While competition from online giant Amazon was certainly one factor in the closure, poor management and massive debt also contributed to the demise of Toys R Us. [35]

Off-Price Retailers

Off-price retailers sell brand name and designer merchandise below regular retail; the products they sell include overruns, irregular products, as well as products from previous seasons. Among examples of off-price retailers are factory outlet stores; close-out retailers, with broad, inconsistent assortments; and single-price retailers. Although this type of retailing is popular in the U.S. and Canada, in the rest of the world, there are only limited possibilities, other than store sales, for purchasing brand names at a discount. Outlet stores have started sprouting up in Europe around 2005, but their prices are not sliced as deeply as on this side of the Atlantic. In Germany, Hugo Boss has an outlet store in southern Germany, close to its factory, and Walter Steiger has an outlet off the main shopping street in Munich, but neither store offers deep discounts. In large European cities, there are outlet malls in the outskirts, but the stores in these malls offer discounts that would not impress American shoppers.

Examples of outlets are Ingolstadt Village, outside of Munich, Germany, with boutiques of designers such as Tommy Hilfiger, Calvin Klein, and Stefanel; Wertheim Village, outside of Würzburg, Germany, with brands such as Rene Lezard, Nike, Lacoste and Samsonite; La Valleé Village, near Paris, France, has boutiques such as Armani Outlet, Burberry, Coach, and Diesel; Shanghai Village, adjacent to Disneyland, China. Consumers purchase discounted products at these outlet shops – at 20 to 30 off full price. Discounts are not substantial because competitors selling these brands at full price in central shopping centers have a strong lobby that prevents discounters from taking over their business. For this same reason, TK Maxx, the European TJ Maxx off-price retailer, has very few name brands for sale in their always-packed stores.

Catalog Showrooms

Catalog showrooms offer high-turnover, brand name goods at discount prices. A typical format for a catalog showroom is one in which customers order from a catalog in the showroom where the product is only displayed and then pick up the merchandise at a designated location. The concept was developed in 1957 by Best Products, which was headquartered in Richmond, Virginia. However, the chain liquidated in 1997, as consumers lost interest in this type of retail marketing format. While this category is on the decline, especially in the U.S., IKEA continues to use this strategy successfully to sell to millions of consumers worldwide. Customers receive a catalog, which is also available in the showroom; based on the offerings displayed in the catalog and in the showroom, customers order in the store the product they would like to purchase and pick it up from a designated location in its unassembled state.

11-6b Food Retailers

Conventional Supermarkets

Food retailers include conventional supermarkets, which are self-service retailers with annual sales greater than $2 million and less than 20,000 square feet of store space. Such supermarkets abound worldwide, with local retailers and regional international retailers most prominent in this retail category. In high-income countries, this format is slowly replaced by competing formats, such as warehouse clubs, convenience stores, and superstores, and discounters such as Aldi and Lidl in Germany – but expanding worldwide – and Trader Joe's in the U.S. In emerging markets, conventional supermarkets are rapidly increasing in number. In India, for example, *kirana*, small neighborhood stores, are increasingly adding merchandise, ultimately becoming conventional supermarkets.

Superstores

The superstores category includes combination stores (food and drug) and hypermarkets (which combine supermarket, discount, and warehouse retailing principles). In the United States, combination stores have been quite successful; all-purpose general discount stores, such as Walmart, are often transformed into superstores to facilitate one-stop shopping for consumers. In their new, enhanced formats, these stores are known as the superstores (Walmart Superstore), and they carry an extensive food selection but have a limited refrigeration space and fresh produce offerings, similar to that offered by a supermarket. Leading worldwide in the superstore category are, in addition to Walmart, France's Carrefour; the Canadian Real; and U.K.'s Tesco. [36]

Warehouse Clubs or Wholesale Clubs

Warehouse clubs, also called wholesale clubs, require members to pay an annual fee and operate in low-overhead, warehouse-type facilities. They offer limited lines of brand name and dealer-brand groceries, apparel, appliances, and other goods at a substantial discount. They sell to final consumers who pay a fee or are affiliated with different institutions, as well as to businesses (in this capacity, they are wholesalers, rather than retailers). This retailing concept is presently pioneered worldwide by Sam's Club (part of Walmart) and Costco.

Sam's Clubs are in China, Brazil (see screenshot below), Puerto Rico, and Mexico and Costco has more than 200 stores overseas, among them, 89 in Canada, 27 in the U.K., 11 in Taiwan, 11 in Korea, 23 in Japan, seven in Australia, 36 in Mexico, and one in Spain.[37] San Diego-based PriceSmart formed joint ventures and licensing agreements with foreign partners to set up wholesale clubs in Latin America and Asia-Pacific countries. Currently, it is the largest warehouse club in Central and South America and the Caribbean, with a presence in Colombia, Costa Rica, El Salvador, Guatemala, Honduras, Nicaragua, Panama, Aruba, Barbados, Dominican Republic, Jamaica, Trinidad and Tobago, and the U.S. Virgin Islands.[38]

Convenience Stores

Convenience stores are small retailers located in residential areas, convenient to consumers. They are open long hours, carry limited lines of higher-turnover necessities, and offer the possibility of a one-stop shopping experience. Formats of convenience stores vary world-wide — from small independent retailers to chains such as 7-Eleven; from large stores offering a one-stop shopping opportunity for convenience goods and fast food to kiosks selling food items and alcoholic beverages obtained through both legal and illegal channels; from convenience stores-cum-pharmacies in a city's town square to seventh-floor apartments with a large opening in the front door selling milk, cheese, bread, and different types of chocolate. Convenience stores abound in both developing and developed countries, with many chains developing in conjunction with gas stations.

11-6c Nonstore Retailing

Digital Retailing

Also known as interactive shopping or online, or electronic retailing, selling through the Internet has quickly become an important retail format. In the Internet retailing category, digital companies and traditional retailers are attempting additional market penetration by making it convenient for loyal customers to purchase their products, as well as attempting market diversification by expanding their market to consumers who otherwise would not normally shop in their particular retail establishment.

JKstock/shutterstock.com

With the increase in the number of Internet users worldwide, providing retailing services through a website becomes much easier. Local retailers can easily become international retailers without making investments in store leases, aesthetics, atmospherics, and so forth.

Internet retailing provides opportunities for retail firms to define their market beyond their target regions. At the same time, it presents dilemmas with regard to customer service and control of the retail transactions (due to international and regional differences in mail reliability and in customer orientation and skill of local service representatives). Many companies with e-commerce capabilities turn away international orders, primarily because they do not have a way to ship the merchandise overseas or lack the skill for processing international shipments.[39]

Shopping via the Internet for consumers in countries where attractive shopping alternatives are available, such as malls and stores with great merchandise assortment and variety, is quite different from shopping in many developing countries, where alternatives are limited, and where both retailers and the products they sell may be inferior. If it were not for Internet retailing, consumers in low- and middle-income countries would be able to purchase higher quality Western goods only if they went abroad.

However, the Internet is rapidly gaining penetration in countries of all levels of development, as follows:[40]

• More than 38 percent of the world's population is online, and more than three billion users, which represents a big jump in countries where there was no fixed service before.

• In North America, 84 percent of the population consists of Internet users, and, in Western Europe, 79 percent of the population are Internet users. In Latin America, Internet about 59 percent of the total population are internet users. On the other hand, Internet users make up only 17 percent of the total population in Sub-Saharan Africa, 39 percent in North Africa and the Middle East, and 28 percent in the emerging markets of Asia-Pacific.

Mobile global penetration is expected to be 71 percent by 2019. In the Asia-Pacific region, mobile Internet device penetration exceeds 100 percent, which means that individuals have multiple subscriptions; in North America, Western Europe, and Central and Latin America, mobile Internet penetration is expected to rise above 100 percent. In Central and Eastern Europe, a 98 percent penetration is forecast by 2019.There are numerous stories describing situations where consumers have to contend with unethical retailers. Whereas brick-and-mortar retailers can be sued in a local court of law for nonperformance, Internet retailers are more elusive; the issue of the appropriate jurisdiction further complicates the situation. In low- and middle- income countries, a safer alternative may be purchasing goods online from established and well-known Western brick-and-mortar retailers.

The Internet also provides a venue for émigrés shopping for their relatives in their home countries as described in International Marketing Illustration 11-3.

International Marketing Illustration 11-3
Retail Opportunities for Émigrés: Repatriating Food and Clothing to Home-Country Relatives

In the past, helping out relatives with money or with food packages was expensive. Traditionally, émigrés living in high-income countries sent money periodically to their relatives in their low-income home country. Typically sent through money wire transfers or by check, the sums were often decimated by fees by the time they reached them. For example, sending a check from the United States would require the recipient in Ecuador, India, or Slovakia to go to a local bank to cash it. The money would be released as late as a month after the check was cashed, and the recipient, who did not normally have an account at the international bank, would be charged hefty fees. The recipient of a $100 check might cash out $70 or less. To get around high transfer fees, in 2018 several companies including Brink's and Amazon began or expanded the issuance of prepaid debit Mastercards in several Latin American markets. These cards do not require the holder to have a checking account and can be replenished in person or via relatively inexpensive wire transfers. The prepaid debit cards also provide local residents access

to financial services and purchases. This is especially important in lower-income countries, where more than half the adults do not have a bank checking account.

In the pre-Internet past, émigrés also helped their families with food packages: Most diaspora newspapers advertised the shipping of consumer products to the home country at competitive prices (they still do today, but the Internet has taken a large bite of their business). Merz Pharmaceuticals, a German pharmaceuticals firm, has been catering to East European émigrés for decades. All one had to do was pick up the phone and order the goods for delivery, paying for a credit card. Because shipping was involved, overall costs were high. (Continued on next page).

Rosen Ivanov Iliev/shutterstock.com

International Marketing Illustration 11-3 (continued)
Retail Opportunities for Émigrés: Repatriating Food and Clothing to Home-Country Relatives

Today, a greater accessibility of goods in the home country, coupled with Internet-facilitated transactions, allows émigrés to order goods for the family at competitive prices and with free shipping for more expensive orders. This variant is so attractive that it is not unusual for émigrés from Latin America and Eastern Europe to purchase food and other necessities for family members in the home country, in some cases as often as three times a month.

To illustrate, shoppers in Oregon can place grocery orders for their relatives in Argentina through Discovirtual.com, an online site of Argentine retailer Disco SA, owned by Dutch chain Royal Ahold. Peruvian supermarket chain E. Wong launched an online store that taps Peruvians abroad shopping for their families, doubling its online transactions in one year. Similarly, Brazil's Pao de Acucar found that it can sell an average of 5,000 grocery items a day through its website. Mexico's Grupo Gigante is also actively pursuing this market.

Latino immigrants and their descendants living in the United States repatriate close to $20 billion yearly. Immigrants from Haiti and Nicaragua remit more than 20 percent of the home-countries' GDP yearly. Somali remittance companies, known as hawala, transfer close to $1 billion a year from Somali diaspora.

Online retailers have good prospects for tapping into the remittance market.

Sources: DiscoVirtual.com.ar, accessed June 29, 2018. Nicole Raymond, Di Pinheiro, and Alejandro Bianchi, "Emigres Send Food Online to Old Country—Retailers Seek to Tap into Billions Repatriated by Latino Immigrants to the U.S.," Wall Street Journal, November 6, 2002, B3; "Mexicans in the U.S. are Sending Home More Money Than Ever" NPR, February 10, 2017; "Amazon Launches First Debit Card in Mexico e-Commerce Push" Reuters, March 13, 2018); and this textbook author's remittance experiences.

Vending Machines

With the advent of the Smart Card, vending machine retailing has become more popular than ever (and, increasingly, more vending machines worldwide accept credit cards). Technology is now facilitating a more interactive consumer relationship, where videos illustrate product use and provide more information. The extent to which vending machines are used as a retail venue varies from country to country. Vending machines are used most in Japan, where they sell just about anything one can think of, including beer, hot food, cold food, ice cream (see Figure 11-14), cameras, and so on. Coke vending machines are ubiquitous (see Figure 11-15 on next page). In fact, in central locations in Japan's major cities, there are so many vending machines that they interfere with pedestrian traffic.

MAHATHIR MOHD YASIN/shutterstock.com

Figure 11-14: *Japanese vending machines offer ice cream, cold drinks, hot food, and beer, as well as many nonfood items.*

Vending machines are encountered in different configurations around the world. In the Netherlands, for instance, one can enter an outfit known as an Automatiek and select sausages, meatballs, salads, and beverages from the different machines, all replenished frequently by a full-time employee. In Munich, Germany, a vending machine for fresh flowers is located in the center of town. In much of the rest of the world, with the exception of the United States and Canada, cigarettes are readily available in the streets at all times of the day. In Europe, condoms are sold in vending machines outside pharmacies.

Figure 12-11 *Cold drink vending machines in Japan, selling Coca-Cola, and Tropicana, as well as local favorite Pocari Sweat.*

Television Home Shopping

The television home shopping category includes cable channels selling to consumers in their homes, infomercials, and direct response advertising shown on broadcast and cable television. Television shopping networks, much like QVC and the Home Shopping Network in the United States, operate in many developed countries. The Home Shopping Network has three international channels, Home Shopping Europe in Germany; SHOP Channel, Japan; and TVSN Ltd. China. And QVC is also present in international markets, in the United Kingdom, Germany, and Japan. Local television home shopping channels are sprouting everywhere, from the United Kingdom, which has many shopping channels — Telewest now owns all the SitUp TV shopping channels — to China, where the largest TV shopping network is Acorn International, in a country where television home shopping is a $2 billion market.[41]

Catalog and Direct Mail Retailing

Retailers of all categories are expanding internationally through catalog sales and direct mail retailing. Marketers continue to use consistent marketing communications worldwide, coordinating their advertising – broadcast, print, and Internet – with direct mail brochures and catalogs. This is surprising, especially in light of the low-cost digital retailing alternative. The reality is that a catalog is bait for customers, much like a store window display. Retailers hope that shoppers will mark the items they like and then head online or in the store to purchase the product. Catalogs today no longer have busy pages with all the merchandise catalogued; instead, they have few pages with merchandise descriptions and larger photos with lifestyle images. Catalogs and direct mail are an expensive proposition for retailers because they entail expensive photoshoots and high postage rates, and they lock retailers into specific trends and merchandise, whereas digital marketing pieces can be updated in minutes.[42]

U.S. retailers use catalogs (Lands' End, Talbotts) to sell to consumers in the United Kingdom. British catalogs have come to the U.S. offering clothing (Boden) and shoes (Shipton & Heneage), offering U.S. shoppers a flat shipping rate of $25. Catalog sales provide challenges to businesses not familiar with local practices. Catalog and internet retailers found that consumers in Japan expect to first receive the product and only then pay for it. Conversely, although Germans are accustomed to buying from catalogs, they are not used

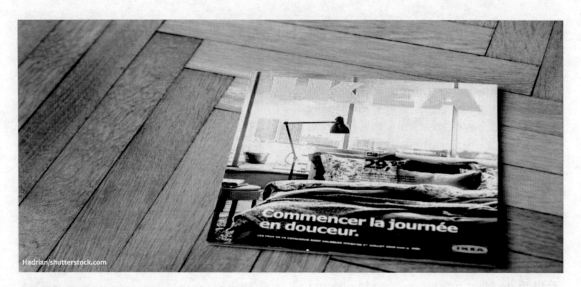

to the privileges considered standard in the U.S. catalog industry, such as 24-hour service, liberal return policies, or even lifetime guarantees from apparel catalogers. Such guarantees were unheard of in Germany, and a group of German retailers took, in the past, Lands' End to court, accusing it of "unfair" competition (and lost).[43]

In some developing countries, however, many obstacles affect catalog retailing. First, the infrastructure must be sufficiently developed to warrant investment. For catalog companies, it means that telephone service and mail service must be reliable. In many countries, consumers must often purchase cellphone service because landlines are inadequate or not available. In addition, the mail system is lax and mail is often intercepted and opened, such that only a portion of a package's contents might be delivered, if at all. Finally, in many countries, average income is a fraction of the average income in developed countries. Thus, products sold via catalog, such as clothing, appliances, housewares, and so on, are prohibitively expensive.

Direct Selling and Network Marketing

In the direct selling retail format, a salesperson, typically an independent distributor, contacts a consumer at a convenient location such as his or her home or workplace, demonstrates product use and benefits, takes orders, and delivers the merchandise. Direct selling is in the growth stage in most of the developing world. Here, a number of impediments restrict firms' ability to successfully carry out their selling activity. Among these impediments are low per-capita income, unreliable postal services, excessive bureaucracy, lack of credit cards, few telephones, and a lack of access to mailing lists.

Direct selling firms are active in growth markets, such as the China and Southeast Asia, Eastern Europe, and Latin America. U.S. direct selling firms, such as Avon, Nu Skin, and Mary Kay Cosmetics, are active in these markets. Latin America is Avon's largest market, representing more than 50 percent of the company annual worldwide sales. While emerging markets like Brazil are often attractive in terms of potential sales, they also illustrate the particular challenges that have bedeviled Avon. These include political instability, economic crises and unemployment, as well as currency devaluations that have cut deeply into profit margins. [44]

Network marketing, or multilevel marketing, is a variation on direct selling and an approach to selling at the same time. It involves signing up sales representatives to go into business for themselves with minimal start-up capital. Their task is to sell more "distributorships"— that is, to identify more sales representatives from their own personal network, to buy the product, and to persuade others to buy the product. Network marketing has been experiencing rapid growth, especially in emerging markets. In South Africa, for example, the poor transportation infrastructure that presents a challenge to many multinationals does not present a problem to network marketing. This and the fit with elements of traditional African culture make network marketing one of the most significant avenues for growth within the post-apartheid economy. It should be noted, however, that these successful distribution models are even more vulnerable than traditional retail formats when emerging markets experience economic downturns or adverse exchange rates.[45] Among the most successful network marketing firms that have international operations are Amway, Herbalife International, and Equinox International.

However, the multilevel marketing industry is not without controversy. It was banned in China from the late 1990s until 2005, where multilevel marketing was considered a pyramid scheme. Today, the Chinese have many restrictions for network marketing. In 2016, Herbalife International reached a settlement with the U.S. Federal Trade Commission, agreeing to a large fine and a revision of their business practices. This settlement allowed the company to avoid criminal charges of operating a pyramid scheme.[45]

11-7 Issues and Trends in International Retailing

Among issues in international retailing are country regulations, which could differ from one market to another, and could have a profound impact on a firm's operations. Protectionist rules in India, for example, have kept out the world's biggest retail names – Walmart Stores, Tesco, Metro, and Carrefour; the retailers were barred legally from setting up and running their own stores until 2012. And, while Walmart bought their joint venture partner and are planning to open large wholesale operations in the near future, and Tesco countered with a partnership with the powerful Tata Group, Carrefour, the retailer who has mastered emerging markets large and small, gave up in 2015, closing its stores in India.[46] To further complicate matters for retailers, in many markets (including China), retail legislation and rules differ from province to province, as well as at the national level.[47] For example, regulations allow foreign retail joint ventures to operate in more cities throughout China and to engage in wholesaling for the first time; however, most rural areas are off limits to international retailers.[48]

Barry Barnes/shutterstock.com

Other types of regulations restrict expansion of superstores and hypermarkets (United Kingdom, France, and Belgium); limit the hours of operation to protect smaller stores (the Netherlands, Spain); require that stores locate in downtown areas (Germany); control disposal of packaging used for transportation (Germany); limit the use of promotional pricing (France, Germany);[49] and limit the period for sales. French companies, for example, rarely offer an extra product free because the amount companies are allowed to give away is minimal. In Germany, offering three products for the price of two or other bundling offers is illegal, and cash discounts to the consumer are limited.

In countries where consumers are not charged duties for products they purchase from a neighboring country (if the neighboring country belongs to the same free trade area, for example), cross-border shopping affects most retailers in the higher-tax countries. The

Karasev Victor/shutterstock.com

United Kingdom, the Irish Republic, and Denmark charge much higher taxes than the rest of the European Union members. To avoid the large value-added tax on most products for personal consumption, consumers in these countries cross borders into countries where this tax is substantially lower. In this sense, consumers' purchase decisions are driven by tax differences rather than by underlying differences in producer

prices, and cross-border shopping causes an inefficient allocation of resources, leading to significant reductions in sales by domestic retailers and manufacturers, reduced profits, and job losses.[50]

In other situations, retailers in neighboring countries suffer from the low taxes imposed by a tax haven nearby. Examples of consumer tax havens are Port Said in Egypt, and Bermuda or the Bahamas in North America, among others. In setting up retail operations overseas, a company must assess and seek the most favorable environment from the taxation perspective.

A combination of protectionist policies and high taxes can also affect retail sales. In Argentina, the government spent millions of dollars to subsidize the local manufacturing of certain consumer electronics items, air conditioners, etc. To further protect the local industries, the government followed a traditional protectionist pattern of imposing high tariffs on imports of competing items. As a result, prices for Argentine consumers are much higher than in neighboring Chile, which has a more open free-market economy. Some Argentine shoppers will even make a long drive to Chile to purchase goods, or travel to Miami to shop for consumer electronics.[51]

In the past, Mexican consumers have routinely shopped on the U.S. side of the borders with Texas and California in search of quality, variety, and novelty. Examples include the McAllen, Texas, area and the Imperial Valley Mall in El Centro, California, located 10 miles north of the Mexican border. The mall targets about one million potential consumers living in Mexicali, Mexico.[52]

11-7a Variation in Retail Practices: A Consumer Perspective

Retail practices vary from one market to another. Consumers in the United States prefer to shop less frequently and purchase products in bulk, whereas consumers in Japan prefer to purchase products in smaller quantities, packaged individually. In Asia, store demonstrations are popular, and in Japan and Korea, Saturday is a major shopping day, when shopping and attending such demonstrations are a family affair. Consumers in Asia and the United Kingdom prefer products of the highest quality and are willing to pay the price. In Argentina and Saudi Arabia, consumers prefer to purchase food products at mom-and-pop stores, rather than at the supermarket, whereas in Mexico consumers continue to go to farmers' markets for fresh produce. Even bugs on fruit are important to consumers in the Philippines; they indicate that the fruit is ripe. Finally, in the United Kingdom, store name is a better indicator of quality for food products than brand name. Hence, private labels are thriving for popular stores.[53]

In the United States, retailing continues to be upended by Amazon. In 2017, the e-commerce giant purchased the Whole Foods Grocery chain, giving them a large brick-and-mortar presence through which to expand the Amazon customer base, including offering same-day grocery delivery services. Other grocery retailers such as Walmart and Kroger are racing to expand their grocery delivery services, allowing consumers to electronically order groceries for delivery within hours. The Kroger grocery store chain is working with a robotics and artificial intelligence firm to design a new specialty unmanned vehicle for the delivery of groceries.[54]

In 2018, Amazon announced yet another new foray into consumer retailing, the delivery of prescriptions. Amazon paid $1 billion in cash to purchase PillPack, a small e-commerce firm that sells prescriptions online to consumers. This purchase has the potential to upend the drugstore industry in the United States and their lucrative prescription business. Predictably, after Amazon's announcement, share prices for two major chains, CVS and Wallgreens Boots Alliance, fell, shaving hundreds of millions of dollars off the firms' market value. (Reportedly, Walmart made an unsuccessful bid to purchase PillPack.)[55]

Finally, also in 2018, Amazon again roiled the retail-sector waters with an announcement that the firm will develop a network of independent package delivery businesses to handle some retail deliveries, called the Delivery Services Partner program. Amazon will allow entrepreneurs to run their own local fleets of up to 40 vans in selected markets with the Amazon Prime logo on the trucks.[56]

11-7b Variation in Retail Practice: Salespeople and Management

Sales service differs greatly from one market to another. Whereas in the United States it is customary to have friendly salespeople waiting on customers, treating them with respect, in many other countries this is not always the case. In Eastern and southeastern Europe, for example, salespeople tend to be curt, bordering on unfriendly. A Pizza Hut employee trained in customer service according to U.S. specifications would sound terribly out of place in much of Eastern Europe.

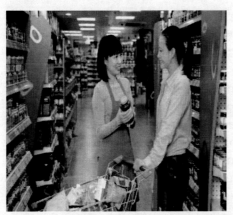
XiXinXing/shutterstock.com

In other examples, in China, the sales staff tend to be overly conscientious. If a customer forgets to pick up the change after a sale is complete, the salesperson will most likely follow him or her into the street to return the change. In other countries, the situation is quite the contrary. Salespeople keep the change and sell only those products that are priced under an even amount so that they can claim they do not have the change if a customer dares ask for it. In countries where there may be shortages of certain products, salespeople are bribed with money and other goods such as coffee, cigarettes, and perfume.

Finally, certain stores charge an admission price to ensure that individuals permitted to enter can actually afford the products sold there (an example is an antique store selling what locally would be considered masterpieces or national treasures). In these stores, it is also appropriate for customers to dress well so that they do not look "suspect." Similarly, not dressing well in environments considered upscale locally (despite the fact that, in most of the world, the respective retail environment would be perceived as average at best) could easily result in denial of service.

Among the trends[56] to watch for in international retailing are those related to technology and consumers. With regard to technology, retailers worldwide are integrating their different customer and supplier databases to create an efficient shopping environment for consumers. In developed countries, new technology, such as Fujitsu's Transaction Solutions' Pervasive Retailing Framework (PRF), is able to coordinate independent retailing applications — such as point-of-sale hardware, wireless shopping cards, and loyalty software — into an efficient customer experience. As customers use their phone to access their loyalty account on the grocer's website, they download their shopping list and the shopping cart guides them through the store, interacting with kiosks at the deli and pharmacy, offering personalized coupons, and helping them proceed to checkout.

Technology is also increasing the transparency of the marketplace. This has an impact on prices, but it also applies to every attribute of the brand mix. The use of child labor, environmentally unfriendly suppliers, and other questionable activities can easily be discovered. Technology also creates highly informed consumers and eliminates the need for retail staff that try to sell consumers products. Finally, technology also means that more consumers will become retailers through auction sites or other e-commerce venues, taking share away from conventional retailers. In emerging markets, there will be faster retail growth as the populations remain relatively young. In addition, there will be two billion middle-class consumers at the end of this decade, most of them in developing countries, with more disposable income to spend on clothing and home goods, rather than just on food products, and their purchases will be greatly facilitated by mobile money. For this reason, more and more specialty stores are successfully pursuing international expansion. In high-income countries, consumer demographics present a problem to retailers, as their aging consumers' spending on services (travel, health care) will increase faster than spending on goods. Moreover, in these countries, customers are taking charge, defining for retailers their preferences for quality, convenience, and low price, making it difficult for retailers to make a solid profit.

Summary

Describe the functions of home-country and host-country intermediaries involved in international distribution. Examples of home-country intermediaries involved in international distribution are export management companies, which specialize in a particular industry; Japanese trading companies, whose operations range from distribution to manufacturing, mining, and technology, and U.S. trading companies, which are export consortia of small businesses; brokers and agents who do not carry titles and export merchants who carry titles to products; cooperative export arrangements, whereby exporters handle other firms' unrelated products on a contractual basis; Webb-Pomerene Associations, which allow competitors to join forces in exporting; and tax-incentive structures, which allow for a portion of a firm's foreign income to be tax exempt. Foreign-country intermediaries involved in logistics are merchant middlemen, who carry title to and have possession of products, and agents and brokers, who do not.

Identify the different facilitators of international distribution and logistics and describe their involvement in the international distribution process. Among facilitators are distribution centers, which use a hub for efficient channeling of operations; transportation companies; freight forwarders and customs brokers, both in the home and the host country, who arrange for transportation, customs clearance, and export documentation; governmental and nongovernmental organizations, such as the International Trade Administration, the Bureau of Export Administration, the Export-Import Bank (currently under re-evaluation by Congress), and the International Chamber of Commerce, which promote and facilitate international involvement of companies.

Address the challenges encountered by distribution in countries of different development levels. Multinationals operating in developing countries often must face challenges related to the transportation infrastructure, containerization (e.g., ports with shallow drafts that cannot handle large vessels), and customs inspections. In both developed and developing countries, multinationals must deal with parallel imports (gray markets), from a low-price market to another market using distribution channels not authorized by the manufacturer. Increasingly, companies are combating such distribution by charging similar prices worldwide, creating products for low markets that are not attractive to the high market, complicating repair and service processes, informing consumers about buying such products, and litigating.

Provide an overview and description of the general merchandise retailing category and offer examples and illustrations. In the general merchandise retailing category are a number of retailers. Specialty stores, offering narrow assortments and deep product lines, are rapidly increasing their presence internationally. From The Gap to Mango to Marks & Spencer, retailers find success well beyond their national borders. Specialized markets are omnipresent worldwide. Department stores are experiencing a decline, with some exceptions. Innovative stores that position themselves creatively have more success. In Asia, the more successful department stores are those that position themselves as European retailers. General merchandise discount stores are rapidly expanding, with great success. Walmart, in particular, has made great strides in conquering international markets. Category specialists, specializing in one product category, are also very successful in their international pursuits. Off-price stores, a staple of U.S. retailing offering brand name products at lower prices, are in great demand in other countries. Recently, such retailers have made substantial inroads into markets in Asia and Europe. Catalog showrooms, selling high-turnover, brand-name goods at discount prices, are also successful internationally, with many competing players. The IKEA "model" has been the most successful to date.

Provide an overview and description of the food retailing category and offer examples and illustrations. Food retailers include conventional supermarkets, which are dominated by national and regional chains. Superstores can be combination stores (food and drug) or hypermarkets, which are successful abroad but are slow to become mainstream retailers in the United States. Warehouse clubs are becoming popular worldwide, and many U.S. retailers in this category are doing well. Convenience stores abound in both developing and developed countries, with many chains developing in conjunction with gas stations.

Provide an overview and description of the nonstore retailing category and offer examples and illustrations. Nonstore retailing is one of the areas with the highest growth and unlimited opportunities. Digital retailing has vastly expanded opportunities for small and medium-sized retailers all over the world. Vending machines are increasing in sophistication and have different formats and capabilities in each market where they are available; the products they can carry also differ. Television home shopping is attracting more audiences and also offers opportunities to brick-and-mortar retailers to expand. Catalog retailers are still strong, expanding rapidly beyond their home-country borders. Direct selling and network marketing are gaining ground rapidly, especially in developing countries.

Address issues related to legislation, taxation, and retailing practices around the world. Retailers have many restrictions imposed on them, and those restrictions vary from one market to another. The restrictions cover hours of operation, sales activity, and pricing techniques; or the restrictions may limit access to local consumers. Retailing practices vary from one market to another. Salespeople may be more courteous and solicitous in some countries, and consumers may be more demanding in certain markets, shop more or less frequently, and may or may not rely on a product's brand name as an indication of quality.

Key Terms

all-purpose discount stores
brokers and agents
building channels
buying offices
catalog retailers
catalog showrooms
category killers
category specialists
combination stores
complementary export agents
complementary export merchants
comprador
convenience stores
conventional supermarkets
cooperative export arrangements
cross-border shopping
department stores
direct mail retailing

direct selling
electronic retailing
established channels
export management companies
export merchants
Export Trading Company (ETC) Act
food retailers
foreign-country intermediaries
general merchandise discount stores
home-country intermediaries
import jobber
keiretsu
hypermarkets
interactive shopping
Internet retailing
logistics alliances
managing agent
manufacturer's export agents

manufacturer's representative
mother henning
merchant middlemen
multilevel marketing
network marketing
Norazi agent
off-price retailers
parallel imports
piggy backing
sogo-shosha
specialized markets
specialty stores
superstores
television home shopping
trading companies
vending machines
warehouse clubs
Webb-Pomerene Associations
wholesale clubs

Discussion Questions

1. Companies can either build new channels or use existing channels in new markets they plan to serve. What are the determinants of this choice? Explain.

2. Who are the different distributors available in your home country? Who can distribute your products abroad?

3. Who are the different distributors in your target market (host country)? Who can manage a company's distribution in the host country?

4. How does the U.S. government help companies in the process of distributing their goods internationally?

5. What types of distribution and logistics challenges do firms face in the process of going international?

6. What is the difference between a specialty store and a category specialist?

7. Describe the state of the department store around the globe. What strategies appear to be more successful for department stores?

8. Hypermarkets are a dominant retailing format in Europe but not in the United States. What are hypermarkets? Give examples of successful hypermarkets worldwide.

9. Direct selling and network marketing have found great success in emerging markets. What is the difference between the two categories of retailers, and how do they gain access to consumers?

10. What are some of the challenges that retailers face in international markets?

Chapter Quiz

True/False

1. Using established channels can be costly for multinational firms, but paying the high price may also erect barriers to entry for competitors.

Answer: True

Rationale: Penetrating markets in China or Japan may mean doing business with the established channel members that dominate the market; the disadvantage of such channel relationships is cost, but the relationship also constitutes a barrier to entry for potential competitors. Coca-Cola and Kraft have benefited from their relationship with the most powerful channel members in these markets. Section 11-1a, "Using Established Channels"

2. Home-country intermediaries are instrumental in providing all international marketing services for firms that otherwise would not be able to enter a foreign market.

Answer: True

Rationale: Companies relying on home-country intermediaries relinquish their control of the marketing mix to their distributors in the target foreign country. Home-country intermediaries provide all the necessary international marketing services for these firms. Section 11-2, "Intermediaries Involved in International Distribution"

3. Buying offices are located in the target market country and carry title to the product.

Answer: False

Rationale: Buying offices consist of buyers located in the firm's home country, representing different firms located abroad. Section 11-2a, "Home-Country Intermediaries"

4. Neither merchant middlemen nor agents and brokers carry title to products.

Answer: True

Rationale: Agents and brokers do not carry title to products. Merchant middlemen usually both carry title to and have physical possession of the products they distribute in the foreign target market. Section 11-2b, "Foreign-Country Intermediaries"

5. Truck transportation handles larger shipments over longer distances.

Answer: False.

Rationale: Truck transportation handles smaller shipments over shorter distances. Most of the local transportation is handled by trucks, which offer high flexibility at competitive rates. Section 11-3a, "International Transportation"

6. General merchandise discount store retailers sell high volumes of merchandise and offer limited services; they also charge lower prices.

Answer: True

Rationale: General merchandise discount retailers sell high volumes of merchandise, offer limited service, and charge lower prices. Section 11-6a, "General Merchandise Retailing"

7. Factory outlet shops are an example of off-price retailers.

Answer: True

Rationale: Among examples of off-price retailers are factory outlet stores and close-out retailers, with broad, inconsistent assortments, as well as single-price retailers. Section 11-6a, "General Merchandise Retailing"

8. Internet purchasing is experience driven in high-income countries.

Answer: False

Rationale: In high-income countries, Internet purchasing is consumption-market driven and not experience driven. Consumers shop to satisfy their needs and wants but do not view Internet surfing as a pleasure trip, as would consumers going to a mall or a store. Section 11-6C, "Nonstore Retailing"

Multiple Choice

1. What services do Japanese trading companies offer their suppliers?
    a. risk reduction
    b. specialization in intermediary services
    c. financial assistance
    d. all of the above

Answer: d is correct.

Rationale: Japanese trading companies offer their suppliers three primary services: specialization in providing intermediary services, risk reduction through extensive information channels, and significant financial assistance. Section 11-2a, "Home-Country Intermediaries"

2. What aspect of international distribution and logistics is facilitated by containerization?
    a. distribution research
    b. freight forwarding
    c. intermodal transportation
    d. government agencies

Answer: c is correct.

Rationale: Intermodal transportation has been facilitated by the use of containers: Goods can be placed into containers, taken by truck to a train-loading facility, transported to a port, and loaded aboard a ship — all using the initial container, providing protection for the products at lower cost. Section 11-3a, "International Transportation"

3. DHL uses hubs that hold products it delivers regularly so it always has them on hand. This is an example of what international distribution and logistics facilitator?
    a. freight forwarders
    b. distribution centers
    c. transportation firms
    d. government agencies

Answer: b is correct.

Rationale: Distribution centers are designed to speed up warehousing and delivery, by channeling operations to one center (hub) that is equipped to handle the distribution of products to their destination. Section 11-3b, "Logistics Facilitators"

4. Which government agency offers export assistance to international firms and, in particular, to small to medium-sized businesses?
    a. U.S. Department of State

b. Bureau of Export Administration
c. U.S. Trade and Development Agency
d. International Trade Administration

Answer: d is correct.

Rationale: The International Trade Administration in the U.S. Department of Commerce offers export assistance to international firms and, in particular, to small to medium-sized businesses. Section 11-3b, "Logistics Facilitators"

5. Which of the following constitutes a possible strategy to combat parallel imports?
a. Charging similar prices worldwide
b. Complicating the repair process for parallel imports
c. Informing customers of problems when buying gray market products
d. All of the above

Answer: d is correct.

Rationale: Possible perils of gray market products might be that the product is new but technically outdated or that the product will not benefit from manufacturer warranties; informing customers of such problems could deter them from purchasing. Similarly, charging the same prices in all markets and complicating the repair process for parallel imports could deter future buyers. Section 11-4b, " Parallel Imports"

6. Retailers that offer a narrow product line and a wide assortment, such as office supply stores, are examples of
a. specialized markets.
b. specialty stores.
c. department stores.
d. all-purpose discount stores.

Answer: b is correct.

Rationale: Retailers that offer a narrow product line and a wide assortment like office supply stores are known as specialty stores; large specialty stores are also known as category specialists or category killers. Section 12-3a, "General Merchandise Retailing"

7. Harrods of London exemplifies which of the following retail formats?
    a.   specialized markets
    b.   all-purpose discount stores
    c.   specialty stores
    d.   department stores

Answer: d is correct.

Rationale: Harrods is a department store, carrying a broad variety of goods and wide assortments. Section 11-6a, "General Merchandise Retailing"

Notes

1. Cui Rong, "Privileged Position," *Far Eastern Economic Review*, Vol. 167, No. 31, August 5, 2004, pp. 46-48.

2. Paul Herbig and Alan T. Shao, "American Sogo Shosha: American Trading Companies in the Twenty-First Century," *Marketing Intelligence & Planning*, Vol. 15, No. 6, 1997, pp. 281–290.

3. *Japan Economics*, "The Business Side of Horizontal and Vertical Keiretsus," March 6, 2015, accessed at http://www.vaioshutdown.com/2015/the-modern-horizontal-and-vertical-keiretsu on October 2, 2015; "Japanese Trading Companies: The Giants That Refused to Die," *The Economist*, Vol. 319, No. 7709, June 1, 1991, pp. 72–73. Lyn S. Amine, Tamer S. Cavusgil, and Robert I. Weinstein, "Japanese Sogo Shosha and the U.S. Export Trading Companies," *Journal of the Academy of Marketing Science*, Vol. 14, No. 3, Fall 1986, pp. 21–32.

4. Ed Crooks, "GE Steps Up Campaign Over ExIm Bank," *Financial Times*, September 17, 2015, accessed at http://www.ft.com/cms/s/0/43a4edde-5d43-11e5-9846-de406ccb37f2.html#axzz3nF1rb8aA on September 28, 2015.

5. "Export Trading Company Act," *U.S. Dept. of Commerce International Trade Administration*, accessed at https://

www.trade.gov/mas/ian/etca/index.asp on June 27, 2018.

6. Ernest R. Larkins and Fenwisk Huss, "Establishing Trade Relations in Russia," *The CPA Journal,* Vol. 65, No. 8, August 1995, pp. 26–31.

7. Ibid

8. https://www.ftc.gov/enforcement/statutes?title=Webb-Pomerene, accessed July 2, 2018.

9. "The Law of International Trade: A Business Overview," *Michigan State University Global Edge,* accessed at https://globaledge.msu.edu/global-resources/trade_law on June 28, 2018. Amy L. Hirter, "Foreign Agents and Distributors: When and How to Use Them," *The Colorado Lawyer,* April 2006, accessed at https://hollandhart.com/files/ForeignAgentsandDistribs.pdf on June 28, 2018.

10. Association of Caribbean States, "Transport, Logistics, and Competitiveness in Latin America and the Caribbean," 2015, accessed at http://www.acs-aec.org/index.php?q=press-center/releases/2015/transport-logistics-and-competitiveness-in-latin-america-and-the-caribbea on September 30, 2015; Joseph Bonney, "Logistics Costs Rise," *The Journal of Commerce Online,* June 6, 2007, 1.

11. "Richmond Marine Terminal," *Port of Virginia,* accessed at http://www.portofvirginia.com/facilities/richmond-marine-terminal-rmt on June 28, 2018. "Virginia Inland Port," *Port of Virginia,* accessed at http://www.portofvirginia.com/facilities/virginia-inland-port-vip on June 28, 2018.

12. Randy R. Irvin, "Pipeline Owners Must Reassess Utility of Undivided-Interest Ownership," *Oil & Gas Journal,* Vol. 99, No. 30, July 23, 2001, pp. 60–65.

13. Larry Rohter, "Vast Pipelines in Amazon Face Challenges Over Protecting Rights and Rivers," *New York Times,* January 21, 2007, 14.

14. Steve Holland and Valerie Volcovici, "Trump Clears Way for Controversial Oil Pipelines," *Reuters,* January 24, 2017, accessed at https://www.reuters.com/article/us-usa-trump-pipeline-idUSKBN15820N on June 28 2017.

15. David Biederman, "Intelligent Island Links the Globe," *Traffic World,* Vol. 264, No. 10, December 4, 2000, pp. 28–31.

16. Richard Foster, "Location, Location, Location: Virginia Attracts Distribution Centers," *Virginia Business,* September 30, 2014, accessed at http://www.virginiabusiness.com/news/article/location-location-location on June 28, 2018.

17. "How to Become a Freight Forwarder in 5 Clear Steps," *Lance Surety Bond Associates,* October 14, 2015, accessed at https://www.suretybonds.org/blog/how-to-become-a-freight-forwarder on June 28, 2018. Laurel Delaney, "Steps to Becoming a Licensed Customs Broker," *The Balance Small Business,* March 30, 2018, accessed at https://www.thebalancesmb.com/becoming-licensed-customs-broker-1953573 on June 28, 2018.

18. Adapted from Prabir K. Bagchi and Helge Virum, "Logistical Alliances: Trends and Prospects in Integrated Europe," *Journal of Business Logistics,* Vol. 19, No. 1, 1998, pp. 191–213.

19. William P. Doyle, "The Panama Canal Expansion Proves Real and Dredging Must Continue," *Maritime Logistics Professional,* July 17, 2017, accessed at https://www.maritimeprofessional.com/blogs/post/the-panama-canal-expansion-proves-real-and-dredging-must-15220 on June 30, 2018.

20. HKTDC Research, "Vietnam's Logistics Market: Overcoming the Challenges," January 28, 2015, accessed at http://economists-pick-research.hktdc.com/business-news/article/Research-Articles/Vietnam-s-Logistics-Market-Overcoming-the-Challenges/rp/en/1/1X000000/1X0A12CI.htm on October 3, 2015,

21. Alexandra Alger, " 'Gray' Watches," *Forbes,* Vol. 160, No. 3, August 11, 1997, p. 151. Matthew B. Myers and David A. Griffith, "Strategies for Combating Gray Market Activity," *Business Horizons,* Vol. 42, No. 6, 1999, pp. 2–8.

22. Deloitte, "Global Powers of Retailing 2015," accessed at https://www2.deloitte.com/content/dam/Deloitte/at/Documents/about-deloitte/global-powers-of-retailing-2018.pdf on July 2, 2018. Suneera Tandon, "A Decade Later, Walmart's Secret e-Commerce Dreams in India are Coming True, *Quartz India,* May 9, 2018, accessed at https://qz.com/1259361/walmart-flipkart-deal-a-timeline-of-walmarts-history-in-india on July 2, 2018.

23. Deloitte, "Global Powers of Retailing 2015," accessed at https://www2.deloitte.com/content/dam/Deloitte/at/Documents/about-deloitte/global-powers-of-retailing-2018.pdf on July 2, 2018.

24. Ibid.

25. Ibid.

26. *Business Standard,* "Retailers Carrefour, Tesco Join Forces in Strategic Alliance," July 2, 2018, accessed on July 2, 2018 at https://www.business-standard.com/article/reuters/retailers-carrefour-tesco-join-forces-in-strategic-alliance-118070200274_1.html

27. Tom Bowley, "Food and Broadline Retailers Crushed by Amazon ……Again," *Stock Charts,* August 25, 2017, accessed at http://stockcharts.com/articles/tradingplaces/2017/08/food-and-broadline-retailers-crushed-by-amazonagain.html on June 29, 2018.

28. shop.mango.com/iframe/faces?state=she_400_US, accessed on October 4, 2015.

29. www.esprit.com, accessed on October 4, 2015.

30. www.harrods.com, accessed on March 12, 2013.

31. Dana-Nicoleta Lascu, Jose Fernandez-Olano, and Thomas D. Giese, "Holiday Shopping: A Cross-Cultural Examination of Spanish and American Consumers," in R. King (ed.), Proceedings of the Fourth Triennial AMS/ACRA National Retailing Conference, 1994, pp. 147–149.

32. Cencosud.com accessed at http://investors.cencosud.com/English/investor-overview/about-us/who-is-cencosud/overview-by-country/default.aspx on june 29, 2018."Falabella (Retail Store,)" *Wikipedia*, accessed at https://en.wikipedia.org/wiki/Falabella_(retail_store) on June 29, 2018. "IKEA Pushes Into South America With Partner Falabella," *Reuters*, May 17, 2018, accessed at https://www.reuters.com/article/us-ikea-falabella/ikea-signs-franchise-agreement-with-falabella-for-peru-chile-and-colombia-idUSKCN1II2W4 on June 29, 2018. Robbie Whelan, "Why So Many Shopping Malls are Being Built in Mexico," *The Wall Street Journal*, February 13, 2018, accessed at   https://www.wsj.com/articles/mexicos-surprising-mall-boom-is-luring-u-s-developers-1518523205 on June 29, 2018. Elizabeth Gonzalez, "Weekly Chart, Latin America's Informal Economy," April 2, 2015, *ASCOA*, accessed at https://www.as-coa.org/articles/weekly-chart-latin-americas-informal-economy on June 29, 2018.

33. Adrianne Pasquarelli, "Retailing Relics Roar Back," *Crain's*, December 8, 2014, accessed at http://www.crainsnewyork.com/article/20141207/RETAIL_APPAREL/141209863/retailing-relics-roar-back on October 6, 2015; Andrew Ness, "Retail Space to Let," The China Business Review, Vol. 26, No. 3, May/June 1999, pp. 44–49; and "China: Shanghai Retail Sector in Transition," International Market Insight Reports, July 26, 1999, pp. 1–4.

34. http://corporate.walmart.com/our-story/our-business/international, accessed on October 5, 2015.

35. Chris Isidore, "Amazon Didn't Kill Toys R Us, Here's What Did," *CNN Money*, March 15, 2018, accessed at http://money.cnn.com/2018/03/15/news/companies/toys-r-us-closing-blame/index.html on June 29, 2018.

36. Deloitte, "Global Powers of Retailing 2015," accessed at https://www2.deloitte.com/content/dam/Deloitte/at/Documents/about-deloitte/global-powers-of-retailing-2018.pdf on July 2, 2018.

37. http://help.samsclub.com/app/answers/detail/a_id/278/~/sam's-club-international, accessed on October 4, 2015.

38. https://shop.pricesmart.com/cr/en/investor, accessed on July 1, 2018.

39. Lynda Radosevich, "Going Global Overnight," InfoWorld, Vol. 21, No. 16, April 19, 1999, pp. 1–3. "Sticking to the Web," Chain Store Age, Vol. 74, No. 7, July 1998, pp. 153–155.

40.*Global Internet Report 2015*, Internet Society, accessed at http://www.internetsociety.org/ globalinternetreport/assets/download/IS_web.pdf on October 8, 2015.

41. Emiko Terazono, "BBC and Channel 4 in Talks Over UKTV Stake Media," Financial Times, June 1, 2005, 20. China Venture News, "Saif Partners Picks China TV Home-Shopping Network as the Next Big IPO," August 15, 2005, www.chinaventurenews.com.

42. Elizabeth Holmes, "Why Online Retailers Like Bonobos, Boden, Athleta Mail So Many Catalogs?" *The Wall Street Journal*, April 16, 2014, accessed at http://www.wsj.com/articles/
SB10001424052702304311204579505532568168984 on October 8, 2015.

43. http://www.bodenusa.com/en-US/Products/Quickshop.aspx, accessed on October 8, 2015. http://www.shipton.com, accessed on October 8, 2015.

44. Trefis Team, "How is Avon Trying to Regain Its Position in Latin America," *NASDAQ Newsletter*, September 28, 2016, accessed at https://www.nasdaq.com/article/how-is-avon-trying-to-regain-its-position-in-latin-america-cm686265 on June 29, 2018.

45. Nathan Bomey and Kevin McCoy, "Herbalife Agrees to $200m Settlement with FTC," *USA Today*, July 15, 2016, accessed at https://www.usatoday.com/story/money/2016/07/15/federal-trade-commission-herbalife/87119208 on June 30, 2018.

46. Bruce Einhorn, "Wal-Mart Tries Again in India," *BloombergBusiness*, October 12, 2014, accessed at http://www.bloomberg.com/bw/articles/2014-10-23/wal-mart-struggles-to-crack-retail-market-in-india on October 4, 2015.

47. Mei Fong, "Avon's Calling, But China Opens Door Only a Crack," Wall Street Journal, February 26, 2007, B1.

48. "China: The Grandest Opening Ever," Chain Store Age, Supplement: "Global Retailing," December 1997, pp. 32–35.

49. See Brenda Sternquist, *International Retailing* 2ed., 2007, New York: Fairchild Books and Visuals; and David Reed, "Country Practice," Marketing Week, Vol. 20, No. 4, July 3, 1997, pp. 45–49.

50. Ian Crawford and Sarah Tanner, "Bringing It All Back Home: Alcohol Taxation and Cross-Border Shopping, Fiscal Studies, Vol. 16, No. 2, May 1995, pp. 94–115.

51. Taos Turner and Paul Kiernan, "How Latin America Pays the Price of Protectionism," *The Wall Street Journal*, November 25, 2016, accessed at https://www.wsj.com/articles/how-latin-america-pays-the-price-of-protectionism -1480089781 on June 30, 2018.

52. Connie Robbins Gentry, "Border Malls," Chain Store Age, Vol. 80, No. 4, April 2004, p. 81.

53. Terry Hennessy, "International Flavors," Progressive Grocer, Vol. 78, No. 8, August 1999, pp. 67–73. Adapted from Deloitte, "Global Powers of Retailing 2015," accessed at http://www2.deloitte.com/content/ dam/ Deloitte/global/Documents/Consumer-Business/gx-cb-global-powers-of-retailing.pdf on October 1, 2015; Stores, "2007 Global Powers of Retailing," Deloitte-Touche Tohmatsu: January 1, 2007.

54. Russell Redman, "Kroger to Pilot Unmanned Grocery Delivery Vehicles," *Supermarket News*, June 28, 2018, accessed at http://www.supermarketnews.com/online-retail/kroger-pilot-unmanned-grocery-delivery-vehicles on June 30, 2018.

55. Sharon Terlep and Laura Stevens, "Amazon Buys Online Pharmacy PillPack for $1 Billion," *The Wall Street Journal*, June 28, 2018, accessed at https://www.wsj.com/articles/amazon-to-buy-online-pharmacy-pillpack-1530191443 on June 30, 2018.

56. Courtney Reagan, "Amazon Reveals a New Plan to Deliver More Packages: Recruit People to Run Small-Scale Delivery Services," CNBC, June 28, 2018, accessed at https://www.cnbc.com/2018/06/27/amazon-is-recruiting-entrepreneurs-to-start-delivery-networks.html on June 30, 2018.

57. Adapted from Deloitte, "Global Powers of Retailing 2015," accessed at http://www2.deloitte.com/content/ dam/Deloitte/global/Documents/Consumer-Business/gx-cb-global-powers-of-retailing.pdf on October 1, 2015; Stores, "2007 Global Powers of Retailing," Deloitte-Touche Tohmatsu: January 1, 2007.

Case 11-1 *Mondelēz China's Distribution Challenges*

Kraft Foods China took on a new identity recently, as Mondelēz China. The company handles all of Kraft's former global snacks business and all the Kraft grocery brands outside of the U.S. Kraft had not yet brought its full product line to China before the changeover, but this is likely to be a priority for the new company, Mondelēz. Kraft's presence in China had increased many times over, with its China business growing from $200 million to $1 billion from 2007 until 2012, before Mondelēz took over the Kraft brands.

One of the greatest challenges for the company remains distribution. Years back, in 2004, Tom Shu, Kraft Foods' warehouse and distribution manager in China, decided to work along with hundreds of other workers, as a day laborer for local logistics companies and to find out how the companies were running the business. He felt that it was important to find out as much as possible about potential logistics providers because he needed to rely on them to handle the movement of Kraft products between production plants, distribution centers, and wholesalers. His insights into China's distribution continue to be useful to Mondelēz today.

Logistics companies are essential for large multinationals and small and medium-sized enterprises alike: They ensure that products arrive on time and in good shape. They also make sure that the manufacturer and the wholesaler do not have to store the product for prolonged periods because this creates additional costs and the potential for merchandise loss. In China, in particular, this is important, as the country's fast economic growth has contributed to serious transport bottlenecks. Although the government attempts to make sure the infrastructure is adequate, building highway networks to adequately serve the needs of the population, it still happens that shipments are stuck in traffic (see Figure 11-16 on next page) or even disappear, as highway robbery of shipments is not unusual.

Kraft partnered with Chinese firms to enter China in the mid-1990s. One of its companies, Kraft Tianmei Foods, in Tianjin, makes Tang instant drink mix and Sugus chews, and the other, Kraft Guangtong Food, in Guangdong, produces Maxwell House coffee. In 2000, as part of the Nabisco acquisition, Kraft gained two more plants, in Beijing and Suzhou, that produce Oreo, Chips Ahoy! and Ritz brands cookies and crackers. Under Mondelēz, the company's portfolio is expanding rapidly today.

Kraft trimmed down its number of regional distribution centers in China from 13 to five to

Figure 11-16: *China has invested massively to improve the road infrastructure. In Beijing, eight-to-ten-lane highways often have traffic jams. In this sprawling city, it is not unusual for a drive across town to take as long as three hours.*   Figure 11-17 *Local officials in China often request additional fees from truck drivers, delaying them and making it hard for them to reach their destination on time. At toll stops, trucks tend to take much longer than other vehicles.*

reduce costs. Each center has networks radiating into several neighboring provinces that are managed by third-party logistics, providing warehousing service and delivering goods to Kraft's designated wholesalers around China. One strategy that has helped the company is to hire mid-size logistics companies, rather than to go with the top companies. In its relationship with the logistics firms, Kraft wanted to be their number one client, to ensure that the company's needs were met first. In China, if a company is the third or fourth largest client, its orders are often delayed when there is a shortage of vehicles.

Mondelez continues to have rigorous delivery and storage standards. Products are sealed in dry-food containers for transport. Once a sales manager approves an order, the logistics firm has only one to three days to deliver, which is not a problem in the United States, but it is in China where roads are often narrow and where local officials often demand additional fees from truck drivers (see Figure 11-17). The reason for the short delivery time is that the company insists on keeping its inventory down at its five warehouses. The highest cost incurred by distribution centers is attributed to inventory, not to management fees.

Another logistics challenge that Mondelēz faces in China is the pilfering of goods transported by rail. Often dozens of boxes are missing at destination. With rail, the company does not have many choices other than to keep its fingers crossed — or to hide the more expensive goods at the bottom of the container.

Yet another challenge is that China is clamping down on overloaded trucks, which will take a big bite out of the company's bottom line. Trucks drive around China with huge loads, a practice adopted by logistics companies to keep costs down, but which poses a threat to road safety. Now, these companies are forced to distribute the same loads over two or three trucks, increasing their costs.

Sources: P. Jinoy Jose, "Growth for Its Own Sake is Dangerous," *Businessline*, August 3, 2014, accessed at abicomplete/docview/1550729899/C2CABE6A5B6A4ABFPQ/3?accountid=14731 on September 29, 2015; Cui Rong, "Privileged Position," *Far Eastern Economic Review*, Vol. 167, No. 31, August 5, 2004, pp. 46–48; "Getting a Foothold in China: Kraft Foods Works on Improving Its Recipe for Distributing Goods," *The Wall Street Journal*, August 3, 2004, A9.

Analysis Suggestions:

1. What types of products in company's product mix can it transport by truck? What are the advantages and disadvantages of truck transportation for the company's China operations?

2. What types of products in the company's product mix can it transport by rail? What are the advantages and disadvantages of rail transportation for the company's China operation?

Case 11-2 Shipping Doo Kingue

Doo Kingue is a baby mountain gorilla, a member of one of the two most endangered species of apes in the world. There are only approximately 880 mountain gorillas alive today, all in the wild in the mountainous forests of northwest Rwanda, southwestern Uganda, and eastern Democratic Republic of Congo. Mountain gorillas in this region are constantly threatened by poaching, continuous encroachment on the national parks for agricultural use, extensive harvesting of wood for fuel, and a landscape covered with land mines as a result of fighting between the different tribes in the region. Doo Kingue, whose tribe perished as a result of water contamination, was able to survive — barely — and is currently experiencing a difficult-to-treat pulmonary infection.

The director of Karisoke Research Center in Volcano National Park in Hawaii, founded by the late American anthropologist Dian Fossey in 1968 and run by the Dian Fossey Gorilla Funds, a U.S. nongovernmental organization, recently approached the National Zoo in Washington, D.C., and asked for help. The Center obtained permission from the regional government of Ruhengeri and the national government of Rwanda to send the gorilla to the National Zoo, provided the zoo takes responsibility for shipping and hospitalization. John James, one of the directors of conservation and science at the zoo, is excited about having a mountain gorilla for its primate exhibit, and Doo Kingue seems like the ideal candidate.

John's plan is to work with one of the transportation companies doing business in sub-Saharan Africa, to bring the gorilla quickly and painlessly to Washington, D.C., and to start aggressive treatment on the pulmonary infection. Clearly, in this decision, time is of the essence. His staff is familiar with some of the companies that provide quick, reliable service for transporting animals, ensuring that they are transported safely to zoos whose mission is focused on animal welfare and on maintaining the earth's biodiversity (see Figure 11-17).

One of the companies he is considering is Live Animal Transport Services (www.pettransport.com), a company with expertise in the relocation of pets and animals, offering services that include housing, transporting, and preparing relevant health certificates and permits. Live Animal Transport Services is a member of the American Zoo Association (AZA), the International Animal Transportation Association (IATA), the International Pet and Animal Transport Association (IPATA), the American Animal Sciences Association (AALAS), the United States Animal Health Association (USAHA), and the U.S. Air Forwarders Association.

Another company that seems a viable candidate for the transportation job is FedEx (www.fedex.com). FedEx has, for example, donated the use of its express transportation network and relocated six endangered polar bears from San Juan, Puerto Rico, to their permanent zoo homes. The company flew the bears from San Juan to the FedEx Hub in Memphis, Tennessee, onboard a DC-10 aircraft. Later in the day, the bears were transloaded to three other aircraft in Memphis to fly to their final destinations near Seattle, Washington; Detroit, Michigan; and Charlotte, North Carolina. FedEx Express used its customs clearance expertise to expedite the animals through U.S. Customs. John found out that FedEx has considerable experience in transporting animals, including elephants, rhinos, lions and gorillas. The company even transported animals to the National Zoo. FedEx provided air transportation, ground support, and logistic expertise to deliver two giant pandas from Chengdu, China, to the National Zoo in Washing-

Figure 11-17 These endangered Grevy Zebras in the Berlin Zoo originate in Kenya and Ethiopia, where there are only 2,000 animals left, due to habitat loss, water shortages, and hunting. The European Conservation Breeding Program ensures that the offspring of these zebras populate European zoos from Lisbon to Moscow.

ton, D.C. FedEx also transported six rare white tigers from Memphis, Tennessee, to Bangkok, Thailand, to ensure that work could continue on an endangered species breeding program.

Sources: WWF Global, "Mountain Gorilla," accessed at http://wwf.panda.org/what_we_do/
endangered_species great_apes/gorillas/mountain_gorilla/ on October 3, 2015; Valerie May, "Animals on the
Move," *Smithonian* Zoogoer, 39(1) 2010, p. 1; http://www.zooberlin.de/index.php?id=210&tx_ttnews[bckPid]
=12&no_cache=1&tx_ttnews [tt_news]=953 (accessed July 12, 2012); www.scienceinafrica.co.za; Paul R. Murphy
and James M. Daley, "Profiling International Freight Forwarders: An Update," *International Journal of Physical
Distribution Logistics Management*, Vol. 31, No. 3, 2001, pp. 152–168; www.fedex.com

Analysis Suggestions:

1. Weigh the advantages and disadvantages of using Live Animal Transport Services and FedEx to transport Doo Kingue to Washington, D.C.

2. Arrange for intermodal transportation for Doo Kingue from Ruhengeri, Rwanda, to Kigali, the capital city of Rwanda, and to the United States. Attempt a few routes by looking at airlines' websites, at the Live Animal Transport Services site, and the FedEx site to find out what markets they serve. Find out how animals can be transported downtown to the National Zoo from Dulles Airport outside of Washington, D.C.

Case 11-3 Stefanel Canada

Jean Luc Rocher, formerly with a leading department store in Montreal, is contemplating opening a clothing specialty store with European flair that would appeal to the city's large middle class. In his many years with various specialty retailers and department stores, he noted the strong appeal of European stores to the local market.

Stylish department stores abound. Holt Renfrew, for instance, founded as a hat shop in Quebec City, is known for its many exclusive designers, branded lines, and its Holt Renfrew Private Brand collections. Also owned by the British Selfridges Group is another popular luxury department store, Ogilvy, soon to be the epicenter of Montreal's luxury market with over 220,000 square feet of high-end offerings. L'Aubainerie offers excellent product selections at competitive prices. Other popular department stores are La Baie d'Hudson and Hoda. In addition, numerous specialty clothing stores draw Canadian consumers and Montreal visitors alike: Gap, Benetton, Abercrombie & Fitch, and Canadian clothing shops are among many retailers present in the city.

Jean Luc knows that Montreal is a mature market for clothing stores but believes that there is sufficient demand for a clothing store that carries with it personality, as well as a history of success in Europe. Ever since his last visit to Europe, where he shopped at Stefanel, a clothing specialty store on Rue de Rennes, in Paris, and on Theatinerstrasse in Munich, Jean Luc has contemplated the idea of bringing the popular chain to Canada.

Stefanel started more than 40 years ago in Ponte di Piave, close to Venice, Italy, where Carlo Stefanel produced knitwear in his factory, the "Maglificio Piave." At first, the company sold its products through Italian wholesalers. In the 1970s, the company diversified to offer sportswear, denimwear, and prêt-à-porter collections, selling the merchandise in modern, stylish retail outlets. The company continues to produce knitwear, which is its core business, in a plant in Salgareda, Italy. In 2000, Stefanel further expanded into Germany in a take-over of Hallhuber GMBH, a clothing retail chain in Munich, and it has a 50 percent stake in Nuance, the leader in airport retailing.

The company's brand is well known in much of Europe: Its stores in many Western European countries are located centrally, in the main downtown shopping centers. They are stylish and have daring ads. Joakim Jonason, the talent behind the provocative Diesel jeans advertisements, is now in charge of the Stefanel advertising account at MADE, a Leo Burnett company. An ad aimed at movie audiences in Europe opens at dawn at the Boom Boom Circus, where the daughter of the dwarf ringmaster has just spent the night with the bearded lady's husband, resulting in chaos, until the husband wakes up from his dream. The tagline used is "Stefanel. Now you wake up." Stefanel uses "Now" in all its ads, on shopping bags, and on its website.

Stefanel also has several stores in East Asia, in Hong Kong, South Korea, Taiwan, and Thailand, and in the Middle East—in Kuwait and the United Arab Emirates. In 2007, it opened its first store in China, in Shenzhen. Stefanel had actually opened a store in China in 1992, but it did not make any headway then due to the immaturity of the Chinese market. It is working in cooperation with Hong Kong High Fashion Group to subsequently expand to Beijing, Shanghai, Macao, and Hong Kong. It is currently solidifying an expansion in the former Eastern Bloc, into Croatia, the Czech Republic, Slovakia, Slovenia, Romania, and Russia. In the Americas, Stefanel is present only in Los Angeles and Chicago in the United States; in Hamilton, Bermuda; and in Santiago de Chile. A retail franchise in Canada may be attractive to the company and appeal to Canadian consumers as smart, casual clothing with European flair.

Jean Luc Rocher is presently consulting with investors to evaluate the likelihood of success of a Stefanel retail outlet in Montreal. He learned that Stefanel has important and costly requirements for new franchises. For example, the stores must be located on the main commercial streets of cities with a population of at least 50,000; they should have a surface area between 120 and 250 square meters and numerous wide store windows. The franchise is permitted to use only Stefanel's furnishings that distinguish the store from those of other companies. Stefanel would provide the franchisee with architects free of charge; with training seminars for the store's personnel; and with shop-window designs, posters, and images. Stefanel will lease software for sales and inventory analysis and the appropriate hardware to ensure coordination and profitability. Although the company protects franchises in the sense that it limits same-store competition, Stefanel has just partnered with Pino Venture to pursue Internet shoppers.

Jean Luc's questions include: What would be the appropriate expansion strategy into the Canadian market? Would his Montreal store be the first leg in the company's international expansion into Canada? Would Stefanel sell other franchises to competitors? To what extent will Internet sales cannibalize Jean Luc's brick-and-mortar operation? How should he most effectively sell the Stefanel franchise to his investor friends?

Sources: http://www.holtrenfrew.com, accessed on October 4, 2015; http://www.hbc.com, accessed on October 4, 2015; http://www.stefanel.it, accessed on October 4, 2015; Jonathan Rothman, "An Expanding Icon, Ogilvy," *YClass Magazine*, accessed at http://www.yclassmagazine.com/#!ogilvy-montreal/c1rb2 on October 4, 2015; China Retail News, "Stefanel Opens First Store in China," May 9, 2007; Laure Wentz, "The World," Advertising Age, Vol. 73, No. 37, September 16, 2002, p. 14.

Analysis Suggestions

1. Identify the retail category of Stefanel.

2. What are some of its competitors worldwide? How is Stefanel different from its competitors?

3. What is the company's international expansion strategy? How does Jean Luc Rocher's proposal fit into the company's expansion plans?

Chapter 12

International Promotional Mix: Advertising, Publicity, Public Relations and Sales Promotions

Promotion is omnipresent in all countries of the world. Promotion has become part of the world landscape, framing highways, lighting crowded downtowns, projecting glamour on walls of slums, and shading street cafés. Advertisers increasingly prefer the Internet and phone apps to reach prospective customers. Services such as Facebook and Google are accessible around the world, offering new opportunities for global promotional campaigns. Promotion is daily life in Dar es Salaam, in the blazing Shanghai skyline at night, and on famous avenues of wanton consumption in Buenos Aires and Manhattan. Promotion is condemned for creating unaffordable consumption desires and celebrated for its creativity and for setting new trends. Unilever can claim both, based on the following illustration of the Dove and Axe campaigns.

Unilever's Advertising Strategy: Dove vs. Axe

"Evolution," Dove's famous viral video, and other new media ads were the big winners at the Cannes Lions International Advertising Festival in 2007. Dove's spot, from Ogilvy, Toronto, was a 60-plus-second spot that barely qualified for the category. It first went viral on the web and garnered more attention than a Super Bowl ad. Dove had the foresight to run the ad just once on TV, so it qualified for the Lions award. The Lions award also reflects a change in the realm of promotion. Most of the awards went to new media (Internet) ads.[1]

The "Evolution" video shows a woman undergoing a complete makeover, from human to billboard model. It presents a succession of stylists poking and lining the face and teasing the hair and a computer, elongating the neck and enhancing the eyes for a billboard-ready look. The ad was part of Dove's "Campaign for Real Beauty." The campaign fights the definition of beauty that uses narrow, stifling stereotypes and tries to build an acceptance that real beauty comes in many shapes, sizes, and ages. The tool the campaign uses is advertising that inspires women and society to think differently about what is defined as beautiful. In the campaign, Dove — a Unilever company specializing in skin, body cleansing, and hair care products — uses the "Evolution" video, as well as other advertisements on television, in magazines, and Internet advertising, to portray women older than 50 as beautiful, whether they are nude or dressed up or down. The company websites in most of Europe, Australia, and New Zealand, as well as in Japan, South Korea, Chile, Canada, and the United States, portray women of all sizes, ethnicities, and ages, with wrinkles, moles, pimples and all. In the Romanian website, the Dove campaign asked women to submit a photo that indicates how beautiful they are for a contest where, if selected, they would win a cruise on the Mediterranean.[2] (continued...)

Interestingly, in 2012 Unilever received the Creative Effectiveness Grand Prix at the Cannes Lions International Advertising Festival for its Axe "Excite" campaign, portraying voluptuous, sexy angels falling upon a small town from the heavens, walking until they stop in front of a man wearing Axe deodorant, and one by one, they rip off their halos and smash them. The tagline states, "Even Angels Will Fall." Unilever, through its advertising agency, BBH London, treaded aggressively into a territory where women were presented in all of the 75 countries where Unilever sells Axe as victims of men's irresistible charms.

The Axe ad used "Bom Chicka Wah Wah," a musical expression associated with pornographic movies, and interpreted as a slang term for a sexual encounter: When a thin, attractive woman smelled Axe on a man nearby, she would blurt out "Bom Chicka Wah Wah." In its online campaign, the company webpages showed a map depicting areas where women fell prey to Axe; viewers were asked to find an area on a local map where they could click and watch women lose their minds... and their clothes.[3]

Much like the Dove advertisements, the Axe ads went viral and received much publicity – positive and negative. When comparing Unilever's two contradictory campaigns, Dove's Real Beauty and Axe's Excite, many are accusing the company of hypocrisy. Is this good marketing? In 2015, a Dove campaign calls for women to renounce the media's narrow, unattainable standards of beauty and to replace them with a message of female empowerment. However, this campaign hit a false note: *The Guardian* reacted to it as follows: "So, sorry to break it to everyone, but your Deep Moisture Nourishing Body Wash doesn't really care about you or your self-esteem. And your cucumber and green tea deodorant doesn't give a damn about nurturing your confidence. Ultimately the aim of campaigns like this is not for you to choose beautiful, it's for you to choose Dove."[4]

The previous Dove/Axe examples illustrate Unilever's creative and controversial approach to promotion, from advertising to sales promotion, to public relations. This chapter discusses the international promotional mix and the international communication process. Of the mix items, the chapter focuses on advertising and illustrates advertising formats, practices, and infrastructure-related issues around the world.

12-1 The International Promotional Mix

The components of the international promotional mix are international advertising, international sales force management, international sales promotion, and public relations and publicity (see Figure 12-1). Companies use the promotional mix to communicate with international consumers about their products and services. In the process of expanding internationally, companies are faced with numerous challenges to their plans for communicating with the world's consumers. Many of the challenges are attributed to differences in culture. As described in Chapter 5, "Cultural Influences on International Marketing," understanding the norms, motivations, attitudes, interests, and opinions of the target market is crucial to company success in marketing to

Figure 12-1 *The International Promotional Mix*

and communicating with different cultures around the globe. Companies also must be prepared to handle the challenges presented by the local media, local advertising infrastructure, and the different layers of government regulating all aspects of communication with the target market.

Section 12-2 describes the international communication process, Section 12-3 presents the topic of international advertising, Section 12-4 addresses *International Publicity and Public Relations*, Section 12-5 addresses *Consumer Sales Promotion Strategies* and Section 12-6 addresses *International Trade Promotion Strategies*. Chapter 13, "International Personal Selling and Personnel Management," will address the remaining element of the international promotional mix.

12-2 The International Communication Process

The international communication process involves using the entire promotional mix to communicate with the final consumer (see Figure 12-2). Regardless of the elements of the promotional mix involved, the communication essentially has the same format. The international sponsor (sender), usually represented by an advertising agency, encodes the sponsor's message into words and images. The message is then translated into the language of the target market and transmitted through a channel of communication, or medium, to the international consumer in the target market (receiver). The medium may be a nonpersonal medium:

· A print medium, such as a newspaper, magazine, billboard, pamphlet, or a point-of-purchase display

· A broadcast medium, such as television and radio

· An interactive medium, such as a website, a computer terminal on the retailer's premises, and increasingly via an app on personal communication devices.

Alternatively, the channel may be a personal medium:

· A salesperson calling on a supplier or a door-to-door salesperson calling on consumers

· A telemarketer calling on consumers (telemarketing)

· A trade show, where one can address questions to an individual who is knowledgeable about the product

Figure 12-2: *The International Communication Process*

The international consumer (receiver) receives the message and decodes it into meaning. Ideally, the meaning of the decoded message should be identical to the meaning of the encoded message. However, noise — all the potential interference in the communication process, particularly noise attributed to cultural differences — can impede communication. During the message transmission and delivery processes, noise can interfere with proper message reception. The sponsor (sender) collects and relies on information regarding the effectiveness of the message (feedback) to evaluate the success of the promotional campaign. Such information may be provided by sales data or by advertising research evaluating message recall rates.

Mikhail Gnatkovskiy/shutterstock.com

Each step of the international communication process presents challenges to the message sponsor beyond those encountered when marketing to home-country consumers. First, when encoding the message, the source determines whether the attitudes, interests, and motivations of consumers in the international target market are different from those in the home-country target market. Manufacturers of Peugeot bicycles in France selling their product in Belgium and the United States need to be aware that consumer motivations behind the purchase differ. In Belgium, the main purpose of using the Peugeot bicycle is transportation. Major cities have bicycle paths on the sidewalks, and pedestrians and automobiles are not allowed to block them. Bicycle paths also have their own signals at intersections. In the countryside, paths, in parallel with the main roads or highways, are reserved for bicycles. A Belgian consumer who purchases a Peugeot bicycle wants a product that is reliable and can perform optimally, regardless of weather. Communication about the product, then, should stress durability, reliability, and quality. In the United States, a Peugeot bicycle is used primarily for recreation. Communication about the product is more likely to be successful if it focuses on a weekend recreational activity and on performance.

Similarly, Pizza Hut in the United States and the United Kingdom is a staple family restaurant for busy families who do not have time to cook. Pizza Hut advertising focuses on deals for the entire family. In Poland, Pizza Hut is the in-place for dinner accompanied by techno music before consumers descend to the downstairs disco in the city of Wroclaw. It is also the place for a business lunch near Warsaw's prestigious Marriott hotel, located strategically between stores selling haute couture. Consequently, communication about Pizza Hut in Poland should not limit itself to a family focus.

When encoding the message, one must ensure that the message is appropriately translated. In the process of translating the message, one should note that language is closely related to advertising strategy. For example, English requires less space in print and less airtime for broadcast advertising. This is one of the reasons it is widely used in advertising (see Figure 12-3 on next page). Translated into German, Dutch, or French, the headline, body copy, and tag line require more space for a print or online advertisement and more airtime for a broadcast ad.

Figure 12-3 *Lucky Strike's cigarettes' English message for German-speaking consumers: "iSmoke" – plays on the statement "I Smoke" and on the name of the trendy iPhone.*

From product name to the entire marketing communication, all must be monitored to ensure that the meanings intended are the meanings conveyed. There is an explosion of naming consultancies, set up as offshoots of advertising agencies, which develop brand names that are intended to work worldwide. Because consumers travel everywhere, it is important that brand names are consistent in any country where they are sold.[5] From names such as the Nova automobile, meaning "no go" in Spanish, to airlines claiming that one will fly "in leather" (translated to "flying naked"), companies have made mistakes when communicating with international consumers.

Sending the message through the appropriate channel is often a challenge. The media infrastructure might be such that the most appropriate medium cannot be successfully used. In countries where mail is less reliable, such as India and many countries in Latin America, it is advisable not to send direct mail containing samples. In other countries where the mailing system is reliable, such as Saudi Arabia, mail might not constitute a traditional medium for sending samples, and a direct mail package might be perceived as suspicious. In Rwanda and Burundi, for the last several decades, radio has been the primary broadcast medium; however, international brands are rarely advertised on this medium. To reach the mass market in these two countries, the primary appropriate communication medium has been the billboard. Furthermore, it is preferable that the advertisement has few words and relies on pictorials to convey the message because many target consumers are illiterate. However, the Internet is inching toward a 10 percent penetration rate in the two countries, and digital marketing might be a viable alternative for communicating with consumers in these countries in the near future.

Latin America represents a growing and appealing market, representing 10 percent of global GDP and a market of 640 million consumers in one of the most urbanized regions in the world. It is also the fourth-largest mobile market in the world and has social media adoption rates higher than the United States. Accordingly, digital and social media are the emerging appropriate channels of communication for sending the message.[6]

The different channels of communication, the programming itself, and noise, as well as audience inattention – another form of noise – could negatively affect the decoding process, such that the target consumer does not fully comprehend the communication. To lessen the impact of these communication impediments, companies do the following:

· Conduct research to evaluate the message in different countries.

· Evaluate the effectiveness of the communication in targeting consumers by using recall tests.

· Evaluate the effectiveness of the communication in getting consumers to purchase the product.

The company then uses this research to modify the message or to design future communication. It should be remembered that, while large multinationals will have extensive in-house market research capabilities, as well as ready access to leading global agencies, the typical small and medium-size exporter (SME) will not. Thus, SMEs often must rely on their in-country sales agents and stocking distributors to develop appropriate advertising strategies. A key point for the exporting SME is to resist the temptation to simply use existing home-country communications, or to just use a basic translation of home-country promotions in an international market. As previously discussed regarding sales and distribution agreements, the SME's home-country communication materials often are inappropriate in international target markets. SMEs must commit to spending the necessary funds to develop promotional strategies tailored to the new international markets.

12-3 Advertising

International advertising is becoming increasingly complex. More local and international companies are competing for consumers who are increasingly sophisticated and demanding. International advertising is defined as a nonpersonal communication by an identified sponsor across international borders, using broadcast, print, or interactive media.

12-3a The Media Infrastructure

The media infrastructure provides different challenges in countries of different levels of economic development. And, even though the media infrastructure is essentially the same in most industrialized countries, challenges still arise in terms of business practices; a medium might not be considered appropriate for advertising. For example, newspapers might not constitute the right medium for advertising a particular product in one country, whereas, in other countries, advertising a particular type of product or service might be restricted or prohibited in media, such as television.

Here would be a good place to note that, in some countries, the choice of particular broadcast, print, or interactive media for advertising or sales promotion is actually a secondary consideration. In Latin America, studies continue to show that consumers are most likely to trust personal recommendations from friends and family. Branded websites were ranked second. One possible interpretation is that these numbers reflect the very high importance Latin Americans place on relationships with family and friends. Latin Americans tend to be very loyal to trusted local and international brands. While social media, broadcast communications, etc. currently rank much lower in the trust index, their standing will undoubtedly rise as personal communication devices expand market penetration in the region.[7]

Media infrastructure challenges are discussed next. However, one additional caution is in order: It is not just the infrastructure that poses challenges in a target market, but even the status of promotion in industry, the extent to which management considers promotion to be an important strategic tool may create obstacles to communication. For example, until the 1990s, advertising was held in low regard in Germany and that posed difficult for businesses that needed a comprehensive communication strategy.

Media Challenges

Some of the challenges firms encounter on the media front are availability, reliability, restrictions, and costs.

Media Availability

An important issue facing the international marketing manager is media availability, the extent to which the media needed for a particular communication exist locally, and if they do exist, how they can be used as needed for the company communication. Certain types of media simply might not be available in a company's target markets. In many countries in sub-Saharan Africa, for example, there are few local television stations, or there may be one or two government-owned or controlled stations that do not permit advertising or that limit advertising to certain times. Although some television owners might have access to online distribution or to international satellite television, especially in the emerging markets in Asia and Latin America, many more cannot afford a satellite dish or a subscription to cable television. Access to these consumers, then, is limited. And, even though more and more consumers have access to Internet advertising worldwide, such access primarily favors consumers from more developed countries, or wealthy consumers and government employees from developing countries. See the following example of media in the Democratic Republic of Congo and Angola.

Media in Angola and the Democratic Republic of Congo [8]

Angola, in southern Africa, has a rapidly growing media sector in a rapidly growing economy. The government is still grappling with the notion of a free media. There are 20 television sets and 68 radio sets per 1,000 people. The state controls all media with a nationwide reach, including the radio, which is the prevalent medium outside the capital city, Luanda. The *Jornal de Angola*, the daily newspaper, and the main television service TPA are both state owned, as is Radio Nacional de Angola (RNA), the only medium that broadcasts in indigenous languages, such as Bantu. Fewer than a dozen private radio stations operate in cities, and a similar number of private weekly newspapers, but they have a limited reach. TV Zimbio is a private television channel. There are over 4.5 million Internet users. Cinema is not a viable advertising medium as there are too few cinemas available, but outdoor advertising offers a full range of opportunities.

In comparison, the Democratic Republic of Congo in eastern Africa is a vast country with a large and comprehensive media industry. There are 20 TV sets and 358 radios per 1,000 people, 50 TV stations, 3 national (one government owned and two private), whereas the rest are regional, mostly private, television stations. The United Nations Mission in DR Congo and a Swiss-based foundation, Fondation Hirondelle, operate Radio Okapi, which aims to bridge political divisions. The BBC broadcasts in five cities, and Radio France Internationale is the most popular news station. There are 170 radio stations, 13 government-owned. There are 175 newspapers and magazines, as well as French and Pan-African magazines. Cinema here is also not a viable advertising medium, but outdoor advertising offers a full range of opportunities. There are more than one million Internet users.

In both countries, consumers who can afford satellite and other pay TV services have access to numerous programs, including programming from the U.S., such as the MTV Base Africa channel, a 24-hour, English-language music television channel, reflecting the tastes and interests of African youths through African and international music videos, primarily rap and hip-hop. MTV is using local management teams to create and market programming that connects with the local audiences. It is currently broadcasting to 48 countries in sub-Saharan Africa, reaching approximately 1.3 million households via the multichannel operators DStv, Trend TV, CTNL, and FSTV.[9]

Media Reliability

Media reliability, the extent to which the existing media reliably reach the target consumer in the intended format and within the intended time frame, is also an important consideration. In some cases, media may be unreliable. Magazine or newspaper issues might not be printed on time, or publishers might accept more advertisements than they can print. The quality of the medium itself

Alf Ribeiro/shutterstock.com

may be questionable. Local newspapers might not be of a high enough quality to print advertising for a global brand. Television stations might go off the air indefinitely at inopportune times, such as when a company's advertisement is scheduled to air. This often happens to small television stations that compete with government stations for viewers' attention.

Media Restrictions

Media restrictions refer to the different limitations that existing media impose on the sponsor. For example, the media could limit the types and number of advertisements aired or published. As mentioned in Chapter 5, "Cultural Influences on International Marketing," advertising in a number of Islamic countries might not permit the portrayal of women, whereas in China and other countries, the media do not readily encourage the advertising of feminine hygiene products. Airtime might be limited as well, and advertising might be clustered and separated from editorial content in newspapers or magazines or from television programming. Many television stations in Europe and South America, broadcast television advertising only between programs, in clusters. Consumers typically choose to engage in other activities during that time. In these countries, firms that need to communicate with visuals in broadcast media may benefit from movie advertising. In Europe, cinema advertisements are shown before films to a captive audience; viewers see about 25 minutes of advertising and just five minutes of movie trailers. Films also have an intermission, when viewers are urged to purchase products that the movie theater offers (soft drinks, popcorn and the like). In many countries where the literacy rate is low, advertising is primarily limited to billboards that display primarily images rather than words, as well as the company logo and brand name.

Media scheduling also constitutes a restriction. Lag times between the submission of the advertisement and printing could reach as much as one year for some publications, primarily due to space restrictions allotted to advertising. Also, a contract that requires a publication or a television station to print or air an advertisement on a particular date is not backed by guarantees in many countries.

Due to the many restrictions imposed on broadcast media, many businesses targeting emerging markets are increasingly using digital media.

Media Costs

Media costs differ greatly among countries, and even within a particular country. Factors that account for this difference range from income per capita of a target market and competition for media by advertisers, to firm status (a local firm is charged less than an international firm in Eastern European countries, China, Cuba, and Vietnam).

Costs are high in countries where the advertising campaign must be translated into multiple languages. India is an interesting case in point. A campaign aimed at a more educated consumer can be communicated effectively in either Hindi or English. To reach the masses in southern India and penetrate this target market, however, translating the advertisements into Malealam, Tamil, and Telegu would be important.

Figure 12-4: Kiosks have many formats. Some are used just for the display of advertising, while others are used for the purpose of retailing – the latter might also carry advertisements.

Media Formats, Features, and Trends around the World

Advertising Posters on Kiosks and Fences: Advertising posters appear on kiosks and fences in the United States to a more limited extent than in much of the rest of the world. In the United States, some kiosks display neighborhood announcements, and construction fences in larger cities display advertisements for plays, concerts, and art exhibits. In much of the rest of the world, especially in low- and medium-income countries, kiosks display large advertisements for the international products they sell, and less prominent advertising for local products and services. Kiosks are valuable and relatively inexpensive communication venues for multinationals (see Figure 12-4). Some kiosks where products are sold may be required to have posters displayed in exchange for having the rights to carry particular brands.

Fences and other display structures are omnipresent in international capitals and small towns alike (see Figure 12-5). In France, the affichiste movement of modern art, whose works are displayed in major museums worldwide, used layers of posters that had been displayed for decades and then torn off walls and placed on canvas.

Advertising on Outdoor Umbrellas: In the United States, outdoor umbrellas, if they contain any information at all, typically display the name of the restaurant where they are located. In other locations worldwide, umbrellas display international brand names, such as Marlboro, Coca-Cola, Pepsi, or regional brands, like Sagres (see Figure 12-6 on next page).

The Omnipresent Billboard: Although billboards are quite common in the United States, in other parts of the

Figure 12-5: Advertisements are ever present in large urban areas.

world they dominate the landscape. Examples of billboard advertisements include elegant advertisements for Coca-Cola in Russia and at the railway station in Barcelona, Spain; ads for new housing developments that promise the good life in Shanghai, where they are allowed (in Beijing, there is always an effort on the part of local government to ban them); or for a new movie in Beijing, just outside the movie theater where it is playing. An especially interesting development is the fact that, increasingly, local ads are of comparable quality and compete effectively with ads of leading multinational firms. This new development is attributed to the proliferation of computer technology and lower technology costs.

Smaller billboards are used in captive environments such as bus and metro stations. Figure 12-7 portrays a billboard used in a bus station.

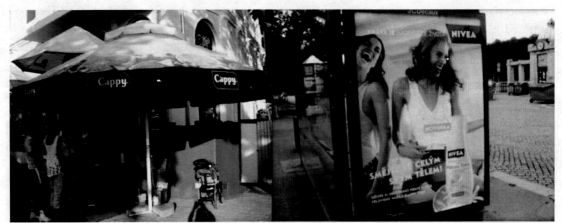

Figure 12-6 *Outdoor umbrellas in Poland compete with colorful local ads and public information.*

Figure 12-7 *Billboards are common in train and bus stations.*

In the booming Hispanic/Latino markets in the United States, the two major Spanish-language television networks are Univision and Telemundo. Programming from both networks is also readily available in Latin America. Telemundo is owned by media giant Comcast and is part of their NBC Universal Division. Univision and Telemundo offer news, entertainment, and sports programming. Telemundo successfully bid $600 million for the Spanish-language world broadcasting rights for the 2018 and 2022 World Cup matches. A staple of television viewing in Hispanic households in the U.S. and Latin America has been the *telenovela*, a racier form of the traditional soap opera. Advertisers have traditionally flocked to these *telenovelas*. In 2018, both Univision and Telemundo began offering edgier and more violent fare in a bid to capture a larger portion of the all-important 18-49 viewing market and their advertising dollars. Some of the newer story lines have been referred to as *narconovelas.* [13]

Magazines such as *Glamour*, *Cosmopolitan*, and *Mademoiselle* are published in languages ranging from Mandarin and Italian to Polish and Japanese. These magazines are vehicles for global, regional, and local advertising campaigns of multinational companies.

Infomercials and Television Shopping Networks

Infomercials and television shopping networks once were primarily a North American phenomenon. Currently, infomercials and television shopping channels exist in much of the industrialized world and in many emerging markets. Not only have QVC and the Home Shopping Network expanded in Europe, Latin America, and Asia, but also local competition is growing rapidly. Home Order Television (HOT) in Germany has created a strategic alliance with Quelle, the catalog store, selling its products to television shoppers, and Acorn in China is the leading local shopping channel in this rapidly growing sales medium.

English in Local Advertising

Section 12-2, "The International Communication Process," stressed some of the benefits of using English for advertising. Other reasons for using English, particularly in advertising by local firms to local consumers, are to stress a cosmopolitan attitude and to endow a product or service with status. Words such as "very quick" are used in advertising for a tire repair service (vulcanizacion) in Ecuador and "super wonderful" to describe the travel bags sold by a company in Poland. This is true also for product and service brand names, such as the Romanian-American University and American Gold for a brand of gold-plated jewelry, when the products or services really have little to do with the Americas. Figures 12-8 through 12-10 show some examples of advertisements using English in non-English–speaking countries, aimed at local consumers. Also, they show some examples of English names for products and retail establishments appealing to local consumers in non-English–speaking countries.

Figure 12-8 (left) Use of English in Estonia, appealing to Estonian consumers, promoting Big Milk ice cream.

Figure 12-9 (above) Swedish brand Zewa sells toilet paper and advises customers, in English, that it is a "big pack" and suggests that they should "open here."

Figure 13-10 A bus advertisement for Chinese consumers: La Maison (with a wants-to-be-French-but-it's-not spelling) and advertised in English: New! opening . . . for a restaurant-cum-cabaret establishment.

Product Placement

Product placement involves placing brands in movies with the purpose of promoting the products to viewers. Studies have found that product placement can produce a greater level of advertising recall than television advertising.[11] Year after year, films exported by the United States have swept the globe and, as a result of the world dominance of Hollywood films, product placement is likely to be a venue providing high exposure for international brands.

However, there are restrictions against product placement. The most restrictive area has been the European Union (EU), where, until recently, product placement has been illegal in many EU countries. And, in spite of changes in EU law in 2007, Hollywood's product-placement continues to be problematic in some countries, whereas, in countries like Denmark, product placement continues to be popular for local shows.

Product Placement in the European Union

In 2007, the European Union's (EU) national governments approved sweeping changes to the bloc's television-broadcasting rules, extending the amount of advertising allowed and allowing product placement in TV shows. The rules now allow product placement, although only for certain programs, such as movies and film series, sports, and light-entertainment programs, and under certain conditions. For example, the products featured must not be too prominent and must come with repeated disclaimers to viewers. In addition, they are banned from children's programs, news programs, and documentaries.

These restrictions apply to all EU programming, including shows created outside the EU, which would mean that it would be difficult or even illegal for broadcasters to show many U.S. programs, which are often laden with product placements. However, member states are able to opt out of such provisions, allowing free reign to product placement, or they can simply opt out of any provisions that might limit product placement.

EU film and TV companies have lobbied hard against product placement, and, in general, for imposing tough limits on Hollywood imports. Of additional concern to European television broadcasters is that the EU has instituted few Internet regulations, and now the broadcasters are facing increased competition from services such as YouTube and mobile-multimedia companies, which places them at a competitive disadvantage.[14]

Advertising Regulations

Advertisers encounter numerous restrictions in their efforts to deliver communication to consumers worldwide. Most regulations are imposed by national (host-country) governments. Alternatively, local firms have established traditions and self-imposed regulations that must be observed by newcomers to the local advertising scene. Among advertising restrictions are the following:

· *Comparative advertising* — In the past, continental Europe condemned comparative advertising as denigration and unfair competition. However, Directive 2006/114/EC of the European Parliament and of the European Council of 12 December, 2006, acknowledged that comparative advertising, when it compares material, relevant, verifiable, and representative features and is not misleading, may be a legitimate means of informing consumers of their advantage. Considerations of comparative advertising should determine if the advertising is detrimental to competitors, distorts competition, or has an adverse effect on consumer choice. It is required that such advertising compare "like with like" – meaning goods and services meeting the same needs or intended for the same purpose and that they objectively compare the products or services. Comparative advertising should take EU trademark law into consideration. As such, firms are not allowed to use competitors' trademarks and other copyrighted materials.[15]

Worldwide, comparative advertising is typically not used, even if laws allow it. Consumers may have difficulty understanding comparative ads. For example, a company that engages in noncomparative advertising in the Arab world may be taking a risk, because the Arabic consumer is not accustomed to them. This lack of exposure to comparative ads, and not a lack of sophistication, may lead to confusion between the advertised brands and ruin the sponsor's message.[16]

· *Advertising to children* — This is a contentious issue in many high-income countries. In the EU, the European Union Directive Concerning Television Broadcasting does not permit advertising that directly exhorts minors to buy a product or a service, that directly encourages minors to persuade their parents to purchase the goods advertised,

that exploits the trust minors place in adults, or that shows minors in dangerous situations. Local law restricts advertising to children further: French law limits the use of children as endorsers in advertising and prohibits the use of children's heroes as endorsers. The French Authority for the Professional Regulation of Advertising (ARPP), the primary regulatory body for marketing communications, requires advertising to be clearly identified as a marketing communication. Advertising is not permitted to undermine the authority of parents and educators, trivialize violence, abuse, or danger, or give the impression that they are acceptable. Regulations regarding advertising targeting children are very specific; the ads:

- Should be at the children's level of understanding;
- Should not mislead about product traits, value, or performance;
- Should not suggest that owning the product would offer an advantage;
- Should not create urgency, suggesting the product might be indispensable;
- Should not suggest that the family can afford it by using terms to indicate a low price.[17]

· *Advertising vice products*—More countries ban the advertising of vice products. A European Union directive prohibits all tobacco advertising.[18]

· *Other regulations*—The French have regulations requiring advertisers (and all broadcasters) to keep the language pure and not to use English terms or anglicized French terms (Franglais). Singapore does not permit advertising that is sexual in nature. The use of sex in advertising is also banned in most Islamic countries. Other challenges are posed by the need to copyright the advertising message in different languages in countries where multiple languages are spoken.

One of the most restrictive marketing regulations in Europe ended in December 2006, a ban on television advertising by supermarkets, hypermarkets, department stores, and other merchants. In January 2007, retailers responded like shoppers, rushing to advertise on television. The purpose of the ban was to safeguard advertising revenue for French local newspapers and to protect small retailers from advertising blitzes by large chains. In 2004, the European Commission forced France to drop the restriction on retailers.

France continues to uphold a restriction regarding the television advertising of films. This restriction is intended to protect French movie producers from big-budget Hollywood marketing.

Before this regulation expired, retailers spent 38 percent of their budget on print ads, 34 percent on radio ads, and 23 percent on outdoor advertising. Television advertising by retailers will have a negative impact on the other media. The print media, however, may retain a competitive edge: To protect them from a free-fall of advertising revenue, advertisers are allowed to include detailed information on product prices and sales in newspapers ads but are prohibited from mentioning prices or sales in their television advertisements.[19]

While it is generally true that monitoring advertising to children is not a top priority in many emerging markets, there is a major concern in Latin America over childhood obesity, considered a pandemic disease. Mexico has the highest rate of childhood obesity in the world, and also the highest per-capita consumption of soda in the world. A high percentage of television food and beverage advertisements in Latin America is directed at children and the family, and this heavy exposure to advertisements for processed foods, snack foods, and sodas has directly led to an increased purchase of these products. This has resulted in new calls for government regulation of advertisements geared towards children. Mexico already steps to reduce the number of allowed television commercials for soft drinks and confectionery items, in favor of products with higher nutrition content. High-calorie food and soda ads are banned on network and cable TV from 2:30 P.M. – 7:30 P.M. on weekdays and 7:30 A.M. to 7:30 P.M. on weekends. Similar restrictions were placed on ads in movie theaters.[20]

12-3b The Advertising Infrastructure

Advertising Agencies

The approach to advertising varies from one company to another, and the strategies used by different companies are numerous. Advertising decisions may be determined based on the product strategy. In one example, Henkel, a leading German manufacturer of household and cleaning products, uses a pan-European approach to advertising. The company achieves efficiency in advertising production and advertising impact by identifying how a particular product addresses target market needs; by assigning that specific need or benefit to one product with one brand name; by assigning a brand to one brand manager and to one agency to develop and market; and by not permitting the use of that individual brand's benefit, name, or creative campaign for any other brand in the company.[21] This strategy results in the use of multiple advertising agencies, depending on the brand involved. Alternatively, the choice of the advertising agency in international markets may be based on a long-standing relationship with a particular agency in the home market. An advertising agency

Kzenon/shutterstock.com

could follow a leading global brand anywhere in the world. This has been the case of McCann Erickson, the advertising agency that has been handling the Coca-Cola account in 60 countries since 1942[22] until recently — it was replaced in a number of markets with its competitor, Leo Burnett.

A company can approach its international advertising strategy using one or more of the following options: developing local ads for the international markets in-house; developing ads using local advertising agencies, home-country agencies, or international advertising agencies with local offices; or using a combination strategy. The home-country agency and the in-house options by themselves are not likely to allow for local participation if they are located away from the target market.

International corporations may opt for either of the following strategies for advertising in a target market:

· Hiring local advertising agencies
· Hiring international advertising agencies
· Hiring local advertising agencies to implement international agency messages

Hiring Local Advertising Agencies

A company that uses a localized strategy, targeting each individual market, is more likely to hire a local advertising agency. Hiring a local advertising agency is appropriate, especially when knowledge of the market is important. The Swedish furniture company IKEA, for example, engaged in a branding campaign aimed at the San Diego market. The company left it up to the San Diego IKEA franchise to hire a firm to build the IKEA brand in the San Diego market. It hired AM Advertising, a Los Angeles firm boasting top local talent.[23] As pointed out earlier in this chapter, SME exporters may use a similar strategy, allowing their local sales agent or stocking distributor to hire an in-country agency to develop appropriate advertising and promotional strategies.

In a relatively uniform market, such as the Latin American market, advertisers often use Spanish and Portuguese to communicate with consumers. When a company advertises to the 25 countries of Latin America and the Caribbean, however, it is preferable to translate into each country's regional dialect to avoid presenting the company as an outsider.[24] A local agency could better design the campaign for each individual market. In addition to its knowledge of the local market, a local agency also offers the advantage of being capable of facilitating interaction with local media and government.

On the negative side, the quality of advertising is not at the level offered by a large international advertising agency. But with the proliferation of technology, local companies, even in developing countries, are increasingly able to provide higher quality graphics, comparable to those produced by larger international advertisers. Nevertheless, if a company decides to hire local advertising agencies, it will not be able to coordinate a global, standardized advertising campaign.

Hiring International Advertising Agencies

If a company uses a standardized (global) strategy for its products or services, it is more likely to use an international agency with local offices that can manage advertising in the respective markets. Most of the leading advertising agencies have branches in important international markets. In Eastern Europe, companies such as Leo Burnett, Young and Rubicam, and Ogilvy & Mather are represented in practically every capital city. For example, J. Walter Thompson is present as J. Walter Thompson/ARK Communications in Prague, the Czech Republic; as Partners J. Walter Thompson Budapest in Hungary; and as Scala JWT Advertising in Bucharest, Romania.

The list of top advertising agency groups worldwide is led by Madison Avenue (New York City) firms (see Table 12-1). Procter & Gamble is the top global advertiser, having topped the advertising spending charts worldwide for years. In 2016, its advertising spending was reported to be $10.5 billion, followed by the South Korean electronics giant, Samsung, at $9.9 billion. Rounding out the top five were European consumer products giants Nestle, Unilever, and L'Oreal. A major story is the huge increase in advertising expenditures by Chinese firms led by Alibaba, the largest Chinese online retailer, internet provider Tencent, and SAIC Motors, the leading Chinese auto production group. In another example of the continued surge in e-commerce, U.S. online retailer Amazon ranked number 11 among top world advertisers, ahead of such U.S. stalwarts as Ford, Coca-Cola, and McDonalds.[25] Most companies are now allocating a significant portion of their marketing budget for online advertising, over traditional methods, and, as a result, agencies are following suit, developing their digital marketing capabilities. The United States continues to dominate the market for online advertising spending with China moving up to number three (see Table 12-2).

Table 12-1 World's Largest Agency Networks

Table 12-2 Countries Spending the Most in Online Advertising

Rank	Company	Worldwide Revenue (US$ billions)	Rank	Country	Media Spending (U.S.$ millions)
1	Accenture Interactive (U.S.)	4.4	1	USA	58.13
2	Young & Rubicam (U.S.)	3.6	2	UK	11.72
3	PWC Digital (U.S.)	3.3	3	China	10.81
4	McCann Worldgroup (U.S.)	3.2	4	Japan	8.32
5	IBM IX (U.S.)	3.0	5	Germany	7.37
6	BBDO Worldwide (U.S.	2.6	6	Australia	5.36
7	Deloitte Digital (U.S.)	2.6	7	France	5.13
8	Publicis Sapient (France)	2.4	8	Russia	4.27
9	Dentsu (Japan)	2.4	9	USA	58.13
10	DDB Worldwide Communications (U.S.)	2.3	10	UK	11.72

Source: *Advertising Age,* "The Agency Report: Consolidated Networks," May 1, 2017, p. 1.

Source: Online advertising revenue in major online advertising markets in 2017 (in billions of US dollars) https://www.statista.com/statistics/246570/largest-online advertising-markets accessed on July 4, 2018.

International advertising agencies benefit from access to the parent company's experience and talent, as well as technology and research capabilities. They also can take advantage of local representatives' expertise and relationships with the media and government. Increasingly, international advertising agencies are present with more than one type of agency in important markets. For example, Rapp Collins Worldwide opened an office of its interactive arm, RAPP Digital, in Brazil. Because Latin America is advanced from the point of view of technology, the market has high potential for creative marketing using interactive services. RAPP worked with BMW to introduce the new Ko Stunt BMW Motorrad, the German automaker's newest motorcycle, by collecting personal stories of participants in the previous São Paulo Motorcycle Trade Show based on the concept "everyone has a story: pilot yours, make life a ride." The stories, collected digitally, were then woven together to present at the motorcycle's formal launch at the Milan's World Motorcycle Exhibition in 2016.[26] In other examples, Grey Global Group is present in Europe with Grey Direct, its direct marketing arm; Grey Desire, a London-based customer relationship management consultancy for Europe;[27] Grey Interactive, GCI (one of the largest public relations firms in the world); and Grey Worldwide, the company's advertising arm.

Hiring Local Advertising Agencies to Implement International Agency Messages

Hiring an international advertising agency with local offices does not preclude the use of local advertising agencies. For example, although Coca-Cola uses leading global agencies to design its message for advertising worldwide, it also encourages each country office to appoint local agencies to implement the brand message. In fact, Interpublic generates ideas at a global level, which are then translated by local marketers as part of Coke's "think global, act local" strategy.[28] International Marketing Illustration 12-1 (on next page) offers insights into the agency choice of one of the corporate sponsors of advertisements, McDonald's.

12-3c The Advertising Strategy

Standardization versus Adaptation in Creating Message Strategies

One of the most important decisions of firms designing their international promotional mix is whether to standardize (globalize) their promotional strategy (standardization of the advertising strategy), to adapt their promotional mix to each country or market (adaptation of the advertising strategy), or to create local campaigns. Practitioners are divided on this issue. Sponsors, as well as advertising agencies, agree that using a standardized strategy world-wide presents substantial advantages. This is most obvious from a cost perspective: Costs are reduced considerably if companies do not need to duplicate the creative effort and the resultant communication campaign in each market. In addition, as product life cycles shrink, companies are pressured to accelerate worldwide rollout of new products. Developing communication strategies for each market would delay launch.[25] Moreover, world consumers are developing common product preferences and increasingly share similar frames of reference with regard to products and consumption because they are exposed to the same sources of influence (broadcast and print media, in particular, as well as blockbuster films and tourists, among others).

High-profile advertisers, including Mercedes-Benz, Hewlett-Packard, Walt Disney, and Coca-Cola, have started, or announced plans to start, worldwide ad campaigns. Some of these marketers have previously eschewed global campaigns or have gone back and forth

International Marketing Illustration 12-1:
The Giant Sponsor and the Small Advertising Boutique

McDonald's surprised the agency world by selecting a small advertising agency to lead its worldwide campaign. It hired the fifteenth largest agency in Germany, Omnicom's Heye & Partner, a company with a reputation for lacking creativity. But Heye, led by chief executive Jurgen Knauss, was able to gain the trust of McDonald's. McDonald's was also ready to take greater risks in its international advertising because its brand outside the United States is relatively young. Today, Heye & Partner is so closely associated with the chain that it is often referred to as the McDonald's agency. Heye also has as clients other top multinationals, such as Johnson & Johnson and Esso (Exxon), but McDonald's, one of the largest ad spenders in the world, is its top client. To best serve this client, Heye employees eat at McDonald's on a regular basis and even work behind the counter.

Going against the German tradition, which shuns humor in advertising, the Heye ads show a man stuck in traffic and a kid in another automobile making faces at him. The man, in revenge, holds up McDonald's fries and eats them demonstratively. This ad is used for most world markets, with exception of the United States. Heye also won the McDonald's competition between several agencies for a tag line— "I'm lovin' it" — and it is used for all the company's ads in English. In another ad, aliens are shown ready to eat humans standing in line at McDonald's, with one urging the other to wait until the humans have eaten the burgers because they taste better afterward. The ads are funny and emotional — and it is difficult to imagine that a German company came up with them. The ad campaign communicates a youthful spirit and the idea that something is changing at McDonald's, something that its franchisees are not especially keen on. Heye also won another award, the GWA Effie award, for the "McDonald's Once One Is One" campaign.

Sources: www.mcdonalds.de/produkte (accessed July 8, 2018); www.mcwww.gwa.de/ Press.1441.0.html, June 2007; Erin White and Shirley Leung, "How Tiny German Shop Landed McDonald's," Wall Street Journal, August 6, 2003, B1; Kate MacArthur, "McD's Sees Growth, But Are Ads a Factor?" Advertising Age, Vol. 74, No. 47, November 24, 2003, p. 3.

360b/shutterstock.com

between local and regional approaches. Now, however, there is clearly a shift in the strategy of multinational firms. Standardization versus adaptation decisions come down to a battle between marketing and sales — marketing emphasizes a global approach, whereas sales insists on being local.[29]

Typically, marketers end up in between, with a consistent overall image, but tailoring the ads for perceived local differences. McDonald's, in the earlier example, has been using this strategy for more than a decade, with its theme "I'm lovin' it."[30] The campaign, however, adapts to appeal to local markets, assuring consumers that McDonald's products are local.

Other companies whose brand identities had become fragmented through regional or country-specific advertising have also moved toward global campaigns. Coca-Cola, for example, has moved to unify its advertising under the theme, "The Coke side of life." Or, companies can have a unique regional theme that appeals to a broad market segment. For

example, Coca-Cola removed its logo from its soda cans in the Muslim world during Ramadan, to encourage people not to judge one another. Its labels then read "Labels are for
cans, not for people."

The auto industry, which has for many years rejected adopting global campaigns,
has also changed its strategy at the insistence of local sales branches. Mercedes hired the
advertising agency BBDO to develop a single global ad campaign for its new C-Class.
Hewlett-Packard rolled out its first global advertising campaign for its personal computer
division, and Disney started a global campaign for its theme parks. This approach makes
sense, as it costs less for one ad agency to create a single global ad campaign than it does
for multiple agencies to create separate campaigns. Moreover, new technology makes it
easier to adapt a global campaign for individual markets, and procurement officials know
this, putting further pressure on agencies to cut costs. Most big marketing campaigns now
include a substantial online presence, and the enormous popularity of social networking
and video-sharing web services means ads and videos quickly zip across borders.[31]

Mercedes-Benz introduced the C-Class
using a comprehensive integrated marketing
campaign, with the slogan "C-for Yourself," developed by the advertising agency BBDO France.
The campaign attempted to convince customers
based on the world of qualities of the new C-Class
sedan, its design, comfort, agility, and safety. Interestingly, Mercedes decided that all communication measures for the C-Class should be geared
toward direct contact with customers and potential buyers. Specifically, magazines and newspapers with high circulation featured ads inviting
customers to test-drive the sedan.[32]

Cinebergshutterstock.com

In Germany, a 30-/40-second television commercial was launched on all prominent
public and commercial stations, featuring the Formula 1 world champion race-car driver Fernando Alonso. At the end of the ad, Alonso, who drives for the Vodafone McLaren Mercedes Formula 1 team, symbolically hands over the keys to a new C-Class to the audience at
home, inviting them to test-drive the vehicle. Mercedes coupled this campaign with the
more local "Exclusive Driving Experience" campaign, which allowed 80 consumers from all
over Europe to experience the C-Class. In Barcelona, participants drove an off-road course
— and King Juan Carlos of Spain and representatives of founding partner Mercedes-Benz
attended the event. Vacationers at Robinson Club Resorts and Westin Hotels & Resorts facilities in Germany, Austria, Scotland, Italy, Spain, Portugal, and Greece were also offered
the opportunity to test drive the new C-Class. In addition to its traditional advertising strategies, Mercedes combined direct communication at driving events with interactive films on
the Internet. The online presentation at www.mercedes-benz.com/c-class allowed viewers
to select the vehicle of their choice and see it displayed against realistic backdrops. The site
also offered several interactive films featuring individuals describing details of the new C-
Class as they took the vehicle for a drive.[33]

Differences between countries, however, might render standardization a challenge,
or even impossible. The following are barriers to advertising standardization:
• The communication infrastructure is one barrier. A particular medium might be inappropriate or not available for advertising.

• International advertising agencies might not serve a particular market.

• Consumer literacy level constitutes another major barrier. Consumers might not be able to read the body copy of the advertisement, so the information conveyed to the consumer should be visual.

• Legal restrictions and industry self-regulation might also impede standardization: Comparative advertising is not permitted in many countries, whereas, in others, such as Korea, Confucianism forbids the public criticism of others.[34]

• Values and purchase motivations differ across countries and cultures, as illustrated in Chapter 5, "Cultural Influences on International Marketing." Targeting consumers with a campaign that stresses the good life, exemplified by driving a luxury car and having a blonde on one's side, might be inappropriate in countries where consumers are living a subsistence existence and just as improper in highly developed, cultured environments. Consumers from collectivist cultures will also question the values suggested by such ads. The decision of whether to standardize is most often contingent on the degree of cultural similarity between the sponsor and the target market. Standardization of communication is recommended when similarity exists between senders and receivers in the communication process.

• Attitudes toward the product or service country of origin create another barrier. Especially in environments where there is some level of hostility toward the United States and its economic and cultural dominance, it might be best not to have an advertising campaign that stresses the product's country of origin.

The elements of the promotional mix are especially difficult to standardize because communication is language- and culture-specific. Latin America presents interesting challenges regarding the standardization versus localization debate for advertising, notwithstanding the common Spanish language. (Portuguese-speaking Brazil is a completely distinct market.) Advertisers should recognize the use of different dialects and accents in the Spanish-speaking Latin American countries. This can be especially important when using voice-over talent in a commercial. In addition, translating English advertisements to Spanish or Portuguese can add up to 20 percent to the recording length, which may necessitate changes to the video images. Finally, many Latin American cultures are more matriarchal than the U.S., and are thus more receptive to female voice-over talent in commercials.[35]

Budgeting Decisions for International Advertising Campaigns

Companies use the following approaches to advertising spending decisions.

Objective-and-Task Method: Companies using the objective-and-task method first identify advertising goals in terms of communication goals such as target audience reach, awareness, comprehension, or even purchase. As a next step, research is conducted to determine the cost of achieving the respective goals. Finally, the necessary sum is allocated for the purpose.

This method is the most popular one used by multinational corporations in the process of deciding on their advertising budgets because it takes into consideration the firms' strategies. A comprehensive international study suggests that this method is more frequently used by firms from Canada and Singapore and less frequently by Swedish and Argentinean firms.[36]

Percent-of-Sales Method: The percent-of-sales method determines the total budget allocated to advertising based on past or projected sales. This method is difficult to adopt for firms entering new markets, which are more likely to benefit from budgeting methods such as competitive parity or objective and task. The problem with this method is that it causes advertising expenditures to decline as sales decline, whereas, at this point, the company should increase advertising spending. For firms that have been in a particular international market for some time, this method is used by almost half of the respondents in a study on transnational advertising practices. This study found that the percent-of-sales method is most popular in Brazil and Hong Kong and less popular in Germany.[37]

Historical Method: Firms using the historical method base their advertising budget on past expenditures, usually giving more weight to more recent expenditures. The percent-of-sales method uses the historical method as a first step, if the percentages allocated to advertising are based on past, rather than projected, sales. This method is not recommended for firms that operate in unstable economic, political, or competitive environments.

Competitive-Parity Method: The competitive-parity method uses competitors' level of advertising spending as benchmarks for a firm's own advertising expenditure. This approach is not recommended for a firm entering a new market and whose brands are not known locally. Moreover, this method suggests that a firm's goals and strategies are identical with those of competitors, which, most likely, is not the case.

Executive-Judgment Method: In the executive-judgment method, executive opinion is used in determining the advertising budget. A third of the responding firms queried in the above-mentioned study reported relying on executive judgment.

All-You-Can-Afford Method: Most small and medium-sized enterprises entering a new market do not have the large budgets of multinational corporations. The all-you-can-afford method best suits the financial limitations of these firms. Unfortunately, this approach completely ignores strategic considerations.

12-4 Publicity and Public Relations

In the past, multinational firms hired advertising agencies and put them in charge of advertising, and the firms themselves handled publicity and sales promotion in-house. Multinationals today hire agencies to coordinate globally all aspects of their communications,

including public relations. All public relations activities, local and international, are contracted to firms with public relations expertise. This fact is readily evident, especially in high-income countries, where a public relations machine stands ready to avert any negative doubts cast on multinationals.

Large multinational law firms are also now actively engaged in working with multinational as well as SME clients on promotional strategies, issues management, damage control, and relationships with local governments. Virtually all major U.S.-based law firms have dedicated consulting and strategic planning sections that include lawyers as well as non-legal consultants on the team. Major law firms have international offices or partnerships with local firms in key markets in order to more effectively serve their business and local public sector clients.

Local companies and local governments in emerging markets, however, often appear to lag behind in their public relations actions, sometimes reacting too late or not at all to negative information. Chinese exports have encountered more than their fair share of negative publicity; at first, they denied any responsibility, which did not serve them well. More recently, the Chinese government has come to understand the importance of acting promptly and accepting responsibility, at times taking it to an extreme, even executing those responsible for manufacturing lethal Chinese products.

China's Export Products Scrutinized

China's exports to the rest of world are soaring. But its reputation in manufacturing safe, high-quality products took a serious plunge a few years ago. China's goal is to sell cars to the West, but it is increasingly drawing the scrutiny of buyers and regulators alike. To date, only Jiangling Motors Corp. has cracked the Western European market. In 2005, its Landwind sport utility vehicle became the first Chinese car offered for sale in Europe, appealing to cost-conscious consumers. Its safety quickly came under scrutiny as a result of a crash test. Jiangling quickly responded by recalling the automobile and addressing the ADAC concerns. However, the crash test prompted the European Commission to closely scrutinize the extent to which Chinese automobiles meet EU safety standards. This did not deter Chinese automobile manufacturers from pursuing a large share of the European and North American market. In 2012, Great Wall Motor opened

the first Chinese manufacturing plant in Europe (Bulgaria), with plans to make automobiles for the European market; to date, the company has only sold its cars in Bulgaria, Macedonia, and Romania. Meanwhile, Landwind is dealing with a new controversy: the Landwind X7, just introduced in 2015, is a copy of the Range Rover Evoque crossover. Tata Motors, the Indian owner of Jaguar Land Rover, is up in arms: the company just built a $1.8 billion factory to build the Evoque – which retails for $72,000 in China, whereas the Landwind X7 retails for $24,000.[38] In other product safety breaches, China did not respond as effectively as it did in the Landwind case. One was melamine in pet food that killed 16 cats and dogs and made thousands of pets sick. Xuzhou Anying Biologic Technology Development, a small agricultural products trader that was the source of the melamine-contaminated wheat gluten, distributed to major pet food suppliers in North America. The gluten was mixed with a chemical that sickened or killed the animals. Another incident involved a Chinese toothpaste that contained diethylene glycol, a poison used in antifreeze, sold in the U.S. and elsewhere. The Chinese argued that small amounts of diethylene glycol can be safely used in toothpaste. What is especially concerning is that this same poison, made in China, contaminated 260,000 bottles of cold medicine in Panama, killing 100 people. In this case, Chinese regulators acknowledged that the two companies engaged in mislabeling.[39]

Will consumers think twice when they purchase Chinese products? Does the brand name lessen consumer concerns about the safety of the product if that product is manufactured in China? With appropriate handling of the situation, which might involve a prompt recall, or rectification, consumers' perceptions of Chinese products might not have suffered. Yet the Chinese have had to learn the importance of public relations. The first step for all the companies involved should have been to immediately rectify the situation. The second step should have been to hire a competent international public relations firm as well as legal counsel to further address consumer concerns. China's State Council eventually strengthened the oversight role of the local government in food safety, and increased fines for firms tampering with product safety, and shut down firms violating safety laws. It even executed a public official who took bribes for overlooking safety violations. However, a more systematic use of public relations in addressing this crisis would have limited the damage incurred in the international public opinion and, specifically, in international consumers' perceptions of Chinese products.

It is important for the firms to carefully manage the elements of the promotional mix to manage such crises. Figure 12-11 illustrates the communication vehicles used by each component of the promotional mix.

Publicity

- Communication about a company and/or the company's products that the company does not pay for. Could be any type pf print article, broadcast message, Tweet, Facebook post or word-of-mouth communication about the company and/or its products.

- Could be either positive or negative messages.

Public Relations

- News releases/letters, press releases, company publications.

- Event sponsorship and presence.

- Corporate advertising.

- Advocacy advertising.

- Public appearances by company representatives.

Sales Promotion

- Consumer sales promotion (includes free samples, coupons, point-of-purchase displays).

- Trade promotion (includes trade discounts, trade shows, and exhibitions).

Figure 12-11: *The publicity, public relations, and sales promotion components of the promotional mix.*

12-4a Publicity

Publicity is communication about a company and/or the company's products that the company does not pay for. In this category falls any type of print article, broadcast message, or word-of-mouth communication about the company and its products. The message may be positive, negative, or a mix of both.

Multinational corporations, in particular, frequently experience negative publicity. In general, there is a negative perception of multinational firm dominance and globalization. Brands that are especially vulnerable are those closely associated in consumers' mind with the country of origin. For example, McDonald's greatest appeal is the image it projects, that of the American way of life. However, its franchises are mostly locally owned, and the franchisees have consciously tried to present a local face. Nevertheless, the company has been the target of anti-American sentiment. In response to Europe's decision to ban hormone-treated beef, the U.S. government imposed high import tariffs on French Roquefort cheese,

Dijon mustard, and foie gras. Some French people retaliated by vandalizing McDonald's restaurants. In their eyes, the company was a symbol of U.S. hegemony, globalization, multinationals, the power of the marketplace, and industrially produced food, all at the expense of individuals' health and French peasants' livelihood.[40] This event, although not McDonald's fault, created a strong sentiment at that time against the company.

      In other examples, driven by anger over U.S. support for Israel, an anti-U.S. boycott started in Egypt and spread to other Arab countries. Local McDonald's franchisees countered, engaging in public relations that portrayed the company as a local company, and tailoring menus to local tastes, introducing the McFalafel sandwich, which was launched with the help of an ad jingle by a famous Egyptian singer, Sha' aban Abdul Raheem, best known for his nationalistic songs. McDonald's franchisees have also contributed to local charities:

eFesenko/shutterstock.com

In Saudi Arabia and Jordan, a portion of sales for a given period was donated to charity. In other public relations efforts, in Indonesia, photos of local franchise owners, wearing traditional Islamic clothing, were posted at the entrance of some restaurants. In Argentina, when antiwar demonstrators blocked the entrances of a number of McDonald's restaurants, the company launched a campaign for the chain with the "Made in Argentina" theme.[41]

      Entire industries can also come under public scrutiny. The well-respected World Health Organization (WHO) warned in 2015 that sausage, ham, other processed meats, as well as red meat, can cause colon, stomach, and other cancers, and that processed meats are in the same danger category as cigarettes or asbestos. This news put many businesses, such as McDonald's and Burger King, under a microscope, as consumers curtailed their consumption of processed foods and red meat.

      The diamond industry is still suffering from the impact of the negative publicity generated by the Warner Bros. action thriller, *Blood Diamond*. The movie moved audiences world-wide with bloody images of diamond smuggling from sub-Saharan Africa during the diamond business' heaviest selling season, in the month of December. The film was set during Sierra Leone's civil war, and it portrayed a soldier turned smuggler chasing a rare pink diamond. The movie portrays smugglers of conflict diamonds, or blood diamonds — the name implies that sales of these diamonds are used to fund wars against legitimate governments. The industry pleaded with Warner Bros. to add disclaimers that voluntary industry reforms have eliminated conflict diamonds from the trade, but the film's producer, Ed Zwick, refused on the basis that the film was set during a time when conflict diamonds were common. In response, the World Diamond Council trade group fought an expensive fight. It launched a $15 million public relations and education campaign to disassociate the images of conflict diamonds from the diamonds the industry sells to wealthy buyers. It claimed that conflict diamonds constituted less than one percent of all diamonds sold, and that it uses the Kimberly Process Certification System, backed by the United Nations, to guarantee that the diamonds sold are not conflict diamonds. Many of the measures the diamond trade has adopted are attributed to this film. [42]

Positive publicity, although difficult to come by, is valuable. Due to its independent nature, it is more credible than advertising. For many years, *Consumer Reports* raved about Tesla's Model S (which retails for more than $120,000) giving the company a great boost in the marketplace. However, in 2015 *Consumer Reports* significantly lowered its ratings, reflecting owners' reports of squeaking noises, engines that needed to be changed, and problems with the car's automatic door handles. Companies work to create positive publicity for their brands using public relations, supporting their local community, and they use the other promotional tools — advertising, sales promotions, and personal selling — to create a positive buzz for the company and the brand. Marketers believe that publicity is a must in international marketing.

12-4b Public Relations

International public relations is a concerted effort to generate goodwill among international publics (community, government, consumers, employees, among others) that are essential to the company. Its main purpose is to generate positive publicity about the company. International public relations is big business. The leading public relations firms are primarily U.S. multinationals – their numbers in the top 14 continues to expand. See Table 12-3.

Table 12-3 The Top Public Relation Firms (Ranked Based on 2017 Worldwide Net Fees)

Firm, City, State	2017 Net Fees	Employees
1. Edelman, New York, NY	$893,591,000	5,940
2. W2O Group, San Francisco, CA	$144,300,000	651
3. APCO Washington, DC	$128,236,300	682
4. FINN, New York, NY	$81,290,000	533
5. ICR, New York, NY	$63,427,224	177
6. Prosek, New York, NY	$40,818,192	137
7. Padilla, Minneapolis, MN	$40,078,469	206
8. Hotwire, New York, NY	$33,249,507	222
9. COYNEPR, New York, NY	$28,000,000	139
10. 5W, New York, NY	$27,538,768	148
11. G&S Business Communications, New York, NY	$27,275,329	146
12. Fahlgren-Mortine, Columbus, Ohio	$26,975,583	160
13. Health Unlimited, New York, NY	$25,890,471	122
14. FWV, Raleigh, NC	$25,241,802	103
15. Racepoint Global, Boston, MA	$25,105,128	148

Source: O'Dwyer, "Worldwide Fees of Top PR Firms With Major U.S. Operations," accessed at http://www.odwyerpr.com/pr_firm_rankings/independents.htm on July 3, 2018.

Much of the growth in public relations expenditures takes place in emerging markets, especially in large emerging markets such as China and India. Many new developments are taking place in the transition economies of Central and Eastern Europe as well, as illustrated in International Marketing Illustration 12-2.

International Marketing Illustration 12-2
Central and Eastern Europe: A Growing Market for Public Relations

Public relations firms are growing rapidly in numbers and in revenue in Central and Eastern Europe. Among some of the obstacles the companies face are the overly close relationships between magazines and public relations companies. Often, companies pay journalists to write stories about them. Public relations agencies control the media, especially the popular lifestyle publications, digital and print, where ads for the holidays and food are portrayed as editorial articles. Sponsoring companies pay for the travel for journalists. And publishers do not permit journalists to write negative stories about the firms that advertise with them.

The reverse situation also presents problems. Media, and newspapers in general, tend to be suspicious of public relations agencies. In fact, media owners are wary of corporations and often view any type of positive publicity as something they should be paid for. Hungarian and Czech newspapers even go as far as to place barriers in front of public relations companies and prevent journalists from having contact with them. When a company executive shares an important tip, he or she is quoted as the representative of an unnamed firm, rather than the representative of an identified firm.

Adding to the difficulties of the public relations firms in the region is that most of their senior executives are younger than 30. They are perceived as inexperienced, and clients have difficulty paying them a fee of 15 percent on top of expenses. It is difficult to justify to clients that public relations involves important work that helps companies remain competitive. Yet, in spite of all the challenges, the public relations industry is growing by leaps and bounds, with local firms increasing in number and successfully competing with leading international firms. This is encouraging because companies and their products are only strengthened by competent public relations. As noted earlier in the chapter, major law firms also have international consulting firms to advise on issues management, government relations, business development, etc.

For example, McGuire Woods Consulting, affiliated with the large Richmond-based law firm, McGuire Woods, recently opened a consulting office in Bucharest to serve clients in Central and Eastern Europe. (Continued on next page.)

Alternatively, negative publicity can be countered and its impact lessened by expert PR. Euro 2012, the European soccer tournament that took place in the Ukraine, could have benefitted from PR expertise. Ukraine worked for two years to prepare for the tournament, built two stadiums and opened four airports at a cost of over $14.5 billion – quite a lot for a former Soviet state. However, just before the games, a former prominent British player stated that it was wrong to hold the Euro games in Poland and the Ukraine because of the racist attitudes there and the risk of coming back home in a coffin. The British Foreign Office followed up and advised fans of African or Asian descent to be careful if attending the games.

Ukraine only has itself to blame for failing to sell itself. Kiev is a fabulous European capital, Ukrainian fans drink a lot of beer, and the country has an illustrious literary history (Bulgakov was born there, Chekhov wrote some of his famous work in Yalta), and much pride in its soccer history, with Dynamo Kiev winning the European cup twice. Ukraine, much like the other countries in Central and Eastern Europe, needs good PR.

JaySi/shutterstock.com

Sources: *The Guardian*, "Euro 2012 turning into PR disaster for Ukraine as racism fears scare off fans," 28 May, 2012, www.guardian.co.uk/football/2012/may/28/euro-2012ukraine-sol-campbell; Maria Vornovitsky, "Advertising Changes in Post-Soviet Russia: Content Analysis," working paper; Katka Krosnar, "Hope for PR in Eastern Europe," *Marketing Magazine*, Vol. 106, No. 2, January 15, 2001, p. 6; Katka Krosnar, "PR Struggles in Eastern Europe," *Market-Magazine*, Vol. 106, No. 1, January 1/8 2001, p. 6, "McGuire Woods Consulting," accessed at http://www.mwcllc.com/reach/international/bucharest.asp on July 3, 2018.

Public relations efforts fall into the following categories:

· News releases/letters, press releases, company publications

· Event sponsorship and presence

· Corporate advertising

· Image advertising

· Advocacy advertising

· Public appearances by company representatives

News Releases/Letters, Press Releases, and Company Publications

Multinational firms must, on a regular basis, communicate with their different publics (home-country, local, and international customers; trade; stockholders; government; and community). When new products are introduced in local markets, company representatives are likely to offer news releases, press releases, or company publications touting the advantages of the new products or services. Companies also use their websites to promote the brand and create excitement about events organized around their brand. In its news and press releases, Mexican Corona beer is touting its European campaign, announcing the Movida Corona parties. These parties revolve around live Latin music and are held at celebrated music venues throughout Europe—in Italy, at Rimini's Bahia Imperial; in Spain, at Madrid's Teatro Kapital; or in the United Kingdom, at London's Ministry of Sound. Corona also announced a campaign including a giant American truck and a mind-blowing laser and video show enhanced by a powerful sound system, which was targeted at Spain, Croatia, Denmark, France, Italy, the United Kingdom, Austria, Switzerland, Sweden, and Germany. In 2014, Movida Corona created a DJ competition that was touted as a great opportunity for DJs to launch their career. It flew DJs to Ibiza, Spain, to play at the grand Pacha party. Competitors were asked to upload a mix of no more than 30 minutes on Mixcloud, tag it with Movida Corona UK, and use the Movida Corona art in the mix.[43]

Event Sponsorship and Presence

Event sponsorship is a growing venue for international marketing communication. Nearly every important international cultural or sports-related event has the backing of multinational corporations. Brands such as Adidas, MasterCard, Visa, Rolex, Coca-Cola, Pepsi, and Heineken, sponsor events ranging from World Cup Soccer to World Cup Cricket to the Davis Cup for tennis. Among the sponsors and partners of the 2018 World Cup were Adidas, Coca-Cola, Budweiser, McDonald's and Visa, but also Russia's Gaz Prom, South Korea's Hyundai Kai Motors, Qatar Airways, China's Wanda Group, Hisense, Mengniu, and Vivo.

Across continents, cultural manifestations are supported by major international brands. For years now, Makedonski Telekom, the Macedonian subsidiary of the German Deutsche Telekom, has sponsored festivals in emerging markets. For example, it sponsors the International Arts Festival AKTO in Bitola, the Ohrid Summer Festival, and the Skopje Jazz Festival, in the capital, Skopje, bringing prominent jazz musicians from all over the world.[44] Tata, the venerable Indian multinational that owns, among so many others, Tata Steel, Land Rover, and Jaguar, is sponsoring numerous events in emerging markets and developed countries alike, from the Ferrari Formula 1 team to the Cardiff Bay 5 Marathon benefitting cystic fibrosis in the United Kingdom.[45]

International sponsorship is so prevalent that it has drawn the attention of artists. Near a bus stop in Kassel, Germany, a kiosk that would normally carry advertisements is actually a work by New York–based artist Hans Haacke displaying quotes from executives telling why they sponsor art shows. Hilmar Kopper, head of Deutsche Bank, says: "Whoever pays, controls." Alain Dominique Perrin, Cartier's head, says: "[Sponsorship] is a tool for shaping public opinion."[46]

Corporate Advertising

Corporate advertising is used to promote the company behind the different brands. One particularly memorable advertisement of this kind in advertising history was designed by Philip Morris International for the Chinese market on the occasion of the Chinese New Year. This ad portrayed traditional Chinese dancers dancing on the Great Wall to the Marlboro theme song, which was still familiar to consumers despite the fact that Marlboro cigarettes are no longer advertised on television. At the end, the ad wished Chinese consumers a happy new year from the Philip Morris companies: "A new year brings a new spirit that spreads upon the land."

In another example, on the occasion of President Horst Kohler of Germany visiting China, a full-page Daimler ad in China's newspaper *China Daily*, avowed: "A German soul, with a heart for China. Embracing the spirit of our commitment to Sino-German relations, Mercedes-Benz wishes President Horst Kohler a pleasant, successful, and prosperous visit to China. With a long industrial heritage, grounded in German technology and expertise, Mercedes-Benz is widely recognized for its passion for innovation and constant pursuit for perfection. This is our heart and soul — and what drives our commitment to China."[47] The ad sounds much like modern Chinese poetry and it resonated well with Chinese consumers, who responded positively to a respectful communication from the prestigious German company.

In other corporate advertising examples, Bombardier Transportation is a Canadian company with a strong presence in Berlin, Germany. Its transportation division alone has more than 9,000 employees. Bombardier partnered with the Berlin Transportation Authority and the German railway system, Deutsche Bahn, to build the Berlin train station, a work of art and ingenious technology. Bombardier enjoys great prominence in the country, and in Berlin, in particular. (See Figure 12-12).

Figure 12-12 Corporate presence: Bombardier, the Canadian aircraft and rail systems manufacturer, advertises in a prime location at the Berlin state-of-the-art train station.

Image Advertising

Image advertising is used to enhance perceptions of a company in a given market. McDonald's used image advertising to combat the negative attitudes of consumers and farmers in France in the late 1990s, when José Bové, a farmer campaigning against globalization, protested against McDonald's by bulldozing down a restaurant. More recently, in 2005, in an event that echoed the McDonald's bulldozing, the police in northern Lille found a stolen plastic figure of Ronald McDonald, dangling beneath a city bridge with a ball and chain attached to one foot. McDonald's reacted promptly in both situations to change the company's image. It intensified advertising campaigns, informing customers more about McDonald's France, what ingredients it used, and what kind of people it employed. The company's strategy was to blur the lines about McDonald's nationality — all the buns, meat, and other ingredients were from France and virtually all the work force was French.[48]

McDonald's is also improving its image on the labor front. In a campaign entitled "McDo = McJob," the company announces that its restaurant directors are supported financially by the company in pursuing a management or business degree. More and more, McDonald's has to maintain its image as a local brand because its main competition is local. The McDonald's restaurant in Syntagma Square, in Athens Greece,

Sharaf Maksumov/shutterstock.com

has plenty of competition from Greek upstarts that serve fast and convenient food and much more — localization and customization.

Next door, is Everest, a local fast food chain that customizes sandwiches, while across the street is Mikel Coffee Company, a local coffee shop chain that also sells sandwiches together with custom-made espresso drinks served by highly trained associates.[49]

These corporate marketing strategies, including press releases, event sponsorship, advertising, and corporate and image advertising, are applicable not only to private-sector corporations and product manufacturers, but also to services providers. Services account for one third of U.S. exports, at $800 billion in 2017. Services cover a wide range of activities including computer, technology and information services, financial services, legal services, international transportation, education, etc. By far the largest component of international services in the United States is international tourism, a $300 billion industry in the U.S. [50]

Inward international tourism spending in the United States is considered a U.S. export, because it represents payments coming into the U.S. from outside the country. The international services industry is also a major source of job creation in the United States, ranging from lower-paying food server positions at tourism sites to lawyers in the United States representing international clients at a fee of $700 an hour. International tourism is an equally important service industry in many countries around the world. International tourism promotion and the famous "Virginia is for Lovers" brand is a big business for Virginia. On the state tourism website, there is a dedicated section for international tourists https://www.virginia.org/international/ with welcoming messages in numerous international languages. Like multinational companies, Virginia Tourism also promotes Virginia via press releases, publications, and advertising, especially to international travel agents. Virginia also maintains a high profile in event sponsorship and presence. Among examples is Virginia's successful invitation to have the popular reality TV series "The Bachelorette" filmed in Richmond in 2018, or Steven Spielberg's movie "Lincoln," a few years earlier. Both helped promote the Virginia brand.

Advocacy Advertising

Advocacy advertising is used by a company to stress a particular point of view. Benetton has always been an advocate — for multiculturalism, for reflections on the existence of death rows, and, more recently, for reflections on climate change. Advocacy advertising is effective, and multinationals like to be known for the causes they embrace and for which they actively advocate.

Public Appearances by Company Representatives

In addition to public appearances to speak on behalf of the firm and its products, company representatives frequently attend international events. There are many opportunities for company representatives to voice concerns and support various causes.

One such event is the World Economic Forum (WEF). The 2018 World Economic Forum took place in Davos, Switzerland. The WEF is typically attended by prominent representatives of industry, such as Microsoft Corp. co-founder Bill Gates, Gao Xiqing, President of the China Investment Corporation, and Doug McMillon, President and Chief Executive Officer, Wal-Mart International, and politicians, such as President Bill Clinton, Vice-President Al Gore, and Prime Minister Tony Blair, as well as local and regional leaders.[51]

12-5 Consumer Sales Promotion

Aside from advertising, personal selling, public relations, and publicity, all other sponsored communications offered to the end consumer or to the trade that stimulate purchases or improve relationships to intermediaries and retailers in the short term fall into the category of sales promotion. Examples of consumer sales promotion are point-of-purchase displays, free samples to initiate trial, other incentives (coupons, cents-off, gifts, product tie-ins) to initiate trial or brand switching, and sweepstakes and contests. Trade promotion examples are trade discounts, sweepstakes and contests, and trade shows.

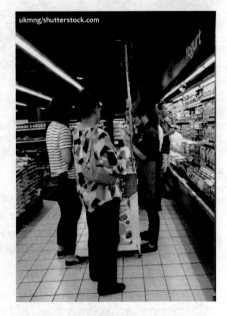
ukmng/shutterstock.com

Sampling is used primarily by food and beverage manufacturers, but can also be used by almost any type of good or service (see Figure 12-13). Free samples are offered in stores, at busy intersections, or at train stations. For example, people arriving with suitcases at Berlin's main train station on a particular day were given packets of Haribo *Gummibären* candy, free newspapers, and fruit drinks.

Coupons are often used to stimulate sales, especially in the short term. Worldwide, most coupons are delivered via direct mail. Coupons are also handed out at events with product samples. North American

Figure 12-13 *In this store, free samples are offered to customers to induce them to try and to purchase their yogurt.*

companies prefer using inserts and print media to distribute coupons because consumers must make an effort to clip and save the coupon. In most other countries, membership in a loyalty program creates a consumer database that companies then use for mailing coupons and other promotions. In Europe, few companies offer coupons. U.S. fast-food restaurants, such as McDonald's and Burger King, appear to offer coupons most frequently in order to gain, and later to maintain, customer loyalty. Their couponing strategy for Europe is similar to that used in the United States. In the case of Burger King, one coupon offers two double-Whoppers and medium-sized fries for €6.49 (regularly priced at €9.88); another coupon offers buy one Big King, get one Big King for free; and a third coupon offers two Crispy Chicken with medium-sized fries for €4.49 (regularly priced at €7.48).

Interestingly, coupon usage is low in Latin America, with fewer than 25 percent of consumers indicating they use coupons. Brazil is the most active market, albeit a modest one. [52]

Premiums offer free merchandise for purchasing a product. In the U.S., premium value is usually high, often a major benefit. When purchasing cosmetics, premiums' value can be as high as that of the purchased product itself. In the rest of the world, such gifts are of low value. For example, a cereal box might carry with it a small "prize," such as toy race car.

Contests and *sweepstakes* allow participants to win prizes. The participant must perform an activity or make a purchase. For example, IKEA in Europe has a contest where one can win €500 in merchandise by filling out a form and answers correctly on Fridays. As mentioned, contests and sweepstakes are against Islamic law, which does not condone gambling.

Figure 12-14 *In many of the countries of the former Soviet Union, the German company Henkel sells its Persil laundry detergent in bundles, along with its Silan fabric softener.*

Bonus packs, with additional merchandise offered at the same price or slightly higher, such as four packs of gum for the price of two, or a bundle of complementary products, are increasingly found in supermarkets outside of North America (see Figure 12-14).

Promotional tie-ins include two products or services within the same promotional offer and they can be intracompany or inter-company. A Toggo children's television channel promotion in Germany and Austria offers parents the opportunity to purchase a children's Toggo cell phone with a GPS function where people can track their children — and phone calls to the parent's phone are free. A city family pass in a European city offers reduced-price access to the zoo, museums, public swimming pools — and, if you can prove that you have low income, you also get a reduction for public transportation. The pass is something that every family can pick up every year.

Frequency programs, also called loyalty programs, are aimed at current customers and are designed to create repeat purchase and loyalty. Such programs abound worldwide. Air-lines in every country have some type of frequency program (e.g., frequent flier miles), and hotel chains offer free rooms and free access to their executive suites for sustained loyalty. Food stores and gas stations offer discounts for members (see Figure 12-15).

Price-offs are reductions in the listed retail price of a product. They are used to attract consumers, and have the greatest impact on price-sensitive shoppers. This is a strategy that is often used for store openings. In one example, a large electronics retailer, Saturn, had advertised the opening of a new store for weeks in a large city in Germany. In addition, consumers were mailed inserts advertising the grand event. At the opening of the five-floor retail establishment, the business was practically mobbed. Women with

Figure 12-15 *In many countries, promotions include a loyalty card that also serves as a membership card.*

baby carriages had no babies seated in them, only merchandise piled high. Men were overwhelmed by the large number of packages they carried all at once to the registers. At the store entrance, there was a tiny convertible automobile and a flat-panel-TV box standing tall and obstructing all rear visibility. The deals were only so-so, but the excitement created by the advance promotion was high.

In the United States, firms also use *rebates* or *refunds*, which are cash reimbursements paid to consumers after they turn in a proof of purchase. These promotions are rarely used outside of North America.

Point-of-purchase displays are popular all over the world, if there is sufficient space for the display. Some could consist of valuable refrigerators with the company's brand name and various shelf structures with the manufacturer's brand name. Others could show the product in action as the train set pictured in Figure 12-16.

Figure 12-16 *This fast train point-of-purchase display was difficult to photograph. Children and parents were congregating around it at all times.*

12-5a Adaptation of Sales Promotion

International sales promotion campaigns fall into one of three strategies, paralleling international advertising and international product marketing strategies: global campaigns, modular campaigns, and local campaigns.

Global Campaigns

Global campaigns were rarely attempted in the past in sales promotion. Now, more and more global campaigns have managed to create excitement for their brands. For example, Virgin Mobile offered their customers a free concert or festival ticket of their choosing when they purchased a new phone – the campaign was a success.[53]

Certain types of sales promotion, such as point-of-purchase displays, lend themselves to a more standardized campaign. They do not rely on words, so different language versions are not necessary. They speak an international language by reinforcing logos and emphasizing brand images visually.[20] Yet, even point-of-purchase displays need some adaptation. Johnnie Walker Scotch whisky has a 200-square-foot point-of-purchase display for its Blue Label at Shanghai's Pudong Airport. In a dark, executive-suite-type setting, with deep blues everywhere, the display is a head turner. In glass cases, very, very special bottles lie next to their very special cases. In the front, at the desk, you can order engraving services for "your passport to luxury." Then, you can plop down a few thousand dollars for one of those pretty bottles, and it is all duty free.

Occasionally, the target market itself may encourage the use of a global, standardized approach. For example, in markets where multiple languages are spoken, and where English is one of the unifying languages, as in the case of India, using English for sales promotion may be appropriate. Even in countries where English is not a language used nationally, such as in Switzerland, using English as the language of the promotion may be a benefit. For example, promotions aimed at Swiss consumers often use English, rather than French, German, or Italian, because two groups of consumers would be offended if a campaign used only one of the three languages spoken in Switzerland.[54]

photobyphm/shutterstock.com

Modular Campaigns

Modular campaigns provide a template that can be varied from market to market.[55] Even in the European market, different strategies are likely to be used in the United Kingdom than in continental Europe. In one example, McDonald's teamed up with the biggest children's TV network in Europe, Fox Kids, to run a Happy Meal push spanning 49 countries. The promotion was coordinated from London, but localized to suit individual countries. Its mission was to entertain, rather than educate, which fits with the objectives set by McDonald's for its Happy Meals. The Happy Meals have a spinning top that integrates a CD, decorated by either Power Rangers, Totally Spies, Gadgets & the Gadgetinis, and Medabots; there are eight premiums to collect—four are straightforward spinning tops and four contain the CD. McDonald's purpose is to get kids in front of computers and improving their information technology skills. If, in some targeted markets, children may not have access to computers . . . at least they are getting a spinner.[56]

Local Campaigns

Local campaigns are tailored to local needs, and retailer cooperation is of particular importance in ensuring that such sales promotion campaigns are successful. In the Netherlands, Albert Heijn appears to be favored as a grocery store where multinationals offer their new products and attempt to initiate consumer trials. The store, part of the Royal Ahold retail conglomerate, offers quality products aimed at the middle and upper-middle class. It was there that Procter & Gamble first introduced Bounty paper towels to Dutch consumers about 10 years ago. Albert Heijn displayed the product prominently using point-of-sale displays located near the cash registers and also offered the product in the paper products section of the stores. Simultaneously, the company mailed samples of Bounty in individual sheets, with different designs, in plastic bags, to selected homes. In another more recent example, Coca-Cola representatives offered free samples of Coke and Coke Light to consumers shopping at Albert Heijn. After sampling Coke in miniature cans, consumers were able to purchase the product with a two-for-the-price-of-one promotion.

12-5b The Online Venue for Sales Promotion

Online sales promotion is quickly becoming a pervasive mode of communication with prospective consumers. Whether the promotion involves sweepstakes, printed coupons, promotional pricing, or other strategies, companies find that consumers around the world respond well to aggressive online promotions. Of course, more and more consumers are doing much of their actual shopping online, too. Most of the agencies now serve their clients by providing to target consumers extensive interactive sales promotion that is in line with the company's other types of communications. Luxury retailing websites rarely advertise sales promotion internationally; however, most use their Facebook pages to post promotions. For example, you can look throughout the Galeries Lafayette – the famed French luxury retailer – and you will not find any trace of promotions most of the time. Go, however, to their Facebook page and you will find plenty of sales promotion. One recent promotion was for ten tickets to the PICASSO.MANIA exhibition at the Grand Palais; if you were to purchase the tickets, each would cost about $16.

On the other hand, KaDeWe, the German luxury retailer, advertised their legendary Halloween Party on Facebook and on its website, with countless culinary delights and fine Veuve Cliquot champagne; access to the party would cost a little over $200 per person. No mention of the party is made on the KaDeWe online shop website, however.

12-5c Legal and Ethical Issues in Consumer Sales Promotion

To a certain degree, adaptation to local markets is necessitated by legal require-ments. Even in economically and politically integrated markets, such as the European Union, sales promotion–related legislation differs from one country to another. In Germany, for example, "buy one, get one free" offers are illegal; in France, premiums are restricted to seven percent of the product's value; and in Belgium, retail sales can run for only a month and prices cannot be cut more than one-third.[57]

In 2001, the European Union attempted to institute sales promotion regulations. However, its efforts were jettisoned by the European Commission after member states failed to reach a consensus. The idea was to create an internal market for sales promotion, allowing advertisers to run identical promotions across the EU. However, the members could not agree on a cap on prize funds and on regulations related to promoting to children. The regulation on sales promotions was designed to break down barriers to across-the-border sales promotions on discounts, premiums, gifts, competitions, and promotional games and to replace them with rules on transparency and information designed to ensure freedom of movement. The purpose of the regulation was to bring the countries with the most restrictive promotions laws, such as France and Belgium, into line with more liberal countries, such as the Italy.[58] In Latin America there are no common sales regulations such as found in the EU. Accordingly, marketers and their support team must sift through regula-tions for each target market.

Sweepstakes based on pure chance are deemed illegal in Holland,[59] Canada, Swe-den, and Belgium,[60] whereas, elsewhere in the world, additional legal requirements for sales promotion strategies diverge. Puerto Rican law, for instance, requires rules for all promo-tions to be printed in both English and Spanish, and both versions should be printed in a general circulation newspaper at least once a week for the duration of the campaign. Que-bec requires sponsors to provide French translations, to pay a duty based on the total value of the prize pool, and to post a bond to run a promotion.[61] All paperwork regarding point-of-sale displays must be legalized by going through embassies in the Middle East, while dis-plays going to Eastern Europe must be marked as not being for resale to avoid additional customs duties.[62]

Often the companies themselves are responsible for creating a bad reputation for sales promotion. Sales promotions aimed at emerging markets over time have been ques-tionable. For example, local consumers wearing fur jackets and hats promoting luxury auto-mobiles, investment funds, expensive cigarettes, and airlines — products and services they could not possibly afford — are common in developing countries in sub-Saharan Africa and Eastern Europe.

Historically, there are also examples of flagrant violations of businesses' ethical re-sponsibilities in their management of sales promotion. A case in point is that of Nestlé, a multinational food-product company, which successfully lured new mothers in sub-Saharan Africa to adopt the company's baby formula. Women dressed as nurses offered free sam-ples to new mothers in maternities, urging them to feed formula to their infants as a re-placement for breast milk. Lack of sanitary conditions for formula preparation, as well as the high cost of the product, ultimately led to the death of many infants. What is especially interesting in this case is the fact that the negative publicity for the company was generated abroad, where consumer groups brought this issue to international media attention, rather than on the African continent.

12-6 International Trade Promotion
(Trade Shows and Exhibitions)

Most sales promotion previously addressed in this chapter is primarily aimed at the final consumer, although sweepstakes and contests, or incentives such as price-offs, can also be aimed at the trade. Trade shows and exhibitions belong to the category of business-to-business promotion. They are also referred to as *international trade promotion* — sales promotion aimed at the trade. Trade shows and exhibitions are held annually; there, companies purchase exhibit space to display and demonstrate their offerings to the target market. There are many trade shows for most industries. You can view different trade shows by searching by date, industry, location, at the U.S. Department of Trade website for the International Trade Administration (www.ita.doc.gov).

Trade shows and exhibitions offer potential buyers and sellers a chance to meet face to face, bringing decision makers to a single location, enabling firms to get their message to a large number of people. In a typical promotional environment, the seller must pitch the product to the buyer. For trade shows and exhibits, however, the visitors are the ones who approach the seller in a neutral location where there is a high probability of meeting every decision maker who will influence the buying decision.[63]

Country and state governments are often involved in ensuring that national companies are represented at important fairs. The Department of Commerce and other U.S. state and regional economic development agencies are actively involved in promoting U.S. companies abroad in trade shows. Usually, the U.S. government shares the cost of the exhibits by sponsoring a national pavilion. State and regional economic development organizations participate in international events to promote their state or region as attractive sites for investment. Fairfax County, Virginia, is a major global technology center, home to many international firms. The Fairfax County Economic Development Authority (FCEDA) markets the region as a business location site at trade events around the world. For example, the FCEDA's regional office in Bangalore, India, recently co-hosted the "US-India Emerging Technologies Forum" to highlight business strategies and investment opportunities in Fairfax County.[64]

As mentioned, trade shows and exhibitions are organized annually or at set intervals and tend to be specialized in one domain. The Frankfurt Book Fair, for example, draws publishers and authors on all topics from around the world every fall to the city of Frankfurt, Germany.

The *documenta* and the Venice Biennale exhibit works of contemporary artists (see Figure 12-17). In other examples, DRUPA is an annual show for the graphic arts industry, and Interkama is an international trade fair for industrial communication, automation, measurement, and analytics. Messe Dusseldorf, in Dusseldorf, Germany, specializes in trade shows for machinery, as well as for the medical, fashion, and services industries.

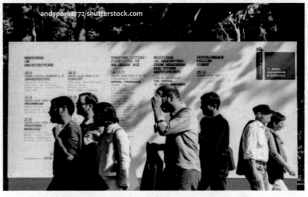

Figure 12-17 The Venice Biennale is one of the most Important venues for showcasing contemporary art and artists. Among its sponsors are Fiat, AMB AMRO and illy coffee.

The World Exposition (the World's Fair) cuts across domains and is one of the most important venues for exhibiting new ideas, technology, and art in an environment where numerous countries are represented. Expo 2005 was organized in Seto, Japan, in the Aichi Prefecture, and Expo 2010 took place in Shanghai, China, with more than 70 million visitors in attendance. Expo 2020 will take place in Dubai, United Arab Emirates.

Summary

Describe the international promotional mix and the international communication process. The components of the international promotional mix are international advertising, international sales force management, international sales promotion, and public relations and publicity. The international communication process involves the sender encoding a message and sending it via a medium to the receiver, who then decodes the message; the goal is to have the message sent be identical to the message received. In an international communications context, the process is complicated by interferences (noise) injected by cultural and language differences between the advertiser, sponsor, and the target audiences.

Explore the international advertising formats and practices around the world. International advertising — defined as a nonpersonal communication by an identified sponsor across international borders, using broadcast, print, and/or interactive media — faces many international challenges. The primary challenge is attributed to the lack of uniformity in media infrastructure, formats, and practices accepted in different markets. Among such challenges are media availability and reliability issues, such as media's inability to work with company deadlines and television going off the air frequently. The media could limit the types and the number of advertisements aired or published, or they might not permit the portrayal of women or advertising of certain products. They also might isolate advertising from programming or from editorial content. Media costs, formats, features, and trends can differ around the world.

Describe the international advertising and media infrastructure and infrastructure-related challenges in different markets. Advertising worldwide is dominated by U.S. advertising agencies, but that is quickly changing. Firms from the United Kingdom and Japan are competing with large full-service agencies from the United States, and boutique advertising agencies worldwide are winning important accounts and awards for quality advertising. Multinationals today have increasing advertising agency choices. Depending on the availability of local talent and capability, companies advertising in international markets have a choice between advertising using a local agency, using an international agency, or using a local agency to advertise international agency messages.

Describe advertising strategies and budgeting decisions and offer examples of international applications. An important decision is whether to use a standardized message worldwide or to adapt the message to local markets. Standardization leads to economies of scale and cost savings; in reality, standardization may not be possible because of variations in the advertising and media infrastructures due to differences in consumer literacy, motivations, or consumer interests, and due to differences in advertising legislation. Advertising budgeting uses one of the following methods: objective-and-task, whereby managers set objectives and then calculate the cost for reaching the objectives; percent-of-sales, whereby the advertising budget is set as a percent of sales; historical, whereby spending is based on past expenditures; competitive-parity, whereby spending is based on competitors' spending; executive-judgment, whereby the firm's executives make the decisions; and the all-you-can-afford method.

Provide an overview of international publicity and the different international public relations activities that can be used to influence it. Publicity is a promotional tool that companies do not pay for; rather, publicity is a result of companies' performance and perception in world markets. For companies conducting business internationally, publicity in one country may have important repercussions on company perception in all the markets where the companies are present. Publicity can be positively influenced by using appropriate public relations tools, such as releasing relevant company publications, press releases, news releases; engaging in appropriate public appearances; and hiring agencies to design image advertising and corporate advertising that reflects company philosophies and strategies. In addition to promoting tangible products and goods, similar strategies are employed to market international services.

Describe the different approaches to international consumer sales promotion and the activities involved. International consumer promotions are becoming popular worldwide. Such activities include point-of-sale displays, free samples to initiate product trial or brand switching, and other incentives (coupons, cents-off, gifts, product tie-ins) designed with the purpose to initiate trial or brand switching. Promotional activities can be global in nature; modular, with some adaptation in select markets; and local, designed with local consumers in mind.

Describe the different approaches to international trade promotion and the different activities involved. International trade promotion, aimed at the business-to-business market, can involve trade shows and exhibitions, as well as trade discounts, sweepstakes, and contests. Trade shows provide a neutral environment where buyer and seller can meet face-to-face in a low-pressure situation in which the buyer is most likely to approach the seller, rather than vice versa.

Key Terms

adaptation of the advertising strategy

all-you-can-afford method

billboards

broadcast medium

channel of communication

competitive-parity method

decoding

encoding

executive-judgment method

feedback

historical method

infomercials

interactive medium

international communication process

international promotional mix

media availability

media infrastructure

media reliability

media restrictions

medium/media noise

nonpersonal medium

objective-and-task method

percent-of-sales method

personal medium

print medium

product placement

receiver

sender

standardization of the advertising strategy

telemarketing

television shopping networks

Discussion Questions

1. Describe the challenges involved in the international communication process and suggest how each challenge could be addressed by a firm's international marketing manager in conjunction with an advertising agency.

2. What are some important traits of the international media infrastructure that are likely to affect local advertising strategies?

3. Describe how media formats, features, and trends differ around the world.

4. What are the advertising agency choices that international companies have for communicating with local markets? Describe each choice, its advantages and disadvantages.

5. Ideally, multinationals should standardize their message worldwide to benefit from economies of scale and other cost savings. What prevents companies from using a standardized message worldwide?

6. How do multinational firms determine their budgets for advertising?

7. Describe the relationship between international public relations activities and international publicity.

8. What are the different public relations tools that an international firm can use to fend off negative publicity?

9. Describe some of the international consumer promotion activities that international firms currently engage in, while addressing ethical issues and international standards involved.

10. How does international business-to-business sales promotion (trade promotion) benefit international companies and target consumers?

Chapter Quiz

True/False

1. In the international communication process, the sender can evaluate the effectiveness of the message with appropriate feedback from the target market.

Answer: True

Rationale: The sender can determine whether the communication program launched to the international target market is effective by evaluating the market response to the communication. Section 12-2, "The International Communication Process"

2. Billboards are used in captive environments such as bus and metro stations.

Answer: True

Rationale: Billboards are used in captive environments such as bus and metro stations. They tend to be smaller than typical outdoor billboards. Section 12-3a, "The Media Infrastructure"

3. *Glamour*, *Cosmopolitan*, and *Mademoiselle* are all examples of global media.

Answer: True

Rationale: Magazines such as *Glamour*, *Cosmopolitan*, and *Mademoiselle* are published in languages ranging from Mandarin and Italian to Polish and Japanese. These magazines are vehicles for global, regional, and local advertising campaigns of multinational companies. Section 12-3a, "The Media Infrastructure"

4. The European Union Directive Concerning Television Broadcasting limits all advertising of tobacco and prescription drug products in all media.

Answer: False

Rationale: The European Union Directive Concerning Television Broadcasting prohibits only tobacco and prescription drug advertisements on television. Section 12-3a, "The Media Infrastructure"

5. Communication about a company that the company does not pay for is defined as publicity.

Answer: True

Rationale: Publicity is defined as a communication about a company and the company's products that the company does not pay for. The communication can be either positive or negative. Section 12-5a, "Publicity"

6. The main purpose of public relations is to generate *positive* publicity about a company.

Answer: True

Rationale: Public relations is defined as a concerted effort on the part of a company to generate goodwill among its publics (community, government, consumers, employees, among others). Section 12-5b, "Public Relations"

7. Companies must consider legal and ethical issues with consumer sales promotions. In Germany, "buy one, get one free" offers are illegal.

Answer: True

Rationale: Companies need to adapt their sales promotions to local markets to conform to legal requirements, which could vary from country to country even in markets where there is regional political and economic integration. Section 12-5c, "Legal and Ethical Issues in Consumer Sales Promotion"

8. Trade shows are an example of consumer sales promotion.

Answer: False

Rationale: Trade shows and exhibitions belong to the category of business-to-business promotion. They are also referred to as international trade promotion — sales promotion aimed at the trade. Section 12-6, "International Trade Promotion (Trade Shows and Exhibitions)"

Multiple Choice

1. Which of the following is a nonpersonal medium of the International Communication Process?

        a. personal selling
        b. trade shows
        c. television
        d. telemarketing

Answer: c is correct.

Rationale: Television is the only nonpersonal medium of the four. Personal selling and trade shows involve the presence of sales people, whereas telemarketing involves the presence of a telemarketer who would be handling the sales call. Section 12-2, "The International Communication Process"

2. Which of the following refers to interference in the communication process attributed to cultural differences, competing messages, and degree of consumer interest?

        a. encoding
        b. decoding
        c. noise
        d. none of the above

Answer: c is correct.

Rationale: Noise refers to all the potential interference in the communication process, particularly noise attributed to cultural differences, which may interfere with proper message reception. Section 12-2, "The International Communication Process"

3. Local newspapers that are unable to produce high enough quality in a print ad for a global brand are an example of what media challenge?

        a. media availability
        b. media costs
        c. media reliability
        d. media restrictions

Answer: c is correct.

Rationale: Media reliability refers to the extent to which the existing media reliably reach the target consumer in the intended format and within the intended time frame. Section 12-3a, "The Media Infrastructure"

4 The budgeting decision that is mostly used by small and medium-sized corporations' campaigns is the
- a. percent-of-sales method.
- b. executive-judgment method.
- c. competitive-parity method
- d. all-you-can-afford method.

Answer: d is correct.

Rationale: Most small and medium-sized firms are limited in terms of their advertising expenditures and cannot afford to copy competitors' strategies or spend enough for the desired impact; consequently, they use the all-you-can-afford method. Section 12-3c, "The Advertising Strategy"

5. Marlboro is one of the official sponsors of Ferrari's Formula 1 team. This is an example of
- a. press release.
- b. company publications.
- c. event sponsorship.
- d. advertising.

Answer: c is correct.

Rationale: Marlboro's sponsorship of the Ferrari team at Formula 1 is an example of event sponsorship public relations. Section 14-1b, "Public Relations"

6. According to the text, what international organization often uses advocacy advertising?
- a. McDonald's
- b. Benetton
- c. Visa
- d. Adidas

Answer: b is correct.

Rationale: Benetton's advertising is an example of advocacy advertising, used by a company to stress a particular point of view. Its current advocacy topic is global warming. Section 12-4b, "Public Relations"

7. Which of the following is an example of sales promotion?
- a. product tie-ins
- b. free samples
- c. cents-off
- d. all of the above

Answer: d is correct.

Rationale: These three promotions are offered to stimulate purchases or improve relationships to intermediaries and retailers in the short term. They fall in the category of sales promotion. Section 12-5, "Consumer Sales Promotion"

Notes

1. Laurel Wentz, "'Evolution' Win Marks Down New Cannes Era," Vol. 78, No. 26, June 25, 2007, pp. 1–2.

2. www.unileverusa.com/brands/hygiene/dovecampaignforrealbeauty, www.dove.de, www.dove.ro, all accessed on May 28, 2012.

3. Rupal Parekh, "Creative Effectiveness Cannes Lion Goes to Unilever's Axe," *Advertising Age*, June 19, 2012, http://adage.com/author/rupal-parekh/4468; Daniel O'Donnell, "Unilever's Dove and Axe: Examples of Hypocrisy or Good Marketing?" Case Study Competition, 2008 (Arthur W. Page Society): 39–51.

4. Arwa Mahdawi, "Sorry Dove, Empowerment Isn't a Personal Care Product" *The Guardian*, April 9, 2015, accessed at http://www.theguardian.com/commentisfree/2015/apr/09/sorry-dove-personal-care-product-choose-beautiful-campaign on October 4, 2015.

5. Sam Solley, "Developing a Name to Work Worldwide," *Marketing*, December 21, 2000, p. 27.

6. Nataly Kelly, "How Marketing Is Evolving in Latin America," *Harvard Business Review*, June 1, 2015, accessed at https://hbr.org/2015/06/how-marketing-is-evolving-in-latin-america on July 1, 2018.

7. "To What Extent Do You Trust the Following Forms Of Advertising/Recommendation," *Statista 2018*, accessed at https://www.statista.com/statistics/222725/consumer-trust-in-advertising-in-latin-america on July 1, 2018.

8. Adapted from BBC News, "Angola Profile: Media," January 16, 2015, accessed at http://www.bbc.com/news/world-africa-13036740 on October 4, 2015; BBC News, "The Democratic Republic of Congo Profile: Media," January 16, 2015, accessed at http://www.bbc.com/news/world-africa-13285760 on August 4, 2015; www.omdmedia.co.za.

9. Anver Versi, "MTV Rolls Out Africa Channel," *African Business*, Vol. 305, January 2005, pp. 58-59.

10. "Panama: New Rules for Outdoor Advertising," *Central American Data*, January 2016, accessed at https://en.centralamericadata.com/en/article/home/Panama_New_Rules_for_Outdoor_Advertising on July 2, 2018.

11. Anita Franklin, "Whose News? Control of the Media in Africa," *Review of African Political Economy*, Vol. 25, No. 78, December 1998, pp. 545–550.

12. Helen Johnstone, "Asian TV Companies Take Lead in Local Content," *Asian Business*, Vol. 32, No. 10, October 1996, pp. 26–33.

13. Keach Hagey, "Inside Telemundo's Battle with Univision for American Hispanics," *The Wall Street Journal*, March 16, 2018, accessed at https://www.wsj.com/articles/inside-telemundos-battle-with-univision-for-american-hispanics-1521198000 on July 2, 2018.

14. See Pola B. Gupta and Kenneth R. Lord, "Product Placement in Movies: The Effect of Prominence and Mode on Audience Recall," *Journal of Current Issues and Research in Advertising*, Vol. 14, No. 1, Spring 1998, pp. 47–59; and Steven J. Gould, Pola B. Gupta, and Sonja Grabner-Kräuter, "Product Placements in Movies: A Cross-Cultural Analysis of Austrian, French, and American Consumers' Attitudes Toward This Emerging International Promotional Medium," *Journal of Advertising*, Vol. 29, No. 4, Winter 2000, pp. 41–68.

15. European Union, "Audiovisual Commercial Communications," accessed at http://ec.europa.eu/digital-agenda/en/audiovisual-commercial-communications on October 12, 2015; Anne Jolis, "EU Backs Rise in Advertising on Broadcast TV," *The Wall Street Journal*, May 25, 2007, B3.

16. European Commission, "Misleading and Comparative Advertising," accessed at http://ec.europa.eu/consumers/consumer_rights/unfair-trade/false-advertising/index_en.htm on October 12, 2015; http://eur-lex.europa.eu accessed on May 31, 2007.

17. Morris Kalliny and Lance Gentry, "Cultural Values Reflected in Arab and American Television Advertising," *Journal of Current Issues and Research in Advertising*, Vol. 29, No. 11, Spring 2007, pp. 15–21.

18. European Union, "UK Advertising Standards Authority research: Children and advertising on social media websites," July 1, 2013, accessed at http://ec.europa.eu/digital-agenda/en/content/uk-advertising-standards-authority-research-children-and-advertising-social-media-websites-0 on October 12, 2015; Dana Lascu, Lalita Manrai, Ajay K. Manrai, and Fabienne Brookman Amissah, "Online Marketing to Children," *Young Consumers*, Vol. 14, No. 1, 2013, pp. 19-40; Ross D. Petty, "Advertising Law in the United States and European Union," *Journal of Public Policy & Marketing*, Vol. 16, No. 1, Spring 1997, pp. 2–13.

19. Ibid.

20. "Childhood Obesity: Mexico Has World's Worst Childhood Obesity," *TRT World, You Tube*, October 12, 2017, accessed at https://www.youtube.com/watch?v=QoyROok4gnE on October 12, 2017. Maggie Hennessy, "Mexico Restricts Junk Food Ads; Time for Rethink on Advertising," *Food Navigator-USA*, July 31, 2014, accessed at https://www.foodnavigator usa.com/Article/2014/07/22/Mexico-restricts-junk-food-ads-time-for-rethink-on-advertising on July 1, 2018. Montserrat Bacardi-Gascon and Arturo Jimenez-Cruz, "TV Food Advertising Geared to Children in Latin American Countries and Hispanics in the USA: A Review," *Nutricion Hospitalaria*, 2015 accessed at http://www.nutricionhospitalaria.com/pdf/8730.pdf on July 1, 2018.

21. William Wells, John Burnett, and Sandra Moriarty, *Advertising Principles and Practice*, Seventh Edition, Upper Saddle River, NY: Prentice Hall, 2006, *Advertising Age*, "10 Biggest Stories of 2003," Vol. 74, No. 51, December 22, 2003, p. 4.

22. Hillary Chura, "Coke Brands IPG as Global Ad Strategist," *Advertising Age*, Vol. 71, No. 50, December 4, 2000, p. 50.

23. David Lipin, "San Diego Ikea Hires a Local Ad Agency," *Adweek*, Vol. 50, No. 51, December 18, 2000, p.4.

24. Peter Rosenwald, "Surveying the Latin American Landscape," *Catalog Age*, Vol. 18, No. 2, February 2001, p. 67.

25. Bradley Johnson, "Advertisers: Spending is Growing (and Surging in China,)" *Ad Age*, December 5, 2017, accessed at http://adage.com/article/cmo-strategy/world-s-largest-advertisers-2017/311484/ on July 4, 2018.

26. http://www.rapp.com/ accessed on July 1, 2018; Cara Beardi, "Grey's Global Desire," *Advertising Age*, Vol. 71, No. 48, November 20, 2000, pp. 22, 24.

27. Cara Beardi, "Grey's Global Desire," *Advertising Age*.

28. Cordella Brabbs, "Can Coke and IPG Truly 'Think Local'?" *Marketing*, December 7, 2000, p. 7.

29. Eric Pfanner, "On Advertising: Passport to Success?" *International Herald Tribune*, August 6, 2006, online edition.

30. Knowledge@Wharton, "McDonald's Sets Out to Conquer the World by Changing Its Image," October 22, 2003, accessed at http://knowledge.wharton.upenn.edu/article/mcdonalds-sets-out-to-conquer-the-world-by-changing-its-image/ on January 5, 2016.

31. Eric Pfanner, "On Advertising: Passport to Success?" *International Herald Tribune*, August 6, 2006, online edition.

32. "C-for Yourself": Mercedes-Benz launches integrated marketing campaign for the new C-Class, Stuttgart, March 19, 2007, Official Press Release, www.mercedes-benz.com/c-class, accessed on October 12, 2012

33. Ibid.

34. Michel Laroche, V. H. Kirpalani, and Rene Darmon, "Determinants of the Control of International Advertising by Headquarters of Multinational Corporations," *Revue Canadienne de l'Administration*, Vol. 16, No. 4, December 1999, pp. 273–290.

35. Fabiano Cid, "Top 10 Multimedia Localization Best Practices for Latin America," *Brand Quarterly*, June 11, 2014, accessed at   http://www.brandquarterly.com/top-10-multimedia-localization-best-practices-latin-america on June 2, 2018.

36. Zahna Caillat and Barbara Mueller, "Observations: The Influence of Culture on American and British Advertising: An Exploratory Comparison of Beer Advertising," *Journal of Advertising Research*, Vol. 36, No. 3, May/June 1996, pp. 79–88.

37. Nicolaos E. Synodinos, Charles F. Keown, and Lawrence W. Jacobs, "Transnational Advertising Practices: A Survey of Leading Brand Advertisers in Fifteen Countries," *Journal of Advertising Research*, Vol. 29, No. 2, April/May 1989, pp. 43–50.

38. Benjamin Zhang, "China's Knockoff Range Rover Is Back – and There's Nothing Jaguar Land Rover Can Do About It," *Business Insider*, April 20, 2015, accessed at http://www.businessinsider.com/jaguar-land-rover-landwind-x7-range-rover-evoque-2015-4 on October 27, 2015; Stephen Power, "EU Lifts the Hood on Chinese Autos; Questions on Safety Abound As China Looks to Become a Major Player in the West," *The Wall Street Journal*, October 7, 2005, 14.

39. David Barboza, "Some Suspect Chemical Mix in Pet Food," *New York Times*, April 12, 2007, A1; Walt Bogdanich, "Toxic Toothpaste Made in China Is Found in the U.S., *New York Times*, June 2, 2007, A1.

40. See Jon Henley, "Flip Flop, "*The New Republic*, Vol. 222, No. 1, January 3, 2000, p. 24.

41. Saleh AlShebil, Abdul A. Rasheed, and Hussam Al-Shammari, "Battling Boycotts: When a Company Is Targeted Simply Because of Its Nationality, What Can It Do?, *MIT Sloan Management Review*, April 27, 2007.

42. Examples adapted from Strategic Sourceror, "Amnesty International Finds Conflict in Blood Diamond Supply Chain, October 7, 2015, accessed at http://www.strategicsourceror.com/2015/10/amnesty-international-report-finds.html on October 28, 2015; *Sources*: T. L. Stanley, "Gem Sellers Launch Blitz Against "Blood Diamond,'" *Advertising Age*, December 11, 2006, 50 (12), p. 12; www. DiamondFacts.org.

43. www.movidacorona.com; www.corona-extra.net, both accessed on October 28, 2015.

44. *Makedonski Telekom*, "Culture and Public Life," www.telekom.mk/en/?z=956 (accessed June 1, 2012).

45. *Autocar*, "Tata to Sponsor Ferrari," www.autocar.co.uk/car-news/industry/tata-sponsor-ferrari (accessed on June 1, 2012); *Cystic Fibrosis Trust*, "Tata Steel Cardiff Bay 5," May 6, 2012, http://www.cftrust.org.uk/help/events/cb5.

46. Thane Peterson and Sandra Dallas, "Tycoons on the Trail of the Next de Kooning," *BusinessWeek*, Vol. 3541, August 25, 1997, p. 16.

47. *China Daily*, May 24, 2007, Special Advertising Insert. John Tagliabue, "A McDonald's Ally in Paris," *New York Times Online*, June 20, 2006.

48. Panos Mourdoukoutas, "Three Trends Haunting McDonald's: Localization, Customization, And Cheap Labor,"

Forbes, June 18, 2015, accessed at http://www.forbes.com/sites/panosmourdoukoutas/2015/06/18/three-trends-haunting-mcdonalds-localization-customization-and-cheap-labor/ on October 28, 2015; http:// ad-sneeze.com/2007/03/01/mcdonalds-france-advert, accessed on April 28, 2012.

49. http://www.colorsmagazine.com/downloads/PDF/COLORS_71.pdf (accessed June 2, 2012)

50. Kimberley Amadeo, "U.S. Imports and Exports: Components and Statistics," *The Balance*, March 3, 2018, accessed at https://www.thebalance.com/u-s-imports-and-exports-components-and-statistics-3306270 on July 3, 2018.

51. Frank Kane, "Six lessons from the Summit on the Global Agenda of the World Economic Forum in Abu Dhabi," *The National*, October 27, 2015, accessed at http://www.thenational.ae/business/economy/six-lessons-from-the-summit-on-the-global-agenda-of-the-world-economic-forum-in-abu-dhabi on October 28, 2015.

52. "Couponing Worldwide," Couponasaurus, 2018, accessed at https://couponasaurus.com/couponing-worldwide/ on July 4, 2018.

53. 4Eon.net, "Most brands are looking for ways to either increase sales or consumer engagement," accessed at http://www.4eon.net/experiential-marketing/consumer-sales-promotions-rewards-incentives/ on October 28, 2015.

54. Daney Parker, "Popular Choice," *Marketing Week*, Vol. 19, No. 10, May 31, 1996, pp. 39–40.

55. Ibid.

56. Suzy Bashford, "McDonald's and Fox Kids," *Promotions & Incentives*, February 2004, pp. 25–27.

57. Ken Gofton, "How Euro Rules Will Change SP," *Marketing*, October 5, 2000, pp. 60–61.

58. *Marketing Week*, "EC Abandons Plan for Sales Promotion Regulations," September 29, 2005, p. 6.

59. Rob Furber, "Centre Shop," *Marketing Week*, Vol. 22, No. 38, October 21, 1999, pp. 51–54.

60. Warner Bernhard, "Crossing the Border," *Brandweek*, Vol. 37, No. 48, December 16, 1996, pp. 37–38.

61. Maxine Lans Retsky, "Global Promotions Are Subject to Local Laws," *Marketing News*, Vol. 31, No. 10, May 12, 1997, p. 8.

62. "News From Our Bangalore Office," *FCEDA Global News*, April 2018, accessed at https://www.fairfaxcountyeda.org/our-global-presence/global-news on July 4, 2018.

Case 12-1 **Selling the Donnelly Brand in Romania**

Donnelly's Cigarettes of Martinsville, Virginia, is planning its international expansion into a rapidly growing market, Central and Eastern Europe. The company sells the popular, low-priced Donnelly brand in select Southern states, but it is currently looking for other venues for selling its brand. Encumbered with tight regulations in the United States, Donnelly is actively seeking markets that offer a higher profit potential than the home market.

Donnelly started out seven decades ago as a tobacco farm that initially sold its products to cigarette manufacturers, such as Philip Morris. It started developing its own brand of tobacco in the 1980s, providing substantial competition to the lower-priced Philip Morris brands. To the Southern U.S. market, Donnelly offers filter cigarettes, light cigarettes, menthol and menthol lights, as well as ultra lights and menthol ultra lights. The company romanticizes the Donnelly brand's indigenous origins, and it pursues profits aggressively by stressing its homegrown quality. In advertising, it stresses the Virginia origins of the tobacco, and its point-of-purchase advertising displays the brand's home-grown characteristics — even though Donnelly imports most of the tobacco from Asia. In its advertising for the U.S. market, Donnelly claims that it uses a large percentage of U.S.-grown tobacco, higher than that of all the Philip Morris brands.

The family patriarch, John Donnelly, a third generation tobacco farmer with impressive business acumen, is presently investigating modes of expansion that are likely to increase company profits. Cigarettes are under scrutiny in the United States, and Donnelly is dealing with lawsuits by individuals claiming that smoking the brand led to health problems. Moreover, in the United States, state governments and localities have started to ban smoking from public buildings, leading many consumers to quit and many others to decide against smoking.

In its plans to expand in Central and Eastern Europe, as with its business in the United States, Donnelly will maintain a hands-on approach to marketing the brand. Research of the business literature revealed that cigarettes are especially popular in Romania, where they are in a profitable late

Bacio/shutterstock.com

growth stage. John Donnelly found this market especially attractive after examining this research.

Romanians have had a long-running love affair with Western cigarettes. Kent cigarettes constituted important commodity money in this market for many decades during the communist rule. Western cigarettes in general were coveted status symbols for Romanian smokers. Today, about 31.3 percent of individuals over 15 years of age smoke, in a country with a population of 22 million, with the highest prevalence in the 25-34 age group. The average age for starting to smoke is just under 19 years old. And 47.1 percent of all smokers smoke between 10 and 20 cigarettes daily. About 34.5 percent of men smoke daily, most in the 25-44 year-old group, whereas 21.9 percent of women smoke daily, with those between 15 and 24 years of age being the heaviest smokers.

As income increases across the board, premium brands are taking an increasing share of the cigarette market, with the highest sales made in the upper mid-price brands, such as Pall Mall, Winston, Lucky Strike, especially mid-tar versions. In response to the growing health awareness of Romanian consumers, both because of improvements to standards of living and public campaigns against smoking, cigarette manufacturers launched new, "reduced harm" varieties of their products.

Excise duty on tobacco is continually rising to reach a level acceptable to the EU; Romanian authorities continue to raise taxes three times a year and will continue to do so more frequently, with higher increases. As a result, the selling of contraband cigarettes has intensified. Contraband cigarettes are usually imported from the Republic of Moldova and Ukraine, countries where taxes are three times lower than in Romania.

Research also revealed that leading Western cigarette manufacturers have set up factories to take advantage of this market. The British tobacco giant B.A.T. Industries PLC built a $70 million factory in Romania in the mid-1990s, designed to produce more than four billion cigarettes a year; the company has a market share of just under 10 percent. R.J. Reynolds Tobacco International, a U.S. firm, opened a large plant there as well. R.J.R. has a 15 percent share of the market. Philip Morris holds an 18 percent share of the Romanian market. The company dominates the Central and Eastern European market for American blend cigarettes, with 70 percent of the market share. It has cigarette plants in the Czech Republic, Kazakhstan, Poland, Hungary, Ukraine, and Russia, but not in Romania. A company manufacturing cigarettes in Romania is Papastratos Cigarette Manufacturing Company of Greece.

A main competitor for Donnelly is the Romanian tobacco company, Galaxy Tobacco, that is currently reinventing itself to appeal to Romanian consumers' nostalgia for traditional Romanian brands, such as Snagov and Carpati. The company holds 50 percent of the market share in Romania. Donnelly believes that this important market segment prefers foreign cigarettes but cannot afford them; once Donnelly sells its affordable U.S. brand to the Romanian market, many consumers smoking Romanian brands are likely to switch to the Donnelly brand.

Donnelly planned to ship the products to Romania from the port of Norfolk, Virginia, and pick them up at the Romanian port of Constanta, on the Black Sea. Even with transportation costs and with the excise duties placed on both local producers and importers and an added tax of 20 percent, the Donnelly brand would still be much cheaper than its other Western competitors. The company is planning to sell its products directly to convenience stores — mom-and-pop types that would agree to lower gross margins, which would keep prices low for Romanian consumers. The major decision that remains for the company is how to advertise in this market. Donnelly presently does all its advertising in-house in the Martinsville office complex. However, John Donnelly believes that it would be risky to use materials produced in-house in a market that is so different from its Southern U.S. market. John Donnelly and his family are now contemplating the choice of an advertising company.

Many of the large multinational ad firms are present in Romania. Among them are Graffiti/BBDO, a division of BBDO Worldwide, among the first international firms to come to Romania; Grey Business Room, a division of Grey Worldwide; Olympic DDB; and Ogilvy Romania. John Donnelly believes that these companies have substantial expertise and capability, but their high costs are likely to infringe on company profits. Their ads would be exceptional in quality and impact, nevertheless.

The alternative would be to hire a local firm. Among prominent local firms are Ager Press S.A., a large formerly state-owned company; Andrei Advertising; Artmedia Group, a full-service advertising agency; Advertigo, a full-service independent agency; and B&C Consulting, a full-service public relations and advertising agency. Donnelly found that two of the firms might be a better fit in terms of capability and expertise.

The first company, Advertigo, is a full-service independent agency founded in 1998, serving a number of Romanian firms and a few prominent international firms and brands. Among them are 121 Marketing, Atlanta (a clothing company with brands such as Wampum Jeans, ATL, and Atlanta), Atlas Trading, Avanti Furs, Corporate Office Solutions, Corona Cosmetics, Creative Paving, and Johnson & Johnson—specifically, the company's baby care products, Carefree, o.b., and Neutrogena brands. The company has experts in media strategies, media planning, copywriting, design, and research, as well as various business specialists. Its services span all media available in Romania.

B&C Consulting is a public relations and advertising strategy offering full service in communications and image consulting. Among its clients are the Romanian government, promoting Romania's image abroad with the B&C Consulting slogan "the strength beside you"; SNP PETROM, the large gas company, promoting its image with the slogan "the essence of movement"; and the popular Supermarket pop-rock group with its slogan "Pop-Rock Made in Supermarket." This young group creates edgy advertisements and memorable slogans in both Romanian and English.

John Donnelly must decide whether to use a global firm or a local firm. His family in Martinsville, the only other individuals with ownership in the company, has difficulty in offering advice. John must decide on the advertising agency before his trip to Romania in two months.

Sources: Euromonitor, "Tobacco in Romania," October 2015, accessed at http://www.euromonitor.com/tobacco-in-romania/report on October 27, 2015; Anastasia Warpinski, "Tobacco Firms Look to Pocket Romania as Push in Central Europe Intensifies," Wall Street Journal, September 19, 1997, C1; http://www.advertigo.ro/; http://www.bcconsulting.ro/Portofoliu.html. This case is fictitious.

Analysis Suggestions

1. Should Donnelly use in-house produced advertising in the Romanian market? Why or why not?

2. What advantages would Donnelly have if it decided to use a U.S. advertising agency present in Romania? What would be the disadvantages of using a U.S. agency?

3. Which advertising agency should Donnelly choose for advertising the Donnelly brand in Romania? Explain.

Case 14-1 *Promoting Coke in South Africa*

Coca-Cola just moved its operating group headquarters from the United Kingdom to Johannesburg, South Africa, to be closer to target consumers. Coca-Cola is the largest consumer goods provider in Africa. To date, the company has grown through close collaboration with its bottling and retail partners. Company headquarters have an aggressive growth plan for the African continent and for South Africa in particular. With a large percentage of the population young and dynamic, this market should be carefully courted.

As part of its efforts to reach this population, Coke set up the Coca-Cola Africa Foundation, in which the company partners with other organizations to build sustainable communities on the continent. To reach young South Africans in particular, the company hired South African artists that would appeal to this segment of the population to participate in a re-mix of the "I'd Like to Buy the World a Coke" theme song as a musical montage of reggae, Kwaito, rap, hip-hop, and hard rock. The ad was part of the "Coke Side of Life" campaign, and the theme song was so popular that radio stations added it to their playlists.

Tony Campbell/shutterstock.com

South Africa was Coca-Cola's first stop on the African continent in 1928. The company set up the first bottling and distribution plant in Johannesburg and has expanded its business in the country ever since, employing more than 10,000 people. The company's presence in South Africa created many more jobs in the country. For every job created by the production and marketing of Coke products, 10 additional jobs, on average, were created in South Africa in related industries.

The Coca-Cola Company sells numerous nonalcoholic brands to South African consumers. Among them are Coca-Cola (with its Light and Vanilla Coke versions), Fanta (with its Orange, Grape, and Pineapple versions), Sprite, Tab, Sparletta, Lemon Twist, Schweppes, Mixers, Fresca, Minute Maid, Powerade, Bibo, Milo, Krest, Splash, Bonaqua, and Vitango. Its product mix in South Africa is more extensive than in the United States because, in South Africa, the company also bought out a number of popular regional competitors.

During its time in Africa, Coca-Cola ran a few successful promotions. First, in 2002, it hired Riverside Technologies in Wilton, Connecticut, to provide ideas on technologic modifications that would set the brand apart. Riverside came up with modules that could be inserted into the packaging; these modules would sing and announce the winner of a Coke promotion. Consumers who purchased the winning cans were instant winners of Panasonic stereo equipment. The winning cans were filled with carbon dioxide and water, to replicate the weight and feel of a real can, and were assembled into the Coke can by Schmalbach-Lubeca Continental Can in Bonn, Germany. Fifty talking cans were produced for the promotion and were distributed nationally. In just the first month of the promotion, sales of Coke cans rose by 3.2 percent, Diet Coke cans by 18.6 percent, and Fanta by 3.8 percent compared with the previous year. This was in line with the theme of the promotion, "This summer only Coca-Cola talks," literally— and figuratively, in terms of sales.

Since 2002, Coca-Cola hasn't had many promotions that delivered a similar impact. In the spring of 2004, for example, the company coordinated with its advertising agencies another promotion that was not as popular with South African consumers. The promotion asked them to nominate the most inspiring person they knew to carry the Olympic Flame in Cape Town. Distributors were unhappy that they were not involved in the promotion, and generally, it was felt that a more aggressive and creative approach was needed to resuscitate Coke sales again.

In early 2006, Coke hired Conceptualise, South Africa's leading promotional marketing specialist, whose area of expertise is the development and implementation of promotional competitions and games. The company developed the Coca-Cola Mega Millions game for the South African market, which has captivated South African consumers. Mega Millions had a game-show format, and it was broadcast live during prime time on one of South Africa's top network channels, SABC 1. In the game, contestants interacted live to win cars and large cash prizes. To enter the game, individuals had to purchase Coca-Cola carbonated drinks, check the label, and find out if they had won a prize. Their number also qualified them to enter into a pool of candidates to become a contestant on the live show — a contestant was drawn during each show from the pool of potential contestants. The Mega Millions game was hugely successful, with 22 million entries over a 4-month period.

Another successful promotion was co-sponsored with the retailer Pick 'n Pay, the 2012 Olympics Pick 'n Pay promotion. Participants were required to purchase a Coke product from any of the retailer's stores and SMS the number at the bottom of their receipt to win as much as 20 million SA Rand in cash. This would cost the individual sending the SMS 1 Rand.

In 2015, Coke organized the Highway Africa Conference, a gathering of journalists, editors, and academics across Africa. The conference provided training to facilitate accurate reporting on health, nutrition, and the environment. "Knowing that media influences health and nutritional perceptions among the public, journalists were taken through various topics in nutrition research such as research methodologies, research validity and reliability, peer review system, ethical clearance and conflict of interest."

Sources: Coca-Cola, " Highway Africa Offers Nutritional Science Workshop to Journalists," accessed at http:// www.coca-cola.co.za/articles/2015_highway_africa.html?cat=3 on October 28, 2015; www.coca-cola.co.za/ upload/ documents/competitions/20120703_OlympicPick_n_Pay_Promo_rules_03_July_2012_FINAL.pdf; www.thecoca-colacompany.com/contactus/faq/africa.html; www.conceptualise.co.za; Andrew Kaplan, "Case Study: Drumming Up Sales," *Beverage World*, Vol. 122, No. 1724, March 15, 2003, p. 99; http://rsa.coca-cola.com; http://www.coc-cola.co.za/.

Analysis Suggestions

1. Evaluate Coke's market position in South Africa relative to other competitors and other businesses.

2. Evaluate the different types of consumer promotions used in South Africa to increase sales for Coca-Cola South Africa. Are there any types of sales promotions that should not have been used in a country characterized by a wealth gap, with a substantial proportion of the population below the poverty line? Explain.

This page is intentionally blank...

Chapter 13

International Personal Selling
and Personnel Management

lmtmphoto/shutterstock.com

International sales representatives are often the frontline personnel in a firm's relationship with an international target market. Their expertise, ability, demeanor, and appearance convey information that is integral to the firm's offering and help shape its relationship with the target market, distributors, suppliers, and government agencies. These representatives may be full-time expatriate employees of the company, crossing cultural divides and bridging cultures on behalf of the firm, often in unfamiliar settings, where the culture and marketing practices differ from those in the sales representatives' home country. Expatriate sales representatives must survive challenges posed by the new environment, adapt to its changing demands, and play by the host-country rules while representing the company.

Local sales representatives face challenges as the company's frontline personnel. As nationals of the host country, they understand the market and its intricacies; as representatives of the company, they must be familiar with the company's home country, its organizational culture, as well as its marketing practices. Local representatives may be full-time employees, or, as is often the case, independent contractors selling the company's goods on a commission basis. This distinction between an employee and an independent contractor is important for the company's relationship with and obligations to the sales representative.

This chapter addresses the management of local and expatriate employees, motivating them for optimal performance, and, for expats, ensuring their successful repatriation.

13-1 International Presence and Personnel Issues

From a company perspective, hiring expatriates or locals is a function of the company's involvement in the market. The company's presence in the market — entry mode — and its commitment to the market are important considerations in determining the size of the sales team and the types of sales representatives the company employs or engages on a contract basis. Companies whose international activities are primarily export-related, and especially SMEs (small medium-sized enterprises), will take a different approach to developing a sales team than would a multinational corporation with a major manufacturing and/or distribution presence in the country. There are numerous definitions for an SME in the United States as well as in the European Union and other countries. In the U.S., one benchmark defines an SME as having less than 500 employees and revenues of less than $25 million.[1]

As firms enter the direct exporting process (as opposed to selling their products to an in-country export-trading company), the company's involvement with the export selling process will expand. New-to-export firms, as well as existing SME exporters targeting a new market, may start the process by sending a company representative to a trade show overseas. U.S. state and regional economic development offices, as well as the U.S. Dept.

of Commerce, may organize the participation of a U.S. delegation at a show. This is designed to encourage and support the smaller, often novice, exporters. Depending on the product or service for export and the target country, these SMEs may use initial visits in a foreign market to locate an in-country international sales representative or a stocking distributor. An in-country sales representative, typically operating on a commission basis, is often the preferred route for exporting customized industrial goods as well as commodities. The in-country agent represents the company and helps negotiate deals but does not take title to the exported goods and typically will not be signing any final sales agreements or contracts.

A stocking distributor is typically the more appropriate market entry strategy for exporters of consumer goods that can be sold by the exporter to the in-country stocking distributor. The stocking distributor takes title to the goods and pays the exporter. The stocking distributor operates almost like a wholesaler and would have the primary responsibility for negotiating in-country sales with retailers and distributing products to them, often from the local distributor's own warehouse.

The home country firm may engage a number of agents or distributors in a country depending on the size of the market, a preference not to grant exclusive sales or distribution rights for the country, etc. With multiple in-country agents or distributors, the home country firm might even hire an in-country manager, a local citizen or an expatriate, to oversee the firm's business in the country. Of course, these models can and do vary. In the case of selling software and other types of professional services, local in-country representation could be via a commission sales agent, distributor, or even a franchise.

An international sales manager based in the exporter's home country will lead the sales effort and may travel to international markets on a regular basis. The company is now becoming much more involved in personal selling. Personal selling is an important component of international marketing communications, especially for business-to-business transactions. Salespeople are the Dior saleswoman selling the French brand in a leased department in a U.S. department store, the representative of the Coke bottler selling Fanta to a Burundi bottled drinks retailer, the Air India ticketing agent at JFK airport in New York, and the Polish manufacturer selling upholstery to the Fiat plant in Italy. Personal selling involves a face-to-face interaction between the seller and the buyer and, in industrial sales, their respective teams. The interaction between the two parties is affected by their national cultures.

Figure 13-1 *An order taker in this health food and organic cosmetics company would have to be highly skilled and familiar with the specifics of the products sold.*

In the international selling context, the order taker, the individual who processes routine orders from the customer, is likely to be a local employee who is familiar with the local customs and culture. Individuals working at the German Reformhaus are highly skilled in selling health foods and cosmetics free of preservatives. In Taiwan, these individuals would also have to be familiar with the local culture, and, in effect, act as a bridge between the German and Taiwanese culture (see Figure 13-1).

Order getters, individuals who actively generate potential leads and persuade customers to purchase the firm's products, can be local or international staff who are highly skilled technically, as well as trained in conducting negotiations. In international marketing, most order getters work in the business-to-business area as field salespeople, going to customers to solicit business.

Order getters selling to other businesses would go to their clients' places of business. In the case of the SME exporter, the order getter and order taker functions could both be handled by the exporter's in-country sales representative, along with administrative support from the exporter's home or regional office. Order getters selling to consumers directly would go to consumers' homes. For example, direct marketers such as Avon and multilevel marketers such as Amway hire salespeople to sell products to their network of friends, and to also recruit new sales personnel for the multilevel sales network.

In developed countries, telemarketing is also popular in selling products. For telemarketing campaigns to be successful, companies need to have access to a reliable telephone system and teleconferencing, and for the culture to accept telemarketing and/or teleconferencing. In the United States and Canada, telemarketing was historically an acceptable form of sales promotion. However, by 2018 U.S. consumers have become increasingly upset with unsolicited telemarketing "junk calls." Consumers now regularly take steps to remove their names and phone numbers from telemarketers' call lists and even electronically block such calls. In North Africa, the Middle East, or even Europe, telemarketing calls, even charity solicitations and opinion polling, are not met with acceptance and do not generate a very good response.

osim Shukurov/shutterstock.com

After a sale is closed, companies sign contracts that address the terms of the transaction, costs involved, and the term of the relationship. In many countries, a written contract does not mean much; sellers and buyers can readily choose to ignore the agreement without any penalty. The legal systems might endorse contracts but not defend them. In many cultures, a contract might have little value, while someone's word may be fully reliable. In many countries outside the United States, trust relationships are expected, and company executives are insulted at the suggestion the agreement should be documented in a written contract.

However, exporters, and especially exporters engaged in long-term distributor contract relationships, should take steps to protect their legal interests. This may include contract language requiring that any disputes be subject to the law of the home country as well as jurisdiction in a court of law in the home country. Another approach could be to require that any contract disputes be subject to international arbitration, perhaps utilizing the International Court of Arbitration, a unit of the International Chamber of Commerce, or a private mediation and arbitration services company.[2]

U.S. companies establishing distributor relationships in a foreign country also need to understand the requirements of the U.S. Foreign Corrupt Practices Act (FCPA) concerning bribes and other illegal payments to foreign public sector officials to secure contracts. The U.S. company may be liable for the actions of a distributor notwithstanding that the U.S. firm would not normally hold title to the goods in question. Similarly, the actions of an in-country sales representative may also expose the U.S. company to FCPA scrutiny, even if the local representative is deemed an independent contractor and not an employee of the company.[3]

As mentioned earlier, an exporter entering a new market may choose to engage a local in-country commission sales agent to represent the home-country firm. The agent solicits and negotiates orders on behalf of the exporter, but does not take title to the goods. As is customary in the United States, the exporter may seek to define this legal relationship with the sales representative as that of an independent contractor who contracts with the company to provide specific services, as opposed to a general employee. However, if the exporter exercises too much control over the sales representative's day-to-day activities or does not properly structure the contract relationship with the in-country representative, the local in-country legal system may deem the representative to be an employee. Employee status would typically require the company to offer more benefits and job protection. In addition, in the event of a termination, the now local "employee" may be eligible for several years' worth of prospective commissions that might have been earned. Exporters are always advised to work with experienced international trade attorneys to draft these legal agreements.[4]

Jojje/shutterstock.com

At the next level of the buyer-seller relationship is the electronic data interchange (EDI) relationship, whereby buying and selling firms are able to share important data on production, inventory, shipping, and purchasing. EDI relationships are possible primarily if the firms have the appropriate resources and trust their local partner with the information. Such relationships entail a very high level of trust because the seller has access to the buying firm's production information and the seller ships the products automatically. EDI relationships are typically single-source relationships, as sellers need to be assured that the buyer is not purchasing products from a competitor — at least as long as the contract is in place. In EDI relationships, switching vendors is a high-cost proposition. In many countries switching vendors is, in fact, difficult. U.S. firms, such as Walmart, expect full information from their suppliers; however, East Asian and European are less inclined to offer full inventory disclosure than U.S. firms.

Multinational firms are also increasingly using extensible markup language (XML) to efficiently manage their supply-chain relationships. The system encodes production, inventory, shipping, and purchasing data and processes the content without human intervention, sharing it with the company's supply chain partners. XML and EDI exist primarily in high-income countries; when firms operate in low-income countries, they often must revert to paper reports, which bring with them inaccuracies, inability to track shipments and ensure timely delivery, and lag time for inventory information. Large firms must often subcontract logistics operations with different companies to ensure timely shipments. Logistics companies, such as Deutsche Post FedEx and UPS, often rekey paper information from clients' suppliers and factories and offer their clients tracking information regarding manufacturing process, shipment, and delivery.

The most committed relationship of the buyer-seller dyad interaction is the strategic partnership, whereby buyers and sellers share information at the highest levels. The seller actively examines product improvements to better serve the needs of the buying firm. The company needs to determine the types of salespeople it should hire for optimal performance. The foreign sales force of the multinational corporation could include *expatriates* (home-country nationals and third-country nationals) and *host-country nationals*.

13-1a Expatriates

merzzie/shutterstock.com

Expatriates working in a particular foreign country belong to two categories: One category is the *home-country national,* an employee who was successful as a sales representative in the home country and has been assigned overseas – for example, a Philip Morris International employee from the company headquarters in Switzerland working at the company's Hong Kong operations. Representing the second category is the *third-country national,* a truly international salesperson, an expatriate who works in numerous countries, such as a Chilean salesman working in Italy, assigned to Unilever's Bulgarian accounts.

Home-Country Nationals

Home-country nationals — *parent-company nationals* — are preferred by companies whose products are at the forefront of technology, and when the selling function relies on extensive training and specialized information. In situations in which a greater interdependence exists between an overseas unit and corporate headquarters, firms are more likely to dispatch home-country nationals. This is also true for situations in which complex operations are involved, there is a greater political risk, and there is a greater level of competition.[5]

A disadvantage of home-country nationals is the high cost. In addition to the regular salary and commission the employee would have received in the home country, additional incentives are standard for international assignments. A cost-of-living allowance, a housing allowance that also covers household help, and an education allowance for children, paying for education at expensive private schools, are standard.

Other perks are an annual or biannual home-leave for the family or an annual visit from immediate family living in the home country. The firm may have to pay for the costs of selling the employee's home, for storing furniture, and for moving household goods overseas, all adding up to a high cost. Even sending an employee overseas for five months can be costly, covering housing in a hotel, an automobile, and a high living allowance. The costs could easily be above $100,000 beyond salary for the five months.

Assignments in expensive world capitals, such as London, Paris (see Figure 13-2 on next page), or Tokyo will result in even higher costs.

Among other disadvantages of hiring home-country nationals are:

• The cultural barriers faced by the home-country nationals in the country of assignment (see Figure 13-3 on next page);

• The expenses involved in training home-country nationals in the culture (and, often, language) of the country of assignment;

• The lack of local personal connections to the important decision makers in the government and the local trade;

Figure 13-2 *Sending a home-country national to Paris
is costly – renting a one bedroom apartment in the
center will easily cost over 2,500 euros per month
unfurnished and without utilities.*   Figure 13-3 *Home country nationals from a U.S.
firm might have difficulty adapting to Asian culture
without understanding the local traditions and language*

• The difficulty of finding quality employees willing to take on international assignments because they are reluctant to uproot their families or because they fear that
they will lose visibility and status at the head office (international companies offer
many incentives to overcome this impediment).

• Using home-country nationals can also send the signal to the local target market
that the company trusts only its own people to run the business. This backfired in the
case of Walmart Stores, which brought their own managers to manage its German
operations, for example. Unlike Walmart, Tesco believes in being fully integrated in
the local environment and hires mostly locals in the higher-profile, management jobs.

When international business began to rapidly expand after World War II, it was common for the multinational company to dispatch home-country nationals to manage local in-
country operations. That was due to control considerations, as well as the fact that it was
difficult to find adequately trained international business management talent in the host
country. That has all changed; now, universities around the world offer sophisticated international business education programs. Accordingly, more large exporters, and especially
multinational firms, prefer to hire local managers and sales personnel. A multinational company may still send expatriates abroad for multi-year assignments, especially when the candidate is being groomed for senior global management responsibilities. Increasingly,
though, multinational firms may send home-country employees abroad for shorter training
stints with the local in-country operation, or even with a key distributor. These short-term
assignments can focus on sales, finance, information systems, etc.

Third-Country Nationals

Third-country nationals are employees working temporarily in an assignment country, who are not nationals of that country or of the country in which the corporate headquarters of the company they work for are located. They are "professional expatriates."
They are accustomed to constantly adapting to new environments. They speak numerous
languages, are familiar with customs and business practices in different environments, and
have learned, through their vast international experience, to adapt optimally for international assignments. In certain countries, third-country nationals are more likely than home-

country nationals and locals to be on international corporations' payrolls. Examples of such countries are the United Arab Emirates and Saudi Arabia, where international companies hire highly skilled employees from India, Pakistan, Egypt, and the Philippines, among others. One study found that expatriates working in Saudi Arabia typically save for future consumption and gear most of their purchases toward home-country consumption.[6] Third-country nationals are also less likely to return early from the foreign assignment due to difficulties in adapting to the local environment.

Often, third-country nationals are competent company employees transferred from a subsidiary of the company operating in another country. Usually, third-country nationals cost less than home-country nationals (but more than locals) and expatriate allowances tend to be lower than those typical for home-country employees. There is at least one exception to this rule: Hiring Emirati employees in the United Arab Emirates requires paying a premium. Most of the professional cadre in the UAE consists of third-country nationals, as local Emiratis constitute only 20 percent of the population.

In the Middle East, many countries have a large proportion of third-country nationals in their labor force. Take, for example, the following case of Oman.

Third-Country Nationals in Oman

In Oman, non-Omanis constitute 44.4 percent of the population, and this is low compared with some other Gulf countries. Omanis make up more than 80 percent of the public-sector labor force, but constitute less than 20 percent of the private-sector workforce, with expatriates primarily from Asia filling mostly unskilled, low-paid jobs, and middle-management positions. But the government is pushing for the "Omanization" of the private sector, pressing for Omanis to replace expatriates.

Marcin Szymczak/shutterstock.com

Reducing the unemployment of Omanis is high on Oman's government's agenda. The country has a young population, with almost 55 percent younger than the age of 20, and 83 percent younger than 35, and many of Oman's young have moved to the cities in search of better job prospects. Today, 70 percent of the population is urban. Most Omanis are Muslim, but, as a result of its trading history, the country is a mixture of races, with a prominent trading family of Indian Hindu descent.[7] The country has a tradition of welcoming foreigners, and the mandate of "Omanization" is surprising to many expatriates.

In the case of both home-country nationals and third-country nationals, many governments, primarily in developing countries, dictate the number (usually a percentage) of foreign nationals that a foreign firm operating is permitted to hire. In the case of third-country nationals, it is not uncommon for local governments to delay visas or otherwise complicate the hiring process. In all these situations, firms are forced to rely heavily on host-country nationals (locals) and may tap into international sales talent and expertise only to a limited extent. One recent development was the announcement by the Saudi Arabian government banning foreign nationals from working in retail and sales positions in several sectors starting in September 2018. The new ruling is part of a larger plan to modernize the Saudi economy, deal with increased unemployment, and create new employment opportunities for both Saudi men and women.[8]

13-1b Host-Country Nationals (Locals)

The local salesperson who works in his or her home country for an international corporation is a host-country national. An example would be the Hungarian brand manager schooled in a university in the United States, working for Procter & Gamble in Hungary. This individual understands the U.S. business environment, has been well trained technically at an accredited U.S. institution, and is willing to return to his/her home country to work for a U.S. multinational firm.

Increasingly, international firms appear to prefer local employees to expatriates. Cost is only one consideration. Frequently, locals with similar levels of education and training are available for employment at a fraction of the cost of expatriates. Host-country nationals also speak the local language and often have a well-developed network within the local industry and government. And, as mentioned in Section 13-1a, "Expatriates," some host governments restrict the number of foreign nationals working in the country. Thus, host-country nationals also fit with the country's employment policies.

mentatdgt/shutterstock.com

Many international firms compete for the types of individuals described here. Although the multinational company deems it appropriate to remunerate host-country nationals below the level of expatriates, not offering them the appropriate motivation to remain with the company increases their risk of flight to a competitor.

13-1c Long-Distance International Selling

Multinationals are increasingly taking a more strategic view of international staffing, exploring a variety of supply-side issues, cost issues, demand-side issues, and career issues, and identifying a portfolio of alternatives to the traditional international assignment. Such alternatives are short-term assignments, commuter assignments, international business travel, and virtual assignments.[9]

Selling via the Internet or mail is an important venue for approaching new customers overseas. Costs of distance selling are lower — companies do not have to dispatch salespeople abroad and spend on cross-cultural training — allowing for greater market coverage. However, distance selling is difficult to coordinate internationally, often largely due to cultural differences.

International retail selling via the Internet is growing substantially. However, there are concerns. According to recent research, only a third of online merchants based in the U.S. offer their products or services internationally. Canada is the strongest international market for U.S. e-commerce retailers, accounting for over 40 percent of international revenues. By contrast, Latin America, with a population of 650 million, accounts for only 12 percent of international revenues. One reason is because almost one half of Latin Americans are unbanked, with no access to debit or credit cards with which to make payments. Fraud, as well extensive local country e-commerce regulations, are also deterrents to the expansion of Internet selling in Latin America, and probably other developing regions as well.[10]

13-2 Managing International Employees

13-2a Managing Relationships

Managing internationals — expatriates and host-country nationals — is no easy task for multinational corporations. Companies that attempt to transplant personnel policies that have proven successful in the home country run into obstacles in different international environments. Establishing quotas, assigning management responsibilities to employees within the firm, or even simply addressing employees by first names could prove to be problematic for the firm.

Figure 13-4 *In some countries, even offering to brave the roads to go to the enterprise on foot, rather than being picked up by the company car, may lead to a loss of status.*

Issues related to culture, such as national character, could come into play. Rolling up one's sleeves and working on the assembly line results in an instant loss of status for the manager in Southeast Asia, Eastern Europe (see Figure 13-4), and South America.

Problems related to social class or caste bring additional challenges. Placing a Dalit, a member of a low-caste group of Hindu India, previously known as "untouchables," in charge of a Brahman in India would be problematic, as would placing someone of peasant origins in charge of someone from the intellectual class in Eastern Europe (even if training and education justify such an assignment).

13-2b Understanding the International Buyer-Seller Relationship

In a personal selling environment, challenges also arise in the international buyer-seller relationship. Certain approaches to selling work better than others. For example, a hard sell is not likely to be successful in most Asian countries, where modesty, a humble attitude, and respect are seen as valuable traits. Looking one's counterpart directly in the eye — a sign of honesty in the United States — is likely to be perceived as an aggressive stance in Asia and Latin America. In one's first encounter with a Chinese counterpart, it is advised that business cards be exchanged. When one takes the Chinese manager's business card, one should do so with both hands and read it, as a sign of respect. The U.S. manager is advised to have business cards written in English and Chinese when dealing with the Chinese. It should be noted, however, that, increasingly, such pleasantries are cut short in the many dynamic business environments in Asia. In a busy work-life environment, sometimes the Chinese will surprise their U.S. counterparts and address bottom-line issues directly, but still gently.

In general, however, it is best to understand the difference between the Western and the Chinese approach to negotiations. While Western business cultures treat communication as an exchange of information — and the communication ends when the deal is over — the Chinese view the negotiation as an inseparable part of building and maintaining business relationships. From the Chinese perspective, building relationships takes time and analysis. From the American perspective, time is money and they need to inform the headquarters that they have a done deal. Not taking into account these differences in approaches to negotiations will invariably lead to a breakdown in the dialogue, with American negotiators viewing the Chinese as inefficient, indirect, and even dishonest, while the Chinese view American negotiators as aggressive, impersonal, and excitable. [11]

In other examples, Italians typically enjoy engaging in the negotiation process and want to feel that they are special customers. They want to feel like they are getting a deal; offering them a bottom-line price at first is a strategy that will most likely meet with failure.[12] The strategy of focusing on closing the deal and aiming toward the next sale is unlikely to work in Latin America, where individuals prefer to take time to build a relationship with suppliers.[13] In this environment, it is best to first socialize, to build a relationship of friendship and trust, preferably involving the family. In the Middle East, this approach also works well, although it most often does not involve the family.

13-1c Understanding Cultural Values and the Relationship between Buyer and Seller

National Character, Organizational Culture, and Personality

The level of psychological overlap in communication between buyer and seller varies across three dimensions: national character, organizational culture, and individual personality.[14] A personal selling situation involves *content* and *style*. Content includes substantive aspects of the interaction, such as suggesting, offering, or negotiating product-specific utilities and expectations, whereas style refers to rituals, format, mannerisms, and ground rules of the buyer and seller during the course of their interaction.[15] An interaction between buyer and seller is satisfactory if the two parties are compatible on these two dimensions.[16] In cross-cultural sales interactions, style is shaped by national character, organizational culture, and the personality of the individuals involved in the interaction.[17]

Zurijeta/shutterstock.com

Chapter 5, "Cultural Influences on International Marketing," described national character in terms of personality traits shared at the national level. The key dimensions identified as constituting national character are individualism, power distance, uncertainty avoidance, and masculinity/femininity.[18] To illustrate, in cross-cultural interactions, individuals from cultures low in power distance negotiating with counterparts from a high power distance environment have to adopt a more formal negotiation style, addressing these individuals by their last name and title, and following their hierarchy protocols.

Compatible organizational styles also contribute to creating a satisfactory interaction between buyer and seller. Organizational culture refers to shared norms and values that guide collective behavior in organizations. Here, too, a match in organizational styles will lead to a more successful relationship between buyers and sellers.

Personality refers to enduring traits that characterize individuals, motivating them to act or react to external stimuli in a particular manner. Congruency within the three dimensions between the buyer and seller is likely to result in the most successful transaction, where-as discrepancy is likely to result in a small chance for success. To have a better chance for success in international markets, a company could select a target market with a national character similar to that of its own home country, or make sure they have adequately researched and understand the national character of the target market, target companies with similar organizational culture, and hire international salespeople with the appropriate personality traits, [19] as described in Section 13-3a, "Recruiting Expatriates."

Low- and High-Context Cultures

As mentioned in Chapter 5, "Cultural Influences on International Marketing," individuals from cultures with a low context of communication use formal, direct communication that is verbally expressed, whereas individuals from cultures with a high context of communication use less verbal information to convey the message, relying instead on cues such as gestures and facial expressions. In the latter case, status of the speaker, individual background, values, associations, and so on are important in completing the message conveyed, thus linking the message to the context in which it was delivered. Negotiators from high-context cultures, such as those of Latin America and Asia, are less programmatic and less rigid, especially in time management, contract signing, and closing deals, whereas negotiators from low-context cultures follow Western logic, with the negotiation terminating when an agreement is formally reached and in writing. [20] Furthermore, individuals from high-context cultures are less confrontational and place greater emphasis on interpersonal interaction than individuals from low-context cultures. [21]

13-2 Successfully Managing Expatriates

International management experts estimate that the cost of a failed expatriate assignment is in the millions of dollars and that more than 80 percent of companies experience expatriate failure, attributed primarily to candidate selection and the inability to adapt to host cultures. [22] The direct costs associated with each expatriate turnover are estimated to be in the hundreds of thousands of dollars. And indirect costs — such as reduced productivity and efficiency, lost sales, reduced market share, diminished competitive position, unstable corporate image, and tarnished corporate reputation — are even greater. [23]

ASDF_MEDIA/shutterstock.com

Firms could attempt to minimize their early return rate by engaging in the appropriate training and development strategies for expatriates. Such strategies should involve the use of effective selection and screening criteria for recruiting expatriates, training them and preparing them for the international assignment, motivating them for peak performance, and ensuring their successful repatriation.

13-3a Recruiting Expatriates

In the process of recruiting expatriates, companies should select those individuals who have traits such as[24]

• An openness and sensitivity to others, cultural sensitivity and awareness, competency in other languages, awareness to relate across cultures, awareness of their own cultural values

• The ability to change their usual behavior in cross-national settings

• A high level of resiliency, as ascertained from the individuals' performance histories

• Extensive international knowledge or willingness to gain it

• A desire to go overseas and willingness to work in areas where there is political instability and a strong anti-American sentiment

Typically, potential recruits for international assignments, from within or outside the company, are given batteries of personality tests and are subjected to interviews to determine their motivation for an international assignment. Those prospects who are primarily interested in completing the assignments to earn promotions are not likely to be as successful as those who are eager to experience different environments.

13-3b Attenuating Culture Shock

Culture shock, which frequently accounts for early repatriation, is defined as a pervasive feeling of anxiety resulting from one's presence in a new, unfamiliar culture (see Figure 13-5). Culture shock could result in feelings of inadequacy, reluctance to experience the environment, and fear of failure. Cross-cultural communication experts advise companies that culture shock can be diminished when employees know what to expect in their new environment. Companies need to provide some familiarity with the physical and social environment (local customs, in particular) to the prospective expatriates to attenuate culture shock.

The family, in particular, must be prepared for the international assignment. Whereas the expatriate employee interacts within the company and has a company culture around him/ her, the spouse and children often find themselves isolated, lacking support. They face different customs, lifestyles, and food (see Figure 13-6).

Experts in culture shock suggest that expatriates who dealt with their culture shock effectively used what is called "stability zones" to which they would retreat when conditions in the host country became overly stressful to them, rather than becoming isolated, lonely, and falling into depression (see Figure 13-7 on next page). Problems, though, arise when those stability zones are not as stable – in fact, they could be dangerous. Take, for example, lesbian, gay, bisexual, transgender, or genderqueer (LGBTQ) expatriates assigned to dangerous locations. While many discriminate themselves out of an international assign-

Figure 13-5 Transplanting an expatriate's family from a quiet, suburban Midwestern town into the heart of Asia is likely to produce culture shock. The close, traditional, elaborately crafted homes here look nothing like the suburban lawns of the expatriate family's previous life.

Figure 13-6 Tourists and locals dine in a restaurant in Hong Kong. Tour guides in China often impress foreigners with stories of restaurants serving monkey brains. Would they go well with fries?

Figure 13-7 *Stability zones are places to which individuals can retreat when conditions in the host country became overly stressful to them. It is always helpful when one has a stability zone that is everywhere in one's new city, and even wraps around local buses—as, in this case, Dunkin' Donuts.*

ment that is important for their career progression, many do not, and go to dangerous locations, facing circumstances that present a threat to their wellbeing or security. In these environments, beyond a "global closet," where one must hide one's sexual orientation – living in separate bedrooms, – LGBTQ employees must seek additional protection from anti-gay laws and propaganda. "Stability zones," essential to the international assignment, may be beyond reach. Employers of LGBTQ employees in Russia have to ensure not only confidentiality regarding one's LGBTQ status, but also access to "stability zones" beyond social media, which could out the employee; these zones might actually mean the guarantee of evacuation for the couple if a crisis arises.[25]

International Marketing Illustration 13-1 addresses issues related to the accompanying spouse and expatriate compensation.

International Marketing Illustration 13-1
The Financial and Legal Cost of the Expatriate Spouse

Expatriate employees often ask their employer to find their spouse a job in the country of assignment. The employer may agree to find the spouse a job either with the same subsidiary or with an affiliate company located within a reasonable geographic proximity.

From a legal perspective, finding employment for a spouse may be problematic for the employer. The marriage may end in divorce, and the company will be in a bind by continuing to accommodate the spouse. Or the spouse can claim that he or she is owed additional salary and compensation because, in fact, he or she is also an expatriate employee. Companies are covered if a written agreement makes clear that the request is, in fact,

an accommodation for the accompanying spouse and that the spouse is not entitled to special benefits.

The company will also find that the costs of bringing the expatriate with an accompanying spouse are much higher than bringing the expatriate alone. Note that this amount does not include other costs, such as the cost of education in private school for the children or hardship allowances. And the cost of living varies greatly, worldwide. Transferring an employee from San Francisco to Zurich could increase the costs to the family by more than a third, based on the cost-of-living comparisons in Table 13-1 (on next page).

Table 13-1 Cost of Living: Worldwide Rankings for Selected Cities

Rank	City	Country	Rank	City	Country
1	Hong Kong	HKSAR	13	New York City	United States
2	Tokyo	Japan	16	Tel Aviv	Israel
3	Zurich	Switzerland	19	London	United Kingdom
4	Singapore	Singapore	26	Dubai	United Arab Emirates
5	Seoul	South Korea	28	San Francisco	United States
6	Luanda	Angola	29	Sydney	Australia
7	Shanghai	China	33	Milan	Italy
8	N'Djamena	Chad	42	Lagos	Nigeria
9	Beijing	China	53	Mumbai	India
10	Bern	Switzerland	58	Sao Paulo	Brazil
11	Geneva	Switzerland	69	Santiago	Chile

Source: Mercer Human Resource Consulting, "2018 Cost of Living City Rankings," accessed at
https://mobilityexchange.mercer.com/Portals/0/Content/Rankings/rankings/col2018f852369/index.html on
July 5, 2018.

13-3c Training for International Assignments

Companies use different strategies in training their employees for international assignments. The strategies range from short courses in cross-cultural communications to extensive cultural immersions. For example, Procter & Gamble, Motorola, Microsoft, and Hewlett-Packard require extensive cross-cultural training courses for their international salespeople, whereas other companies require employees to read books and other materials on the cultures before departure for the sales mission.[26] When the Abril Group, a diversified media company, sends its salespeople to Brazil, a country where it does much of its business, it requires them to participate in a 10-day Portuguese immersion program, studying the country's language, culture, and customs.[27]

In training expatriates for international assignments, a company must assess the fit between the individual salesperson and the client the person will call on. See International Marketing Illustration 13-2 (on next page) for a number of important cultural elements that must influence the recruitment and selection of sales force personnel.

13-3d Motivating Expatriates

The success of an international assignment is predicated on a high degree of motivation. The intrinsic (internal) aspects of motivation for an international assignment are addressed in the recruiting process, which ensures that only those candidates who have the appropriate traits (see Section 13-3a, "Recruiting Expatriates") are deployed. The company controls the extrinsic aspects of motivation, such as compensation, leave and family policies, career incentives, and so on.

In terms of compensation, certain companies attempt to use uniform policies

International Marketing Illustration 13-2
Hiring the Right Person for a Company's International Sales Force

A number of cultural elements are important to consider in the process of recruiting and selecting international sales force personnel. Among them are the ethnic composition of the sales force and the religious orientation and social class of the employees, as well as their gender:

• Ethnic composition — Managers should be aware of the ethnic composition in the country and match the salespeople with the customers appropriately; this is especially important in countries where there is cultural and ethnic diversity, such as India and Indonesia, and where the ethnic groups do not get along well.

• Religious orientation — Managers should match individuals with similar religious backgrounds to have the greatest impact.

• Social class — Countries with long social histories base social class on different criteria, such as seniority (Japan and other Asian countries), caste (India), or other criteria of which the marketer should be aware.

• Education — In many countries — Japan and most countries in Europe, for example — educational systems are more elitist, and an appropriate match based on education is essential for optimal appeal to the target market.

• Gender status and sexual orientation — Many countries keep women in the background and do not involve them in business. Consequently, it would be a mistake to have women in a sales force that sells products to male decision makers in countries such as Japan and most of the countries of North Africa and the Middle East. Similarly, sexual orientation confidentiality must be ensured for LGBTQ employees.

After determining the cultural match, select only those expatriates evaluated as having the highest probability of cultural adaptation and prepare them with in-depth cross-cultural communication training. In addition, enhance their transition with additional support and host-country assistants and help integrate the expatriates into the host country.

Sources: Ruth McPhail and Yvonne McNulty, "Lies, Duplicity, and Fake Second Bedrooms: A Study of LGBTQ Expatriates' Experiences in Dangerous Locations," *European Academy of Management* (EURAM) Conference, June 2015, Warsaw, Poland, accessed at http://www.researchgate.net/profile/Yvonne_Mcnulty3/publication/269106838_Lies_duplicity_and
fake_second_bedrooms_A_study_of_LGBT_expatriates_experiences_in_
dangerous_locations/links/556573d508ae94e957205c70.pdf on October 31, 2015; Jean McFarland, "Culture Shock," Benefits Canada, Vol. 30, No. 1, January 2006, p. 31; Robert H. Sims and Mike Schraeder, "An Examination of Salient Factors Affecting Expatriate Culture Shock," Journal of Business and Management, Vol. 10, No. 1, Spring 2004, pp. 73–87; Jeffrey E. Lewin and Wesley J. Johnson, "International Salesforce Management: A Relationship Perspective," *Journal of Business and Industrial Marketing*, Vol. 12, No. 3/4, 1997, p. 236.

world-wide. More frequently, though, other companies offer numerous compensation incentives above those used for assignments in the home country, thus making the international assignment attractive. Some of the incentives are described next.

Cost-of-Living Adjustment/Post Adjustment

For many companies, the cost-of-living adjustment is above and beyond that justified by the local conditions. This type of compensation, also referred to as post adjustment, includes payment for household help, such as maids, cooks, gardeners, night watchmen, and so forth.

Housing Allowance

Often, companies cover part or the entire cost of housing for the expatriate employees while abroad (see Figure 13-8 on next page). The housing allowance will most likely also cover the cost of staying at a quality hotel until housing becomes available.

Education Allowance

The education allowance covers the cost of children's education at an international private school. U.S. companies pay the education allowance for their employees primarily so that they will be on par with employees working for European multinationals. Many European firms pay for high-quality education for their employees' children, regardless of whether they are in their home country or overseas, and for as long as they are attending school.

Figure 13-8: *This house is very similar to the typical expat houses in Bucharest. They tend to be large, have servants' quarters, and they might or might not look particularly well maintained.*

Home-Leave Allowance

The home-leave allowance pays for the family abroad to vacation in the home country. The company also may pay for the children remaining in the home country to attend school and to visit the family member or members posted abroad.

Moving Allowance

Household moving expenses to the country of assignment are usually covered. The moving allowance also may cover storage in the home country. Some companies also arrange for the sale of the expatriate's home, often incurring losses if the housing market is in a slump.

Repatriation Allowance

The repatriation allowance covers expenses for moving back to the home country. In addition, the repatriation allowance may consist of a considerable sum paid to the expatriate simply for completing the international assignment.

Other Types of Allowances

Expatriates also can benefit from other types of allowances. Such allowances may, for example, cover family membership in a social or health club designed primarily for expatriates and for well-to-do locals.

Noncompensation incentives are important. Multinational corporations frequently offer as incentive to the expatriate a guaranteed promotion in the company ranks on his or her successful return from the country of assignment. Companies also must address career-related concerns of the accompanying spouse. In an effort to recruit the best candidates for international posting, companies often offer spouses positions in the companies congruent with their talents and objectives to ensure the continuity of their careers.

13-3e Obstacles to the International Sales Mission

Once in the country of assignment, expatriates must learn the culture quickly and not gravitate toward home-country expatriates.[28] When they are living in the expatriate community, however, such situations may be unavoidable. First, if the expatriates are assigned to a country where restrictions are imposed on interactions with foreigners, such as Saudi Arabia, China, and Cuba, the expatriate community is likely to be the only forum for social interaction.

Expatriates may be drawn toward their home-country expatriate community in other countries as well. For example, for U.S. expatriates, many home-country offices and representatives play an important part. Among them are the United States embassy, the various other offices present in a particular country in conjunction with the embassy (the United States Information Agency, the United States Agency for International Development, the Fulbright Office), as well as others associated with the embassy — the cultural, the military, and the commercial attaché. One responsibility of U.S. officers within these respective positions and structures is to organize activities that involve the participation of U.S. expatriates. Expatriates are invited to various functions, activities, and celebrations to participate and to represent the United States. Often, there are even American schools for expatriates' children and American clubs. The Marine House, which houses the marines stationed at the embassy, periodically shows American movies, accompanied by receptions. Most often, a recreation center is open to American expatriates so that they can play pool, watch American football games, and reminisce about life in America.

At the very least, one can find a website that unites expatriates in a particular region. Expat Forums is such an example, helping individuals cope with their foreign assignments and compare benefits, other company practices, and costs. Although the forum is open to any participants, most are U.S. expatriates. Other sites aimed at expatriates help them to "live abroad as they would in their home country," as expatries-france.com, a website aimed at French expatriates, claimed with its original slogan.

All these factors have the potential to impede expatriates' immersion in the local culture. An extreme outcome would be the expatriate who is isolated and lives primarily for his or her return to the home country. The only motivation for this individual's international presence is strictly monetary or is linked to the international assignment as a precondition for promotion. Individuals in this predicament are more likely to fail than those who actively participate in the life and culture of the host country.

Yet another extreme is the expatriate who has "gone native." In extreme cases, this individual may refuse to return to the home country, insisting on remaining abroad in the company's service, and in some situations even serving locals to the detriment of the company.

13-3f Repatriation Issues

On repatriation, expatriates often find themselves working in a company that has changed drastically during their absence. They find that their corner offices are occupied by their former underlings or by professionals new to the company and that they do not quite fit into their new work environment. They also suffer a loss of status in their home environment. Whereas, during their international assignment, expatriates and their families were involved in a close, elite social environment that was reserved for the local international community, on return, they often find themselves to be no more than average dwellers in nondescript suburbia. At this point, they may experience reverse culture shock, a feeling of anxiety associated with a longing for the international environment left behind or fear of not adapting in the new environment and losing one's job due to lack of fit.

Companies often try to soften the reverse culture shock experienced by expatriates, especially professional expatriates, who are often reluctant to return to their home country. An expat from a low-income country, spoiled by Western abundance and supermarkets and stores loaded with merchandise during his assignment abroad, will be shocked to go back home, where the infrastructure is in bad shape, and where Western-style merchandise of any kind is scarce and comes at a premium price. See Figure 13-9.

Figure 13-9: A low-income country expat used to a consumerist lifestyle in the West, being able to purchase products at low prices just about anywhere, may have difficulty repatriating to his homeland, where Western products and conveniences are scarce and come at a premium.

Strategies used by companies to better prepare the expatriates for repatriation involve offering a substantial incentive package, such as a raise on return; guaranteeing a promotion; and providing a repatriation grant.

One of the most important actions of the company may be to keep the expatriates "in the loop" for the duration of their assignments.[29] This can be accomplished by flying them back to headquarters on a regular basis, preferably for extended stays, and keeping them on a regular mailing list for intra-office and intra-company communication. Expat Forums recommends ongoing communication to avoid the renegade syndrome and the "out-of-sight, out-of-mind" mind-set, and arranging for a mentor in upper management.

Summary

Describe the differences between agents and distributors and potential management issues. As companies enter the international market, there is a continuum of engagement ranging from limited participation via a trade show, to the appointment of an international sales manager with responsibilities for in-country agents and/or distributors. Agents and distributors have different responsibilities and present different legal and personnel challenges for the company in the local market.

Examine companies' expatriate management strategies. Managing international employees requires using appropriate personnel management policies, a process complicated by obstacles presented by the international environment. Decisions such as assigning management responsibilities to employees, establishing quotas, or even simply addressing employees by their first names could prove to be a challenge. To further complicate matters, local culture and national character affects relationships between management at each tier of the organization, as does social class or caste.

Describe the different types of employees suited for a company's international operations. A company hires three types of employees for its international operations. Expatriates are home-country nationals groomed from within the firm's national operations. These employees are familiar with firm policy, operations, goals, and objectives and are likely to best represent company interests. Third-country nationals are professional expatriates who adapt easily regardless of the environment to which they were assigned. On the downside, they need to learn both about the local environment and the company's culture, procedures, and goals. Locals (host-country nationals) are familiar with the host-country operating environment and have relationships already established with the national government and other important agency representatives. They also are the employees most likely to sell out the company by creating a local competitor.

Address issues related to expatriate management, such as motivating international employees and ensuring successful assignment performance and repatriation. To ensure top performance, companies need to appropriately train and motivate expatriates. Training in the local language, however superficial, may benefit the expatriates, as does cultural training; both minimize culture shock. Appropriate motivation also improves performance. Some typical perks for expatriates are a housing allowance, moving allowance, education allowance, post-adjustment pay, and home-leave pay. In addition, the employees should be prepared for re-entry in the firm and home country at the end of the assignment to minimize reverse culture shock.

Key Terms

cost-of-living adjustment
culture shock
education allowance
electronic data interchange (EDI)
expatriate
extensible markup language (XML)
home-country national
home-leave allowance

host-country national
housing allowance
individual personality
international buyer-seller relationship
moving allowance
national and regional character
order getter
order taker

organizational culture
post adjustment
repatriation
repatriation allowance
reverse culture shock
strategic partnership
third-country national

Discussion Questions

1. Describe the three types of employees a company is likely to send to a foreign post. What are their strengths and weaknesses?

2. Discuss some of the management and culture-related challenges involved in international sales force management. How do companies address those challenges?

3. How do international companies select and train employees for international assignments?

4. What are some of the methods that international firms use to motivate employees for international assignments, and how do these companies ensure that employees face minimal culture shock on repatriation?

Chapter Quiz

True/False

1. A third-country national is also known as a local.

Answer: False

Rationale: A third-country national is an expatriate working in a country other than his/her home country or the home country of the company. Section 13-1a, "Expatriates"

2. An advantage of hiring home-country nationals for international operations is that they are less expensive for the company.

Answer: False

Rationale: Home-country nationals are the most expensive expatriates the company can send on an international assignment. They are preferred by companies whose products are at the forefront of technology and when the selling function relies on extensive training and highly specialized information. Section 13-1a, "Expatriates"

3. Expatriates working in a particular foreign country are either home-country nationals or host-country nationals.

Answer: False

Rationale: Expatriates working in a particular foreign country belong to two categories: one category is the home-country national, and the other is the third-country national. Section 13-1a, "Expatriates"

4. Organizational culture refers to personality traits shared at the national level.

Answer: False

Rationale: Organizational culture refers to shared norms and values that guide collective behavior in organizations. Section 13-2c, "Understanding Cultural Values and the Relationship between Buyer and Seller"

5. Reverse culture shock is a feeling of anxiety experienced after returning to the home country.

Answer: True

Rationale: Reverse culture shock is a general feeling of anxiety associated with a longing for the international environment left behind or fear of not adapting in the new environment and losing one's job due to lack of fit. Section 13-3f," Repatriation Issues"

6. In low-context cultures, what is said is precisely what is meant.

Answer: True

Rationale: In low-context cultures, what is said is precisely what is meant. In high-context cultures, the context of the message, including the characteristics and role of the sender, is equally meaningful. Section 13-2c, "Understanding Cultural Values and the Relationship between Buyer and Seller"

Multiple Choice

1. In Asian countries, what approach to selling would work best?

      a. Confident, persuasive

      b. Modest, exhibiting a humble attitude

      c. Serious, formal hard sell

      d. None of the above

Answer: b is correct.

Rationale: A hard sell is not likely to be successful in most Asian countries, where modesty, a humble attitude, and respect are seen as valuable traits. Section 13-2b, "Understanding the International Buyer-Seller Relationship"

2. What are some preferred traits of expatriates?

      a. Sensitivity to others

      b. Willingness to gain international knowledge

      c. High level of resiliency

      d. All of the above

Answer: d is correct.

Rationale: In the process of recruiting expatriates, companies should select individuals who have cultural sensitivity and awareness, the ability to change their behavior in cross-national settings, a high level of resiliency, extensive international knowledge or willingness to gain it, and a desire to go overseas. Section 13-3a, "Recruiting Expatriates"

3. How do companies motivate expatriates?

      a. Guaranteed promotion

      b. Travel and other allowances

      c. Finding spouses employment in the country of assignment

      d. All of the above

Answer: d is correct.

Rationale: The intrinsic aspects of motivation for an international assignment are addressed in the recruiting process, which ensures that only those candidates who have the appropriate traits are sent overseas. The company controls the extrinsic aspects of motivation, such as compensation, leave and family policies, and career incentives. Section 13-3d, "Motivating Expatriates"

4. To relieve reverse culture shock, companies can

      a. keep an employee updated with office e-mails.

      b. offer promotion on return to the home country.

      c. fly an expatriate back regularly for meetings.

      d. all of the above

Answer: d is correct.

Rationale: In addition to keeping in close contact with the expatriate throughout the assignment period, companies use certain strategies to prepare him or her for repatriation, such as updating the employee on changes in the organization, flying the expatriate back to the home country often, and offering a promotion on return. Section 13-3f, "Repatriation Issues"

Notes

1. "Small and Medium-Sized Enterprises: Overview of Participation in U.S. Exports," *United States International Trade Commission,* January 2010, accessed at https://www.usitc.gov/publications/332/pub4125.pdf on July 5, 2018.

2. "Negotiating Governing Law and Dispute Resolution Clauses in International Commercial Contracts," *Lexology,* November 24, 2010, accessed at https://www.lexology.com/library/detail.aspx?g=08a41896-6b21-47fa-91ed-25f9f4b216ce on July 5, 2018. "ICC International Court of Arbitration," *International Chamber of Commerce,* accessed at https://iccwbo.org/dispute-resolution-services/icc-international-court-arbitration/ on July 5, 2018.

3. Amy L. Hirter, "Foreign Agents and Distributors: When and How to Use Them," *The Colorado Lawyer,* April 2006, accessed at https://hollandhart.com/files/ForeignAgentsandDistribs.pdf on July 5, 2018.

4. Ibid.

5. Nakiye Boyacigiller, "The Role of Expatriates in the Management of Interdependence, Complexity and Risk in Multinational Corporations," *Journal of International Business Studies,* Vol. 22, No. 3, Third Quarter 1991, pp. 357–381.

6. Dana-Nicoleta Lascu, Lalita A. Manrai, and Sugandha Kamalapuri, "Purchase Behavior of Expatriate Consumers in Saudi Arabia: An Exploratory Study," in W. D. Herrington and R. Taylor (eds.), *Marketing Advances in Theory, Practice, and Education,* Mount Pleasant, MI: Society for Marketing Advances,1998, pp. 128–134.

7. The Times of Oman, "Oman's Population Crosses 4.25 million, October 12, 2015, accessed at http://www.timesofoman.com/article/69475/Oman/Expatriates-made-up-444-per-cent-of-Oman's-total-population on October 28, 2015; "Oman: Population," *EIU ViewsWire,* June 1, 2007.

8. Samuel Osborne, "Saudi Arabia Bans Foreigners From Certain Jobs to Give Citizens More Employment Opportunities, *Independent,* January 31, 2018, accessed at https://www.independent.co.uk/news/world/middle-east/saudi-arabia-foreign-workers-ban-jobs-retail-sales-citizens-nationals-employment-opportunities-a8187531.html on July 5, 2018.

9. David G. Collings, Hugh Scullion, and Michael J. Morley, "Changing Patterns of Global Staffing in the Multinational Enterprise: Challenges to the Conventional Expatriate Assignment and Emerging Alternatives," *Journal of World Business,* Vol. 42, No. 2, June 2007, pp. 198–208.

10. "E-commerce in Latin America: Challenges, Opportunities and Rewards," *Allpago,* February 7, 2018, accessed at https://www.allpago.com/2018/02/e-commerce-latin-america-challenges-opportunities-rewards/ on July 5, 2018.

11. Clyde D. Stoltenberg, "Doing Business in China: Culture and Practice," *Thunderbird International Business Review,* Vol. 45, No. 2, March/April 2003, p. 245.

12. John L. Graham and N. Mark Lam, "The Chinese Negotiation," *Harvard Business Review,* Vol. 81, No. 10, October 2003, p. 82.

13. Cynthia Kemper, "Global Sales Success Depends on Cultural Insight," *World Trade,* Vol. 11, No. 5, May 1998, pp. S2–S4.

14. Erika Rasmusson, "Can Your Reps Sell Overseas?" *Sales and Marketing Management,* Vol. 150, No. 2, February 1998, p. 110.

15. Sudhir H. Kale and John Barnes, "Understanding the Domain of Cross-National Buyer-Seller Interactions," *Journal of International Business Studies,* Vol. 23, No. 1, First Quarter 1992, pp. 101–131.

16. Jagdish N. Sheth, "Cross-Cultural Influences on the Buyer-Seller Interaction/Negotiation Process," *Asia Pacific Journal of Management,* Vol. 1, No. 1, 1983, pp. 46–55.

17. Rosann L. Spiro and Barton A. Weitz, "Adaptive Selling: Conceptualization, Measurement, and Nomological Validity," *Journal of Marketing Research,* Vol. 16, No. 3, August 1990, pp. 355–369; Kale and Barnes, "Understanding the Domain," pp. 101–131.

18. Kale and Barnes, "Understanding the Domain," pp. 101–131.

19. Geert Hofstede, *Culture's Consequences: International Differences in Work-Related Values,* London: Sage Publications, 1980.

20. Kale and Barnes, "Understanding the Domain," pp. 101–131.

21. Alma Mintu-Wimsatt and Julie B. Gassenheimer, "The Moderating Effect of Cultural Context in Buyer-Seller Negotiation," *Journal of Personal Selling Sales Management*, Vol. 20, No. 1, Winter 1999, pp. 1–9.

22. Ibid.

23. See Edward Hall, *Beyond Culture*, Garden City: NY: Anchor Press/Double Day, 1976; and Mintu-Wimsatt and Gassenheimer, "The Moderating Effect," pp. 1–9.

24. Jean McFarland, "Culture Shock," *Benefits Canada*, Vol. 30, No. 1, January 2006, p. 31.

25. Earl Naumann, "A Conceptual Model of Expatriate Turnover," *Journal of International Business Studies*, Vol. 23, No. 3, Third Quarter 1992, pp. 499–531.

26. See David M. Noer, *Multinational People Management*, Washington, D.C.: Bureau of National Affairs, 1975; Nancy J. Adler and John L. Graham, "Cross-Cultural Interaction: The International Comparison Fallacy?" *Journal of International Business Studies*, Vol. 20, No. 3, Third Quarter 1989, pp. 515–537; Stephen J. Simurda, "Finding an International Sales Manager," *Northeast International Business*, Vol. 1, No. 3, 1988, pp. 15–16; Rasmusson, "Can Your Reps," p. 110.

27. Ruth McPhail and Yvonne McNulty, "Lies, Duplicity, and Fake Second Bedrooms: A Study of LGBTQ Expatriates' Experiences in Dangerous Locations," European Academy of Management (EURAM) Conference, June 2015, Warsaw, Poland, accessed at http://www.researchgate.net/profile/Yvonne_Mcnulty3/ publication/269106838_Lies_duplicity_andfake_second_bedrooms_A_study_of_LGBT_expatriates_experiences_in_dangerous_locations/links/556573d508ae94e957205c70.pdf on October 31, 2015; Robert H. Sims and Mike Schraeder, "An Examination of Salient Factors Affecting Expatriate Culture Shock," *Journal of Business and Management*, Vol. 10, No. 1, Spring 2004, pp. 73–87.

28. Kemper, "Global Sales Success," pp. S2–S4.

29. Rasmusson, "Can Your Reps," p. 110.

30. Lambeth Hochwald, "Luring Execs Overseas," *Sales and Marketing Management*, Vol. 152, No. 2, February 2000, p. 101.

Case 13-1 *Manufacturing in China: Information Technology Challenges*

Each year, millions of GT, Mongoose, Pacific, Schwinn, and other bicycles traveled from Chinese factories to U.S. distribution centers owned by manufacturer Pacific Cycle LLC. Shipping the products was the easy part. The difficult part was moving the data and tracking the items as they moved from suppliers to manufacturing sites in China, and, from there, to Chinese ports. Today, Pacific has some help from Exel LLC, a third-party logistics company based in the United Kingdom, which gathers the data from the suppliers and factories, rekeys it into its own systems, and then uses

Gorodenkoff/shutterstock.com

EDI to transmit the data back to Pacific Cycle. Errors show up in five percent of the 4,000 documents Exel generates for Pacific Cycle, which can cause delays at U.S. customs if there are discrepancies between the shipments and the paperwork — and delays can translate into lost business.

For companies doing business in emerging markets, it often happens that the information technology infrastructure is considerably less sophisticated than the one they use — or the technology infrastructure might not even be there. But China is becoming the manufacturing giant serving the world, thanks to its competent, low-cost labor. Import and export volume is experiencing an explosion, at more

than $1,000 billion yearly, and growing at more than 30 percent a year. However, the country has an immature information technology infrastructure, which, coupled with expensive inland transportation and the high price of land for building logistics hubs, increases the cost of doing business there. Compared with Europe, Japan, and the United States, the logistics cost per GDP is much higher — more than 50 percent higher.

One of the reasons for the high cost of logistics is that Chinese government mandates dictate everything from where companies can set up factories to the use of trucking and freight-forwarding companies, which are licensed by the government and permitted to transport goods in

China. And companies cannot force these logistics providers, which have very low profit margins to begin with, to adopt expensive EDI connectivity. In fact, most do not even know what EDI is.

Multinationals would incur high costs setting up their own logistics operations— something China has allowed since 2004. For the moment, a model that works is that set up by large international logistics firms operating in China, such as DHL, FedEx, and UPS. They offer services similar to Exel's, rekeying paper-based data and using EDI to help companies track their orders and monitor warehousing and shipping information related to their Chinese operations.

Often, multinationals have to compensate for the lack of a seamless logistics infrastructure by pairing with more logistics firms. Celestica, a company manufacturing electronics equipment for Hewlett-Packard, IBM, and Nortel Networks, relies on Exel, Kuehne & Nagel, Menlo Worldwide, and Panalpina to help it stay connected to local suppliers and carriers via EDI or XML; these logistics firms run more than 10 vendor-managed inventory hubs for Celestica, all of them located right in its manufacturing facilities. This reduces their lead time for inventory, increases responsiveness, and reduces material liabilities.

GM has invested more than $1.6 billion in China in the past 10 years to build its own technology and physical infrastructure, and yet it continues to dispatch "milk runs," where supplier pickup and delivery instructions are given on paper to drivers of the local transportation companies GM employs, ensuring just-in-time delivery. The Chinese suppliers use GM's Internet portal to log on and check inventory status and to alert GM when orders have been picked up by local carriers.

Auto-parts supplier Delphi Inc., in China since 1993, has 11 factories in the country, and more than 200 Chinese and approximately 250 overseas suppliers support Delphi's operations in China. Some Chinese carriers are developing information technology capabilities that will improve documentation for customs and electronic invoicing, but the process is slow. The company installed software that helps partners efficiently navigate the congested roads and report on whereabouts; the software is also used by the company's suppliers in Europe, Mexico, and North America.

FedEx has built a supply-chain logistics service in Asia that ships a half-million pounds of goods daily from China to the United States and Europe. It has a logistics distribution center in Shanghai, among several others in Asia, that manages everything for customers from orders and inventory to the transport network, with EDI and XML technology systems. The FedEx EC-Inventory Visibility and FedEx EC-Warehouse Management, both Internet-based systems, update and validate orders placed against quantities in the distribution center, track and trace customer orders and shipments, maintain shipping and billing data, and detail purchase history. Their goal is to reduce costs for customers through sophisticated monitoring and reporting systems: They offer automatic notification of low-stock items and replace paperwork with online entries.

UPS had been the market leader in logistics in China until recently, when it was overtaken by the German Deutsche Post DHL, whose operations in China are worth $5.15 billion, and whose turnover in China is equal to the combined turnover of UPS, FedEx, and TNT. UPS has 33 large, wholly owned branch offices that serve more than 330 cities in China, and has plans for expansion and for building further connections between ground and air services, offering several flights a week connecting Shanghai and the United States, and other Asian flights from Shanghai to Japan and the Philippines, as well as to European cities. In 2009, the company opened its $20 million new hub at Shanghai Pudong International Airport. UPS flies Boeing MD-11s and 747s to China and plans to add more 747s — the hub is serviced by eight 747-400s. The new hub was designed to handle 17,000 items an hour, and it employs more than 1,000 people. With these new capabilities, it is able to offer more efficient information technology interfacing to its multinational clients manufacturing products in China.

Sources: China Times, "DHL, FedEx, UPS set to do battle in Chinese logistics market, July 19, 2012, www.wantchinatimes.com/news-subclass-cnt.aspx?MainCatID=0&cid=1502&id=20120719000049; Gareth Powell, "UPS Plans New Air Hub in China," *China Economic Review*, online edition, April 19, 2007; Robert Malone, "UPS Targets China," *Forbes.com*, October 2, 2006; Laurie Sullivan, "Road Work in China," *Information Week*, August 30, 2004, Vol. 1003, pp. 30–34.

Analysis Suggestions:

1. What efficiencies do Electronic Data Interchange systems provide in the relationship between buyers and sellers?
2. What are some of the logistics-related challenges and costs encountered by multinational firms manufacturing in China?
3. How does EDI lower the costs of manufacturing in China?

Case 13-2 *The Expatriate Spouse: Managing Change*

Geena Sorenson, a former Madison Avenue advertising executive and spouse of a U.S. expatriate from his company's New York headquarters, assigned to Shanghai, found herself looking forward to her first home leave scheduled in exactly nine months. She missed visiting her circle of friends and former classmates at New York University, spending her Saturday mornings at the Chelsea art galleries, buying her bagels hot at Tal Bagels, and experiencing the quiet trepidations of the city on a Sunday morning. Instead, she was counting the hours until her return, unable to fit into the local environment of an equally vivacious Shanghai. She felt much like the lonely characters of the movie *Lost in Translation,* unable to understand her environment, spending long hours in a high-rise apartment, and waiting on her busy husband, who was rarely home.

Reading the different journals and magazines for expatriates and looking at the readily available online literature, she found that the cost of sending a family to an international location is as high as $1 million. And yet companies are not as skillful in the selection and preparation procedure as one might think. A foreign assignment presents problems for the entire family, but, perhaps, more so in China, where twice as many expats are leaving the country rather than arriving in China. Some of the reasons could be expiring work contracts, but there are other reasons, including the rising costs of living and the apocalyptic pollution, which makes cities unlivable.

Geena could relate. The employee should be capable of coping and learning how to lead, motivate, and work with staff from other cultures. The spouse, if female, may have to deal with living in a male-dominated culture. It is often likely that her world is limited to the local expatriate community. China, which is by far the most popular new destination for foreign assignments, is quite a problematic posting because expats face not only language and cultural barriers, but also challenges when it comes to housing, transportation, education, and medical care.

Geena also found that, in spite of China's status as an important destination for expatriates, the number of its expatriates is decreasing, primarily for two reasons. One, expatriates are increasingly hired on local terms, without the traditional expat package. Expatriates tend to have less pay and a shorter-term package and thus are less likely to accept the assignment. And, two, jobs are increasingly going to well-trained nationals.

In her search, Geena discovered a website, Expats in China, which offered an overview of the expatriate life in China, similar to the materials provided by her husband's company in the training materials for the assignment. Apparently, after South Koreans, U.S. citizens are the second largest group of nearly 600,000 foreigners living on the Chinese mainland. She also found useful referrals for various services she could potentially use in the future, a digest of the local and national news from various sources, but not much else. Other expatriate sites were also only marginally useful.

Beer5020/shutterstock.com

Using her entrepreneurial skills, Geena decided to create an agency that would address the needs of spouses like her, attempting to understand the local environment, but also longing for her home country. The purpose of the agency would be to facilitate integration and dialogue about integration in a society that is culturally dissimilar.

Sources: The Wall Street Journal, "Twice As Many Expatriates Leaving China Than Arriving," accessed at http://blogs.wsj.com/chinarealtime/2015/02/09/twice-as-many-expatriates-leaving-china-than-arriving-moving-company-says/ on October 31, 2015; Calum MacLeod, "U.S. expatriates pursue American dream in China," *USA Today,* July 12, 2011, www.usatoday.com/news/world/2011-07-12-Americans-China-dreams-transplants_n.htm; Rensia Melles, "Lost in Translation," *Canadian HR Reporter,* Vol. 17, No. 5, March 8, 2004, p. 14; "Hong Kong, A Classic Case of Expatriate Change," *International Money Marketing,* March 2004, p. 16; "Where Next for the Expat?" *International Money Marketing,* March 2004, p. 14; http://www.expatsinchina.com/.

This case is fictitious.

Analysis Suggestions

1. Is Geena experiencing culture shock? Explain. If the answer is yes, what can she do to lessen its impact?

2. What are the costs of bringing a spouse along for an assignment? Would the company be better off if the spouse remained in the home country? Explain.

3. How should Geena's agency help in addressing the needs of expatriate spouses? Offer ideas and activities that would benefit the large group of spouses accompanying expatriates in China.

This page is intentionally blank...

Chapter 14

International Pricing Strategies

docstockmedia/shutterstock.com

Pricing is especially important in international marketing strategy. Pricing decisions can often lead to an immediate reaction on the part of a product or service buyer. Pricing affects product positioning, market segmentation, demand management, and market share dynamics.[1] The international pricing decision is complex. Variables internal to the firm, such as the location of plants and factory utilization rates, as well as variables external to the firm, such as the economic climate, customers' price sensitivity, and barriers to entry, must be evaluated before determining the final price. Pricing decisions are further affected by companies' market experience, market share, exchange rates, tariffs, inflation, financing, and government intervention in pricing.[2]

This chapter addresses challenges that international firms face internally when setting prices. It also addresses the impact of the international competitive, political and legal, and economic and financial environment on firm pricing decisions. Finally, it evaluates pricing policies of firms for different international markets.

14-1 Pricing Decisions and Procedures

Pricing decisions are determined by the location of production facilities and the companies' abilities to track costs.

14-1a Production Facilities

Production facilities are important *internal* — within the firm's control — decision-making factors in international pricing strategy. The location of production facilities determines the extent to which companies can control costs and price their products competitively. Multinationals usually can afford to shift production to take advantage of lower costs and exchange rates, whereas small to medium-sized firms are often limited to exporting as the only venue for product distribution.[3] Companies sometimes price themselves out of the market in certain countries, especially if they do not shift production to a low-labor-cost, low-tax, and/or low-tariff country. As an example, Marc Controls purchases raw materials in Korea, China, and India to lower the price of its products and ships them to the United States for manufacturing; its products are competitively priced when sold on the German market, but they are still considered over-priced in most of Asia.[4]

Important aspects related to firms' production facilities are factory capacity utilization, internal cost structures, and the market contribution rate:[5]

- Factory capacity utilization: Firms with factories operating at full capacity are able to spread fixed costs over more units, and thus have more flexibility in their pricing strategies. On the other hand, firms with factories operating at less-than-full capacity have high costs to contend with and do not have much price flexibility.

- Internal cost structures: Some firms have more advantageous cost structures than others. For example, firms with production facilities in countries that have an abundance of cheap labor have an advantage over firms with production facilities in countries that have no excess labor. Also, firms that exploit technological advantages have cost advantages that ultimately have an impact on their pricing strategies. Mul-

>

tinational firms manufacturing and selling products in the same country would also likely have advantages because there would be minimal concerns about foreign exchange fluctuations as well as tariffs.

• Market contribution rate: This is the percentage of total firm profits from a particular product. This product will garner more attention than a less-lucrative product and thus affect pricing decisions.

14-1b Ability to Keep Track of Costs

Product components are likely manufactured in different countries. Often, the final products are assembled in a particular country, which is usually not the company's home country, and then sold all over the world. It is thus difficult to keep track of product costs. However, with improvement in information technology and electronic data interchange (EDI) systems, which are increasingly coordinated throughout the supply chain, firms are better able to track product costs in emerging markets and even in lower-income countries.

Foreign trade zones (FTZs) can be used to manage supply chain costs in the manufacturing process. Manufacturing companies can assemble items inside a FTZ using domestic and imported components. The manufacturer often can realize savings where the tariff on the finished product is less than the tariffs on the various imported components. Moreover, tariffs are not paid on the finished goods until they leave the FTZ site. If the finished product is then exported to another country, typically no tariffs are incurred in the country of manufacture. STIHL, the major German chainsaw and outdoor equipment company, uses an FTZ at their U.S. manufacturing site in Virginia Beach, Virginia. Finished goods are also exported to South America and other key markets from the STIHL FTZ in Virginia. [6]

14-2 Environment-Related Challenges and Pricing Decisions

Pricing decisions are affected by all the external elements in a company's international environment. An international company must react effectively to changes in the competitive environment, in the political and legal environment, and in the economic and financial environment. Figure 14-1 addresses examples of different challenges in the international firm's environment that affect the firm's pricing decisions.

The Competitive Environment	• Gray market/parallel imports as a competitive threat • Dumping as a competitive threat
The Political and Legal Environment	• Transfer pricing • The competitive price of protectionism
The Economic and Financial Environment	• Inflationary pressure on price • The competitive price of protectionism • Shortage of hard currency and countertrade

Figure 14-1: Environmental factors affecting pricing decisions.

14-2a The Competitive Environment

Competition

International and local competition often pose concerns to multinational firms and SME exporters. Competitors' offerings and the price sensitivity of customers influence the firm's pricing decisions. Also, if consumers face a high cost to switch from one product to another, firms have to price their offering low enough to have the customers switch to their brand. But, if the firm is operating where barriers to entry, such as nontariff barriers, patents, or technological advantages, are high, they can retain relatively high prices without fear of competition.[7] Finally, if competition can keep product prices low by manufacturing in a low-labor-cost country, then the firm must meet this challenge and maintain a low price, potentially at a loss.

In retailing and other service environments, companies often are challenged by local competitors offering legal copycat products at a much lower price. For example, Pizza Hut is challenged in every market in Poland by a local pizza chain offering almost identical products, such as Neapolitan pizza, at a price lower than Pizza Hut's. Challenges at the retail level may be difficult to identify. For example, in some markets, retailers price products just under an even number so that the cashier can keep any change. In Egypt and Romania, retailers are unlikely to give back small change. There, a company using even pricing will be at a disadvantage because retailers will choose to sell competitors' products – even if that company's prices are lower.

Gray Market/Parallel Imports as a Competitive Threat

A firm engaging in a differential pricing strategy could be vulnerable to competition from unauthorized channels. In fact, differential pricing (price discrimination) by the manufacturer has been identified as a main cause of parallel importing—diverting products purchased in a low-price market to other markets (parallel imports) by means of a distribution system not authorized by the manufacturer, otherwise known as a gray market.[8] (see Figure 14-2).

A manufacturer might charge different prices in different markets for the same product:

• To meet the needs of target consumers who have a limited purchasing power.

• To keep the product price competitive in markets actively targeted by competition.

• Due to changes in the exchange rate in countries where the products are sold; the product is likely to be cheaper in the countries with the weakest currency.

• Due to the fact that it offers discounts to wholesalers buying higher quantities.

• Due to differences in wholesale prices in different markets; for example, wholesale prices for luxury goods are high in the U.S. compared to the rest of the world.

• Due to differences in taxes the company has to pay in different countries.

Figure 14-2 *This Mercedes A-170 crossover automobile could be brought to the United States, adapted according to the Department of Transportation requirements, and then resold at a small profit — a reasonable price would be $30,000. It would appeal to U.S. consumers who would like to pay much less than $60,000, the price of the smallest Mercedes station wagon or crossover available in the U.S. market. This automobile would be sold as a parallel import, through a channel that Mercedes did not authorize. Don't wear out any parts, though, because all the parts would have to be shipped from Stuttgart, Germany.*

If lower-priced products aimed for a low-price market are diverted into a high-price market, where they more expensive, then the company loses profits in the high-price market, the authorized distributors lose a substantial part of their business, and the local government in the high-price market is deprived of the higher taxes for the expensive products. For this reason, companies and governments actively fight against parallel imports.

Gray markets or parallel imports are common in the United Kingdom and elsewhere in the world (see International Marketing Illustration 14-1).

International Marketing Illustration 14-1 Parallel Imports: A Perspective

In the United Kingdom, one can buy Coke produced for the Middle East, Russian Head & Shoulders shampoo, South African Colgate toothpaste, and Brazilian Dove soap. Tesco even purchased Levi Strauss jeans in the United States to sell them at a discount in its U.K. stores, selling 15,000 pairs a week for half the price charged in specialty stores approved by Levi Strauss. Levi Strauss filed a lawsuit at the European Court of Justice, joined by Davidoff, the perfume maker. The Court ruled that selling Levis meant for U.S. consumers was illegal. Tesco and the public were outraged: Tesco was seen as attempting to level an uneven ground where jeans were sold as premium goods in Europe and as mass-merchandise in the U.S., cheating U.K. consumers. Levi Strauss attempts to explain that it is costly to sell jeans in the U.K. because of the limited retail space were met with skepticism. Levi Strauss then agreed to introduce lower-priced jeans under the Signature brand name at Tesco, at about $40 a pair — a fraction of the price of its regular jeans.

Gray market cellphones constitute 13 percent of the global mobile handset business. In Kenya, for example, 70 percent of the cellphones on the market are gray market. These numbers are expected to increase despite regional lock-outs to prevent use in any market other than the one intended. In India, an estimated eight million handsets are imported monthly through a gray market, circumventing import taxes of 25 percent.

Sources: Harichandan Arakali, "With No Android One, Cheap Gray-Market Smartphones Flood Africa," International Business Times, February 3, 2015, accessed at http://www.ibtimes.com/no-android-one-cheap-gray-market-smartphones-flood-africa-1803954 on November 2, 2015; Green World Investor, "India's massive illegal Grey Market for mobile phones raises concerns,"19 July, 2010, www.greenworldinvestor.com/2010/07/19/indias-massive-illegal-grey-market-for-mobile-phones-raises-concerns; "Market Report: Parallel Lines," In-Store, September 2003, p. 21; "Business: Trouser Suit; Parallel Imports," The Economist, Vol. 361, No. 8249, November 24, 2001, p. 76.

Dumping as a Competitive Threat

Firms also can face challenges from companies dumping products in their target market. Dumping is an important factor affecting pricing decisions. The World Trade Organization (WTO) states that, if a company exports a product at a price lower than the price it normally charges on its own home market, or at or below cost, it is said to be 'dumping' the product. A typical example of dumping involves a foreign company that enjoys high prices and high profits at home as a result of trade barriers against imports. The company uses those profits to sell at much lower prices in foreign markets to build market share and suppress the profitability of competitors with open home markets. Another common scenario is dumping of industrial commodities such as steel, aluminum, etc. as part of a government policy to control the world market for the product and also to maintain high employment levels in in the producing country's aging factories. The Chinese steel industry policy offers such an example.[9]

According to the World Trade Organization (WTO), dumping should be condemned if it threatens to cause injury to an established industry in a particular market and if it delays the establishment of a viable domestic industry. It should be noted that the WTO Agreement does not regulate the actions of companies engaged in dumping; its focus is on how governments choose to react or not react to dumping. It disciplines dumping actions.[10]

Antidumping policies differ somewhat from country to country. China, according to its Antidumping and Anti-Subsidy Regulations set forth by the State Council, defines dumping as the subsidization of exports resulting in substantial injury, or the threat of substantial injury, to an established domestic industry, or substantially impeding the establishment of a comparable domestic industry. According to Chinese law, dumping is involved if a product is sold at a price below its normal value, where normal value may be based on production costs plus reasonable expenses and profit or on the comparable price in the exporting country for an identical or like product. If there is no comparable price for the product in the exporting country, reference is made to the price at which the exporter sells a similar product in a third country.[11]

Similarly, the United States Department of Commerce, the government branch responsible for determining whether products are dumped on the U.S. market, considers that dumping takes place if products are priced only minimally above cost or at prices below those charged in the producing country. The European Commission, in charge of antidumping regulation in the European Union (EU), has mandated that antidumping investigations show that:

• There is evidence of dumping by the exporting producers in the country or countries concerned;
• The industry concerned in the EU has suffered material injury;
• There is a causal link between the dumping and the injury assessed;
• The measures imposed are not against the EU interest.

Once it is determined that the above conditions have been met, penalties will take the form of *ad valorem* duties, i.e., duties are set as a percentage of the product's monetary value.[12]

Dumping challenges and charges abound. Vietnam faced 100 anti-dumping lawsuits against its exports in 2015 alone, for products such as fiber boards, steel, iron, bicycle tires and tubes – with India most recently initiating anti-dumping investigations for imports of AA batteries exported from Vietnam. China, Japan, and South Korea have often been challenged for dumping products in the United States and Europe. China has been accused of dumping everything from shrimp to household goods, from tissue paper to furniture and television sets. In 2011, seven American makers of solar panels filed a broad trade case in Washington against the Chinese solar industry, accusing it of using billions of dollars in government subsidies to help gain sales in the American market and dumping the solar panels in the United States for less than it cost to manufacture and ship them. The Commerce Department found several Chinese solar-panel companies guilty of dumping and slapped 31 percent tariffs on their products.[13]

As established by the WTO, after determining that price discrimination did indeed occur and that a particular local industry was injured by the dumping activity, governments are entitled to impose antidumping duties on the merchandise. Similar to these are countervailing duties, which are imposed on subsidized products imported into the country.

Such subsidizing could, for example, take the form of government aid in the processes of production and distribution.

The question of unfair subsidies for Boeing has been an often-disputed issue in the United States. For years, groups in the U.S. and abroad have questioned the loan guarantees received by Boeing from the Export-Import Bank of the United States. These guarantees have helped Boeing close deals with international purchasers of jet aircraft, primarily commercial airlines. Boeing has been the largest recipient of Export-Import Bank funding. Some officials allege that the loan guarantees and other forms of federal government support for Boeing are unfair and illegal subsidies. U.S. politicians in both major parties have argued that the "corporate welfare" Boeing receives should be terminated along with the Export-Import Bank itself.[14]

Lightspring/shutterstock.com

In 2018, the United States launched a major new anti-dumping tariff initiative against imports of Chinese steel, imposing a 25 percent tariff. China produces over 50 percent of the world's steel, while the U.S. share has fallen to less than 5 percent. The tariff is part of a larger effort by the U.S. to address the entire trade relationship with China, and the substantial U.S. trade deficit. Allegations include Chinese theft of intellectual property, artificial currency manipulation favoring Chinese exports, and ongoing subsidies to protect Chinese steel and other manufacturers. U.S. domestic political considerations are also a factor; the U.S. steel industry is highly visible, with a significant presence in several major U.S. states.[15]

Enforcement of antidumping regulation is particularly intense when the economy is not faring well and when price competition is intense. In the recent past, the United States Department of Commerce and the International Trade Commission scrutinized numerous importers' pricing practices, using strict criteria to determine whether the importer had committed price discrimination and, if so, if it resulted in injury to a particular local industry. Electronics, textiles, and steel originating in countries from Japan and Russia to China and Mexico have been at the center of antidumping action in the past decades. In the case of Mexico, the U.S. administration imposed prohibitive and unreasonable antidumping duties on imports of cement, in spite of the shortage of cement in the United States – but the conflict was quickly resolved.

In spite of more strict enforcement, companies continue to be affected by pricing actions of importers taking advantage of loopholes in the antidumping legislation. To avoid price discrimination charges, the importers modify their products slightly so as not to permit them to be directly compared with products sold in other countries at higher prices.

14-2b The Political and Legal Environment

Governments regulate prices charged by multinational firms. Regulations and restrictions exist with regard to many pricing decisions, ranging from dumping to setting limits on wholesalers' gross margins and on the product's retail price. As mentioned in Chapter 12, "International Retailing," Walmart has been challenged in the European Union for charging prices that are too low (just above cost) and that drive competition out of business. Price promotions are severely restricted, limiting the manufacturers' ability to boost sales in the short term and to help retailers renew their inventories.

Multinational companies also are affected by local government subsidies to local manufacturers, in particular to producers of agricultural products and to exporting firms. Subsidies lower the price charged in international markets for products and challenge the competitive position of firms operating in the same industry. Finally, governments can also impose tariffs and other duties on products in certain industries, especially if those industries are in infancy in the respective countries. Governments defend such action under the infant industry argument, which permits setting high tariffs on imports that challenge emerging local producers.

In general, governments use numerous strategies in their attempts to restrict the repatriation of profits by multinationals and to tax or to encourage the reinvestment of profits. One way that companies can bypass such restrictions is through the use of transfer pricing.

Transfer Pricing

Transfer pricing is a pricing strategy used in intra-firm sales: The pricing of products in the process of conducting transactions between units of the same corporation that are within or beyond the national borders of the parent company is known as transfer pricing and regarded as a legitimate business opportunity by transnational corporations.[16] Developing countries often bring the issue of transfer pricing to the attention of international trade bodies as a strategy that could help a multinational company under-report profits and decrease its tax burden in countries where it has foreign direct investment, thus evading taxation. Instead of pricing products at cost, products can be priced *at market level*, known as market-based transfer pricing, where the price reflects the price products sell for in a particular market; *at cost*, known as cost-based transfer pricing, where the cost reflects not the cost incurred by the company, but the estimated opportunity cost of the product; or products can be priced using a combination of the two strategies.

The Price of Protectionism

Protectionism adds to the final price paid by consumers. In spite of the Uruguay Round Agreement on trade liberalization and the strides made subsequently by the World Trade Organization, protectionist actions continue to increase the costs of goods, and hence the price for the final consumer. Europe's economy, for example, is almost as protected as it was ten years ago, and its costs are as high as seven percent of the gross domestic product of the European Union — some $600 billion.

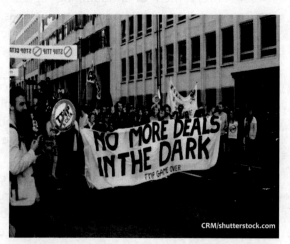

CRM/shutterstock.com

To illustrate, the EU's banana-import restrictions cost European consumers up to $2 billion a year, or about 55 cents per kilogram of bananas. In other examples, European beef farmers receive large subsidies, while tariffs of up to 125 percent are imposed on beef imports; in addition, the EU has a ban on hormone-treated beef from the United States. The costs incurred by European beef consumers for subsidies, tariffs, and other restrictions amount to $14.6 billion a year in the form of higher prices and taxes, or around $1.60 per kilogram of beef. These figures are high in the United States as well, especially in service industries such as shipping and banking.[17]

Latin America is another region where protectionism continues to affect trade and overall economic development. Throughout the twentieth century several Latin American countries instituted import substitution policies to protect local, often wildly-inefficient industries, from international competition. Protectionism was been a feature of populist governments in Argentina, Brazil, Mexico, etc. These measures included tariffs, various non-tariff barriers, and outright bans on certain imports. Predictably, consumers have suffered from higher prices and inferior goods. Protectionism in Latin America also affects services. A recent example is the 2017 proposal by discount carrier Norwegian Airlines to offer domestic airline service in Argentina in competition with the state-owned Aerolineas Argentinas, which would lead to fares slashed in half or more! Predictably, labor unions and other groups opposed the plan as unfair and not in the best interests of Argentina.[18]

14-2c The Economic and Financial Environment

Inflationary Pressures on Price

An inflationary environment places strong pressures on companies to lower prices. Often, pricing competitively may mean that companies are not producing a profit. During inflationary periods, firms often find that they must decide between maintaining a competitive presence in a market and weathering the downside of the economic cycle or abandoning the market, which is a high-cost, high-risk proposition. Companies operating in Latin America in the 1980s and early 1990s often faced challenges posed by inflation. In the United States and Europe, inflationary fears emerged as a result of the rapid increase in gasoline prices in 2006 and 2007.

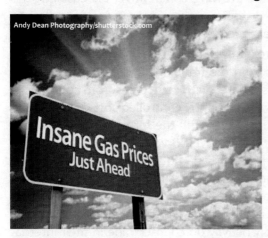

Price inflation and the resulting local currency devaluation leads businesses to set prices in a more stable hard currency. Even individual sellers set prices in hard currency – in Romania, a EU member not part of the Eurozone, home sale prices are specified in euros.

Fluctuating Exchange Rates

Fluctuating exchange rates provide both challenges and opportunities to global firms. Companies that do not pay attention to fluctuations in exchange rates could find their profits are greatly eroded during the time lapse between contract negotiations and product delivery. Including a percentage that covers exchange rate fluctuations when specifying the product price is one strategy companies use to address the unpredictability of such fluctuations.

Traditionally, firms specified all transactions in a strong, stable, hard currency, usually the U.S. dollar. A dollar-pricing strategy could help an exporter protect profit margins on a sale in a country with a volatile local currency subject to devaluations. However, future orders from local buyers are likely to drop as their costs of acquiring dollars become prohibitive and prices from the exporter become uncompetitive with other suppliers.

After the U.S. dollar's ups and downs in the 1970s and 1980s, however, other currencies have emerged as standards for exchanges. Increasingly, pricing decisions are facilitated by the advent of successful venues for regional integration, such as the European Union and the Southern Cone Common Market (Mercosur). Member countries have adopted a single currency in the case of the European Union. The advent of the euro in the European Union has greatly facilitated transactions in the region. However, in recent years, some Eurozone-member countries have actively considered dropping the euro and returning to their local currency. Greece is one example. Several Greek leaders have proposed a return to the drachma, in order to improve Greece's export competitiveness vis-à-vis other European countries and encourage more international travelers to visit the country. [19]

Shortage of Hard Currency and Countertrade

Developing countries face a significant shortage of hard currency reserves. Hard currency is currency that is accepted for payment by any international seller; soft currency is currency that is kept at a high artificial exchange rate, overvalued, and controlled by the national government. This situation, compounded by the inability to borrow from international banks or other sources such as the International Monetary Fund, has led developing countries to resort to countertrade to remain active in international trade and to address the needs of local consumers. Moreover, as global markets are growing competitive, increasingly, the balance of power is shifting from sellers to buyers. In the process, buyers require sellers to engage in reciprocal purchases, known as countertrade. [20]

Countertrade involves selling a product to a buyer and agreeing to accept, in return for payment, products from the buyer's firm or from the trade agency or an institution of the buyer. Countertrade has been traditionally associated with companies from countries in the former Soviet Bloc and from other countries with a tightly controlled soft currency. The classic countertrade example is the one initiated by Pepsi with the former Soviet Union. In the late 1960s, Nikita Khrushchev, then president of the Soviet Union, was impressed by the taste of Pepsi and agreed to an exchange of Pepsi syrup and bottling equipment in return for Stolichnaya vodka. This exchange was an example of successful countertrade conducted over decades. And countertrade is on the increase worldwide; it is estimated that the percentage of the total world trade financed through countertrade transactions is just more than 20 percent. [21] Many developing countries rely heavily on countertrade in their international trade activity. For example, as much as 70 percent of Russian industrial activity involves barter. [22]

It should be noted that countertrade is an important venue for firms in developed countries as well. For example, firms in the United States and Western Europe use counter-trade exchanges routinely. [23]

The Position of the U.S. Government on Countertrade

The United States, in line with the mandates of the General Agreement on Tariffs and Trade (GATT) and the WTO, has a policy that opposes government-mandated countertrade. The U.S. government interferes only in the case of firms that operate with U.S.-government financing or firms that have contracts with the U.S. government. In this case, the U.S. government could compromise the competitive position of U.S. firms, which are at a disadvantage compared with their Japanese and European competitors. However, the U.S. government does not deter firms from engaging in countertrade with private parties.

Furthermore, the U.S. government supports countertrade for the sale of weapons and air-craft (countertrade is prevalent in the trade of defense equipment) and for agricultural sur-plus.[24]

Countertrade Brokers

Often, countertrade is conducted with the help of countertrade brokers because it is rare that a perfect match can exist for product exchanges, and because the exchanges are complex. Exchanges range from paying sausages to rock stars for their performances to bringing French high fashion to Russian consumers by selling quality Russian crystal to Saudi merchants. Numerous companies specialize in brokering barter deals. Located in financial centers, such as London and New York, as well as in countries with traditions of brokering barter trade, such as Sweden, these brokers put together intricate exchanges.

Advantages of Countertrade

Countertrade offers substantial advantages to the involved parties. Countertrade allows firms from industrialized countries to sell their products in markets in the developing world that otherwise would not be accessible. Many countries that have a shortage of hard currency and that otherwise cannot secure bank loans to finance imports restrict the import of products considered nonessential by using foreign exchange controls and other barriers. Countertrade can help an exporting company bypass such restrictions.

In addition to offering an opportunity to many developing countries to participate in trade, countertrade also offers individuals from developing countries access to consumer products. Developing countries' governments tend to favor *heavy* industry imports and to restrict *light* industry imports, especially soft consumer goods. Countertrade offers develop-ing countries' consumers access to brand-name clothing, appliances, and music concerts.

Disadvantages of Countertrade

Among the disadvantages of countertrade are the following:[25]

- Companies countertrading with an indebted nation may find that foreign lenders have prior claim on goods offered as part of the countertrading agreement.
- Countertrade arrangements often restrict profit margins, and during negotiations, price setting is difficult because not all cost factors are known in advance.
- Countertrade practices encourage economic inefficiency and are a cumbersome.
- Prices are distorted as deliveries, which could take place over time, are made without reference to changes in technology, taste, quality, market structure, or com-peting products.
- Companies may receive inferior quality products as payment because rigorous quali-ty control may not be a practice in the trading partner's enterprise.
- Exchange partners can, in the long term, become competitors.
- Countertrade agreements often require long and expensive negotiations.

Often, the goods firms receive as payment are unrelated to the products they sell, and the firms have no expertise in marketing these products. For example, Caterpillar Trac-tor received Algerian wine in exchange for its products but was unable to sell it in the U.S. market.

Types of Countertrade

The different types of countertrade usually involve monetary exchange to a certain degree. Barter is the only type of exchange that does not involve monetary exchange. At the next level are clearing agreements and switch trading, which involve the transfer of currency, usually a mutually agreed-on hard currency. All other types of countertrade are based on direct monetary exchange.

Photobank/shutterstock.com

Barter

Barter can be traced back for centuries as a form of exchange. It involves a simple, nonmonetized exchange of goods or services between two parties. Although no money is involved in the exchange, the parties calculate the value of the goods in a particular currency and attempt to achieve value parity for the exchanged goods.

Clearing Agreement

A clearing agreement, also known as a **clearing account,** is a somewhat complex form of countertrade. Under this form of countertrade, a third party, usually a barter agent or some other type of broker, creates clearing accounts that represent trade credits for the respective parties, and companies trade in and out as necessary.[26] Under a clearing agreement, countries are likely to trade products up to a certain amount stated in a particular, mutually agreed-on hard currency and within a given time frame. When an imbalance occurs and one country owes money to the other, **swing credits** are paid in an agreed-on hard currency, known as the **clearing currency.**

Switch Trading

Switch trading involves buying a party's position in a countertrade in exchange for hard currency and selling it to another customer. Professional switch trading firms purchase products that are not accepted by the seller as payment for products and, for a commission, sell them on the market at a discount.

Compensation

Compensation involves payment in products and in cash, usually in a mutually agreed-on convertible currency. The firm compensated using this system is at lesser risk — especially if the proportion of cash is high — than the firm that is entirely dependent on the sale of the products it receives from the trading partner.

Counterpurchase

Counterpurchase involves two exchanges that are paid for in cash. As such, counter-purchase involves two parallel contracts, hence, its name of **parallel barter.** The seller agrees to purchase products that usually are unrelated to its business from the buyer and sell them on international markets. The purchase could be for the total sum of the products sold or for a fraction thereof. The exporter agrees to buy goods from a shopping list provided by the importer. The list typically consists of light manufactures and consumer goods. In a few historical examples, Volkswagen sold 10,000 cars to the former East Germany and agreed to purchase, over a period of two years, goods for the value of the automobiles, from a list of goods provided by the East German government. And, in another classic countertrade example whereby Pepsi sold its syrup to Russia in the late 1960s, the export agreement stated that Pepsi would subsequently import Stolichnaya vodka to be sold in the United States.[27]

The advantage of counterpurchase is that, typically, the seller is paid up front, in cash. The seller also has a specified, limited period (usually no more than a year) to sell the goods obtained through the exchange. Many governments of developing countries mandate counterpurchase as a requirement for firms exporting products to them.

Offset Purchase

Offset purchases involve large hard-currency purchases, such as the purchase of defense equipment, airplanes, telecommunications networks, railway or road building, and other expensive civil engineering projects, by a developing country. The seller agrees, in return for the sale of its offering, to purchase products that are valued at a certain percentage of the sale, ranging from 20 percent, which is quite typical, to as much as 100 percent for highly competitive deals. Among the advantages of offsets are reduced currency requirements, increased economic activity, and increased sales volume of both the product for the seller and of corresponding products for the buyer and improved technology development throughout the country. And, in addition to the direct economic benefit to the buyer, offset purchases also provide indirect economic benefit to the country, as the offset provides a vehicle to increase a country's technology base, allowing the country to develop a competitive position in a well-established international market. In one example of an offset transaction, the Taiwanese government spent roughly $16 billion for purchasing Patriot missiles, P-3 long-range antisubmarine planes, and diesel-engine submarines from the United States through the Foreign Military Sales (FMS) program, and the U.S., in turn, received offset credits.[28]

Buyback Agreements

In a buyback agreement, the seller builds and provides a turnkey plant, as well as the manufacturing know-how, the necessary equipment, patents, and licenses necessary for production and distribution of the product. The seller is paid up front part of the cost of the plant in an agreed-on convertible currency, which is typically obtained by borrowing from international banks or the International Monetary Fund. The seller agrees to purchase specific quantities of the plant's output over an extended period of time. An advantage of this type of countertrade to the seller is that it has the know-how in terms of marketing and distributing the products because the company operates in a similar business.

A buyback agreement that raised eyebrows was Royal Dutch Shell's Iranian deal. The company defied the U.S. government restrictions on trade with Iran and established a buy-back agreement worth $10 billion with the National Iranian Oil Company to produce liquefied natural gas from the Iranian South Pars oil field.[29]

14-3 International Pricing Decisions

14-3a Price Setting

Setting prices internationally tends to be intuition-and experience-driven and highly decentralized. The skill in pricing lies in exploiting differences in consumers' willingness to pay for products and services. Consequently, it is important for marketing managers to be familiar with the price elasticity of their products in a particular international market.[30]

Important determinants of the final price are currency fluctuations. Managers must decide what their reactions should be to currency fluctuations: Should they adjust their prices based on these fluctuations, or should they fix the prices on their home country currency or the currency in the country of production? Should they pass on price increases to customers or choose a lower profit? Due to the instability of currencies, many sales contracts have exchange rate clauses that address exchange rate fluctuations and exchange risk. Periodic examinations of exchange rate trends determine the adjustments necessary to align prices accordingly.

Additional important determinants of the final price are the terms of sale and the terms of payment to the ultimate buyer, as well as various suppliers in the chain of distribution. The terms of sale determine what is and what is not included in the price quotation and when the seller takes possession of the goods. In a business-to-business environment, a buyer can correctly evaluate price deals on their face value only when fully taking into account the terms of sale and the terms of payment, including the possible extension of credit offered by the seller. Consequently, these considerations constitute important competitive tools when quoting prices; it is helpful to be aware not only of the prices that competitors set, but also the terms of sale and terms of payment quoted. Moreover, it is important to note that businesses in certain markets may have a preference for one type or category of quote over another, and that certain markets may not be suitable risks for trade financing.

The terms of sale are stated using Incoterms — the International Commercial Terms, described in International Marketing Illustration 14-2. As a general trend, marketers and exporters tend to be more inclined to quote more inclusive terms — the D-terms described in the illustration in order to be proactive with their customers and competitive with other suppliers.

International Marketing Illustration 14-2 Terms of Sale

Incoterms apply both to domestic and to international transactions. They were first devised by the International Chamber of Commerce (ICC, based in Paris, France) in 1936 and, since then, have been updated a number of times, most recently in the year 2010. These terms of sale are also referred to as "Incoterms 2010."

The terms are further organized into E-terms, implying that the seller makes the goods available at the seller's plant, factory, or place of business. The E-term EXW — Ex Works (factory, warehouse, etc.) — states that the title and risk pass to the buyer from the seller's factory, plant, or warehouse. The seller's merchandise is not cleared for export, and the seller does not load merchandise on a vehicle. Ex Works is used for any mode of transportation, and it requires the minimum responsibility of the seller.

Prices are also quoted using F-terms, meaning that the seller delivers goods to the carrier that the buyer appoints. Among the F-terms are FCA — Free Carrier (a place after the origin point) — whereby the title and risk pass to the buyer at the point when the seller

delivers goods that have been cleared for export to the carrier designated by the buyer. The seller loads the goods on the buyer's vehicle, and the buyer receives the seller's arriving vehicle unloaded. A product that is delivered FAS — Free Alongside Ship (at port, after all port charges)— requires the title and risk to pass to the buyer after the merchandise is delivered alongside the ship by the seller. This term is used for sea or inland waterway transportation. The seller is in charge of export clearance. FOB — Free on Board (port, after all port charges) — means that the title and risk pass to the buyer once delivered on board the ship by the seller — after the goods pass the ship's rail. This term is used for sea or inland waterway transportation. The seller is in charge of export clearance.

Sebastian Kaullitzki/shutterstock.com

C-terms denote that the seller must arrange for transportation without assuming the risk of loss. *CFR — Cost and Freight* (destination port) — means that the title, risk, and insurance cost pass to the buyer when delivered on board the ship by the seller. The seller pays transportation costs to the destination port. *CIF—Cost, Insurance, and Freight* (destination port)—means that the title, risk, and insurance costs pass to the buyer when delivered on board the ship by the seller. The seller pays transportation and insurance costs to the destination port. CFR and CIF are used for sea or inland waterway transportation. *CPT — Carriage Paid To* (place at destination; includes all port charges) — means that the title, risk, and insurance costs pass to the buyer when delivered to the carrier or seller. The seller pays transportation and insurance costs to the destination port. A product delivered *CIP — Carriage and Insurance Paid To* (place at destination; includes all port charges) — means that title and risk pass to the buyer when delivered to the carrier or seller. The seller pays transportation and insurance costs to the destination port. Both CIP and CPT are used for any mode of transportation, and the seller is obligated to clear the goods for export.

D-terms imply that the seller bears all the costs and risks to bring the goods to a location agreed on by the buyers. *DAF — Delivered to Frontier* (border of country) — means that the title and risk pass to the buyer who is responsible for import clearance. This term is used for any mode of transportation. *DES — Delivered Ex Ship* (on board ship to destination port) — means that the title, risk, and responsibility for vessel unloading and import clearance pass to the buyer when the seller delivers goods on board the ship to the destination port. *DEQ — Delivered Ex Quay* (Wharf), Duty Paid (destination port, includes duties and taxes but not destination charges and delivery) — means that the title and risk pass to the buyer when delivered on board the ship at the destination by the seller. The buyer clears the merchandise for import and pays for all formalities, duties, taxes, and other charges. The seller delivers goods on dock at the destination and clears merchandise for import. The terms *DES* and *DEQ* are used for sea or inland waterway transportation.

DDU — Delivered Duty Unpaid (destination; excludes all duties and taxes) — means that the title, risk, and responsibility for the vessel's discharge and import clearance pass to the buyer when delivered on board the ship at the destination point by the seller. Finally, *DDP—Delivered Duty Paid* (buyer's door; includes all charges — means that the title and risk pass to the buyer when the seller delivers goods to the destination. The seller is responsible for import clearance. The terms *DDU* and *DDP* are used for any mode of transportation.

Now consider three identical shipments with identical prices for each shipment, quoted for EXW (Dieburg, Germany), CIF (Norfolk, Virginia), and DDP (Norfolk, Virginia) for Stihl merchandise shipped from Dieburg, Germany, to Norfolk, Virginia. The best deal for the buyer is the DDP (Norfolk).

Sources: International Chamber of Commerce, "The New 2010 Incoterms Rules," accessed at http://www.iccwbo.org/products-and-services/trade facilitation/incoterms-2010/ on November 2, 2015; International Chamber of Commerce, *Incoterms 2000,* Paris: ICC Publishing, 2000; John Murray, Jr. "Risk, Title, and Incoterms," *Purchasing,* Vol. 132, No. 10, June 19, 2003, p. 26; John Shuman, "Incoterms 2000," *Business Credit,* Vol. 102, No. 7, July/August 2000, p. 50.

Other determinants of the final price are the terms of payment offered by the seller. The ability of a seller to offer or arrange extended payment terms can be the "make or break" factor for a foreign buyer receiving competitive offers from other suppliers. Financing terms are critical for transactions ranging from cosmetics to industrial machinery and even jet aircraft.

The methods of payment are determined by the company's reasons for going international, the company's strategy in the market, and its expected return. The company must find out what forms of payment are preferred in a market and are acceptable to the buyer;

this information will also shed light on the partner's financial strength.[31] However, obtaining verifiable or audited financial statements on a foreign buyer can be a major challenge. Similarly, information on buyers from local credit bureaus may not be available. International Marketing Illustration 14-3 examines the terms of payment in international transactions.

International Marketing Illustration 14-3 Terms of Payment

Buyers and sellers can agree to a number of payment methods in transactions:

Cash in Advance — This is the most advantageous payment option for the seller, but not for the buyer. It is used for sellers' markets primarily or for high-risk buyer environments.

Open Account — This method entails delivering goods or services without a guarantee of payment; the buyer and seller have conducted transactions in the past, and there is an expectation of continued business for both. The Basic Open Account entails payment reasonably soon after the shipment arrives or within an agreed-on period. This method is risky for the seller, who must choose buyers well.

Consignment with Open Account — Sellers can reduce risk with an Open Account because they still own the merchandise. However, the costs of recovering the goods are high in international transactions. This method is rarely used in international sales transactions.

Documentary Collection — With this method, title and possession pass to the buyer when the documents attesting to the title and the shipping documents pass as well. These documents can be a bill of lading, a commercial invoice, an insurance certificate, or a certificate of origin. The payment document, known as a bill of exchange or draft, requiring the buyer to pay immediately (sight draft) or at a specified time (time draft), is sent through the seller's bank to the buyer's bank after the goods have been shipped. The buyer then pays the draft, the documents are released to the buyer, and the buyer can take possession of the goods.

Letter of Credit (L/C)—With this method, the L/C is opened by the buyer's bank, which guarantees to pay the seller for the merchandise upon the presentation of the required documents in the L/C that provide evidence of shipment, title to the goods, and adherence to the purchase order, and even an inspection certificate, if stipulated.

As with a documentary collection, the L/C may call for either a sight draft or time draft with payment at a later date to the supplier. The bank releases the funds when all the conditions of the L/C are met. Most L/Cs are irrevocable: neither party can change them without the consent of the other parties to the transaction, including the banks. When an L/C is issued by a foreign bank, it is "advised" via the seller's bank or another bank in the seller's country. At this point, the seller's commercial risk is that of the issuing bank in the foreign country. While this may be an acceptable risk in a number of cases, the seller may request that the L/C be "confirmed" by a bank in the seller's country. With a confirmation, the seller's credit risk is now the confirming bank in seller's country. If a letter of credit is to be confirmed, that is part of the original L/C. Unless an inspection certificate of the merchandise is one of the required documents under the letter of credit, the entire L/C transaction is based strictly on the conformity of the documents with the terms of the L/C. Therefore, a buyer cannot open a shipping container and inspect the goods prior to payment by the bank to the seller. Any commercial disputes between the buyer and seller concerning the merchandise would be addressed independently of the L/C transaction.

The risk of selling to international buyers, especially using cash in advance or on open account, can be alleviated by purchasing insurance using the many different sources discussed in Chapter 2, "An Overview of the International Marketing Environment."

Source: Adapted from "Getting Paid or What's a Transaction For?" *World Trade*, Vol. 12, No. 9, 1999, pp 42-48; Justin Pritchard, "How a Letter of Credit Works-Protection for Payments," *The Balance*, February 9, 2018, accessed at https://www.thebalance.com/how-letters-of-credit-work-315201 on July 9, 2018.

To illustrate, assume a company in Virginia is selling a container of cosmetics to their distributor in Santiago, Chile. Upon receipt of the container, the distributor will have to take the container to a warehouse, break out the shipment, repackage the items, and sell the products to Chilean retailers. With tighter sales or payment terms, the Chilean distributor's cash flow may become stretched while waiting for proceeds from the sale of the cosmetics to the Chilean retail stores. From the point of view of the distributor, "net 30" or some other short-term credit extension is preferable as it allows the distributor to complete the retail transactions and get paid. This, however, means the Virginia exporter is carrying the credit risk of the Chilean buyer unless the seller has arranged credit insurance on the international accounts receivable on the books. In short, exporters should only consider extending open account terms to better buyers in countries with an established banking system with available funds to pay the U.S. supplier.

This issue of extended payment terms is even more critical in the sale of specialized machinery and other major industrial equipment, including jet aircraft. In these cases, buyers will often insist on extended payment terms beyond the normal short-term credit terms of payment at sight to 180 days. Buyers need time to put the machinery or aircraft to work in order to generate sales and cash flow to help pay for the purchase.

In setting prices, companies need to examine existing competition, the labor market and materials costs, the buying power of consumers, and the goal of the company with regard to the respective target market. The company may price products higher or lower in the home market; it could engage in aggressive export pricing, skimming, or penetration pricing; or it could use standardized pricing worldwide or local pricing. These strategies are described next.

Prices Higher in the Home Market

Setting prices higher in the home market than in the international market is justified by one or a combination of the following reasons:

- A lower labor or raw material cost in the international market
- Strong local competition in the international market
- A lower buying power of host-country consumers relative to consumers in the company's home market
- A firm's goal to increase market share by using a penetration pricing strategy in the international market, as is most likely in the example offered in Figure 14-3.

Prices Lower in the Home Country

Setting prices lower in the home country, compared with company prices in the international market, is justified by one or a combination of the following reasons:

Figure 14-3 Companies selling bottled water in the Czech Republic find that they have to price water at a lower price point in order to be able to compete with quality local competitors and gain market share.

• There may be no cost advantages to producing overseas, such as economies of scale and labor to justify a lower price.

• There may be few or no challenges from competition in the international market.

• The market potential might be limited.

• Buyers in the international market can afford the higher price.

One strategy used by multinational firms to penetrate an attractive international market is aggressive export pricing.

14-3b Aggressive Export Pricing

To gain market share and to remain competitive in international markets, companies often engage in aggressive export pricing. One example of aggressive export pricing is dynamic incremental pricing, whereby a company assumes that it will have certain fixed costs whether or not it exports its products overseas. As such, the company does not factor in its international price marketing and promotion costs or its full overhead for domestic distribution. The price is based on variable international marketing and promotion costs, which allows the company to be more competitive.[32] The company allows for the product cost to reflect only the *variable cost* of taking the product abroad (thus using variable-cost pricing), rather than the *full cost* of the product (that is, full-cost pricing). Companies from Japan, Taiwan, and South Korea exporting semiconductor chips to the United States gained high market share rankings using aggressive export pricing.[33]

Figure 14-4 Even pricing for Japanese fruit.

Similarly, products in China are mostly priced evenly, though the currency there is on a closer parity to the dollar and the euro, at about seven yuan to the dollar. Consumer research shows that consumers in high context, non-Western cultures were found to be less prone to the illusion of low price or gain created by odd price endings, and more likely offended by perceived attempts to "fool" them. Thus, Western firms must be cautious replicating odd pricing practices in non-Western markets. Even pricing is thought to be a "safer" format for the Chinese and the Japanese (see Figure 14-4).[34]

On the other hand, and contrary to the pricing theory discussed earlier, in Taiwan, odd prices appear to be predominant (see Figure 14-5 on next page). Even in luxury markets, sales signs abound and information on price-cutting is everywhere.

Finally, odd prices are very common in the European Union. At first, just after the adoption of the euro, prices were pretty strange, with endings all over the place. European retailers wanted to prove to their consumers that they diligently transformed prices based on the original currency (franc, deutsche mark, lira) to the euro. Subsequently, odd-pricing strategies became prevalent. Figure 14-6 illustrates the strategy of a warehouse club — prices on top are wholesale prices, prices below are retail prices.

Figure 14-5 *In Taiwan, most prices advertised are odd prices.*

Figure 14-6 *Cheap wine, odd prices. Prices at a wholesale club: wholesale prices with corresponding retail prices below. Note that retail prices are primarily odd prices.*

14-3c Penetration Pricing and Skimming Strategies

Multinationals that have sales-based objectives, attempting to gain a high sales volume, are likely to use penetration pricing. Firms using this strategy price the product at first below the price of competitors to quickly penetrate the market at their competitors' expense. Compaq, now HP, was able to quickly capture the European market by using this strategy. In the Netherlands, for example, Compaq offered deals unmatched by any brand name competitor and coupled this pricing strategy with excellent warranties and support.

Alternatively, firms may have pricing objectives that are centered on generating a high profit and recovering the costs of product development quickly. Companies thus use a skimming strategy, pricing the product above that of competitors, when competition is minimal. In general, consumers responding to skimming strategies are more concerned with quality, uniqueness, and status, rather than price.

Summary

Identify pricing-related internal challenges facing international firms. Product pricing is partially determined by the location of the production facilities. Companies that do not move production to take advantage of low-cost labor are likely to price themselves out of the market. Because products are manufactured in one country, assembled in another, and then modified in yet another country, keeping track of product costs is difficult. Companies need to keep track of costs and ensure that the maximum profitability is achieved.

Identify pricing-related challenges imposed by competition on international firms. Products can face challenges from legitimate competitors; from gray markets, whereby a company's products from a low-priced market are sold through unauthorized channels in a high-priced market, competing with authorized distributors; and from dumping activities of competitors who price their products below cost to gain competitive advantage.

Identify pricing-related challenges imposed by the political and legal environment on international firms. Governments often regulate prices charged by multinationals, thus setting limits on wholesalers' gross margins and on the products' retail price and restricting price promotions. Governments can impose tariffs and other duties, thereby increasing the prices charged by the international firm.

Identify pricing-related challenges imposed by the economic and financial environment on international firms. Multinational companies are facing many challenges, among them inflationary pressures on price, fluctuating exchange rates, and even the inability of governments to guarantee payment in hard currency. For the latter, a viable solution is countertrade, whereby a company accepts payment in kind, in product output of a company or in some other format, in return for the products it sells or for setting up operational factories in the respective country.

Address international pricing decisions of international firms. International firms use different pricing strategies in different markets. They may set prices higher in the home country if they want to penetrate new international markets or if the international markets cannot afford high prices. Or prices may be higher in international markets if those markets can afford it and pricing is in line with competitors' pricing, or if the international markets are not perceived as offering viable long-term opportunities. Companies need to make decisions such as determining whether aggressive export pricing is an appropriate strategy or whether they should use standardized prices throughout or local prices in their target markets.

Key Terms

aggressive export pricing	countervailing duties	offset purchase
antidumping duties	dumping	parallel barter
barter	dynamic incremental pricing	parallel imports
buyback agreements	grey market	penetration pricing
clearing account	hard currency	skimming strategy
clearing currency	Incoterms	soft currency
compensation	infant industry argument	standardized pricing
cost-based transfer pricing	letter of credit	swing credits
counterpurchase	local pricing	switch trading
countertrade	market-based transfer pricing	transfer pricing

Discussion Questions

1. What are gray markets? How do distributors using parallel imports affect a multinational firm's operations in the target market?

2. What is dumping? Why do international companies use dumping strategies in select target markets?

3. Countertrade helps a company do business in markets that otherwise would be inaccessible. What are the different approaches to countertrade that a manufacturer of telecommunications equipment could use to penetrate such markets?

4. What are the different motivations behind a company setting prices higher or lower in the home country?

Chapter Quiz

True/False

1. Dumping is defined as selling products at or below cost to get rid of excess inventory and to undermine competition.

Answer: True

Rationale: Dumping is defined as selling products at or below cost to get rid of excess inventory and to undermine competition. Section 14-2a, "The Competitive Environment"

2. Dumping represents a problem if it threatens to cause injury to an established industry in a particular market and if it delays the establishment of a viable domestic industry.

Answer: True

Rationale: According to the World Trade Organization, dumping should be condemned if it threatens to cause injury to an established industry in a particular market and if it delays the establishment of a viable domestic industry. Section 14-2a, "The Competitive Environment"

3. Hard currency is currency that is accepted for payment by any international seller.

Answer: True

Rationale: Hard currency is currency that is accepted for payment by any international seller, and soft currency is currency that is kept at a high artificial exchange rate, overvalued, and controlled by the national government. Section 14-2c, "The Economic and Financial Environment"

4. Countries with a shortage of soft currency reserves are more likely to engage in counter-trade.

Answer: False

Rationale: Countries with a shortage of *hard* currency reserves are more likely to engage in countertrade. Section 14-2c, "The Economic and Financial Environment"

5. Aggressive export pricing involves pricing products below market price to penetrate new markets.

Answer: True

Rationale: Aggressive export pricing is defined as pricing below market to penetrate new markets; a downside of exports priced well below fair market value is that they might place the company at risk for dumping challenges. Section 14-3b, "Aggressive Export Pricing"

Multiple Choice

1. Which of the following is NOT an external economic or financial factor affecting pricing decisions?
   a. inflation pressure on price
   b. shortage of hard currency
   c. transfer pricing
   d. fluctuating exchange rates

Answer: c is correct.

Rationale: Inflationary pressures, shortage of hard currency, and fluctuating exchange rates constitute external economic and financial factors that the company does not control. Transfer pricing is a pricing strategy that the firm can use for intra-firm sales. Section 14-2c, "The Economic and Financial Environment"

2. A manufacturer may charge different prices in different markets for the same product
   a. to meet target market needs.
   b. due to changes in the exchange rate.

    c. due to differences in wholesale prices.

    d. all of the above

Answer: d is correct.

Rationale: A manufacturer can charge different prices in different markets for the same product to meet the needs of target consumers who have a limited purchasing power, to keep the product price competitive in markets that are actively targeted by competition, to meet the needs of consumers in the countries with the weakest currency, and to address differences in wholesale prices in different markets. Section 14-2a, "The Competitive Environment"

3. What company was responsible for initiating a countertrade relationship with the Soviet Union in the late 1960s?

    a. McDonald's

    b. Pepsi

    c. Philip Morris

    d. none of the above

Answer: b is correct.

Rationale: Pepsi initiated countertrade with the Soviet Union, agreeing to an exchange of Pepsi syrup and bottling equipment in return for international distribution rights to Stolichnaya vodka. Section 14-2c, "The Economic and Financial Environment"

4. What type of countertrade involves buying a party's position in a countertrade in exchange for hard currency and selling it to another customer?

    a. compensation

    b. switch trading

    c. counter purchase

    d. offset purchase

Answer: b correct.

Rationale: Switch trading involves buying a party's position in a countertrade in exchange for hard currency and selling it to another customer. Professional switch trading firms typically purchase products that are not accepted by the seller as payment for products and, for a commission, sell them on the market at a discount. Section 14-2c, "The Economic and Financial Environment"

5. If a firm's objectives are centered on generating high profit and recovering product development costs quickly, it is likely to use which one of the following international pricing strategies?

    a. skimming

    b. penetration pricing

    c. standardized pricing

    d. competitive pricing

Answer: a is correct.

Rationale: A skimming strategy is used when competition is limited. This allows the firm to price the product higher than competitors, allowing for a higher profit margin. Section 14-3d, "Penetration Pricing and Skimming Strategies"

Notes

1. Terry Clark, Masaaki Kotabe, and Dan Rajaratnam, "Exchange Rate Pass-Through and International Pricing Strategy: A Conceptual Framework and Research Propositions," *Journal of International Business Studies*, Vol. 30, No. 2, Second Quarter 1999, pp. 249–268.

2. Howard Forman and James M. Hunt, "Pricing Issues in Industrial Marketing," *Industrial Marketing Management*, 34, 2, February 2005, 133-146.

3. Virginia Citrano, "The Right Price," *CFO*, Vol. 8, No. 5, May 1992, pp. 71–72.

4. Ibid.

5. Discussion of internal factors adapted from Howard Forman and James M. Hunt, "Pricing Issues in Industrial Marketing," *Industrial Marketing Management*, Vol. 34, No. 2, February 2005, pp. 133–146.

6. "National Assn. of Foreign Trade Zones 2017 Annual Report," accessed at https://www.naftz.org/wp-content/uploads/2018/02/2017-Annual-Report.pdf on July 6, 2018.

7. Forman and Hunt, "Pricing Issues in Industrial Marketing."

8. For an additional discussion on parallel imports, see Chapter 11, "Managing International Marketing Channels."

9. "China Deploys State Power to Dominate Global Steel Industry," *Industry Today*, Volume 14, Issue 1, 2011, accessed at https://industrytoday.com/article/china-deploys-state-power-to-dominate-global-steel-industry on July 7, 2018.

10. World Trade Organization, "Anti-Dumping," accessed at https://www.wto.org/english/tratop_e/adp_e/adp_e.htm on November 2, 2015; Greg Mastel, "The U.S. Steel Industry and Antidumping Law," *Challenge*, Vol. 42, No. 3, May/June 1999, pp. 84–94.

11. Lester Ross and Susan Ning, "Modern Protectionism: China's Own Antidumping Regulations," *The China Business Review*, Vol. 27, No. 3, May/June 2000, pp. 30–33.

12. European Commission, "Anti-Dumping," accessed at http://ec.europa.eu/trade/policy/accessing-markets/trade-defence/actions-against-imports-into-the-eu/anti-dumping/ on November 2, 2015.

13. Viet Nam News, "Anti-dumping Lawsuits Weigh Down VN Exports," accessed at http://vietnamnews.vn/economy/277970/anti-dumping-lawsuits-weigh-down-vn-exports.html on November 2, 2015; Keith Johnson and Cassandra Sweet, "U.S. Imposes Tariffs on China Solar Panels, *The Wall Street Journal*, May 18, 2012, online.wsj.com; Philip Scott Andrews, "U.S. Solar Panel Makers Say China Violated Trade Rules, *The New York Times*, October 19, 2011, www.nytimes.com.

14. "Aircraft Financing 'Robust' but Exim Bank needs Reinstatement, Boeing Says," *Leeham News and Comment*, March 5, 2018, accessed at https://leehamnews.com/2018/03/05/aircraft-financing-robust-exim-bank-news-reinstatement-boeing-says on July 8, 2018.

15. Jim Zarroli, "China Churns Out Half the World's Steel, And Other Steelmakers Feel Pinched," *NPR*, March 8, 2018, accessed at https://www.npr.org/2018/03/08/591637097/china-churns-out-half-the-worlds-steel-and-other-steelmakers-feel-pinched on July 7, 2018. "The U.S.-China Trade Relationship: A Dispute in Five Charts," *Bloomberg News*, July 6, 2018, accessed at https://www.bloomberg.com/news/articles/2018-07-06/the-u-s-china-trade-relationship-a-dispute-in-five-charts on July 7, 2018.

16. Messaoud Mehafdi, "The Ethics of International Transfer Pricing," *Journal of Business Ethics*, Vol. 28, No. 4, December 2000, pp. 365–381.

17. Examples from *The Economist*, "Finance and Economics: Europe's Burden," Vol. 351, No. 8120, May 22, 1999, p. 84.

18. Taos Turner and Paul Kiernan, "How Latin America Pays the Price of Protectionism," *The Wall Street Journal*, November 25, 2016, accessed at https://www.wsj.com/articles/how-latin-america-pays-the-price-of-protectionism-1480089781 on July 7, 2018. Taos Turner, "Argentina Wants Cheap Flights, but not Too Cheap," *The Wall Street Journal*, December 23, 2017, accessed at https://www.wsj.com/articles/argentina-wants-cheap-flightsbut-not-too-cheap-1514030401 on July 7, 2018.

19. Jack Ewing, "Weighing the Fallout of a Greek Exit From the Euro," *The New York Times*, July 9, 2015, accessed at https://www.nytimes.com/2015/07/10/business/international/drachma-grexit-eurozone.html on July 7, 2018.

20. Dorothy A. Paun, Larry D. Compeau, and Dhruv Grewal, "A Model of the Influence of Marketing Objectives on Pricing Strategies in International Countertrade," *Journal of Public Policy & Marketing*, Vol. 16, No. 1, Spring 1997, pp. 69–82.

21. Derren Young, "The Extent of FTSE Companies Are Using Countertrade Strategically as a Method of Internationalization," PSU Paper, accessed at http://citeseerx.ist.psu.edu/viewdoc/download?doi=10.1.1.453.843&rep=rep1&type=pdf on November 4, 2015; Sam C. Okoroafo, "Determinants of LDC-Mandated Countertrade," *International Marketing Review*, Vol. 5, Winter 1988, pp. 16–24.

22. David Woodruff, *Money Unmade: Barter and the Fate of Russian Capitalism*, Ithaca: NY: Cornell University Press, 2000..

23. Derren Young, "The Extent of FTSE Companies Are Using Countertrade Strategically as a Method of Internationalization," Pennsylvania State University Working Paper, accessed at http://citeseerx.ist.psu.edu/viewdoc/

download?doi=10.1.1.453.843&rep=rep1&type=pdf on November 4, 2015; John P. Angelidis and Nabil A. Ibrahim, "Countertrading between United States and Western European Firms: An Empirical Analysis of the Benefits and Pitfalls," *International Journal of Management*, Vol. 18, No. 2, 2001, p. 252.

24. Paun, Compeau, and Grewal, "A Model of the Influence of Marketing Objectives," pp. 69–82.

25. Nabil A. Ibrahim and John P. Angelidis, "Countertrading with Eastern Europe: A Comparative Analysis of the Benefits and Pitfalls," *International Journal of Commerce & Management*, Vol. 6, No. 3/4, 1996, pp. 22–40.

26. Plank, Reid, and Bates, "Barter: An Alternative," p. 52.

27. Derren Young, "The Extent of FTSE Companies Are Using Countertrade Strategically as a Method of Internationalization"; Jean F. Hennart, "Some Empirical Dimensions of Countertrade," *Journal of International Business Studies*," Vol. 21, No. 2, Second Quarter 1990, pp. 243–270.

28. Chyan Yang and Tsung-cheng Wang, "Multi-Criteria Analysis of Offset Execution Strategies in Defense Trade: A Case in Taiwan," *Journal of American Academy of Business*, September 2006, Vol. 10, No. 1, pp. 179-185.

29. Terry Macalister, "Shell Defies US Pressure and Signs £5bn Iranian Gas Deal," *The Guardian Unlimited*, online edition, January 29, 2007.

30. Howard Forman and James M. Hunt, "Pricing Issues in Industrial Marketing," *Industrial Marketing Management*, Vol. 34, No. 2, February 2005, pp. 133–146.

31. "Getting Paid or What's a Transaction For?" *World Trade*, Vol. 12, No. 9, 1999, pp. 42–48.

32. Barbara Stottinger, "Strategic Export Pricing: A Long and Winding Road," *Journal of International Marketing*, Vol. 9, No. 1, 2001, pp. 40–63.

33. Citrano, "The Right Price," pp. 71–72.

34. Adam Nguyen, Roger M. Heeler, and Zinaida Taran, "High-Low Context Cultures and Price-Ending Practices," *Journal of Product and Brand Management*, Vol. 16, No. 3, 2007, p. 206.

Case 14-1 *Travel Turkey: Pricing Decisions in a Changing Environment*

Erdogan Eser, a former hotel sales manager with Golden Tulip Hotels, decided to return to his home country, Turkey, to establish a travel agency called Travel Turkey. With an office in Taksim Square in the center of Istanbul, the travel agency is a broker between foreign tour operators and lodging operators in Turkey. Lodging operators — managers of hotels, bed and breakfasts, inns, and resorts — have voiced concerns about foreign tour operators, especially about the lack of guarantees regarding occupancy. Foreign tour operators also felt that their needs were not addressed by lodging operators. As a broker, Erdogan would address concerns and benefit each party by creating optimal matches. Travel Turkey will benefit from Erdogan's many years in the travel industry and from his extensive network in the travel business. Even though Turkey has experienced its own economic and political problems, the country remains attractive to tourists and is a preferred destination for many tourist groups.

Turkey's tourism has experienced a boom since the early 1980s. Turkey is an attractive destination, at the crossroads of Asia and Europe, with centuries-old cultural and historical sites, a dynamic destination of sun, seas, and archeological sites. The government offers incentives to businesses to increase bed capacity.

Viacheslav Lopatin/shutterstock.com

The major players in Turkey's expanding tourism are Western European package tour operators, one of Erdogan's main target markets. These operators coordinate their activities with airlines and travel agencies in France, Germany, and the United Kingdom, in particular. The relationship between Turkish lodging operators and the European tour operators is not always smooth: A study of 200 Turkish lodging operators revealed the difficulties that are often encountered in their relationship with Western tour operators (see table).

Types of Problems	Number of Times Cited
Cancellations	113
Delayed payments	126
Pressure to accept low prices	129
Artificial price competition	129
Reduced number of rooms blocked	118
Requests for complimentary rooms	65
Requests for last-minute reservations	116

Erdogan Eser will also target U.S. travel agencies, especially church groups visiting European capitals — a market that, in spite of safety concerns, remains relatively solid. There are still concerns and numerous reports that Americans are verbally attacked on the street in much of Europe by locals who oppose U.S. military policies around the world. Newspapers advise U.S. travelers: If you're heading overseas, be prepared to have discussions with people who think America is the devil. In fact, the United States Department of State is encouraging the departure of U.S. government family members from certain areas in Turkey, such as the Hatay, Kilis, Gaziantep, Sanliurfa, Sirnak, Diyarbakir, Van, Siirt, Mus, Mardin, Batman, Bingol, Tunceli, Hakkari, Bitlis, and Elazig provinces, in Southeastern Turkey.

One of the concerns in Turkey is the seasonality of tourism. Most tourists visit Turkey between the months of June and October. August is the high season, the hottest month, with temperatures hovering in the 90s, and with high humidity. This tendency is entrenched and there is little variation over time. A major concern for tourists is that Turkey is currently going through a period of instability, with the year 2018 particularly marked by increased civil unrest, a faltering economy, and authoritarianism on the rise.

Despite these developments, Erdogan feels that the right price would bring U.S. tourists to the shores of the Bosporus, in Western Turkey. After all, Greece and Turkey are among the hottest destinations for Christians: The ruins of Ephesus in Turkey, where Mary is said to have spent her last days, are especially popular. Travel Turkey could partner with Travel Dynamics International, which specializes in these types of tours.

Another important target market is the Eastern European travel operators who coordinate shopping trips to Istanbul. Eastern European consumers often take short trips to Istanbul to purchase quality leather products of Turkish provenance and knockoffs of top international brands. They may purchase products for their own and their family's use, or they may purchase for resale. Regardless, the buses always return to Russia, Ukraine, and Romania full of merchandise.

Erdogan's plans are to assure lodging operators of high occupancy levels and obtain large discounts. He will then assure tour operators of rooms at reasonable rates that would meet their needs. For example, for a week in Istanbul, he would arrange with the Conrad hotel, the Ciragan Palace (a Kempinski Hotels property), and Swissôtel to book 100 rooms, each at 70 euros. For spending a week at one of these hotels, he would charge the tour operators as follows:

• Western European tour operators would pay 100 euros per room per night.

• Eastern European tour operators would pay 90 euros per room per night.

• U.S. tour operators would pay $130 per room per night.

One of the first to meet Erdogan in his capacity as travel agent, a U.S. tour operator, Jack Maloney, who heads a church travel agency in Cincinnati, Ohio, was concerned that the dollar price for the three hotels was rather high. His feeling was that because his Ukrainian colleague, another tour operator, was charged only 90 euros, his business should be charged the same amount. Moreover, even a tourist off the street would be able to book a room at the Conrad, for instance, for only $150 for a Conrad Saver rate — not much more than the deal he was getting. True, those are all premium properties and five-star hotels, but charging different prices for the East European operators seemed unfair, and Jack's travel agency would not be able to make a sufficient profit.

As a result of this meeting, Erdogan Eser decided to rethink his pricing strategy. Were there any international laws that did not allow him to charge different prices to different clients? This was never a concern in Turkey. And, at his previous job with the Hilton, charging different rates was customary. Was it ethical to give a break to the Eastern European tour operators? Was it unethical to charge the U.S. operators higher amounts?

Sources: *Euromonitor International,* "Travel Turkey: Industry Overview," September 18, 2015, accessed at http://www.portal.euromonitor.com.newman.richmond.edu:2048/portal/analysis/tab on November 4, 2015; United States Department of State, "Turkey Travel Warning," September 3, 2015, accessed at http:// travel.state.gov/ content/passports/en/alertswarnings/turkey-travel-warning.html on November 4, 2015; Marco R. della Cava, "Ugly Sentiments Sting American Tourists as Europeans Cite Frustrations with U.S. Policy," *USA Today,* March 4, 2003, 1–2; Gene Sloan, "Cruise Lines Are Forced to Bail Again," *USA Today,* March 4, 2003, 10b; Dan Reed, "American Wants to Get the Low-Fare Word Out," *USA Today,* March 4, 2003, 8A; Elizabeth Bernstein, "The Other Holy Lands—Spiritual Tourists Skip Israel for Sites in Cuba, Turkey; Keeping Kosher in China," *The Wall Street* , December 6, 2002, W4; Kurtulus Karamustafa, "Marketing Channel Relationships: Turkey's Resort Purveyors' Interactions with International Tour Operators," *Cornell Hotel and Restaurant Administration Quarterly,* Vol. 41, No. 4, 2000, pp. 21–32.

Analysis Suggestions

1. Are there any legal or ethical concerns that might preclude Travel Turkey to charge different prices to different travel agents for the same room? Is it ethical or legal to charge different prices based on the home country of the tour operators and their respective tourists?

2. What can Erdogan do if the dollar continues to fall relative to the euro?

3. How can Travel Turkey ensure against foreign exchange risk and maintain its Eastern European and U.S. clients?

This page is intentionally blank...

Part 5

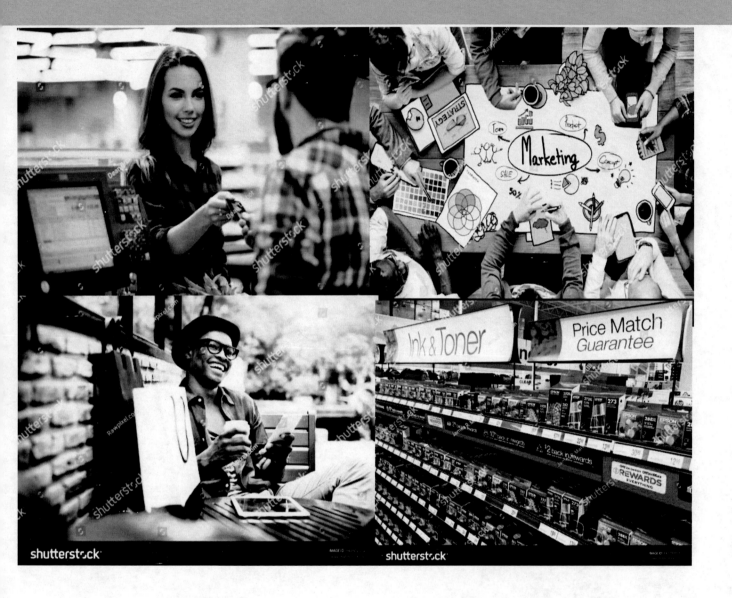

International Marketing Strategy: **Implementation**

Chapter 15

Organizing and Controlling International Marketing Operations and Perspectives for the Future

Learning Objectives

After studying
this chapter,
you should be able to:

- Identify the factors in a firm's external and internal environment that determine the organizational design best suited for international operations.

- Describe different organizational designs and offer examples of designs that different international firms have adopted.

- Identify formal and informal controls necessary to ensure that company operations are in line with company goals and objectives as stated in the strategic plan.

Chapter Outline

Multinational companies must focus on many aspects of strategic planning, both short and long term. This includes planning for contingencies such as natural disasters or sudden political upheavals in key markets. Companies have some contingency plans in place; however, what if the contingency is a fundamental change in attitudes and perceptions about globalization and international business? This was the scenario in 2018. There was a worldwide re-examination and even backlash against globalization and international trade, increasingly directed at multinational companies and government trade policies. It led to significant new controversies, beginning with the imposition of new tariffs on steel and aluminum imports by the U.S. While this initial tariff hike focused largely on China, it has since morphed into a whole series of tariffs and retaliatory tariffs involving the United States and key trading partners around the world. There was even active talk about the possibility of a global tariff war not seen since the early 1930s. The new tariff barriers imposed by the United States led to retaliatory tariffs on a wide range of U.S. exports ranging from Harley-Davidson motorcycles to soybeans. The consequences for the global economy from an expanded and protracted tariff battle were dire.[1]

On the political front, populism along with anti-international business policies had an unexpected resurgence. Mexico elected a leftist populist candidate as president and gave his new political party large majorities in the Mexican congress. Among the goals for the new administration was curtailing oil exploration agreements with multinational oil companies and revisions to NAFTA. It is uncertain how this election will affect the currently-stalled negotiations with the United States over the future of NAFTA. These new and unchartered global business waters present major challenges to multinational corporations, as well as SME (small-medium enterprise) exporters.[2]

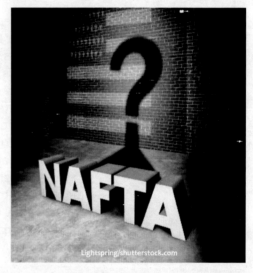

Lightspring/shutterstock.com

Multinational companies are confronted with aggressive competition for markets worldwide. To meet the challenges of intensifying competition, multinationals have been forced to alter their organizational structures and to adapt their standards to the new environment, aligning executive compensation with the companies' new goals. Ford, responding to rapid changes in the global economy, implemented a major reorganization, ending competing regional fiefdoms by consolidating engineering, design, and development within new global divisions. Motorola, faced with aggressive Asian competitors and falling profits, adopted a similar plan, replacing decentralized and competing businesses with three distinct global groups focusing on retail customers such as cell phone users, telecommunications companies, and government and industrial clients. Procter & Gamble initiated the broadest overhaul in its industry, transforming four business units based on geographic regions into seven global entities based on product lines such as baby care or food and beverage. Subsequently, in 2014, it sold off several units, such as pet-care (to Mars), and in pursuit of cost cuts, higher cash flow, and profit growth, it reorganized yet again its brands into twelve segments.[3]

In 2018 General Electric, in response to poor earnings and falling share prices, began a wholesale reorganization of the corporation. This included selling off major business units such as lighting products, medical equipment, and locomotive manufacturing. GE would no longer be a conglomerate with wide-ranging operations in finance and manufacturing, but rather a trimmed-down operation focused on a few key business areas including jet engines and power generation.[4]

Latin American-based multinational companies are also developing new strategies to expand operations in multiple countries in order to target the growing middle-class market. Dubbed the *multilatinas,* these diverse multinationals, whose offerings range from consumer goods and telecommunications, to banking and technology, are developing strong regional markets, often competing with European and U.S. multinationals that have been present in the Latin American market for many years. Companies such as LATAM airline and the Falabella department store chain are now major players in a number of key South American markets. These business trends are especially important for Latin America as the region moves away from old economic models largely based on commodities exports.[5]

As the international arena is becoming highly competitive, companies need to reorganize to more effectively meet challenges and communicate with key target consumers, as demonstrated in the following case of Micro Focus.

Micro Focus

Micro Focus, formerly the Borland Software Corp., a leading application life cycle management vendor, fully reorganized its international operations. The company's goal was to become more customer focused and accelerate its application life cycle management (ALM) strategy, thus streamlining operations and better aligning its resources in the enterprise. In the re-scoping of the company's international operations, it engaged in geographic consolidation, thus achieving cost savings.

In this business, there is a need for collaboration between sales, presales, and services, and for close collaboration with partners in the supply chain. Thus, Micro Focus also combined its customer service and research and development (R&D) functions, organizing them into an overall function that would respond more quickly to customer support requests.[6]

This chapter addresses the process of organizing for international marketing and controlling international operations, offering examples of organizational structures of firms worldwide. It also provides an overview of future developments in international marketing, with a focus on Internet-related trends.

15-1 Organizing for International Marketing Operations

Firms need to consider organizational designs that fit with their external environment and with company characteristics and goals. Organizational design is determined by numerous factors in a firm's operating environments. Among such factors are those in each

Petr Vaclavek/shutterstock.com

firm's environment, such as competition, environmental stability, similarity with the home country, common regional traits and regional integration, and availability of qualified labor. Factors within the firm also affect organizational design — in particular, the priority given to internationalization. These factors are described in Sections 15-1a, "Factors in the Firm's Environment," and 15-1b, "Factors within the Firm."

15-1a Factors in the Firm's Environment

Competitive Environment

In environments characterized by intense competition, where decisions must be made quickly to counter competitive moves, a decentralized organization would allow for the most immediate reaction. In a decentralized organization, each subsidiary operates as a profit center and has full charge of its market. Such an organization permits direct offense on competition or immediate defensive action in reaction to competitive moves. High flexibility is essential to react to changes quickly. However, even in a highly competitive international environment, centralization helps firms avoid duplication and lower costs. Activities such as finance and research and development benefit from centralization. Even firms that have at one point adopted a decentralized model to compete effectively in the international market have rethought their strategies and opted for a centralized model. Section 15-2d, "The Matrix Structure," addresses changes at Philips, a multi-national company that decided to move from a decentralized organization to a centralized organization to effectively compete internationally.

Environmental Stability

Countries characterized by unstable political and legal environments or those where government policies are unstable, countries characterized by high inflation and high unemployment, and countries with an unstable currency, all require companies to adapt quickly to the changing environment. Such companies must be able to take immediate action to adapt to the new environment and need an organizational structure that allows them to react quickly.

Environmental Similarity with the Home Country

Companies operating in countries that are similar to their home country are likely to use similar strategies. These companies would opt for an organization that integrates operations between the home and host countries.

Common Regional Traits and Regional Integration

Companies can organize their operations with a regional focus in countries that share language, religion, or other cultural similarities; countries that share a border; or countries that are members of a regional alliance.

Availability of Local Qualified Labor

Companies operating in countries with ample educated and qualified labor delegate more control to local operations and have organizational structures that allow for more local control.

15-1b Factors within the Firm

Organizational design also is determined by company traits. A firm that considers internationalization a priority is likely to have an organizational structure with regional divisions in charge of particular countries. Other organizations involved in international business might have only an international division that oversees international operations. Companies with a low volume of export sales might have only a small international sales department. Of course, these are relative terms. To an SME firm with $10 million of annual sales, with exports accounting for 15 percent, international business is very important; in fact, the emergence of SME exporters has been one of the major international business success stories in the U.S. and several other countries. You do not have to be a *Fortune 500* company to succeed in international business.[7]

Companies are likely to maintain their organizational structure when they go international. A hierarchical and centralized organization is likely to have a centralized international organization. An organization structured on the basis of product lines is also likely to maintain this structure for its international operations.

15-2 Examining International Organizational Designs

Multinational companies use five types of formal structures in their international organizational designs: international divisions, worldwide regional divisions, product divisions, the matrix structure, and the holacracy structure.

15-2a The International Division Structure

Firms with an international division structure have a domestic division and an international division. When firms become involved in international business by exporting products overseas, they usually assign responsibility for international operations to an export department – this is an export department structure. As their international involvement increases, they will most likely have an international division in charge of international operations. These firms are still primarily focused on domestic operations, but their international operations are important, at the same level with other divisions. In an international division structure, all foreign subsidiaries report directly to a single division responsible for international operations, which is separate from the one responsible for domestic operations.

15-2b The Worldwide Regional Division Structure

A worldwide regional division structure configures operations either by geographic region or by country. Under this model, subsidiaries report directly to the single division responsible for operations in the country or geographic region. Although this structure allows for some duplication of activities and thus might increase costs, managers consider this organization to be effective in creating competitive advantage for the firm.[8] A particular advantage of the worldwide regional division structure is that it is better equipped to immediately process and respond to country-specific information and conditions than other formal structures— at some cost to product-related information — because of its strong regional focus.[9]

Frito-Lay, which belongs to the Pepsi family of companies, has a worldwide regional division structure. The Frito-Lay Company, headquartered in the United States, oversees all the functional areas (i.e., marketing, manufacturing, research and development, finance, etc.). The regional divisions — Frito-Lay North America, headquartered in Plano, Texas; Frito-Lay Europe/ Africa/Middle East, headquartered in Geneva, Switzerland; and Frito-Lay Latin America/Asia Pacific/Australia — oversee all regional operations, country subsidiaries, and offices (see Figure 15-1 on next page).

Aitor Serra Martin/shutterstock.com

This type of structure is helpful for firms that have similar congruent product lines or services, such as Frito-Lay. The Guggenheim museum also has this type of structure, with the Guggenheim New York (the main museum and Guggenheim Soho); Guggenheim Venice (Italy); Guggenheim Bilbao (Spain); Guggenheim Berlin (Germany); and the Guggenheim Virtual Museum, an online museum for virtual exhibitions and artists' projects.

Figure 15-1 *Worldwide regional division structure: Frito-Lay.*

15-2c The Product Division Structure

In a regional or worldwide product division structure, subsidiaries report to the product division (strategic business unit) with responsibility for the particular products. In the past, this structure was common for high-tech companies or multinational companies with diversified portfolios. However, increasingly, this format is replaced by the matrix structure. Even companies that once were identified as typical examples of the product division structure, such as Sun Microsystems and Whirlpool, have adopted a matrix structure.

15-2d The Matrix Structure

The matrix structure takes into account the multiple dimensions involved in doing business internationally — functional areas, product, and region/country. In a matrix structure, two dimensions are integrated such that each operational unit reports to both region/country managers and product managers.

Many large multinationals have had a matrix structure for decades, among them Philips Electronics, Unilever, Electrolux, IBM, and Procter & Gamble. And, in recent years, many more multinationals have adopted this organizational structure, among them, BASF, Disney, and Rockwell International. This type of format works especially well for firms that have global brands as well as local brands. Such companies need to coordinate marketing activities world-wide involving the global brands, and need to focus on the local market for the local brands.

Unilever's matrix structure is organized based on products (home and personal care, home care, foods, refreshment products and Best foods products) and on regions around the world. Its divisions are Home & Personal Care, Africa, Middle East & Turkey; Home & Personal Care, Asia; Home & Personal Care, Europe; Home & Personal Care, North America/Latin America; Unilever Bestfoods Africa, Middle East & Turkey; Foodservice; Ice Cream and Frozen Foods; Latin America & SlimFast worldwide; Unilever Bestfoods, Asia; Unilever Bestfoods, Europe; and Unilever Bestfoods, North America. Today, the company retains its matrix organization, in a simplified form, based on products (personal care, home care, foods, and refreshment) and regions (emerging markets). They focus their resources on growing the brands in each category, and they are committed to aggressive growth in emerging markets, as they are assessed to have good long-term growth prospects.[10]

In another example of a matrix structure, Philips is organized into three divisions (see Figure 15-2), each run separately. The divisions are Philips Lighting, Philips Consumer Lifestyle, and Philips Healthcare. The company initially ran its operations in different regions, with production, sales, and marketing coordinated separately for North America, Latin America, Asia, Africa, and Europe for each of the five divisions. In addition, the company had a separate division for research and development.

Figure 15-2 *The Philips organization: The organization runs its divisions—Philips Lighting, Philips Health Care, and Philips Lifestyle—separately.*

Philips has been streamlining operations through a concerted effort to centralize its global operations. The company has reduced the number of divisions (more recently, from five to three) and its business units. It created teams in each division and outsourced its customer service department. Table 15-1 identifies the divisions of Philips. To illustrate, Philips Consumer Electronics, one of the company's former five divisions, reduced the number of business units from seven to three, the number of creation teams from 21 to 12, and made other important changes, such as aligning research and development roadmaps and outsourcing and sharing service centers and consumer services. Subsequently, its Philips Consumer Electronics division merged with Philips Domestic Appliances and Personal Care divisions to form Philips Consumer Lifestyles.

Table 15-1 *A Comparison between the Organization for Consumer Electronics at Philips in 2003 and 2012*

2003 Organization for Consumer Electronics	2012 Organization for Consumer Electronics
Decentralized business planning, logistics, and accounting	Centralized business planning, logistics, and accounting
7 business units	3 business units
21 creation teams	12 creation teams
Individual R&D approach for each team	Aligned R&D roadmaps
Distinct regional marketing programs	Coherent global marketing approaches
Undifferentiated business models	Business model adapted to life cycle
In-house infrastructure	Outsourced, shared service centers
Large, company-owned consumer service organization	Outsourced consumer service

Source: Adapted from www.philips.com

Philips Lighting, another Philips division and its principal business historically, reorganized around the different subdivisions: luminaries, lamps, lighting electronics, and automotive and special lighting (see Figure 15-3).

Figure 15-3 *The Philips Lighting organizational chart.*

15-2e The Holacracy Structure

Holacracy starts from the premise that there are many firms worldwide that are poorly managed because of the popular belief that management should be the responsibility of the few people at the top. There is increasing agreement that tomorrow's corporations' success will require a form of distributed management. A holacracy is an example of distributive management. A holacracy is a more comprehensive approach to structuring, governing, and running the organization. It replaces the top-down control with the distribution of power throughout the company. The organization chart becomes circular, and people take on more than one role, moving in teams/circles, without any thought to the organizational hierarchy. Under holacracy, the management hierarchy remains in place, but it becomes more fluid. Management is viewed as an operating system for distributing power and leadership throughout the organization.[11]

Companies such as Zappos and Medium in the U.S., Endenburg Elektrotechniek and MyWheels in the Netherlands, and Terra Viva Group in Brazil are among the many companies that adopted a holacracy structure, and it is expected that many more will follow suit.

15-3 Controlling International Marketing Operations

Controls are necessary to ensure that international company operations are in line with company goals and objectives, as stated in the company's strategic plan. Yet, controlling international operations and ensuring that performance standards are met throughout the company are complex tasks. Adding to the complexity are the following:

• Local units and a regional focus often add intermediate levels of management and staffing that further complicate the management, communication, and evaluation processes.

• Multinational companies are likely to have subsidiaries and branch offices in countries where the external environment is changing at different rates, having a different impact on company operations. Thus, standards and measures instituted for evaluation purposes are often not comparable across countries.

• Given the distance of subsidiaries from headquarters, there is a tendency to resist influence in both directions, such that subsidiaries often fight to retain autonomy in decision making and performance evaluation, while the headquarters may resist input from the subsidiaries in the planning and evaluation process.

Difficulties imposed by the complexity of the international management context can, to a certain extent, be offset by instituting the appropriate formal and informal controls.

15-3a Formal Controls

Instituting formal controls involves the following process:

· Establishing performance standards
· Measuring performance
· Addressing discrepancies

Establishing Performance Standards

The first step in establishing formal controls involves establishing performance standards in light of the company's projected market potential. Parameters must be developed in the strategic plan for evaluating dimensions of the external environment for the purpose of setting standards based on that potential. The evaluation must include a continual assessment of competitive intensity (local and international competitors in the market), political stability, developments in the economy, regional and local trade, and other developments that directly affect company performance. In many emerging economies, currencies have fluctuated widely over the past few years, and many of these economies have seen major political overhauls. Hence, it is difficult to accurately measure outcomes and evaluate managerial performance. Moreover, postprivatization restructuring may take a long time to complete and may produce soft outcomes, so outcome measurability becomes problematic, thereby complicating management evaluation.[12]

Measuring Performance

Actual performance is measured based on established standards. At this point, measures such as sales, profit, and market share are assessed for the target market in a particular country or region and measured against previous performance or against competitors. These assessments are compared with company goals and objectives for the target market as expressed in the company plan.

cigdem/shutterstock.com

Addressing Discrepancies

At the final stage of this process, discrepancies between standards and performance are corrected. If the standards were unreasonable or were not reached due to unanticipated changes in the external environment, they will be adjusted accordingly for the next assessment period. Lessons from the company's experience in other parts of the world and lessons learned from other companies' experiences are useful at this stage. For example, studies have found that the performance of European and Japanese multinationals is positively correlated with corporate policies emphasizing innovation and product designs that are standardized globally but adapted locally. A company that may be keen on a standardized international product strategy may benefit from adapting its offer to suit local preferences. The company may also need to offer more innovative products to the target market. Both the local adaptation strategy and the focus on innovation need to be coordinated with company headquarters. In fact, for many firms, innovation takes place at the company's national headquarters. For example, Procter & Gamble has 26 innovation centers worldwide, with 8,000 employees, and invests $2 billion annually in research development.[13]

15-3b Informal Controls

In addition to the controls described in Section 15-3a, "Formal Controls," companies also can use informal controls to ensure that there is a fit between the standards and actual performance. The following are examples of informal controls a company can use:

• Establishing frequent contact between the home-country headquarters and the regional or local office. Such contact serves as a means to better coordinate activities and ensure clear communication of expectations in both directions.

• Rotating managers to different assignments to obtain the maximum benefit from international experience. One often-used strategy is to hire third-country managers (from a country other than the home or the host country) to oversee new or problematic operations. These individuals have the flexibility and experience but not the biases created by an association with the home or host country of the company. In general, moving expatriates from one subsidiary to another offers valuable exchange in information to be used as input into the control function.

• Training the employees and inculcating a management culture that is consistent with company goals and objectives. Management development training can be used to share the mission and objectives of the company expressed in the relevant performance terms. For example, a company can focus on company growth or profitability objectives, innovation, the relationship with the target customer, or any other dimension that the company deems important.

15-4 International Marketing: Some Future Perspectives

The world economy has experienced revolutionary changes in the past few decades with the growth of the technology sector. The Internet and related technologies have expanded the realm of international marketing and dramatically increased access to new markets. World markets are expected to continue to benefit from the expansion in opportunities facilitated by e-commerce.

In 2018, well over 4.1 billion people worldwide used the internet, with only 8.3 percent of those in North America. In comparison, in 2007, just 491 million people used the internet, with almost one-third of those in the United States. Table 15-2 (on next page) provides statistics on eight regions in terms of Internet penetration of the home market. The largest penetration of the population is in North America, at 95 percent, followed by Europe, at 85.2 percent, and Australia/Oceania, at 68.9 percent. Developing regions including Africa and Latin America recorded substantial gains. The usage rate in Africa almost tripled in six years.[14]

Differences exist with regard to Internet usage. For example, Americans are more active on political news sites than Canadians. On the other hand, Canadians are more likely to view entertainment websites, more active on humor websites, more active on gaming sites, and sports. In addition, Canadians are more active in online banking and more involved with online trading.[15]

World Regions	Population (2018 est.)	Internet Users	Penetration (% Population)	Users %
Africa	1,287,914,329	453,329,534	35.2 %	10.9 %
Asia	4,207,588,157	2,023,630,194	48.1%	48.7 %
Europe	827,650,849	704,833,752	85.2%	17.0 %
Middle East	254,438,981	164,037,259	64.5%	3.9%
North America	363,844,662	345,660,847	95.0 %	8.3%
Latin America / Carib.	652,047,996	437,001,277	67.0 %	10.5 %
Oceania / Australia	41,273,454	28,439,277	68.9%	0.7 %
WORLD TOTAL	7,634,758,428	4,156,932,140	54.4 %	100.0 %

Table 15-2 Internet Use in the Different World Regions

The differences are even greater between American and Japanese consumers, who are used to handling many more transactions than their counterparts in the United States on the Internet, through high-tech vending machines and other interactive media.

It is expected that e-commerce will increase dramatically worldwide. The adoption of the internet will continue to be the most rapid in highly industrialized countries, where it will soon have 100 percent penetration. It will be rapid in emerging markets and especially in those markets where English is widely spoken; and countries such as China, Brazil, India, and many countries in Latin America anticipate significant increases in usage.

Online sales have increased exponentially over the past decade, as online retailers expand to new markets, and as brick-and-mortar retailers enter new markets through e-commerce. Established brick-and-mortar multinationals such as Walmart continue to expand their online offerings, while online leaders Amazon of the U.S. and China's Alibaba are expanding rapidly and contemplating a brick-and-mortar presence. Shipping is improving rapidly, and transactions are quickly becoming more secure, as the Internet is upending the global payments market, especially for personal transactions and remittances, and as the global economy moves towards a cashless society. Mobile wallets and other form of e-payments, such as prepaid debit cards not linked to a commercial bank account, are enabling more consumers in developing countries to participate in the local economy and obtain credit. In Africa, one in 10 adults, about 100 million people, use mobile-money services, including 26 million people in Kenya alone, almost half the population. More than half of the world's current mobile-money platforms are in sub-Saharan Africa.[16]

StudioByTheSea/shutterstock

The internet has been an internationalization driver because it offers companies the advantage of reaching customers worldwide. Yet, despite broad access worldwide, even companies with the best e-commerce capabilities, are not equipped to handle online sales and turn away international orders because they lack processes in place to fill them, or because language and cultural barriers hinder basic communication. They may also have difficulty handling the destination country's import and tax regulations or export controls in the home country. Also, payment systems are cumbersome, and there is a high rate of credit

Figure 15-4 Lhasa, Tibet, has been off limits to marketers until recently.

card theft, adding to the company's risk. Additional risk is posed by online security and data protection.

Many changes will take place in the product arena, where product life cycles will continue their current trend of acceleration. International firms must be prepared for rapid new product introductions simultaneously in world markets, regardless of the markets' levels of development. In Tibet, one of the most remote areas in China, separated by the mainland by impassable mountain ranges, is undergoing rapid change. In the past decade, train access has facilitated transportation to the region and planes land and take off continually from Lhasa Airport. Moreover, access to Internet is both rapid and convenient, allowing consumers to purchase products that before were off limits. See Figure 15-4.

In other developments, the battle for market share for market leaders often takes place in emerging markets. When new products such as new smartphone models are introduced, emerging markets have become important battlegrounds and, for many offerings, they are projected to become primary battle grounds in the future.

As the world population grows, there will be a significant change in consumption, with environmental concerns becoming critical. Pollution and the shortage of raw materials will place constraints on marketers, who will adapt strategies to respond to consumers' and governments' environmental demands (see Figure 15-5). A case in point is Starbucks, which,

in 2018, announced plans to phase out the use of plastic straws in all of their 28,000 coffee shops. Environmental and consumer groups are also targeting the use of plastic utensils in fast-food restaurants.[17]

With regard to distribution, companies will continue to pursue measures to reduce costs by adopting just-in-time inventory systems and creating product flows rather than stocks. They will also coordinate their inventory systems with suppliers and clients through improved versions of or alternatives to electronic data interchange.

Figure 15-5 China's cities are heavily polluted. To see the blue sky, one has to fly (high).

In terms of promotion, firms will compete on their ability to produce themes that resonate with world consumers, and most efforts will be in the area of integrating their messages. Integrated marketing communications are already standard for both international consumer product companies and for business-to-business communications, although, increasingly, consumers are expecting more micro-targeting, even in emerging markets.

Entertainment will be especially important when communicating with consumers in all retailing environments (see International Marketing Illustration 15-1).

International Marketing Illustration 15-1
Shoppertainment: The Future of Retailing Worldwide

Brand experiences are the future of marketing. Shoppertainment is the logical blend of retailing and leisure that increases the guests' length of stay and thus the total spending on the retailer's premises. World retail and consumer brands will aim to create entertaining in-store environments that delight customers and increase repeat visits and spending.

Shoppertainment takes different forms. A factory outlet center in Livingston, Scotland, has one of the largest indoor Ferris wheels in the world. A large shopping center in Kent, England has a prayer "Quiet Room" with hair- and feet-washing facilities for Muslim guests. Girl Heaven has hot pink, glitter-flecked floors and training counters that teach teens the latest nightclub dance moves and makeup and hairstyle trends. Themed food courts, onsite jugglers and face painters, shuttle trains to parking lots, and on-site day-care centers are all the rage. Large bookstores partner with Starbucks and other chains to attract shoppers who linger to consume, leaf through magazines, and purchase books. Starbucks reinvented itself as a brand that speaks to consumers in a way that is uniquely relevant to their stage of life, self-image, culture, or specific shopping motivation. Here, customers get more than coffee: They get great service and music and a comfortable upbeat meeting place where many peers show up. Together, these elements create a social club of consumption that is the unique Starbucks experience. And the Starbucks experience is continuously reinventing itself to appeal to its target market, with music and film and with new food, coffee, and tea offerings that are characterized by unique and innovative personalities, which allow Starbucks to appeal to a broad base.

Brick-and-mortar retailers worldwide are competing with online shopping and e-commerce, especially in developed countries. They are also competing for shoppers with limited time who expect a memorable and pleasant shopping experience. Retailers are now creating relevant digital content that drives sales, presenting it on large screens and on interactive in-store displays. For example, Burberry's London store transforms into an entertainment destination every season, presenting their latest collection through catwalks on large screens; they also enable consumers to order their products in the store using an iPad. In other examples, leading grocery retailer Tesco is today the number one grocery brand in Korea, offering a virtual store in the subway system, allowing commuters to order their groceries from a wall while waiting for their train.

Be Panya/shutterstock.com

Sources: *InMoment*, "Going Beyond Omnichannel in the 'Shoppertainment' Era," March 25, 2014, accessed at http://www.inmoment.com/blog/going beyond-omnichannel-in-the-shoppertainment-era/ on November 9, 2015; *2007 Global Powers of Retailing*, Deloitte, Touche, and Tohmatsu, www.stores.com; Allyson L. Stewart-Allen, "Europe Says 'That's Shoppertainment,'" *Marketing News*, Vol. 33, No. 17, August 16, 1999, p. 7.

Finally, the future will be characterized by greater price competition and broader price alignment, as local businesses and multinationals compete over markets. However, this competitive surge is likely to be accompanied by increased governmental scrutiny, especially in middle- and low-income countries.

Summary

Identify the factors in a firm's external and internal environment that determine the organizational design best suited for international operations. Organizational design is determined externally by the competitive environment: Intense competition requires a company to react quickly, and it can do so effectively if it has a decentralized structure. Companies operating in environments plagued by high inflation, unemployment, and political instability must be organized to be able to react quickly to changes. Multinational companies are likely to have similar operating structures to those in their home country if the countries where they operate are culturally similar to their own country. Companies that have competent, educated, local employees are likely to delegate more control to local operations. Companies that operate in a region with common traits, or within a regional bloc, will most likely organize the company with a regional focus. Firm traits such as degree of focus on international operations or its organization in the home country also have an impact on organizational structure.

Describe different organizational designs and offer examples of designs that different international firms have adopted. The five organizational designs for international operations are the international division structure, for firms with limited international involvement that are likely to have an export department; firms with a worldwide regional division structure, which operate either by region or by country; firms with a product division structure, where subsidiaries report to the product division with responsibility for the respective product; firms with a matrix structure, which combine functional areas, product, and region in their organization; and, a more recent phenomenon, the holacracy structure, a form of distributed management whereby the organization chart becomes circular, and people take on more than one role, moving in teams/circles, without any thought to the organizational hierarchy.

Identify formal and informal controls necessary to ensure that company operations are in line with company goals and objectives as stated in the strategic plan. Formal controls involve establishing performance standards, measuring performance, and addressing discrepancies by either changing the standards to correct for differences in market traits or changing executive compensation to reflect firm priorities. Informal controls involve maintaining contact between headquarters and international operations, rotating managers to share experience with new operations, and appropriately indoctrinating new employees in the company's culture.

Key Terms

formal controls	ture	performance standards
holacracy	matrix structure	product division structure
informal controls	organizational design	worldwide regional division
international division struc-	organizational structure	structure

Discussion Questions

1. List the factors that influence organizational design. Describe how each factor influences the design.

2. Compare the international division structure and the regional division structure. What would make a company move from an international division structure to a regional division structure?

3. How does the matrix structure differ from the other four organizational structures? Explain.

4. Discuss the formal and informal controls used to ensure that international marketing operations are in line with company goals and objectives.

Chapter Quiz

True/False

1. Companies operating in countries characterized by unstable political environments or countries where government policies are unstable need an organizational structure that allows them to react quickly.

Answer: True

Rationale: Companies operating in politically unstable countries need an organizational structure that allows them to react quickly; they need to be able to take immediate action to adapt to the new environments. Section 15-1a, "Factors in the Firm's Environment"

2. Companies operating in countries that have ample educated and qualified labor are more likely to be centralized.

Answer: False

Rationale: Companies operating in countries that have ample educated and qualified labor delegate more control to local operations and have organizational structures that allow for more local control. Section 15-1a, "Factors in the Firm's Environment"

3. A worldwide regional division structure has two main divisions: the domestic division and the international division.

Answer: False

Rationale: A worldwide regional division structure configures operations either by geographic region or by country. Section 15-2b, "The Worldwide Regional Division Structure"

4. An advantage of the worldwide regional division structure is that it is better equipped to immediately process and respond to country-specific information and conditions than other formal structures.

Answer: True

Rationale: A particular advantage of the worldwide regional division structure is that it is better equipped to immediately process and respond to country-specific information and conditions than other formal structures—at some cost to product-related information—because of its strong regional focus. Section 15-2b, "The Worldwide Regional Division Structure"

5. In a regional or worldwide matrix division structure, subsidiaries report to the product division (strategic business unit) with responsibility for the particular products.

Answer: False

Rationale: In a regional or worldwide product division structure, subsidiaries report to the product division (strategic business unit) with responsibility for the particular products. Section 15-2c, "The Product Division Structure"

6. Informal controls are used in international marketing to ensure that international company operations are in line with company goals and objectives.

Answer: True

Rationale: Informal controls, such as coordinating activities and ensuring clear communication of expectations, rotating managers to different assignments to obtain the maximum benefit from international experience, and training employees and inculcating a management culture that is consistent with company goals and objectives, are used in international marketing to ensure that international company operations are in line with company goals and objectives. Section 15-3b, "Informal Controls"

Multiple Choice

1. Which of the following companies has a worldwide regional division structure?
    a. Frito-Lay
    b. Coke
    c. Eli Lilly
    d. None of the above

Answer: a is correct.

Rationale: Frito-Lay has a worldwide regional division structure. The Frito-Lay Company, headquartered in the United States, oversees all the functional areas (i.e., marketing, manufacturing, research and development, finance, etc.). The regional divisions — Frito-Lay North America, headquartered in the United States; Frito-Lay Europe/Africa/Middle East, headquartered in Geneva, Switzerland; and Frito-Lay Latin America/Asia Pacific/Australia — oversee all regional operations, country subsidiaries, and offices.
Section 15-2b, "The Worldwide Regional Division Structure"

2. Which of the following companies has a matrix structure?
    a. IBM
    b. Unilever
    c. Disney
    d. All of the above

Answer: d is correct.

Rationale: The matrix format works especially well for firms that have global brands as well as local brands; such companies need to coordinate marketing activities worldwide involving the global brands and need to focus on the local market for the local brands.
Section 15-2d, "The Matrix Structure"

3. What is the process for instituting formal controls?
    a. Measuring performance, establishing standards, addressing discrepancies
    b. Establishing standards, measuring performance, addressing discrepancies
    c. Addressing discrepancies, establishing standards, measuring performance
    d. None of the above

Answer: b is correct.

Rationale: The first step in establishing formal controls involves establishing performance standards in light of the company's projected market potential. The next step involves measuring performance and comparing with the standards.
Section 15-3a, "Formal Controls"

4. In spite of extensive Internet access worldwide, companies are not equipped to handle sales due to
    a. language and cultural barriers.
    b. difficulty handling the destination country's import and tax regulations.
    c. difficulty in handling export controls in the home country.
    d. all of the above

Answer: d is correct.

Rationale: Many potential transactions are turned away annually by companies doing business on the Internet due to language and cultural barriers, difficulties handling the destination country's import and tax regulations, or export controls in the home country. In addition, payment mechanisms are cumbersome, and there is a high rate of credit card theft. Section 15-4, "International Marketing: Future Perspectives"

Endnotes

1. Greg Ip, "U.S. Exporters Will Be a Surprise Loser in Tariff Fight," *The Wall Street Journal*, July 9, 2018, accessed at https://www.wsj.com/articles/how-tariffs-hit-u-s-exports-not-just-imports-1531128600?mod=hp_lead_pos2 on July 9, 2018.

2. "Mexico Election: Lopez Obrador Vows Profound Change after Win," *BBC News*, July 2, 2018, accessed at https://www.bbc.com/news/world-latin-america-44677829 on July 9, 2018.

3. Gerelyn Terzon, "Procter & Gamble – Will Lafley's Breakup Plan Jump-Start PG?" *Investorplace*, August 4, 2014, accessed at http://investorplace.com/2014/08/aj-lafley-procter-gamble-pg-stock/2/#.Vju3WUv72g0 on November 5, 2015; Jeffrey E. Garten, "Cutting Fat Won't Be Enough to Survive This Crisis," *BusinessWeek*, No. 3603, November 9, 1998, p. 26.

4. Aprana Narayanan, "This is the Latest Asset GE is Selling Off as Giant Shrinks Further," *Investor's Business Daily*, April 2, 2018, accessed at https://www.investors.com/news/ge-sells-1-billion-health-software-assets-amid-breakup-talk/ on July 9, 2018.

5. Marcos Aguiar, "Why Multilatinas Hold the Key to Latin America's Economic Future," *Boston Consulting Group*, March 15, 2018, accessed at https://www.bcg.com/en-us/publications/2018/why-multilatinas-hold-key-latin-america-economic-future.aspx on July 10, 2018.

6. Micro Focus, "About Micro Focus," accessed at http://www.borland.com/en-GB/About on November 5, 2015; Jason Stamper, "Borland Slashes Staff in Reorganization," Datamonitor, online edition, May 4, 2006.

7. Natalie Soroka, "Small and Medium-Sized Enterprises Reaching New Markets," *Tradeology: U.S. Dept. of Commerce*, May 2, 2017 accessed at https://www.commerce.gov/news/blog/2017/05/small-and-medium-sized-enterprises-reaching-new-markets on July 9, 2018.

8. Allen J. Morrison, David A. Ricks, and Kendall Roth, "Globalization versus Regionalization: Which Way for the Multinational?" *Organizational Dynamics*, Vol. 19, No. 3, Winter 1991, pp. 17–29.

9. Bruce T. Lamont, V. Sambamurthy, Kimberly M. Ellis, and Paul G. Simmonds, "The Influence of Organizational Structure on the Information Received by Corporate Strategists of Multinational Enterprises," *Management International Review*, Vol. 40, No. 3, Third Quarter 2000, pp. 231–252.

10. Unilever, "Our Strategic Focus," accessed at https://www.unilever.com/about/who-we-are/our-strategy/ accessed on June 29, 2018. Unilever.com, accessed on July 12, 2018.

11. Georges Romme, "The Big Misconceptions Holding Holacracy Back," *Harvard Business Review*, September 10, 2015, accessed at https://hbr.org/2015/09/the-big-misconceptions-holding-holacracy-back on July 12, 2018.

12. Ravi Dharwadkar, Gerard George, and Pamela Brandes, "Privatization in Emerging Economies: An Agency Theory Perspective," *Academy of Management: The Academy of Management Review*, Vol. 25, No. 3, July 2000, pp. 650– 669; Masaaki Kotabe, *Global Sourcing Strategy: R&D, Manufacturing, and Marketing*, New York: Quorum Books, 1992.

13. *Forbes*, "How Procter & Gamble Keeps Its Innovation Edge," April 12, 2012, accessed at http://www.forbes.com/ sites/innovatorsdna/2012/04/12/how-procter-gamble-keeps-its-innovation-edge/ on November 9, 2015.

14. Internet World Statistics, June 2018, accessed at www.internetworldstats.com/stats.htm on July 12, 2018.

15. Rob Gerlsbeck, "Are Canadians and Americans Different Online Too?" *Marketing*, Vol. 112, No. 6, March 26, 2007, p. 10.

16. Matina Stevis-Gridneff, "An Isolated Country Runs on Mobile Money ," *The Wall Street Journal*, July 6, 2018, accessed at https://www.wsj.com/articles/an-isolated-country-runs-on-mobile-money-1530882001?mod=searchresults&page=1&pos=3 on July 11, 2018.

17. Alana Wise, Caroline Hroncich, "Starbucks to Phase out Plastic Straws as Opposition to Them Grows," *Reuters*, July 9, 2018, accessed at https://www.reuters.com/article/us-starbucks-straws/starbucks-to-phase-out-plastic-straws-as-opposition-to-them-grows-idUSKBN1JZ12H on July 11, 2018.

Case 15-1 *Qantas' New Organizational Design*

In 2012 Qantas decided to split its company into domestic and international divisions with different CEOs, as well as separate operational and commercial plans for each business. Simon Hickey, CEO of Qantas' frequent flyer program at the time, became the CEO of Qantas International, while Lyell Strambi, who was the group executive for airline operations, was named CEO for the domestic business. The advantage of their new international division structure is that both divisions were able to focus on their individual priorities and market positions. The international and domestic segments of Qantas were targeting different consumers, thus allowing the company to develop businesses to develop in line with their individual markets and goals.

Before the split, the domestic sector was making $552 million in profits, while the international business experienced losses of $216 million. If the company had continued as one entity, it would have had to focus its efforts on decreasing international losses. This strategy, however, would have led to the domestic segment of the airline suffering because the company's resources would have been diverted to competing internationally. With an international division structure, Qantas Domestic could continue its high performance, while Qantas International could address the challenges posed by the high fuel prices and oversupply of flights to Australia attributed to the Emirates and Etihad airlines, leading to a drastic fall in ticket prices – the oversupply affected only international flights, and not the domestic airline's profits.

This international division structure was at first a five-year plan for Qantas, a test to find out if it could continue to increase the domestic airline's profits and turn the international-market losses into profits. Indeed, in 2017, the company reported that it had the second highest performance in its 97-year history. Qantas gained an advantage over both local and global competitors, which has allowed it to increase its profits to $327 million for Qantas International and $645 for Qantas Domestic. After deciding on the international division structure, Qantas' stock almost tripled within two years and the company's value has continued to increase.

A primary goal for the company when it decided to pursue an international division structure was to decrease costs within the company and the different sectors. After the separation of international from domestic operations, Qantas advanced a three-year plan to cut costs by switching aircraft depending on the length of the hauls, and reducing staff. These changes led to a $2.1 billion cut in costs, as well as a great improvement in operating efficiencies. The company plans on continuing this trend with its use of technology, supplier cost improvements, and a reduction in indirect costs. To reduce costs, Qantas believes that is has to be sustainable and innovative, which will help it gain an advantage over its many competitors. For example, in 2017, it introduced its 787-9 aircraft, with a 20 percent saving in fuel consumption; it is also a smaller plane, which will help the company increase revenues.

After the international and domestic division split, Qantas International was able to more effectively compete with other airlines. It improved its routes and cut out unprofitable routes, as well as reduced the number of seats available on flights by 0.7 percent. This made the airline more competitive and allowed it to increase its profits. Other airlines, including Qantas' biggest competitor, Virgin Airways, reported losses for the same years that Qantas International began reporting profits.

Qantas has six subsidiary companies, which include QantasLink, Q Catering, Qantas Freight, Express Ground Handling, Qantas Holidays, and Jetstar. QantasLink is a regional airline with about 56 destinations all over Australia and can be used in connection with both Qantas Domestic and International flights. The Q Catering Group is made up of two catering businesses: Q Catering and Snap Fresh. Q Catering designs, produces, and delivers meals for airplanes while Snap Fresh is a research development kitchen in Queensland; there, employees create menus for the airlines in order to best meet consumers' needs. Qantas Freight serves as Australia's biggest air freight business, as it delivers about 4,000 items to over 500 destinations all over the world every day. Once the cargo lands in its destination country, Qantas Freight even has partners that will transport the goods on the road so door-to-door services are possible. This is a highly efficient way to deliver goods to consumers all over the world. The Express Ground Handling subsidiary of Qantas is a ground handling service for Jetstar, among other regional airlines. Qantas Holidays organizes sporting events and shows, offering very competitively-priced promotions. This subsidiary acts as a travel agency for visitors to Australia. Lastly, Jetstar is a low-priced airline that offers leisure flights globally, allowing consumers looking for low fares to travel in a cost-efficient manner. The six subsidiaries report to international operations. By having this division among domestic and international airlines, it creates a clear responsibility for these subsidiaries and allows Qantas to have a better focus on them.

Sources: Chong, J. (2017). Qantas targeting $400 million in annual savings over next three years. *Australian Aviation*. Retrieved at http://australianaviation.com.au/2017/05/qantas-targeting-400-million-in-annual-savings-over-next-three-years/ Freed, J. (2015). The five reasons Qantas is back in the black. *The Sydney Morning Herald*. Retrieved from https://www.smh.com.au/business/companies/the-five-reasons-qantas-is-back-in-the-black-20150224-13nbws.html. Pash, C. (2014). Here's how Qantas is setting up its international services for a partial sale. *Business Insider Australia*. Retrieved from https://www.businessinsider.com.au/it-looks-like-qantas-is-setting-up-its-international-services-for-a-partial-sale-2014-8. Pash, C. (2017). The Qantas turnaround is complete. *Business Insider Australia*. Retrieved from https://www.businessinsider.com.au/the-qantas-turnaround-is-complete-2017-8. Qantas announces $852m profit, second best in airline's 97-year history. (2017, August 25). Retrieved on July 03, 2018 from https://www.news.com.au/travel/travel-updates/qantas-is-losing-money-despite-852m-profit-as-it-announces-buyback/news-story/d21731fe33e3464ab0e18dbef132c860. Qantas group full year 2017 financial result. (2017, August 25). Retrieved July 03, 2018 from https://www.qantasnewsroom.com.au/media-releases/qantas-group-full-year-2017-financial-result. Qantas group strategy update. Retrieved on July 02, 2018, from https://www.qantasnewsroom.com.au/media-releases/qantas-group-strategy-update-2. Qantas splits domestic, international wings. (2012). *The Sydney Morning Herald*. Retrieved from https://www.smh.com.au/business/qantas-splits-domestic-international-wings-20120522-1z250.html. Qantas transformation plan boosts customer advocacy. (2014, August 24). Retrieved July 01, 2018, from http://www.adnews.com.au/news/qantas-transformation-plan-boosts-customer-advocacy. Qantas turnaround plan delivers record annual profit. (2016). *Irish Times*. Retrieved from https://www.irishtimes.com/business/transport-and-tourism/qantas-turnaround-plan-delivers-record-annual-profit-1.2766609. Somasundaram, N. (2012). Qantas to separate international business in turnaround plan. *Reuters*. Retrieved from https://www.reuters.com/article/uk-qantas-separation/qantas-to-separate-international-business-in-turnaround-plan-idUSLNE84L00L20120522. Subsidiary companies. Retrieved July 02, 2018, from https://www.qantas.com/travel/airlines/subsidiaries/global/en.

Analysis Suggestions:

1. Describe Qantas' organizational design.

2. Did Qantas operate more efficiently before it adopted an international division structure?

3. What are some advantages of Qantas' International Division organization?

Case 15-2 *iPhone: A Gem – But Not without Controversy*

What is made in China, looks really cute, and left many leading European companies with their "nose out of joint" because they were initially rejected as its partners? Here is another hint: It combines a mobile phone, a widescreen iPod, and an Internet device into a handheld device, with full-screen web browsing, a multi-touch screen, and useful applications, such as GPS and wireless streaming of YouTube videos. It is the product that came with so much buzz in 2007, when it was introduced, that bloggers called it the "Jesus Phone," a product that sold by the hundreds of thousands before it was even available on the market. It is, of course, the iPhone.

With the iPhone, Apple muscled its way into one of the world's most brutally competitive markets, rattling the cell phone industry's most dominant players by producing the number one must-have mobile phone on the market, a true innovation that changed consumer expectations about the capabilities of a smart phone.

The Service Provider Controversy: A Historical Perspective

The first controversy that engaged the iPhone even before it was out on the market was its choice of providers during the first two years. In the United States, it limited its access to AT&T, America's largest wireless phone company. In Europe, multinational powerhouses Vodafone, France Telecom, Spain's Telefónica, and Germany's Deutsche Telekom's T-Mobile clamored for the honor to be the iPhone carriers. The stakes were high: The winner would sell more than six million iPhones over three years, and, most likely, half of that would be new service contracts. Speculations that Vodafone would get the deal sent its stock soaring. And then its stock took a dive when it was announced that Vodafone was off the list.

The European countries where the iPhone was launched are the same countries where Apple chose to launch its iTunes music stores: Germany, France, and the United Kingdom. And the winning service providers were Deutsche Telekom's T-Mobile in Germany, France Telecom's Orange net-

GuadiLab/shutterstock.com

work in France, and Spain's Telefónica's O2 network in the United Kingdom. Each provider is the largest in the three respective countries. However, industry experts believe that it would have been in Apple's best interest to have more than one operator distribute the phone because the European market is much more fragmented than the market in the United States. Moreover, T-Mobile has little or no presence in Italy, Spain, or France, whereas Vodafone is present in all European markets and beyond.

In the negotiations, one of the main concerns was that Apple's deals were much more onerous than previous agreements with other handset makers. For example, in the United States, the agreement between Apple and AT&T clearly put Apple in the driving seat, giving it a share of the customer revenue, which was substantial, as the iPhone was priced at $499 for the 4 GB model and $599 for the 8 GB model. In Europe, the iPhone is priced at €450 for the 8 GB model in the three countries. Moreover, for European customers, the iPhone ran on the same 2.5G data connection network as U.S. phones did in 2007, instead of on the faster 3G technology common in Europe at that time.

The provider controversy was eventually resolved and the product is now carried by the previously slighted providers, and by many carriers in emerging markets. In fact, the iPhone is performing phenomenally well even in markets where it was believed that consumers might not be able to afford it. In 2015, Apple's total revenue was $233.72 billion, up from $24.67 billion in 2011. In China alone, it sold well over 100 million iPhones in 2011, with the Chinese market accounting for about 20 percent of Apple's revenues.

The Labor Controversy

Among the companies that benefited the most from iPhone's success were a handful of Taiwanese companies known only by a few consumers or investors. Apple does not manufacture most of its products. Instead it hires manufacturing specialists — Taiwanese companies with extensive operations in China that assemble Apple's gadgets based on Apple's designs. They use parts from many suppliers throughout Asia who are running complex and labor-intensive production lines in China. Among these companies is Foxconn International Holdings Ltd., the Hong Kong unit of Hon Hai Precision Industry Co., the world's biggest electronics contract manufacturer by revenue. Hon Hai is in charge of handling the iPhone's assembly. Catcher Technology Co., which makes stainless-metal casing increasingly popular for cell phones and notebook personal computers, is supplying iPhone's casing. Other Taiwanese companies involved in the manufacturing of the iPhone are Primax Electronics Ltd., which makes digital camera modules for cell phones; Entery Industrial Co., a maker of connectors that join other components; and Unimicron Technology Corp., which makes printed circuit boards.

Manufacturing the iPhone in China and Taiwan allows Apple to reap immense profits and to keep prices relatively competitive. Apparently, however, this comes at a cost to the workers and to Apple's image. In China, workers assembling iPhones work in harsh conditions, facing daily hazards and deadly safety conditions. Employees, some of them under-age, are often forced to work excessive overtime, seven days a week. Their legs swell until they can barely walk, and they live in dorms that are overcrowded at supplier's Foxconn's factories in Chengdu and Shenzhen. Suppliers in particular have falsified records and have improperly disposed of hazardous waste. In 2010, 137 workers working for a supplier in eastern China were injured after they were ordered to use a poisonous chemical to clean the phone's screens, and, in 2011, there were two explosions at iPad factories that killed four people and injured 77. At Foxconn's Chengdu factory, banners on the walls state "Work hard on the job today or work hard to find a job tomorrow." There, some workers worked as much as 12 hour days, or they worked back-to-back shifts to manufacture the iPhone. Apple claims it is strict with violators, terminating suppliers if they do not rectify the violations. In reality, fewer than 15 suppliers have been terminated for such violations since 2007.

The Tax Controversy

Apple's earnings in 2012 were about $45.6 billion, but the taxes the company paid were minimal, compared to other companies. Apple's headquarters are in Cupertino, California, but it has an office in Reno Nevada to collect the company's profits, to take advantage of Nevada's tax rate, zero (compared with California's, at 8.84 percent). Apple similarly sidesteps income taxes on its worldwide gains by using subsidiaries in low-tax havens, such as Ireland, the Netherlands, Luxembourg and the British Virgin Islands – in some of these places, it has little more than a letterbox or a small office.

As a technology giant, Apple benefits from tax codes written for the industrial age which are not as well suited for the digital age. Much of its profit comes from royalties on intellectual property, such as patents, software, apps, and downloaded songs and ringtones. Such profits are easier to move to low-tax states and countries.

Apple pioneered an accounting technique known as the "Double Irish With a Dutch Sandwich," which helped it lower its taxes by routing profits through Irish and Dutch subsidiaries and from there to the Caribbean, a tactic used by many other imitators today. If it had not used these tactics, Apple would have had to pay about $2.4 billion more in taxes in 2011. The company paid $3.3 billion in taxes on profits of $34.2 billion, at a tax rate of 9.8 percent. In comparison, Walmart Stores paid $5.9 billion in taxes on profits of $24.4 billion, at a tax rate of 24 percent.

The Rest of the Controversies

With the iPhone, it has been another year, another controversy. In 2014, it was Bendgate, where the iPhone 6+ would bend if one tried really hard; in 2013, it was security research firms' ability to crack the new Touch ID fingerprint sensor; in 2012, it was the disastrous launch of Apple Mapps as the standard mapping service; and so on. More recently, in 2015, a controversy centered on Apple's dual sourcing of its A9 processor – one is better than the other. The one manufactured by Taiwan Semiconductor is better than the one manufactured by Samsung, leading to a longer battery life ... an important distinction.

Apple is quickly advancing to an early maturity stage, as evidenced by its decision to provide its technologically advanced iPhone X versions at prices discounted by over $300 in 2018. As it perfects its existing technology and rapidly adopts new ones, such as the three cameras on iPhone X plus, Apple will surely face new challenges – and reap great profits.

Sources: Gordon Kelley, "iPhone Exclusive: Apple's New Designs 'Confirmed,'" *Forbes*, June 10, 2018, accessed at https://www.forbes.com/sites/gordonkelly/2018/06/10/apple-iphone-x-plus-design-triple-camera-new-iphone-x-price-specs-cost/#3800b5757b06 on July 10, 2018. *The Motley Fool*, "This Year's iPhone Controversy: Chipgate," October 10, 2015, accessed at http:// www.fool.com/investing/general/2015/10/10/this-years-iphone-controversy-chipgate.aspx on November 8, 2015; Statista.com, "Apple's global revenue from 1st quarter 2005 to 4th quarter 2015, accessed at http://www.statista.com/statistics/263426/apples-global-revenue-since-1st-quarter-2005/ on November 8, 2015; Nick Wingfield, "Apple Profit Rises on Higher iPhone and iPad Sales," *The New York Times*, April 24, 2012, www.nytimes.com; Charles Duhigg and David Barboza, "In China, Human Costs Are Built Into an iPad," January 25, 2012, www.nytimes.com; Charles Duhigg and David Kocieniewski, "How Apple Sidesteps Billions in Taxes," *The New York Times*, April 28, 2012, www.nytimes.com; Mark Halper, "Can Nokia Beat iPhone at Its Own Tunes?" *Fortune*, Vol. 156, No. 3, August 6, 2007, p. 12; Andrew Parker and Maija Palmer, "O2 Near iPhone Partnership," *FT.com*, July 5, 2007; *Financial Express*, "Genius Behind the iPhone Hype," July 2, 2007; *Marketing Week*, "T-Mobile Looks Set to Win Euro Distribution Rights for the iPhone," May 10, 2007, 8; Peter H. Lewis, "How Apple Kept Its iPhone Secrets, *CNN Money*, January 12, 2007; Jason Dean and Chiu Piling, "Taiwan Makers May Wring Big Profits from iPhone," *Wall Street Journal*, January 11, 2007, C1; Owen Thomas, "Apple: Hello, iPhone," *CNN Money*, January 9 2007.

Analysis Suggestions:

1. Describe iPhone's international presence. Discuss iPhone's entry modes during the introduction phase.

2. How is Apple leveraging its competitive advantage in each of the international markets discussed?

3. A firm's viability in international markets is predicated on offering a coveted product at a reasonable cost. How is Apple attempting to keep costs at a reasonable level and yet still provide staggering profits for investors? Comment on the strategies the company is using and on their long-term viability.

Appendices

A International Marketing Plan

B Glossary

C Index

Appendix A

The International Marketing Plan

OVERVIEW

The international marketing plan is an essential element of a company's strategic plan because it is an effort to maintain a fit between company objectives and capabilities and the continuously changing international environment. Students are advised to first focus on corporate planning and, subsequently, on the specific international marketing strategy.

The steps outlined in this blueprint are general and should be adapted based on the information available and based on the industry and on the country conditions at the time of the analysis.

STEP 1 ANALYZING THE COMPANY AND COUNTRY BACKGROUND

As a first step, the marketing plan should include a brief company background, with a focus on the product that will be marketed internationally and the country where the product will be introduced.

The company should rely on its mission statement to articulate its vision and principles for its international endeavors, underscoring the distinctive differentiating aspects of the business and the company's approach to its different stakeholders: consumers, employees, society. It should rely on its overall goals and objectives to create the specific goals and objectives for the international market. The company objectives may be to enter new international markets or to increase market share in its existing markets. Or they may involve focusing on research and development in order to bring leading-edge technology to the marketplace worldwide. Objectives can also be expressed in terms of societal outcomes, such as increasing literacy or reducing world hunger, depending on the focus of the business.

The ultimate organizational goal is creating profit for the company and wealth for its shareholders. Company goals could include increasing productivity and production volume; lowering labor costs by moving production to countries with low-cost labor; maximizing consumption of consumers worldwide; and, as a result, increasing sales.

In the process of achieving these organizational goals, companies compete to offer a wide variety of goods and services and a maximum number of choices for consumers. As they compete, they lower prices that consumers pay for their products to gain market share.

This step of the analysis could include the following information:

- Brief profile of the company
- Brief product profile
- Brief country background
- Rationale for introducing the product to the respective country

STEP 2 ANALYZING THE ENVIRONMENT

In the second step, the local and regional environment must be assessed to evaluate the country and target market attractiveness. At this stage, the local economy and the trade, political, and legal infrastructures are evaluated to determine the extent to which investing in the country constitutes a sound decision. The sociocultural environment also is assessed to identify the most viable marketing strategy to use in the respective country. Finally, the competitive environment is examined. Here, the competitive intensity (local and international) and the existing and potential barriers to entry imposed by the competition are evaluated to determine the resources needed for market penetration.

This step of the analysis could include the information on the following topics:

Economic and Trade Analysis

Population statistics and relevance of demographics to company plans

Economic development statistics (GNP, GDP, economic growth) and relevance to company plans

Overview of industrial and agricultural sectors, national resources, and labor

Analysis of transportation and telecommunication infrastructure

General analysis of the marketing support structure:

> Distribution and logistics
>
> Promotion infrastructure
>
> Marketing research suppliers

Trade trends:

> Membership in regional and international trade organizations
>
> Trade patterns (imports, exports, foreign direct investment) and rate of growth
>
> Barriers to trade

Political and Legal Analysis

Political stability:

> Legitimacy of political elite
>
> Diversity of ethnic groups with divergent interests
>
> Degree of political repression
>
> Nationalism
>
> Stability of government policies

Type of legal system

Transparency of the legal system

Degree of ambiguity of commercial laws

Degree to which laws are followed and enforced

Sociocultural Analysis

Languages and dialects and implications for marketing

Social institutions and implications for the company:

> Family
>
> Social class
>
> Social status
>
> Social groups and group dynamics

Religion, norms, and value systems and marketing implications

Target Market and Competitive Analysis

Target consumer analysis (product use, shopping behavior)

Existing distribution patterns for product category and availability of local distributors (wholesalers, retailers, logistics companies)

Existing promotion patterns for product category and availability of local promotion talent and media

Degree of competitive intensity

Competitor marketing strategies

Competitive barriers

STEP 3 EVALUATING THE INTERNATIONAL BUSINESS PORTFOLIO

The third step involves evaluating the different strategic business units of the international company. At this stage, the company must identify the products that have great promise in the marketplace and
need additional resources, the products that are performing well in a mature market, and those that are
not and must be divested. Establishing a strategic fit with the market is essential. Companies may have the
resources to support a particular strategic business unit, but if the unit does not fit with the company's
long-term goals, or if selling the unit would generate resources that could be invested to further the company's goals, the company may consider selling this particular business. Companies periodically review
their different businesses and make decisions on whether to acquire new ones or divest those that might
be unprofitable or that do not represent a good fit with the company.

Each business unit must develop its own mission statement, focusing on the strategic fit between
resources and the company goals with regard to its international target markets. The mission statement
of the business unit should be more specific than the corporate mission statement, focusing on the brand
or product itself.

An important step in the analysis process involves identifying the company's strengths, weaknesses, opportunities, and threats (SWOT). Students should first examine the microenvironment of marketing,
addressing its strengths and weaknesses; more specifically, students should examine strengths and weaknesses related to the company, consumers, suppliers, intermediaries, and other facilitators of marketing
functions, as well as those of the competition. Next, students should examine threats and opportunities in
the international sociodemographic and cultural environment, the economic and natural environment, the
technological environment, and the political and legal environment. To facilitate the analysis, students can
use Table A-1 and Table A-2 for each region or country.

STEP 4 DEVELOPING THE INTERNATIONAL MARKETING PLAN

The marketing plan focuses on the strategic business unit the company has selected: a product or
service that the company has proposed to analyze. It involves the following topics:

Setting marketing objectives (express objectives in terms of sales, profit, and market share) based
on corporate goals and objectives and market potential:

Product Decisions:

> Decisions on standardization versus adaptation

> Product mix decisions (short and long term) for the market

Promotion Decisions:

> Advertising objectives

> Media decisions

> Message decisions

Distribution Decisions:

> Decisions on whether to use existing channels or to build distribution

> Decisions on wholesalers, retailers, warehousing, and logistics firms

> Logistics decisions (intermodal transportation, freight forwarders, customs brokers, insurance
> agents, other facilitators)

Pricing Decisions:

> Identifying local market traits and needs and product cost

> Assessing the potential impact of fluctuating exchange rates and government exchange controls
> on price.

> Developing an international marketing budget based on cost

Identifying human and capital resources needed for local operations

Identifying International Marketing Objectives

Marketing objectives could be defined in terms of dollar sales or units sold, profit, or in terms of market share.

Defining the Marketing Strategy

The marketing strategy involves identifying international segments that are similar with regard to key traits and those who would respond well to a product and related marketing mix (market segmentation); selecting the segments that the company can serve most efficiently and developing products tailored to each (market targeting); and offering the products to the market, communicating, through the marketing mix, product traits and benefits that differentiate it in the consumer's mind (market positioning).

At this stage, students should identify the different international market segments, select the segments that represent the best fit with the company goals and objectives for the respective international market, and design the strategies aimed to serve these segments more effectively than competitors.

Developing the Marketing Mix for the International Market

At this stage, international marketing mix decisions address product, price, promotion, and distribution strategies that will be used for entering the international target market and the controls needed to evaluate marketing performance.

Product: Decide on design, features, brand name, packaging, and service components for a particular market. Refer to Chapter 9, "Products and Services: Branding Decisions in International Markets," and Chapter 10, "International Product and Service Strategies."

Place: Decide on the types of channels used, market coverage, assortment, transportation and logistics, and inventory management. Refer to Chapter 11, "Managing International Distribution Operations and Logistics," and Chapter 12, "International Retailing."

Price: Decide on the price, discounts, and credit terms. Refer to Chapter 16, "International Pricing Strategy."

Promotion: Decide on advertising, personal selling, sales promotion, public relations, and publicity that the company should pursue. Refer to Chapter 13, "The International Promotional Mix and Advertising Strategies," Chapter 14, "International Publicity, Public Relations, and Sales Promotion Strategies," and Chapter 15, "International Personal Selling and Personnel Management."

Table A-1	Microenvironment, Country A	
	List of Strengths	**List of Weaknesses**
Company		
Consumers		
Suppliers		
Intermediaries		
Other facilitators		
Competition		

Table A-2	Macroenvironment, Country A	
	List of Threats	**List of Opportunities**
Sociodemographic and cultural environment		
Economic environment		
Natural environment		
Technological environment		
Political environment		
Legal environment		

STEP 5 ESTABLISHING METHODS FOR IMPLEMENTATION AND CONTROL OF THE INTERNATIONAL OPERATION

Students should suggest how marketing plans can be turned into marketing action programs to accomplish the international marketing objectives.

The company will set performance standards and related controls to ensure that performance is in line with market potential given the country-specific operating environment.

This step of the analysis could include the following information:

• Standards for operation in light of market potential

• Proposed performance measures in light of goals and objectives

• Methods for addressing discrepancies

Appendix B Glossary of Key Terms

A

accessibility: The ability to communicate with the international target market.

acculturation: The act of learning a new culture; encompasses intercultural interaction and adaptation.

actionability: The extent to which the target market segment is responsive to the marketing strategies used.

adaptation: The strategy of altering a product to better meet the needs of a local market.

adaptation of the advertising strategy: The act of changing a company's promotional mix to each country or market or creating local campaigns.

adiaphoras: The norms that refer to customs that a foreign national may engage in but is not necessarily expected to do so.

advertising effectiveness research: Studies conducted to examine the effectiveness and appropriateness of advertisements aimed at individual markets.

advocacy advertising: Advertising a particular position or point of view.

African Development Bank: A bank, headquartered in Abidjan, Ivory Coast, that has as a primary goal poverty reduction in Africa, providing support and expertise in agriculture, human resources, and health services, with an emphasis on small business. (See www.afdb.org.)

aggressive export pricing: A pricing strategy that prices products below market price to penetrate new markets.

all-purpose discount stores: General merchandise discount stores that offer a wide variety of merchandise and limited depth.

all-you-can-afford method: The process of allocating the maximum amount possible to advertising; this method is used by small and medium-sized corporations.

analogy method: A method for estimation that relies on developments and findings in similar markets or where the product is in the same life cycle stage.

Andean Common Market (AnCom): A trade group of the Andean countries that aspires to become a common market; it is currently in the process of agreeing on common external tariffs. (See www.comunidadandina.org.)

antidumping: Legislation designed to counter unfair price competition; lengthy antidumping investigations can also serve as an impediment to trade.

antidumping duties: Duties that must be paid by firms as a punishment for engaging in unfair price competition.

antitrust laws: Laws designed to prevent anticompetitive activities, such as the creation of monopolies and cartels.

appearances: An individual's physical attire and overall grooming.

applications positioning: The marketing of a precise product application that is differentiated in the consumers' minds from other products that have a more general use.

arbitration: Binding procedure for conflict resolution involving an independent third party; a faster and less costly procedure than a lawsuit.

ASEAN Free Trade Area (AFTA): A free trade agreement signed by members of the Association of Southeast Asian Nations (ASEAN). (See www.aseansec.org.)

Asian Development Bank: A bank, headquartered in Manila, the Philippines, that focuses on the private sector in Asia, sponsoring projects aimed at increasing access to technology and improving the functioning of government in the region. (See www.adb.org.)

Asia-Pacific Economic Cooperation (APEC): A trade group including all major economies of the Asia-Pacific region, it is a forum for economic cooperation and has as its goal the gradual reduction of barriers to trade and investment between member countries. (See www.apec.org.)

assimilation: The act of abandoning all home-country traditions while learning a new culture.

Association of Southeast Asian Nations (ASEAN): A successful example of integration in Asia, creating an environment that promotes mutual involvement in industrial development in the region and a free trade area composed of Brunei, Cambodia, Indonesia, Laos, Malaysia, Myanmar, the Philippines, Singapore, Thailand, and Vietnam. (See www.aseansec.org.)

attribute/benefit positioning: Positioning that communicates product attributes and benefits, differentiating each brand from the other company brands and from those of competitors.

automatic import license: A license granted freely to importing companies but may be used by government for the purpose of import surveillance, thus discouraging import surges, imposing administrative and financial burdens on importers, and delaying shipment.

B

back translation: The translation of translated text back into its original language, by a different individual, to ensure that the instrument has been translated as intended.

barter: A simple, nonmonetized exchange of goods and services between two parties.

benefit segmentation: The process of identifying international market segments based on important differences between the benefits sought by the target market from purchasing a particular product.

big emerging markets (BEMs): Large markets characterized by rapid economic development and high potential; big emerging markets set the pace for the economy in their geographic region.

bilateral agreement: Regional trade cooperation between two countries aimed at reducing or eliminating trade barriers for all or for selected products.

billboards: Advertisements in public areas appearing on large posters or electronic panels.

blocked currency: A strategy that does not allow importers to exchange local currency for the seller's currency or a currency that the seller is willing to accept as payment (hard currency).

bourgeoisie: A dominant social class, which, according to Marxist-Leninist theory, establishes lucrative means of production and achieves high productivity at the expense of exploited workers.

boycott: An action calling for a ban on consumption of all goods associated with a particular company or country.

brand awareness research: Research investigating how consumers' knowledge and recognition of a brand name affect their purchasing behavior.

brand name counterfeiting: Selling counterfeit products as brand name originals.

brand name generation and testing: The testing of brand names and logos; necessary when companies market their products internationally.

broadcast medium: A nonpersonal channel of communication such as television or radio.

brokers and agents: Intermediaries who bring international buyers and sellers together; they do not carry title to the product.

building channels: Creating new distribution channels, especially necessary in situations where there are no channels at all, or there are no channels that conform to the needs of the company.

buyback agreements: Agreements whereby the seller builds and provides a turnkey plant and is paid up front part of the cost of the plant in an agreed on convertible currency; in return, the seller agrees to purchase specific quantities of the plant's output over an extended period of time.

buyer behavior research: Research examining brand preferences and brand attitudes.

buying offices: Buyers representing different firms located abroad.

C

capitalism: A stage of economic and political development, which, according to Marxist-Leninist theory, is characterized, in its early stages, by an emerging bourgeoisie, the shift of production from the agrarian sector to the industrial sector, and, in its later stages, by imperialism, where capital loses its national identity by crossing borders and establishing monopolies.

catalog retailers: Retailers selling products through mail catalogs.

catalog showrooms: Showrooms displaying the products of catalog retailers, offering high turnover, brand name goods at discount prices.

category killers: Large general merchandise discount stores that carry a narrow variety of merchandise and a wide assortment; also called category specialists or stores with category dominance.

category specialists: Large general merchandise discount stores that carry a narrow variety of merchandise and a wide assortment; also called category killers.

causal research: Research that examines cause-and-effect relationships.

Central American Common Market (CACM): An economic agreement between Central American countries; this agreement includes plans for forming a regional economic union similar to the European Union and to advance regional and international trade.

channel of communication: The medium used to communicate a message about a product to the consumer.

channel performance and coverage studies: Studies investigating whether existing channels are appropriate for communication, if channels exist at all, or whether they are appropriate for international marketing communications.

chronemics: The timing of verbal exchanges.

clearing account: A complex form of countertrade whereby countries trade products up to a certain amount stated in a particular, mutually–agreed on hard currency and within a given time frame, and, when an imbalance occurs and one country owes money to the other, swing credits are paid in an agreed on hard currency, known as the clearing currency; also called a clearing agreement.

clearing currency: The agreed on currency used to pay swing credits in a clearing account or agreement.

code law: Comprehensive written laws that specify what constitutes legal behavior.

collectivism: The degree to which individuals prefer to act in the interest of the group, rather than in their own self-interest.

combination stores: Medium-sized retail stores that combine food and drug retailing.

common law: Laws that are based on prior court rulings (legal precedents).

common market: A market composed of member countries, characterized by the unrestricted movement of goods, labor, and capital.

Common Market for Eastern and Southern Africa (COMESA): An agreement between 20 member countries aimed at achieving economic integration; COMESA is currently eliminating all tariff and nontariff barriers to trade and is in the process of adopting common external tariffs.

Commonwealth of Independent States (CIS): A political agreement between the twelve non-Baltic countries of the former Soviet Union. (See www.cis.minsk.by.)

communism: A stage in economic and political development, which, according to Marxist-Leninist theory, is characterized by state and cooperative ownership of all means of production and property.

company publications: Public relations publications that describe the products of a company to potential customers and summarize financial achievements.

comparative advantage: The premise that countries benefit from specialization in an industry where they have comparative advantage and from trading with one another.

compensation: The payment in products and in cash, usually in a mutually –agreed on convertible currency.

competitive pricing analyses: Pricing studies that determine the price the market will bear for the respective product category.

competitive-parity method: The strategy of using competitors' level of advertising spending as a benchmark for the company's own advertising expenditures.

competitor positioning: The process of comparing the firm's brand with those of competitors, directly or indirectly.

complementary export agents: Firms that export other firms' products that are complementary to their offerings, along with their own products, for a fee/commission.

complementary export merchants: Distributors who take title to the complementary products distributed and are compensated in the form of a discount.

comprador: A foreign agent with an exclusive arrangement with a company, representing its operations in a particular country; also referred to as a managing agent.

concentrated targeting: The process of selecting only one market segment and targeting it with a single brand.

concept development and testing studies: Concept tests usually performed in developed countries evaluating the product/service offering and the related marketing mix in light of the different international target markets.

conceptual equivalence: The extent to which meanings remain the same in different cultural environments.

confiscation: The foreign government seizure of company assets and investors' assets without any compensation.

consortia: A company created with the participation of three or more companies; allowed in underserved markets or in domains where the government and the marketplace can control its monopolistic activity.

consumer segmentation studies: Research conducted to identify market segment profiles.

content analysis: Method that assesses the content of advertisements in a medium with verbal and visual content.

continuous innovation: Product innovation where there is no disruption in consumption patterns; such innovations involve product alterations such as new flavors or new products that are improvements over the old offerings.

contract manufacturing: A relationship between two companies wherein one company contracts with another to manufacture products according to the contracting company's specifications and for a specified period of time.

controlled test marketing: Test marketing that involves offering a new product to a group of stores and evaluating the market's reaction to it.

convenience stores: Small retailers located in residential areas, open long hours, and carrying limited lines of high-turnover necessities.

conventional supermarkets: Self-service food retailers with annual sales of more than $2 million and with an area less than 20,000 square feet.

cooperative export arrangements: Agreements that involve the use of a distribution system of exporters with established systems of selling abroad, who agree to handle the export function of a noncompeting (but not necessarily unrelated) company on a contractual basis; also called mother henning or piggybacking.

cooperative exporting: Using the distribution system of exporters with established systems of selling abroad who agree to handle the export function of a noncompeting (but not necessarily unrelated) company on a contractual basis; also called mother henning and piggybacking.

copyright: The rights to an original work of art (literature, music, film, design, and other works), enabling the owner to reproduce, sell, perform, or film the work.

core product strategy: The strategy of using the same standard core product/service worldwide, but varying certain aspects of the offering (product ingredients, advertising) from market to market.

corporate advertising: A type of advertising that is used to promote the company behind the different brands.

corruption laws: Laws designed to prevent multinational corporations from using unethical means to obtain competitive advantage in a particular market.

cost analyses: Methods used for projecting the cost of research.

cost-based transfer pricing: A pricing strategy used in intra-firm sales for commercial transactions between units of the same corporation, within or beyond the national borders of the parent company, where the costs reflect the estimated opportunity costs of the product.

cost-of-living adjustment: A compensation incentive whereby the company adjusts expatriate salaries to reflect the cost of living in the new environment at standards in the expatriate's home country; also called post-adjustment.

Council of Ministers: The decision-making body (the legislature) of the European Union, composed of one minister from each member country.

Council of Mutual Economic Assistance (CMEA): A trade agreement between the countries of the Soviet Bloc that disintegrated after the fall of communism. CMEA was an economic body similar in nature to a free trade area and approached what would be considered a political union.

Council of Nations: The constitutional council of the European Union consisting of representatives from parliaments of EU member states. (See www.europa.eu.int.)

counterpurchase: A form of trade that involves two exchanges paid for in cash; it involves two parallel contracts whereby the seller agrees to purchase products that are usually unrelated to its business from the buyer and sell them on international markets; also called parallel barter.

countertrade: A form of trade whereby a company sells a product to a buyer and agrees to accept, in return for payment, products from the buyer's firm or from the trade agency/institution of the buyer.

countervailing duties: Duties imposed on subsidized products imported into a country.

countervailing duty actions: Investigations initiated to determine whether imports are sold below fair prices as a result of foreign subsidies and the subsequent establishment of measures to offset subsidies.

country of manufacture: The country in which a particular product is manufactured.

country of origin: The country with which a particular product or service is associated.

creeping expropriation: A situation characterized by bureaucratic red tape and corruption, an unreliable judicial system, and shifting regulations, where foreign government actions discourage foreign investment, especially investment in nonessential sectors.

cross-border shopping: Purchasing products from a neighboring country where the consumers may be charged lower duties.

cultural variability: The classification of cultures on a number of dimensions, or continuums; Hofstede classified cultures on the dimensions of collectivism, masculinity, power distance, and uncertainty avoidance.

culture: The continuously evolving totality of learned and shared meanings, rituals, norms, and traditions among the members of an organization or society.

culture shock: A pervasive feeling of anxiety resulting from one's presence in a new, unfamiliar culture.

currency and capital flow controls: All protectionist activities involving the control of capital and hard currency flows in and out of a particular country.

customs union: A market composed of member countries imposing identical import duties and sharing import regulations.

D

data collection instrument: The instrument used to collect data, such as a printed questionnaire, a paper-and-pencil measure, or an electronic measurement device.

decentering: The successive translation (by different translators) of an instrument between the original language and the language of administration with the purpose of obtaining an instrument that is closest in meaning to the original.

decision support system: A coordinated collection of data, systems, tools, and techniques, complemented by supporting software and hardware designed for the gathering and interpretation of business and environmental data.

decline stage: The stage of the international product life cycle in which products are rapidly losing ground to new technologies or product alternatives, causing a decrease in sales and profits.

decoding: The process whereby the target consumer receives the message from the advertiser and translates it into meaningful information.

degree of product/service newness: The extent to which a product is new to the market in general or to a group of consumers.

Delphi method: A method of forecasting sales by asking a number of experts to estimate market performance, aggregating the results, and sharing this information with the said experts; the process is repeated several times, until a consensus is reached.

demographic segmentation: The process of identifying market segments based on age, gender, race, income, education, occupation, social class, life cycle stage, and household size.

department stores: General retailers that offer a broad variety of goods and wide assortments.

depth interview: A qualitative research method involving extensive interviews aimed at discovering consumer motivations, feelings, and attitudes toward an issue of concern to the sponsor using unstructured interrogation.

descriptive research: All research methods observing or describing phenomena.

design counterfeiting: Copying designs or scents of another company.

designing and developing the product: Developing product prototypes and giving the product a name, a brand identity, and a marketing mix; a step in the new product development process.

developed countries (also high-income countries): Highly industrialized countries with well-developed service sectors, mature markets, and intense competition; they are characterized by the World Bank as high-income, with a GNP per capita of US $9,266 and greater.

developing and evaluating concepts: Determining how consumers will perceive and use a new product; a step in the new product development process.

developing countries (also low-income countries): Countries that are primarily agrarian, often neglected or underserved by large multinationals, and characterized by the World Bank as low-income countries, with a GNP per capita of less than US$755.

differential exchange rate: The rate imposed by the local government to promote imports of desirable and necessary goods; it also can be the difference between the black market exchange rate and the official government rate.

differential response: The extent to which international market segments respond differently to marketing strategies.

differentiated targeting: A targeting strategy identifying market segments with different preferences for a particular product category and targeting each segment with different brands and different marketing strategies.

diffusion process: The process by which a product is adopted by consumers worldwide.

direct exporting: An export entry mode whereby a firm handles its own exports, usually with the help of an in-house exporting department.

direct mail retailing: Retailing using catalogs and other direct mail, instead of brick-and-mortar stores.

direct selling: Selling that involves a salesperson, typically an independent distributor, contacting a consumer at a convenient location—at his or her home or workplace, demonstrating product use and benefits, taking orders, and delivering the merchandise.

distribution alliance: A nonequity relationship between two firms, in which one firm handles the other's distribution or some aspect of the distribution process.

domestic marketing: Marketing that is focused solely on domestic consumers and on the home-country environment.

domestication: The process initiated by a foreign government leading to the gradual transfer of ownership and management to locals.

drive-to-maturity stage: A stage in economic development, described by Rostow, as characterized by the technological and entrepreneurial skill to produce anything society chooses to produce.

drivers in the business environment: Elements in the business environment, such as competition, technology, and labor costs, causing the firm to become involved internationally.

dumping: Selling products below cost to get rid of excess inventory and to undermine competition.

dynamic incremental pricing: A pricing strategy whereby a company assumes that it will have certain fixed costs whether or not it exports its products overseas and does not factor in its international price marketing and promotion costs or its full overhead for domestic distribution.

dynamically continuous innovation: Innovation that does not alter significantly consumer behavior but still entails a change in the consumption pattern.

E

early adopters: Consumers who purchase a product early in its product life cycle and who tend to be opinion leaders in their communities who take risks, but with greater discernment than innovators; they account for 13.5 percent of the total market.

early majority: Consumers who enjoy the status of being among the first in their peer group to purchase a popular product; they account for 34 percent of the total market.

ecology: The manner in which society adapts to its habitat (i.e., the distribution of resources within an industrialized country versus a developing country); the desire for efficiency, space-saving devices, or green products.

Economic Community of West African States (ECOWAS): A free trade agreement that strives to achieve economic integration in West Africa; domination by Nigeria, civil unrest, and regional conflict have served as impediments in the group's success. (See www.ecowas.int.)

education allowance: A compensation incentive whereby the company agrees to cover the cost of children's education at an international private school in the country of assignment or at a boarding school in the expatriate's home country.

electronic data interchange (EDI): Relationship whereby buying and selling firms are able to share important data on production, inventory, shipping, and purchasing.

electronic retailing: Selling through the Internet using websites to increase market penetration and market diversification; also called interactive home shopping and Internet retailing.

embargo: The prohibition of all business deals with the country that is the target of the embargo that is endorsed or initiated by the company's home country.

emerging markets (also middle-income countries): Countries that are developing rapidly and have great economic potential; the World Bank characterizes them as middle-income countries, with a GNP per capita of US$766 to US$9,265.

emic instrument: A data collection instrument constructed for each nationality to measure a particular factor; it is the best measure for culture-specific phenomena.

employment protection: Protection of local employment by not granting import licenses for products competing with similar locally produced goods.

encoding: The process whereby the advertiser puts the company's message about the product into words and images that are aimed at the target consumer.

enculturation: The process by which individuals learn the beliefs and behaviors endorsed by their own culture.

entry mode: The approach to international expansion a company chooses based on desired control and on the risk it can afford.

established channels: Distribution channels that already exist in a particular market.

ethnocentric orientation: Company strategies consistent with the belief that domestic strategies, techniques, and personnel are superior to foreign ones and therefore provide the most effective framework for the company's overseas involvement; companies adopting this perspective view international operations and customers as secondary to domestic operations and customers.

ethnocentrism: The belief that one's culture is superior to another and that strategies used in one's home country (presumably a developed country) will work just as well internationally.

etic instrument: A culture-free data collection instrument that can be used to measure the same phenomenon in different cultures.

Euroland: The nickname of the European Monetary Union. (See www.europa.eu.int.)

European Atomic Energy Community: A precursor to the European Union, it addressed issues related to the use and control of atomic energy.

European Bank for Reconstruction and Development: A bank headquartered in London, United Kingdom, which has as main goals reforming and strengthening markets in the transition economies of Central and Eastern Europe. (See www.ebrd.com.)

European Central Bank: The bank of the European Union charged with enacting monetary policy for the twelve countries that share a common currency, the euro. (See www.europa.eu.int.)

European Coal and Steel Community: An agreement that represents an early attempt at tariff reduction between members of the European Union.

European Commission: The body of the European Union in charge of initiating and supervising the execution of laws and policies. (See www.europa.eu.int.)

European Council: The highest policy-making body of the European Union. (See www.europa.eu.int.)

European Court of Justice: The Supreme Court–equivalent of the European Union. (See www.europa.eu.int.)

European Exchange Rate Mechanism (ERM): A precursor of the euro, a float that included the euro, the then-theoretical currency of the European Union; the float allowed for variability in each currency.

European Free Trade Association (EFTA): A free trade agreement between Iceland, Liechtenstein, Norway, and Switzerland; previously, Sweden, Austria, and Finland were also members, but they have since joined the European Union. (See www.efta.int.)

European Monetary Union (EMU): A union composed of the members of the European Union who adhere to the joint monetary policy enacted by the European Central Bank and who have adopted the euro as the single currency. (See www.europa.eu.int.)

European Parliament: The Parliament of the European Union, composed of members elected every 5 years by direct universal suffrage; seats in the Parliament are allocated among member states based on their population. (See www.europa.eu.int.)

European Union: An economic union consisting of most of the Western European countries; it is the only agreement that has achieved full economic integration and is now pursuing political integration. (See www.europa.eu.int.)

event sponsorship: The financial support of cultural or sports-related events; companies use these events to get positive publicity.

exclusives: The norms that refer to activities that are appropriate only for locals and from which individuals from a foreign country are excluded.

executive-judgment method: A budgeting process that allocates the company's advertising budget based on the opinions of executives.

expatriate: An employee working in a foreign country.

experimental research: Research that examines cause-and-effect relationships; it has the highest validity and reliability of all types of research.

exploratory research: Research conducted early in the research process that helps further define a problem or identify additional problems that need to be investigated.

export management companies: Companies specializing in the export function for client companies in a particular industry.

export marketing: Involvement in international marketing limited to the exporting function; although the firm actively seeks international clients, it considers the international market an extension of the domestic market and does not give it special consideration.

export merchants: Intermediaries who take title to and possession of the products they carry; they are responsible for shipping and marketing the products to the target market.

Export Trading Company Act: Legislation, passed in 1982, that encourages the formation of export trading companies by competing firms to promote U.S. exports without violating antitrust regulation.

expropriation: The foreign government seizure of company assets with partial reimbursement, usually not at market value.

extensible markup language (XML): System that encodes data on production, inventory, shipping, and purchasing and processes the content without human intervention, sharing it with the company's supply chain partners.

external secondary data: Data collected for purposes other than the problem at hand.

F

feedback: Information regarding the effectiveness of a company's message.

femininity: The degree to which a national culture is characterized by nurturing, rather than assertive, values.

feudalism: A stage in economic and political development, which, according to Marxist-Leninist theory, is characterized by the dominance of feudal lords, who own the land and its dwellers.

firm-specific drivers: Elements specific to the firm, such as product life cycle, causing the firm to become involved internationally.

focus group interview: A qualitative research approach investigating a research question using a moderator to guide discussion within a group of subjects recruited to meet certain characteristics.

food retailers: Retailers selling primarily food products.

foreign consumer culture positioning: The positioning of a particular brand as symbolic of a desired foreign culture.

Foreign Corrupt Practices Act: Legislation that makes it illegal for companies and their representatives to bribe government officials and other politicians or candidates to political office, either directly or through third parties.

foreign exchange permit: A permit that is generally provided by a country's Central Bank in conjunction with the Department of Trade (Ministry of Foreign Trade) and that gives priority to imports of goods considered to be in the national interest.

foreign trade zones: Tax-free areas in a country that are not considered part of the respective country in terms of import regulations and restrictions.

foreign-country intermediaries: Intermediaries who help distribute products in a target foreign market.

formal controls: Systematic controls, such as performance standards and measurement, used in international marketing to ensure that international company operations are in line with company goals and objectives.

franchisee: The recipient party to a franchise who pays royalties in return for the right to use the franchisor's brand name and related trademarks.

franchising: The main international entry mode for the service industry, whereby the franchisor gives the franchisee the right to use its brand name and all related trademarks in return for royalties.

franchisor: The owner of the franchise who gives the franchisee the right to use its brand name and all related trademarks and its business know-how, such as secret recipes and customer interfacing techniques, in return for royalties.

free trade agreement: An agreement whose goal is the reduction in, or even elimination of, customs duties and other trade barriers on all goods and services traded between member countries.

Free Trade Area of the Americas (FTAA): A plan to create a free trade association by 2005 that would comprise all member countries of the 34 democratic nations of North, Central, and South America. (See www.ftaa-alca.org.)

functional equivalence: The difference in the purposes for which products may be used in different country environments.

G

gender roles: The roles that women and men are expected to hold in a society.

General Agreement on Tariffs and Trade (GATT): The international trade agreement promoting trade and eliminating trade barriers, opening markets to international business, and creating a forum for resolving trade disputes; GATT issues are now addressed by the World Trade Organization. (See www.wto.org.)

general merchandise discount stores: Retailers that sell high volumes of merchandise, offer limited service, and charge lower prices.

generating new product ideas: Seeking ideas using different strategies as the first step in the new product development process.

geocentric orientation: Company strategies that are consistent with the belief that the entire world, without national and regional distinctions, constitutes a potential market with identifiable, homogeneous segments that need to be addressed differentially.

geographic segmentation: Market segmentation based on geographic location, such as country or region.

gift giving: The norms regarding the gifts that are appropriate to give to others.

global campaign: A worldwide standardized advertising campaign that is not adjusted to different target markets.

global consumer culture positioning: Marketing programs appealing to individuals who want to be part of a global consumer culture by purchasing a brand that is a symbol of that culture.

global consumers: The homogeneous consumer group worldwide sharing similar interests and product/brand preferences.

global elite: A psychodemographic group worldwide characterized by high income and desire for status brands and exclusive distribution.

global gay and lesbian segment: A psychodemographic group worldwide characterized by higher disposable income and high loyalty to brands positioned as gay-friendly.

global localization: The practice of global branding and localized marketing adaptation to differences in local culture, legislation, and even production capabilities.

global marketing: International marketing activities that do not have a country or region focus and that are possibly due to the emergence of global consumer segments and efficient global allocation of company talent and resources.

global standardization: The standardization of products across markets and, ultimately, to the standardization of the marketing mix worldwide; more commonly called glocalization.

global youth segment: A psychodemographic global group of teenagers considered to be astute consumers with precise desires for brand name clothing products and entertainment.

glocalization: The standardization of products across markets and, ultimately, the standardization of the marketing mix worldwide; also called global standardization.

grey market: A distribution system not authorized by the manufacturer whereby the products purchased in a low-price market are diverted to other markets; also called parallel imports.

greenfielding: Developing a brand new subsidiary.

growth stage: The stage of the international product life cycle characterized by increasing competition and rapid product adoption by the target market.

H

haptics: The use of touch while conversing.

hard currency: Currency that is accepted for payment by any international seller.

high mass consumption: A stage in economic development, described by Rostow, as characterized by leading sectors shifting toward durable goods.

high-context cultures: Cultures in which the context of a message—the message source, the source's standing in society or in a group, his or her expertise, tone of voice, and body language—are all meaningful parts of the message.

high-income countries: Highly industrialized countries with well-developed service sectors, mature markets, and intense competition, with a GNP per capita of US$10,726 and greater.

historical method: An approach to budgeting that is based on past expenditures, usually giving more weight to more recent expenditures.

home-country intermediaries: Intermediaries in the home country.

home-country laws: Laws of a company's home country that follow the international company all over the world.

home-country national: A local employee who works in his or her home country for the international corporation.

home-leave allowance: A compensation incentive that pays for the expatriate and his or her family to vacation in the home country.

host-country laws: Local laws; laws of the different countries where a company operates.

host-country national: A local employee who works in his or her home country for the international corporation.

housing allowance: A compensation incentive whereby the company covers part of or the entire cost of housing for the expatriate employee while abroad.

hypermarkets: Large retail stores that combine supermarket, discount, and warehouse retailing principles.

I

ideology: The manner in which individuals relate to their environment and to others, including their attitudes toward time, space, possessions, and referent others.

image advertising: An advertising campaign that enhances perceptions of a company in a given market by creating a positive impression on the target consumers.

imperatives: The norms referring to what individuals must or must not do in a certain culture.

imperialism: A stage of economic and political development, in which, according to Marxist-Leninist theory, capital loses its national identity by crossing borders.

import jobber: A merchant intermediary who purchases commodity goods from the manufacturer to sell to the trade (wholesaler, retailer, business-to-business client) in the target market.

import quota: The maximum quantity (unit limit) or value of a product that may be imported during a specified period.

import/export: Analysis research that aids companies in identifying the necessary logistics that serve their needs in a timely and cost-effective manner.

Incoterms (International Commercial Terms): Terms of sale used in transactions.

indirect exporting: An export entry mode whereby a company sells its products in the company's home country to intermediaries who, in turn, sell the product overseas.

individual personality: Enduring traits that characterize individuals, motivating them to act or react to external stimuli in a particular manner.

individualism: The degree to which people in a country prefer to act as individuals, in their self-interest.

infant industry argument: A protectionist strategy aimed at protecting a national industry in its infancy from powerful international competitors.

infomercials: Long television advertisements (one-half to 1 full hour in length) that are positioned as programming.

informal controls: Systematic controls, such as dialogue between the headquarters and the international field operations, used in international marketing to ensure that international company operations are in line with company goals and objectives.

innovation: A product new to the world.

innovators: Risk takers who can afford to pay the higher purchase price charged by companies during the introduction stage of a product; they account for 2.5 percent of the total market.

intellectual property rights: Laws protecting the rights of the inventor or of the firm employing the inventor to use and sell an invention for a specified period of time.

interactive home shopping: A venue for selling through the Internet using websites to increase market penetration and market diversification; also called electronic retailing and Internet retailing.

interactive medium: A nonpersonal channel of communication such as a Web page or a computer terminal on the retailer's premises.

Inter-American Development Bank: A bank headquartered in Washington, D.C., aiding companies in the Americas that do not ordinarily deal with the large development banks; this bank is involved in funding private sector projects, modernizing governments, strengthening institutions, and eliminating technology barriers. (See www.iadb.org.)

internal secondary data: Data collected by a company to address a problem not related to the current research question.

international buyer-seller relationship: The distribution between the buyer and the individual involved in personal selling.

international communication process: The communication process that takes place between the product sponsor and the international target market.

international division structure: An organizational structure whereby firms have separate domestic and international divisions.

international laws: Rules and regulations that countries agree to abide by, addressing agreements among countries with regard to trade, protection of property, and other issues in the political and economic sphere.

international market potential studies: Studies conducted to evaluate the potential that a particular country offers for a company.

international marketing: The processes involved in the creation, production, distribution, promotion, and pricing of products, services, ideas, and experiences for international markets; these processes require a substantial focus on international consumers in a particular country or countries.

international marketing research: The systematic design, collection, recording, analysis, interpretation, and reporting of information pertinent to a particular marketing decision facing a company operating internationally.

International Monetary Fund (IMF): Traditionally the lender of last resort; the IMF also has assumed the position of mediator between debtors and creditors, imposing stabilization programs; debt-reduction guidelines; ceilings for bank credit, budget deficit, borrowing, and international reserves; and development programs for borrowing countries. (See www.imf.org.)

international product life cycle (IPLC): A product life cycle theory, which states that firms from developed countries engage in domestic production in the early stage of the product life cycle, marketing the product to industrialized countries; as the product reaches maturity, product specifications and the manufacturing process stabilize, price competition becomes intense, and markets in developing countries become essential to the firm's success.

international promotional mix: The different modes of communication with international consumers about products and services, using international advertising, international sales force management, international sales promotion, public relations, and publicity.

international public relations: A concerted effort on the part of a company to generate goodwill among international publics that are essential to the company; its main purpose is to generate positive publicity about the company.

Internet retailing: Selling through the Internet using websites to increase market penetration and market diversification; also called interactive home shopping and electronic retailing.

introduction stage: The first stage of the international product life cycle when products are developed and marketed in industrialized countries.

Islamic law: A system of law based on the interpretation of the Koran, Islam's holy book, and on interpretations of the practices and sayings of the prophet Muhammad.

ISO 9000 certification: Certification that specifies that the organization must meet customer and regulatory requirements and follow its policies and procedures while advancing quality through continuous improvement.

ISO 14000 certification: Certification that a company follows guidelines that discourage firms from engaging in hazardous environmental practices, and ensures that corporate policies promoting environmentally sound, efficiency-embracing, innovative technologies and processes will contribute to establishing twenty-first century production and distribution systems that are far less environmentally degrading.

J

joint venture: A corporate entity created with the participation of two companies that share equity, capital, and labor.

jurisdiction: The country and legal body where a particular dispute should be adjudicated, according to the country's law, or according to the legal body's principles, respectively.

jury of expert opinion: An approach to sales forecasting based on the opinion of different experts.

K

keiretsu: A Japanese trading firm that consists of families of firms with interlocking stakes in one another.

kinesics: The movement of part of the body to communicate.

L

lag countries: Countries where a product or service is adopted after already being introduced in lead countries.

laggards: Consumers who are the last to adopt new products and do so only in late maturity because they are risk averse and conservative in their spending; they account for 16 percent of the total market.

language: The vehicle used for communication in a particular culture; includes spoken and written language and nonverbal communication.

late majority: Individuals of limited means who are likely to adopt products only if the products are widely popular and the risk associated with buying them is minimal; they account for 34 percent of the total market.

Latin American Free Trade Association (LAFTA): An attempt by Latin American countries to establish a free trade association; its demise is attributed to the economic disparity between member countries and to protectionist policies.

Latin American Integration Association (LAIA): Latin America's largest trade agreement striving to establish bilateral and multilateral agreements aimed at reducing tariff and nontariff barriers.

launching the product internationally: Introducing a new product to the international market as the last step in the new product development process.

lead countries: Countries where a product or service is first introduced and adopted.

licensee: The purchaser of the license who pays royalties to the licensor for the rights to use the licensor's technology, know-how, and brand name.

licensing: An international entry mode that involves a licensor, who shares the brand name, technology, and know-how with a licensee in return for royalties.

licensor: The owner of a product license who agrees to share know-how, technology, and brand name with the licensee in return for royalties.

local campaign: An advertising campaign that is tailored to local needs; especially used in markets that media cannot easily reach.

local consumer culture positioning: Positioning that associates the brand with local cultural meanings, reflecting the local culture, and portrayed as consumed by locals and depicted as locally produced for local people.

local content requirement: A protectionist measure requiring that a certain percentage of the products imported are locally produced.

local pricing: A pricing strategy in which different prices are charged in different markets, reflecting differences in consumer purchase power, distribution costs, tax systems, or other market traits.

logistics alliances: Distribution alliances between two firms involving product transportation and warehousing.

low-context cultures: Cultures in which what is said is precisely what is meant so that the verbal message carries the full meaning of the sentence.

low-income countries: Countries that are primarily agrarian, with a GNP per capita of less than US$875.

M

Maastricht Treaty: The treaty credited with establishing the European Union, eliminating all tariffs; establishing common external tariffs; allowing for the free movement of capital and labor within its territory; and setting regulations involving common trade policies, common agricultural and industrial policies, and common monetary and fiscal policies between member countries. (See www.europa.eu.int.)

managing agent: A foreign agent who has an exclusive arrangement with a company, representing its operations in a particular country.

mandatory adaptation: The adaptation of products to local requirements so that the products can legally and physically function in the specific country environment.

manufacturer's export agents: Agents in the firm's home country handling the exporting function of a certain manufacturer on a commission, per deal, basis.

manufacturer's representative: An agent who represents the manufacturer exclusively in the foreign target market.

manufacturing alliance: A nonequity relationship between two firms, in which one firm handles the other's manufacturing or some aspect of the manufacturing process.

maquiladora: Customs-privileged contract manufacturing facilities in Mexico that take advantage of low-cost labor.

market-based transfer pricing: A pricing strategy used in intra-firm sales for commercial transactions between units of the same corporation, within or beyond the national borders of the parent company, whereby products are priced at market cost, rather than at the cost incurred by the company.

marketing alliance: A nonequity relationship between two firms, in which one firm handles the other's marketing or some aspect of the marketing process.

Marxist-Leninist development model: A development model attributed to Karl Marx and Vladimir Lenin that maps the development of society from an agrarian, traditional society to a society characterized by shared ownership of the means and outcomes of production and an equitable resource allocation; advancement from one stage to another is based on class struggle and transfer of ownership from one class to another and, ultimately, to the state.

masculinity: The degree to which a national culture is characterized by assertiveness, rather than nurturing.

materialism: Individuals' degree of concern with material possessions.

matrix structure: An organizational structure whereby each operational unit reports to both region/country managers and product managers.

maturity stage: A stage of the international product life cycle characterized by a slowdown in sales growth as the product is adopted by most target consumers and by a leveling or decline in profits primarily due to intense price competition.

measurability: The ability to estimate the size of a market segment.

media availability: The extent to which media are available to communicate with target consumers.

media infrastructure: The media vehicles and their structure in an international target market.

media reliability: The probability of the media to air advertising messages on time, at an acceptable quality, and with the agreed on frequency.

media research: Studies that evaluate media availability and appropriateness of the medium for a company's message.

media restrictions: Legal or self-imposed restrictions on the types and the number of advertisements aired or published.

mediation: Nonbinding procedure for conflict resolution involving an independent third party.

medium/media: The channel(s) of communication that a company uses to send to the target consumer a message about its product or services.

merchant middlemen: Different intermediaries who carry the manufacturer's product line in a particular country; they both carry title to and have physical possession of the products they distribute.

middle-income countries: Countries with emerging markets and great potential, with a GNP per capita of US$875 to US$10,725.

Ministry of Foreign Affairs: The international institutional equivalent of the Department of State; it coordinates a country's involvement in international relations.

Ministry of Trade: The international institutional equivalent of the Department of Commerce; it coordinates a country's international trade relations.

modification: The alteration of an existing company product.

modular adaptation: The localization across markets of the product by offering parts (modules) that can be assembled worldwide in different configurations, depending on the needs of the market.

modular campaign: An advertising campaign that provides a template that is varied and customized from market to market.

monetary union: A form of economic integration characterized by the establishment of a common central bank enacting monetary policy for the group.

monochronic time: The interpretation of time as linear, such that individuals do one thing at a time, and in sequence.

monopolistic capitalism: A stage of economic and political development, in which, according to Marxist-Leninist theory, multinational companies establish monopolies and expand internationally with the goal of subjugating developing countries.

mother henning: Using the distribution system of exporters with established systems of selling abroad who agree to handle the export function of a noncompeting (but not necessarily unrelated) company on a contractual basis; also called piggybacking and cooperative exporting.

moving allowance: A compensation incentive whereby the company pays for the household moving expenses to the country of assignment and, at the end of the assignment, back to the home country.

multilateral forums and agreements: Agreements that involve multiple countries, have an informal structure, and do not necessarily have regional integration as their goal.

multilevel marketing: Using acquaintance networks through an alternative distribution structure for the purpose of distribution; also called network marketing.

multinational marketing: Marketing in different countries without coordinating across operations.

N

national and regional character: A set of behavior and personality characteristics shared by individuals of a certain country or region.

nationalism: An expression of fierce nationalist sentiment in a country where a company is operating, which poses an implicit threat to the company and its operations.

nationalization: The takeover of company assets by a foreign government with the aim of creating a government-run industry.

network marketing: Using acquaintance networks through an alternative distribution structure for the purpose of distribution; also called multilevel marketing.

new item in an existing product line: A new brand that the company offers to the market in an existing product line.

new line: A new product category offered by the company.

new product to existing company: A new product that the company offers to the market; the product competes with similar competitor offerings.

new product to existing market: A product never before offered to the market.

news releases: Statements issued to the public to introduce a new product, touting its advantages; any other information shared with the media.

noise: All the potential interference in the communication process.

nonautomatic import license: A license issued on a discretionary basis to restrict imports of a given product or from a particular country.

nonmandatory adaptation: The strategy of adapting a product to better meet the needs of the local market, without being required to do so.

nonpersonal medium: A channel of communication such as a print medium, a broadcast medium, or an interactive medium that does not involve contact between the seller and the consumer.

nontariff barriers: All measures, other than traditional tariffs, used to distort trade flows, used to increase prices of imports, and thus favor domestic over foreign products.

nonverbal communication: All communication that is not written or spoken; includes body language, gestures, facial expressions, eye contact, and silence.

Norazi agent: An export agent dealing in illegal and grey market products.

norms: Rules that dictate what is right or wrong, acceptable or unacceptable in a society.

North American Free Trade Agreement (NAFTA): An agreement between the United States, Canada, and Mexico, aiming to eliminate tariff and nontariff barriers between the countries. (See www.nafta-sec-alena.org.)

North Atlantic Treaty Organization (NATO): A military agreement between countries that were initially not part of the Soviet Bloc. (See www.nato.int.)

O

objective-and-task method: An advertising budgeting method in which the company first identifies advertising goals, conducts research to determine the cost of achieving the respective goals, and allocates the necessary sum for the purpose.

observational research: A research approach used frequently in international markets, whereby subjects are observed interacting with a product and the related components of the marketing mix.

obstacles to internationalization: Impediments that the firm may encounter in the process of internationalizing.

oculesics: The use or avoidance of eye contact during communication.

off-price retailers: Retailers who sell brand name products and designer merchandise below regular retail prices.

offset purchase: A large, hard-currency purchase, such as the purchase of defense equipment, airplanes, telecommunications networks, railway or road building and other expensive civil engineering projects whereby the seller agrees, in return to purchase products that are valued at a certain percentage of the sale.

offshore assembly plants: Plants located in customs-privileged bonded areas in countries with low labor costs, where products are manipulated and re-exported.

olfactions: The use of odors to convey messages.

open-ended questions: Questions with free-format responses that the respondent can address as he or she sees appropriate.

order getter: Individual who actively generates potential leads and persuades customers to purchase the firm's products.

order taker: An individual who processes routine sales orders from the customer.

orderly market arrangements: Protectionist measures involving intricate processes for establishing quotas in the textile and apparel industries.

Organization for Economic Co-operation and Development (OECD): An economic multilateral agreement. (See www.oecdobserver.org.)

Organization of the Petroleum Exporting Countries (OPEC): Industry-specific (oil) multilateral agreement aimed at managing the output and price of oil. (See www.opec.com.)

organizational culture: The shared norms and values that guide collective behavior in organizations and enduring traits that characterize individuals, motivating them to act or react to stimuli in the organization and in the environment in a particular manner.

organizational design: The organization of reporting and coordination within a company.

organizational structure: The outcome of the organization of reporting and coordination within a company.

orientations: Individuals' positioning relative to their counterparts during conversation.

outsourcing (also known as offshoring): The strategic use of outside resources to perform activities that are usually handled by internal staff and resources.

Overseas Private Investment Corporation (OPIC): U.S. government corporation that provides loans, guarantees, and insurance to U.S. corporations investing in countries that present high political risk.

P

paralinguistics: The nonverbal aspects of speech that include intonation, accents, and the quality of voice.

parallel barter: A form of trade that involves two exchanges that are paid for in cash; it involves two parallel contracts whereby the seller agrees to purchase products that are usually unrelated to its business from the buyer and sell them on international markets; also called counterpurchase.

parallel imports: A distribution system not authorized by the manufacturer whereby the products purchased in a low-price market are diverted to other markets; also called grey market.

parallel translation: The process of translating the original instrument by different translators and comparing the translations.

paratariff measures: Additional, nontariff fees that increase the costs of imports in a manner similar to tariffs.

patent: Protection of the rights of the inventor or of the firm employing the inventor to use and sell an invention for a specified period of time.

penetration pricing: A pricing strategy in which a product is first priced below the price of competitors' products to quickly penetrate the market at the competitors' expense and then raised to target levels.

percent-of-sales method: An advertising budgeting method that determines the total budget allocated to advertising on the basis of past or projected sales.

performance standards: A priori measures against which firm performance is evaluated.

performing a product business analysis: Calculating projected costs such as return on investment and cash flow and determining the fixed and variable costs for the long term.

Permanent-Normal-Trade-Relations status (PNTR): Trade status that grants equal tax treatment on imported products from most countries, with the exception of rogue nations.

personal medium: A communication channel that involves contact between the seller and the consumer.

piggybacking: Using the distribution system of exporters with established systems of selling abroad who agree to handle the export function of a noncompeting (but not necessarily unrelated) company on a contractual basis; also called mother henning and cooperative exporting.

plant/warehouse location studies: Studies that evaluate the appropriateness of plant or warehouse location to ensure that it is in accordance with the limitations of the national environment and with the needs of a company.

point-of-sale–based projections: Market share and other relevant market dimensions assessed by the use of store scanners in weekly and biweekly store audits.

political risk: The risk associated with actions of local, regional, and parastatal governing bodies affecting the international company, and with the overall economic and political stability within a particular country.

political union: The highest level of regional integration; it assumes a viable economic integration and involves the establishment of viable common governing bodies, legislative bodies, and enforcement powers.

polycentric orientation: Company strategies predicated on the assumption that each country's market is unique and should be addressed individually, with a country-specific marketing mix.

polychronic time: The interpretation of time as fluid, such that individuals can accomplish multiple tasks at once.

post-adjustment: A compensation incentive whereby the company adjusts expatriate salaries to reflect the cost of living in the new environment at standards in the expatriate's home country; also called cost-of-living adjustment.

postures: Individuals' physical postures during conversation.

power distance: The manner in which interpersonal relationships are formed when differences in power are perceived.

press releases: Statements issued to the press to communicate news about a company and its products.

price controls: Strategies requiring a product to sell for a particular price in the local market; price control strategies are typically used to increase the prices of imports to match the minimum prices of local competition.

price elasticity studies: Studies examining the extent to which a particular market is price sensitive.

price/quality positioning: A strategy whereby products and services are positioned as offering the best value for the money.

primary data: Data collected for the purpose of addressing the problem at hand.

primitive society: The first stage of economic and political development, characterized, according to Marxist-Leninist theory, by the joint tribal ownership of primitive means of production centered on agricultural tasks.

print medium: A nonpersonal channel of communication such as a newspaper, magazine, billboard, pamphlet, or point-of-purchase display.

private labels: Brands sold under the brand name of a retailer or some other distributor.

product class positioning: A strategy used to differentiate a company as a leader in a product category, as defined by the respective company.

product consistency: The extent to which a company's different product lines are related, use the same distribution channels, and have the same final consumers.

product depth: The number of different offerings for a particular brand.

product division structure: An organizational structure whereby subsidiaries report to the product division (strategic business unit) with responsibility for the particular products.

product length: The total number of brands in the product mix.

product line: All the brands the company offers in the same product category.

product mix: The complete assortment of products that a company offers to its target international consumers.

product packaging design studies: Studies that evaluate consumers' reaction to a package, the extent to which the package adequately communicates information to the consumer, and the distribution implications of the package.

product placement: The strategy of placing brands in movies with the purpose of promoting the products to viewers.

product testing: Studies that estimate product preference and performance in a given market.

product user positioning: A positioning strategy that focuses on the product user, rather than on the product.

product width: The total number of product lines that a company offers to its target international consumers.

product-country stereotypes: Product-specific stereotypes that associate the country of origin as a certification of quality.

profit analyses studies: Studies that estimate product profit in specific international markets.

protection of markets with excess labor: The erection of barriers to imports of products competing with local offerings in an effort to protect local jobs.

protection of markets with excess productive capacity: A protectionist measure used to prevent foreign buyouts, invoking the protection of local labor.

protectionism: All actions by national and local governments aimed at protecting local markets from foreign competitors.

proxemics: The amount of physical space individuals require to feel comfortable in the process of communication.

psychographic segmentation: The use of values, attitudes, interests, and other cultural variables to segment consumers.

public appearances: Company representatives' public involvement, speaking on behalf of the international firm and its products.

publicity: Any communication about a company and the company's products that the company does not pay for; may be positive or negative.

purchase behavior studies: Research aimed at evaluating consumers' reaction to and interaction with a company's products.

Q

qualitative research: Research that uses nonsystematic processes, such as nonrandom sampling and open-ended data, as well as involves the researcher as participant.

quantitative research: A structured type of research that involves either descriptive research approaches, such as survey research, or causal research approaches, such as experiments.

R

radical innovation: The creation of new industries or new standards of management, manufacturing, and servicing that represent fundamental changes for consumers, entailing departures from established consumption.

receiver: The target market that receives the advertising message from a sender.

regiocentric orientation: Company strategies that view world regions as distinct markets that share economic, political, and cultural traits that will respond to a regionwide marketing approach.

regional standardization: The use of a uniform marketing strategy within a particular region.

reliability: The extent to which data is likely to be free from random error and yield consistent results.

religion: A society's relationship to the supernatural.

repatriation: The return of the expatriate employee to the home country.

repatriation allowance: A compensation incentive whereby the company covers expenses involved in moving back to the home country, as well as a large sum paid for successfully completing the international assignment in some cases.

research approach: The method used to collect data.

reverse culture shock: Anxiety experienced after returning to the home country, associated with a longing for the international environment left behind and with the difficulty of readjusting to the home country and to corporate life at one's firm.

Rostow modernization model: An economic development model attributed to Rostow, according to which each stage of economic advance is a function of productivity, economic exchange, technological improvements, and income.

S

sales force compensation, quota, and territory studies: Different studies pertaining to personal selling activities; they are crucial in helping to determine the appropriate strategies for certain international markets.

sales force composite estimates: Research studies wherein sales forecasts are based on the personal observations and forecasts of the local sales force.

sales forecast: Projected sales for a particular territory.

sales potential studies: Studies forecasting optimal sales performance.

sales promotion: Sponsored communications to the target consumer or trade segment that stimulate purchases or improve relationships with intermediaries.

sample size: The number of study participants necessary to obtain a high study reliability.

sampling frame: The list from which sample units are selected.

sampling procedure: A decision involving the selection of sampling units.

sampling unit: The entity included in the study; it may be individuals or representatives belonging to particular groups.

sanctions: Punitive trade restrictions applied by a country or a group of countries against another country for noncompliance.

screening new product ideas: Eliminating product ideas that do not fit with the target consumers and the overall mission of the organization.

secondary data: Data collected to address a problem other than the problem at hand.

segmentation: The process of identifying consumers and international markets that are similar with regard to key traits, such as product-related needs and wants, and that would respond well to a product and related marketing mix.

self-reference criterion: Individuals' conscious and unconscious reference to their own national culture, to home-country norms and values, and to their knowledge and experience in the process of making decisions in the host country.

sender: The sponsor of an advertisement, usually represented by an advertising agency, who encodes the message into words and images and communicates it to the target market.

service barriers: Barriers encountered by services in different markets, such as requirements for local certification, local providers, and other requirements that favor local over international service providers.

simulated test marketing: Test marketing simulating purchase environments where samples of target consumers are observed in their product-related decision-making process.

skimming strategy: A pricing strategy in which a product is priced above that of competitors' products, when competition is minimal, to quickly recoup investments; consumers responding to skimming strategies are more concerned with quality, uniqueness, and status, rather than price.

slavery-based society: A stage of economic and political development, which, according to Marxist-Leninist theory, emerges as a result of tribes' dominance over other tribes: Dominant tribes claim ownership of conquered tribes and their property.

social structure: The organization of relationships in a society.

socialism: A transition stage of economic and political development, characterized, according to Marxist-Leninist theory, by the disappearance of private property and its replacement with collective, state property.

soft currency: Currency that is kept at a high artificial exchange rate, overvalued, and controlled by the national central bank.

sogo-shosha: A large Japanese trading company that specializes in providing intermediary services, risk reduction through extensive information channels, and significant financial assistance to manufacturing firms.

South African Customs Union (SACU): A customs union that includes Botswana, Swaziland, Lesotho, and Namibia. The group's main trading partner is South Africa, and member countries have partially or entirely tied their currencies to the South African rand.

Southern African Development Community (SADC): A free trade organization that promotes economic cooperation among a coalition of 14 of Africa's more affluent and developed nations, designed to foster increased economic and governmental stability through the use of collective peace-keeping forces.

Southern Cone Common Market (Mercosur): A free trade agreement in South America that has met with considerable success; Mercosur is presently in the process of becoming a viable customs union. (See www.mercosur.org.uy.)

special economic zones: Customs-privileged manufacturing facilities in China where multinational companies can take advantage of low-cost labor.

specialized markets: Markets that contain specialty stores specializing in a particular product category.

specialty stores: Retailers that offer a narrow product line and wide assortment.

spoken/written language: The language used in conversation/the language used in written communications.

stability over time: The extent to which preferences are stable, rather than changing, in a market segment.

standardization of the advertising strategy: The process of globalizing a company's promotional strategy so that it is uniform in all its target markets.

standardized pricing: A pricing strategy in which the same price is charged for a product regardless of local market conditions.

standards as barriers to trade: Trade barriers imposing performance, environmental, or other requirements that are primarily aimed at imports.

status concern: The value placed on symbols of status and on the attainment of high status in a society.

strategic alliance: Any type of relationship between one or more companies attempting to reach joint corporate and market-related goals; term used to refer to most nonequity alliances.

studies of premiums, coupons, and deals: Studies that help identify the practices in each target country where a promotion is planned by investigating the practice and legality of premiums, coupons, and special deals.

substantiality: The extent to which the market is large enough to warrant investment.

superstores: Large retailers such as combination stores or hypermarkets that sell food, drugs, and other products.

survey research: Descriptive research that involves the administration of personal, telephone, or mail questionnaires.

swing credits: Amounts paid within the framework of a clearing agreement by the country that owes money to the other when an imbalance occurs.

switch trading: The process of buying a party's position in a countertrade in exchange for hard currency and selling it to another customer.

T

take-off: A stage in economic development described by Rostow as one in which economic growth becomes the norm and improvements in production lead to the emergence of leading sectors.

target market: Consumers and international markets that are similar in aspects relevant to the company.

target marketing: The process of focusing on those segments that the company can serve most effectively and designing products, services, and marketing programs with these segments in mind.

tariffs: Taxes imposed on goods entering a country.

telemarketing: A personal channel of communication that involves a salesperson calling on consumers.

television home shopping: Retailing through cable channels selling to consumers in their homes, through infomercials, and through direct response advertising shown on broadcast and cable television.

television shopping networks: Cable channels that sell products to a television audience.

test marketing: Testing new-product performance in a limited area of a national or regional target market to estimate product performance in the respective country or region.

third-country national: An employee working in the country of assignment who is not a national of that country nor of the country in which the corporate headquarters of the company he or she works for are located.

time orientation: The manner in which individuals view time in relation to accomplishing tasks.

time series and econometric models: Models that use the data of past performance to predict future market demand.

trade secrets: Intellectual property such as know-how, formulas, special blends, and other elements that are not registered, and are thus not protected by law.

trade shows and exhibitions: Business-to-business promotions that usually are held annually in formats where companies purchase exhibit space to display and demonstrate their offerings to the target market.

trademark: A brand name, mark, symbol, motto, or slogan that identifies a particular manufacturer's brand and distinguishes it from the competitors' brands in the same product category.

Trade-Related Aspects of Intellectual Property Rights (TRIPS): An international agreement, under the World Trade Organization, that sets out minimum standards for the legal protection of intellectual property. (See www.wto.org.)

trading companies: Large companies that specialize in providing intermediary services, risk reduction through extensive information channels, and significant financial assistance to manufacturing firms.

traditional society: A stage in economic development defined by Rostow as one in which the economy is dominated by agriculture and relatively few exchange transactions occur.

transfer pricing: A pricing strategy used in intra-firm sales for commercial transactions between units of the same corporation, within or beyond the national borders of the parent company.

transitional society: A stage in the economic development process described by Rostow as characterized by increased productivity in agriculture and by the emergence of modern manufacturing.

trialability: The ability of the consumer to experience a product with minimal effort.

U

uncertainty avoidance: The extent to which individuals are threatened by uncertainty, risk, and ambiguous situations and thus adopt beliefs, behaviors, and institutions that help them to avoid the uncertainty.

undifferentiated targeting: A targeting strategy aiming the product at the market using a single strategy, regardless of the number of segments.

United Nations organizations: The totality of United Nations bodies created to maintain international peace and security; to develop relations among nations; to achieve international cooperation in solving international economic, social, cultural, or humanitarian problems; and to encourage respect for human rights and fundamental freedoms using the venues offered by the different UN organizations. (See www.un.org.)

United States Agency for International Development (USAID): An independent agency of the federal government that supports the economic development of and trade with developing countries aligned politically with the United States. (See www.usaid.gov.)

United States Department of Commerce: The U.S. governmental agency that oversees and promotes trade, offering export assistance and counseling to U.S. businesses involved in international trade, providing country information and country specialists, and bringing buyers and sellers together.

United States Department of State: The foreign affairs arm of the United States government, in charge of promoting relations with other governments. (See www.state.gov.)

usage segmentation: The process of segmenting markets based on the extent to which consumers are nonusers, occasional users, medium users, and heavy users of a product.

use positioning: The process of marketing a precise product application that differentiates it in the consumers' minds from other products that have a more general use.

user status segmentation: The process of determining the status as users of competitors' products, ex-users, potential users, first-time users, and regular users.

V

validity: The extent to which data collected is free from bias.

values: Enduring beliefs about a specific mode of conduct or desirable end-state that guide the selection or evaluation of behavior.

vending machines: Interactive modes of retailing convenience goods.

voluntary export restraints: A government's self-imposed export quotas to a particular country that are established to avoid more severe protectionist action by the respective importing country.

voluntary import expansion: A government's response to protectionist threats from another country whereby it agrees to open markets to imports and to increase foreign access to a domestic market to avoid more severe protectionist action.

W

warehouse clubs: Stores that require members to pay an annual fee operating in low-overhead, warehouse-type facilities, offering limited lines of brand name and dealer-brand groceries, apparel, appliances, and other goods at a substantial discount; also known as wholesale clubs.

Webb-Pomerene Associations: Associations of competing companies that are granted immunity from antitrust prosecution and that join resources and efforts to export internationally.

West African Economic and Monetary Union (WAEMU): One of the first attempts at economic integration in Africa. Although it is successful as a monetary union that has adopted a single currency, trade is quite modest within the WAEMU. (See www.dakarcom.com/EconReports/econ_waemu.htm.)

wholesale clubs: Stores that require members to pay an annual fee operating in low-overhead, warehouse-type facilities, offering limited lines of brand name and dealer-brand groceries, apparel, appliances, and other goods at a substantial discount; also known as warehouse clubs.

wholly owned subsidiary: The entry mode that affords the highest level of control and presents the highest level of risk to a company; it involves establishing a new company that is a citizen of the country where the subsidiary is established.

World Bank: The World Bank Group, headquartered in Washington, D.C., that is one of the largest sources of funds for development assistance aimed at the poorest countries worldwide. (See www.worldbank.org.)

World Trade Organization (WTO): The largest and most influential international trade organization whose primary goal is ensure the free flow of trade; WTO's agreements (negotiated and signed by member countries, ratified in their parliaments) represent trade rules and regulations and act as contracts guaranteeing countries trade rights and binding governments to trade policies. (See www.wto.org.)

Appendix C

Company and Brand Index

Appendix C

Subject Index

Page numbers in italics indicate illustrations. A t indicates a table.